ENCYCLOPEDIA OF CONTEMPORARY LGBTQ LITERATURE OF THE UNITED STATES

ENCYCLOPEDIA OF CONTEMPORARY LGBTQ LITERATURE OF THE UNITED STATES

VOLUME 1: A–L

Edited by Emmanuel S. Nelson

Greenwood Press
An Imprint of ABC-CLIO, LLC

A B C CLIO

Santa Barbara, California • Denver, Colorado • Oxford, England

Copyright 2009 by Emmanuel S. Nelson

Library of Congress Cataloging-in-Publication Data

Encyclopedia of contemporary LGBTQ literature of the United States / edited by Emmanuel S. Nelson.
    p. cm.
    Includes bibliographical references and index.
    ISBN 978–0–313–34859–4 (set : hard copy : alk. paper) — ISBN 978–0–313–34861–7 (vol. 1 : hard copy :
    alk. paper) — ISBN 978–0–313–34863–1 (vol. 2 : hard copy : alk. paper) — ISBN 978–0–313–34860–0
    (set : ebook) — ISBN 978–0–313–34862–4 (vol. 1 : ebook) — ISBN 978–0–313–34864–8 (vol. 2 : ebook)
1. American literature—20th century—Bio-bibliography—Dictionaries. 2. Sexual minorities' writings, American
—Bibliography. 3. Sexual minorities—United States—Intellectual life—Dictionaries. 4. Sexual minorities in literature—Dictionaries. I. Nelson, Emmanuel S. (Emmanuel Sampath), 1954– II. Title: Encyclopedia of contemporary
lesbian, gay, bisexual, transgender, and queer literature of the United States.
PS153.S39E53   2009
810.9'92066—dc22   2009010181
[B]

13 12 11 10 09 1 2 3 4 5

This book is also available on the World Wide Web as an eBook.
Visit www.abc-clio.com for details.

ABC-CLIO, LLC
130 Cremona Drive, P.O. Box 1911
Santa Barbara, California 93116-1911

This book is printed on acid-free paper ∞

Manufactured in the United States of America

For Trevor again, with love

CONTENTS

ALPHABETICAL LIST OF ENTRIES

GUIDE TO RELATED TOPICS

Gay Literature
AIDS Literature
Alameddine, Rabih
Albee, Edward
Ali, Agha Shahid
Als, Hilton
Alumit, Noel
Alvarez, Aldo
Amisano, David Christopher
Angels in America
Antler
Ashbery, John
Autobiography, Gay
Baldwin, James
Baron, Jeff
Barr, James
Beam, Jeffery
Beierle, Andrew W. M.
Belton, Don
Bergman, David
Blanco, Richard
Boyd, Randy
Boykin, Keith O.
Bram, Christopher
Britton, Donald
Broughton, James
Bumbalo, Victor
Burroughs, Augusten
Burroughs, William S.
Busch, Charles

Caffé Cino
Camp
Campo, Raphael
Cañón, James
Cassells, Cyrus
Champagne, John
Chee, Alexander
Children's Literature, Gay
Coe, Christopher
Cole, Henri
Coming Out Narratives, Gay Male
Cooper, Bernard
Cooper, Dennis
Corn, Alfred
Covino, Peter
Cox, Christopher
Crowley, Mart
Cunningham, Michael
Currier, Jameson
Curzon, Daniel
Dancer from the Dance
Davis, Christopher
Delany, Samuel R.
Dhalla, Ghalib Shiraz
Dixon, Melvin
Dlugos, Tim
Donaghe, Ronald L.
Drake, David
Drama, Gay
Duncan, Robert

PREFACE

Certain foundational texts, such as encyclopedias, sourcebooks, and dictionaries, are indispensable for legitimizing as well as institutionalizing any distinct and emergent field of knowledge. Such books collect, organize, and present primary data about the subject. By doing so, they help define the new discipline, create a necessary knowledge base, and provide an epistemological framework that can be shared by students and scholars in the field. They serve as instruments for advanced inquiry; they facilitate dialogue within and across disciplines. Such works, therefore, are vital for the relatively young field of lesbian, gay, bisexual, transgender, and queer (LGBTQ) studies. Those of us who have a scholarly commitment to this dynamic new field must continue to consolidate its gains, expand its knowledge base, and claim its intellectual grounds. This two-volume *Encyclopedia of Contemporary LGBTQ Literature of the United States* is intended as a significant contribution to that ongoing project.

This *Encyclopedia* is unique in its scope. Though there are quite a few sourcebooks and reference volumes that focus on key areas within LGBTQ literary studies (for example, Greenwood's *Contemporary Lesbian Writers of the United States* [1993] and *Contemporary Gay American Poets and Playwrights* [2003]), this two-volume *Encyclopedia* is the first reference work that seeks to offer a comprehensive and inclusive introduction to gay, lesbian, bisexual, transgender, and queer writing in the contemporary United States. The more than 300 entries in the two volumes address topics as diverse as lesbian autobiography, African American gay literature, transgender young adult literature, bisexual novel, and queer theory. A vast majority of the entries are on individual authors. Some of the writers are major figures with international name recognition; some others are lesser-known or emerging new artists. The author entries range in length from about 500 to 2,000 words, depending on the relative importance of the writers. There are a few entries on seminal texts (for example, Tony Kushner's *Angels in America*) and several entries on topics that have compelling relevance to our deeper understanding of LGBTQ literature (for example, Heterosexuality, Lesbianism, Transgenderism, Bisexuality, Stonewall Riots). There are two substantial entries on queer pedagogy as well. The focus of the *Encyclopedia* is on contemporary literature: mostly works published since 1980. However, I have included major entries on two writers who cannot be strictly defined as contemporary—James Baldwin and Tennessee Williams—because of their foundational roles in the development of LGBTQ literature.

Yet the central objective of this *Encyclopedia* is not to define a contemporary LGBTQ literary canon; its primary goal is to provide reliable, thorough, and up-to-date information on hundreds of authors, texts, and topics. Advanced scholars will find this a useful research tool. Its user-friendly style, format, and level of complexity, however, make it accessible to a much broader audience that includes high school students and their teachers, community college as well as undergraduate students, and intellectually curious general readers and patrons of the public library. If you are a scholar researching the literature of AIDS, you will find here a succinct entry on that topic. If, on the other hand, you are researching the works of an individual author, such as Audre Lorde or Gloria Evangelina Anzaldúa, you will be able to find in this *Encyclopedia* concisely crafted entries on their lives and works; those entries will also direct you to other entries in this *Encyclopedia* that you will find useful. If you are an instructor interested in introducing your students to lesbian poetry or young adult gay fiction, you will not only find lively overviews of those specific subjects but also useful entries on a range of closely related topics. And if you are a general reader curious about gay film or bisexual stereotypes or transgender autobiography, you will find in this *Encyclopedia* thoughtful and accessible commentaries on those subjects.

Accessibility, in fact, is a salient feature of this reference work: I have made every effort to make it as reader-friendly as possible. The entries, for example, are arranged in alphabetical order. If you have a particular author or topic in mind, you may go directly to that entry. You may also consult the two elaborate tables of content: the first one lists all entries alphabetically; the second lists them, alphabetically, under various topical categories. You will also find the index useful. It is located at the end of Volume 2 of the *Encyclopedia*. Look under Walker, Alice, for example, to find the main entry on her as well as any other substantive discussion of her in the book.

Furthermore, the entries themselves are designed to facilitate cross-referencing. For instance, whenever an author who is also the subject of an entry is first mentioned within another entry, his or her name appears in bold. Whenever a topic (for example, Graphic Novel, Gay; Homophobia) on which there is a separate entry is first mentioned within another entry, the words appear in bold. Many entries also conclude with the "*See also*" feature: the entry on Adrienne Rich, for example, invites the reader to see also the longer entries on Poetry, Lesbian and Lesbian Literature, Jewish American to gain an understanding of Rich's significance in wider contexts.

Over 120 scholars have contributed to this *Encyclopedia,* so the entries reflect a wide spectrum of styles, perspectives, and approaches. However, the entries themselves follow a standard format. An entry on an individual author, for example, begins with the author's name (last name first), followed by the year of birth and, when applicable, the year of death. The opening line is always a phrase that identifies the author and the genre(s) in which she or he has published. It is followed by brief biographical information; the rest of the entry offers a judicious discussion of the author's major works and themes. When the title of the text by the author is first mentioned, its year of publication is indicated parenthetically. If brief quotations from primary sources are introduced, page numbers are not included, largely because multiple editions of works are often available and page numbers would therefore be misleading. However, direct quotations from secondary sources are documented, and the sources are listed in the Further Reading section that follows all entries. Entries on general topics also follow a standard pattern; they allude to major events, figures, and texts as well as provide relevant historical background information. Those entries, too, conclude with a Further Reading section.

All Further Reading sections direct interested readers to the most useful secondary materials available on the topic. Given the constraints of space, contributors were specifically instructed to list only the most significant and accessible secondary sources, both print and Internet. Entries on topics that have received substantial critical attention have several entries listed in the Further Reading section. However, entries on authors who are yet to be discovered by a wide audience may have only a couple of book reviews. I have made a deliberate attempt to give bisexual and transgender topics the same level of serious attention that gay and lesbian topics receive, but there are some inevitable gaps. For example, there are entries on gay as well as lesbian poetry, but there is not yet a sufficiently large body of bisexual or transgender poetry now to warrant entries. It is quite possible for a future edition of this *Encyclopedia* to include entries on those topics.

I would like to take this opportunity to thank all the contributors to this project. They have been generous in sharing their knowledge and thoroughly professional in handling the assignments. I wish to express my special gratitude to Marylynne Diggs, whose lively and perceptive introduction follows this Preface. Finally, I would like to thank George Butler, who commissioned this project for Greenwood Press, and Greenwood's editorial staff who expertly guided it to its successful completion.

INTRODUCTION

Lesbian, gay, bisexual, transgender, and queer (LGBTQ) literature is arguably one of the most exciting fields of study in the Humanities today. Although literary studies is often assumed to be relatively static, English departments dedicated to the study of literature have seen enormous change in the last three decades, and the emergence of LGBTQ literature as a legitimate academic field has contributed to that growth. A college student would have been hard-pressed to find a course in gay or lesbian literature before the 1980s. Indeed, faculty rarely chose such specialties; instead they often carved out specializations in authors whose work or life suggested a queer identity, but who were also well recognized, canonical authors, such as Walt Whitman, Gertrude Stein, Virginia Woolf, or James Baldwin. Today, however, most major colleges and universities have faculty who have specialized in LGBTQ Studies in English, History, Sociology, or Women's Studies. The number of English departments offering courses in LGBTQ literature grows every year, with a significant number of community colleges and small regional state schools contributing to these offerings. Perhaps we should not be so surprised that the field has become a regular part of literature curricula. While LGBTQ literature may sound like a very specific niche, the field is full of exciting discussions about fundamental questions in history, culture, and aesthetics and provides a perfect example of the intersections between literary and cultural practice.

Despite the relatively recent development as an acknowledged academic field, LGBTQ history and literature have deep roots and complicated genealogies. When one considers that texts from Ancient Greece to the medieval and Renaissance periods, including the Bible, represent same-sex love and gender variation, it is tempting to claim that queer identity is as old as human history, and in some ways, it is. Clearly there have always been people who loved others of the same sex or who experienced their gender or sex to be at variance from their anatomy. However, a more sophisticated approach to understanding both *history* and *identity* reveals a far more complicated picture. Identity does not exist in a vacuum; in fact, it takes shape in relation to cultural norms and definitions. These norms and definitions change over time and across cultures. For example, in Ancient

Athenian society, sex between men had very different meanings, norms, and social functions than it does today. Even when we omit consideration of international and historical cultures, narrowing our focus to the United States in the modern era, the differences remain staggering in part because contemporary American culture is diverse to begin with. In many Native American cultures of the past and the present, the gender variations of *two-spirit* individuals hold a place of reverence in both tribal society and literature. Some African American men who sleep with men do not identify themselves as gay, in part because the gay culture has been represented as a predominantly Caucasian culture. Even within specific racial demographics, cultural norms for sexuality and gender expression in the United States of the 1850s differed dramatically from the norms of the 1950s and 1960s, which were worlds away from the 1980s and 1990s. A more relevant point for today's readers is that all of these decades were remarkably different from the first decades of the twenty-first century, in which this *Encyclopedia* is taking shape.

Understanding the implications of these culturally and historically specific identities requires some understanding of the concept of Social Constructionism, and in particular, the debate between Constructionism and Essentialism. This debate is frequently confused with the more familiar nature versus nurture debate, which also gets invoked in LGBTQ studies, so clarifying that distinction is a good first step. The nature versus nurture debate focuses on what causes certain behaviors or identity characteristics in people. In the case of sexuality, those who believe nature determines sexual orientation might use experiments in genetics, endocrinology, or physiology to prove the connection. Those who believe that nurture is the causal factor might examine the effects of socialization or life experiences to explain why some people identify as gay, lesbian, bisexual, or transgender and others do not. The nature/nurture debate is frequently used to claim that sexual orientation is either fixed at birth or a choice. Settling this debate has been a goal of both queer allies and their opposition, in part because rights and protected class status have more frequently been granted to those with no choice over the characteristics for which they face discrimination. Lack of choice is not always the basis for protected status, as we can see in the protections afforded religion or political affiliation, for example. Moreover, a liberty that grants freedom to be only that which one has no choice but to be is a very strange application of the concept of liberty. However, many believe settling that issue will settle the political debates over LGBTQ rights.

While this debate is interesting, the debate between Essentialism and Constructionism is more relevant to LGBTQ literature. Although many texts could be cited as foundations for social constructionist positions, the three most influential, especially with respect to sexuality and gender, are Michel Foucault's *The History of Sexuality, Volume 1* (1978), Jeffrey Weeks's *Sexuality and Its Discontents* (1985), and Diana Fuss's *Essentially Speaking* (1990), all of which assiduously illustrate that identity, particularly sexual identity, is not *essential* but *constructed*. Both Weeks and Foucault noted that prior to the late nineteenth century, homosexuality did not exist as a discrete category of identity determined by sexual behaviors. Of course, same-sex love existed, but it did not constitute an identity. Only in the late nineteenth century, with the emergence of a new medical science known as sexology, was the homosexual, as we currently understand that concept, created. Note the use of the word *created* in the preceding sentence. The idea that a discourse, a body of knowledge, *creates or constructs* an identity as a particular cultural concept is the basis of Social Construction theory. In contrast, Essentialism is based on the belief that behaviors and their corresponding cultural identities and significance are intrinsic, or essential.

According to this theory, an intrinsic connection exists between homosexual identity and the cultural interpretation of it. As such, essentialists would argue that homosexuality is an intrinsically negative deviation from a fundamentally correct norm of heterosexuality and is not merely a matter of cultural definitions and norms. Thus, while the nature/nurture debate considers *why people are attracted* to a particular sex or *experience* a particular gender identity, the Essentialism/Constructionism debate considers *the basis on which society interprets those human differences.*

The Essentialism/Constructionism debate might seem esoteric and philosophical, and perhaps even less important than the nature/nurture debate, but its politics are far-reaching and arguably more progressive. Think about it this way: if one believes that the connections between homosexual behavior, individual identity, and social disapproval are intrinsic to the essence of homosexuality, then there is no basis for claiming that cultural attitudes are unjustified. If, on the other hand, the connections between homosexuality, identity, and social disapproval are socially constructed, then the social construct itself, the discourses that created it, and, more importantly, the laws that have promoted discrimination on that basis can be critiqued. Perhaps nowhere was the political impact of Social Constructionism more visible than in the landmark *Lawrence et al. v. Texas* case in which the United States Supreme Court overturned sodomy laws. Justice Anthony Kennedy noted in the majority opinion that not only is it false to claim that homosexuality has been universally denounced, but that "the concept of the homosexual as a distinct category of person did not emerge until the late 19th century" (*Lawrence et al. v. Texas*). Kennedy cited as evidence the work of historians Jonathan Katz as well as John D'Emilio and Estelle B. Freedman.

This complexity in the concepts of both history and identity enable us to appreciate fully how LGBTQ identity and literature developed over time in the United States. In the early nineteenth century, it was not uncommon for both men and women to have same-sex relationships that would, today, be considered quite queer. At the time, these relationships were defined as romantic friendship and were relatively accepted aspects of American social life (Martin; Faderman). Over the last third of the nineteenth century, medical discourse, produced by an international community of academics and practitioners, began addressing same-sex desire and gender variations as forms of a psychological and physiological pathology. Initially, these medical studies had as a primary objective repealing British and German sodomy laws on the basis that they punished what should be considered an illness, not a crime. Although their intentions might have been to promote understanding and decriminalization, the idea of sexual pathology solidified and led to numerous terms for variations from the mythical norm of absolute heterosexuality and perfectly binary feminine and masculine gender expression corresponding to a perfectly matched anatomical sex. Terminology began to expand exponentially as minute variations in sexual orientation and gender expression were regarded as needing a separate category and etiology, resulting in a voluminous taxonomy of sexuality and gender. By the early twentieth century, American physicians would have been familiar with more variations in sexual and gender identity than we have today.

These new terms and their cultural connection with illness made LGBTQ people truly *queer,* in the sense that we were considered fundamentally different from a norm and, as a result, in need of some kind of intervention. The twentieth century saw a gradual reduction in the range of identity categories as the general public, and to some extent the queer community itself, began to assume a correlation between homosexuality and gender variant expression. In fact, by the 1950s and 1960s, homosexuality became, to most of the public, a fairly simple pair of identity categories: (a) girlish boys who like boys or (b) mannish women who like women. Not only did homosexuality and gender variation become part of the same identity, but after World War II, they were associated with socialism, political subversion, and treason as well. It was as if those who dared to embrace their sexual or gender identity, rather than seek forgiveness and treatment for it, were seen by mainstream society as a danger to everything America stood for. While this might sound somewhat silly today, the exigencies of the Great Depression and World War II had suspended traditional ideas of femininity, masculinity, family, and work. For two decades, Americans fought to survive economic chaos or to provide material for "the war effort" in factories where women assumed jobs left vacant by men joining the armed forces. That era saw the emasculation of men, first through unemployment and then through wartime dismemberment; this coincided with the coming-of-age of a generation of women socialized to be independent and well paid. In such a context, homosexuality seemed like an impediment to restoring a fractured, threatened social order that had been romanticized through nostalgia for "the old days." By the late 1940s and early 1950s, anything that did not fit that romanticized norm of the family with a working father and homemaking mother seemed to many a direct and audacious challenge to the very safety of the nation.

Of course, even during the "ultranormal" fifties, there were revolutionaries, those not represented in the mid-century sitcoms many now assume to be culturally representative. Whether Beat Generation bohemians or other nonconformists, these rebels would build alliances, creating movements that would dramatically reshape the cultural landscape of the decades to come. By the late 1960s, a counterculture of civil rights activists, hippies, and intellectuals had begun to form, forging fragile alliances between the black community, young college students of all races, hippies exploring communal living and psychotropic drugs, antiwar protestors, and feminists. Represented in all of these groups were queer people of various identities. From homosexual-identified Bayard Rustin, a close member of Martin Luther King, Jr.'s inner circle, to lesbian feminists such as Barbara Smith concerned about the place of lesbians and women of color in the second wave of the feminist movement, to Beat Generation poets turned hippies such as Allen Ginsberg, queer folk were a central part of a broad, countercultural movement. Perhaps just as significantly, as early as 1965, gay civil servants, including Frank Kameny, and other homosexual activists, including Barbara Gittings, were walking picket lines in standard men's and women's business attire looking as mainstream as any bureaucrat while protesting the State Department's ban on homosexuality in government employment. These were, as many documentaries attest, interesting times.

In the 1970s and 1980s, when the sexual revolution had begun to pay off for women and queer folk, the "gay rights" movement made regular but slow and narrow progress. Many rights were achieved in part by distancing gay men and lesbians from the bisexual, butch/femme, gender variant, and transsexual aspects of the community, thus further dividing an already small minority against itself. In addition, the newly formalized rights came in part by debunking mid-century stereotypes while creating mainstream images that would in hindsight begin to look like new gay and lesbian orthodoxies. Paradoxically, the emerging homogenized gay culture and lesbian culture seemed internally alienated. By the 1980s, gay men had a well-developed macho image and a highly stylized drag culture that was offensive to many lesbian feminists, while the radicalism of the "womyn's community" seemed antimale to many gay men; gender variance was perceived by many as an antiquated reaction to heterosexual expectations and traditional gender norms. The result was a tacit distrust among gay men, lesbians, and transgender people that seemed to make coalition building unlikely.

The AIDS crisis would change all of this during the 1980s. The lesbian community, with an established place in feminist social welfare organizations and the health care professions, rallied to the defense of gay men at a time when the men's community was exhausting its political and psychological energies in a battle of epic proportions. Young men were dying quickly, and an unsympathetic president was in the White House; the times called for dramatic action. Groups such as ACT UP (AIDS Coalition to Unleash Power) and Queer Nation emerged, building a new queer coalition that radicalized its political practices and redefined its sense of community. In fact, the cultural discourse of the 1990s was largely dedicated to *queering* the presumed homogeneity of the "gay community" as it had been called for much of the 1970s and 1980s. The terminology for academic programs, historical and literary texts, and advocacy and political action groups evolved over the course of 15 years, altering the queer labels from simply "gay" to "gay and lesbian" to "GLB" and "GLBT," which reorganized into a more feminist-sensitive "LGBT," settling in the early twenty-first century into "LGBTQ."

This transformation in terminology and political practice was an invigorating, reciprocal amalgamation with the growing academic discourse. Personal and political practice problematized categories of academic study, and academic study transformed the language of identity politics in the queer community. Even revisionist historical approaches were critiqued by queer academics who interpreted history and culture differently. Cherished studies that labeled gender variant figures of the past as gay or lesbian were critiqued as ethnocentric appropriations of transgendered people's predecessors. Queer theory began to climb the tower of academia, sometimes challenging and sometimes bringing with it an older generation of intellectuals for whom the radically deconstructive approach to identity as mutable, a matter of performance, was sometimes unsettling. Indeed, even the phrase "queer theory" was difficult for some academics to accept; many saw the term *queer* as essentially an epithet, hardly worth reclaiming at all. Others, connecting the term with the early years of Queer Nation, initially a fairly male dominated organization, saw the broader use of the term as lacking inclusivity. As theory became increasingly important in literary and cultural studies in general, its impact on LGBT literature is hardly surprising; nonetheless, the initial reciprocal relationship between theory and practice began to break down as activists bemoaned the inscrutable density of queer theory texts. The work of theorists such as Judith Butler, Eve Kosofsky Sedgwick, and Michael Warner were embraced by many, but rejected by some who saw their language as inaccessible. Time has settled the dust, and many intentionally accessible texts, notably the work of Annemarie Jagose, Nikki Sullivan, and Riki Wilchins, have explained the complexities of queer theory.

These evolutions in the field of queer theory might seem disconnected from the world of LGBT literature. After all, theory is not fiction, not poetry, not autobiography; however, understanding any work of literature requires an understanding of the cultural contexts in which it was written and in which it has been read. Literature is not so much an expression of individual creativity, the work of an author who exists in isolation from time or space, remaining untouched by the cultural currents that energize the world, but rather a textual representation or cultural artifact that is a product of a person, place, and time, but which will also always be read through the lenses of both the past and the present.

Moreover, understanding the complexity of queer theorizing helps readers understand why particular texts might be classified LGBTQ literature. After all, what constitutes a gay, transgendered, or queer text? Is it determined by the sexual or gender identity of the author, by the inclusion of queer characters or themes, by the subversive syntax or semantics of the language itself, or is it determined by the approach taken by the reader? For that matter, what constitutes "literature" or a "text"? Is literature limited to the written word, or can it exist more temporally as spoken word? Must it even be verbal, or can the body itself become a text? Over the last 20 years, one thing has become certain: all of these interpretations of LGBTQ literature are possible.

When we place these elements of literary study within the diversity of authors and their work, the field begins to look wonderfully limitless. Even in modern American LGBT literature, spectacular diversity exists. Queer writers include a full spectrum of racial, religious, gender, and sexual differences. Throughout the twentieth century, queer authors have been African American and Christian, Native American and urban, rural and working poor, intellectuals and artists, and in some cases, all of these things combined. When we add the diversity of historically specific identities, the demographics become even more complex. Queer literature includes early twentieth century autobiographical writers such as Earl Lind/Jennie June who identify as inverts, a label hardly recognized today. We include pseudonymous writers such as Diana Frederics, calling herself both a lesbian and a member of "the third sex," conflating distinct contemporary identities. We even explore the work of writers such as Alice Dunbar Nelson and Nella Larsen, biracial African American authors whose apparently heterosexual characters *passed* as white and in doing so expressed a complex lexicon of the closet that shows how just how tenuously a writer may be tied to the queer canon. When one adds to this list writers as renowned as James Baldwin, Tennessee Williams, Allen Ginsberg, Truman Capote, Gore Vidal, William S. Burroughs, Christopher Isherwood, Rita Mae Brown, and Tony Kushner, the seemingly inexhaustible diversity of queer writers looks even more intriguing.

Part of what makes this literature so exciting is its thematic and aesthetic diversity. When reading literature written in the 1900–1950s, one cannot help but be struck by the prominence of autobiographies, novels, and short stories influenced by the psychological discourses of the time. The autobiography, having its roots in both spiritual autobiography and conversion narratives as well as medical case histories, became a likely avenue to write about developing a sense of self and finding a place on the margins of society—misunderstood but understandable. Whether these narratives took the form of autobiography or the novel, the emphasis in many was on the role of stereotypes in both self perception and representation to others. Writers frequently felt a responsibility to create a representative persona without conforming to a stereotype or creating a new one. They frequently represented the realities of the closet, but sometimes did so only metaphorically. Writers such as Willa Cather, Angelina Grimke Weld, Wallace Thurman, Robert McAlmon, and Hart Crane all received critical acclaim, sometimes to the degree that their subject matter remained allusive. Other writers, published by small presses and cycling in and out of print for decades, remain less known, including Gale Wilhelm. The challenges of coming out and getting published and of signification without oversimplification led more experimental writers of narrative to turn both forms upside down, as did Richard Bruce Nugent with the jazz-inspired "Smoke, Lilies, and Jade" (1926) and Gertrude Stein with *The Autobiography of Alice B. Toklas* (1933) and pieces such as "Miss Furr and Miss Skeene" (1922). In some cases, poetry was a refuge for allusive work. The freedom from narrative and character description and the flexibility of lyric allowed the expression of what might have seemed inexpressible for some poets and what could never be held back for others. Amy Lowell wrote love poetry addressed to a gender-free "you." Edna St. Vincent Millay's poetry remains an interesting study in queer identity and expression, and Langston Hughes's work similarly invites interpretations of homoeroticism, particularly in poems that reflect moments of visual recognition and longing between men. Of course, Allen Ginsberg's long poem "Howl" (1956) would break the allusiveness and begin a new era of unrepressed expression of sexual identity, an era that would include the out and proud work of poets Pat Parker, Adrienne Rich, and Audre Lorde.

During the last half of the twentieth century, a prolific literary culture would develop, first feeding the hunger of queer readers who longed to find in books a community more diverse than their own, and finally, representing the thriving queer culture of communities everywhere. The lesbian pulp fiction of mid-century, though ostensibly intended for a straight male audience, gave lesbian readers fictional friends, even if initially they seemed to commiserate their outcast status rather than celebrate their identities. Jane Rule's *Desert of the Heart* (1964), May Sarton's *Mrs. Stevens Hears the Mermaids Singing* (1965), Anne Bannon's Beebo Brinker series, as well as Isabel Miller's *A Place for Us* (1969), later reissued under the more familiar title *Patience & Sarah* (1972), began the 1960s transition from pulp to more popular fiction with lesbian readers as the intended audience. While critics were reclaiming writers of the past, new writers, such as Judy Grahn, Minnie Bruce Pratt, and Lee Lynch, were building an impressive body of popular fiction for women. The lesbian literature of the 1970s and 1980s would create worlds where families of origin were gleefully replaced by positive families of choice, and where butch/femme characters remained a model for queer readers, albeit out of sight from most mainstream audiences. Some lesbian fiction did find a broader audience, most notably Rita Mae Brown's *Rubyfruit Jungle* (1973), which remains the best-selling lesbian novel of all time. Eventually, lesbian literature would include such forms as the comic strip, such as Alison Bechdel's popular series, *Dykes to Watch Out For* (1983). By the 1980s, small presses such as Naiad, Kitchen Table, Aunt Lute, and Firebrand were established, promoting more positive lesbian, feminist literature, especially by women of color. During this period, Cherríe Moraga, Gloria Evangelina Anzaldúa, Paula Gunn Allen, Ann Allen Shockley, Kitty Tsui, Jewelle Gomez, and other women of color wrote some of the most highly acclaimed work of the latter part of the century.

During this same period, gay men's literature saw a different trajectory but eventually developed a similarly multicultural body of work. Rather than building on a pulp fiction foundation, men's literature built upon the critical acclaim of Tennessee Williams, Truman Capote, Gore Vidal, and other mid-century queer men in the United States and abroad. Several literary magazines, including *Christopher Street,* provided a forum for gay poetry and fiction. Edmund White, Andrew Holleran, Paul Monette, David Leavitt, and Armistead Maupin were among the most widely read. As AIDS began to take its toll on the gay community, it became a more central theme of gay literature. The work of Larry Kramer, Randy Shilts, David B. Feinberg, and Tony Kushner received significant attention, and a resurgence of political activism saw an increased sensitivity to issues of race and class in the community. In particular, the voices of gay African Americans and Asian-Pacific Islanders gained an audience. This new body of literature reflected an emerging brotherhood whose racial and class differences would be only partly leveled by the disease. During the 1980s and 1990s, AIDS would claim the lives of notable African

American authors Joseph Beam, Melvin Dixon, Marlon Riggs, Essex Hemphill, and Assoto Saint and white writers Allen Barnett, Randy Shilts, and George Whitmore. The literature of AIDS turned toward more spiritual and philosophical themes exploring the meaning of life, the limits of the body, and the fragile ties that bind all of us to each other and to Earth.

More recently LGBTQ literature in America has grown through the diversification in publishing, in academic discourse, and in queer communities across the country, resulting in an impressive collection of transgendered and gender queer autobiographies and essay collections, including the work of Leslie Feinberg and Patrick Califia; novels that cross boundaries of time, race, gender, and language, such as Tom Spanbauer's taboo-breaking novel *The Man Who Fell in Love with the Moon* (2000); and poetry, prose, drama, and graphic novels published electronically—not to mention prolific, annually issued volumes of queer erotica. It is safe to say that currently there are no limits to the literature being written or to what can be read. While the political climate from 2000 to 2008 may go down in history as among the most conservative and combative in over 50 years, the climate for publishing and consuming queer literature has perhaps never been better.

If you are interested in reading queer literature, either as a form of entertainment or as an academic and intellectual endeavor, there is an enormous body of work that will keep your attention for as long as you like. The study of LGBTQ literature is not entirely separate from the study of all American literature; any course in American literature, whether taught at the high school or college level, will include writers whose lives and work are addressed in this *Encyclopedia,* and any course in queer literature will include some of the biggest names in the traditional American literary canon. Nonetheless, reading these writers in the context of LGBTQ history and culture changes what we notice, the connections we make, and the patterns we are inspired to articulate. Readers who identify as LGBTQ will find pieces that give context and meaning to their experiences and that broaden their minds by viewing queerness through a wider angle lens. Readers who have little or no affiliation with queer communities will gain insight into experiences and cultures they only barely understand and might not understand at all were it not for the volumes written to help bridge differences in how we see ourselves, how we live our lives, and how we fit into American culture at large.

Further Reading

Butler, Judith. *Bodies That Matter: On the Discursive Limits of "Sex."* New York: Routledge, 1993.

D'Emilio, John, and Estelle B. Freedman. *Intimate Matters: A History of Sexuality in America.* New York: Harper and Row, 1988.

Faderman, Lillian. *Surpassing the Love of Men: Romantic Friendship and Love between Women from the Renaissance to the Present.* New York: Morrow, 1981.

Foucault, Michel. *The History of Sexuality, Volume 1: An Introduction.* New York: Random House, 1978.

Fuss, Dianna. *Essentially Speaking: Feminism, Nature, and Difference.* New York: Routledge, 1990.

Halperin, David. *One Hundred Years of Homosexuality: The New Ancient World.* New York: Routledge, 1990.

Jagose, Annamarie. *Queer Theory: An Introduction.* New York: NYU Press, 1997.

Katz, Jonathan Ned. *The Invention of Heterosexuality.* New York: Plume, 1996.

Martin, Robert K. "Knights Errant and Gothic Seducers: The Representation of Male Friendship in Nineteenth Century America." In *Hidden from History: Reclaiming the Gay and Lesbian Past*. Edited by Martin Bauml Duberman, Martha Vicinus, and George Chauncey, Jr. New York: NAL, 1989, pp. 169–82.

Sedgwick, Eve Kosofsky. *Epistemology of the Closet*. Berkeley: University of California Press, 1990.

Sullivan, Nikki. *A Critical Introduction to Queer Theory*. New York: NYU Press, 2003.

Warner, Michael, ed. *Fear of a Queer Planet: Queer Politics and Social Theory*. Minneapolis: University of Minnesota Press, 1993.

Weeks, Jeffrey. *Sexuality and Its Discontents: Meanings, Myths, and Modern Sexualities*. London: Routledge and Kegan Paul, 1985.

Wilchins, Riki. *Queer Theory, Gender Theory: An Instant Primer*. Boston: Alyson, 2004.

Marylynne Diggs

A

AIDS Literature

After American investigators uncovered HIV/AIDS in 1981, numerous people wrote about the illness's politics, problems, and fatalities as a form of response. Those who have written about AIDS include experienced authors and novices alike, such as activists, critics, novelists, playwrights, and poets, among others. As such, the literature of AIDS is largely defined by its great multiplicity in both provenance and style. Among the various authors who write about AIDS, many self-identify as lesbian, **gay**, bisexual, transgender, and **queer**. Indeed, there has been a long-standing history between these communities and AIDS-related writing because many of these same authors experienced the illness firsthand. In this way, a voluminous amount of AIDS-related literature has been written by lesbian, gay, bisexual, transgender, and queer (LGBTQ) authors, and in part, their work builds upon the ideas of the **gay rights movement**. Critics and writers discuss these phenomena in a myriad of ways; for instance, many critics articulate how the virus and the medical syndrome it causes are experienced *intimately* and *publicly*. Even though AIDS is often perceived by many as being a private matter, the illness is often couched in public contexts, such as debates of congressional legislation and spaces of cultural life, such as print media, film, and activism.

AIDS literature has been influenced by a wide range of intimate and public happenings, including political efforts, such as that of the Gay Men's Health Crisis and the AIDS Coalition to Unleash Power (ACT UP). These groups have sought to bring the illness into the public spotlight through direct-action methods to instigate change and disrupt silence. Other activists have aimed to educate about problems, such as the stereotype that only queers contract AIDS. These activists educate that lesbians, gays, bisexuals, transgendered people, and queers are not the only ones who are affected and infected by the virus. For such activists, public stigma and uncertainty about AIDS is troubling because the illness is a global struggle, and approximately 40 million people worldwide experience the illness personally. These precarious circumstances are made clear by a

2006 report issued by the United Nations (http://vitalvoicesonline.org/blog/hivaids/), which estimates that more than 8,000 people die from it everyday. In light of these dire straits, the problem of public inaction is a common theme in AIDS literature. Likewise, some texts show the themes of militancy and protest as a means to gain a voice in the public sphere, escape the **closet**, and react against cultural denial.

Notions of voice and memory are prominent in AIDS literature because they are a means to articulate an identity publicly, inform others about infection, and understand the political exile forced upon queers. Hence, visions of the human voice have become a foundation for self-determination, social empowerment, and critiquing the **homophobia** and stigma dealt to them by intolerant majority cultures and AIDS-phobic groups. This is not to say that AIDS literature is only about voices though, since much LGBTQ-related literature about AIDS tends to present imagery concerning the intimacies of the human body. This literature has rendered storylines about caretakers of the AIDS-afflicted body, the physical effects wrought by AIDS medicines, and the challenges of AIDS-related sexuality. Still, texts about AIDS do not isolate the body from the mind, which is to say, the works show the body and the mind as intersecting through the emotion and pain faced by people with AIDS. The emotional resonances of AIDS literature imply much about the illness. The theme of emotion in the context of AIDS attaches much seriousness and power to the epidemic and thus points out how the disease alters one's life in intimately personal but also public terms.

Sentiments such as the above are legible in several of the first AIDS-related texts that grabbed public attention in the early 1980s. For instance, **Paul Reed**'s novel *Facing It: A Novel of Aids* (1984) and Robert Chesley's play *Night Sweat* (1984) were among the first works to engage actively in portraying the AIDS crisis, but to date, they have not received the same attention as that of **William M. Hoffman**'s successful play, *As Is,* which made its New York debut in 1985. This play portrayed the emotional experiences of a gay male protagonist living with AIDS. Hoffman's play went on to win the 1985 Drama Desk Award for Outstanding New Play that same year. Another playwright, **Larry Kramer**, similarly launched his AIDS play, *The Normal Heart*, in 1985; Kramer's work was a booming success, and he himself became known as an activist, co-founding two AIDS-related organizations: the Gay Men's Health Crisis and ACT UP (AIDS Coalition to Unleash Power). Kramer went on to become one of the most recognized figures in the American epidemic's cultural history. In that same year, the queer African American writer **Samuel R. Delany** published his book *Flight from Neveryon,* which featured a vision of the HIV/AIDS epidemic as a significant issue faced within the larger text's own imaginary fantasy world.

Likewise, the African American gay writer Craig Harris made a groundbreaking contribution to gay African American literature in the collected volume *In the Life: A Black Gay Anthology.* Similar to Kramer, Harris is now lionized for his activism and educating about AIDS. Thereafter in 1987, the journalist Randy Shilts published his 613-page chronicle *And the Band Played On: Politics, People, and the AIDS Epidemic,* which was later adapted to a film directed by Roger Spottiswoode. Shilts's account became a best seller and was nominated for the National Book Critics Circle Award, among other honors. Around the same time, the author **Armistead Maupin** received public attention for his representations of AIDS in his *Tales of the City* series, which includes *Babycakes* (1984), *Significant Others* (1987), and *Sure of You* (1989). A similarly notable text from this time was **Harvey Fierstein**'s *Safe Sex*—a group of three one-act plays that shows AIDS indirectly, but foregrounds the perils of unprotected intercourse and intimate involvement. For poetry at this time, Mark Doty's work *Turtle, Swan* (1987) and **Paul Monette**'s *Love Alone: Eighteen Elegies for Rog* (1988) portrayed the gay life of HIV/AIDS.

By and large, Doty's work has been praised for its honesty, and Monette's work has been acclaimed for its realism. The genuineness of feeling and the grim reality captured in these works are echoed in another major work by Monette: *Borrowed Time: An AIDS Memoir* (1988), which narrates intimate moments between Monette and his partner, Roger Horwitz. Like many other LGBTQ writers, Monette became a well-known public figure, who fostered consciousness-raising and aimed to end homophobia. Monette's brand of intimacy and reality was portrayed in **Christopher Davis**'s *Valley of the Shadow* (1988) insofar as it narrated the relationship of two gay men facing AIDS together in a relationship. This rather ubiquitous trope of gay male trouble with AIDS was reiterated in **George Whitmore**'s *Someone Was Here: Profiles in the AIDS Epidemic* (1988); his text gives lifelike portraits based on people he met, thereby further grounding AIDS literature in realism. He is noted today for partaking in the **Violet Quill Club**, which was a group of seven gay writers, who read and commented on one another's work.

Another famed voice in this group was **Robert Ferro**, who wrote the novel *Second Son* (1988). Ferro's **gay novel** gives a magisterial treatment about the AIDS epidemic, showing an iconography of family, social status, and love between men. During this same time, works of drama, such as Harry Kondoleon's play *Zero Positive* (1988) and Richard Greenberg's play *Eastern Standard* (1988) similarly addressed the health crisis, but to this day, have not received the same lionizing as some gay writers. Another member of the Violet Quill, **Andrew Holleran**, published a volume of essays at this time—*Ground Zero* (1988)—that poignantly tells tales of both the survivors and souls lost to the epidemic. Andrew Holleran, which is the pseudonym of Eric Garber, is known as one of the prominent voices in not only AIDS-related literature, but also the queer literature of **camp** aesthetics. Similar in its stature, but far more political is Larry Kramer's drama *Just Say No* (1988), a critique of political administrations of the time, which are accused of ignoring AIDS. The reputations of Holleran, Ferro, and Kramer can be said to trump some of the other AIDS-based work of this time, which includes Joel Redon's *Bloodstream* (1988), a memoir of a gay man living with AIDS, and a novel by journalist **John Weir**: *The Irreversible Decline of Eddie Socket* (1989). Weir's piece contrasts with that of Redon and Kramer in that, while it similarly narrates the AIDS epidemic, it instead employs some elements of humor.

Another work that made use of comedic elements was **David B. Feinberg**'s novel *Eighty-Sixed* (1989)—a novel that is mostly built around the frenetic character B. J. Rosenthal, a gay man who greatly fears HIV. The 1989 tome *Poets for Life: Seventy-Six Poets Respond to AIDS* expands the archive of AIDS representation since it offers a space for seldom-heard identities like lesbian writers, such as **Adrienne Rich**, and also the gay African American writer **Melvin Dixon**. Edited by Michael Klein, *Poets for Life* also includes famed writers, such as Mark Doty, **Allen Ginsberg**, Paul Monette, and other significant voices. In 1988, another giant of queer literature—**Edmund White**—published a collection of stories with British writer Adam Mars-Jones, titled *Darker Proof: Stories from a Crisis;* it consists of seven stories narrating the lives of several characters living with AIDS. As a Violet Quill member, White's work has a reputation for its honesty in portraying queer AIDS life; relatedly, **Christopher Bram**'s text *In Memory of Angel Clare* (1989) narrates a fictional account of loss felt by a group of friends and an AIDS widower who remember their friend Angel, a New York filmmaker. Bram's work is significant because it explores how memory relates to AIDS cultures. Further, Larry Kramer's project, ***Reports from the Holocaust: The Making of an AIDS Activist***, is a collection of writings from the 1980s that also remembers the ruins wrought by the virus. In contrast to these memories, **Larry Duplechan**'s *Tangled up in Blue* (1989) narrates a fictional predicament of a married woman, Maggie, who learns of her bisexual husband's relationship with their gay HIV-positive friend, Crockett. Also in 1989, the famed AIDS activist Michael Lynch published his now well-known work *These Waves of Dying Friends: Poems,* which is a collection about mourning.

The poetry of Ron Schreiber equally narrates the American AIDS epidemic insofar as his work, *John: Poems* (1989), speaks to the loss of a loved one; this great exemplar of gay poetry has been linked to the poet's life partner, John MacDonald, who died of AIDS. This theme of loss is further developed in Allen Barnett's 1990 collection of stories, *The Body and Its Dangers and Other Stories,* which establishes an aesthetic of gay community life. Critics suggest that Barnett's story "The *Times* as It Knows Us" is the most excellent of the six stories, but each of them arguably shows substantial merit. This aesthetic of community similarly plays out in **Sarah Schulman**'s famed novel, *People in Trouble* (1991), which narrates the experiences of lesbian life and AIDS activism in New York City. This work made Schulman known as an outstanding lesbian novelist; moreover, she has participated extensively in activism and has achieved in the fields of dramaturgy and journalism. She is also a co-founder of the Lesbian Avengers, a group of activists who sought to inform the public about AIDS. Another well-regarded playwright of this period is **Terrence McNally**, who is known for scribing the play *André's Mother* (1990). McNally's work is greatly revered for its representation of a gay man who grieves and reconnects with the lost loved one's mother.

The motif of family, and reorienting the heterosexual family dynamic, is a common theme in much of the LGBTQ narratives about the HIV/AIDS epidemic. For instance, in the AIDS-related text *A Home at the End of the World* (1990) by the gay novelist **Michael Cunningham**, a queering of the family paradigm takes place. Although Cunningham's novel mostly portrays the relations of a family (or union) of three, the latter portions of Cunningham's novel notably concern a male figure who dies of AIDS. This family dynamic is also interwoven through Paul Monette's *Afterlife* (1990), which portrays the lives and musings of three gay men whose partners have died from AIDS-related complications. Similarly, Paul Gervais's novel *Extraordinary People* (1991) narrates the family experience of two gay brothers, one of whom has AIDS, and it tells of the siblings' relationships with their partners. While these convey the relations of family and AIDS, others have constructed forms of family through community relations. For instance, Rachel Hada's *Unending Dialogue: Voices from an AIDS Poetry Workshop* (1991) builds a family-like collective through the words of eight participants from the Gay Men's Health Crisis.

Another gay **anthology**, *Brother to Brother: New Writings by Black Gay Men,* similarly fosters a sense of community within the African American landscape of gay life and AIDS. Edited by **Essex Hemphill** and originally started up by Joseph Beam, this text provides several powerful poetic and prose visions of the AIDS epidemic in the United States. Of significant interest are the entries by Walter Rico Burrell, Melvin Dixon, David Frechette, Craig G. Harris, and Marlon Riggs. The sensibility of community and family represented here indeed fractures in David Wojnarowicz's *Close to the Knives: A Memoir of Disintegration* (1991) and David B. Feinberg's *Spontaneous Combustion* (1991). Each of these illuminates the troubling chaos inflicted by AIDS on the body and subject. Feinberg's book conveys a sequel to his earlier work about B. J., while Wojnarowicz writes an acerbic and segmented commentary on life with AIDS and other destructive elements. Wojnarowicz became a renowned activist and critic because of his propensity to critique conservatives who disapproved of his work. Community is also shown to a certain degree in Peter McGehee's sui generis novel *Boys Like Us* (1992), which presents the story of a man named Zero MacNoo, an Arkansas man who cares for a friend who lives with AIDS.

The narrative of *Boys Like Us* is elaborated in McGehee's sequel *Sweetheart* (1992) where readers perceive the cavorting of Zero MacNoo who continues to give campy commentary on life. After *Sweetheart*, another sequel followed—*Labour of Love* (1993)—but this time, it was written from McGehee's notes by his partner, Doug Wilson. Like that of McGehee's sequels, Larry Kramer's play *The Destiny of Me* (1992) further develops the life of his protagonist Ned Weeks from *The Normal Heart*, showing Ned as a voluble patient receiving treatment at the National Institutes of Health. In contrast to these more politicized and innovative visions of AIDS, Richard Hall's collection of stories in *Fidelities* (1992) focuses on working through the draining emotions that arise in AIDS-related death. Like that of Hall's work, Paul A. Sergios's work, *One Boy at War* (1993), plumbs the depths of the personal by narrating the challenges that an HIV-positive gay man faces as he attempts to find emotional and medical remedies. Furthermore, **Fenton Johnson**'s *Scissors, Paper, Rock* (1993) and **Jameson Currier**'s *Dancing on the Moon* (1993) capture the feeling of everyday life. That is to say, Johnson's work represents the quotidian of gay protagonist Raphael as he dies, and he follows up this work in 1997 when he writes his memoir, *Geography of the Heart*. For Currier, his work is a collection of short stories that tells about how AIDS has complexly remade the relationships of gay men in parts of America.

In 1993, another milestone volume, *Sojourner: Black Gay Voices in the Age of AIDS*, debuted, providing a collection of writings by black Americans experiencing AIDS; edited by B. Michael Hunter, the anthology does much to unsettle the stereotype that only white gay men contract AIDS. In other words, while such works as *Jeffrey* (1998) by Paul Rudnick and **Angels in America**: *Millennium Approaches* (1991) and *Perestroika* (1993) by **Tony Kushner** have been, on the one hand, complicated for largely portraying AIDS as a gay white man's disease, on the other hand, these works have been critically acclaimed for their achievements in artistry. Like McGehee's novels, *Jeffrey* similarly uses camp humor to process AIDS tensions, while in Kushner's *Angels in America*, the texts utilize fantastic and supernatural elements. Kushner's work won the 1993 Pulitzer Prize for best drama. Unlike the works of Kushner and Rudnick, the novels *Tim and Pete* (1993) by James Robert Baker and Christopher Coe's *Such Times* (1993) relate more extreme visions of AIDS, illustrating the taxing elements of sickness. This same harsh realism is portrayed in Peter Cameron's *The Weekend* (1994) and Rebecca Brown's novel *The Gifts of the Body* (1994), where Cameron shows the pain of surviving beyond the dead and Browning tells of an unnamed woman health care worker who visits the homes of those living with HIV/AIDS.

The difficult intimacies in Browning's work also appear in much of this time's **gay autobiography**, such as Susan Bergman's memoir, *Anonymity* (1994), and Harry Kondoleon's semiautobiographical novel, *Diary of a Lost Boy* (1994). Bergman tells of her father's closeting as a homosexual and death from AIDS, while Kondoleon's novel paints a complex portrait of Hector Diaz, a man dying of AIDS. This realism is similarly presented in Marci Blackman and Trebor Healey's anthology, *Beyond Definition: New Writing from Gay and Lesbian San Francisco* (1994). Blackman and Healey's dynamic collection includes Edward Wolf's AIDS poem, "Garden," and Robert Kaplan's "AIDS Death #54911"—both of which give provocative visions of AIDS. In the genre of autobiography, David B. Feinberg's work *Queer and Loathing: Rants and Raves of a Raging AIDS Clone* (1994) brings together a collection of essays about his own HIV-positive status, using dark humor to mitigate the challenges of living with HIV in public. In the following year, the Olympic champion diver Greg Louganis co-wrote his autobiography, *Breaking the Surface* (1995), with Eric Marcus; in it, Louganis speaks of how he articulated his HIV-positive status and his self-doubts as a gay athlete in the public spotlight. Another gay athlete, Dr. Tom Waddell, contributed material for *Gay Olympian* (1995), which was written by sports writer Dick Schapp; the text shows Waddell's life as an HIV-positive co-founder of the Gay Games.

The gay poetry of this time similarly builds upon the autobiographical insofar as Mark Doty's collection of poems, *Atlantis* (1995), includes a spate of the poems that are said to be linked to the AIDS-related death of Doty's partner. Akin to that of Doty, the poetry of **Tim Dlugos**—*Powerless: Selected Poems, 1973–1990* (1996)—explains what happens after Dlugos's diagnosis. This work is edited by the well-known gay poet **David Trinidad**. Relatedly, the collection of writings in *Things Shaped in Passing: More "Poets for Life"* (1997), which is edited by Michael Klein and Richard J. McCann, presents the work of 42 American poets; this noteworthy work further fosters the work begun in the earlier *Poets for Life* (1992). Also, the poet Mark Doty published his memoir, *Heaven's Coast* (1996), most of which concerned the loss of his partner, Wally, and others to AIDS. Similarly, the gay poet **Rafael Campo** published his collection of poems *What the Body Told* (1996), which continued his consideration of gay Latino life—a project he began in the collection *The Other Man Was Me* (1994). Campo further expanded his repertoire with his memoir, *The Poetry of Healing* (1997), which presents his life as a doctor to people living with AIDS. Also in 1997, the widely read writer Jamaica Kincaid published her memoir, *My Brother,* which reflected on the death of her gay brother, Devon, who died of AIDS in Antigua at the age of 33. Like that of Kincaid's memoir, Edmund White's *The Farewell Symphony* (1997) is also said to use autobiographical elements, showing a character who, like White himself, travels to Paris, France, amid the epidemic in the 1980s.

The works of **Alfred Corn** and Amy Hoffman similarly present poignant commentaries on the U.S. AIDS epidemic in 1997; that is, the poet Corn presents readers with a novel about a writer who attempts to move beyond the death of his partner in *Part of His Story* (1997). In the memoir *Hospital Time* (1997), Hoffman tells of caring for her gay friend Mike who is dying of AIDS. Additionally, the poet Miguel Algarín presents a memoir-like collection—*Love Is Hard Work* (1997)—a work comprised of poems about New York's queer Hispanic milieu of AIDS. Further, Allan Gurganus wrote *Plays Well with Others* (1997)—a novel that tells of three artists, two men and a woman, who go to New York in hopes of making something for themselves. In the following year, 1998, the gay poet **David Bergman** published his work of poetry, *Heroic Measures,* which reflects on the minutia of everyday life and builds a larger picture of AIDS life. Another gay writer, Michael Cunningham, wrote the Pulitzer Prize winning *The Hours* (1998), which narrates the story of several characters, including the gay artist, Richard, who is dying of AIDS. In 1999, Clifford Chase published another AIDS memoir, *The Hurry-*

Up Song: Memoir of Losing My Brother, a work that depicts a gay man who sees his gay brother die from AIDS.

Following in the tradition of memoir, Kate Scannell's autobiography, *Death of the Good Doctor* (1999), tells of Scannell's doctoring experiences with several queer figures in a California AIDS ward during the late 1980s. Of similar importance is Daniel Baxter's *The Least of These My Brethren* (1998)—it tells of a doctor's experiences in an AIDS ward, where readers learn of transgender sex workers. Also in 1999, the award-winning **Jim Grimsley** published the novel *Comfort and Joy,* which narrates the difficulties of gays in family life. In the following year, Edmund White published two works that prominently display AIDS-related life: a novel, *The Married Man* (2000), and a short story, "A Venice Story," in the 2000 edition of *Men on Men: Best New Gay Fiction for the Millennium.* Another significant work of fiction, *Interesting Monsters,* was published in 2001 by a Puerto Rican American author, **Aldo Alvarez**, and it details the story of a queer man, Dean, who develops HIV/AIDS. Also in 2001, Fritz and Etta Mae Mutti connected their AIDS-related experiences to the beliefs of Methodists in a family memoir, *Dancing in a Wheelchair.* Another compelling collection of stories about AIDS-related medicine— *AIDS Doctors*—was published in 2002 by the authors Ronald Bayer and Gerald M. Oppenheimer.

The literature of AIDS between 2003 and 2004 is noticeably missing, but the writing of AIDS reappears in 2005 with Larry Kramer's *The Tragedy of Today's Gays*—a collection of Kramer's writings concerning the so-called political inaction of young gay people. Another autobiographical work published at this time was Joan Nelson's *Before, During and After AIDS* (2004), which recounts her son's experience with the illness. Similarly, in 2006, the landmark collection *Not in My Family: AIDS in the African-American Community* (2006)—compiled by Gil Robertson—thus brings to the fore personal and political reflections of AIDS among black Americans. Also in 2006, the great writer Andrew Holleran returned to the public spotlight with another AIDS-related novel, *Grief;* in this work, Holleran portrays the life of a gay man whose life is changed and defined by AIDS in several ways. Another work from 2007 is Armistead Maupin's *Michael Tolliver Lives,* which continues with some of the plot and characters—such as the HIV-positive Mouse —that first appeared in his series, *Tales of the City.* Finally, Richard Canning's collection *Vital Signs: Essential AIDS Fiction* (2007) is a comprehensive anthology that brings together some of the first works about AIDS and several more recent ones as well.

Further Reading

Kruger, Steven F. *AIDS Narratives: Gender and Sexuality, Fiction and Science.* New York & London: Garland Publishing, 1996.

Murphy, Timothy F., and Suzanne Poirier. *Writing AIDS: Gay Literature, Language and Analysis.* New York: Columbia University Press, 1993.

Nelson, Emmanuel S. *AIDS: The Literary Response.* New York: Twayne, 1992.

Pastore, Judith, ed. *Confronting AIDS through Literature: The Responsibilities of Representation.* Champaign: University of Illinois Press, 1993.

Román, David. *Acts of Intervention: Performance, Gay Culture, and AIDS.* Bloomington: Indiana University, 1998.

Ed Chamberlain

AIDS Memorial Quilt, The

The concept behind the quilt is credited to Cleve Jones, a **gay** activist who worked as a student intern under Harvey Milk. Jones got the idea of the quilt when, as part of a memorial parade in San Francisco honoring Milk in 1985, the marchers carried placards of names of people who had died of AIDS. Inspired by the display of public grief and collective mourning, on June 28, 1987, Jones along with other members of the Castro community displayed a quilt with about 40 panels from the mayor's office at City Hall on the occasion of the Lesbian and Gay Freedom Day Parade. The act not only commemorated the thousands who were dying of AIDS, but also functioned as a public response to state-sanctioned homophobia and government apathy to the disease. Following this display, Jones along with several other members of the community created the NAMES Project Foundation after the overwhelming public and nationwide response to the AIDS Memorial Quilt.

The same year, the Quilt was first displayed at the National Mall in Washington, D.C., on October 11 not far from the Vietnam Veterans Memorial, with approximately 2,000 panels and covering an area the size of two football fields. The location of the display was significant in that the Quilt attempted to occupy, both literally and ideologically, a national space through which a process of remembering and grieving could begin to take place. The very decision to use the medium of the quilt could be seen as an attempt to work within a cultural form that is an essential part of American heritage. The use of the Quilt thus functions as a recognition that the loss of gay lives constitutes a larger loss to the nation itself.

The Quilt continues to grow with various local chapters and international affiliates. As a work of art, it is unique in that it is a text that has multiple authors and continues to grow (a painful reminder that the disease is far from "over"). Critiques of the Quilt have ranged from the suggestion that this form of activism concentrates energies on the dead rather than on those who are still living with AIDS, that it focuses too narrowly on the experience of gay men, and that it marginalizes the experience of those outside U.S. borders, especially when the scope of the epidemic has acquired global dimensions. Nevertheless, the Quilt still remains a poignant reminder of loss that is not limited only to the **queer** community. It also recognizes the potency of art as activism: the Quilt has raised over $4,000,000 for people living with AIDS.

Further Reading

Elsley, Judy. "The Rhetoric of the NAMES Project AIDS Quilt: Reading the Text(ile)." In *AIDS: The Literary Response,* edited by Emmanuel S. Nelson, 187–96. New York: Twayne Publishers, 1992.

Hawkins, S. Peter. "Naming Names: The Art of Memory and the NAMES Project AIDS Quilt." *Critical Inquiry* 19, no. 4 (Summer, 1993): 752–79.

Ruskin, Cindy. *The Quilt: Stories from the NAMES Project.* New York: Pocket Books, 1988.

Nishant Shahani

Alameddine, Rabih (b. 1959)

Pioneering Lebanese American novelist. The oldest son of a Lebanese Druze family, Rabih Alameddine was born on October 24, 1959, in Amman, Jordan. His father was born in Caracas, Venezuela, and his mother in Jerusalem, Palestine. Alameddine grew up in Kuwait, spending the summers in Aitat—a small Druze village of his father's ancestors in Mount Lebanon—until he was 10 when he left Kuwait to live with his aunt in Beirut to receive a better education. His parents and two younger sisters followed in 1974. His father retired from Kuwait, built his dream house in his village, and wished to enjoy the fruits of his emigrant experience. These fruits quickly soured. The war in Lebanon erupted in 1975, and Alameddine was sent to boarding school in England. In 1977 he moved to Los Angeles to attend the University of California. He graduated with a degree in mechanical engineering and tried to move back to Lebanon, which proved disastrous: in 1982 the Israeli army invaded the country and the American battleship USS *New Jersey* destroyed his father's dream house with one 16-inch shell. Alameddine returned to the United States and attended business school at the University of San Francisco, graduating with an M.B.A. in 1984. Finance and marketing held his interest even less than engineering. In 1988, when he again attempted living in Lebanon, the Syrian army launched a major bombing campaign.

In 1992 Alameddine took up painting. He had his first solo show in New York in 1994 and in London a year later. Alameddine began writing his first novel, *Koolaids: The Art of War,* in 1996 in San Francisco. The publication of *Koolaids* in 1998 brought immediate recognition to Alameddine. A collection of short stories, *The Perv: Stories,* followed in 1999, but critics have largely ignored it despite the success of *Koolaids. I, the Divine: A Novel in First Chapters* was published in 2001. Like *Koolaids,* it was both critically and commercially successful. Alameddine spent the next six years working on a big novel, *The Hakawati* (The Storyteller).

Alameddine was the recipient of a Guggenheim Fellowship in 2002. He taught creative writing at the American University of Beirut. Alameddine writes insightful essays on contemporary culture and politics (" 'Allah' vs. 'God': Using English to Separate the Two Has Become a Dangerous Practice," *Los Angeles Times,* April 6, 2008). He wrote the introduction to *Homophobia: Views and Positions,* the first book in Arabic to address **homophobia** directly. He currently lives in San Francisco and Beirut.

Critics have been writing about this rising Arab American **gay** writer, but Alameddine disagrees with these labels. "I'm both an Arab and an American, although I have a problem with hyphenated identities, so I don't consider myself an Arab American . . . . I am both us and them. Or more accurately, neither" (Hout 220). Although he is out as a gay man, he does not define himself as a gay writer; he considers himself simply a writer.

His first novel, *Koolaids,* draws a parallel between the AIDS epidemic in the United States and the Civil War in Lebanon, examining the similar effects these disparate events have on the characters. Despite the gloomy topics of this work, Alameddine's humor and style make it a joyous read. As Steven Salaita illustrates, "*Koolaids* utilizes a fragmented narrative to subvert a host of truisms about the Lebanese Civil War, Arab America, homosexuality, immigration, and the AIDS epidemic." *Koolaids'* defining features are "its lack of a defining feature" and "its dissolution of . . . modernist politics" (75). *Koolaids* "is so forthrightly realistic," Salaita adds (78). No book "achieves quite the same level of thematic and poetic complexity . . . it is completely globalized while remaining vigorously local" (74).

Alameddine's second book, *The Perv,* encompasses eight short stories with themes of bigotry, racism, sexual identity, migration, AIDS, the Lebanese War, and death. "Unlike much postcolonial and postwar fiction, neither book is politically motivated nor is concerned with advancing a definition of nationalism or patriotism" (Hout 221). The centerpiece and most troubling story—to some readers—is "The Perv," a self-justifying pedophile's explicit account of his correspondence with a Lebanese American boy.

In some stories in *The Perv,* Alameddine breaks out of **queer** themes. The female protagonist in "Whore" is a Druze painter who tries to figure out where she fits in her family and the world. This story is Alameddine's favorite, and he claims he is closer to the protagonist than all his other characters. The Druze funeral and the graphic sex scene in "Whore" highlight Alameddine's skillful use of language.

His second novel, *I, the Divine,* is subtitled "A Novel in First Chapters." Its protagonist, Sarah, is a Druze woman who, like Alameddine, lived in Lebanon and the United States and has struggled with her relationships and marriages, mirrored in her struggle to write her memoir. She continually rewrites the first chapter from various angles, revealing her character in subtle and not so subtle ways. It eventually becomes clear that a major issue in her difficulties is a violent episode in her life that she struggles to confront: her abduction by a taxicab driver in war-torn Beirut. Alameddine also brings in two queer characters: Sarah's best friend, a Massachusetts Institute of Technology graduate, who is lesbian and happily living in a nurturing relationship, and Sarah's half-brother who is openly and unapologetically gay.

Alameddine uses different writing methods and styles, but the brevity and the fragmentation seem a constant in his first three books. The plots of *Koolaids* and *I, the Divine* are "non-linear and fragmentary, structurally reflecting the ravages of war and the shattered lives of the characters" (Hassan 36). Alameddine also uses polyvocal narration from multiple perspectives.

After the success of his first two novels, Alameddine spent many years on *The Hakawati,* probably his masterpiece, published in 2008. Alameddine gives a modern twist to classic tales borrowed from various sources, such as the Old Testament, the Koran, and *A Thousand and One Nights.* In *The Hakawati,* the framing narrative "concerns a young man's trip from Los Angeles to his father's deathbed in Beirut. There he and his relatives exchange jokes, tear-jerking tales, cliffhangers and legends during the weeks of their vigil" (Adams 8). Some of their stories are contemporary—a great-grandfather falling in love, the 1967 Israeli-Arab war, and the homosexuality of a favorite uncle.

Alameddine uses his talent, wit, humor, and style to write captivating stories that both entertain and show the reader the world from an outsider's perspective, a perspective that can disrupt racism, homophobia, and other forms of prejudice.

Further Reading

Adams, Lorraine. "Once Upon Many Times." *New York Times,* May 18, 2008, 8.

Hassan, Wail S. "Of Lions and Storytelling." *Aljadid: A Review and Record of Arab Culture and Arts* 10, nos. 46/47 (Winter–Spring 2004): 36–37.

Hout, Syrine C. "Memory, Home, and Exile in Contemporary Anglophone Lebanese Fiction." *Critique: Studies in Contemporary Fiction* 46, no. 3 (March 22, 2005): 219–33.

Salaita, Steven. *Arab American Literary Fictions, Cultures, and Politics.* New York: Palgrave Macmillan, 2007.

Bassam Kassab

Albee, Edward (b. 1928)

Playwright, director, and teacher. Edward Albee is generally regarded as one of the most important American playwrights of the twentieth century. Using educated middle-class characters, the openly **gay** Albee explores the anxiety and unfulfilled promise at the heart of the American bourgeois in his four masterpieces, *The Zoo Story* (1958), *Who's Afraid of Virginia Woolf?* (1962), *A Delicate Balance* (1966), and *Three Tall Women* (1991), as well as in a host of other highly regarded works.

Born in Washington, D.C., in 1928, Albee was adopted by Reed and Frances Cotter Albee of Larchmont, New York. Albee's father does not figure prominently in the playwright's biography; he seems to have been literally and figuratively absent. Frances Cotter Albee, however, provides the grist for much of Albee's work. A wealthy socialite unable or unwilling to understand her son, Frances Cotter Albee's anger and indignation fueled her young son's rebellion as he experienced expulsion from two schools before graduating from Choate in 1946. His habitual absences from class and his refusal to attend chapel resulted in his expulsion from Trinity School in his first year, and a subsequent confrontation with his mother left them estranged. She would turn up again and again in his work, however, becoming his primary muse and the subject of *Three Tall Women*. He moved to Greenwich Village in 1949 and began writing.

In 1959, Albee's *The Zoo Story* premiered in West Berlin after several rejections from New York producers. It premiered in the United States at the Provincetown Playhouse in 1960 on a double bill with Samuel Beckett's *Krapp's Last Tape*. Perhaps because of *The Zoo Story*'s initial pairing with the Beckett play and because of the seemingly random, unlikely encounter of Peter and Jerry, *The Zoo Story*'s two characters, early critics of the play often categorized it as a rare example of American absurdism from the school of Eugène Ionesco. Though this categorization has largely stuck, some later critics have seen the characters' encounter as possibly occurring at a gay pickup spot in Central Park. In the play, Jerry, a young, rootless outsider, encounters Peter, a middle-aged exemplar of the middle class, sitting on a bench in Central Park. Jerry engages Peter in a lengthy conversation in which Jerry reveals the sometimes outrageous eccentricities of his bohemian lifestyle while pulling information from Peter about the banality of his bourgeois life. The play culminates in a shocking moment of violence in which Albee uses Peter as a surrogate for the audience as he leaves the stage with an imperative to begin thinking about himself and the construct of his world in new ways.

Albee made his Broadway debut in 1962 with *Who's Afraid of Virginia Woolf?* Its initial run featured Arthur Hill and Uta Hagen in legendary, Tony-winning performances as George and Martha, a middle-aged, upper-middle-class couple living in the ivy-covered realm of academia, who invite a new up-and-coming faculty member from George's university and his wife home for an alcohol-soaked evening of vicious parlor games and wound-picking. The production won five Tony Awards, including one for Best Play, and has been revived twice on Broadway since its original run: in 1976 with George Grizzard and Colleen Dewhurst and in 2005 with Bill Irwin (Tony Award for Best Actor) and Kathleen Turner. The 1965 film version with Richard Burton and Elizabeth Taylor won five Academy Awards, including Best Actress in a Leading Role for Taylor and Best Actress in a Supporting Role for Sandy Dennis. Many important literary figures, including Richard Schechner, Robert Brustein, and Philip Roth, accused Albee in the early 1960s of using his plays—particularly *Virginia Woolf*—of veiling gay subjects, applying adjectives such as "ghastly" and "pansy" to it. Sometimes a Martha is really a Martha, however, and a more responsible, less homophobic reading of the play will see that the unfulfilled promise of George and Martha's marriage and their creation and destruction of an imaginary son is a warning to the young visitors, Nick and Honey, as well as to the audience that sacrificing independent thought and action to conformism and avarice leads only to the death of the self.

Many critics who admired *Virginia Woolf* nonetheless missed many of its intricacies, seeing only a brilliantly worded alcoholic domestic dispute. Consequently, many of them saw his following works as self-conscious and pretentious. *Tiny Alice* (1964), for example, with its theme of the limitation of the human mind in grappling with the idea of God, met with bafflement from many critics, who blamed their confusion on Albee's "pretension" rather than on their expectations for another *Virginia Woolf*. His next play, *A Delicate Balance* (1966), fared better, winning a Best Featured Actress Tony for Marian Seldes, who would become perhaps the finest interpreter of Albee's work, and the Pulitzer Prize for Drama. Dealing again with white, middle-class anxiety, Albee sets his play in the home of Tobias and Agnes, a well-to-do couple, who have never gotten over the death of their son Teddy. Living with them is Agnes's alcoholic sister Claire and their recently arrived and much divorced daughter Julia. The already uneasy atmosphere of the home is further unsettled by the arrival of Tobias and Agnes's friends Harry and Edna, a similar upper-middle-class couple, who have fled their home in terror of something unnamed and seek refuge with their friends, who politely offer sanctuary without asking embarrassing questions. Adapted for the screen in 1973, the play was revived successfully on Broadway in 1996, winning Tony Awards for Best Revival of a Play, Best Actor (George Grizzard), and Best Director (Gerald Gutierrez).

Though *Seascape* (1975) would win Albee a second Pulitzer Prize for Drama, his work continued to divide critics throughout the 1970s and 1980s. Though he was widely recognized as one of America's greatest playwrights, Albee's critics continued to find his work inaccessible and mannered. Meanwhile, Albee became more and more involved with production of his plays, demanding approval of directors, designers, and actors, even understudies. He directed many of his works and continued to mentor new playwrights, a task he had passionately undertaken since the 1960s. In the 1990s, critical doubt seemed to dissipate rapidly with the success of *Three Tall Women,* Albee's third Pulitzer-Prize winner.

Three Tall Women premiered in Berlin in 1991 and debuted in America in Woodstock in 1992. Based on Albee's own mother, the main character, A, is a woman in her 90s reflecting on her life with its joys and pitfalls, including an estrangement from her gay son. B, a middle-aged woman, and C, a younger woman, interact with A but also clearly serve as doppelgangers for her at different points in her life. Through understanding the evolution of the character from C to A, we understand the reaction of her son to her shallow, entrenched values and his self-fashioning in response to his anger toward her. The 1994 New York City production earned Albee nearly universal raves and prompted critical reevaluation of his previous works.

Further Reading

Bigsby, C. W. E., ed. *Edward Albee*. Englewood Cliffs, NJ: Prentice-Hall, 1975.
Kolin, Philip C. *Conversations with Edward Albee*. Jackson: University Press of Mississippi, 1988.
Mann, Bruce J., ed. *Edward Albee: A Casebook*. New York: Routledge, 2003.
McCarthy, Gerry. *Edward Albee*. New York: St. Martin's Press, 1987.

Sinfield, Alan. *Out on Stage: Lesbian and Gay Theatre in the Twentieth Century.* New Haven: Yale University Press, 1999.

Jeff Godsey

Ali, Agha Shahid (1949–2001)

Poet, translator, editor, scholar, anthologist, and professor. The son of Agha Ali and Sufia Nomani, Agha Shahid Ali was born February 4, 1949, in New Delhi. Ali was himself a "multicultural" person: raised both in New Delhi and Kashmir, the beautiful but war-torn region still in dispute between India and Pakistan (a subject of great import in his later poetry), and for a time in Muncie, Indiana, where his father attended graduate school, Ali grew up in multiple traditions, including Muslim, Hindu, and Western cultures, and with four languages, Kashmiri, Persian, Urdu, and English, the language of his poetry. All these were to be influences in both his life and his poetics. After completing a B.A. degree from the University of Kashmir, Srinagar, in 1968 and an M.A. in English from the University of Delhi in 1970, Ali worked as a lecturer in English at the University of Delhi from 1970 to 1975. During this time he published a chapbook of poems, *Bone Sculpture,* in 1972. He then moved to the United States and worked as an instructor at Pennsylvania State University throughout his time in graduate school. In 1979, Ali published another chapbook in India, *In Memory of Begum Akhtar and Other Poems,* a collection that showcases Ali's knowledge of and love for the ancient Persian lyric form of the ghazal, of which Begum Akhtar was the greatest singer; Ali would popularize this form for U.S. audiences in his later and best work. He earned an M.A. in English in 1981 and a Ph.D. in 1984 from Pennsylvania State University; and in 1985, Ali earned an M.F.A. from the University of Arizona where he worked as a graduate assistant from 1983 to his graduation. During this time he also received a number of honors for his work, including Bread Loaf Writers' Conference scholarships in 1982 and 1983 and an Academy of American Poets Prize and a Pennsylvania Council on the Arts Fellowship in 1983. After completing graduate school, he published a scholarly work, *T. S. Eliot as Editor* in 1986. The year 1987 saw the publication of two Ali collections in the United States: *A Walk through the Yellow Pages,* a chapbook; and *The Half-Inch Himalayas,* his first full-length collection. In this breakthrough collection are poems that the critic Maimuna Dali Islam calls "transimmigrant writings" (260), poetry that demonstrates the poet's and his poetry's roots in more than one culture, existing together and independently of both Kashmiri and North American cultures; this can be said of all of Ali's poems from this date forward. In this year, Ali also won an Ingram Merrill Foundation Fellowship. From 1987 to 1993, Ali worked as an Assistant Professor of English and Creative Writing at Hamilton College, taking time in 1989 to teach as Visiting Professor of Creative Writing at the State University of New York, Binghamton, in 1989. In 1991, Ali's major collection appeared, *A Nostalgist's Map of America.* This book, the first of his three final and most important books, can be read as one long love letter to a deceased friend; as an understanding of land's importance; and as homage to the work of Emily Dickinson, many of whose lines Ali reworks into his own poems, and to that of the painter Georgia O'Keefe. This book also establishes the great subjects on which Ali would write the remainder of his life: exile, loss, recovery, and love. Viking published a selection of Ali's poetry in 1992, *The Beloved Witness: Selected Poems.* From 1993 to his death he would serve as Director of Creative Writing at the University of Massachusetts at Amherst. In 1997, Ali published, *The Country without a Post Office,* an important collection deploring the violence done to Kashmir (understanding that violence as connected to other violence worldwide) and revealing Ali's mastery of a variety of forms, including the villanelle, sestina, pantoum, and, of course, the ghazal. Ali brought out an anthology, *Ravishing DisUnities: Real Ghazals in English,* in 2000, both to correct the misuse of the ghazal by poets in English and to demonstrate how the form can be accomplished correctly. *Rooms Are Never Finished* appeared in 2001 with the important canzone "Lenox Hill," a work detailing his sorrow over his mother's death. This collection was nominated for the National Book Award. Ali died from brain cancer on December 8, 2001. A posthumous collection, *Call Me Ishmael Tonight: A Book of Ghazals,* appeared in 2003, confirming Ali's greatness in the ghazal, the form he loved so much and for which he will be known.

Further Reading

Hayahsi, Robert T. "Beyond Walden Pond: Asian American Literature and the Limits of Ecocriticism." In *Coming into Contact: Explorations in Ecocritical Theory and Practice,* edited by Anne Merrill Ingram et al., 58–75. Athens: University of Georgia Press, 2007.

Islam, Maimuna Dali. "A Way in the World of an Asian American Existence: Agha Shahid Ali's Transimmigrant Spacing of North American and India/Kashmir." In *Transnational Asian American Literature: Sites and Transits,* edited by Shirley Goek-Lin Lim et al., 257–73. Philadelphia: Temple University Press, 2006.

Needham, Lawrence. "Agha Shahid Ali." In *Dictionary of Literary Biography. Volume 323: South Asian Writers in English,* edited by Fakrul Alam, 9–14. Detroit: Thomson, 2006.

Newman, Amy. " 'Separation's Geography': Agha Shahid Ali's Scholarship of Evanescence." *The Hollins Critic* 43, no. 2 (April 2006): 1–14.

Billy Clem

Allegra, Donna (b. 1953)

Contemporary African American lesbian poet and essayist. The oldest of two children, Donna Allegra was born in Brooklyn. Her parents separated when she was nine, and Allegra and her brother, Chad, lived with their father. She was estranged from her mother for most of her life and only began to reconnect with her shortly before her mother's death. She was also estranged from her father shortly after high school. Allegra always felt that she did not meet her mother's standards and that neither of her parents accepted her for who she was. She attended Bennington College but graduated from New York University with a B.A. in dramatic literature, theater history, and cinema in 1977. To support her budding writing and dancing career, Allegra trained and worked as an electrician in the construction industry. Her life in a male-centered workplace has clearly influenced her understanding of **gender** politics. She lives in the East Village in New York City where she is currently a full-time writer and dancer.

Donna Allegra has been extensively published in feminist and lesbian/**gay** as well as straight magazines, newspapers, journals, and periodicals. Her work has also appeared in collected works alongside her contemporaries. Allegra has written theater, book, film, and dance reviews for several newspapers. Until recently, her writings had not been published as a collection, and she is yet to receive significant critical attention.

Allegra released her first and only collection of short stories in 2000 entitled *Witness to the League of Blond Hip Hop Dancers.* The collection features 13 stories in which all but one are set in a dance studio in New York City. Each is narrated in the first person by an African American lesbian; many of the stories explore the intersection of sexual desire and racial difference. While the mainstream critical reception of the work was not enthusiastic, Allegra has in recent years become an increasingly visible presence in New York City's informal literary circles public readings and café gatherings.

Further Reading

Pinson, Luvenia. "Donna Allegra." In *Contemporary Lesbian Writers of the United States: A Bio-Bibliographical Critical Sourcebook,* edited by Sandra Pollack and Denise D. Knight, 1–4. Westport, CT: Greenwood Press, 1993.

Donna Dvoracek

Allen, Paula Gunn (b. 1939)

One of the foremost scholars of Native American literature as well as a talented poet, novelist, and essayist. Paula Marie Francis was born in Albuquerque, New Mexico, to Elias Lee and Ethel Haines Gottlieb ('Tu'u-we'ta, "like a song") Francis on October 24, 1939. Raised in Cubero, New Mexico, a Spanish-Mexican land grant village abutting the Laguna and Acoma Indian reservations and the Cibola National Forest, Allen was the third of five children. She refers to herself as a "multicultural event," recalling her Pueblo/Sioux/Scottish American ancestry from her mother and her Lebanese American heritage from her father. These influences account for her ability to bridge perspectives and offer understandings across cultures, religions, and worldviews.

For most of her schooling, Allen attended a Sisters of Charity boarding school in Albuquerque, graduating in 1957. She received a bachelor's degree in English (1966) and a Master of Fine Arts in Creative Writing (1968) from the University of Oregon. In 1975, she received her doctorate in American Studies with an emphasis on Native American literature from the University of New Mexico. However, Allen's personal and professional life was often difficult. She had three marriages and five children before fully realizing that she was lesbian. She had difficulties with editors and professors who wanted her to fit conventional Western literary standards and to disregard her Native American aesthetics.

Allen is the author of numerous volumes of poetry. Because of her multicultural background, Allen can draw upon varying poetic rhythms and structures that emanate from such sources as country and western music, Pueblo corn dances, Catholic masses, Mozart, Italian opera, and Arabic chanting. Allen became interested in writing in high school when she discovered Gertrude Stein, whom she read extensively and tried to copy. Other influences were Euramerican writers such as William Carlos Williams, Robert Creeley, Charles Olson, **Allen Ginsberg**, Denise Levertov, **Adrienne Rich**, Patricia Clark Smith, and E. A. Mares. It was not until she was finishing up her M.F.A. in Oregon that she had any exposure to Native American writers. Feeling isolated and suicidal, Allen says that the presence of a Santee Sioux friend and the discovery of N. Scott Momaday's *House Made of Dawn* (1968) were what helped her to continue.

In addition to being a poet and novelist, Allen is recognized as a major scholar, literary critic, and teacher of Native American literature. She has held teaching positions at San Francisco State University, the University of New Mexico, and the University of California at Berkeley and at Los Angeles. Allen's 1983 *Studies in American Indian Literature:*

Critical Essays and Course Designs, an important text in the field, has an extensive bibliography in addition to information on teaching Native American literatures. *The Sacred Hoop: Recovering the Feminine in American Indian Traditions,* 1986, exhibits Allen's belief in the power of the oral tradition embodied in contemporary Native American literature to effect healing, survival, and continuance that underlies all of her work. It also contains her groundbreaking essay, "Hwame, Koshkalaka, and the Rest: Lesbians in American Indian Cultures," which has served to stimulate a new perspective on research on sexuality and **gender** among tribal groups.

Allen was awarded a National Endowment for the Arts writing fellowship in 1978, and she received a postdoctoral fellowship grant from the Ford Foundation–National Research Council in 1984. She is an activist involved with such movements as antinuclear and antiwar, gay and lesbian, as well as feminist. She is especially well known on the West Coast for her participation in **gay** and lesbian communities. She won an honorable mention from the National Book Award before Columbus Foundation for her 1982 book of poetry, *Shadow Country.* Allen uses the theme of shadows—the not dark and not light—to bridge her experience of mixed heritage as she attempts to respond to the world in its variety. In addition lesbian themes appear in her poetry. Poems such as "Koshkalaka (Ceremonial Dyke)" and "Beloved Women" address Native American lesbian themes while "Some Like Indians Endure" compares society's treatment of Native Americans to that of lesbians.

She won an American Book Award in 1990 for *Spider Woman's Granddaughters: Traditional Tales and Contemporary Writings by Native American Women,* an attempt to correct the lack of stories by and/or about Native Women in literature collections. She also won the 1990 Native Prize for Literature. In her 1991 *Grandmother of the Light: A Medicine Woman's Sourcebook,* Allen expands her interest in the ritual experience of women as exhibited in the traditional stories. She traces the stages in a woman's spiritual path using Native American stories as models for walking in the sacred way. More recently, she has extended her interest in Native American writing by publishing collections of Native writing: *Voice of the Turtle: American Indian Literature 1900–1970* (1994) and *Song of the Turtle: American Literature 1974–1994* (1996). In 2007, Allen won a Lannan Literary Writing Fellowship that honors writers of work of exceptional quality—a fine tribute to her long writing career.

A major theme of Allen's work is delineation and restoration of her Laguna Pueblo woman-centered culture, lost because of the incursion of Euramerican culture. She comes from a culture in which the descent is matrilineal; the women owned the houses and the major deities are female. In a startling article in *Sinister Wisdom* in 1984, "Who Is Your Mother? Red Roots of White Feminism," she articulated Native American contributions to democracy and feminism, countering a popular idea that societies in which women's power was equal to men's never existed.

She has also been a major champion to restore the place of Native American gays and lesbians in the community. These ideas were first published in 1981 in a groundbreaking essay in *Conditions,* "Beloved Women: Lesbians in American Indian Cultures" and then reworked for the *Sacred Hoop.* Further, her work abounds with the mythic dimensions of women's relationship to the sacred, as well as the struggles of contemporary Native American women. Her 1983 novel, *The Woman Who Owned the Shadows,* has a woman character of mixed ancestry reclaiming a Native American woman's spiritual tradition that includes being open to same-sex relationships. Through her poetry, novel, essays, collections of stories, and activism, Allen has made a major contribution to Native American literary studies, American literature, women's studies, and gay and lesbian studies.

See also Lesbian Literature, Native American

Further Reading

Hanson, Elizabeth J. *Paula Gunn Allen*. Boise, ID: Boise State University, 1990.

Keating, AnaLouise. *Women Reading Women Writing: Self-Invention in Paula Gunn Allen, Gloria Anzaldua and Audre Lorde*. Philadelphia: Temple University Press, 1996.

Van Dyke, Annette. "The Journey Back to Female Roots: A Laguna Pueblo Model." In *Lesbian Texts and Contexts,* edited by Karla Jay and Joanne Glasgow, 339–54. New York: New York University Press, 1990.

Annette Van Dyke

Allison, Dorothy (b. 1949)

Lesbian American writer and feminist. Dorothy Allison was born on April 11, 1949, in Greenville, South Carolina, to an unwed mother who was only 15 and working as a waitress to support herself and her baby. Allison had a difficult childhood of dire poverty and social exclusion, living with her mother and an abusive stepfather who discouraged her from attending school. Allison's eventual confrontation of her stepfather's sexual, physical, and emotional abuse led to a years-long estrangement from her mother. She was the first in her family to graduate from high school, eventually earning her B.A. from Florida Presbyterian College, which she was able to attend with support from a National Merit Scholarship. In 1979, she studied anthropology at The New School for Social Research in New York City. While in college, Allison became active in the women's movement, and she credits the support of her fellow feminists with allowing her to heal from her childhood experiences, reconcile with her mother and other family members, and begin writing. Allison remained deeply involved with both the feminist and lesbian and **gay** movements during the 1970s and 1980s, not only drawn to the political fight for women's equality, but also the cultural milieu of lesbian feminism at the time, serving as an editor and contributing author of the award-winning feminist, gay, and lesbian literary journals *Quest, Conditions,* and *Outlook.* The focus of these journals was not only writing that reflected women's, gay, or lesbian experiences, but also leftist political concerns such as the class struggle, socialism, and the political empowerment of sexual minorities. Allison first published a chapbook of poetry in 1983 entitled *The Women Who Hate Me* and in 1988 lesbian publishing house Firebrand Books published a critically acclaimed collection of her short stories, *Trash,* which won two Lambda Literary awards and the American Library Association Award for Gay and Lesbian Writing. From that point on, Allison's literary reputation continued to grow within the gay community. The publication of *Bastard Out of Carolina* (1992), a semiautobiographical account of growing up poor and illegitimate in the southern United States in which the protagonist suffers emotional, physical, and sexual abuse at the hands of her stepfather, brought her mainstream attention for the first time, including a glowing full-page review in *The New York Review of Books;* the novel went on to become a best seller. *Bastard Out of Carolina* has been translated into more than a dozen languages and made into a television movie, in spite of its graphic depictions of poverty and childhood sexual abuse, which many readers found shocking.

Because of this, the book attracted controversy when a film version starring Anjelica Huston was shown on the Showtime network in 1996 and was subsequently banned from ever being shown or sold in Canada. Allison's second novel, *Cavedweller* (1998), also chronicled the experiences of a woman in the Deep South, but this time the protagonist is herself a mother. *Cavedweller* was also very successful and was adapted for the stage and, in 2003, a movie. Allison has also received widespread critical acclaim for her other literary works, including her memoir *Two or Three Things I Know for Sure* (1995) and a short story collection *Trash* (1988), which was republished in an expanded version in 2002; it included a new short story entitled "Compassion" that received numerous awards, including being selected as one of 2003's Best American Short Stories. In addition to her work as a novelist, poet, short story writer, and memoirist, Allison has remained engaged with the feminist movement that first inspired her to write, as well as contemporary **queer theory**. In *Skin: Talking about Sex, Class & Literature* (1994), she brings her autobiography to bear on wider social issues. Through a combination of essays, short fiction, and performance pieces, Allison describes her political beliefs and identifies herself as an outsider, whose background as a poor, working-class southerner, a feminist, and a lesbian simultaneously raise her awareness of—and freedom to transcend—the invisible boundaries that define what it means to belong to any of these categories, or to none of them. Currently, Allison lives in California with her partner Alix and son Wolf. She frequently serves as a lecturer, writer in residence, and writing teacher and mentor at colleges and universities in the United States and Europe.

Further Reading

Dorothy Allison Homepage. February, 2008. http://www.dorothyallison.net/.
Gilmore, Leigh. *Trauma and Testimony.* Ithaca, NY: Cornell University Press, 2001.

Michele Erfer

Als, Hilton (b. 1961)

African American theater critic, columnist, screenwriter, and autobiographer. Born in the Flatbush district of Brooklyn, New York, to Marie Als, an immigrant woman from Barbados, Hilton Als is the middle child, born between an older sister and a younger brother. By the time Als was eight years old, he had expressed a desire to become a writer. He attended public school but, uncomfortable in the structured environment, he often cut classes to go to the library. Encouraged by his mother's love for reading and an English teacher, he began secretly writing serious prose when he was 13 years old, which also coincided with his bourgeoning sexual difference, signified by his flair for dramatic fashion. Later, after majoring in art history at Columbia University and dropping out to become a secretary for the *New York Village Voice,* Als began realizing his dream of being a writer. After writing his first piece on New York writer Ian Frazier, Als moved from secretary to contributor. It was his refreshing memoir *The Women* (1998), a personal and psychological study that poignantly showcases the role gender and race play in establishing sexual identity, that further elevated his status as a noteworthy writer. In his nonfiction novel, Als reveals a writerly genius that challenges the personal memoir as a form, the limitations of essential blackness, and the stifling disengagement with gender and sexuality by African American political communities. Creating theoretical and personal tropes such as "the Negress" and "the Auntie Man," Als discusses the relationship with his Caribbean mother and other black women throughout the text. While Als documents the influence of many black women in his life, one of the most important relationships in his life came from a black male.

From the age of 15 until he was 19 years old, Hilton Als was engaged in an intimate relationship with the illustrious poet, playwright, and theater scholar Owen Dodson. It was during this time that Dodson became a lover and the first professional mentor to Als. Dodson's competitive distaste for and identification with women, as well as his Harlem Renaissance influences, made him a unique role model. In Als's assessment of Dodson's commitment and crushing self-sacrifice to New Negro politics, readers learn of how Als finds his own voice and understanding of blackness for the late twentieth century. It is a voice that has been valued and rewarded for its originality and tenacity.

Als won the prestigious 2002–2003 George Jean Nathan Award for Dramatic Criticism. Scholars from Cornell University, Yale University, and Princeton University awarded Als the $100,000 prize for his efforts in theater criticism. He is the former editor of *Vibe* magazine and a former staff writer of the *Village Voice*. He became a frequent freelance contributor to *The New Yorker* magazine's "Talk of the Town" section. In 1996, he became a regular contributor and in 2002 a critic for its theater section. In 2000, he won the prestigious Guggenheim Fellowship for Creative Writing. In 2007, the New York Association of Black Journalists awarded him first place in two categories: "Magazine Critique/Review" and "Magazine Arts and Entertainment."

In addition to *The Women*, Als wrote *The Group* (2001). He co-authored (with David Margolick and Ellis Marsalis) *Strange Fruit: The Biography of a Song*. He co-edited (with Darryl A. Turner) *White Noise: The Eminem Collection*. He has contributed to various magazines and newspapers: *Essence, Interview, Nation, New York Times Magazine, The New Yorker, Out, Vibe,* and the *New York Village Voice*. He also was a contributor to the Whitney Museum Catalogs (1994). Beyond print media, he wrote the screenplays for *Swoon* (1991) and the groundbreaking film *Looking for Langston* (1989). He also served as co-writer (with Turner) of *Don't Explain,* a screenplay being produced by Christine Vachon at Killer Films, producers of the films *Boys Don't Cry* and *Hedwig and the Angry Inch*.

Further Reading

Als, Hilton. *The Women.* New York: Farrar, Straus, and Giroux. 1998.
Jones, Jacqueline C. "Hilton Als." In *African American Autobiographers: A Sourcebook,* edited by Emmanuel S. Nelson, 5–9. Westport, CT: Greenwood Press, 2002.
Kelley, Adam. "In Profile." *Advocate* 722 (October 1996): 74–76.

L. H. Stallings

Alther, Lisa (b. 1944)

Author of five best-selling novels, a memoir, essays, and short stories. Lisa Alther's fiction, filled with quirky characters and wry humor, depicts women struggling with identity and societal pressures while often discovering strength and sexuality along the way. Her female characters, from teens to middle age, defy labels and stereotypes of sexual orientation and often find themselves through the love of other women.

One of five children of John Shelton, a Virginia doctor, and Alice Margaret Reed, an upstate New Yorker and English teacher, Lisa (pronounced Liza) Alther was born in Kingsport, Tennessee, on July 23, 1944. Educated in public schools in east Tennessee, Alther went on to graduate from Wellesley College in 1966 with a B.A. in English literature. On August 26 that year, she married Richard Philip Alther, a painter from New Jersey, at a large wedding in Tennessee. The couple moved to New York City and later to a Vermont farm where Lisa raised their one daughter, Sara Halsey, after their divorce. Alther worked for Atheneum Publishers in New York and taught as a visiting lecturer in southern fiction at St. Michael's College in Winooski, Vermont. After living in Paris and London, Alther currently divides her time between homes in New York City and Hinesburg, Vermont.

After 250 rejections, Alther's first novel, *Kinflicks,* was published in 1976. The book not only became a best seller, but has also gone through over 29 paperback reprintings and has been translated into over 15 other languages. Alther drew heavily on her Tennessee roots for the story. The book's alternating chapters detail the life of Ginny Babcock Bliss during her present-day vigil by her dying mother's bedside in rural Tennessee and her varied past and love life from high school to adulthood. Ginny reinvents herself for each of her lovers, including her lesbian relationship that ends tragically when her lover is killed. Ginny's flashback episodes are filled with humorous antics and hilarious dialogue, a drastic contrast with the grim reality of her mother's approaching death. As Ginny fights through kudzu each day on the farm, she begins to slowly reclaim her own life while reconciling herself to losing her mother.

Alther has written four other novels since *Kinflicks,* each with intriguing characters struggling with identity and sexuality. *Original Sins* (1981), also set in Tennessee, follows the story of five individuals from youth to adulthood. Like Ginny of *Kinflicks,* Emily, one of the primary characters in *Original Sins,* moves north and becomes increasingly aware of her lesbian identity. Alther uses a third-person narrator to comment on many southern issues, including racism and religion. *Other Women* (1984) and *Bedrock* (1990), both set in Vermont, depict the struggle of older protagonists. Carolyn Kelley of *Other Women* is a single mother and lesbian whose story is told through her meetings with her therapist. *Bedrock*'s Clea Shawn, a married mother of two children, decides to buy a home in a small Vermont town during her mid-life crisis. While struggling to restore the home and find stability in her life, Clea slowly discovers that she is in love with her longtime friend, Elka. Jude, the main character of *Five Minutes in Heaven* (1996), like Alther, moves from Tennessee to New York City and then to Paris. Jude is rather androgynous and, like so many Alther characters, is on a quest for identity and love.

Her most recent work, *Kinfolks: Falling Off the Family Tree* (2007), is a memoir recounting Alther's search for identity much like the exploration that her characters experience. With two of her novels set in the South and others embracing a small community, Alther's southern roots continue to entwine with her rural Vermont farm life. This memoir sheds light on the geography of this identity crisis experienced at an early age with a mother from New York and a father from Virginia. The feelings of isolation, confused identity, and struggle between worlds are very much a function of Alther's fiction as they have been a part of her life.

Further Reading

Ferguson, Mary Anne. "Lisa Alther." In *Contemporary Fiction Writers of the South: A Bio-Bibliographical Sourcebook,* edited by Joseph M. Flora and Robert Bain, 22–31. Westport, CT: Greenwood Press, 1993.

Hall, Joan Lord. "Symbiosis and Separation in Lisa Alther's Kinflicks." *Arizona Quarterly* 38 (Winter 1982): 336–46.

Pond, Wayne J. "Lisa Alther: Healing Laughter." In *Appalachia and Beyond: Conversations with Writers from the Mountain South,* edited by John Lang, 275–91. Knoxville: University of Tennessee Press, 2006.

Ruth R. Caillouet

Alumit, Noel (b. 1968)

Author, creative writing instructor, playwright, and performance artist. Noel Alumit was born in the Philippines, the second of four children. He immigrated to the United States as a toddler when his mother obtained a job in Boston. In the early 1970s, the family settled in Los Angeles, which Alumit continues to call home.

Alumit's adolescence was marked by a strong belief in his creativity—he obtained a theatrical agent at age 15—and certainty regarding his sexual orientation; however, it was not until he was pursuing a drama degree at the University of Southern California that he began to accept his sexual orientation. Drawing upon a love of the theatrical and his personal experiences, Alumit found success in performance art, writing several critically acclaimed pieces including "The Rice Room: Scenes from a Bar," an examination of the lives of **gay** Asian men.

Longing to explore the creative process more deeply, Alumit abandoned the collaborative nature of performance work and tried writing longer pieces. He discovered the "Emerging Voices" writing program sponsored by PEN (Poets, Playwrights, Editors, Essayists, and Novelists) USA West. The PEN, designed to develop writing talents from underserved communities, seemed ideal for Alumit, a Filipino gay man raised in the inner city. After submitting pages from a draft novel, he was accepted into the six-month course and emerged a writer. Those draft pages became Alumit's first novel, *Letters to Montgomery Clift*.

Letters concerns the young Filipino Bong-Bong, sent to the United States to escape the Marcos regime. Living with a neglectful aunt devoted to writing letters to dead ancestors, Bong-Bong yearns to reunite with his parents. He finds solace in Montgomery Clift movies and begins writing the letters that constitute the novel's epistolary style. Through the letters, Alumit weaves a coming-of-age and coming out story addressing immigration, class, and the horrific effects of the Marcos dictatorship. Ultimately, the book's message is about finding the faith to face life's disappointments.

Alumit relied upon personal influences and experiences to produce *Letters*. Compelled to write about society's underdogs, Alumit was influenced by the fantasy elements in Maurice Sendak's works, which fit nicely with the Hollywood upbringing that allowed Alumit to idolize Clift in real life. Judy Blume's misfit characters were translated by Alumit into Bong-Bong's marginalized status as a gay Filipino youth. Alumit's first novel received favorable reviews and garnered several awards, including the American Library Association's **Stonewall** Book Award, the **Violet Quill** Award, and the Global Filipino Literary Award, was nominated for the Lambda Literary Award, the PEN West Coast Award, and received several other accolades.

Since the success of *Letters,* Alumit has penned an additional novel, *Talking to the Moon* (2007), contributed pieces to anthologies and magazines, and served as guest editor for *Blithe House Quarterly* and as adjunct instructor at UCLA's Extension Writer's Program. Currently, he is working on a third novel.

Further Reading

Bunn, Austin. "Montgomery and Me." *The Advocate* (July 9, 2002): 38–39.

Dhalla, Ghalir Shiraz. "For Saints and Sinners: First-Time Novelist Noel Alumit Writes to the Dead." *Asianweek* 23, no. 35 (April 24, 2002): 25.

Matheson, Whitney. "Tragedy Inspires Alumit's 'I Love You.'" *USA Today* (August 15, 2002): D5.

Ellen Bosman

Alvarez, Aldo (b. 1965)

Innovative short story writer and publisher. Aldo Alvarez's biggest contribution to lesbian, **gay**, bisexual, transgender, and **queer** (LGBTQ) literature is highlighting the myriad voices that exist in queer fiction through his journal *Blithe House Quarterly*. Aldo Alvarez was born January 16, 1965, and raised in Mayagüez, Puerto Rico. Although his parents spoke only Spanish, they raised Alvarez to be bilingual. By first grade he was able to read, speak, and write in English. His parents also made sure to send Alvarez and his siblings to private schools. Alvarez pinpoints his ninth grade English teacher as the source of much of his inspiration. In this class, Alvarez's teacher acquainted him with the works of writers such as James Joyce, Saki, and Kurt Vonnegut. However, when Alvarez came to the United States, his stance on cultural understandings was so mixed that he felt as if he belonged to neither. Despite this newfound perplexity, Alvarez's love of language became clear. He earned his bachelor's degree from Xavier University, his master's in Creative Writing from Columbia University, and his doctorate in English from Binghamton University.

There is no one word to describe Alvarez's writing style, as his writing is as varied as his literary influences. Alvarez has received awards for not only his unique writing style but also his impact on the LGBTQ literary community. Alvarez was the recipient in 2004 for the Trailblazer's Award and a 2002 Nominee for the **Violet Quill** Award. Alvarez is the founder, executive editor, and publisher of *Blithe House Quarterly*, which was nominated for the Gay & Lesbian Alliance Against Defamation (GLAAD) Media Award and recognized by *Out* magazine as a leading medium for queer fiction. Currently, Alvarez lives, writes, publishes, and teaches in Chicago. He is a professor of English at Wilbur Wright College and Northwestern University. Recently, Alvarez was a Visiting Writer at Indiana University at Bloomington.

Alvarez's most notable work of fiction is *Interesting Monsters* (2001). The highest praises for the collection are its selection as one of the best short story collections of Fall 2001 by the *Washington Post* Book World and being listed in *OUT Magazine*'s December 2001 issue as one of the 100 greatest LGBTQ success stories. The subject of much favorable review, *Interesting Monsters* is a collection of short stories. However, some critics argue that the work is actually a well-constructed novel. Most of the stories are linked together by the relationship of Mark Piper and Dean Rodriguez. Mark is a former rock star turned producer, slightly homophobic initially, and in his 40s. Dean, an antiques dealer, has AIDS and moves back to Puerto Rico for his remaining days of life. The reader learns that the titular monsters are not specific characters but characteristics of society: prejudice and hatred. Alvarez, in an interview conducted by Jarrett Walker of *Pif Magazine*, expresses how Mark and Dean complement each other as Mark is someone no longer cherished or deemed useful to society and Dean is in a profession that highlights the beauty of items that have been devalued by people. The mix of linear and nonlinear plots in *Interesting Monsters* and just as eclectic characters pushes the boundaries of traditional fiction.

Alvarez's writing at times reads like the magical realism of Gabriel García Márquez or the fantasy of Jorge Luis Borges. Prose poem "Tokens" (2006), though brief, gives an interesting depiction of what can be done when one realizes the skill that anthropomorphism and/or personification requires. "Tokens" includes an iron, a shoe, a top hat, a sports car, and a thimble that reflect or comment on aspects of life.

Alvarez is prolific in writing short stories. "Property Values" (1995) has been reprinted in several publications. "Property" is based on the characters Mark and Dean from *Interesting Monsters* in Puerto Rico. The story is told from the point of view of a real estate broker, Claudia, who is literally appalled when she learns that her clients are gay. In the end, Claudia is made to look the fool. "Flatware" (1997) chronicles some experiences and thoughts a teacher has. This short story is reprinted as "Property Values." More recent works include "Up Close" (2002), "A Private Amusement" (2002), "Quintessence" (2001), and "Losing Count" (2000).

Further Reading

Heintz, Kurt. "Blithe House Quarterly: Publishing Queer Fiction Online." e-poets.network. May 21, 2004. e-poets network. http://www.e-poets.net/PlainText/page04-003.shtml.

Walker, Jarrett. "Interview with Aldo Alvarez." *Pif Magazine.* May 1, 2002. Amazon.com. http://www.pifmagazine.com/SID/200/.

Stephanie B. Crosby

Amisano, David Christopher (b. 1972)

Commercial writer and novelist. David Christopher Amisano's very beginning was an oddity; his parents, told that they could not have biological children, had just adopted a son when his mother became pregnant with him. He was born April 23, 1972, in Memphis, Tennessee. Raised in a loving but staunchly conservative Christian environment, Amisano spent his Sundays in church and sang in his Southern Baptist Church's youth ensemble. He earned a bachelor's degree in Spanish Language and Literature from the University of Memphis, as well as a touch of worldly ways via his membership in Pi Kappa Phi Fraternity. Baptized in his church's teachings of homosexuality as a damnable sin, Amisano married his high school sweetheart shortly after college graduation. The marriage dissolved within two years as he accepted his homosexuality and came out to himself, his family, and friends.

Amisano then took off, quite literally, becoming a flight attendant based in San Francisco. This was a time not only for self-actualization, but a means of character study that would later serve as a personal vault for his work. Having slain many of his demons, he moved back to Memphis and resumed his college career of banking and corporate training instruction. It was during this time that he met his partner Art Cavalier. Their two-year relationship ended tragically with Art's death from cancer at the age of 27. Amisano was to channel his grief, as well as a dim spark of hope, into his work.

The loss of his partner forced Amisano into a new phase, and he relocated to south Florida in 2000. His days were immersed in the corporate world and his evenings were spent writing, primarily short stories and online articles.

In 2007, Amisano published *An Imperfect Arrangement,* a quasi-autobiographical novel of Alex Palini, a 35-year-old **gay** man in search of genuine love and adventure. Palini's partner Ayers had passed away three years prior, and Palini has taken up with his younger boyfriend Stephen, also known as Disposable Boy. Palini lives in a 1920s apartment building in midtown Memphis, as Amisano himself did, referring to himself as a "good Southern boy." Palini's lost happiness since Ayers's passing arrives in a new neighbor, Rick Monette. Yet the path to joy is fraught with confusion, longing, and a touch of southern gay gothic.

Despite the loss of his partner and the struggle of coming out in a conservative, religious environment, Amisano's work remains anchored in hope. His characters fall in love, obtain the happiness they yearn for, and give the reader a piece of happily ever after. The use of sarcasm and humor is commonplace in his work and tempers any sweetness. His result is a world that anyone, gay or straight, would want to own.

Further Reading

Review of *An Imperfect Arrangement. Kirkus Reviews.* June 22, 2007. www.kirkusreviews.com/kirkusreviews/search/article_display.jsp?vnu_content_id=1003628708.

Trisha Patton Gurley

Androgyny

The word originates from the Greek *andro* (man) and *gyne* (woman) and refers to a state or condition of the merging of feminine and masculine traits or of having no differentiation between the two. This dual definition creates problems in determining the primary and secondary meanings of the term. Hermaphrodite lies on the fringe of the concept of androgyny because of its peripheral association with the physiological/physical ambiguity of the sex organs. Androgyny as a psychological blending of masculine and feminine characteristics within one individual serves as the primary meaning of the concept. The spectrum of the possibilities in such blending of masculine and feminine traits in a single individual can range from the harmonious and balanced to the one-sided and distorted and anything in between, consequently affecting variations in behavior, emotions, attitudes, and social roles. The interplay between sexuality, **gender**, and identity reshapes the intricate complexities of the notion of androgyny and reflects much of the theoretical and scholarly work on androgyny in the twentieth century.

The blurring of the boundaries between the traditionally imposed binary oppositions of masculine and feminine inspired a long-lasting aesthetic-philosophical, mythological, and literary interest in the notion of androgyny. Androgyny had been a popular cultural construct in many mythological, religious, and philosophical doctrines starting from Hinduism and Taoism and reaching to alchemy, Kabbalah, Gnosticism, and beyond. In her study *Androgyny: Toward a New Theory of Sexuality* (1977), June Singer, a Jungian psychoanalyst, points out that the idea of androgyny has been recurrent in many cultural traditions, thus revealing the manifestations of the collective unconscious.

Androgyny often was used as a symbol of the empowering psychosexual union of male self and female other. Such presentation of androgyny involved a desire to usurp specific gender characteristics without erasing gender demarcations entirely. The assumption of the unification of the sexes based on the fusion of the silent and passive female and the active and dominant male characterized many representations of androgyny well into the nineteenth century. In her famous book *Romantic Androgyny: The Women Within* (1990), Diane Long Hoeveler argues that "the androgynous fantasy demanded that women be essentially different from man and therefore a complementary force, but sexual differences institutionalized as gender roles have always been culturally understood as ideologies that justify inequality" (5).

However, in the late nineteenth and early twentieth centuries, new discoveries in sexology, psychology, anthropology, and creative explorations of sexuality in literature challenged and destabilized the hierarchical, binary relation between the sexes. Sigmund Freud's influential theory of bisexuality in his *Three Essays on the Theory of Sexuality* (1905), Carl Jung's theory of anima and animus in his *Two Essays on Analytical Psychology* (1916), American sexologists G. Frank Lydston and J. G. Kiernan's theory of innate hermaphroditism, and artistic experiments with psychosexual imagination in William Faulkner, Virginia Woolf, James Joyce, H. D., and Sherwood Anderson all prepared the ground for the blurring of gender demarcations. In her essay collection, *Moments of Being* (1939), Virginia Woolf's canonical literary motto about the androgynous mind proclaims the essential nature of "some collaboration" that "has to take place in the mind between the woman and the man before the act of creation can be accomplished" ("A Sketch of the Past" 104). The new vision of androgyny as a fluid and flexible exchange of masculine and feminine characteristics brings about the rapprochement of the sexes; the sexual indeterminacy reflects the range of proportions in which the masculine and feminine coexist in the individual. "There are innumerable reasons for this growing sense of sexual indeterminacy, among them the suffrage movement, the new science of anthropology and its discovery of primitive matriarchy, and the effects of the Industrial Revolution and the First World War—specifically the entrance of rising numbers of women in traditionally male professions," Lisa Rado observes in her book, *The Modern Androgyne Imagination* (10).

Despite the early enthusiasm about androgyny among intellectuals and artists, American society as a whole seemed unprepared to accept the fluidity and indeterminacy of gender roles. The highly conservative social environment during the 1930s and 1950s advocated the strict codification of gendered representation and sexual morality. It explains why Alfred C. Kinsey's works on sexual behavior, *Sexual Behavior in the Human Male* (1948) and *Sexual Behavior in the Human Female* (1953), caused a revolution in sexual awareness and an eager interest in human sexuality. Historians argue that the conservative periods of the 1930s and 1950s characterized by puritanical and strictly conditioned sexual behaviors led to the explosion of the Sexual Revolution in the 1960s.

As a result, the stifling and limiting gender paradigms of the earlier years started collapsing and morphing into the newly defined androgynous representations of identity. In the early 1970s, a famous feminist psychologist, Sandra Lipsitz Bem, introduced the concept of "psychological androgyny" to describe those men and women whose behavior, motivation, and self-concept transcended the traditionally defined gender roles in society. In one of her later articles "Androgyny and Gender Schema Theory: A Conceptual and Empirical Integration" (1984), she defines the androgynous individual as the one whose personality combines both masculine and feminine elements.

Other notable works on androgyny explore androgyny as a rhetorical embodiment of male-female unity and androgyny as a free exchange of gender roles. Carolyn Heilbrun's highly acclaimed book, *Toward a Recognition of Androgyny* (1982), defines androgyny as "a movement away from sexual polarization and the prison of gender toward a world in which individual roles and modes of personal behavior can be freely chosen" (ix). In her book *Androgyny and the Denial of Difference* (1992), Kari Weil views androgyny as an aesthetic union of masculine and feminine, that is, the self and the other, through language. The problem the author poses is whether or not the androgynous mentality/discourse transgresses and transcends the boundaries of sexual difference and identity.

As reconstructions of traditional gender categories open new opportunities for self-exploration and self-realization, androgyny lies at the center of such cultural, aesthetic, and psychological transformations. Challenging or redefining the very notion of self and identity, the ambivalent power of androgyny seems to have a potential to simultaneously suppress and validate the difference within—of man within woman and/or woman within man. The latest approach to androgyny focuses on the affirmation of difference, not a confirmation of sameness and blurred identity, thus questioning and destabilizing the traditional understanding of androgyny as a fusion and nondifferentiation between masculine and feminine aspects. In her book *Androgynous Imagination of Difference* (2007), Alla Boldina emphasizes that the recognition of androgyny as a genuine interplay between masculine and feminine elements within a single individual and the dynamic dialogue between the equally valid male and female modes of being, feeling, and perceiving can bring about the birth of a new consciousness based on the union of difference and respect for subjectivity. Is it indeed a possibility that reflects our own revisions of masculinities and femininities?

Further Reading

Boldina, Alla. *Androgynous Imagination of Difference.* VDM Verlag: Dr. Muller, 2007.

Heilbrun, Carolyn. *Toward a Recognition of Androgyny.* New York: Norton, 1982.

Hoeveler, Diane. *Romantic Androgyny: The Women Within.* University Park: Pennsylvania State University Press, 1990.

Rado, Lisa. *The Modern Androgyne Imagination: A Failed Sublime.* Charlottesville: University Press of Virginia, 2000.

Singer, June. *Androgyny: Toward a New Theory of Sexuality.* New York: Anchor Books, 1977.

Weil, Kari. *Androgyny and the Denial of Difference.* Charlottesville: University Press of Virginia, 1992.

Woolf, Virginia. *Moments of Being,* edited by Jeanne Schulkind. New York: Harcourt, 1976.

Alla Boldina

Angels in America

Tony Kushner's groundbreaking, extraordinarily imaginative, and highly acclaimed play *Angels in America: A Gay Fantasia on National Themes* actually comprises two separate but linked plays: *Part One: Millennium Approaches* and *Part Two: Perestroika*. However, Kushner notes that the two plays are very different, with the second moving forward from the first, and that, if staged together, this difference should be clear to the audience. *Angels in America* is distinctively theatrical, not least because it uses a cast of only eight actors to play several roles and also employs several split scenes. The play is set in New York City in the mid-1980s, a time when AIDS was emerging as a major national health epidemic but was largely ignored by the Reagan administration, and when funding for many social programs was being slashed, including those for the homeless and the mentally ill.

Part One: Millennium Approaches is composed of three acts: "Bad News" (Oct.–Nov. 1985), "In Vitro" (Dec. 1986–Jan. 1986), and "Not-Yet-Conscious, Forward Dawning" (Jan. 1986). The play centers primarily around two couples, one **gay** and one straight, with other storylines intertwined as well. The central character, Prior Walter, is dying of AIDS, and the inability of his lover, Louis Ironson, to deal with the horror and ugliness of the illness leads him to move out, enduring guilt and self-loathing for abandoning Prior. Joe Pitt and his wife, Harper, are Mormons who have emigrated from Utah to Brooklyn, where Joe works as chief clerk for a judge in the Federal Court of Appeals. Joe, a staunch Republican, is a repressed homosexual who is gradually forced to come to terms with his real identity, while Harper, a Valium addict who is prone to hallucinations and fantasies, suspects her husband's latent sexuality. Both are conflicted, given that homosexuality and addiction are against the Mormon religion.

Joe's mentor, the McCarthyist lawyer Roy Cohn, is also a **closet**ed homosexual who, by the end of the play, is also dying of AIDS, though he refuses to acknowledge it as anything more than liver cancer. Cohn offers Joe a promotion to a Justice Department position in Washington, although the real reason he wants Joe to accept the job is so that Cohn will have an inside connection to help him escape impending disbarment, due to his shady legal practices. The idealistic Joe, shocked that Cohn would expect him to engage in illegal behavior, refuses the job, and he is even more outraged when he learns of Cohn's illicit conspiracy in the execution of accused American traitors Julius and Ethel Rosenberg. Another character in the play is an African American ex-drag queen and nurse named Belize, who provides comfort to Prior after Louis has left him, and who ironically administers to Cohn in his hospital room, despite his hatred of the man. Belize, in fact, serves as the key moral voice in the play, a unifying figure who demonstrates compassion and forgiveness for all.

In the course of the play, Joe becomes involved with Louis, and at one point, he calls his mother, Hannah, in the middle of the night, from a phone booth in Central Park, to tell her that he is gay. Shocked but determined, Hannah puts her Salt Lake City house up for sale and travels to Brooklyn to try and salvage her son and to take care of Harper. Meanwhile, as Cohn's illness worsens, he is haunted by the ghost of Ethel Rosenberg. Likewise, as Prior continues to deteriorate, he is visited by the ghosts of his ancestors, two Priors among dozens in a lineage that reaches back to the Mayflower, even perhaps as far back as the eleventh century. Prior also imagines that his nurse is speaking in Hebrew, sees a vision of a great steel book emerging from the hospital floor, and periodically hears the Voice of the Angel, who tells him that he is a prophet and whose resplendent appearance marks the end of the play.

Part Two: Perestroika comprises five acts: "Spooj" (Jan. 1986), "The Epistle" (Feb. 1986), "Borborygmi (The Squirming Facts Exceed the Squamous Mind)" (Feb. 1986), "John Brown's Body" (Feb. 1986), and "Heaven, I'm in Heaven" (Feb. 1986), followed by an Epilogue. Kushner considers this play, which concerns how the characters learn to move forward and let go of the past with grace and dignity, to be essentially a comedy. *Perestroika* opens with the World's Oldest Living Bolshevik speaking at the Kremlin, questioning whether people can indeed change, whether humanity can survive without a theory akin to Marxism, or whether the world is in fact doomed. This opening scene ends with a transition to the end of *Part One: Millennium Approaches,* where Prior cowers in his bed below the imposing figure of the Angel.

Much of *Perestroika* illuminates the dissolutions that occurred in *Millennium*. One scene depicts Harper in a hallucinatory Antarctica with her travel agent, Mr. Lies, where she chews down a pine tree to burn for warmth, but the scene dissipates into Brooklyn, where Harper is arrested for stealing the tree from the Botanical Gardens. Joe has moved in with Louis, though the two will eventually come to blows—literally—when Louis discovers that Joe has written "legal" decisions that betrayed gay people. Roy Cohn is by now in the hospital, where he again sees the ghost of Ethel Rosenberg, who gleefully informs Roy that he has been officially disbarred. Roy also blackmails Martin Heller, a Justice Department cohort who appears in *Millennium,* into securing for him a large quantity of the coveted AIDS drug AZT, a stash that Belize smuggles away after Roy dies.

In another scene, Prior tells Belize about the Angel, who has now revealed his/her message that God abandoned the human race on April 18, 1906, the day of the Great San Francisco Earthquake, being fed up with humankind's incessant need for change. The Angel's advice is to stay put, a proposition Belize considers malevolent and that is, as *Perestroika* demonstrates, impossible, since people are capable only of forward movement.

Meanwhile, Hannah has signed on as a volunteer at the Mormon Visitors Center in Manhattan, which features a Diorama Room depicting the westward migration of the Mormons. In a scene here with Prior and Harper, the dummy of the father figure in the Diorama turns into Joe, and Louis also enters the stage. The dummy of the mother figure leaves the theater with Harper, and the two women are later seen on the Brooklyn Promenade, where the mother describes the male domination of the Mormon passage.

In the final act of *Perestroika,* the Angel appears in Prior's hospital room, dressed in black, and engages him in a wrestling match reflecting the Biblical scene of Jacob's similar struggle. A brilliant ladder appears, and the Angel demands that Prior return to Heaven the Book he received in *Millennium*. Prior does so, only to discover that Heaven looks much like the aftermath of the San Francisco earthquake, and he decides he wants to return to Earth. When he awakens in his bed, he tells Hannah and the others that he has had a dream in which they appeared, a parody of Dorothy's dream recollection at the end of *The Wizard of Oz*. Louis comes to Prior's room, asking forgiveness and wanting to come back, but Prior rejects him; similarly, at the Pitts' home in Brooklyn, Harper tells Joe that she is leaving him. Act 5 ends with Joe alone in Brooklyn and Harper in a window seat on a plane bound for San Francisco.

The play's Epilogue, *Bethesda,* takes place in February 1990 at the statue of that name in Central Park, with Prior, Louis, Belize, and Hannah sitting on its edge. Momentous events have occurred in the intervening years: the fall of the Berlin Wall (1989), the demise of the Nicolae Ceauçescu regime (Romania), and Mikhail Gorbachev's initiation to restructure the Soviet economy: Perestroika. Prior has continued to live with AIDS; Louis tells the story of the healing powers of Bethesda Angel; Hannah predicts that when the Millennium comes, the fountain's mythical waters will flow once again; and the play ends on a forward note that the time has come for a new kind of society.

Kushner's sweeping epic is so richly textured and layered that many themes emerge, including **gender** politics, community, power, exile, history, race, love and loss, isolation and abandonment, loyalty and friendship, justice and democracy, illness, forgiveness, and salvation. The play's subtitle highlights two primary themes: "gay" and "national," and Kushner tackles these broad topics by focusing on individuals and their situations. *Angels in America* unflinchingly confronts the AIDS crisis from both a personal and a social perspective, so that the private becomes public. The disease ravaging Prior and

Roy is analogous to that wracking America in the 1980s—the government's abandonment of the poor, the sick, and the homeless—while the notion of homophobia embraces not only homosexuals but all marginalized people. Roy Cohn exemplifies this private/public connection as he denies his gay identity and his disease—noting that he is defined by his power, not his homosexuality—while using his political clout for ignoble ends, though he claims patriotism. Joe, too, despite his moral shortcomings, wrestles with the contradiction between his sexual identity and his religious background, as well as with the desire to further his career while maintaining political integrity.

Another prominent theme involves isolation, abandonment, and a loss of connections. People are cut loose from their moorings and set adrift in a world of uncertainty and instability. Louis abandons Prior; Harper, Joe, and Hannah all leave Utah but struggle to reconcile their own roots with their lives in New York; the Mormons themselves emigrated westward, while the Jews emigrated to the United States, where they have attempted to retain and recreate their old world. Harper constantly feels alone, escaping through imaginary journeys, though it is she who ultimately abandons Joe. Perhaps the homeless woman in the Bronx, one of the first people Hannah encounters in New York, best exemplifies all of "Reagan's children" who have been left to fend for themselves.

While *Part One: Millennium Approaches* traces the dissolution of community, *Part Two: Perestroika* begins the mending process, suggesting some answers to the questions posed in *Part One* and bringing to characters a sense of self-realization. Belize enlists Louis to recite a Jewish prayer for the dead over Roy, despite Belize's hatred of the man; Hannah has accepted both her son and Prior as homosexuals; Harper leaves to find her own life, while world events have started to reshape the political landscape. As Prior makes clear, the world must move forward, and humankind must take upon itself the responsibility to carve out a new world and a new mythology.

Kushner's theatricality, particularly his use of split scenes, underscores the divisions and conflicts the characters face throughout *Angels in America*. For example, in one split scene, Joe and Harper are at home, while Louis is in Prior's hospital room. Joe is trying to persuade Harper to relocate to Washington, implying that he may go there without her, while Louis tells Prior that he is moving out. In a mutual dream scene, Harper tells Prior that he is, deep inside, free of disease, while Prior reveals to Harper that her husband is a homosexual. The double and triple castings that Kushner employs further highlight the connections among the characters, in a time when connections are being broken. Hannah, a devout Mormon, also plays a rabbi, Roy's doctor, Ethel Rosenberg, and the World's Oldest Bolshevik, thus blurring the boundaries between religion, sexuality, and politics. The character of Mr. Lies, Harper's imaginary travel agent friend who spirits her away from her loneliness, also plays Belize, the nurse who ministers to the sufferings of others. Throughout *Angels in America,* Kushner freely mixes realistic scenes with those of fantasy, which Kushner makes clear should be theatrical illusion in the tradition of Bertolt Brecht, whose work deeply influenced this and other of Kushner's works.

Angels in America is credited with opening the doors for gay drama that reaches beyond the domestic realm that had been its primary territory, but it has also impacted other kinds of theater, particularly plays that resonate with the merging of public and private and with the reexamination of history. Kushner's own subsequent works, including *Homebody/Kabul* and *Caroline, or Change,* illustrate this connection, as does Moisés Kaufman's *The Laramie Project,* which addresses how a town copes with the horrific murder of a young gay student and gradually learns to heal through the sense of community.

Angels in America reaped numerous honors, including the Pulitzer Prize for Drama, the Tony Award for Best Play, the Drama Desk Award, Britain's *Evening Standard* Award, the New York Drama Critics' Circle Award, and the Los Angeles Drama Critics Circle Award.
See also AIDS Literature; Drama, Gay

Further Reading

Bloom, Harold, ed. *Tony Kushner.* Philadelphia: Chelsea House Publishers, 2005.

Geis, Deborah R., and Steven F. Kruger, eds. *Approaching the Millenium: Essays on* Angels in America. Ann Arbor: University of Michigan Press, 1997.

Vorlicky, Robert, ed. *Tony Kushner in Conversation.* Ann Arbor: University of Michigan Press, 1998.

Karen Charmaine Blansfield

Anthologies

Writings by and about gay men and lesbians have always had a place in the history of American literature. However, it was not until the increase of **queer** literary magazines and small presses in the late 1970s and early 1980s that the writings of **gay** men and lesbians came into full view of the American public and along with that, acceptance. Anthologies gathered the works of new and established writers from around the country. But more importantly they created a sense of community among readers and other writers and provided to these communities an education in gay and lesbian life and viewpoints that would not have otherwise been obtainable.

One of the most significant anthologies to appear after 1980 was *Men on Men: Best New Gay Fiction* (1986). It was edited by George Stambolian and featured many writers from the **Violet Quill Club** such as **Edmund White**, **Felice Picano**, and **Andrew Holleran**. While this was never intended to be anything more than a single edition, its success has led to a new collection being published every two years.

In 1986 Alyson Publications released *In the Life: A Black Gay Anthology.* Edited by Joseph Beam, the stories not only explored what it meant to be gay, but more importantly what it meant to be gay and black. Each story is a reflection on the struggles and of hope for building a stronger black gay community.

A second anthology published by Alyson in 1991 once again introduced readers to the voices of the black gay man. *Brother to Brother: Collected Writings by Black Gay Men* was originally begun by Joseph Beam, but completed by **Essex Hemphill** after Beam's death to AIDS in 1988. Through the talents and personal narratives of these authors, these collected stories addressed the emerging black gay sensibility of the late 1980s.

While the late 1980s established a place in American publishing for gay and lesbian writing, it was not until the 1990s that the full spectrum of queer writing could be shown. *The Faber Book of Gay Short Fiction* (1991), edited by Edmund White, not only introduced readers to current and new writers, it also stepped back in time, reintroducing the rich and varied stories of writers from the past. Authors such as Henry James, **Tennessee Williams**, and **Gore Vidal** were showcased alongside such currently influential authors as **David Leavitt**, **Dennis Cooper**, and **Allan Gurganus**.

By the mid-1990s gay and lesbian writing had found a solid place in American literature. It was also during this time that straight-identified men and women began to write about the gay and lesbian experience as well. *The Penguin Book of Gay Short Stories* (1994), edited by David Leavitt and Mark Mitchell, was one of the first anthologies of its time to feature writings on the gay male experience of identity, and relationships with lovers, friends, and family by both gay and straight authors. Alongside this anthology came *The Penguin Book of Lesbian Short Fiction* (1991), edited by Margaret Reynolds. Unlike its gay counterpart, this collection spanned a full century of lesbian writing. From a 1897 short story by Sarah Orne Jewett, through the 1930s with works by Radclyffe Hall and into contemporary authors such as **Jewelle Gomez**, **Dorothy Allison**, and Pat Califia.

As gay men and lesbian's writings became more visible in the mid-1990s, another path of queer writing began to take shape. *Am I Blue?: Coming Out from the Silence* (1994), published by HarperCollins and edited by Marion Dane Bauer, was the first anthology of young adult fiction to be devoted to gay and lesbian themes. Subjects such as coming out, self-discovery, and **homophobia** were addressed by an impressive list of popular children's authors such as M. E. Kerr, **Nancy Garden**, and William Sleator.

Following in its success, *Not the Only One: Lesbian & Gay Fiction for Teens* (1995) was published by Alyson Publications. Edited by Tony Grima, the collection was aimed at teens in grades 10 through 12 and featured a variety of stories about gay and lesbian youth dealing with everyday issues. It was also during the mid-1990s that another genre of gay and lesbian writing resurfaced and has had an impressive impact on gay and lesbian publishing to this day. *Best Gay Erotica* (1996) has been published annually since its debut by Cleis Press and has featured the works of some of the best contemporary authors including William J. Mann, D. Travers Scott, Dale Chase, Richard Labonte, and Simon Sheppard. Its lesbian counterpart, *Best Lesbian Erotica* (1996), has also been published annually with such featured authors as Sacchi Green, Rachel Kramer Bussel, and Tristan Taormino.

Bésame Mucho (1999) is a collection of 17 stories about gay life from the viewpoint of Latin American men. Published by Painted Leaf Press and edited by Jaime Manrique and Jesse Dorris, its stories range from a transsexual finding real love for the first time to the fear of loneliness after realizing one's sexual orientation. This collection features works by Alex R. Silva, Joel Villalón, and Emanuel Xavier.

As if on cue, the millennium brought with it a new style of intense, cutting-edge writing. Two of the leading publishers for this new area of fiction were Arsenal Pulp Press and Suspect Thoughts Press. *Queer Fear* (2000), edited by Michael Rowe and published by Arsenal Pulp, was one of the first anthologies to take the horror genre away from the stereotypical male antagonist and the female victim by turning the tables and making the protagonist clearly and visibly gay. The collection features works by William J. Mann, Michael Thomas Ford, Becky N. Southwell, and Douglas Clegg.

Of the Flesh: Dangerous New Fiction (2001), edited by Greg Wharton and published by Suspect Thoughts Press, is another anthology that pushed the boundaries of queer literature in another direction. Written by some of the most well-respected writers of erotica, Ian Phillips, M. Christian, and Simon Sheppard, these stories focus on the extreme and often dangerous side of queer sex, desire, and lust.

Nonfiction anthologies have also played a significant role in gay and lesbian literature, especially with the boom in queer and gender studies programs in many of America's colleges and universities. These anthologies like their fictional counterpart cover a wide range of topics from the theoretical to the narrative.

The Lesbian and Gay Studies Reader (1993), published by Routledge and edited by Henry Abelove, Michele Aina Barale, and David M. Halperin, offers a diverse and often challenging look into this new and expanding field of queer studies.

Queer Studies: A Lesbian, Gay, Bisexual, and Transgender Anthology (1996), published by New York University Press, was written as an introduction to queer studies programs; the anthology takes a look at how **queer theory** is defined and how it can build and expand political activism.

Finding the Real Me: True Tales of Sex and Gender Diversity (2003), published by Jossey-Bass, was edited by Tracie O'Keefe and Katrina Fox. These first-person narrative accounts from transgender individuals document their struggles to become who they are. Among the many stories is a moving account by Vera Sepulveda entitled "Confessions of a She-Male Merchant Marine."

With the nation's eye on same-sex marriage in the early twenty-first century, *I Do, I Don't: Queers on Marriage* (2004), published by Suspect Thoughts Press and edited by Greg Wharton and Ian Philips, brought together a collection of personal essays, poetry, love letters, and sermons surrounding this highly debated topic. It won the 2004 Lambda Literary Award for best nonfiction anthology.

Black Queer Studies: A Critical Anthology (2005), published by Duke University Press and edited by E. Patrick Johnson and Mae G. Henderson, focuses on current issues of racism in the gay community to issues around the depiction of black gays and lesbians in films.

Whether told in a narrative style for entertainment, stimulation, or education, the gay and lesbian anthology has had a rich and vibrant history among American literature. From the days of the gay liberation movement in the early 1980s to the changes that the gay and lesbian community faced during the 1990s, we have witnessed stories of love, friendship, and dying, as well as a development of intense, edgy narratives and personal essays of struggles and integration. Regardless of the story, whether fictional or not, the gay and lesbian anthology has played an important role in sharing our stories and our lives with others and will without a doubt continue to play an important role in our lives as we move further into the twenty-first century.

Further Reading

Carbado, Devon W., Dwight A. McBride, Donald Weise, and Evelyn C. White, eds. *Black Like Us: A Century of Lesbian, Gay, and Bisexual African American Fiction*. San Francisco: Cleis Press, 2002.

Sheppard, Simon. *Homosex: Sixty Years of Gay Erotica*. New York: Carroll & Graf, 2007.

Summers, Claude J., ed. *The Gay and Lesbian Literary Heritage*. New York: Henry Holt and Company, 1995.

Woods, Gregory. *A History of Gay Literature: The Male Tradition*. New Haven, CT: Yale University Press, 1998.

William Holden

Antler (b. 1946)

Notable poet/activist. Born in 1946 in Wauwatosa, Minnesota, the poet Antler's unusually appropriate name was ceremonially bestowed at age 18. His birth name is Brad Burdick. He continues to live in Milwaukee with his partner, poet Jeff Poniewaz, and spends at least two months of each year in the wilderness. Antler earned a bachelor's degree in Anthropology (1970) and a master's in English (1973) at the University of Wisconsin campus at Milwaukee and also attended the Iowa Writers' Workshop. He has taught at Esalen Institute, Omega Institute, Antioch College, and the Jack Kerouac School of Disembodied Poetics. Recipient of the Walt Whitman Award (1985), Antler also was the Poet Laureate of Milwaukee (2002, 2003) and received the Major Achievement Award from the Council for Wisconsin Writers (2003). Widely heralded as heir to Walt Whitman, and championed by **Allen Ginsberg**, his poetry and personality celebrate an ecology of orgasmic unity and Eros in wilderness.

A startling personal and explosive visionary attack against the realization of William Blake's Satanic mills, Antler's first book, *Factory* (1980), written while working for the Continental Can Company, won the Walt Whitman prize. It began his career as a planetary poet. His frank, lusty, generous, green, almost tribal, voice contrasts poetry, the body, the wild, and the cosmos with the assaults of the insatiably intolerant, unjust, militaristic, antisexual establishment. In *Last Words* (1986), which won the Witter Bynner Poetry Prize (1987) from the American Academy and Institute of Arts and Letters, Antler further developed his social critique suffusing his outrage with a meditative Whitmanesque empathy and Ginsberesque hedonism.

Antler: The Selected Poems (2000) gathered work from the previous books as well as from a larger unpublished work, Ever-Expanding Wilderness. Antler's robust, joyous, child-like enthusiasm for the body and uninhibited sex mirrors **James Broughton**'s buoyant poems; but unlike Broughton's mythically sacred sexual play, Antler's poems depict sexual holiness through an even more candid physicality. Semen becomes less an elixir and more potently real. The young boys in Antler's poems express the adolescent abandon and curiosity, which come with the youthful discovery of sexuality and all the sensations it brings.

Antler's uncompromisingly Utopian, flamboyant, melodramatic, and even, at times, over-the-top style adds surprisingly to his poetry's allure. His inventive metaphors, driving rhythms, and timeless spiritual sincerity bring a holistic, yet wholly entertaining, energy to contemporary gay poetry. His unique use of language—a hypnotic and somehow elegant combination of the surreal, the feral, the shamanistic, and the colorful—places him in the ranks of the great American originals such as Walt Whitman and Emily Dickinson.

Further Reading

"Craft Interview with Antler." *New York Quarterly* 52 (1993): 14–31; Kolker, Julia. "Antler (Interview)." *Riverwest Currents.* October 2004. http://www.riverwestcurrents.org/2004/October/002225.html.

Lewis, Brandon. "Antler: Learning the Constellations (Interview)." *Porcupine Literary Arts Magazine* 7.2 (n.d.). http://www.porcupineliteraryarts.com/antler.html.

Nelson, Howard. "The Work of Antler." In *Twayne Companion to Contemporary Literature in English,* edited by R. H. W. Dillard and Amanda Cockrell, 21–34. New York: Twayne Publishers, 2003.

Jeffery Beam

Anzaldúa, Gloria Evangelina (1942–2004)

Feminist visionary, spiritual activist, poet-philosopher, fiction writer, and early architect of **queer theory**. As one of the first openly **queer** Chicana authors, Gloria Evangelina Anzaldúa has played a key role in redefining contemporary lesbian and Chicana/o identities; by defining herself as a queer Chicana, she emphasized both that lesbian identity cannot be defined exclusively in Anglo-American terms and that Chicano identity cannot be defined exclusively in heterosexual or male terms.

Born on September 26, 1942, in Raymondville, Texas, to Urbano and Amelia Anzaldúa, Gloria Anzaldúa was the oldest of four children. Anzaldúa had deep roots in south Texas; her parents were sixth-generation Mexicanos, and she spent the first half of her life in this area. Due to a rare hormonal imbalance, Anzaldúa began menstruating while still an infant and went through puberty when only six years old. Throughout her childhood, she was marked by this physical difference in ways that profoundly shaped her perspective on queer identity. Punished in grade school for her inability to speak English, Anzaldúa eventually emerged as an exceptional student and a voracious reader. She defiantly majored in English at college, where she also obtained her certificate in secondary education. After graduating from Pan American University in 1968, she taught public school for several years while attending the University of Texas, Austin, each summer. In 1972 she received her M.A. in English and Education and in 1973 worked for a year in Indiana where she served as the liaison between the public school system and migrant farm workers' children. During this time, she took her first creative writing course and began to write seriously. In 1974 Anzaldúa enrolled in the doctoral program in Comparative Literature at the University of Texas, Austin, where she was introduced to feminism, "**gay** life," and Chicano Studies. Throughout the 1970s, Anzaldúa participated in various political movements, including the Chicano movement, the farm workers movement, the antiwar movement, the civil rights movement, and the women's movement. Her work with these movements enabled her to comprehend more thoroughly the limitations to oppositional politics that focused on a single issue.

In 1977 Anzaldúa resolved to devote her life to her writing and moved from Austin, Texas, to northern California where she became intensely involved in the San Francisco literary scene. Despite severe economic hardships, she took only part-time jobs so that she could devote the majority of her time to her writing. Around this time, she began identifying as queer. In 1979, after being repeatedly tokenized and in other ways ignored because of her status as a nonwhite, or "Third World," writer, Anzaldúa decided to edit a collection of writings by women of color and invited **Cherríe Moraga** to work with her on this project. Their collection, *This Bridge Called My Back: Writings by Radical Women of Color,* broke new ground in feminist studies, women-of-color studies, and queer studies. After spending several years on the East Coast, primarily in New York City, Anzaldúa returned to California in 1985, living first in San Francisco and finally in Santa Cruz where she passed away in May 2004 of diabetes-related complications.

Throughout her career, Anzaldúa was critical of the term "lesbian" and preferred to describe herself and her work as "queer." As she explains in her 1990 essay, "To(o) Queer the Writer—Loca, escritora y chicana," because the term "lesbian" has often been used in ethnocentric ways to refer exclusively to "white"-raced women, it erases her specific identity and desires. Instead, she prefers the ambiguity of the term "queer," with its working-class roots, or Spanish terms such as "patlache," "tortillera," and "mita' y mita.'"

Anzaldúa offers an expansive definition of queer identity. Unlike many authors, she refused to focus exclusively on sexuality (or on any other identity category). In all of her writings, she moved among issues of class, color, **gender**, language, physical (dis)abilities, religion, and sexuality. Rather than examine sexuality by itself, she locates and anchors her sexuality in other aspects of her identity, such as culture, race/ethnicity, class, and spirituality. By so doing, she challenges conventional Western concepts of identity, as well as contemporary forms of identity politics. As such, Anzaldúa offers one of the earliest and most complex articulations of intersectional identity.

A versatile author, Anzaldúa published poetry, theoretical essays, short stories, autobiographical narratives, interviews, children's books, and multigenre anthologies. She won a number of awards, including the Before Columbus Foundation American Book Award, the Lamda Lesbian Small Book Press Award, a National Endowment for the Arts Fiction Award, the Lesbian Rights Award, the Sappho Award of Distinction, and the American Studies Association's Bode-Pearson Lifetime Achievement Award.

Borderlands/La Frontera: The New Mestiza (1987) is Anzaldúa's most widely acclaimed book. Named one of the 100 Best Books of the Century by both *Hungry Mind Review* and *Utne Reader, Borderlands/La Frontera* combines autobiography with poetry, history, mythology, social critique, and philosophy, creating a new genre that Anzaldúa called "autohistoria-teoría." Anzaldúa coined this term to describe women-of-color interventions into and transformations of traditional Western autobiographical forms. Unlike conventional autobiography, which focuses on the individual life, autohistoria-teoría blends individual and collective biography with a variety of genres and forms of theorizing.

Borderlands/La Frontera is divided into two parts: the first half contains seven mixed-genre essays that combine autobiography with history, social protest, poetry, and revisionist mythmaking. The second half contains 38 poems, divided into six sections. Like the mixed-genre essays, the poems depict a wide variety of issues and scenes, ranging from intimate self-definition to critiques of systemic racism/sexism. In poems such as "Immaculate, Inviolate: Como Ella" Anzaldúa draws on her family's history to explore heteronormativity's negative impact on women; and in poems such as "Interface," she offers unique twists on conventional love poetry. Although scholars rarely acknowledge *Borderlands'* groundbreaking contributions to queer theory, this text has significantly impacted the ways contemporary scholars think about border issues, the concept of the Borderlands, ethnic/gender/sexual identities, and conventional literary forms.

Anzaldúa also edited or co-edited three anthologies. Her first co-edited anthology, *This Bridge Called My Back: Writings by Radical Women of Color* (1981), is a groundbreaking collection of essays, letters, and poems widely recognized as a premiere multicultural feminist text. Co-edited with Cherríe Moraga, this multigenre anthology offers a classic illustration of intersectional theory and serves as a crucial reminder that U.S. feminism is not and never has been a white, heterosexual, middle-class women's movement. *This Bridge Called My Back* also includes "La Prieta," Anzaldúa's first published theorization of queer identity, politics, and ethics—framed within her innovative theory of "El Mundo Zurdo," or "The Left-Handed World." Anzaldúa's theory of El Mundo Zurdo represents inclusionary identity formation and alliance-building based on affinity, self-selection, and a relational approach to difference. Anzaldúa's second anthology, *Making Face, Making Soul/Haciendo Caras: Creative and Critical Perspectives by Women of Color* (1990), makes important contributions to women-of-color studies and includes pieces from a variety of genres. Most recently, Anzaldúa co-edited *This Bridge We Call Home: Radical Visions for Transformation* (2002), a collection of theoretical and creative essays, short stories, poems, e-mail conversations, and artwork offering a bold new vision of women-of-color consciousness for the twenty-first century. Co-edited with AnaLouise Keating, this anthology illustrates the growth in Anzaldúa's vision of social change as well as the expansion of her definition of queer identity. Written by women and men—both "of color" and white—

This Bridge We Call Home transforms existing identity categories and develops new forms of feminist theorizing and action, or what Anzaldúa calls "spiritual activism." Anzaldúa began exploring transgender issues in her unpublished writings from the 1970s, and this collection includes contributions by transgender people.

Anzaldúa has also written two bilingual children's books, *Friends from the Other Side/ Amigos del otro lado* (1993) and *Prietita and the Ghost Woman/ Prietita y la Llorona* (1995). Focusing on a strong female protagonist, both books challenge conventional gender roles. Anzaldúa has also published a collection of interviews, *Interviews/Entrevistas* (2000), offering intimate biographical details and useful information about her theories and writings. In her most recent writings, including many that will be published posthumously, Anzaldúa expands previous theories of queer identities and ethics, creating radically transformative politics and innovative, inclusionary models of identity formation.

See also Autobiography, Lesbian; Lesbian Literature, Mexican American

Further Reading

Alarcón, Norma. "Chicana Feminism: In the Tracks of 'The' Native Woman." In *Living Chicana Theory*, edited by Carla Trujillo, 371–82. Berkeley, CA: Third Woman Press, 1998.

Barnard, Ian. "Gloria Anzaldúa Queer Mestisaje." *MELUS: Journal for the Study of the Multi-Ethnic Literature of the United States* 22 (1997): 35–53.

Garber, Linda. " 'Caught in the Crossfire Between Camps': Gloria Anzaldúa." *Identity Poetics: Race, Class, and the Lesbian-Feminist Roots of Queer Theory*. New York: Columbia University Press, 2001. 147–75.

Keating, AnaLouise. *Women Reading Women Writing: Self-Invention in Paula Gunn Allen, Gloria Anzaldúa, and Audre Lorde*. Philadelphia: Temple University Press, 1996.

———, ed. *EntreMundos/AmongWorlds: New Perspectives on Gloria E. Anzaldúa*. New York: Palgrave Macmillan, 2005.

Norton, Jody. "Transchildren, Changelings, and Fairies: Living the Dream and Surviving the Nightmare in Contemporary America." *This Bridge We Call Home: Radical Visions of Transformation*, edited by Gloria E. Anzaldúa and AnaLouise Keating, 145–54. New York: Routledge, 2002.

AnaLouise Keating

Arnold, June Fairfax Davis (1926–1982)

Novelist and publisher. Born on October 26, 1926, in South Carolina to wealthy, affluent parents, Robert Cowan and Cad Davis, Arnold lived a privileged life. She moved to Houston, Texas, as a young girl where she began her education at Kinkaid School. She next attended Bryn Mawr in Pennsylvania, a college preparatory school for girls. For her undergraduate education, Arnold chose Vassar College, where she remained for one year before moving to Houston and earning her B.A. at Rice University in 1948. During that time, Arnold was presented at the Allegro Club's Debutante Ball in 1947. In 1953, she married a Rice classmate, Gilbert Harrington Arnold, and had four children before she divorced and moved to New York City's Greenwich Village with her children to pursue a writing career, which she insisted was secondary to her other interests. In 1958, she earned a Master's Degree in Literature, also from Rice University.

Arnold quickly acclimated herself to the open atmosphere of Greenwich Village. She established her identity as a feminist lesbian and began a long-term relationship with Parke Bowman, an attorney. She also began taking writing courses at the New School for Social Research and published her first novel, *Applesauce,* in 1967, which echoed her own past in its treatments of the ways that women change once they become wives and how they are expected to fulfill a variety of roles at once.

Sometime after the publication of her first novel, Arnold moved to Vermont where, in 1973, she founded a women's press, Daughters, Inc., with Parke Bowman, novelist **Bertha Harris**, and activist Charlotte Bunch. Before declaring bankruptcy five years after its foundation, the press published 30 novels dealing with lesbian themes including **Rita Mae Brown**'s pioneering *Rubyfruit Jungle* (1973). Daughters, Inc. was also responsible for publishing Arnold's next two novels, *The Cook and the Carpenter: A Novel by the Carpenter* (1973) and *Sister Gin* (1975). The former is the story of a community of women who support and nurture one another. It depicts characters whose genders remain anonymous (pronouns are replaced with na/nan) until the end of the novel. The latter is Arnold's best-known novel and details the difficulties that Su and Bettina (white, southern, lesbian lovers) face as they age. Set in North Carolina during the early 1970s, the women and their close circle of friends and relatives deal openly with issues such as menopause (a focal point), alcoholism, and sexuality. They are quite comical, even managing to dish out their own brand of vigilante justice. The novel has been both praised and criticized for its experimental, nonlinear, and impressionistic style.

Arnold did more than write novels. She frequently contributed to popular and unconventional periodicals, including the New York *Village Voice* and *Sister Courage*. She also helped to organize the first Women in Print Conference, held in Omaha, Nebraska, in 1976. She served as a member of the Texas Institute of Letters, the National Organization for Women, and PEN (Poets, Playwrights, Editors, Essayists, and Novelists), the worldwide association of writers.

Once Daughters, Inc. closed in 1978, Arnold moved to Houston with Bowman, where she began work on *Baby Houston* (1987), her final novel. Set in Houston, long before it became the huge city of today, it is a tribute to her mother, told in her mother's voice. It depicts the mother-daughter relationship as volatile yet peculiarly loving. Interestingly (and ironically), the widowed mother's name is Baby, and the name seems well suited to the character. Throughout the novel, Baby and her youngest daughter, Hallie, fight continuously over everything having to do with both their lives and, while there is never any resolution, the arguments provide a detailed portrait of what it means to be a mother (and a daughter). There is obviously something very personal lurking in the text, which turns out to be its strength as well as its weakness. Arnold's descriptions of Baby— her personality and style—are intricate and thoughtfully considered, but despite that, one is left with the feeling that they just cannot get at all of the intimacies that informed the work.

As a publisher and writer, Arnold was a pioneer. She was known for creating complicated, multidimensional characters and writing about subjects that were not commonly addressed in mainstream fiction. In addition, she was known for establishing a women's press that published groundbreaking lesbian fiction. June Arnold died prematurely of cancer on March 11, 1982. She was 55.

Further Reading

Marcus, Jane. Afterword. *Sister Gin.* By June Arnold. New York: Feminist Press, 1989. 217–34.

Sherri Foster

Arobateau, Red Jordan (b. 1943)

Self-published novelist, playwright, poet, essayist, and visual artist of black **queer** underclass life and culture. Red Jordan Arobateau was born in Chicago, Illinois, on November 15, 1943. Born and raised as a girl, Arobateau, later in adult life, has identified as a female-to-male transsexual. Arguably Red Jordan Arobateau is the first and probably most prolific female-to-male transsexual writer of African American descent. Arobateau was born the only child of a Honduras father who immigrated to Chicago in the 1930s and a light-skinned college-educated black woman. They later married. In a community with few Spanish-speaking people and even fewer interracial married couples, Arobateau grew up in an emotionally fragile family. His parents separated when he was 17, and because he had always been closer to his father he chose to live with him and never saw his mother again. By 1967, tired of the Chicago police force's harassment of **gay**s and lesbians and his failure at finding a comfortable lesbian, gay, bisexual, transgender, and **queer** (LGBTQ) community, he moved to the more gay-friendly San Francisco.

Reflective of Arobateau's creativity and boldness in self-evolution, Arobateau created his pseudonym from an amalgamation of familial and personal experiences. He took on his maternal grandmother's surname, Jordan, because of its connection to the black side of the family and its Biblical symbolism. He then added an "A" to his given surname, Robateau. After a former hairdresser and lover dyed his head red, he chose that for his first name because it conveyed his attention to passion and eroticism as a writer. Arobateau began writing at the age of 13. Because his books have never been published by a major or smaller press, he has lived in poverty most of his life. To finance his self-publishing, he worked various jobs: newspaper deliverer, office clerk, factory laborer, telemarketer, karate teacher, postal worker, nurse's aide, cashier, cook, and janitor. He has resided in the Bayside area of California, alternating between Oakland and San Francisco for the last 35 years

Influential lesbian writer **Ann Allen Shockley** once wrote of Arobateau as "a different kind of lesbian writer" (1979, 139). This is the best description of the writer's work that prominently features lesbian prostitutes, drug dealers, hustlers, transsexual bikers, and lesbian motorcycle gangs as characters immersed in street language and culture. Arobateau's fiction has more in common with Iceberg Slim and Donald Goines than **Audre Lorde** or Ann Allen Shockley. Arobateau is the author of 40 novels, six short story collections, three volumes of poetry, several plays, and a contributor to several edited lesbian and transsexual anthologies. Early in his writing career and before his **gender** reassignment surgery, Arobateau identified as a butch lesbian. At the age of 15, after skimming through a dime-store pulp novel with a passage about a lesbian in it, Arobateau saw herself in the representation and began identifying as lesbian. After many years of feeling a sense of difference and alienation, Arobateau sensed that his orientation as a butch lesbian was not his true self. He soon began identifying as transgendered and, after having a gender reassignment surgery, defined himself as transsexual in the 1990s.

Arobateau's mixed-race heritage has been an important part of his life and writing career. As someone who looks white, but who primary identifies as black, Arobateau has discussed and written about the politics of passing, mongrelness, and isolation in his non-fiction essays and autobiography. In some of Arobateau's fiction, mixed-race politics become a part of the characters and the stories that he creates. At one point, he belonged to the Mongrels, a West Coast group of mixed-race women. Although he embraced and accepted black culture, his identification with his father determined many other aspects of his life. Having been an atheist for the early part of his adult life, he became a Christian after his father, a devout Christian, died. Much of his poetry reflected his religious beliefs, and he continued to write sexually explicit fiction focused on the queer underclass.

Some of Arobateau's most notable works include *The Bars across Heaven* (1975), *Ho Stroll* (1975), *The Big Change: A Transsexual Novel* (1976), *Five Stories* (1977), and *Jailhouse Stud* (1977). Though Arobateau had been writing for years, the lesbian community has been especially important in bringing Arobateau's work to a larger audience. In 1982, black lesbian journal *Sinister Wisdom* took the initiative of highlighting the streetwriter's work by featuring an interview between Red Jordan Arobateau and established black lesbian writer Ann Allen Shockley. To date, the interview is one of the most complete biographical assessments of the same-sex dimensions of the author's life in print. Arobateau has been featured in two documentaries: *Before Stonewall* (1984) and *Nobody's People; Portrait of a Christian Pornographer* (1992). He continues to write and publish.

Further Reading

Arobateau, Red Jordan. "Nobody's People." In *Daughters of Africa: An International Anthology of Words and Writings by Women of African Descent from the Ancient Egyptian to the Present,* edited by Margaret Busby, 593–603. New York: Ballantine Books, 1992.

———. "They Say I Write Sex for Money." In *Whores and Other Feminists,* edited by Jill Nagle, 191–95. New York: Routledge, 1997.

Shockley, Ann Allen. "The Black Lesbian in American Literature: An Overview." *Conditions 5 2,* no. 2 (Autumn 1979): 133–42.

———. "A Different Kind of Black Lesbian Writer: Red Jordan Arobateau." *Sinister Wisdom* 21 (1982): 35–39.

L. H. Stallings

Ashbery, John (b. 1927)

Major American poet of the first rank. John Ashbery's mostly farm-bound childhood in upstate New York was lonely and ordinary, excepting the tragic loss of his older brother from leukemia when Ashbery was 13. Ashbery attended Deerfield Academy, then matriculated at Harvard, where he wrote poems, served on the *Harvard Advocate,* and became friends with fellow poets Frank O'Hara and Kenneth Koch. (Ashbery, O'Hara, and Koch, along with **James Schuyler** and Barbara Guest, would later be tagged as poetry's "New York School.") Ashbery's first major book of poems, *Some Trees* (1956), was selected by W. H. Auden for the Yale Series of Younger Poets, chosen over O'Hara's manuscript. O'Hara, however, held no grudge and later reviewed the book generously in *Poetry* magazine, calling it "the most beautiful first book to appear in America since Wallace Stevens' *Harmonium*" (313). The comparison was apt; Ashbery's greatest supporter, literary critic Harold Bloom, has called the second half of the twentieth century the age of Ashbery, as the first half had been the age of Stevens.

Ashbery is now so celebrated, it is difficult to imagine a time when he wrote in obscurity. Yet the austere sonorities, surreal tableaux, and illogical associative leaps of *Some Trees* mostly befuddled readers (including Auden, who in introduction for the book expressed reservations about Ashbery's surrealism). Ashbery's second book, *The Tennis Court Oath* (1962), written while Ashbery was living in Paris, was even more off-putting. The book's centerpiece, the long poem "Europe," was composed largely from fragments from an English-language children's book. Ashbery has said that with *The Tennis Court Oath,* he was attempting to reexamine poetry by taking it apart. Ashbery's expatriation in France had the effect of making him see language as something by turns foreign yet intimate (in the case of French), as familiar yet estranged (in the case of English). *The Tennis Court Oath* would finally provide inspiration to L=A=N=G=U=A=G=E poets, such as Charles Bernstein, for whom Ashbery's use of collage foreground language's material properties, much as Pollock's paintings emphasize painterliness over any recognizable figure or subject matter. (Indeed, parsing "subject matter" in Ashbery's elusive work is often fruitless; it is better to listen for the "how said" than the "what said.")

Though Ashbery has to some degree disowned the extreme experimentalism of *The Tennis Court Oath,* he would continue to develop "other realities," marrying his surrealist impulses to a wistful, occasionally ironic romanticism. Ashbery's third book, *Rivers and Mountains* (1966), was seen as a return to form and was nominated for a National Book Award. "Soonest Mended," from Ashbery's fourth book, *The Double Dream of Spring* (1970), is the single poem that best crystallizes the early Ashbery idiom. Allegedly written for Frank O'Hara, who died in 1966, "Soonest Mended" is elegiac in tone and, though abstract in overview, is braided with memorable Keatsian phrases and moving particulars. *Three Poems* (1972), Ashbery's fifth major book, provided the poet with another departure. The length of a short novel, the eponymous three poems are in fact prose meditations, drier and more discursive in tone—akin to Darwin's prose—than the rich, condensed lyricism typical of, say, Arthur Rimbaud's prose poetry. Here and elsewhere, Ashbery's finds poetic power in his deviation from genre conventions, even within a genre—prose poetry—already seen as experimental or marginal.

Ashbery's breakthrough would finally come in 1976 with his book *Self-Portrait in a Convex Mirror,* winner of the Pulitzer Prize, the National Book Award, and the National Book Critics Circle Award. Ashbery's book-award hat trick transformed him, seemingly overnight, into a literary celebrity. The book's long title poem concerns Parmigianino's 1524 self-portrait, which the painter made by gazing on his reflection in the titular convex mirror. "Self-Portrait in a Convex Mirror" is more essayistic in tone and ostensibly logical in structure—as if Ashbery were impersonating an unusually sensitive cicerone—without sacrificing any of Ashbery's felicities of phrase or feeling. Poets, it has often been said, write about painters to test precepts about their own art making. Thus, Ashbery's choice of a painter as realistic as Parmigianino to reflect and refract his own artistic practice is a surprising move, though his choice of such a canonical, conservative subject may account for the wider readership and acceptance this poem garnered Ashbery.

Ashbery's next volume, *Houseboat Days* (1977), is perhaps his most consistently excellent, interesting, and representative volume and is thus an ideal starting point for the reader unfamiliar with his work. (Ashbery's 1984 *Selected Poems* is also indispensable in this regard.) *Houseboat Days* also contains a number of small masterpieces: "Wet Casements," "Syringa," "Daffy Duck in Hollywood," and two *ars poetica* (poems that address the writer's own practice): "And *Ut Pictura Poesis* Is Her Name" and "What Is Poetry." Ashbery, even at his peak, refused to rest on his laurels. His next volume, *As We Know* (1979), contains his most experimental and impossible work: the long poem "Litany," written in two columns meant to be read simultaneously. The volume also contains "My Erotic Double," one of the few poems of this period to take up and pursue homosexuality as a subject—though treated, as always, with Ashbery's customary irony.

At least one critic, John Shoptaw, has tied Ashbery's evasive poetic style to his sexual discretion, forged in the formative McCarthyism of the early 1950s, when homosexuality was publicly condemned and self-identified homosexuals feared government retribution (Ashbery had registered as homosexual to avoid the draft). Ashbery's early poem, "The Thinnest Shadow," obliquely addresses the poet's need, at this time, to banish **gay** subject matter to the shadows. Only in the 1970s would Ashbery begin incorporating more explicit gay subject matter, and even then in coded form, as with "The Fairies' Song," in *The Vermont Notebook* (1976). Because Ashbery is not a directly autobiographical poet, such omissions do not seem notable in themselves—they are typical of Ashbery's mode, which is generally untethered from narrative and more interested in the movement of thought than in the calcification of identity. Yet it seems likely that Ashbery developed this aesthetic approach—writing "anybody's autobiography" rather than his own—in response to the virulent **homophobia** of his early adulthood.

In his last decades, Ashbery has continued to be a strong and prolific writer. Though *Flow Chart* (1998), Ashbery's 215-page book-length magnum opus was a divisive work —some critics find it unmoored and tiresome—it is nevertheless an important testament to Ashbery's restless need to innovate. In his late 70s and now 80s, Ashbery has increased his rate of productivity, writing shorter, more accessible poems that are alternately parodic and tender. The ebbing of life and love are Ashbery's growing concerns in these works, collected in *Notes from the Air* (2007), which offers a generous collection of the writing done between 1984, when Ashbery's *Selected Poems* was assembled, and the poet's 80th year. Though many readers continue to reject Ashbery's work as "nonsense" or "gibberish," his influence on the culture has been vast and transformative, even beyond the borders of poetry. Many musicians and filmmakers have cited Ashbery as a seminal influence, and in 2007 Ashbery was chosen, at the age of 80, as Music Television's (MTV) first poet laureate.

Further Reading

Bloom, Harold, ed. *John Ashbery.* New York: Chelsea House, 1995.
Lehman, David. *The Last Avant-Garde: The Making of the New York School of Poets.* New York: Doubleday, 1998.
O'Hara, Frank. "Rare Modern." *Poetry* 89, no. 5 (Feb. 1957): 307–16.
Shoptaw, John. *On the Outside Looking Out: John Ashbery's Poetry.* Cambridge, MA: Harvard University Press, 1994.

Christopher Schmidt

Autobiography, Bisexual

In the late twentieth century, bisexuals began to claim their unique voice in literature, distinguishing themselves from both heterosexuals and homosexuals. Earlier twentieth-century biographical writing tended to focus on homosexuality, subsuming the voices of bisexual people. Often bisexuals were seen as confused about their true orientation or trying to maintain heterosexual privilege by engaging in relationships with opposite sex partners. Even bisexuals described themselves in ways that indicated their ambivalence with available sexual labels. Many bisexuals who became involved in a same-sex relationship after being in a heterosexual relationship describe themselves as **gay** or lesbian rather than bisexual. Although Wendy W. Fairey was in a long-term marriage and had children before committing herself to a relationship with a woman, in her essay "Mind and Body" in *A Woman Like That: Lesbian and Bisexual Writers Tell Their Coming Out Stories* (1999) edited by Joan Larkin, Fairey describes the term bisexual as a more or less appropriate identifier given her history and "abiding illusions." The illusion is that she could love a man again after finding her sexual identity in relationships with women. Unlike Fairey, Rupert Everett does not claim any illusions that he would be able to become involved with a woman in the future. Everett's *Red Carpets and Other Banana Skins* (2006) describes his bisexual relationships including a long-term sexual relationship with a woman, described as an adventure rather than a real interest. He has since described himself as homosexual.

In the late twentieth century, more works were published that included the B in LGBTQ (lesbian, gay, bisexual, transgender, **queer**). In spite of the recognition of **bisexuality** as a distinct sexual orientation, there continues to be few books that respect the idiosyncratic perspective that bisexual men and women have. Even in the nascent twenty-first century, most anthologies tend to focus on the gay and lesbian experience, rather than addressing the LGBTQ experience. There are some collections that acknowledge and explore the differences between lesbians and bisexual women, and between gay and bisexual men.

Some of these are coming out stories, personal accounts of discovering and acknowledging one's sexuality. *A Woman Like That: Lesbian and Bisexual Writers Tell Their Coming Out Stories* focuses primarily on lesbian experiences, although a very few narratives discuss bisexual themes. Most of the mentions of bisexuality are secondary rather than the focus of the piece. A good example is "A Vision" by Rebecca Brown. Brown begins her story by describing her developing interest in older women. Later, Brown says that when she went to college, she had sex with boys and girls her own age. That is the only mention of her bisexuality.

Out & About Campus: Personal Accounts by Lesbian, Gay, Bisexual, & Transgendered College Students (2000), co-edited by Kim Howard and Steven Drukman, is a collection of personal accounts by LGBTQ college students. This compilation contains narratives by students who are bisexual and clear about their sexual orientation. While many of these are coming out stories, the book is of interest because it does not limit itself to gays and lesbians, but acknowledges the bisexual experience as unique. "Teamwork" by Lisa Walter is an account of the coming out of a biracial, bisexual woman during her freshman year of college. "Creating Familia" by Gabriela Rodriguez, a bisexual Latina, describes her struggles within the LGBTQ community because of antibisexual sentiment. Rodriguez uses the word lesbian to describe herself, although it is obvious that she sees herself as bisexual. There is a notable difference in the experiences of older and younger women. Older women seem more likely to have been involved with men and then in exclusive relationships with women while the younger women seem more flexible in their sexual preferences. That critical difference may be related to the eras in which each group came to maturity. Women who matured in the 1950–1970s had less societal acceptance and more overt pressure to conform to heterosexual norms, while younger women had a slightly more accepting culture as they found their way through the sexual labyrinth in high school and college.

By the twenty-first century, bisexual autobiography had moved from passing mentions in manuscripts to mainstream publishing. The publication of *Black, White and Jewish* (2000) by Rebecca Walker marked a turning point in the availability of autobiography by self-identified bisexuals. Walker, the daughter of Pulitzer prize–winning black author **Alice Walker** and Jewish/white civil rights lawyer Mel Leventhal, brings to the discussion a number of perspectives. Walker looks at the ways race, culture, class, and sexuality have informed and shaped her life. She discusses her struggles at being accepted by relatives and friends as well as her own struggle for identity as a black/white, Jewish, bisexual woman. Walker describes her coming out moment as nonexistent. Instead, Walker describes herself as having an unquestioned fluid sexuality throughout her life. During a lengthy relationship with well-known musician Meshell Ndegeocello and while co-parenting her child, Walker decided to become pregnant herself. She did not have a child and the relationship later dissolved. Afterward, Walker met her current male partner and had a son. She wrote about the experience of becoming a parent in *Baby Love* (2007). Walker blurs the politics of **gender** by writing about her relationships in ways that give few clues about gender.

More recently, other bisexuals have begun writing well-received memoirs, including Farley Granger's *Include Me Out: My Life from Goldwyn to Broadway* (2006). Granger frankly discusses his relationships with both men and women while refusing to categorize himself as either homosexual or bisexual.

Further Reading

Burleson, William E. *Bi America: Myths, Truths and Struggles of an Invisible Community.* New York: Harrington Park Press, 2005.

Hutchins, Loraine, and Lani Kaahumanu, eds. *Bi Any Other Name.* Los Angeles: Alyson Books, 1990.

Ochs, Robyn, and Sarah Rowley, eds. *Getting Bi: Voices of Bisexuals around the World.* Boston: Bisexual Resource Center, 2005.

Orndorff, Kata, ed. *Bi Lives: Bisexual Women Tell Their Stories.* Tucson, AZ: See Sharp Press, 1999.

Patricia L. T. Camp

Autobiography, Gay

A relatively recent subgenre that has developed from the traditional autobiography. Like the originating genre, **gay** autobiography narrates the life and times of its author; however, it departs from the conventional sexual mores and traditional moral values found in the autobiography to specifically present gay lived experience.

As autobiographical scholars have noted, beginning with St. Augustine's *Confessions* and continuing through the *Confessions* of Jean-Jacques Rousseau, the autobiography has tended in content and structure to largely serve as an upper-class white heterosexual Christian male narrative. Although this tendency originated in other nations, its continuity can be detected in American literature, most notably in *The Autobiography of Benjamin Franklin,* where the autobiography's moral concerns are combined with a desire to cultivate future Americans, particularly from the perspective of a father training his son. This narrative hegemony has delimited autobiographical writing for all minority groups; however, it is has been particularly restrictive for gay men, whose individual access to patriarchal privilege is more precarious than is often presumed. Compared to other historically marginalized groups, such as African Americans, nonhomosexual women, Native Americans, who began publishing autobiographical works in the nineteenth century, gay American autobiography largely did not find its way into print until the second half of the twentieth century. Moreover, gay autobiography has also been problematically intertwined with the changing moral, scientific, and political discourses about homosexuality, which further delimit the gay autobiographical impulse through the discursive demands of the **closet**, the case study, and the process of coming out. For this reason, any rigorous effort to explore the phenomenon of gay autobiography must deploy a broad understanding of autobiographical narratives to include the memoir, the diary, and other first-person narratives that similarly perform the project of gay life writing.

Claude Hartland wrote America's arguably first gay autobiography *The Story of a Life* in 1901. Hartland's pseudonymous autobiography deploys a rhetorically rich first-person narration that performs a medical and a moral pathological subjectivity while simultaneously invoking sympathy. It achieves this goal by deploying the medical discourses surrounding homosexuality while simultaneously resisting them with literary techniques that express something of the gay individual beneath the dehumanizing discourses. Hartland's autobiography performs this function through its use of the case history, and this narrative strategy stems from the work of Britain's Richard von Krafft-Ebing's *Psychopathia Sexualis* (1886) and Havelock Ellis's *Sexual Inversion* (1896), which each used medical case histories to explore the subject matter of men who preferred same-sex sexual experiences from a scientific perspective. Earl Lind's *Autobiography of an Androgyne* (1918), which like *The Story of a Life* was published by a medical publisher, functions similarly as an early gay autobiography that uses the narrative device of the case history to express something of the gay subjectivity behind it. The similar strategic narration behind both Hartland's and Lind's autobiographies establishes a continuity in gay American autobiography—the tactical narration of the gay self.

The gay autobiography does not fully develop in America until the mid-twentieth century when, after a series of political and historical events, the gay life writer began to take authorial control of his individual lived experience and its narrative patterns. In *Telling Sexual Stories* (1994), Ken Plummer asserts narrative development is the product of the parallel and parasitic development of the individual and his or her culture, and the profusion of gay autobiographies following the cultural events of the mid-twentieth century appears to support this assertion. The political organization of 1950s homophile rights groups, such as the Mattachine Society and the Daughters of Bilitis, coupled with gatherings for gay and lesbian equality throughout the 1960s, such as the annual July 4th meetings held from 1965 to 1969 in front of Philadelphia's Independence Hall, signaled the emergence of an organizing and burgeoning LGBT community. This subcultural zeitgeist found its literal and figurative touchstone in the June 1969 **Stonewall Riots**, which have come to serve as the birth date for the modern **gay rights movement** in America.

The post-Stonewall era prompted a retrospective and contemporaneous chronicling of the gay lived experience, and this difference fell along generational lines. For a generation of gay men, who were already middle-aged, the post-Stonewall freedoms allowed for the chronicling of what gay life was like prior to the emergence of a free and more visible gay culture. Martin Duberman's *Cures: A Gay Man's Odyssey* (1991) chronicles Duberman's complex personal and professional pre-Stonewall experiences, as he struggled with self-acceptance, **homophobia**, and psychotherapy. Duberman followed his pre-

Stonewall chronicling with *Midlife Queer: Autobiography of a Decade 1971–1981* (1996), which records his participation in and subsequent disillusionment with the post-Stonewall gay rights movement. Although Duberman's autobiographical work documents experiences shared by many gay men within his generation, Alan Helms's *Young Man from the Provinces: A Gay Life before Stonewall* (1995) illustrates the dangers of interpreting a minority culture's experience through any one individual narrative. From his childhood in Maryland through his young adulthood, Helms's chronicling of pre-Stonewall Manhattan reflects his experiences within the urban gay culture of 1950 and 1960s Manhattan. The multifaceted understanding of pre-Stonewall gay life offered by Duberman's and Helm's autobiographical works is further expanded by Ned Rorem's *The New York Diary* (1967) and Donald Vining's *A Gay Diary* (1979), both of which initiated multivolume autobiographical projects. **Samuel R. Delany**'s *The Motion of Light in Water: Sex and Science Fiction Writing in the East Village, 1957–1965* (1988) presents yet another distinct autobiographical chronicling of pre–Stonewall gay life. Delany's autobiography specifically reflects upon his childhood in Harlem and his adulthood living in the Bohemian enclave of New York City's Lower East Side. **John Rechy**'s *About My Life and the Kept Woman* (2008), which chronicles Mexican American Rechy's upbringing in Texas, is another significant chronicling of pre-Stonewall gay life, particularly for its discussion of homosexuality beyond the confines of New York City. The post-Stonewall chronicling of pre-Stonewall life even included Jeb Alexander's posthumously published *Jeb and Dash: A Diary of Gay Life 1918–1945* (1994). This book, which excerpts 50 volumes of private diary writing, documents gay life in Washington, D.C., and evidences a determined pre-Stonewall gay life writing impulse.

For the generation of gay men whose emergence into adulthood was contemporaneous with the events of Stonewall, the gay autobiographical impulse chronicled the newly found freedoms of the emerging gay culture, which often included the process of coming out and migrating to the gay urban center. However, there were still frequent narrative concessions behind the individual gay autobiography, suggesting something of the enduring cultural stigma behind the revelation of homosexuality in post-Stonewall America. This point is illustrated by John Reid's *The Best Little Boy in the World* (1973), which appeared under the author's real name Andrew Tobias only in 1993. The continuing risks surrounding gay autobiography may have sublimated the gay autobiographical impulse to fiction, resulting in what **Edmund White** terms autofiction. This fictionalized form of the autobiography performs the gay life writing impulse while simultaneously providing the protective buffer of fiction. Although this literary technique is not unique to the gay autobiographer, its productivity is particularly appealing to the gay life writer, who must narrate a minority perspective to a historically resistant, if not hostile, majority. White pioneered this hybrid genre with a trilogy of gay autobiographical novels: *A Boy's Own Story* (1982), *The Beautiful Room Is Empty* (1988), and *The Married Man* (2000). Eventually, White produced a traditional autobiography: *My Lives: An Autobiography* (2006). Similarly, **Felice Picano** produced a trilogy of autobiographical novels: *Ambidextrous: The Secret Lives of Children* (1985), *Men Who Loved Me: A Memoir in the Form of a Novel* (1989), and *A House on the Ocean, a House on the Bay* (1997). Like White, Picano also eventually produced a more traditional autobiography: *Art and Sex in Greenwich Village: A Memoir of Gay Literary Life after Stonewall* (2007).

The post-Stonewall gay life writing impulse continues with younger writers, whose gay autobiographies are uniquely different, for in addition to the freedom to narrate the gay self more openly and directly, they also tend to be written more contemporaneously to the lived experiences they narrate. Notably among these are Aaron Fricke's *Reflections of a Rock Lobster* (1981) and **Kenny Fries**'s *Body, Remember: A Memoir* (1997). Fries's autobiography is particularly notable as its life writing impulse grapples with multiple concerns of identity, including sexuality, religion, and disability.

Plummer's assertion regarding the interconnected nature of personal narratives and cultural developments takes on profound significance during the age of AIDS, and the HIV pandemic has profoundly impacted the gay autobiography. This impact has been reflected in the life writing of people living with AIDS, as well as in their caregivers' life writings. The effect on caregivers can be seen in the autobiographical works of **Paul Monette** and Mark Doty, both of whom wrote memoirs chronicling their partner's dying and death before writing their own autobiographies. Monette's *Borrowed Time: An AIDS Memoir* (1988) chronicles the decline of his partner Rog, and *Becoming a Man: Half a Life Story* (1992) offers a more traditional autobiographical recounting of Monette's own life. Doty's *Heaven's Coast* (1996) recounts the illness and death of his partner Wally, and *Firebird* (1999) is an autobiography of Doty's childhood.

Perhaps the most profound impact the HIV virus has had on gay autobiography is best reflected in the life writing of people living with the virus, and the AIDS pandemic can be seen to have profoundly altered the content and structure of the gay autobiographical impulse. This influence is powerfully illustrated by **Paul Reed**'s *The Q Journal: A Treatment Diary* (1991), which records his day-to-day experiences during an experimental HIV drug trial. Reed's diary, with its oft brief and interrupted entries, literally narrates the impact of AIDS via its structure and content. This impact also appears to have served as a fulcrum for writing that is as experimental as it is autobiographical. This experimentalism is most clearly seen in the autobiographical writings of David Wojnarowicz. Wojnarowicz's *Close to the Knives: A Memoir of Disintegration* (1991) is a pastiche of personal essays that read like viral vignettes to narrate his childhood to his homelessness and subsequent artistic success in New York City. His *Memories That Smell Like Gasoline* (1992) is an experimental mixed media autobiographical narrative that blends prose, prints, and paintings. The depth of Wojnarowicz's life writing impulse is perhaps best evidenced in the posthumously published *In the Shadow of the American Dream* (1998), which collects excerpts of the diaries he kept from 1971 to 1991. The mixed media impulse of Wojnarowicz's work continues with John Dugdale's *Life's Evening Hour* (2000), which blends prose with photographs to express the self-portraiture of a blinded artist, who happens to be a gay man with HIV.

Gay American autobiography has not been exclusive to the upper-class gay white male, for in addition to Delany and Rechy, the subgenre reflects a wider multicultural purview. American immigrant and gay Cuban exile Renaldo Arenas's *Before Night Falls* (1993) records the events that led to his expatriation and subsequent death from AIDS, and African American author **E. Lynn Harris**'s *What Becomes of the Brokenhearted* (2003) chronicles his closeted childhood through his emergence as a best-selling author. Nor has the gay autobiography been the exclusive domain of the gay artist. **Richard Rodriguez**'s *Days of Obligation: An Argument with My Mexican Father* (1992) is a collection of autobiographical essays that address his homosexuality in a chapter titled "Late Victorians," and Tab Hunter's *Tab Hunter Confidential: The Making of a Movie Star* (2005) details the repressed homosexuality behind the 1950 Hollywood idol's public persona. The development of the gay autobiography has even included the sports world, and since

Glen Burke's *Out at Home: The Glenn Burke Story* (1995), Billy Bean published *Going the Other Way: Lessons from a Life In and Out of Major League Baseball* (2003), and John Amaechi published *Man in the Middle* (2007).

Further Reading

Cohler, Bertram. *Writing Desire: Sixty Years of Gay Autobiography.* Madison: University of Wisconsin Press, 2007.

Robinson, Paul. *Gay Lives: Homosexual Autobiography from John Addington Symonds to Paul Monette.* Chicago: University of Chicago Press, 1999.

Mark John Isola

Autobiography, Lesbian

Lesbian autobiography first came into existence over 100 years ago and appears to be the earliest expressive vehicle for lesbian modernism. As lesbians could not tell their stories coherently, and therefore articulate their identities, in "straight" form, the "straight" was made over in the image of social parody and **camp** travesty. Lesbian counternarratives created lesbian and **queer** solidarity through clever "talk-backs" to the moralizing straights and preachers and reformers. The rise of medical sexologist and Freudian theories of homosexual identity as maladjusted, diseased, and perverse prompted more elaborate responses in the lesbian autobiographical counternarratives in the work of lesbian modernists such as Gertrude Stein, Djuna Barnes, and Margaret Anderson. While these writers have been accused of veiling and hiding **lesbianism** through the use of code language, they also and equally rejected the language of medicine and, in addition, relished the capacity to talk their lives and loves in the demotic subculture lingo that the straight readers could not see or censor.

From these beginnings as camp parody and "talk-back" at the straights in the code they could not understand, in the 1970s lesbian autobiography became articulated as the coming out story, in which an inauthentic silenced self was replaced by an authentic and self-affirming lesbian identity. Since lesbian identity was an ethic of choice and solidarity, lesbians of color created narratives that articulated the complexities and contradictions of those multiply marginalized, not only by their lesbianism, but also often by racism, color, class, language, or education. The fact that lesbians of color could not be "one thing" or move toward the dream of completely authentic lesbian selfhood, which was imagined as the separation of lesbians from society, enabled other lesbian writers to reconsider the meanings, manifestations, and narrative logics of lesbian identity. Recognizing that sexual identity does not represent the truth of human nature, for in extended narrative sexual identity can be articulated only through the nests of particulars that humanize. Performance artists represent lesbian identity through camp, political parody, and anticonsumer culture, while others are articulating lesbian autobiography in political action, and narratives that explore the dynamics of familial **homophobia** and the economic and political contexts in which lesbian relationships and communities exist.

In her modernist context, Gertrude Stein draws several lesbian autobiographical counternarratives, none as richly pleasurable as *The Autobiography of Alice B. Toklas* (1931), which gave Stein fame and celebrity. Surprisingly, in this experimental narrative, which has about as much resemblance to the cosmos of Freudian psychology as Ruth and Naomi have to Electra and Clytemnestra, Stein does not write her own story. Rather, she narrates the story of Alice, her wife, but still attributes its authorship to her wife. Crossing the boundaries between story and narrator, biography and autobiography, and author (Stein) and subject (Toklas), there is no chaotic codependence here, as Freud and his followers would have predicted. Instead, it would seem that the marriage or union between these two women is the subject, and Stein models for us the joyous difference that lesbian authorship of lesbian narrative means. In her expansive three-volume autobiography, Margaret Anderson represents what lesbian artistic identity and bohemianism require as demonstrations of character, and a creatively resourceful poverty that refurbishes a decayed cottage in the then bucolic landscape of Long Island. Anderson seems joyous in her lesbian identity, despite the melancholic displays of her girlfriends. They are connected through their journey, their modernist aesthetic passion, and the pleasure they take in ingenuity, discovery, and self-reliance. The foe they face is, in this context, consumer capitalism and crass greed. Whereas Anderson backgrounds her lovers in her partially autobiographical novel *Nightwood* (1930), Djuna Barnes explores the passion and anguish of a lesbian relationship between two Americans in a Europe descending into the maelstrom of Fascism. Robin creates her counternarrative from her refusal to speak about her past, her occasional prostitution and disinterest in monogamy, and her desertion of her husband, a Jew passing as a Gentile, after she has her child. Nora frantically wants an "ordinary" monogamous albeit lesbian relationship, while Robin, radiating the allure of her Marlene Dietrich–like raffish beauty, seduces as she pleases. Indeed, Robin returns to Nora and walks out of a lesbian relationship with Jenny Petherbridge because she steals Robin and has not developed an independent lesbian self or narrative. Perhaps the most direct statement that lesbian Modernists saw the articulation of lesbian autobiography as a prerequisite for lesbianism understood as an act of artistic creation, this idea of lesbian self-narrative as art has persisted. Anomie and alienation are not "lesbian" problems, but rather the conditions of Fascism, and Nora and Robin take refuge in the countercultural night world inhabited by circus people, prostitutes, dissidents, the poor, and Matthew O'Connor, lesbian, Jennie, attempts to steal from Nora the lesbian autobiographical narrative she lacks but wants. In the end, Nora and Robin do escape back to America, but remain locked in isolation.

The lesbian modernist critique of medical sexologist and Freudian narrative remained an artistic matter, and in the 1970s these earlier works seemed coded and obscure to lesbian feminists who defined lesbianism politically and wanted dialogue, openness, culture, and community. Lesbian social reality needed public identification, which developed into the definitive autobiographical form, the coming out narrative. **Rita Mae Brown**'s novel ***Rubyfruit Jungle*** (1973) became an enormous best seller, and the plucky, sassy, attractive Molly Bolt modeled coming out for readers. The distinguished poet **Adrienne Rich** came out and lent her eloquence and probity to lesbian autobiographical narrative in "Split at the Root: An Essay on Jewish Identity" (1982), her encounter with her Jewish identity, the assimilation of American Jews, including her father, and the relations between her lesbian and Jewish identities. *The Coming Out Stories* (1974), an important collection, represented coming out as collective affirmation and celebration. However, coming out was a struggle toward a moment, and soon much writing became bland, filled with commendable lesbians who had healthy relationships and the right political views. At the same time, **May Sarton** was seen as too tepid, despite her later work on chronic illness and lesbian loss and mourning, and Kate Millett as too negative for writing about lesbian love embroiled in tragedy.

The lesbian at the center of lesbian autobiographical narrative had become doctrinaire, narrow, and intolerant. However, in the 1980s, two lesbians of color, in company with others, produced brilliant works that transformed lesbian autobiography: **Audre Lorde**'s *Zami: A New Spelling of My Name* (1983) and **Gloria Evangelina Anzaldúa**'s *Borderlands: La Frontera* (1987). Lorde, a distinguished poet, called her work a "biomytholography" for combining myth, biography, and history—an unlikely trio for standard Western autobiography, and one designed to dash hot pepper into assumptions about the constitutive elements of autobiography. The protagonist as a girl suffers harsh punishment from her mother, rent by her helplessness before the blows of racism. Having ethically disqualified the rhetoric of positive lesbian representation, she redefines lesbian as strong emotional bonds between women, not sexual passion. At this stage, one wonders what the protagonist will do with the pains she has inherited. She stands beneath the blows and stands within the representation of lived experience until, when overwhelmed, she resorts to the mythic African goddesses she has inherited from her ancestors. She knows that they impose absolute order on the world, and sometimes she needs them. As for Anzaldúa, *Borderlands* inscribes the geography of mixture and marginalization, performing hybridization as an initiation into her uncanny childhood, the world of Native American and Catholic myth, snake rituals, and her terror, as an adult lesbian, of returning home. Evoked in Spanish and English, in this land queers and **gay**s become part of the lesbian autobiography of the borderlands, alive to the creative possibilities but also the violent passions that inflame the border.

Anzaldúa takes the journey back home, to homophobia, to the homophobic familial matrix of sibling enmity, the betrayal of love for all. This trip would nurture the maturity and critical reflection of lesbian autobiographical narrative. In *Bastard Out of Carolina* (1991), **Dorothy Allison** represents return to her place of origin, telling the harrowing story of Bone's abuse at the hands of Daddy Glen, and, in the end, her Aunt Rae, a lesbian and the only responsible adult in the book, gives her a home when her mother abandons her for Daddy Glen. In *Skin: Talking about Sex, Class, and Literature* (1993) and elsewhere, Allison analyzes, from an autobiographical perspective, how illiteracy, violence, and poverty shape the sexuality of poor white southern women. Another southerner, the distinguished poet and novelist **Minnie Bruce Pratt**, describes how she almost lost her sons when she came out in *Crimes against Nature* (1991), where she also explores racism, censorship, antisemitism, and transsexual rights. Pratt, a self-defined femme, has had a long-term relationship with **Leslie Feinberg**, a working-class, Jewish, transsexual activist whose autobiographical novel, *Stone Butch Blues* (1993), reveals the violence inflicted repeatedly on her as a butch "he/she," and the struggles for survival, inclusion, and political affirmation. Along with **Joan Nestle**, the Jewish founder of the Lesbian Herstory Archives and editor of *The Persistent Desire: A Femme-Butch Reader* (1992), these writers articulate the range of **gender** roles, sexual practice, and sex identity/identification. In the wake of AIDS, assaults on abortion rights, and the cultures to which they give voice, these writers sometimes assume the role of sex educators, advisors, and promoters. Yet, none constructs models of lesbian identity as sexual practice that approach the devotions of time, focus, and cultivated practiced demanded by Patrick Califia-Rice, formerly Pat Califia. Once self-identified as a butch lesbian and now as gay male, this author seeks uninhabited territories and bends an individual life into an autobiographical narrative devoted to sadomasochism and leather practice, ritual, pleasure, and polemic.

The proliferation and range of lesbian autobiography reveals its importance and appeal. There are celebrities and mothers, ex-nuns and rabbis, sex workers and athletes, musicians and actresses, cancer and sexual trauma survivors, Jewish and Native Americans, African Americans and Hispanics, elderly and rural, and more, including sex experts, political activists, and participants in historical events, political groups, or specific cultures.

This abundant lesbian autobiographical narrative, which has extended to the writer-celebrity-culture maven reports, interviews, and reviews on the Web site www .afterellen.com cannot hide that between 1998 and 2008, the number of American lesbian-authored works of fiction published by major or mainstream publishing houses dwindled and almost stopped. **Sarah Schulman**, an acclaimed writer with an established reputation, waited 10 years for the publication of her novel *The Child* (2008). Sandra Bernhard critiques inane consumer culture in her performance art, which uses camp parody and pastiche to represent her identities as Jewish lesbian mother and actress. *I'm Still Here . . . Damn It!* (1999) opens with Bernhard on a stage with gorgeous light, wearing nothing but a sheer slip, and hugely pregnant. This glowing representation of lesbian motherhood stands alone, and she moves into biting camp parodies of celebrities, consumer products, and the White House, ending with a Jewish prayer for Israel. And the lesbian comic strip artist **Alison Bechdel** published her lesbian autobiographical graphic novel, *The Fun Home: A Family Tragicomic* (2006). The college-age protagonist comes out as a lesbian and, returning home, tells her parents. All seems fine. But two weeks later, her father, whom she discovers was a gay man, dies in a freak accident that could have easily been avoided. Was he too careless in the wrong moment? Is her father, having suffered in the **closet**, so grief struck when he finds out his daughter is a lesbian who will suffer as he has that he takes his life? Does her declaration make him unbearably aware of the futility of his life?

Lesbian autobiography has redefined, questioned, and re-represented both "lesbian" and "autobiography," considering the relations among memory, narrative constructs, communities, and history, and how extended narrative articulates and defines lesbian identity in and through the multiple identities, contexts, histories, memories, situations, and concerns of the subject. Recent lesbian autobiographical narrative in performance art, historical documentation, examinations of families of origin, and political struggle indicate the current directions of this durable genre of modern lesbian literature.

Further Reading

Gale, Maggie Barbara, and Vivien Gardner. *Auto/biography and Identity: Women, Theater, and Performance.* Manchester, UK: Manchester University Press, 2004.

Gilmore, Leigh. "A Signature of Lesbian Autobiography." *Autobiographics: A Feminist Theory of Women's Self-Representation.* Cornell, NY: Cornell University Press, 1994. 199–223.

Johnson, Georgia. *The Formation of 20th Century Queer Autobiography.* New York: Palgrave MacMillan, 2007.

Martin, Biddy. "Lesbian Identity and Autobiographical Difference(s)." In *Women, Autobiography, Theory: A Reader,* edited by Sidonie Smith and Julia Watson, 380–92. Madison: University of Wisconsin Press, 1998.

Martindale, Kathleen. *Un/popular Culture: Lesbian Writings after the Sex Wars.* Albany: State University of New York Press, 1997.

Corinne E. Blackmer

Autobiography, Transgender

Transgender autobiography is a body of literature that consists of narratives that articulate and empower the transgender or transsexual autobiographical voice. Transgendered
and transsexual individuals have *gender dysphoria* (a condition characterized by intense,
often painful, feelings that one's assigned sex does not match one's **gender**). Gender dysphoria is clinically diagnosed, not without controversy, in the West as *gender identity disorder.* Transgendered people live full time as the gender they feel themselves to be and
may undergo sexual reassignment surgery to transition from one sex to another. As testimonies to transsexual and transgender experience, transgender autobiographies give voice
to an ever-shifting range of gendered identities and experiences, some of which may or
may not involve medical treatment, **queer** sexuality, or the embrace of "trans" terminology or politics.

Most critics chart the rise of the transgender autobiography as a twentieth-century phenomenon, although more dated texts certainly lend themselves to this genre, despite their
sometimes questionable authenticity. Various historical pressures, including the rise of the
scientific field of sexology in the first decades of the twentieth century and the Sexual Revolution of the 1960s, helped construct "transsexual" and "transgender" identities as well
as a reading public hungry for narratives written from the social margins. As a mode of
political discourse, transgender autobiography has been an effective tool in arguing for
transgender rights and recognition.

Early Transgender Autobiographical Narratives. Although the term "transsexual" was
coined in 1910 by German sexologist Magnus Hirschfeld, transsexual identity more fully
developed in the 1950s in psychiatric and medical diagnoses. However, critics continue to
debate the historical origins of transsexual and transgender people. No doubt, medical
discourse and technology have been a primary force in the definition and construction
of transgender subjects; but, people who cross sex and gender boundaries have existed
across cultures and across time.

Most early accounts of trans-like behavior (such as the story of Megilla who changes to
Megillus in Lucian's *Dialogue of the Courtesans*) are written in third person and are next to
impossible to confirm. But first-person trans narratives do exist prior to the medical and
scientific carving out of a transsexual identity, not to mention before the development
of medical and scientific technology for sexual reassignment surgeries. This latter point
gestures to the question of what to include in a genre that has come to emphasize a specific
form of transition that is reliant on recently developed technology.

For instance, the phenomenon of "passing women" throughout history presents a number of narratives that deliver a transgender voice prior to the social formation of distinctly
transsexual or transgender identities. Such narratives illustrate the complicated politics of
claiming certain narratives and lives as "trans." Catalina de Erauso (1592–1650), a Spanish adventurer, duelist, and marvel, lived as Francisco de Loyola for nearly all of her life.
The flamboyant autobiography details life as a swashbuckling soldier complete with
romances with women and bouts with the law.

Traditionally, the autobiography of Lili Elbe (1882–1931) is cited as the first book-
length account of transsexuality. Elbe was a male-born Danish painter who identified
and lived as a woman beginning in the 1920s. Elbe underwent five operations, which were
very experimental at the time, as part of her transition, including a surgery intended to
allow her to carry a child. When her transition was made public, the European press
seized on her story, prompting Elbe to arrange for an autobiographical rendering of her

life. Based on diary entries, letters, and dictation, *Man into Woman: An Authentic Record of a Change of Sex* was prepared by her friend Ernst Ludwig Hathorn Jacobson and published in 1933. The book has since been recognized as one of the first books to distinguish homosexuality from transsexuality.

Contemporary Transgender Autobiographies. Like Elbe's, many transgender autobiographies have emerged from public scandals involving the author's outing as transsexual. In this sense, telling one's story, or testifying to one's truth, becomes an empowering act for transsexual and transgender people. While many trans people were not open or political about their status (preferring to live stealth as their chosen gender), the publication of more and more trans autobiographies slowly helped to politicize trans identity and create a new gender identity that trans people increasingly embraced.

The transsexual autobiography *Roberta Cowell's Story* (1954) similarly erupted from sensationalized publicity and was in fact first published as a magazine serial. Cowell is known as Britain's first transsexual. She shared a close friendship with female-to-male (FTM) transsexual Michael Dillon. Two years after Cowell's publication, Christine Jorgensen became an overnight celebrity when the story about her sexual reassignment surgeries broke. An article in New York's *Daily News* proclaimed "Ex-GI Becomes Blonde Bombshell," and Jorgensen was hounded by journalists everywhere she went. As the first transsexual to receive so much press in the United States, Jorgensen comfortably eased into life as a public figure and performer. Largely because of her dignified and articulate reaction to the controversy that surrounded her, Jorgensen became a catalyst for a new transsexual visibility—one that demanded education, research, and recognition. She released a confessional interview record, *Christine Jorgensen Reveals* (1958), in her first response to the public that was eager to hear her story. Her autobiography was published in 1967 and adapted as a film, *The Christine Jorgensen Story* (1970).

Despite the publicity that swirled around these trans autobiographies of the late 1950s through the 1970s, very few accounts of FTM transsexuals were either recorded in the press or published. Mario Martino's *Emergence: A Transsexual Autobiography* (1977) is one of the earliest autobiographical chronicles of FTM life. Martino describes how his traditional Catholic background informed his struggle with gender and his decision to undergo a mastectomy and phalloplasty.

The 1990s, with its insistent focus on **multiculturalism** and diversity, saw the publication of a more overtly politicized transgender autobiography. **Leslie Feinberg**'s semiautobiographical *Stone Butch Blues* (1993) and **Kate Bornstein**'s collection *Gender Outlaw: On Men, Women, and the Rest of Us* (1994) represent a new generation of transgendered people. In these texts and others, authors, activists, and educators Feinberg and Bornstein complicate notions that transsexuals are "trapped in the wrong body" and present alternative narratives to those modeled on the clear transition from one definitive gender to the other.

On the heels of these publications, the publication of trans narratives exploded, especially in the United States. Examples include Jamison Green's *Becoming a Visible Man* (1998), Deirdre McCloskey's *Crossing* (1999), and Max Wolf Valerio's *The Testosterone Files* (2006).

Critical Issues in Transgender Autobiography. Transgender academic Jay Prosser has critiqued the postmodern scholarly attention that has been granted to the transsexual autobiographical narrative. He argues that the focus of such inquiries might more usefully be focused on the trans autobiography as "body narrative" rather than as a narrative of transition. In this sense, transgender autobiographies, in both subversive and hegemonic ways, force readers to encounter a materiality that perhaps other texts do not. As chronicles about embodiment and the body, Prosser claims these autobiographies and narratives disrupt an array of binaries by highlighting the transitional spaces between them.

As definitions of transgender and genderqueer identities expand and as transgender rights and visibility increase, the genre of transgender autobiography will no doubt continue to shift as new generations of trans people tell their stories.

Further Reading

Green, Jamison. *Becoming a Visible Man.* Nashville, TN: Vanderbilt University Press, 2004.
Jorgensen, Christine. 1967. *Christine Jorgensen: A Personal Autobiography.* San Francisco: Cleis Press, 2000.
McCloskey, Deirdre. *Crossing: A Memoir.* Chicago: University of Chicago Press, 1999.
Prosser, Jay. *Second Skins: The Body Narratives of Transsexuality.* New York: Columbia University Press, 1998.
Valerio, Max Wolf. *The Testosterone Files: My Hormonal and Social Transformation from Female to Male.* Emeryville, CA: Seal Press, 2006.

Emma Crandall

Awards, LGBTQ Literature

The rapid development of lesbian, **gay**, bisexual, transgender, and **queer** (LGBTQ) literature is a relatively contemporary occurrence. Prior to 1969, the conservative social climate was not conducive to LGBTQ writers, whose stories faced opposition from publishers and both parties feared censorship or legal charges of obscenity. As a result, authors employed various self-censorship techniques, such as encoding stories within acceptable parameters or simply refusing to publish. Walt Whitman, for example, disguised same-sex attraction inside a story about temperance in *Franklin Evans,* while E. M. Forster never sought publication of *Maurice* during his lifetime. Publishers asked authors such as Vin Packer to alter stories and even avoided works of nonfiction, such as Jeannette Howard Foster's *Sex Variant Women in Literature* (1958), for fear of controversy.

Within this social climate it was possible for LGBTQ writers to receive recognition in the form of book awards. Notable LGBTQ book award winners include Willa Cather who won the nation's oldest literary prize, the Pulitzer Prize for literature in 1923. W. H. Auden garnered a Pulitzer for poetry in 1948, and **Tennessee Williams** received two Pulitzers for drama in 1948 and 1956. The National Book Award also honored writers such as Newton Arvin (1951), Rachel Carson (1952), and Janet Flanner (1966). It would be many years before an openly LGBTQ author writing about LGBTQ themes would win one of these prestigious awards.

LGBTQ literature began emerging from this dark, underground period with the 1969 **Stonewall Riots**, generally considered the birth of the modern LGBTQ civil rights movement. The increasing visibility of the community led to greater demand for LGBTQ literature and gave rise to a variety of entities responsible for heightening the awareness of LGBTQ literature through book awards, including professional associations, nonprofit foundations, corporations, and individuals.

Professional Associations. The earliest LGBTQ professional organization arose within a field intimately connected to the promotion of reading and literature, the American Library Association (ALA), and this organization established the first LGBTQ literary award. The Task Force on Gay Liberation, consisting of a handful of librarians and activist-bibliographer Barbara Gittings, created the Gay Book Award in 1971 and honored Isabel Miller for *Patience & Sarah* (1972). Since those early days when winners were selected by consensus, the award has undergone several changes. By 1981 the quantity of eligible literature had increased substantially, and formal rules were created to pave the way for official recognition by the ALA in 1986. Expanded to include a nonfiction category in 1990, the two prizes were collectively renamed the Stonewall Book Awards in 2002. The Stonewall's limitation to two categories lends the award a measure of prestige and ensures such a rigorous competition that only three authors have won the award more than once.

A similarly competitive award recognizes scholarly literature. In 1986, the Society of Lesbian and Gay Anthropologists of the American Anthropological Association established an award, the Ruth Benedict Prize, for scholarly literature with an anthropological perspective. Esther Newton and Stephen O. Murray are two prominent winners of this annual prize given to single authored and edited volumes.

Like the Benedict Prize, the Publishing Triangle Awards (PTAs) were established by a group of professionals, the Association of Lesbians and Gay Men in Publishing. Since 1989, the annual PTAs have recognized writers with cash awards in a seven categories.

For a brief period between 1996 and 2002, a group of book industry professionals sponsored the Firecracker Alternative Book Awards. The multicategory awards, although not exclusive to LGBTQ literature, acknowledged controversial or insurrectionary works and included an award for the best sex book. The precise reason for the award's demise is unclear, though sponsorship and funding may have been a factor.

Nonprofit Foundations. Creating a nonprofit organization is one method to secure sponsorship and funding in the competitive world of book awards. The Lambda Literary Foundation began in 1988 expressly to support LGBTQ literature; book awards form the cornerstone of that agenda. Presented annually in 21 categories that have varied over the years, the Lambdas are distinctive for initiating the first LGBTQ awards dedicated to children's literature, poetry, romance, science fiction/fantasy, and several other genres. Unlike many other awards, an author or publisher may self-nominate by paying an entry fee and titles may appear in numerous categories. These rules ensure a lengthy and diverse winners' list, repeat winners in the same year, and the entry fee generates financial capital to promote the awards in media venues.

A relative newcomer to book awards, the Gaylactic Spectrum Awards was created in 1996 to distinguish science fiction, fantasy, and horror books with positive LGBTQ content. Within this narrow field, the annual cash awards are presented in three categories: best novel, best short fiction, and best work in another medium, such as comic books.

Corporations. Corporate sponsorship of awards is a potentially tenuous situation. While financial capital enhances an award's prestige, sponsorship by a commercial publisher may represent a conflict of interest and the awards process may not be entirely transparent. Nevertheless, the existence of this type of award is noteworthy because sponsorship is derived from non-LGBTQ publishers.

Independent Publisher magazine sponsors the annual IPPY Awards. Presented in 55 categories since 1996, independently published works of LGBTQ fiction and nonfiction compete against each other in these entry-fee-based awards. The preponderance of categories and the predisposition to independently published works ensures a broad range of entries, but often results in lesser known, self-published authors as winners.

The ForeWord Magazine Book Awards have been competing with the IPPYs since 1999. Like the IPPYs, these awards require an entry fee and are targeted to independently published titles; however, these awards treat LGBTQ fiction and nonfiction in separate categories.

Emerging writers are honored by the **Violet Quill** Award. Named after a circle of gay writers, the cash award is presented annually by the InsightOut Book Club, a Book-of-the-Month Club affiliate. Little is known about the awards' history; however, winners are selected by the InsightOut staff and receive monetary prizes.

Individuals. For a variety of reasons, individuals have opted to promote literature through book awards. The most common motivations for this support are a personal love of literature and the desire to memorialize a loved one. In several instances, these motivations have combined to create awards. The Ferro-Grumley Awards are funded by the estates of novelists-life partners **Robert Ferro** and **Michael Grumley**. The entry-fee-based awards are devoted solely to literary fiction. Since its establishment in 1990, the annual award has recognized one male and one female author. The following year saw the establishment of the James Tiptree, Jr. Memorial Award. While not exclusively dedicated to LGBTQ literature, Tiptrees honor the spirit of LGBTQ literature by recognizing science fiction or fantasy works that subvert **gender** norms. Named after James Tiptree, a pseudonym for Alice B. Sheldon, this annual award carries a cash prize. Playwright-filmmaker Arch Brown created the Arch and Bruce Brown Foundation Awards in 1996 to memorialize his life partner, Bruce Allen Brown. Dedicated to recognizing works with historical content, cash awards are granted in three annually rotating categories, including short story, fiction, and playwriting. The Foundation also issues grants supporting historically based theater productions. Given the award's narrow focus, the majority of winners are lesser-known writers

The newest LGBTQ book awards grew out of reader appreciation. Two of these awards are devoted to fostering lesbian authors and literature. The Alice B. Reader's Appreciation Award, named after Alice B. Toklas, began in 2000 as an effort to recognize a body of work by a single author. Winners receive a monetary prize and commemorative medallions. In 2005, the Golden Crown Literary Society formed a network of authors, readers, and volunteers from the publishing industry to promote lesbian fiction. The Society's first effort was the formation of a book award, the Goldie. Focusing on three categories, romance/erotica; science fiction/fantasy; and mystery/action/adventure/thriller, judges select three winners.

Conclusion. The types of awards, award-granting agencies, criteria for nomination, and form of award are many and varied. Awards may recognize multiple types of literature published in a given year, honor a single author for a body of work, or be devoted to a specific genre of literature. Considered as a group, these book awards signify the success of LGBTQ literature; the substantial overlap among winners demonstrates the prominent writers of the genre, such as Lillian Faderman, **Leslie Feinberg**, Jim Grimsley, Alan Hollinghurst, **Joan Nestle**, **Sarah Schulman**, Colm Tóibín, **Edmund White**, and many others. As the publishing industry moves into the twenty-first century and electronic books gain popularity, literary awards will continue to be coveted by authors as forms of recognition and validation, desired by publishers as marketing tools, and valued by readers as indicators of quality.

Further Reading

Alice B. Reader's Appreciation Award: http://www.alicebawards.org/; and Bruce Brown Foundation Awards: http://www.aabbfoundation.org.

ForeWord Magazine Book of the Year Awards: http://www.forewordmagazine.net/awards.asp.

Gaylactic Spectrum Awards: http://www.spectrumawards.org.

Goldie Awards: http://www.goldencrown.org/awards.html.

Independent Publisher Book Awards: http://www.independentpublisher.com/ipland/LearnMore.php.

Lambda Literary Awards: http://www.lambdalit.org.

Publishing Triangle Awards: http://www.publishingtriangle.org/awards.asp.

Ruth Benedict Prize: http://www.uvm.edu/~dlrh/solga/prizes/Benedict/benhistory.html.

Stonewall Awards: http://www.ala.org/ala/glbtrt/stonewall/stonewallbook.htm.

Tiptree Awards: http://www.tiptree.org.

Ellen Bosman

B

Baldwin, James (1924–1987)

Major African American **gay** novelist, essayist, playwright, poet, and civil rights activist. The circumstances of James Baldwin's birth were unremarkable. He was born on August 2, 1924, at Harlem Hospital in New York City to a poor, unmarried, 20-year-old woman named Emma Berdis Jones. But his death 63 years later on December 1, 1987, at his home in southern France was an event reported on the front pages of newspapers around the world. Indeed, his journey from a difficult childhood in Harlem to his eventual status as a celebrity-artist with a large and loyal international audience constitutes one of the most compelling life stories of the twentieth century.

Baldwin's early years were deeply troubled. Three years after his birth, his mother married David Baldwin, many years her senior, who was a laborer and a fundamentalist Baptist minister. With him she had eight children. Her husband, meanwhile, grew increasingly angry, abusive, and violent; soon he began to terrorize his wife and children. James, presumably because he was a stepchild, became a favorite target for the elder Baldwin's violent outbursts. This problematic relationship with his stepfather would haunt Baldwin for many years to come.

At age 14 Baldwin underwent an experience of spiritual conversion—an experience vividly recreated in his first and explicitly autobiographical novel, *Go Tell It on the Mountain;* for the next three years he was a teenage minister who preached in evangelical churches in and around Harlem. He left the church at age 17, but the three years in the ministry were crucial to his personal and artistic development. Though he formally abandoned the pulpit when he was 17, he remained very much a preacher for the rest of his life. The language of the church—the Biblical imagery and cadences, the grand rhetorical strategies of the African American pulpit oratory—left its unmistakable imprint on his distinct prose style. The social and theoretical imperatives of African American Protestantism fundamentally shaped his vision and granted urgency and authority to his message.

Soon after graduation from DeWitt Clinton High School in Brooklyn in 1942, Baldwin became a laborer at a railroad construction site across the Hudson River in New Jersey. Although he had been subjected to racial taunts and occasional racial violence in New York City, he was totally unprepared for the brutally racist hostility that greeted him in New Jersey. A long series of encounters with petty apartheid culminated in a spectacular incident at a diner that Baldwin later recounted in his classic essay "Notes of a Native Son." Soon he relocated to Greenwich Village, supported himself by doing a variety of odd jobs—he was at times a busboy, a waiter, and an elevator operator—and started to write. His book reviews and essays began to appear in some of the most prestigious journals in the Eastern intellectual establishment. He was gaining attention. But everyday encounters with racism, coupled with his growing awareness of the personal and political implications of his homosexuality, left him deeply unsettled. In a frantic attempt to escape what he felt was impending madness, Baldwin, with the money he had received as part of a Rosenwald Fellowship, purchased a one-way ticket to Paris. He was 24, spoke no French, and had only $40 in his pocket when he landed in Paris on November 11, 1948. Thus began his transatlantic exile, which would continue, on and off, for the rest of his life.

Given the many dilemmas generated by Baldwin's profound sense of racial, sexual, and artistic exclusion from his homeland, expatriation for him was not only a desirable option but a compelling necessity. In Baldwin's own words, he left the United States "to survive the fury of the color problem" (*Nobody Knows My Name* 17). He wanted to be a writer, and the United States did not seem to him to be a congenial place to become one. But it is important to acknowledge the sexual dimension of his exile as well. When he left for France in 1948, he was fleeing not only the racial lunacy of his country but also the personal troubles of his sexuality. Indeed, his flight to France was a flight away from American sexual codes. In France he met and fell in love with Lucien Happersberger, with whom he forged one of the enduring relationships of his life. France, then, became a liberatory space where Baldwin could jettison American scripts of masculinity, a place where he could begin charting the troublesome geography of his homosexual longing.

Race and sexuality—two of Baldwin's primary preoccupations—became the subject of his first major works: *Go Tell It on the Mountain* (1953), *Notes of a Native Son* (1955), and *Giovanni's Room* (1956). In 1957, seeking personal involvement in the burgeoning civil rights movement, he returned to the United States. During the 1960s, perhaps the finest decade in Baldwin's career, Baldwin emerged as a most eloquent civil rights activist. Though an angry prophet, he advocated not a program of violence but a path of reconciliation, forgiveness, and love. With such a message, often articulated in precise and elegant prose, he soon drew a very large American and international audience. Works such as *Nobody Knows My Name, Another Country, Blues for Mister Charlie,* and *Tell Me How Long the Train's Been Gone,* all published during the 1960s, made him one of the preeminent artists of his generation.

During the 1970s, though still quite prolific, Baldwin began to show signs of exhaustion. The civil rights movement largely over, the reception of Baldwin's message began to grow less enthusiastic. The emergence of African American women writers such as **Alice Walker** and Toni Morrison during the late 1970s and 1980s meant that he no longer held the center stage of the literary scene. His failing health, coupled with heavy drinking, began to compromise the quality of his writing. Too, he clearly became disillusioned with the emergence of the New Right in American politics, the election and landslide reelection of Ronald Reagan to the White House, and the escalation of racial animosities —though he continued to insist, even during the reactionary 1980s, on his vision of an America free of its racial pathologies and sexual hypocrisies.

Baldwin chose to die in France. In December 1987, after an emotional funeral service at The Cathedral of St. John the Divine in New York City, attended by thousands of friends and admirers, the casket carrying his frail body was driven through the streets of Harlem—the streets of his troubled childhood. Baldwin's journey ended at Ferncliff Cemetery, a few miles outside the city.

Go Tell It on the Mountain, a modern classic and perhaps Baldwin's magnum opus, was published in 1953. Given the abundant evidence of autobiographical material present in the narrative, *Go Tell* is arguably a record of the author's attempt to come to terms with the given of his complex inheritance. But *Go Tell* is much more than an autobiographical tale. Imbued with an epic sense of history and resonant with elaborate Biblical imagery, it is a universal story of initiation, of coming-of-age, and of a young man's struggle to forge an autonomous identity in opposition to surrounding authority figures.

Go Tell is divided into three parts. Book I focuses on the consciousness of the adolescent protagonist, John Grimes. Part II, the longest of the three, follows a historical-generational pattern: subdivided unto "Florence's Prayer," "Gabriel's Prayer," and "Elizabeth's Prayer," it familiarizes the reader with the personal histories of the three characters through flashbacks. Although John is unaware of the personal struggles of Florence, his aunt, Gabriel, his raging father, and Elizabeth, his mother, the reader is given a telescopically expanding vision of the protagonist's familial and racial histories that have shaped his identity. The three "Prayers" provide a broad framework for the novel's central situation, John's search for self; they also collectively reveal the historical essence of African American experience. As we understand the protagonist's history, we grasp the various forces that inform his inheritance, the interconnectedness of the past and the present, the link between history and self. Book III culminates in John's spiritual conversion, his acceptance of the Holy Spirit, before the altar of the Temple of the Fire Baptized.

Because critics in general have privileged the novel's racial content, many have failed to acknowledge fully the sexual aspect of John's struggle for self-definition. *Go Tell*, in fact, offers one of the most sensitive portrayals of the developing adolescent consciousness in American fiction. The first suggestion of John's homosexual leanings becomes evident when he keeps staring at Elisha, as the 17-year-old Sunday school teacher explains a Biblical lesson. John finds himself "admiring the timbre of Elisha's voice, much deeper and manlier than his own, admiring the leanness and grace, the strength, the darkness of Elisha in his Sunday suit" (13). When Elisha dances in a state of religious frenzy, the adolescent protagonist is fascinated by the "muscles leaping and swelling in his long, dark neck" and his thighs, which move "terribly against the cloth of his suit" (16). John and Elisha's playful wrestling on the church floor, too, has obvious sexual overtones. After the wrestling, the protagonist stares "in a dull paralysis of terror at the body of Elisha" and looks at the older boy's face with "questions he would never ask" (54). Toward the end of the novel, after John's spiritual conversion, he touches Elisha's arm and finds himself "trembling" (220). He looks at his Sunday school teacher and struggles "to tell him something . . . all that could never be said" (220). When Elisha places a "holy kiss" on John's forehead, the new convert views it as a "seal ineffaceable forever" (221), thereby suggesting a new awareness on his part. Thus, Baldwin hints at the doubts, anxieties, and moments of dim excitement that accompany John's sexual awakening.

This theme of sexual identity dominates Baldwin's second novel, *Giovanni's Room* (1956). Prior to the publication of this work, Baldwin had already established himself as an eloquent essayist and gifted novelist. Readers and critics had come to recognize him as an insightful interpreter of the African American experience. Therefore, *Giovanni's Room,* with its all-white cast and its focus on the issue of sexual identity, disappointed and disturbed many. But publishing such a novel in the mid-1950s was a singular act of courage and defiance on the part of Baldwin, because by doing so he risked his career and the possibility of alienating a substantial segment of his audience. Yet now, more than four decades after its publication, *Giovanni's Room* remains a classic piece of American gay fiction.

As much a Jamesian tale of expatriation and its discontents as a lyrical novel of remembrance and atonement, *Giovanni's Room* begins with David, the narrator, standing at the window of a great house in the south of France as the night falls "and dreading the most terrible morning" (7) of his life. An American in his late 20s, he has fled to France to escape the haunting memories of his dead mother, an irresponsible father, and an adolescent homosexual encounter. In Paris, after a brief affair with Hella, an American drifter who soon leaves for Spain, he reluctantly falls in love with Giovanni, a handsome young Italian. But David remains sexually confused: he is simultaneously attracted to, and repelled by, his lover; sometimes he goes out alone to "find a girl, any girl at all" (126) to reassure himself that he is, indeed, capable of functioning heterosexually. When Hella returns to Paris from Spain, David leaves Giovanni to resume his difficult relationship with her. Abandoned by his only close friend, Giovanni resorts to prostitution to pay for his room and food. In a rather sensational turn of events, Giovanni murders Guillaume, an employer who humiliates and exploits him. Soon Giovanni is caught, tried, found guilty, and sentenced to death. On the eve of his execution the narrative begins; in an extended flashback David reconstructs his relationship with Giovanni and his own role in pushing Giovanni to his present plight.

Its despair and violent conclusion notwithstanding, *Giovanni's Room* is a bittersweet remembrance of a gay romance. In it Baldwin reveals one of the primary dilemmas of the American gay male: on one hand, he is faced with rigid social definitions of masculinity and cultural expectations of heterosexual conduct; on the other hand, he has to deal with his sexual feelings for other men, feelings that militate against all the belief systems that he has, for the most part, internalized. The crisis resulting from such a conflict provides the central drama of Baldwin's second novel.

This inability to love authentically resurfaces as a dominant theme in *Another Country* (1962), Baldwin's best-selling third major work of fiction. Here Baldwin, for the first time, explicitly combines racial and sexual protest. Though an angry work, it nevertheless embodies Baldwin's vision of "another country"—a new Jerusalem, an imaginary America —free of repressive racial boundaries and sexual categories.

Another Country is a complex narrative, structured to reveal Baldwin's outrage with maximum force. It has a multiethnic cast of eight major characters: Rufus is a black jazz musician; Leona is a poor white from the South; Ida, Rufus's sister, is an angry and ambitious blues singer; Vivaldo, an aspiring writer of Irish and Italian background, is a friend of Rufus and a lover of Ida; Richard, a Polish American of working-class origins, is a friend of Vivaldo and a fairly successful novelist; his wife, Cass, is a white Anglo-Saxon Protestant from a wealthy New England family; Eric, a southern white male, is an actor; and Yves, a former Parisian prostitute, is Eric's lover. All the women are exclusively heterosexual. Among the male characters, Rufus and Vivaldo are bisexual, although they generally prefer women; Eric and Yves are also bisexual, but their primary attraction is to men; and Richard, the least likable character, is the novel's one exclusively heterosexual male. These regionally, economically, ethnically, and sexually diverse characters constitute a microcosmic America; Baldwin's exploration of the conflicts among them, then, is a commentary on the larger tensions in American society.

In *Another Country* Baldwin argues, on one hand, that labels and categories warp human relationships, that racial histories inform individual encounters, that the politics of color shapes even the most casual of cross-racial connections. Yet, on the other hand, Baldwin insists that labels and categories are merely artificial constructions, that history can, indeed, be transcended, that color has no intrinsic validity in any genuinely human terms. "Another country," then, is a territory without barriers, a place where individuals can connect with one another unhindered by any imposed labels. But that country is not merely a geographical place but also a symbolic space within ourselves—a space where we may imaginatively transcend national, racial, and sexual categories.

For a pre-**Stonewall** novel, the treatment of homosexuality in *Another Country* is remarkably sophisticated. Refreshingly absent is the ubiquitous Freudian pattern of ineffectual fathers, overprotective mothers, and homosexually inclined sons that recurs insistently in many "gay" American novels published before the 1970s. Here homosexuality is hardly an occasion for panic or reason for guilt. True, it causes suffering, as it does in the case of Eric, but in Baldwin's theology suffering can lead to redemptive self-knowledge, to a more humane understanding of the self and the other. Gayness, therefore, has redemptive potential. Significantly, *Another Country* is one of the very few pre-Stonewall novels in which gay romance does not terminate in murder or suicide; on the contrary, the relationship between Eric and Yves at the end of the narrative reveals at least tentative signs of wholeness and durability.

That homosexuality may contain redemptive possibilities is developed even more vigorously in Baldwin's fourth novel, *Tell Me How Long the Train's Been Gone* (1968). It is the story of Leo Proudhammer, a bisexual, 39-year-old, highly successful black actor. While recuperating in a San Francisco hospital from a massive heart attack, Leo looks back on his eventful life—from his bleak childhood in a rat-infested Harlem tenement house to his present status as a phenomenally successful actor. He recalls his romantic involvement with Barbara, a white actress, and the disapproval of a racist society that destroyed that romance. He elaborately remembers his relationship with black Christopher, a young militant committed to radical change. The story is narrated entirely through Leo's flashbacks, with shorter flashbacks embedded within larger ones. Leo examines his life, seeking a pattern that would grant at least a semblance of order to the accumulated anarchy of his experience. He wants to invest his suffering "with a coherence and authority" (99). This larger quest unifies his extended and sometimes disjointed recollections.

Many of Baldwin's thematic concerns—such as the failure of love, the loneliness of the artist, the maiming impact of racism on individuals and on relationships—resurface in *Tell Me*. Once again, Baldwin casts the gay character in a redemptive role. Black Christopher's name itself, for example, suggests his role as a racial savior; his absolute commitment to revolutionary politics shows that he is part of the transforming process that is challenging and changing America. But Christopher is also comfortably and confidently gay. By combining black militancy and gay sexuality in Christopher's character, Baldwin suggests that there is no fundamental conflict between the two. One is tempted, of course, to speculate whether Baldwin, in creating Christopher's character, is defensively responding to the hostile criticism that the gay content of *Giovanni's Room* and *Another Country* elicited from homophobic black militants such as Eldridge Cleaver and Amiri Baraka.

Baldwin's fifth novel, *If Beale Street Could Talk,* was published in 1974. A poignant love story, it is a relatively short novel that centers around an unborn baby, its unwed mother and unjustly jailed father, and the families of the parents. The story is told in the first person by the mother of the baby, Clementine "Tish" Rivers, a 19-year-old who lives with her parents and sister in Harlem. The father of the baby she is carrying is Alonzo "Fonny" Hunt, a self-taught sculptor.

Through Tish's recollections we are familiarized with the action antecedent to the novel's beginning: Tish and Fonny fall in love and plan to get married, but their hopes are shattered when Victoria, an emotionally disturbed Puerto Rican woman, falsely accuses Fonny of raping her. Despite flimsy evidence, Fonny is imprisoned without bail. The novel begins with Tish's visit to the Tombs, the jail where Fonny is held, to inform him of her pregnancy; it ends just prior to the birth of the baby. The events of the intervening months constitute the bulk of the narrative.

Structured as a blues lament, *If Beale Street Could Talk* focuses on the unsuccessful attempt by Tish and her family members to gain Fonny's release from jail. The plot allows Baldwin to explore the complex links between racism and sexuality, the insidiously racist nature of the American judicial system, the moral bankruptcy of institutionalized religion, and the redemptive potential of unconditional love. Conspicuously absent in this novel, however, is one of Baldwin's major preoccupations: the theme of homosexual desire.

Just Above My Head (1979), Baldwin's sixth and final novel, centers around the life of Arthur Montana, a black gay gospel singer, as seen through the eyes of his surviving brother, Hall Montana, a 48-year-old advertising executive. Arthur, at age 39, was found dead of a heart attack in a men's room of a London pub. Hall's thoughts about Arthur's life and death are triggered by his 15-year-old son's question of why his friends at school refer to his musically renowned uncle Arthur as a "faggot." Troubled by his son's query, Hall begins to reconstruct the past—his brother's and his own—in an attempt to understand their particular fates so that he may face "both love and death" (407).

Hall's elaborate recollections offer vivid pictures of Arthur's troubled life as well as the narrator's own evolving attitude toward the content and meaning of his deceased sibling's life. At the core of the narrative is Arthur's anguished search for love; central to the novel, therefore, is the subject of homosexuality. What is noteworthy here is Baldwin's treatment of that subject. Unlike some of his earlier novels, *Just Above My Head* reveals a relaxed and more sophisticated attitude toward gay sexuality: Baldwin treats it less self-consciously, less polemically, and less stridently. The gay theme, in fact, is more smoothly woven into the narrative; and it is presented as an essentially unsensational, though problematic, element in Arthur's search for identity and meaning.

Though there is consensus that James Baldwin is one of the most gifted essayists of the twentieth century, his reputation as a novelist remains contested. Many fans of Baldwin are wildly enthusiastic about Baldwin's fiction and shy away from identifying his artistic lapses or interrogating the ideological assumptions that inform his narratives. But many critics are openly hostile to Baldwin: often their criticism is tinged with racism or **homophobia** or both. Only a few critics appear to make a conscious effort to be balanced in their perspectives and fair in their assessments of Baldwin's achievement as a novelist. Perhaps the fact that Baldwin continues to provoke a broad spectrum of intellectual and emotional responses in itself is a measure of his provocative relevance and value as an artist.

Go Tell It on the Mountain, Baldwin's first novel, continues to be his most celebrated work. It has spawned more scholarship than any of his other works. Critics are nearly unanimous in acknowledging its nearly epic vision, complex narrative design, hauntingly eloquent prose, and sharp psychological insights. *Giovanni's Room,* however, disappointed many reviewers: the absence of African American characters baffled some; the focus on homosexual relationships annoyed others. For example, James Ivy, commenting on *Giovanni's Room* in the respected and often politically progressive black periodical *The Crisis,* begins his review—sarcastically titled "The Faerie Queenes"—by announcing that in this novel Baldwin "tackles the scabrous subject of homosexual love" and concludes by asserting that it is a "pity that so much brilliant writing should be lavished on a relationship that by its very nature is bound to be sterile and debasing" (123). *Another Country,* which generated several favorable reviews, also elicited considerable hostility: critics such as Robert Root and Roderick Nordell were repulsed by the graphic depictions of interracial and homosexual lovemaking. Such hostility reaches its nearly hysterical proportions in Eldridge Cleaver's infamous essay titled "Notes on a Native Son," in which he prefaces his vicious attack on Baldwin with the following declaration: "Homosexuality is a sickness, just as baby-rape and wanting to be the head of the General Motors" (110). However, Addison Gayle, Jr., promptly came to Baldwin's defense: in an essay aptly titled "A Defense of James Baldwin," he offers a convincing retort to the irresponsible criticism leveled against Baldwin by Eldridge Cleaver, Robert A. Bone, and others.

The receptions accorded the other three novels by Baldwin were similar. While some reviewers were enthusiastic, others were condescending or downright hostile. Such trends continue in more recent scholarship as well. Trudier Harris, in her *Black Women in the Fiction of James Baldwin,* sees him as a spokesperson for African American patriarchy. However, several gay male critics praise him for his brilliant and progressive deconstructions of the conventional views of human sexuality. It is safe, then, to state that the mixed reception accorded Baldwin's fiction points to the need for a thorough reevaluation and judicious reassessment of the meaning of Baldwin's work and his significance as a twentieth-century cultural phenomenon.

See also Gay Literature, African American

Further Reading

Adams, Stephen. *The Homosexual as Hero in Contemporary Fiction.* London: Vision Press, 1980.

Bergman, David. *Gaiety Transfigured: Gay Self-Representation in American Literature.* Madison: University of Wisconsin Press, 1991.

Bloom, Harold, ed. *James Baldwin.* New York: Chelsea House, 1996.

Cederstrom, Lorelei. "Love, Race and Sex in the Novels of James Baldwin." *Mosaic* 17, no. 2 (1986): 175–88.

Cleaver, Eldridge. "Notes on a Native Son." *Soul on Ice.* New York: Dell, 1968. 77–111.

Foster, David. " 'Cause My House Fell Down: The Theme of the Fall in Baldwin's Novels." *Critique: Studies in Modem Fiction* 13 (1971): 50–62.

Gayle, Addison, Jr. "A Defense of James Baldwin." *College Language Association Journal* 10 (March 1967): 201–8.

Harris, Trudier. *Black Women in the Fiction of James Baldwin.* Knoxville: University of Tennessee Press, 1985.

Ivy, James. "The Faerie Queenes." *The Crisis* 64 (February 1957): 123.

Kinnamon, Keneth, ed. *James Baldwin: A Collection of Critical Essays.* Englewood Cliffs, NJ: Prentice-Hall, 1974.

Macebuh, Stanley. *James Baldwin: A Critical Study.* New York: Third World Press, 1973.

Mengay, Donald. "*Giovanni's Room* and the (Re)Contextualization of Difference." *Genders* 17 (Fall 1993): 59–70.

Nelson, Emmanuel. "Continents of Desire: James Baldwin and the Pleasures of Exile." *James White Review* (Fall 1996): 8, 16.

———. "Critical Deviance: Homophobia and the Reception of James Baldwin's Fiction." *Journal of American Culture* 14, no. 3 (Fall 1991): 91–96.

———. "James Baldwin's Vision of Otherness and Community." *MELUS* 10, no. 2 (1983): 27–31.

Nordell, Roderick. "Old and New Novels on Racial Themes." *Christian Science Monitor* July 19, 1962: 11.

O'Daniel, Therman, ed. *James Baldwin: A Critical Evaluation.* Washington, DC: Howard University Press, 1977.

Porter, Horace. *Stealing the Fire: The Art and Protest of James Baldwin.* Middletown, CT: Wesleyan University Press, 1989.

Pratt, Lewis. *James Baldwin.* Boston: Twayne, 1978.

Root, Robert. Review of *Another Country* by James Baldwin. *Christian Century* 7 (1962): 1354–55.

Rowdan, Terry. "A Play of Abstractions: Race, Sexuality, and Community in James Baldwin's *Another Country.*" *Southern Review* 19, no. 1 (Winter 1993): 41–50.

Spurlin, William. "Rhetorical Hermeneutics and Gay Identity Politics: Rethinking American Cultural Studies." *Reconceptualizing American Literary/Cultural Studies.* New York: Garland, 1996. 169–83.

Standley, Fred, and Nancy Burt. *Critical Essays on James Baldwin.* Boston: G. K. Hall, 1988.

Standley, Fred, and Louis Pratt. *Conversations with James Baldwin.* Jackson: University Press of Mississippi, 1989.

Trope, Quincy, ed. *James Baldwin: The Legacy.* New York: Simon and Schuster, 1989.

Washington, Bryan. *The Politics of Exile: Ideology in Henry James, F. Scott Fitzgerald, and James Baldwin.* Boston: Northeastern University Press, 1995.

Emmanuel S. Nelson

Baron, Jeff (b. 1952).

Award-winning playwright, screenwriter, and television writer, as well as producer, director, and lyricist. Jeff Baron was born in New Jersey on October 18, 1952. He was exposed to theater while quite young, attending productions in New York City and regional theaters with his parents. He pursued his interests at Northwestern University, where he earned a degree in television and film production in 1974. While there, Baron wrote and directed an evening of comedy, *Tennis Elbow,* and contributed songs and sketches to various shows, including *Waa-Mu,* the campus musical. After graduation, Baron moved to New York, undertaking corporate work and later earning an M.B.A. from Harvard in 1978. Subsequent jobs left Baron little time to write, though he did contribute to publications including the **gay** newspaper *No Bad News,* the Canadian *T.O. Magazine* and *Toronto Magazine, Travel + Leisure, New York Magazine, Dallas City Magazine,* and *New York Daily News.*

In 1982, Baron wrote, directed, produced, and hosted *The Jeff Baron Show,* a weekly Atlanta cable show that ran for 25 episodes and that proved to be a crucial turning point for him. Leaving his successful corporate career, Baron returned to New York, where he wrote his first screenplay, *Jersey Girl*. It was quickly optioned by Marcia Nasatir, producer of *The Big Chill*, and while it was never produced, it gained Baron entrée into the film world. Three subsequent screenplays—*Maid of Honor, Custody,* and *House Swap*—were also promptly picked up by major studios, though are as yet unproduced. Baron wrote and directed *The Bruce Diet*, a short film that won the CINE Golden Eagle Award and was featured at film festivals worldwide. Other short works include the film *Goodbye* and two plays, *Bless Me, Father*—commissioned and produced in New York as part of an evening of plays about September 11, 2001—and *Give 'em an Inch*. Baron's television writing credits include *Sisters, The Tracey Ullman Show, A Year in the Life, Almost Grown,* and *Aaron's Way,* as well as scripts for Disney, Nickelodeon, and Showtime. He also composed the libretto for *Escape,* an original opera commissioned by the Los Angeles Opera through a grant from the National Endowment for the Arts, and he directed the world premiere at Carnegie Hall of *Song of Martina,* a comic opera he wrote with Dean X. Johnson.

Baron's plays focus primarily on family relationships and conflicts, friendship, romance, sex, and the need for human connection. His most celebrated play by far is his critically acclaimed *Visiting Mr. Green* (1996), which has been produced in nearly 40 countries, including tours in England, Germany, Spain, Croatia, and Argentina. The play, starring Eli Wallach in its New York debut, explores the edgy relationship between the belligerent, 86-year-old title character and a 29-year-old corporate hotshot, Ross Gardiner, who nearly hit Green with his car. Gardiner is sentenced to assist Mr. Green weekly for six months, and the play traces the evolution of feelings between the two men, as well as the recognition and reconciliation of individual prejudices. *Visiting Mr. Green* is autobiographical in that Ross Gardiner is based largely on Baron, and Mr. Green was inspired by Baron's grandmother. The play gave him the opportunity to imagine, among other things, the coming out conversation he never had with his grandmother.

Baron's second play, *Mother's Day* (1995), deals more overtly with family issues, with the daughter of the main character bringing home her lesbian partner for the celebration of this Hallmark Card day. As with *Mr. Green,* repressed family conflicts are unearthed and a final reconciliation seems imminent. *Mr. & Mrs. God* (2001), originally titled *Mr. & Mrs. G,* departs noticeably from the more conventional structures of Baron's earlier plays, using a nonrealistic framework to explore the concepts of free will and monogamy through a look into the lives of two couples—one straight and one gay. Collaborating with Moe Angelos, one of the Obie Award–winning Five Lesbian Brothers, Baron wrote *Edna and Joe Forever* (2004), a screwball comedy about an unassuming handywoman who inherits a billion dollars. *Brothers-in-Law* (2005) has two central characters who, in 12 years, have barely spoken to one another, until the funeral of their mutual mother-in-law, yielding unexpected results. *What Goes Around . . .* (2006), featuring six characters played by three actors, is an experimental foray divided into four plays, each of which can be performed separately and which, together or apart, provide a sense of understanding, familiarity, and finality. Baron has written both a straight and a gay version of this play.

Baron's newest, as yet untitled play, is a personal work that deals very theatrically with the loss of his father as a young boy. His future plans include writing and directing film, collaborating with artists he has met working internationally in theater.

Further Reading

American Theatre Wing. "Working in the Theatre: Playwright and Director." Host Isabelle Stevenson. April 1998. CUNY-TV. January 18, 2008. http://www.americantheatrewing.org/seminars/detail/playwright_and_director_04_98.

Baron, Jeff. Home page. January 18, 2008. http://www.jeffbaron.net/.

Blansfield, Karen C. "Jeff Baron." In *Contemporary Gay American Poets and Playwrights: An A-to-Z Guide,* edited by Emmanuel S. Nelson, 11–18. Westport, CT: Greenwood Press, 2003.

Karen Charmaine Blansfield

Barr, James (aka James Fugaté, 1922–1995)

Novelist, playwright, and homophile activist. James Barr was the pen name of James Fugaté. Barr's background is somewhat unclear: he was born in an oil town in Oklahoma or Texas to an absent father and a mother who died shortly after giving birth. He was adopted by a well-to-do Kansas family. In World War II, Barr served in the U.S. Navy. In 1952 he was discharged from the navy when it became known that he had authored *Quatrefoil* (1950), the novel for which he is perhaps best known. The story of *Quatrefoil* is one that matches closely the assimilationist goals of the homophile movement of the 1950s, presenting two male characters in a monogamous loving relationship. The lengthy novel was strikingly different from much of the literary representation of gay men at the time, which usually featured curt tales of tragedy, social exclusion, and even suicide. *Quatrefoil* has been criticized, however, for pandering to the heterosexual status quo because the two main characters are well educated and wealthy, able to understand their relationship as a sort of idealized extension of ancient notions of manly love, and disdainful of other homosexuals who do not share their privilege. Barr's collection of short stories, *Derricks* (1951), has a much earthier tone as the stories present a variety of viewpoints. Barr himself spent some years of his life working in and around the oil fields of Oklahoma and Texas, and it is difficult to avoid imagining that at least some of the elements of the stories are not autobiographical to a degree. Both *Quatrefoil* and *Derricks* present characters who are not necessarily pathological but whose lives hold the same difficulties and rewards as anyone else's.

The navy discharge seemed to politicize Barr, and he became active in the homophile movement, contributing stories and essays to *One Magazine* and other homophile publications. Many of these submissions belie Barr's commitment to a "status quo" form of homosexuality as his publications cover such topics as being homosexual in small-town America, a defense of effeminate gay men, and various critical pieces on the psychology of homosexuality, including one in which he seems to suggest that early psychoanalytic treatment might help homosexuals achieve "normalcy." By the mid-1950s, Barr's writing had earned him no small reputation, though his attitude toward homosexuality remained one of ambivalence.

In *The Occasional Man* (1966), Barr moved beyond the classical tropes used to describe same-sex love in *Quatrefoil* and attempts to represent the diversity of **gay** life. In the novel, a 40-year-old man adjusts to single life after a 15-year relationship ends. Adjusting to his new status, he encounters four very different sorts of men: a decadent and aged European count, a young drifter, the black owner of a gay pub, and a working-class straight man with whom the main character has a sexual affair. The end of Barr's life is clouded in some of the same mystery as the beginning. He left New York City and returned to Kansas where he died in 1995. Many of his papers are housed at Wichita State University in Wichita, Kansas.

Further Reading

Kennedy, Hubert. "*Quatrefoil* Broke New Ground." *Harvard Gay and Lesbian Review* 3, no. 1 (Winter 1996): 22–24.

———. "A Touch of Royalty: Gay Author James Barr." San Francisco: Peremptory Publications Ebook, 2002. http://home.pacbell.net/dendy/Barr.pdf.

Milton W. Wendland

Bashir, Samiya (b. 1970)

Poet, author, activist, editor, and freelance journalist. Born in Ypsilanti, Michigan, on October 27, 1970, Samiya Adelle Abdirahman Mohammed Bashir, the eldest of six children, is of both Somali and African American descent. Her parents, Pamela Adelle Hilliard and Abdirahman Mohammed Bashir, met at Eastern Michigan University.

An avid young reader, Bashir was writing short stories and journaling from age three. She maintained all of her creative work and personal stories in one journal from that time until she arrived in Los Angeles, at age 19. Los Angeles marked a significant turning point in Bashir's life. She came out of the **closet**, got involved in **gay** theater circles, and returned to her poetry after an adolescent hiatus. Inspired by the work of **June Jordan**, she moved up to the Bay Area following the Los Angeles Riots in 1992 and went to study with Poetry for the People Project at the University of California (UC) at Berkeley. She was an active poet in the burgeoning spoken word scene, reading in The Upper Room in San Francisco while simultaneously working as a poetry teacher and promotions consultant for various black performance groups. Bashir was Poet Laureate of the University of California in 1994, the same year she graduated *magna cum laude* from UC-Berkeley with a degree in Literature of American Ethnic Cultures. In 1995, she worked with a collective of black lesbian and bisexual artists and performers to organize The Black Girl Collective, putting on dozens of Pride events throughout the Bay Area where Bashir continued to read and perform her work until moving to New York City in 1997 where she worked as a writer and editor for publications such as *Ms. Magazine, Black Issues Book Review,* and *Curve* magazine.

Bashir has self-described her aesthetic as a conversation between "lightning and tornadoes, the wind and the water" (Fullwood 16). Heavily influenced by writers **James Baldwin** and June Jordan, as well as popular culture, multiple spiritual and religious practices, and family, Bashir is an artist uncomfortable with the status quo and with essential ideas of belonging and place. She is constantly engaging multiple perspectives and approaches to her work, unsatisfied with the idea of going into anything "head on." As an activist, Bashir frames and moves arts and civil rights struggles into multiple spaces, advocating through language and presence, for a more just world. As a poet, her work is constantly engaged with "telling the truth"—whether it be about her state of desire, loss, uncontrollable life circumstances, or politics. Bashir's language is embedded in the multiple landscapes of her life experience: from the frail and fraught family relationships of childhood to the radical politics and identities of the Bay Area, and the love, lust, and personal and political heartbreaks of New York City.

Bashir is the author of *Where the Apple Falls: Poems* (2005—Runner-Up, National Best Poetry Book, Urban Spectrum; Finalist, Lambda Literary Award in Poetry), editor of *Best*

Black Women's Erotica 2 (2003), and co-editor, with Tony Medina and Quraysh Ali Lan-sana, of *Role Call: A Generational Anthology of Social & Political Black Literature & Art* (2002).

Role Call is a thorough and brilliant exposition of the works of critical artists and writers of Bashir's generation, marking not just the context of Bashir's life, but also the vision she holds for other artists and activists.

She has also published three chapbook poetry collections: *Wearing Shorts on the First Day of Spring, American Visa,* and *Teasing Crow & Other Haiku.* Her poetry, stories, articles, essays, and editorial work have been featured in numerous publications including *Bum Rush the Page: A Def Poetry Jam, Other Countries: Voices Rising, Callaloo, Essence, Obsidian III, Cave Canem #7, Poetry for the People: A Revolutionary Blueprint, Contemporary American Women Poets, The San Francisco Bay Guardian,* and *Vibe,* among others.

Bashir is a Cave Canem Fellow and a founding organizer of Fire & Ink, a writer's festival for LGBTQ writers of African descent. She has also won numerous other awards including the Astraea Foundation Lesbian Poetry Award, the SF Guardian Poetry 1996 Award, and the National Association of PEN Women Poet's Choice Award.

Further Reading

Benjamin, Debra A. Review of "Role Call: A Generational Anthology of Social & Political Black Literature & Art." *Gathering of the Tribes Magazine* 9 (2004), http://www.tribes.org.

Enszer, Julie R. "Writing Our Lesbian Lives in Poetry." *Sinister Wisdom* 70 (Spring 2007): 14.

Fullwood, Steven G. "Samiya Bashir: Interviewed." In *Carry The Word: A Bibliography of LGBT Books,* edited by Steven G. Fullwood, 15–19. Washington DC/New York: RedBone Press/Vintage Entity Press, 2007.

Ana-Maurine Lara

Beam, Jeffery (b. 1953)

One of the South's most prolific poets, Jeffery Beam is admired for the unique character of his work and for his exceptional ability to connect with an audience at readings. In spite of working full time as a librarian, over the past three decades Beam has persistently composed, published, performed, edited, criticized, and promoted poetry with unflagging devotion. The literary and artistic community of Chapel Hill has welcomed Beam and provided the tireless collaborator project partners from music, graphic arts, film, and photography. Nationally recognized as an advocate for LGBTQ writing, Beam is poetry editor of *The Oyster Boy Review* and has written for a number of reference books and had reviews appear in over 30 regional and national publications. He has nevertheless remained in a small southern community, convinced that he belongs there by right and because of his ability to contribute to the richer life of the place.

A graduate of University of North Carolina (UNC) at Charlotte, Beam grew up in Kannapolis, North Carolina, in a typically southern environment of textile mills, evangelical Protestantism, and immersion in the natural world. Beam began working for the UNC library in Chapel Hill after college and rose through the ranks to become Assistant to the Botany Librarian. His library career has blended well with his interest in the natural world. Anchored in the Objectivist tradition of William Carlos Williams and influenced by the Black Mountain poets, Beam's writing reflects the courage to avoid the current fashion and persistently seek to call his reader's attention to simple, earthy images. As Beam himself said in an interview in *Nantahala Review,* he strives for "elevated, yet common language" that will put his work "not in the mainstream—but in the mystical stream of poetry" (Roberts 12). Emphasizing natural images does not exclude spirituality as a major theme of Beam's writing, but Beam's efforts at the metaphysical are most fruitful when he implies an intuitive spirituality, free of the structure of religion or myth, contained in the everyday images of the natural world. Beam's poems are always charged with an intuitive spirituality just below the surface, waiting for discovery.

Critics have reacted enthusiastically to Jeffery Beam's work, especially since the publication of *Midwinter Fires* (1990). According to Dale Neal, "Beam brings to his poems the quality of a psalm or pagan hymn" and "locates the energy beneath the surface of his poems" (A10). Kenny Fries noted that *The Fountain* (1992) shows Beam's tendency to "draw on many traditions at once" and that the poet "is led by the natural, by intuition, by his senses" (38). This critical acceptance continued through Beam's collaborations, such as the art song series *Life of the Bee* (2001) with composer Lee Hoiby, and his recent experiments with very short forms in the online book *Gospel Earth* (2006) and *Poems Small and Not So Small* (2006).

Beam's double compact disk set *What We Have Lost: New & Selected Poems* (2002) is an impressive multimedia effort that combines art, music, photographs, and recorded readings with the text of his books—published and unpublished—to that date. This compendium presents Beam's work and approaches art in a depth far beyond that supported by a collection of poems alone. A noteworthy feature of the production is the chance to hear Beam reading or singing his poems. He has excellent range in his reading, communicating his own emotions or portraying those of a character as would an accomplished actor.

The best of Beam's work, however, is included in *The Beautiful Tendons: Uncollected* **Queer** *Poems 1977–2006,* published by Lethe Press and White Crane Institute for their *White Crane Wisdom Series* in 2008. Unexpected discovery is always evident in Beam's treatment of homoeroticism. In *Tendons* as well as in the earlier *Submergences* (1997), he celebrates discovering the hidden sensuality of male flesh, conveying a combination of wonder, fear, and delight that connects desire and discovery. As a mature poet, Beam's world— simple, natural images infused with the spiritual—is also a world charged with sensuality and desire. Beam's acceptance of his erotic self allows him to represent its longing in images that suggest it is a perfectly fitting product of the natural world.

Further Reading

Dillon, Cy. "Jeffery Beam." In *Contemporary Gay American Poets and Playwrights: An A-to-Z Guide,* edited by Emmanuel S. Nelson, 19–24. Westport, CT: Greenwood Press, 2003.
———. "Jeffery Beam: A Life in Poetry." *Virginia Libraries* 50, no. 2 (April 2004): 6–10.
Fries, Kenny. Review of *The Fountain. San Francisco Bay Review* July 2, 1992, 38.
Neal, Dale. Review of *Midwinter Fires. Asheville Citizen-Times* April 22, 1990, A10.
Roberts, Mark A. "Jeffery Beam: An Interview." *Nantahala Review* 2, no. 1 (Spring 2003): 12–14.

Cy Dillon

Bechdel, Alison (b. 1960)

American cartoonist and graphic memoirist. Alison Bechdel was born to Helen and Bruce Allen Bechdel in Lock Haven, Pennsylvania. Both Bechdel's parents were teachers, and her father was also a part-time funeral home director, a family business that gave Bechdel the title of her award-winning memoir, *Fun Home: A Family Tragicomic* (2006). After matriculating at Simon's Rock College, Bechdel transferred to Oberlin College, where she majored in art. After graduating in 1981, Bechdel lived briefly in New York City, then in St. Paul, Minnesota, before settling outside Burlington, Vermont, where she currently lives with her partner, Amy Rubin.

Bechdel's groundbreaking serial comic strip, *Dykes to Watch Out For,* has been appearing nationwide in alternative newspapers and magazines since 1983. Beginning with a single panel submitted to *Womannews* in 1983, *Dykes to Watch Out For* has since generated over 500 episodes, collected into 11 separate volumes. The series explores, in highly compact, information-rich panels, the comings and goings of an ever-enlarging cast of **queer** and nonqueer characters who steel themselves to the trials of living a liberal life in conservative America.

A roundup of a few major cast members of *Dykes to Watch Out For* will give a sense of the comic strip's breadth. Mo, the strip's protagonist—she is also the character who bears the greatest physical resemblance to Bechdel—is an erstwhile bookstore employee, now a librarian. Mo's current partner, Sydney, is a breast-cancer survivor and academic whose interest in nonmonogamy leads her to an affair with a fellow professor, a dalliance that Mo countenances with progressive, if not exactly saintly, forbearance. Another couple, Clarice and Toni, an environmental lawyer and an accountant, are splitting up but continue to parent Toni's teenaged son Raffi together. Another teenager in Mo's extended circle, Janis, née Jonas, wants to delay puberty with a round of hormone therapy.

In its 25-year history, *Dykes to Watch Out For* has touched on many of the important themes of queer culture, including same-sex parenting, loss of sexual desire, breast cancer, nonmonogamy, and transgender issues. It has done so with the sharp character delineation and episodic narrative of a Victorian serial novel, but with a sharp eye for social detail and a biting political commentary uniquely Bechdel's. Since the election of George W. Bush in 2000, the series has taken an increasingly political stance; an episode rarely passes without a buried reference to the war in Iraq or other crimes of the Bush administration.

Fun Home: A Family Tragicomic is Bechdel's beautifully realized graphic memoir, named *Time* magazine's 2006 Book of the Year and nominated for a National Book Critics Circle Award—the first memoir in comics format ever bestowed the honor. *Fun Home* chronicles Bechdel's childhood experiences with her **closet**ed **gay** father, killed by a truck after Bechdel's mother announced her intentions to divorce him. Bechdel had been largely ignorant of her father's homosexuality until she came out to him, just months before her father's accident/suicide. Bechdel is acutely aware of the situation's many interlocking ironies, which she exploits to stunning dramatic effect. Changing social mores allowed Bechdel to realize a sexuality that her father struggled to conceal (often trysting with babysitters and handymen in front of his children's eyes). Yet Bechdel owed her very life to her father's decision to engage in this heterosexual masquerade. She writes, "If my father had 'come out' in his youth, if he had not met and married my mother . . . where would that leave me?" (38).

Bechdel's precise, almost cinematic drawings temper *Fun Home*'s literary pretensions. Yet as much as the memoir is a meditation on sexuality, it is also a book unabashedly in love with other books. James Joyce's *Ulysses* plays a pivotal role in the communication between father and daughter, and Bechdel reads her family's saga through a host of literary and mythical stories: Marcel Proust's *Remembrance of Things Past,* F. Scott Fitzgerald's *The*

Great Gatsby, the story of Daedalus and Icarus, and Homer's *Odyssey.* While reading was an important component of Bechdel's sexual self-discovery—Colette and Kate Millett—books provided her father with an escape from the stifling confines of domestic life.

Bechdel's depiction of her father is perhaps the book's great strength. Though his death is undeniably sad, Bechdel does not flinch from portraying her father as the conflicted, unsympathetic character he was: prissy, mean, cold, obsessed with appearances—a stereotype of the closeted gay man that Bechdel gives depth and roundness of character, in the process showing us the psychic tolls of the closet.

See also Graphic Novel, Lesbian

Further Reading

Arsdale, Sarah Van. "Drawing on Life: Alison Bechdel Shows and Tells." *Lambda Book Report: A Review of Contemporary Gay and Lesbian Literature* 6, no. 12 (1998 July): 1, 6–7.

Chute, Hillary. "An Interview with Alison Bechdel." *MFS: Modern Fiction Studies* 52, no. 4 (2006 Winter): 1004–13.

Deahl, Rachel. "Alison Bechdel." *Publishers Weekly* 253, no. 23 (2006 June 5): 25–26.

Klorman, Renee. "Confessions, Comix, and Miscellaneous Alison Bechdel." *off our backs* 28, no. 5 (1998 May): 1, 7.

Christopher Schmidt

Becker, Robin (b. 1951)

Editor, professor, and an important contemporary poet. Author of six volumes of poetry, Robin Becker is known for lyrical narrative poetry on place, desire, loss, and identities such as lesbian, feminist, and Jewish. Born in 1951 in Philadelphia, Pennsylvania, Becker earned a B.A. (1973) and an M.A. (1976) from Boston University. Becker taught creative writing for 17 years at the Massachusetts Institute of Technology and now teaches as an associate professor at the Pennsylvania State University in the M.F.A. program. She currently serves as poetry editor for *Women's Review of Books,* which features her poetry column "Field Notes." Her poems and book reviews have appeared in *American Poetry Review,* the *Boston Globe, Gettysburg Review, Ploughshares,* and other magazines and journals.

Becker was an out lesbian poet from the beginning of her publishing history. Currents of **queer** desire and identity run through her creative works. Becker's first book, *Personal Effects* (1979), featured a series of her poems as well as those from two other poets, Helena Minton and Marilyn Zuckerman. Her first solo poetry collection, *Backtalk* (1982), includes poems on place ("North"), class ("A Good Education"), desire ("Women in Love," "Studies from Life," and "Morning Poem"), and time ("On Not Being Able to Imagine the Future" and "Vermant/January"). Becker's next collection, *Giacometti's Dog* (1990), contains poems about place, such as Philadelphia, Venice, India, France, the Southwest, Florida, and loss, desire, and trust.

In 1996 Becker won the Lambda Literary Award for *All-American Girl.* Poems in this volume contemplate lesbian and Jewish identity and locales Becker has lived and traveled. Desire found and love loss play a central role in *All-American Girl* (1996) as family members are lost (both Becker's sister and father died by suicide), lovers are held and left, and childhood seems distant now from Becker's stance in middle age. In "Solar" Becker compares the desert to a butch, "A History of Sexual Preference" imagines experiencing eighteenth-century America while on a school trip with a girlfriend, and "The Elimination of First Thoughts" ponders those who are not ruled by desire. Other poems such as "Haircut on Via di Mezzo" suggest that it is impossible to live in the closet.

Becker's next two books take their titles from works by the nineteenth-century painter Rosa Bonheur. Lambda Literary Award finalist *The Horse Fair* (2000) contains, like *The Domain of Perfect Affection* (2006), many ekphrastic poetry or poems based on visual arts. The title poem explores and draws attention to the lesbians in the recent historic past, mainly the life of Rosa Bonheur. Poems in this collection also ponder the brevity of life and aging ("Solstice Bay," "Autumn Song," and "In Praise of the Basset Hound") as well as sadness and grief ("The Grief of Trees," "Dylan's Fault," and "Sad Sestina"). In between *The Horse Fair* and *The Domain of Perfect Affection,* Becker published *Venetian Blue* (2002), a limited edition chapbook published by the Frick Art & Historical Center in Pittsburgh.

In *The Domain of Perfect Affection* (2006), Becker addresses readers who already know the speaker's lesbian and feminist identity, given her nearly two-decade publishing prowess as a lesbain poet. For example, "Ok, Tucker" describes the persona's relationship to a dog, the mediating creature between her and her lover. Themes of affection and the body are in poems such as "Late Butch-Femme," "Mail Order," and "Salon." Becker employs formal traditions in the pantoum "Birds of Prey" and the found poem "Qualities Boys Like Best in Girls."

Becker has received many fellowships and awards such as the Massachusetts Artist Foundation Fellowship in Poetry (1985), a Fellowship in Poetry from The National Endowment for the Arts (1990), a Fellowship from The Bunting Institute of Radcliffe College (1995–1996), the Virginia Faulkner Award for Excellence in Writing from *Prairie Schooner* (1997), the George W. Atherton Award for Excellence in Teaching (2000), four Pushcart Prize nominations (2001, 2002, 2003, 2004), and the Strousse Award, *Prairie Schooner* (2001).

Her residencies include a Visiting Scholar at the Center for Lesbian & Gay Studies at the City University of New York (1998) and the William Steeple Davis Artist-in-Residence (2000–2001). She serves on the editorial board for the *Prairie Schooner* Book Award Series in Poetry, the advisory board for Arktoi Books (from Red Hen Press), and the board of directors for Jewish Poetry Awards at Judah L. Magnes Museum in San Francisco.

Further Reading

Enszer, Julie R. "Robin Becker." *Lambda Book Report* 14, no. 3 (Fall 2006): 24–25.
Stewart, Robert. "Description and Speculation: An Interview with Robin Becker." *New Letters* 70, no. 1 (2003–2004): 91–103.

Laura Madeline Wiseman

Beierle, Andrew W. M. (b. 1951)

American journalist and novelist. Andrew W. M. Beierle was born August 5, 1951, in Brooklyn, New York. The family left the city in 1953 amid the first post–World War II suburban exodus, settling in Bucks County, Pennsylvania. Following the 1961 death of his mother, Beierle faced a tumultuous adolescence in the care of his alcoholic father.

Neighbors became caregivers following a period of neglect, and Beierle was placed in foster care from 1964 to 1965, an episode etched acidly in his debut novel, *The Winter of Our Discothèque* (2002).

Beierle's high school journalism teacher, Susan Lowell Butler, set him on his career path in 1968 when she recommended him for a scholarship to the Blair Summer School for Journalism, a rigorous six-week precollege program. He later earned a journalism scholarship to the Pennsylvania State University, where he became managing editor of the *Daily Collegian*. It was at Penn State that he began work on the short story that some 30 years later would become *The Winter of Our Discothèque*.

Upon graduation, Beierle became a reporter for the *Orlando Sentinel*. Florida provided the setting for the first one-third of *The Winter of Our Discothèque,* and the state's lush tropical environment may have influenced Beierle's cinematic prose. He later became a medical writer at Brown University and for 26 years was editor of *Emory Magazine* in Atlanta.

In 2000, Beierle's short story "Gravity" was first runner-up in the inaugural Richard Hall Memorial Short Story Contest sponsored by the Lambda Literary Foundation, and his short story "La Vie Sexuelle des Monstres" was one of 10 unranked finalists. Beierle was the only author out of more than 100 entrants to place two stories in the top 13 honored by Lambda. "Gravity" later appeared in the *Harrington Gay Men's Fiction Quarterly,* and "La Vie Sexuelle des Monstres," expanded and retitled, became his second novel, *First Person Plural* (2007).

The Winter of Our Discothèque is both humorous and portentous. The title is a sly allusion to the opening line of Shakespeare's *Richard the Third* and also reflects on the time period covered by the novel: the pre-AIDS "Golden Age" of **gay** life. The "winter" of discothèques is meant to foreshadow their demise as a significant cultural phenomenon in the aftermath of AIDS, and the fire that destroys the discothèque at the end of the novel can be read as a metaphor for the AIDS epidemic and its impact on gay life in the 1980s.

The Winter of Our Discothèque won a 2002 Lambda Literary Award, was named a "notable title" by *Publishers Weekly,* and was selected as an offering of the InsightOut Book Club. It was also excerpted on the *Out Magazine* Web site and was featured in an article in the August 2002 *Lambda Book Report.* An excerpt from *The Winter of Our Discothèque* appears in the 2001 anthology *Rebel Yell: Stories by Contemporary Southern Gay Authors* as the short story "Pump Jockey."

Beierle wrote his second novel, *First Person Plural,* over the course of five years (2000–2005), workshopping the material at the Sewanee, Bread Loaf, Napa Valley, and *Kenyon Review* writers' conferences with the personal guidance of Alice McDermott, **Randall Kenan**, Claire Messud, and Christopher Tilghman, respectively. Its prose style is significantly different from that of his debut work—direct, spare, almost journalistic.

First Person Plural deals with the intimate lives of an extremely rare set of conjoined twins of the type *dicephalus* ("two-headed"). Owen and Porter Jamison are separate individuals from the neck up but share a single body. As they grow to adulthood, their differences become more pronounced: Porter is outgoing and charismatic while Owen is cerebral and artistic. Eventually, a greater distinction emerges, as Owen gradually comes to realize that he is gay.

First Person Plural was short-listed for the 2007 Lambda Literary Award in Men's Fiction. The novel was also a September 2007 Main Selection of the InsightOut Book Club, was named one of the 10 best books of the year by Richard Labonté on the Web site *Books to Watch Out For,* and shared the title of best men's fiction of 2007 with **Sarah Schulman**'s *The Child* on the Web site *AfterElton.com.*

Further Reading

Schmidt, Linsey. "Freaks 'R' Us: Inhabiting Alien Characters." *Bookseller Chick,* July 10, 2007. http://booksellerchick.blogspot.com/2007/07/freaks-r-us-inhabiting-alien-characters.html.

Jameson Currier

Belton, Don (b. 1956)

African American **gay** novelist. The major themes of the work of African American writer and editor Don Belton include the gulf between real and represented masculinity, the impossibility of living without love, and home and the quest for sanctuary. His friendships with black gay writers **James Baldwin**, **Melvin Dixon**, **Randall Kenan**, **Essex Hemphill**, and the filmmaker Marlon Riggs influenced the exploration of the potential of a range of caring relationships between men in his writing.

Born in Philadelphia, Pennsylvania, Belton's family valued stories, songs, and the art of conversation and encouraged him to express himself from an early age, supplying him with books, paper, art supplies, music, and his own desk and chair. He graduated from Bennington College in 1981 and received an M.A. from Hollins College in 1982. He met and was befriended by James Baldwin in New York while an undergraduate at Bennington, a further encouragement for him to write.

Belton published the novel *Almost Midnight* in 1986. Set in the Hill section of Newark, New Jersey, the novel details the conflicting attempts to determine the truth about a legendary light-skinned African American preacher, "Daddy" Sam Poole, by the various women in his life. Founder of the successful "Metaphysical Church of the Divine Investigation," the mystery of Daddy Poole remains unanswered by the novel's end, and the women cannot separate themselves from their memories of him.

Belton's peripatetic teaching career has led to extensive travel in the United States and abroad, including Ireland, France, Brazil, England, Italy, and the Ivory Coast. The friendships he developed during this period with African American novelists Melvin Dixon and Randall Kenan, the filmmaker Marlon Riggs, and poet Essex Hemphill encouraged him to focus his work on black male relationships, leading to the anthology *Speak My Name* (1997).

A reaction to a number of issues concerning African Americans in the 1990s from the "cultural wars" and the Million Man March of October 1995 to the violence and despair in the inner cities and the "New Male" movement led by Robert Bly and Sam Keen that held little interest in African American male representation, *Speak My Name* features a range of short fiction and essays that counter distorted images of African American men. Including work by established and emerging writers and scholars Amiri Baraka, Henry Louis Gates, Jr., Robin D. G. Kelley, Walter Mosley, John Edgar Wideman, August Wilson, and others, the anthology explores unconventional, nonmainstream expressions of black masculinity. An interview/conversation among Belton, gay British filmmaker Isaac Julien, and poet Essex Hemphill also critiques heterosexism and debates whether traditional visions of "black unity" can include gay men.

A former reporter at *Newsweek*, Don Belton has also written articles for *Black Film Review*, the *Philadelphia Inquirer*, the *Advocate*, and *Utne Reader*. His short stories have appeared in the *Indiana Review, Black Literature Forum, Breaking Ice: An Anthology of Contemporary African-American Fiction*, and *Calling the Wind: An Anthology of the Twentieth Century African-American Short Story*. He has been a Fellow at the MacDowell Colony and Yaddo. His awards include a Lila Wallace International Travel and Research Grant, a Bellagio/Rockefeller Foundation Fellowship, and a Dance Advance/Pew Charitable Trust Grant for Dramaturgy. Belton has taught literature and fiction writing at Macalester College, the University of Michigan, Ann Arbor, Bennington College, and Temple University and has lectured widely abroad including in the Ivory Coast (sponsored by Arts America/United States Information Agency), at the Sorbonne, and at the University of São Paulo, Brazil. Currently at work on his second novel, Belton lives in Bloomington, Indiana, where he teaches in the Graduate Creative Writing Program at Indiana University.

Further Reading

Anderson, Elijah. "Manhood Under Pressure." *New York Times Book Review*, March 3, 1996, 22.

Baker-Fletcher, G. Kasimu. "Macho Deconstructed." *Cross Currents* 46, no. 4 (Winter 1996/1997): 565.

Belton, Don. "How to Make Love to a White Man." *Transition: An International Review* 7, no. 1 (1998): 164–75.

Hogue, W. Lawrence. "Chapter Ten: Voodoo, A Different American Experience, and Don Belton's *Almost Midnight*." *The African American Male, Writing and Difference: A Polycentric Approach to African American Literature, Criticism, and History*. Albany: State University of New York Press, 2003. 225–51.

Seaman, Donna. "Speak My Name: Black Men on Masculinity and the American Dream." *Booklist* 92, 9–10 (January 1, 1996): 756.

Reginald Harris

Bergman, David (b. 1950)

Influential American poet, critic, and anthologist of contemporary **gay** male literature. Born in Fitchburg, Massachusetts, on March 13, 1950, David Bergman graduated from Kenyon College in 1972 before obtaining his doctoral degree in English Literature from The Johns Hopkins University in 1977. He is currently Professor of English at Towson State University, where he teaches courses in modern American poetry, Victorian literature, and autobiography. Bergman has not hesitated to self-identify as gay and, in fact, regularly publishes autobiographically inflected essays, such as those that appear in *Queer 13: Lesbian and Gay Writers Recall Seventh Grade* (1996) and *Boys Like Us: Gay Writers Tell Their Coming Out Stories* (1996). He also wrote the foreword to Richard Canning's *Gay Fiction Speaks: Conversations with Gay Novelists* (2001).

Bergman is best known for his work as editor and historian, especially regarding the writers involved in the **Violet Quill Club**, a gay writing group in New York City in 1980 and 1981. In the edited collection *The Violet Quill Reader: The Emergence of Gay Writing after **Stonewall*** (1994), Bergman amasses essays, stories, and correspondences, some previously unpublished, in the first full-length text devoted to the group. His most recent book, a social history of the group entitled *The Violet Hour: The Violet Quill and* *the Making of Gay Culture* (2004), traces the connections between these authors and the development of the culture of gay liberation from Stonewall through the AIDS epidemic. As Bergman thoughtfully demonstrates, the work of the Violet Quill embodies the multiple experiences and engagements of its members' generation, from suffering and grief through caregiving and activism. In his representation of the political and aesthetic responses of the Violet Quill members to their rapidly changing circumstance, Bergman too serves as a witness to the AIDS epidemic and the multiple modes of response enacted by gay men against its physiological ravages and social marginalization.

In addition to publications in journals such as *The American Scholar* and *American Literary History,* Bergman has authored an expansive study of the evolution of gay men's literary self-representations entitled *Gaiety Transfigured: Gay Self-Representation in American Literature* (1991). He frames his study through a focus on both individual authors, such as Walt Whitman, Herman Melville, **Tennessee Williams**, **James Baldwin**, F. O. Matthiessen, **Larry Kramer**, and **Andrew Holleran**, and broader themes, such as AIDS, antigay witchhunts, **camp** aesthetics, and multicultural engagements. The book was selected as an Outstanding Academic Book of the Year by *Choice* magazine.

Bergman has also edited the works of individual authors, such as **Edmund White**'s essays on politics and culture in *The Burning Library: Essays by Edmund White* (1994) and **John Ashbery**'s art reviews for the *International Herald Tribune* (Paris), *ARTnews, The New Yorker,* and *Newsweek* in *Reported Sightings: Art Chronicles 1957–87* (1989). He has also edited *Camp Grounds: Style and Homosexuality* (1993), a collection of 16 essays that explore the engagement between style and homosexuality, as manifest in multiple cultural modes. Bergman served as the editor for the biennial series *Men on Men: Best New Gay Fiction* until 2000, when the collection won the Lambda Literary Award for fiction anthologies, and he continues to co-edit *Out Lives: Lesbian and Gay Autobiographies* with Joan Larkin.

Bergman is an accomplished poet in his own right, winning the George Elliston Poetry Prize for *Cracking the Code* (1985), in which he meditates upon the intersections of the body, religion, and myth, as well as the institutes—including literary traditions—that transmit their relevant knowledge. His second book of poetry, *Heroic Measures* (1998)— containing the previously released chapbook entitled *The Care and Treatment of Pain* (1994), with the addition of heretofore unpublished work—also addresses the connections among pain, death, and beauty. The first section explores AIDS-related losses with an emphasis on male relationships that then shifts into a focus on art and religious myth, before culminating with a turn toward family, in which Bergman reflects on parental structures, aging, and his own childhood. His poetry has been published in *The Gay & Lesbian Review, The Kenyon Review, Men's Style, The New Republic, The New Criterion,* and *The Paris Review.*

Further Reading

English, Hugh. Review of *Gaiety Transfigured. American Literature* 64, no. 4 (Dec. 1992): 846–47.

Gilgun, John. Review of *Heroic Measures. Lambda Book Review* 7, no. 4 (Nov. 1998): 32.

Najarian, James. "David Bergman." *Contemporary Gay American Poets and Playwrights,* edited by Emmanuel S. Nelson, 25–28. Westport, CT: Greenwood Press, 2003.

O'Toole, Sean. Review of *The Violet Hour. Journal of the History of Sexuality* 14, no. 3 (2005): 333–37.

Stephanie Youngblood

Birtha, Becky (b. 1948)

Notable black lesbian-feminist poet and fiction writer. Born in Hampton, Virginia, in 1948, Becky Birtha was raised in Philadelphia, the setting for several of her best-loved stories. She began college at Case Western Reserve University, but dropped out and moved to Berkeley for a year at the height of the protests (1969–1970). Returning East, she earned a BS in Child Studies from State University of New York at Buffalo in 1973 and an MFA in Creative Writing from Vermont College in 1984. She has worked in educational settings from preschool to colleges, as a legal librarian, and, most recently, for an adoption organization. Birtha was granted a Pennsylvania Council of the Arts Individual Fellowship in Literature in 1985 and was awarded both a National Endowment for the Arts Creative Writing Fellowship and a Pushcart Prize in 1988.

Best known for her two well-received collections of short stories, *For Nights Like This One* (1983) and *Lover's Choice* (1987), Birtha is also a prolific and widely anthologized poet, with a collection, *The Forbidden Poems,* published in 1991. Her work was of signal importance to the development of lesbian-feminist literature in the late 1970s and the 1980s, appearing in such movement journals as *Sinister Wisdom, Conditions, Sojourner, Paragraph, Focus, Women: A Journal of Liberation,* and *Azalea: A Magazine by Third-World Lesbians* and in Barbara Smith's groundbreaking collection *Home Girls: A Black Feminist Anthology* (1983). Also important to the cross-genre, multiethnic movement that would come to be called woman of color feminism, Birtha's poems and stories complement the iconic contributions of poet-theorists such as **Audre Lorde**, **June Jordan**, **Gloria Evangelina Anzaldúa**, and **Cherríe Moraga**, offering quieter evocations of loss, difference, beauty, and strength in everyday life.

Attentive to the depth, complexity, and diversity of African American experience, Birtha draws on her own Cherokee, Catawba, African, and Irish roots, and also her Quaker ethics, to develop nuanced and emotionally resonant portrayals of interracial relationships, cross-class encounters, childlessness, motherhood, desire, and self-sustenance. Throughout, she is alert to both the vulnerability and the resilience of human connection across time, space, race, and age, capturing an adolescent's glimpse of life-altering possibilities in two strangers' stolen kiss in the story "Johnnieruth," for example; the endurance of a love beyond death in the quietly moving "In the Life"; and the small acts and daily practice of lesbian world-making in such poems as "My Vision of a Women's Community."

Although her work has appeared in mainstream venues including the *Iowa Review* and received positive notices from the *Times Literary Supplement* and *Publishers Weekly,* the demise of many feminist networks, presses, and bookstores has cost Birtha her access to an enthusiastic readership. However, her commitment to children's issues, African American history, and her own creative process continues to find expression, most recently in the award-winning children's book *Grandmama's Pride* (2005).

Further Reading

Bogus, SDiane. "All of Our Art for Our Sake." *Sinister Wisdom* 27 (Fall 1984): 92–106.

Marks, Rebecca. "Becky Birtha." In *Contemporary Lesbian Writers of the United States: A Bio-Bibliographical Critical Sourcebook,* edited by Sandra Pollack and Denise D. Knight, 53–56. Westport, CT: Greenwood Press, 1993.

Pullin, Faith. "Acts of Reclamation." *Times Literary Supplement* 4444 (June 3, 1988): 623.

Review of *The Forbidden Poems. Publishers Weekly* (February 1, 1991): 77.

Kim Emery

Bisexuality

Bisexuality has a long and complicated history within scholarly, sexological, and activist communities. In the nineteenth century, bisexuality had more of the meaning "intersex" as it is contemporarily understood, that is, physically pertaining to both sexes. However, over the years, the term morphed to mean sexual, erotic, and physical attraction to both sexes. In recent years, some use the term to connote the capacity for being attracted to more than one sex/gender grouping. The term is significant for the ways in which it challenges monosexism. Monosexism is the idea that sexuality is a black-or-white, **gay** or straight, binary. In fact, sexuality, like gender, is perhaps better described as a continuum with a variety of possible gradations.

Many people misunderstand the phenomenon of bisexuality. There are a variety of myths perpetrated against the bisexual community. Biphobia, the prejudice toward as well as fear and hatred of bisexual people, is a common problem in both the heterosexual and lesbian/gay communities. There are people who believe bisexuality does not exist and that one is either heterosexual or homosexual. They believe bisexuals are "fence-sitters" who cannot commit to a "real" sexual orientation. They believe that bisexuals are conduits for sexually transmitted diseases into the "innocent" heterosexual community. And often they believe that bisexuality is a phase before one comes out of the closet "fully" as lesbian or gay. Some gays and lesbians believe that bisexuals are just not accepting their gayness because they are trying to cling to some vestige of heterosexual privilege. To counter these inaccurate and harmful stereotypes, the bisexual community has formed a social and political movement to combat biphobia and strengthen people's pride in their bisexuality, as well as proffer accurate and positive information.

One of the milestones in the fight for bisexual liberation was the publication of what many refer to as the "bi bible," *Bi Any Other Name* (1996). This unique volume gives voice to over 70 diverse bisexuals to tell about their lived experiences as bisexual people. In the introduction, the editors passionately write:

> Bisexual people—by any other name, by every other name—have lived and loved since the beginning of time. Yet we're told we don't exist. That we're really heterosexual or really gay, that nothing exists except these two extremes . . . It is time for bisexuals to speak out, in our own voices, and initiate dialogue with the diverse communities we call home (xx).

The book also helps to counter the above myths and proffer accurate information about the realities and complexities of bisexual existence.

However, the term also has its critics. Given the "sexual" part of bisexual, some fear that those who hear the term will place too much importance on physical/sexual/erotic attraction and not enough on other forms of attraction such as mental, emotional, intellectual, or spiritual. In a heterosexist society, all forms of nonheteronormative sexualities are overly associated with carnal sexuality. People see **queer**/gay/bisexual identities as all about "sex." Further, there is no litmus test for being a bisexual. One could have slept with only members of one gender, or be a "virgin" who has not experienced any form of sexuality. Bisexuality is not about sexual practice but about identity.

In addition, in the English language, the prefix "bi" means "two." Therefore, bisexuality in a strict linguistic sense means attraction to "both" sexes/genders, which some feel reinforces the gender binary, that is, the idea that there are two and only two genders. Given the contributions of transgender and intersex liberation, some have redefined bisexual to mean attraction to more than one gender, rather than to the fixed number of "two." However, for some this still does not go far enough in recognizing the complex diversity of multiple gender identities and expressions. Others have opted for terms such as multisexual, omnisexual, or pansexual to call attention to the limitless number of genders to which one can be emotionally, physically, sexually, or spiritually attracted.

As with lesbian and gay literary critics, bisexual studies scholars, as well as activists, have been engaged in a search for bisexual characters in film (see Bryant) and literature, as well as biographical information about the lives of bisexual authors. Bisexual scholarship and activism have helped to propel the bisexual community forward and given all of society a more accurate and inclusive vision of human sexuality.

Further Reading

Bi Academic Intervention, eds. *The Bisexual Imaginary: Representation, Identity and Desire.* London: Cassell, 1997.

Bryant, Wayne. *Bisexual Characters in Film.* Binghamton, NY: Haworth Press, 1997.

Esterberg, Kristin. *Lesbian and Bisexual Identities.* Philadelphia: Temple University Press, 1997.

Hemmings, Clare. *Bisexual Spaces.* New York: Routledge, 2002.

Hutchins, Loraine, and Lani Kaahumanu. *Bi Any Other Name: Bisexual People Speak Out.* Boston: Alyson Publications, 1991.

Klein, Fritz. *The Bisexual Option.* Binghamton, NY: Haworth Press, 1993.

Rust, Paula C. Rodriguez. *Bisexuality in the United States: A Social Science Reader.* New York: Columbia University Press, 2000.

Joelle Ruby Ryan

Blanco, Richard (b. 1968)

Poet, essayist, and memoirist. The youngest son of Geysa Claudia Valdez-Blanco and Carlos Emilio Blanco, Richard Blanco was born on February 15, 1968, and is of Cuban dissent.

In Cuba, Blanco's father, Carlos, served in the Naval Academy, from which he was about to graduate when Fidel Castro's regime came to power in 1959, culminating the long Cuban Revolution's battle against one dictatorship only to replace it with Fidel Castro's regime. Blanco's parents had by that time already met and chose to have a military wedding despite the fact that the Castro dissolved the Cuban Naval Academy, thereby preventing Carlos's graduation. Blanco's mother was the only member of a large, economically challenged family to attend college. She worked as a grade school teacher. Richard was born in Spain, and less than two months later the Blanco family immigrated to the United States where Blanco's father became an accountant, his mother a bank teller. The family, like so many others, was divided into those who remained in Cuba and those who left.

Exile and search for a home is not surprisingly, then, the major theme of Blanco's writing. *City of a Hundred Fires* (1998), which won the Agnes Lynch Starrett Poetry Prize from the University of Pittsburgh Press, is dedicated to his father, who died in 1990, and is filled with portraits of the Blanco family and other members of Miami's Cuban enclave. The portraits are loving and sympathetic, but never sentimental or bombastic, though they often bear a political undercurrent. When Blanco turns his poetic eye toward himself, the resulting poems are a literature of coming-of-age through assimiliation into

American culture rather than a literature of coming-of-age via a struggle with his sexuality. *Directions to the Beach of the Dead* (2005) continues to elegize Blanco's father and sympathetically capture his family and fellow Cuban exiles. However, as Blanco, a man approaching middle age, travels the world and makes a pilgrimage to Cuba, as he settles in the various American cities where he has worked as both a civil engineer and a teacher of writing, the poems engage in a philosophical inquiry into the unstable meaning of words such as "place" and "home." Blanco again and again questions what words like "home" mean when, for example, the "home" that his mother remembers growing up in is, in reality, a place that is constantly in flux. Indeed, it is through his urbanity that Blanco's sexuality exerts itself in his poems—poems often written in poetic form, poems that sometimes contain both English and Spanish, and poems that make references to Friedrich Nietzsche and Rainer Maria Rilke alongside references to Cuban toast and *café con leche*. Nevertheless, one must turn to Blanco's essays for somewhat fuller discussions of the author's sexuality.

Essays such as "The Pines at El Farito, 1513–2008" and "Imaginary America," for instance, briefly discuss the verbal abuse Blanco faced when he was a child from a grandmother and other family members who found him lacking in masculinity, as well as young Blanco's fascination with **camp**y American television shows such as *Bewitched*. Today, the handsome Blanco is an embodiment of masculinity (his broad muscular back is pictured in artful photographs on *Directions to the Beach of the Dead* and on his Web site), and essays such as "The Pines at El Farito" briefly make reference to Blanco's long-term relationship, all of which go some way toward explaining why Blanco's poems and essays are not characterized by the themes of longing and loneliness, the explorations of sexual desire, that mark so much of the **gay** poetry of Blanco's generation. In e-mail interviews with this author, however, Blanco has confessed that his family habitually repressed emotions, and that, after attempting **heterosexuality**, his eventual coming out led to a temporary rift between Blanco and his mother. These biographical matters suggest there is considerable room for exploration of new subject matter and evolving themes as Blanco moves forward in his already bright career.

Further Reading

Blanco, Richard. "Miami after La Revolución." *Indiana Review* 26, no. 1 (Summer 2004): 123–33.
Gonzalez, Ray. "City of a Hundred Fires." *The Bloomsbury Review* 20, no. 2 (March/April 2000): 20.
Wyatt, Sarah. "Directions to the Beach of the Dead." *Indiana Review* 28, no. 1 (Summer 2006): 170–72.

Steven Cordova

Bloch, Alice (b. 1947)

Author, poet, and memoirist. Alice Bloch's writing frequently deals with the complexities of identifying as Jewish, feminist, and lesbian. Born in Youngstown, Ohio, in 1947, Bloch studied at the University of Michigan, Cornell University, and the Hebrew University of Jerusalem. During her 20s she spent two years in Israel, before returning to live in the United States. Bloch was a co-founder of Gay Liberation House in New York City, an editor of *The Lesbian Tide,* and she published her first book in 1981: *Lifetime Guarantee:*

A Journey through Loss and Survival, an account of her younger sister's death from leukemia. A novel, *The Law of Return,* followed in 1983, and Bloch's poetry, short stories, and articles have appeared in various feminist and lesbian periodicals and a number of anthologies.

In *Lifetime Guarantee* Bloch enacts a posthumous collaboration with Barbara, the sister whose death the book memorializes. Bloch's account of her sister's battle with leukemia is interspersed with Barbara's own notes, poems, and letters. In this way the book's time frame exceeds the span of Barbara's life, and Bloch records the continuing psychological effects of her sister's death. Barbara's death alters Bloch's perspective on her family history, and the narrative doubles back to reevaluate certain incidents in her childhood. Therefore, while each chapter is identified by a sequential year, the text is temporally complex. Bloch has described the process of revisiting, commenting upon, and interpreting her family's past in this book as "Talmudic," thus identifying her personal history as part of a larger Jewish history.

In *Lifetime Guarantee* the crisis of her sister's illness provides a lens through which Bloch can examine not only their sibling relationship, but also the larger family dynamics of power, blame, love, and obligation. Barbara's death is not the only one with which Bloch contends in the book, but the text proves to be as much a recounting of Bloch's own coming-of-age, and coming to knowledge of herself, as it is a memoir of her sister, father, and mother. *Lifetime Guarantee* follows Bloch's literal and figurative journey away from her family home toward an affirmative lesbian identity and a greater understanding of the **gender**ed politics of her upbringing. As the book's subtitle suggests, Bloch writes a positive testimony to her survival, as well as a moving account of her losses.

The same structuring concern with physical and psychological journeys is evident in *The Law of Return.* The novel is highly autobiographical in its account of the protagonist's negotiation of her Jewish identity, her sexuality, and the place of women in Orthodox Judaism. As in *Lifetime Guarantee,* Bloch interrogates ideas of home, community, and belonging; the text also examines the interlocking and mutually reinforcing patriarchal institutions of organized religion, the nation-state, and heterosexual marriage.

The Law of Return tells the story of Elisheva Rogin, daughter of a liberal Jewish American family, and her attempt to find a place where she feels at home. Religiously ill at ease in the United States, she travels to Israel. Here she gains a deeper understanding of her faith and delights in the people and landscapes she encounters, but comes to notice deep-rooted class divisions and the subservient role of women in Israeli society. Elisheva's increasing awareness of her lesbian desires also runs counter to the fact that she is frequently told that a good Orthodox Israeli woman is a wife and mother. Elisheva eventually returns to the United States, breaks her engagement to an Orthodox **gay** man, and becomes involved in a gay rights organization. The narrative alternates between the first and third person, and between the past and present tense, suggesting the complex and shifting identity positions with which Elisheva contends. Ultimately, as with *Lifetime Guarantee,* the protagonist's journey concludes in a committed lesbian relationship, and Elisheva returns to visit Israel with her partner, engaging with the country on different terms. The novel charts a move away from Orthodox Judaism, but insists on Elisheva's persistent sense of belonging to a larger Jewish culture and history, along with a new sense of belonging to a community of women and lesbians.

See also Lesbian Literature, Jewish American

Further Reading

Newman, Felice. "A Lesbian Understanding of Israel and Judiasm." *off our backs* 13, no. 6 (June 1983): 19.

Sturgis, Susanna J. "An Interview with Alice Bloch." *off our backs* 11, no. 11 (December 1981): 22.

———. Review of *Lifetime Guarantee. off our backs* 11, no. 11 (December 1981): 22.

White, Em L. "Alice Bloch." In *Contemporary Lesbian Writers of the United States: A Bio-Bibliographical Critical Sourcebook,* edited by Sandra Pollack and Denise D. Knight, 61–64. Westport, CT: Greenwood Press, 1993.

Zimmerman, Bonnie. *The Safe Sea of Women: Lesbian Fiction 1969–1989.* Boston: Beacon Press, 1990.

Liz Vine

Bogus, SDiane Adams (b. 1946)

Publisher, author, professor, and winner of various literary awards: Walser Fellow, Lambda Literary Award, Innovator of the Year, 1992–1993, and the Peninsula Black Writers Award, 1992. The daughter of Lawrence Thomas Waterhouse and Florence (Adams) Bogus, SDiane (pronounced es-di-ann) Adams Bogus was born in 1946 in Chicago, Illinois. Bogus has published a variety of essays, short stories, and poems. With a B.A. from Stillman College and an M.A. from Syracuse University, a Ph.D. from Miami University, and currently a professor at De Anza College, Bogus boasts a literary career rich in diversity and experience. A celebrated poet and essayist of the lesbian and black community, she has earned a name for herself as one of the United States' most popular black, lesbian writers.

A central topic in her work is the cultural, intellectual, and artistic space occupied by the African American women artists in contemporary United States. In her widely popular book of poems *I'm Off to See the Goddamn Wizard, Alright!* (1971), she comments on the unique title and its significance. The reference to L. Frank Baum's *The Wonderful Wizard of Oz* (1900) and the ominous role of the Wizard is Bogus's critique of the all-knowing, powerful yet fraudulent character that she views as symbolic of white hegemonic culture. In the preface and poems Bogus deconstructs the black perception of white fairy tales and stories in attempt to resolve her "happily ever after" as a black woman in a white nation. Shortly after its publication, Bogus earned her Ph.D. from Miami University and went on to publish a number of collections of poetry, short stories. and essays. Perhaps her most well-known collection of poems is *Woman in the Moon* (1971), her second book of poems to be published; this is a collection of poems that center around Bogus's favorite themes: love and loving, friendship, and the hope and despair that accompany these relationships. The book is also highly acclaimed for its social and political critiques on the treatment of women in our society. Bogus writes without sentimentality as she simultaneously condemns and commends the world we live in. Bogus's collection of poems and essays entitled *Dykehands Sutras Erotic and Lyric* (1989) received attention for its graphic sexual expression. Bogus prefaces with a warning that some readers may find the book offensive because of its sexual explicitness but does not apologize for her honest accounts of the day-to-day struggles of being a lesbian. Once again, focusing on spirituality, politics, and the struggles of love, Bogus proves herself to be both insightful and diverse in her writing in the various genres that complete this collection. *The Chant of the Women of Magdalena* (1990) and *For the Love of Men* (1991) are her most current collected works of poetry and prose to be published. She has contributed to a variety of anthologies including *Intricate Passions* (1989), *Lesbian Bedtime Stories* (1990), and *Happy Endings* (1993). She has also published in various periodicals throughout her career including *Literature Forum, Black American Magazine,* and *Women's Review of Books.*

Bogus identifies Toni Morrison, **Ann Allen Shockley**, **Alice Walker**, and **Audre Lorde** as inspiring examples but has acknowledged **James Baldwin** as the writer who has influenced her the most. In addition to teaching, she also regularly performs her poetry and conducts poetry workshops. Bogus also owns and operates a publishing company, Woman in the Moon, which has published eight of her own works. She credits many of her ideas to her maintenance of a journal dating back to 1962 composed of pieces of prose, poems, and essays on the four principal themes of her life: religion, writing, teaching, and love.

Further Reading

Castle, Terry. *The Apparitional Lesbian.* New York: Columbia University Press. 1995.

Dandridge, Rita B. "SDiane Adams Bogus." In *Contemporary Lesbian Writers of the United States: A Bio-Bibliographical Critical Sourcebook,* edited by Sandra Pollack and Denise D. Knight, 65–69. Westport, CT: Greenwood Press, 1993.

Gil-Gomez, Ellen. *Performing La Mestiza: Textual Representations of Lesbians of Color and the Negotiation of Identities: Literary Criticism and Cultural Theory: The Interaction of Text and Society.* New York: Routledge, 2000.

Suzanne C. Farah

Bornstein, Kate (b. 1948)

Celebrated **queer** transgendered author, playwright, activist, performance artist, and **gender** theorist. Kate Bornstein was born with the name Albert on March 15, 1948, just outside of Fargo, North Dakota. Her father was a Lutheran minister, and her mother, Bornstein says on her Web site (www.katebornstein.com), was Miss Betty Crocker, 1939. She is perhaps one of the most widely read and widely taught gender theorists in the world; her books are taught in over 100 colleges and universities both in the United States and overseas. Known for her strong stage presence and glorious wit, Bornstein has also become one of the most cherished college and university solo performers since her first book, *Gender Outlaw: On Men, Women and the Rest of Us* (1994), was published. Part gender theory, part cultural criticism, part memoir, and part a gathering of political, spiritual, and pop culture texts, this book is a cohesive and highly theoretical collage in which Bornstein argues for the cultural and social creation not only of gender roles and gender, but of sex itself. In this first book, Bornstein narrates the emotional and physical changes related to her sex change in 1986, while also challenging the very grounds on which she based her own decision to have this change: these grounds being the notion that if one is not a man, one must then be a woman. Bornstein both celebrates one's right to change and rechange the body and challenges the very meaning of bodies themselves. Her critique of the binary gender system (she likens it to an addiction or cult) leads quite compellingly to a complicated and fresh understanding of sexuality in which sexual preference (Bornstein prefers this term to its more fate-driven "sexual orientation") is based on many factors—very few of which actually have to do with gender itself. The book also includes a printing of Bornstein's play *Hidden: A Gender.*

Bornstein's second book, *My Gender Workbook* (1998), was an interactive extension of her first book. This book included illustrations by Diane DiMassa and a series of sharp and comic gender aptitude tests—the first of which one can find widely cited and posted on various internet Web sites that promote gender studies and **queer theory**. While Bornstein's gender workbook is quite radical, she is quite gentle with her readers; Bornstein's work is perhaps most celebrated for its ability to draw in readers who might have little to no exposure to gender theory or to queer studies in general. The book contains challenging and thought-provoking exercises for both the theoretical novice and the widely read gender studies guru.

While Bornstein does spend much of her time writing books, plays, and performance pieces, she has also worked as an activist for queer youth in school and shelters throughout the United States. Her book *Hello, Cruel World: 101 Alternatives to Suicide for Teens, Freaks & Other Outlaws* (2006) is most direct in illustrating the inextricable link between her creative and critical work and her work as an activist and advocate for queer youth. While this book is marketed as a self-help book (which it is in many ways), it is also a direct answer to the question of what theory can do for our lives. Bornstein introduces herself in the opening pages and expands her theories on gender and gender terrorism out to look closely at the culture of bullying and its striking connection to the political climate of the United States. She goes on to list her 101 alternatives to suicide—most of which are radically different from any self-help book anyone has seen thus far. Bornstein rates the alternatives based on how safe they are, how legal, how difficult, and how effective. Her goal with this text is not only to help the lives of young people in need but also to ask us to reimagine who the teenager even is—how we think about youth and adolescence. Underground zines played a large role in helping to circulate this book to the youth who desperately need it; it went into second printing in 2008.

Bornstein has also published *Nearly Roadkill* (1996), a cyber romance action novel with Caitlin Sullivan. Bornstein's autobiography, which details her life as a transgendered person and her experiences with the Church of Scientology, is forthcoming from Seven Stories Press. The book is entitled "Kate Bornstein Is a Queer and Pleasant Danger." She lives in New York City with her partner, Barbara Carrellas, who is the author of *Urban Tantra: Sacred Sex for the Twenty-First Century* (2007) and *Luxurious Loving: Tantric Inspirations for Passion and Pleasure* (2006).

Further Reading

Felner, Julie. "Woman, Man, Both, Neither?" Review of *Gender Outlaw. Ms.* 5, no. 1 (1994): 77–78.

Freiwald, Bina Toledo. "Becoming and Be/longing: Kate Bornstein's *Gender Outlaw* and *My Gender Workbook*." *Biography: An Interdisciplinary Quarterly* 24, no. 1 (2001): 35–56.

Jervis, Lisa. "Review of *Hello Cruel World: 101 Alternatives to Suicide for Teens, Freaks, and Other Outlaws*." *Bitch Magazine* 34 (2007): 83–84.

Stacey Waite

Boyd, Randy (b. 1962)

African American **gay** author and publisher. Randy Boyd reflects many of the concerns of his personal life: sports and **homophobia**, racism, and discrimination against those diagnosed with HIV. Writing in a variety of genres, his work focuses on nonstereotypical gay men, often in interracial or intergenerational relationships, and has been nominated for five Lambda Literary Awards.

Born in Indianapolis, Indiana, Randy Boyd graduated from the University of California at Los Angeles in 1985, the same year he was diagnosed with HIV. He created West Beach Books to publish his own novels and the work of others. Boyd's first novel, *Uprising,* appeared in 2001. A thriller involving an interracial trio of famous but **closet**ed celebrities from the worlds of business, popular music, and sports who secretly unite to assassinate a homophobic U.S. Senator, modeled after Jesse Helms, it was a Lambda Literary Award finalist for Best Men's Mystery and Best Small Press Title. Echoing Thomas Mann's *Death in Venice,* Boyd's second novel, *Bridge across the Ocean* (2001), centers on the budding friendship and attraction between a vacationing gay black man with HIV and two straight white teenaged boys. It, too, was a Lambda Best Small Press Title finalist.

Mixing mystery with science fiction, *The Devil Inside* (2002) used the story of a man uncovering his lovers' secrets to dissect issues of discrimination within the gay male community. It was a Gaylactic Spectrum Award nominee for Best Science Fiction novel, and Lambda Awards for Men's Mystery and Best Small Press Title.

Boyd's longest and most ambitious novel, *Walt Loves the Bearcat* (2007) was a Lambda Best Romance nominee. The story of the 21-year-long obsession of a black college cheerleader for a white quarterback, who later becomes the first professional athlete to come out of the closet in mid-career, the love story also deals with issues of interracial relationships, homophobia in the sports world, and living with AIDS. There are numerous parallels between aspects of the main character's journey and the author's life.

Boyd is also an editor: he guest edited *Best Gay Erotica 2001;* from 2001 to 2003, he served as the editor of the annual anthology *Buttmen* that celebrated the beauty of the male buttocks. Short stories by Boyd have appeared in *Certain Voices: Short Stories about Gay Men* (1991), *Flesh and the Word: An Anthology of Erotic Writing* (1993), *Sojourner: Black Gay Voices in the Age of AIDS* (1993), *Ma-Ka Diasporic Juks: Contemporary Writing by Queers of African Descent* (1998), and *Freedom in This Village: Black Gay Men's Writing 1969 to the Present* (2004).

An avid sportsman, Boyd has been a columnist for the gay sports Web site *Outsports.* In a 2001 article he speculated about the sexuality of 10 players in the National Basketball Association. One of the men on the list, John Amaechi, went public about his homosexuality in February 2007. A contributor to *Kujisource,* the publication of the Black AIDS Institute, Boyd's nonfiction has been featured in *Au Courant,* the *Washington Blade, Frontiers, The Gay & Lesbian Review, Lambda Book Report,* and the anthology *Friends and Lovers: Gay Men Write about the Families They Create* (1996). He lives in Southern California with his dog, Boomer, named after the mascot of Boyd's hometown basketball team, the Indiana Pacers.

Further Reading

http://westbeachbooks.com/randy.html.

Reginald Harris

Boykin, Keith O. (b. 1965)

African American author, activist, political commentator, and blogger. Keith Oliver Boykin has focused his career and writings on the struggles for equality of and within the black and **gay**, lesbian, bisexual, and transgendered communities, and to enhancing communication among them.

Born in St. Louis, Missouri, in 1965, Boykin has been a high achiever for much of his life: president of the student government, an editor of the school newspaper, award-winning debater, and member of the varsity track team in high school; an exchange student at the Universidad de Granada in Spain; and a member of a championship-contending track team at Dartmouth College. After graduation, Boykin became a press aide in the presidential campaign of Democratic candidate Michael Dukakis and was subsequently named the campaign's Georgia state press secretary. Following the defeat of Dukakis in the 1988 election, Boykin briefly taught high school English and social studies in Georgia before applying to Harvard Law School. At Harvard, he served as an editor of the *Harvard Civil Rights–Civil Liberties Law Review* and was a leader in the Coalition for Civil Rights, a student group dedicated to the cause of a more diverse faculty. It was also at Harvard that he came to terms with his sexual orientation.

After graduating from Harvard in 1992 and briefly working in a San Francisco law firm, Boykin joined the staff of Bill Clinton's presidential campaign as Midwest press director. Following Clinton's victory in the general election, Boykin served as Special Assistant to the President and Director of News Analysis and later Director of Specialty Media. In April 1993 Boykin helped arrange the first face-to-face meeting between a sitting president and leaders of the gay, lesbian, bisexual, and transgendered community. Boykin took part in the Oval Office session, which included members of the National Gay and Lesbian Task Force, the Black Gay and Lesbian Leadership Forum, and the March on Washington Committee.

Boykin left the White House in January 1995 in order to write his first book, *One More River to Cross: Black & Gay in America* (1996). In this memoir, Boykin recounted his experiences as a member of both the black and gay communities and explored the wider subjects of the often tense relationship between the two groups as well as their shared struggles for equality in American society.

In late 1995 Boykin became the executive director of the National Black Lesbian and Gay Leadership Forum, speaking out on issues of concern to the black LGBTQ community and leading a group of black gay men in the 1995 Million Man March. He made frequent appearances on television and radio programs helping to increase black LGBTQ visibility before leaving the organization in 1998 to work on his second book, *Respecting the Soul: Daily Reflections for Black Lesbians and Gays* (1999). The inspirational daybook features monthly themes and daily motivational quotes from famous African Americans with Boykin's commentary, and suggestions for action. It won the 1999 Lambda Literary Award for Spirituality.

Appointed by President Clinton to be part of the presidential trade delegation to Zimbabwe in 1997, Boykin was on the political science faculty of American University from 1999 to 2001 before moving to New York, where he founded the National Black Justice Coalition, which has become the largest African American LGBTQ rights group in the nation. President of the Board from 2003–2006, he continues to serve as an emeritus member.

In 2004, Boykin was part of the Showtime cable network's *American Candidate,* competing in a simulated presidential campaign, with his life partner, Nathan Williams, participating as campaign manager. He continues to be a regular commentator on black and gay and lesbian issues on numerous television and radio programs, including *Paula Zahn*

Now, The Montel Williams Show, The Tom Joyner Morning Show, Fox News, and National Public Radio. Boykin has written for the *New York Village Voice, San Francisco Chronicle, The Advocate,* and other newspapers and magazines, and his syndicated column appears in gay and lesbian newspapers around the country, including the *New York Blade* and *Atlanta Southern Voice.*

Boykin was scheduled to speak at the Reverend Louis Farrakhan's follow-up to the Million Man March, the Millions More March, in Washington in 2005, but was barred by the executive director of the march, Rev. Willie F. Wilson. Known for his antigay sermons, Wilson alleged that Boykin had failed to meet certain conditions required in order to speak, but would not say what these conditions were.

In response to J. L. King's *On the Down Low: A Journey into the Lives of "Straight" Black Men Who Sleep with Men* (2004), Boykin wrote *Beyond the Down Low: Sex, Lies, and Denial in Black America* (2005). Discussing African American attitudes toward sexuality in general and homosexuality in particular, he urged greater openness on the part of the black community. In 2006, Boykin served as co-host on the Black Entertainment Television's "BET-J Network" talk show *My Two Cents.* Boykin won a gold medal in wrestling at the 2006 Gay Games; he authored a popular blog until February 2008, when he became editor in chief of *The Daily Voice,* an African American news and opinion Web site.

Further Reading

Boykin, Keith. Home page. http://www.keithboykin.com/index.
"Boykin, Keith." *Contemporary Authors.* Vol. 139. Detroit: Gale Research Company, 2005. 45–48.
"The 'Down Low' in Life and Legend: An Interview with Keith Boykin." *The Gay & Lesbian Review Worldwide* 12, no. 6 (November–December 2005): 34–36.

Reginald Harris

Boylan, Jennifer Finney (b. 1958)

Transgendered American novelist, memoirist, and teacher, who published under the name James Finney Boylan until **gender** transition from male to female in 2001.

Jennifer (James) Finney Boylan was born in Valley Forge, Pennsylvania, in 1958. She grew up in Philadelphia's affluent western suburbs and attended the exclusive Haverford School. She graduated from Wesleyan University in 1980. Following graduation, Boylan worked in New York City at several editorial jobs in magazine and book publishing until 1986, when she entered the graduate writing program at Johns Hopkins University. In 1988, she was hired to teach writing and literature at Colby College, in Waterville, Maine. At Colby, she has served as director of the creative writing program.

Boylan's first book was a collection of short stories, *Remind Me to Murder You Later* (1988). The book earned good reviews and also praise from established writers such as John Barth and **Edward Albee**. It was followed in 1991 by *The Planets,* a novel structured very loosely on Gustav Holst's orchestral suite of 1914. The story concerns several eccentric characters from the mining town of Centralia, Pennsylvania, where an underground coal fire has been burning since 1962. Their adventures are continued in Boylan's next novel, *The Constellations* (1994). *Getting In* (1997) is a comic novel about four high school students who seek admission to elite colleges.

At least in terms of its tone, Boylan's fiction owes clear debts to the work of John Kennedy O'Toole and Kurt Vonnegut. Her stories and novels successfully explore the precarious balance between the tragic and the absurd. But occasionally in these books, perspective seems to be lost; *Getting In,* for example, implicitly participates in the authority of the elitist system it ostensibly seeks to critique. Nevertheless, Boylan discovered and honed a refined sense of character in her fiction that would serve her very well in the next stage of her writing.

Following her gender transition, Boylan's writing shifted from fiction to memoir. If only on the strength of its finely structured episodes, *She's Not There: A Life in Two Genders* (2003) would stand apart from other books in the emerging genre of transgender autobiography. In the defining episode of the book, 10-year-old Jimmy Boylan stands on a jetty in a hurricane, hoping that somehow love will cure him of his desire to be a girl. The book is further distinguished by Boylan's capacity to examine her own thoughts and motives in a way that is unburdened by narcissism and self-congratulation: "There were times when it was as if I were trying to prove I was truly female by oppressing *myself*" (156).

She's Not There was followed in 2008 by *I'm Looking Through You: Growing Up Haunted.* This chronicle of her family relationships and examination of the costs and rewards of personal authenticity is her most successful attempt to date to balance the tragic and the absurd. In the story, her sister's outright rejection of Jenny is stunningly awful, while the zany antics of a group of amateur ghostbusters are genuinely funny because the telling seems so uncalculated.

As her friend, writer Richard Russo, has suggested, Boylan's writing is drawn to the archetype of the hero quest, in which the revelation of the true identity of the hero is both a central theme and the prevailing structural element of the narrative. In interviews, she has often stated her intention to return to the writing of fiction, and she has expressed her distrust of gender theory and theorists. Her trust in story, rather than theory, sets her apart from most of her generation of academics, for whom the gender binary is a universal, defining principle.

Since the publication of *She's Not There,* Boylan has attained a degree of celebrity through her appearances on television talk shows, such as *The Oprah Winfrey Show* and *Larry King Live.* As a result, she has been in increased demand as a speaker on college campuses and at academic conferences. She has become one of the most visible, public faces and voices among transgender people. While her public interviews have tended to focus for the most part on her individual experiences as a transgender woman writer, she has also spoken as a committed advocate for the legal rights and fundamental dignity of all gender-variant people. Her dedication to these principles was evident in an address she delivered in 2007 to a group of transgender people and their allies, who were gathered in Washington, D.C., to lobby for inclusion in the proposed Employment Non-Discrimination Act.

See also Autobiography, Transgender

Further Reading

Maslin, Janet. "A Novelist Creates a New Identity." Review of *She's Not There: A Life in Two Genders,* by Jennifer Finney Boylan. *New York Times,* July 28, 2003, E6.

Posner, Jennifer. "Gender Immigrant: A Conversation with Jennifer Finney Boylan." *Women's Review of Books* 21, no. 7 (2004): 5–7.

Abby Connelly

Bram, Christopher (b. 1952)

Contemporary **gay** American novelist. The work of prolific novelist Christopher Bram often deals with issues of gay sexuality in a variety of historical periods and contexts, from Hollywood in the 1930s to New York in the 1970s and 1980s, and with society's impact on ordinary gay and straight lives. Noted for his novelistic skill, craftsmanship, and imagination, his work uses a focus on plot and emotionally accurate character development to offer new perspectives on social mores from a gay perspective, combined with humor and a complex moral vision. His work often features characters who are creative artists, and conventional as well as unconventional families.

Born in Buffalo, New York, in 1952, Bram grew up in Kempsville, Virginia, in the Norfolk–Virginia Beach area. He graduated from the College of William and Mary in 1974 with a B.A. in English and moved to New York City in 1978. A 2001 Guggenheim Fellow, he received the Bill Whitehead Award for Lifetime Achievement from the Publishing Triangle in 2003.

Bram's short story, "Aphrodisiac," appeared in *Christopher Street* in 1979 and was the title work of a collection of fiction from the journal collected in 1980. His first three novels explore gay life and issues in New York at different time periods: *Surprising Myself* (1987), a coming out story as well as a love story set in the 1970s; *Hold Tight* (1988) set in the early 1940s; and *In Memory of Angel Clare* (1989) set in the 1980s. *Hold Tight* offers an unusual, hustler's-eye-view of spying and governmental intrigue during World War II as filtered through the sensibility of its gay Texan protagonist. *In Memory of Angel Clare* focuses unsentimentally on the AIDS crisis and a variety of characters isolated by guilt and denial.

His subsequent novels traveled beyond New York and included more explicit political content: the U.S. Foreign Service and the Vietnam War in *Almost History* (1992) and a media-obsessed Washington, D.C., in *Gossip* (1997). Bram's best-known work, *Father of Frankenstein* (1995), is a fictional account of the final years of British expatriate movie director James Whale, whose homosexuality limited his Hollywood career. *Father of Frankenstein* was made into the movie *Gods and Monsters* (1998) starring Sir Ian McKellen and Brendan Fraser. Bill Condon won an Academy Award for his adaptation of Bram's novel and directed the film.

Bram's most ambitious novel, the 500-page *The Notorious Dr. August: His Real Life and Crimes,* appeared in 2000. It was set in both the United States and Europe from the end of the Civil War to the early years of the twentieth century. Shifting in time and place, the novel dramatizes dilemmas of interracial relationships, spirituality, and sexual identity through characters that inhabit Bram's detailed recreation of a Victorian Age that has yet to create clinically labeled sexual identities.

Bram returned to contemporary America with *Lives of the Circus Animals* (2003), a comic and sexual satire set in the world of the New York theater community, and to his native Virginia in *Exiles in America* (2006), focusing on relationships, discrimination, and terrorist fears in a small college town at the beginning of the Iraq War.

Although primarily a novelist, Bram's essays and critical writing have also appeared in many publications, including *Hometowns: Gay Men Write about Where They Belong* (1991), *We Must Love One Another Or Die: The Life and Legacies of Larry Kramer* (1998), and *Boys Like Us: Gay Writers Tell Their Coming Out Stories* (1996), the *Lambda Book Report, New York Newsday,* and the *New York Times Book Review*. His writing appears in and he wrote the introduction to *Particular Voices: Portraits of Gay and Lesbian Writers*

(1997) and was guest editor of the collection *Best Gay Erotica 1998*. He has reviewed movies for the *New York Native* and *Premiere* magazine and has also written several screenplays, including two shorts that were directed by his partner, Draper Shreeve.

Further Reading

"Bram, Christopher." *Contemporary Authors, New Revision Series,* Vol. 86. Detroit: Gale Research Company, 2000. 29–31.

Bronksi, Michael. "Bram, Christopher." In *Gay & Lesbian Literature,* edited by Sharon Malinowski, 50–51. New York: St. James Press, 1998.

Canning, Richard. *Hear Us Out: Conversations with Gay Novelists.* New York: Columbia University Press, 2003. 59–87.

Gambone, Philip. *Something Inside: Conversations with Gay Fiction Writers.* Madison: University of Wisconsin Press, 1999. 91–106.

Reginald Harris

Britton, Donald (1951–1994)

Poet. Donald Britton was a little-known but very talented poet who died of AIDS. He published one book, *Italy,* with poet and novelist **Dennis Cooper**'s Little Caesar Press in 1981. His work was also included in a few anthologies, including the **gay** poetry anthology *The Son of the Male Muse* (1983) and in literary journals. Sadly, his work has since sunk into neglect.

Donald Britton was associated with what has come to be known as the third-generation of New York poets, many of them gay, among them Joe Brainard, Dennis Cooper, Douglas Crase, **Tim Dlugos**, Kenward Elmslie, Brad Gooch, Steve Hamilton, and Bernard Welt. AIDS had a strong impact on this group: both Britton and Dlugos died of the disease, and the survivors have long since gone their separate ways.

Donald Britton's poems frequently explore not just what it might mean to be someone else, but what it might mean to be no one, or everyone. While there is often an "I," that pronoun sometimes serves as no more than a point of view, a place from which the poem sets out. As in T. S. Eliot's "The Love Song of J. Alfred Prufrock" or *The Waste Land* (another poem without an identifiable "speaker"), the "you" that flickers in and out of the poems can be the beloved, a friend, a doppelganger, or the reader, or all of them by turns. There is thus, despite the poems' lack of a fixed or defined self or persona, a sense of intimacy, and an emotional openness made more effective by the surface reticence.

In his only statement on his work, the commentary on his poem "Winter Garden" in the anthology *Ecstatic Occasions, Expedient Forms,* edited by poet David Lehman, Britton writes that the formal rigor of the poem lies "in my attempt to 'non-personalize' or psychologically denature the poem—to detach it from any single speaker or communication context, yet maintain the illusion of a coherent, at times elegant discourse" (20). Britton writes that "Winter Garden" has "no 'speaker,' no 'voice,' no 'persona,' no 'point of view'" (20). This is not true of all of his poems, but in all of them there is a distance from even the most personal and intense emotions, which are objectified rather than treated as an individual's possessions or characterizing features.

Many of Donald Britton's poems do not have immediately identifiable "topics," though they do have places: they are not subject centered in either sense of the word. Britton does not usually write about himself, or any version of himself, but rather about states of mind as it moves through the world. His poems trace out the meanderings of embodied consciousness, teasing out the links between bodily experience and consciousness. In this sense Britton's poetry can be considered phenomenological, investigating the nature of experience itself. The mind that these poems explore is particular and even individual, but it is not personalized in the post-Confessional manner, but abstracted and generalized, much as in the work of **John Ashbery**, who is the single strongest influence on Britton's poetry. (Ashbery wrote a blurb for *Italy,* as did the novelist **Edmund White**.) Britton's poems wear the outfit of self lightly, and rarely singularly; they explore not just what it might mean to be someone else, but what it might mean to be no one at all, or everyone. For Britton, selfhood was something best dispersed or at least shared. This refusal to hold onto the self as a personal possession may be the source of the paradoxical intimacy of these seemingly impersonal poems.

Britton is a follower not only of John Ashbery but of the French Symbolist poets, especially Stéphane Mallarmé, who sought a pure poetry, a poetry in, of, and for itself. As Britton writes in *Ecstatic Occasions, Expedient Forms,* his poems are a way "to project oneself toward that point where one's words cease to comment on *any* experience, but become an experience in and of themselves: empty of discursive content, perhaps, but full of all manner of things *language* wants to say, but people usually don't" (20). Britton's work explores what one of his poems calls the "White Space" where language and music merge.

Further Reading

Britton, Donald. "Winter Garden." *Ecstatic Occasions, Expedient Forms: 85 Leading Contemporary Poets Select and Comment on Their Poems,* edited by David Lehman. 2nd ed. Ann Arbor: University of Michigan Press, 1996.

Shepherd, Reginald. "Donald Britton." In *Contemporary Gay American Poets and Playwrights: An A–Z Guide,* edited by Emmanuel S. Nelson, 38–42. Westport, CT: Greenwood Press, 2003.

Reginald Shepherd

Broughton, James (1913–1999)

Acclaimed avant-garde filmmaker, poet, playwright, memoirist, and mystic. James Richard Broughton was born on November 10, 1913, to Irwin and Olga Jungbluth Broughton in Modesta, California. His father, a wealthy banker, died in the 1918 influenza epidemic when Broughton was five, and his neurotic domineering mother married again. His stepfather sent him to military school in order to make a man of him. Instead he began writing poetry and had his first **gay** experience.

Broughton ran away from college to join the merchant marines, but later returned to Stanford to earn his B.A. (1936). He also studied at The New School for Social Research. He married Susanna Hart in 1962, fathering a daughter, Serena, and son, Orion; he divorced Hart in 1973. In 1974 he married the artist Joel Singer and began a legendary life of collaboration in film, poetry, and lovemaking. He died of heart failure on May 17, 1999, in Port Townsend, Washington.

Broughton's precocious creativity blossomed after a visitation, at the age of three, by a god-like boy, Hermy. The name "Big Joy," given to him by publisher and close friend Jonathan Williams, alluded to his perpetually sunny disposition and his Dionysian pansexual positivism. Considered the father of the West Coast experimental film movement, Broughton was also a member of the San Francisco Poetry Renaissance. He also became well-known as Sister Sermoneta of San Francisco's Sisters of Perpetual Indulgence.

In *The Pleasure Garden* (1953), a puritanical Minister of Public Behavior attempts to squelch the joyful romping of the garden's visitors by turning it into a cemetery. A portly fairy godmother leads a rebellion against all unhappiness and unites all the lost lovers. *The Bed* (1968) broke the taboo of frontal nudity in film, winning many international prizes, including Guggenheim Fellowships (1971 and 1973) and National Endowment for the Arts (1976) awards. In it an empty bed lands in a meadow. Various characters materialize on it; Broughton appears as Pan serenading the naked celebrants. *Nuptiae* (1969), inspired by his own three-day wedding to Hart, depicts a wedding celebrating the alchemical unification of opposites. *The Golden Positions* (1970) venerates the body and the body's unions. *This Is It* (1971) is a Zen fable involving a wandering talking ball, the voice of God, and a wondering boy-child, played by Broughton's young son. The second and fourth films made with Singer are paeans to the gay body. Brougthon recites his poem by the same name in the *Song of the Godbody* (1977) as the camera closely scans his body. *Hermes Bird* (1979) shows Singer's penis erecting in slow motion.

The book *Ecstasies* (1983), a hymn to sexual divinity, celebrates Broughton's union with Singer. Beginning with *Graffiti for the Johns of Heaven* (1982), the poems explore the Divine Body, the unification of dark and light, joyful sexual adventurousness, and culminate in the death poems of Broughton's last years. These poems frame *Packing Up for Paradise* (1997), ensuring Broughton's place among the great poetic mystics.

In the late 1980s and early 1990s Broughton published his memoirs: a philosophic memoir of his life as a filmmaker, *Making Light of It* (1992); *Coming Unbuttoned* (1993), a revised edition of *The Androgyne Journal* (1991), as well as a collection of aphorisms. In these works he offers his accumulated wisdom on living, art, and spirituality.

Spiritual autobiography through play, ecstasy, myth, and alchemical transformation characterizes Broughton's 23 films, 10 plays, 26 books of poetry, and 8 works of nonfiction. During the later part of his life, retrospectives of his film work were held in New York, London, Paris, Montreal, and elsewhere. In 1989 Broughton received the Maya Deren Award for lifetime achievement from The American Film Institute. In 1991 *Special Deliveries* was nominated for a Lambda Literary Award. He also received a lifetime achievement award from the National Poetry Association.

Further Reading

Beam, Jeffery. "James Broughton." In *Contemporary Gay American Poets and Playwrights: An A–Z Guide*, edited by Emmanuel S. Nelson, 43–53. Westport, CT: Greenwood Press, 2003.

Cory, Jim. "Androgyne in the Soul: An Interview." *American Writing* 9 (1994): 22–32.

"Craft Interview with James Broughton." *New York Quarterly* 42 (1990): 23–32.

Foley, Jack. "Big Joy: Octogenarian, An Interview with James Broughton" *Alsop Review.* http://www.alsopreview.com/columns/foley/jfbroughton.html.

Goodman, Martin. "Free to Die Laughing: From an Interview." *Archipelago* 4 (2000) : 1–2. http://www.archipelago.org/vol4-1/broughton.htm.

Morris, Gary. "Laughing Pan: James Broughton." *Bright Lights Film Journal* 27 (January 27, 2000). http://www.brightlightsfilm.com/27/broughton.html.

Jeffery Beam

Broumas, Olga (b. 1949)

Greek American poet and professor of creative writing. Olga Broumas was born on May 6, 1949, on the island of Syros, Greece. Her father, orphaned at two years old and raised by seaside villagers, fought in World War II in Africa and was wounded just before the war ended. He found himself waking up in Alexandria, Egypt, where he met Broumas's mother who was working as a 16-year-old nurse's aide. They married in less than a year, and a few years later Olga Broumas was born. While Broumas spent two short years in the United States in Washington, D.C., during elementary school, she spent the rest of her childhood and adolescence in Greece. She published her first book of poems at the age of 17. She then traveled to the United States again on a Fulbright Scholarship to study architecture at the University of Pennsylvania where she received her bachelor's degree in 1969. She moved on to study writing at the University of Oregon where she earned her Master of Fine Arts degree. Broumas then moved to Provincetown, Massachusetts, to be closer to the ocean. There, she and several friends founded Freehand, Inc.—a school for female writers and photographers. In this group, Broumas further developed her body-centered approach to teaching writing and to thinking about writing. Freehand disbanded in 1987. Not surprisingly, Broumas would go on to further cultivate her interest in body healing and in the jazz saxophone; these interests certainly call attention to both the curative and musical nature of her writing.

Olga Broumas has now become a renowned and prolific writer, becoming the first nonnative speaker of English to win the Yale Younger Poets Prize for her first collection of poems entitled *Beginning with O* (1977). Stanley Kunitz selected her collection and praised the eroticism, sensuality, and integration with Greek myth that so defines Broumas's work as a poet. A groundbreaking book in terms of its explicit sexuality, *Beginning with O* marked Broumas as a sharp and powerful lesbian writer. Some critics even credit her with the invention of the feminist lesbian lyric. She would continue writing and publish four more books of poems. *Soie Sauvage* (1979) is a quiet, introspective, and lyrical collection of poems highlighting Broumas's attention both to body and to sound. She writes a series of poems with the word *landscape* in their titles ("Landscape with Leaves and Figure," "Landscape with Next of Kin," and so forth). Part Zen parables, part love poem, and part musical score, these poems try to locate their subjects in body and Earth; they try to tie all sensuality and corporeality to the landscape itself. Even the poets, John Berryman named one of them, appear in these landscapes. In this sense, Broumas becomes also a kind of painter; she composes images resting there to be seen. *Pastoral Jazz* (1983) continues to explore these themes but seems located more specifically as a book of longing, of deep grief and loss. Broumas would publish one more sole collection, *Perpetua* (1989) before her collected poems would appear in *Rave* (1999). It is striking to note how little criticism has been written about Broumas's work despite being an award-winning and celebrated lesbian poet. This is perhaps connected to a kind of invisibility of the feminine lesbian artist who, as time goes on, will continue to be made more and more visible not merely as artist or writer but also as a mind worthy of careful and critical attention.

Broumas is also known as an inveterate collaborator. She has co-authored several books and finds pleasure in working with other writers and artists. She published two notable collaborative collections: *Black Holes, Black Stockings* (1995) with Jane Miller and *Sappho's Gymnasium* (1994) with T. Begley. In addition, Broumas has published several translations of Nobel Prize winning Greek poet Odysseas Elytis, who died in 1996. She has been a committed teacher of writing and poetry for many years and has taught in various creative writing programs including the University of Idaho and Goddard College. Broumas has been teaching poetry and creative writing at Brandeis University since 1990. She is now the director of the university's Creative Writing Program.

Further Reading

Carruthers, Mary J. "The Re-Vision of the Muse: Adrienne Rich, Audre Lorde, Judy Grahn, Olga Broumas." *Hudson Review* 36, no. 2 (Summer 1983): 293–322.

Carter, Kate. "Olga Broumas." *Contemporary Lesbian Writers of the United States: A Bio-Bibliographical Critical Sourcebook,* edited by Sandra Pollack and Denise D. Knight, 89–93. Westport, CT: Greenwood 1993.

Hammond, Karla. "An Interview with Olga Broumas." *Northwest Review* 18, no. 3 (1980): 33–44.

Horton, Diane "Scarlet Liturgies: The Poetry of Olga Broumas." *North Dakota Quarterly* 55, no. 4 (Fall 1987): 322–47.

Ingram, Claudia. "Sappho's Legacy: The Collaborative Testimony of Olga Broumas and T. Begley." *Tulsa Studies in Women's Literature* 19, no. 1 (Spring 2000): 105–20.

Stacey Waite

Brown, Rita Mae (b. 1944)

Influential and controversial novelist, lesbian feminist, activist, and poet. The author of over 37 books, Rita Mae Brown also is an Emmy-nominated screenwriter. She is best known for the following works: *The Hand That Cradles the Rock* (1971), **Rubyfruit Jungle** (1973), *A Plain Brown Wrapper* (1976), *Southern Discomfort* (1982), *Starting from Scratch: A Different Kind of Writer's Manual* (1988), *Venus Envy* (1993), *Rita Will: Memoir of a Literary Rabble-Rouser* (1997), the Jane Arnold novel series, and the Mrs. Murphy novel series. In the early 1970s Brown co-founded the journal *Quest: A Feminist Quarterly* (1973–1984). She claims to co-author the Mrs. Murphy mystery series with her cat, Sneaky Pie Brown. This series includes the first and most well known of the series, *Wish You Were Here* (1990). As of 2008, she continues to add to the Mrs. Murphy and Jane Arnold series, often producing more than one book per year for each series.

Brown's early works addressed themes of lesbian sexuality, race and racism in the American South, civil rights, and women's rights. Her most recent works are predominantly works of fiction, mostly mysteries, and have animals as the central characters; many of her recent novels are set in the American South. The transition from fighting strenuously for a broad spectrum of civil rights in the 1960s and 1970s, as well as addressing themes of lesbian sexuality and lesbian rights on a more intellectual level in the 1970s, to writing fiction and mystery novels in the 1980s to the present leads some critics to suggest that Brown has become more politically conservative. Yet Brown remains very outspoken on a host of issues: lesbian and **gay** rights, racism, and animal rights. As evidence of her continued advocacy for gays and lesbians, in her recent memoir, *Rita Will,* she writes, "Nobody cares about gay people. Black folks don't want their **queer**s, white people can't stand theirs. Rich people send theirs to psychiatrists. Poor people kick theirs out on the street. Nobody wants us. I want us. We've got to stand up for one another" (18).

While not her first work, *Rubyfruit Jungle* (1973) was a "groundbreaking lesbian novel" (Sachs) and is the work Brown is most revered for to this day. It is ubiquitous in classes that address sexuality, gay/lesbian/bisexual/transgender issues, women's studies, and often literature classes. Yet it almost did not happen. Major publishing houses turned it down, but Brown was paid $1,000 by the small Daughters Press for the rights to the book; due to word of mouth the book became a best seller, going on to sell millions of copies. The book remains in print and is published by Bantam Books; Brown now owns the rights to the book. *Rubyfruit Jungle* "may well be the most widely read lesbian novel ever written" and was "embraced by the lesbian-feminist movement" (Highleyman). Brown denies that the book is autobiographical but admits there are aspects of Molly Bolt's (the protagonist) life that are similar to her own life. The book is viewed as groundbreaking because it features a "happy, unapologetic lesbian protagonist—unlike the tradition of lesbian novels" (Highleyman). This positive outlook on lesbianism caused a lot of turmoil and potential danger, according to Brown. As she states in her memoir, *Rubyfruit Jungle* "brought . . . a ton of hate mail, numerous threats on my life including two bomb threats, increased outrage from the conservative wing of the feminist movement and scorn from the radical dykes. Straight people were mad because I was gay. The dykes were mad because I wasn't gay enough" (41).

Brown was born in Hanover, Pennsylvania, to an unwed teenage mother. She was adopted by the Brown family and spent her early childhood in Pennsylvania. She and her family moved to Florida when she was 11. At age 16 she "had her first sexual experience with a girlfriend from school" (Highleyman). She went to the University of Florida on a scholarship, but was expelled due to what the university administration said was her involvement in the civil rights movement. Brown subsequently lost her scholarship and hitchhiked to New York, living in a car, continuing to write, and later being accepted to New York University (NYU), where she also was awarded a scholarship. She holds a B.A. from NYU in English and Classics, a certificate from the New York School of Visual Arts in Cinematography, and a Ph.D. in Political Science from the Institute for Policy Studies.

While at NYU Brown was active in the U.S. civil rights, women's rights, and gay liberation movements during the 1960s. She started the NYU chapter of the Student Homophile League; the League was the first gay campus group in the United States and was created at Columbia University (Highleyman). Brown also participated in the **Stonewall Riots** in New York City in the summer of 1969.

Brown also was a founding member of the Radicalesbians in 1970. Founding the Radicalesbians was a reaction to being kicked out of the National Organization for Women (NOW) after pressing the organization to pay more attention to lesbian issues and rights. The tension over lesbian issues at NOW came to a head when Betty Friedan, founder and president of NOW, announced at a meeting in 1969 that "lesbians posed 'a lavender menace' to the progress of feminism" and that "anything that might distract from that goal—messy issues like challenging **homophobia** or questioning **heterosexuality**—were a threat to women's common concern [. . .]. By singling out lesbians, Friedan unwittingly set the stage for the emergence of lesbian feminists" (Daly and Stockwell 24). Friedan's comments led Brown and others to descend "on NOW's Second Congress to Unite Women in 1970—which had conspicuously left lesbian issues off its agenda. In a crowded room full of women, they cut the lights, and when they came back up, Brown and company wore purple LAVENDER MENACE t-shirts and passed out their manifesto, 'The Woman-Identified Woman' " (Daly and Stockwell 25). "The Woman-Identified Woman" was a "declaration of the theoretical connections between **lesbianism** and feminism" (Valk 304). These actions and her push for more attention to lesbian issues led to Brown's expulsion from NOW and her founding of the Radicalesbians in 1970 and the Furies, a lesbian separatist organization in Washington, D.C.

The Furies were a separatist lesbian feminist collective; its legacy has had a resonating effect on the feminist movement and more specifically on the **gay rights movement**. The group members lived together, worked together, published a monthly newspaper, and taught workshops. The Furies forced the feminist movement to confront its hetero-sexism and take real notice of lesbian feminists and their unique perspectives. The Furies' goal was not to work *with* the larger feminist movement but to "form their own move-ment in order to be taken seriously, to stop straight women from oppressing us, and to force straight women to deal with their own Lesbianism" (Valk 310). The Furies focused on larger, political and social, change rather than personal awakenings as many parts of the feminist movement did. Otherwise, "we spend the rest of our lives in a maze of per-sonal experience with no plan to get out of those experiences of oppression" (Valk 320). Yet their passionate commitment to political change led some to label the atmosphere at the Furies as dogmatic and authoritarian. Brown stated the environment there was akin to "the dynamic of a fascist state" (Valk 325). She was expelled from the group (preceded by two other members). Following Brown's expulsion, interpersonal conflicts and political differences "regarding how to organize a mass movement caused conflict both within the collective and with other women" (Valk 304), leading the group to break up. After they disbanded, some members of the Furies (including Brown) joined together to publish the journal *Quest*, which was published from 1973 to 1982. Those who published *Quest* seemed to have learned from the problems of the Furies: *Quest* included contributions from a variety of writers including women of color, academics, and activists and addressed a wider range of issues (Valk).

After the decline of the lesbian feminist movement and having finished graduate school, Brown moved to Los Angeles and gained success as a television and film screen-writer. She later returned to the East Coast of the United States and now resides in Char-lottesville, Virginia. In addition to authoring over 37 books, Brown has also served as a Visiting Faculty member at the University of Nebraska from 2004 to 2006.

See also Novel, Lesbian

Further Reading

Brown, Rita Mae. *Rita Will: Memoir of a Literary Rabble-Rouser.* New York: Bantam Books, 1997.

Daly, Meg, and Anne Stockwell. "Fear of Flying . . . to the White House." *The Advocate,* January 15, 2008, 24–26.

Highleyman, Liz. "Rita Mae Brown: Art Mirrors Life." *Lesbian News* (December 2004): 34.

Kattelman, Beth A. *glbtq: An Encyclopedia of Gay, Lesbian, Bisexual, Transgender, and Queer Cul-ture.* http://www.glbtq.com/literature/brown_rm.html (accessed May 20, 2008).

Sachs, Andrea. "Rita Mae Brown: Loves Cats, Hates Marriage." 2008. http://www.time.com/time/arts/article/0,8599,1723482,00.html (accessed May 20, 2008).

Valk, Anne M. "Living a Feminist Lifestyle: The Intersection of Theory and Action in a Lesbian Feminist Collective." *Feminist Studies* 28, no. 2 (2002): 303–32.

Emily C. Martin-Hondros

Bumbalo, Victor (b. 1946)

Italian American **gay** playwright. Bumbalo's multifaceted contribution to gay theater began in 1979. His plays focus on some of the defining themes of gay life: coming out, relationship woes, the effects of AIDS on victims and their loved ones, and the sporadic evolution of gay tolerance.

Niagara Falls (1979) is a two-part comedy in which the nameless gay son is the ghostly hero. The plot revolves around sister Jackie's wedding and how some members of the family come to understand themselves because of the crisis their gay son creates when he comes home with his lover to attend Jackie's wedding.

The play opens in Connie and Johnny Poletti's kitchen the morning of Jackie's wedding, as they discuss the dilemma their gay son's arrival with his lover poses. Bumbalo renders the stereotypical Italian American couple with genuine affection and hilarious precision: they are melodramatic, superstitious, strongly patriarchal, and devoutly Catholic. However, since family is of paramount importance, somehow the Polettis, with Connie's urging, learn how to venture into and navigate difficult new territory thus liberating themselves from self-imposed cultural confines.

Meant to invoke and mock a tired but hilarious stereotype, part two takes place on Jackie and Vinnie's wedding night at the less than edenic Shangri-La Motor Inn. Jackie is grieving and saying her rosary because she regrets having married Vinnie, a stereotypical Italian American. Eventually, with the help of Fred, the gay desk clerk, Vinnie capitulates to Jackie and their marriage is salvaged. The gay brother has inspired the women to voice their own desires and find more joy in their lives.

Adam and the Experts (1990) is about the ramifications of AIDS in the gay community. Eddie is HIV-positive, and Adam is his best friend and neurotic caregiver. Both men are angry and afraid. When Eddie breaks the news to Adam, Eddie ends up consoling Adam. As there is no manual for how to cope with the crisis caused by AIDS, Adam attempts, frenetically, to prolong Eddie's life by reading all the literature available on AIDS cures, and locating expert after expert. Eddie dreads Adam's suggestions. He wants dignity and peace in what remains of his life. The play ends with Eddie's death and the lingering tragedy of lives cut short.

Kitchen Duty (1981) depicts a broken love affair and the struggle of being homosexual in a predominantly heterosexual world. *After Eleven* (1983) is an examination of a gay couple trying to sustain their relationship during the throes of a midlife crisis. Two short plays, *Show* (1992) and *Tell* (1993), also deal with AIDS.

What Are Tuesdays Like? (1994) takes place on the Tuesdays reserved for HIV-positive patients in the waiting room of a hospital. Their conversations demonstrate the plight of AIDS victims, the incremental bond that forms among people who share the same fate. Each character experiences denial, courage, anger, and fear, which sometimes gives way to madness. All of them "used to" do or be something else; now they are only AIDS patients, fighting for survival.

Questa (2006) is the story of Paul who, while seeking erotic pleasure in an alley, inadvertently commits murder, a result of his long-simmering rage gone awry. He runs to his sister, Susan, who tries to persuade him to be ethical and report the incident. He does not, and the two of them become victims of their hideous secret. Joy dissipates from their lives that have already been teetering on the miserable.

Event by tragic event, peacefulness has been obliterated from the lives of all the characters. Incestuously intertwined, their lives are all demarcated by this particular catastrophe. Susan's husband, Nicholas, was the best friend of Paul's deceased lover. Then Paul becomes obsessed with making friends with Lori, the mother of the man he killed. Lori is having an active affair with a priest. She quits her job as a hairdresser in despair over her son's death and her erroneous belief that he was the victim of a gay bashing. Lori's ex-boss and Paul eventually engage in a quasi-romantic affair. And to keep the moral balance, Daniel, a wise, experienced, sympathetic, street person—who is also complicit because he witnessed the entire scene—explains the justification for the characters' aberrant behavior. Finally, this play demonstrates the difficulty of finding and keeping joy and peace in one's life in a world ravaged by adversity.

Bumbalo honestly and humorously presents relevant issues, providing a point of reference for and validity to gay life, an important contribution to gay and AIDS literature.

Further Reading

Massa, Suzanne Hotte. "Victor Bumbalo." In *Contemporary Gay American Poets and Playwrights: An A-to-Z Guide,* edited by Emmanuel S. Nelson, 54–60. Westport, CT: Greenwood Press, 2003.

Suzanne Hotte Massa

Burroughs, Augusten (b. 1965)

Successful **gay** memoirist and essayist. Born Christopher Robison in Pittsburgh, Pennsylvania, on October 23, 1965, Augusten Xon Burroughs is the son of the late John G. Robison, a philosophy professor at the University of Massachusetts at Amherst, and the poet Margaret Robison and the younger brother of John Robison. Burroughs has stated that the fourth grade was the last year of formal education he actually completed; however, he went on to earn his General Education Diploma at the age of 17. At the age of 19 he moved to San Francisco to work as an advertising copywriter and later shifted his career focus to writing.

Burroughs has established a successful career by writing about his dysfunctional family situation when he was young and his lived experiences since then. The disconcerting details of his adolescent experiences are presented in *Running with Scissors* (2002), the best-selling memoir for which Burroughs is best known, which reveals how his biological mother turned him over to be raised by her unorthodox, eccentric psychiatrist and the man's very unconventional family (sample moments in the book feature a dog-food-munching parental figure and a private room called "the masturbatorium"). Although Burroughs called this family the "Finches" in this memoir, various members of the real-life foster family brought a lawsuit against Burroughs and his publisher in August 2005, claiming that several of the book's conversations and events were fabricated and painted a false, damaging picture of their lives and living conditions when Burroughs was with them. (Burroughs maintains that his work is entirely accurate and the lawsuit was settled out of court.) The book was made into a 2006 feature film, starring Alec Baldwin, Annette Bening, Joseph Cross (as Augusten), Joseph Fiennes, Gwyneth Paltrow, and Evan Rachel Wood and directed by Ryan Murphy.

Burroughs's first book, *Sellevision* (2000), a satire of home shopping channels that he wrote in one week while experiencing alcohol poisoning, is the only novel he has published to date. Themes raised in that novel are explored in greater depth in his memoir *Dry* (2003), which explores the drinking problem he developed while working as an advertising executive, his time spent in a gay-friendly rehabilitation center to overcome his alcoholism, and his experiences watching his best friend die from AIDS. Although

Burroughs actually wrote this memoir prior to *Running with Scissors,* his publisher opted to release *Scissors* first in order to adhere to the chronology of the author's life. *A Wolf at the Table: A Memoir of My Father* (2008), his most recent work, revisits Burroughs's childhood years preceding his parents' divorce (beginning with his earliest memories when he was just 18 months old) and explores his strained relationship with, and desire to win the affections of, his biological father, who rejected him. Unlike his previous memoirs, Burroughs emphasizes that *A Wolf at the Table* is entirely serious, rather than witty and the sort of dark comedy that his readers may have come to expect.

In addition to those book projects, Burroughs has to date published two collections of essays: *Magical Thinking: True Stories* (2003) and *Possible Side Effects* (2006). The former explores the author's reflections on his various life experiences, ranging from his unsuccessful efforts as a child actor to dating an undertaker. The latter presents additional reflections on Burroughs's experiences in the advertising profession, adventures with his dogs, and his addiction to nicotine gum, along with introductory comments stating that some of the events presented have been altered a bit (a similar introductory blurb appears in *Dry*).

In interviews, Burroughs has stated that he feels a cathartic need to write and that, before he was old enough to do so, he would tape record his thoughts on a regular basis. He says he feels fortunate to have lived a life full of odd experiences that provides him with endless interesting material upon which to draw and that his brother, a gifted storyteller, has influenced him as a writer. To date, Burroughs's books have been published in more than a dozen countries. He has also served as the narrator for the audio editions of his various works.

Further Reading

Abbott, Charlotte. "Daddy Dearest." *The Advocate,* May 6, 2008, 61–63.

Bahr, David. "Dry, but Flying High." *Publishers Weekly* 251, no. 41 (October 11, 2004): 52.

Leddy, Chuck. "Family Sues over Alleged Portrayal in Memoir." *Writer* 118, no. 12 (December 2005): 9.

Peregrin, Tony. "Augusten Burroughs On and Off the Wagon." *Gay and Lesbian Review Worldwide* 10, no. 5 (September/October 2003): 22.

Saricks, Joyce. Review of *Possible Side Effects,* by Augusten Burroughs. *Booklist* 102, nos. 19–20 (June 1–15, 2006): 110.

Kylo-Patrick R. Hart

Burroughs, William S. (1914–1997)

American avant-garde novelist, essayist, social critic, and influential member of the Beat Generation. The younger of two sons of Mortimer Perry Burroughs and Laura Hammon Lee, William Seward Burroughs was born on February 5, 1914, in St. Louis, Missouri. Burroughs's grandfather was the founder of the Burroughs Adding Machine Company, which grew into the Burroughs Corporation; the author's father owned a gift shop, Cobblestone Gardens, and his mother was the daughter of a minister whose family claimed heritage to the Civil War general Robert E. Lee.

Throughout his life, Burroughs demonstrated an avid nature for the wanderlust and nonconformist lifestyle. This desire for rootlessness and for experimentation on life's edges was often expressed through travel, sex, drugs, and art.

Burroughs's early life was marked by rebellion against traditional social mores. He first attended John Burroughs Elementary in St. Louis, but after the young student failed to fit in, his parents sent him to the Los Alamos Ranch School in New Mexico where they hoped the boy would be toughened up and become manlier. He soon ran afoul of the new school's codes by experimenting with homosexuality and using drugs and was swiftly expelled. After later finishing Taylor High School in 1932, Burroughs enrolled at Harvard University to study art. From the Harvard campus, Burroughs made frequent trips to the **gay** subculture in New York City. He frequented the homosexual life found in the bars of Greenwich Village and Harlem. He graduated from Harvard in 1936.

After college, Burroughs spent the next several years tramping through Europe, particularly Austria and Hungary, where he ensconced himself in alternative lifestyles, encountering a spectrum of people from the bourgeoisie to exiles and drifters. These were the early years in Europe of World War II. One notable story from this European exile focuses on his acquaintance, the young woman Ilse Klapper, a German Jew fleeing the Nazi regime. Burroughs married her, allowing the woman legally to emigrate to the United States. They later divorced. Years later, he would return to London and Paris to find himself in the midst of a cultural war known as the Beats.

Back in the United States in 1939, Burroughs held a series of odd jobs briefly. His emotional health declined, bringing worry to his parents. He was subject to spontaneous and violent acts. In one instance, he severed the last joint of his left little finger to impress a man with whom he was infatuated. This personal episode made its way into his early fiction as the short story "The Finger" and would prefigure later destructive behavior.

The bombing of Pearl Harbor on December 7, 1941, during World War II brought Burroughs to the decision to enlist in the army in early 1942. The strict discipline forced on him as a military foot soldier drove him again into bouts of depression. His mother rescued him by gaining his discharge on grounds of mental instability.

While awaiting his discharge from the army, Burroughs met a Chicago soldier also awaiting release, and once Burroughs was free, he moved to Chicago to join his friend. There he held numerous odd jobs, including that of a pest exterminator. Tiring of Chicago, Burroughs left for New York with two old friends from St. Louis—Lucien Carr, a University of Chicago student, and David Krammerer, Carr's homosexual partner.

The year 1944 marks the emergence of Burroughs and the Beat Generation and a long decade of flights from legal authorities. In New York, Burroughs met Joan Vollmer, who would later infamously die by his hand in Mexico. They shared an apartment with Jack Kerouac and Edie Parker, Kerouac's first wife. Vollmer's daughter from a previous marriage was also part of the household. During these years, Burroughs became addicted to morphine and was arrested for selling heroin and forging narcotic prescriptions to support his drug habit. Vollmer also fell into drug addiction, and Burroughs and Kerouac faced criminal charges for failing to report the murder of David Kammerer by Lucien Carr.

Again aided by his parents, Burroughs escaped prosecution in New York and returned to St. Louis. Eventually, Vollmer and Burroughs traveled to Texas, where their son William S. Burroughs, Jr., was born in 1947. Burroughs was soon arrested again, this time in Louisiana, when police suspected that he and **Allen Ginsberg** were smuggling marijuana into the United States from Mexico. Burroughs, followed later by his then common law wife Vollmer and their two children, fled to Mexico to wait out the statute of limitations on the felony charges.

Burroughs's years in Mexico were punctuated with triumph and tragedy. His wild and erratic behavior brought an end to Vollmer's life. In a drunken game of William Tell at a party in Mexico City in 1951, Burroughs failed at an attempt to shoot an apple off Vollmer's head. She was killed instantly. Burroughs was charged with homicide, but through a series of bribes he was able to flee Mexico and return to his parents' home in St. Louis. He was convicted in absentia.

It was in Mexico in the 1950s that Burroughs began his intensive writing. He remarked that Joan's death was a catalyst to his creative surge and artistic commitment. He penned such counterculture works as *Queer* (written 1951–1952, published 1985) and *Junkie: Confessions of an Unredeemed Drug Addict* (1953). *Queer* grew out of a series of letters the author had written to Ginsberg, who became a lifelong friend and supporter of Burroughs's artistic expression. Under Ginsberg's encouragement, Burroughs launched into the writing of *Junkie*. Ace Books published the novel under the pen name William Lee. Later that same decade while he was in Tangier and Paris, Burroughs finished and published *Naked Lunch* (1959), arguably the author's best-known work.

Naked Lunch was largely written in Tangier, where Burroughs had earlier fled to escape another series of drug charges in the United States. Paul Bowles's fictional accounts of the Moroccan city ignited Burroughs's interest to expatriate to North Africa. Published in Paris in 1959, *Naked Lunch* reveals an advanced modernistic writing style in depicting a struggle between two societies: an underground world and an advancing, self-destructive technological culture. Burroughs's writing technique eschewed standard narrative devices, employing instead abrupt and disjointed descriptions and scenes, chapters arranged randomly, and a stream of consciousness style that some readers have compared to hallucinations. In hurrying the manuscript to the French publisher, Burroughs sent the manuscript in pieces, not arranging the parts in any particular order. The published result was a random order of the parts, chosen by the printer. Burroughs later remarked that he liked the randomness better than the intended original sequence.

Publication of *Naked Lunch* met with praise and denunciation. The novel ran afoul of U.S. censors, most publicly in the Commonwealth of Massachusetts, for its explicit sex, drug usage, and violence, resulting in a famous obscenity trial that was eventually decided in favor of the author by the Massachusetts Supreme Court. Despite the censorship, underground presses made copies of the book available. However, it was not until 1962 that the work was published in North America. Praise came from many writers and artists, including novelist Norman Mailer who remarked that Burroughs was possibly the most talented American writer and the inimitable spokesman for the Beat Generation.

The Beat Generation describes the exploding cultural and artistic phenomena of the late 1950s and early 1960s that appeared on the horizon, largely defined by countercultural writers and their works: Jack Kerouac's *On the Road* (1957), William S. Burroughs's *Naked Lunch* (1959), and Allen Ginsberg's *Howl and Other Poems* (1956). Other members of the pre-hippie crowd included Gregory Corso, Peter and Lafcadio Orlovsky, and Michael McClure. These were writers, artists, musicians, and self-appointed gurus and philosophers who largely lived the alternative life they wrote about. Members of the Beat Generation acquired the label new bohemian hedonists who, somewhat like the Dadaists of the early twentieth century, idolized nonconformity, antiestablishment, and spontaneous actions in life and art. *Naked Lunch* was featured in *Life* magazine in 1959, in part to highlight the popular Beat movement.

The 1960s were a productive decade for Burroughs. He published *The Soft Machine* (1961), *The Ticket That Exploded* (1962), *Dead Fingers Talk* (1963), *Nova Express* (1964), and *The Last Words of Dutch Schultz* (1969). Longer later works include *The Wild Boys: A Book of the Dead* (1971), *Cities of the Red Night* (1981), *The Place of Dead Roads* (1983), and *My Education: A Book of Dreams* (1995). Also published was *The Yage Letters* (1963), a work comprised of the letters between Burroughs and Ginsberg, issued by San Francisco's City Lights Books.

Burroughs moved to Lawrence, Kansas, in 1981 and lived near the University of Kansas, just outside of Kansas City, the remainder of his life. In 1984 he signed a multibook contract with Viking Press, a deal including the rights to the unpublished novel *Queer*. He was inducted into the American Academy and Institute of Arts and Letters in 1983. Burroughs died on August 2, 1997, at the age of 83, from a heart attack.

Among American novelists, Burroughs remains regarded by many as one of the most influential in terms of his dissent against conventional standards and his honesty in prose. Others consider him a cult author, where the myth made up from his ideas and personal stories flies far above the prosaic prose.

Further Reading

Bartlett, Lee, ed. *The Beats: Essays in Criticism.* Jefferson, NC: McFarland, 1981.

Burroughs, William S. *Burroughs Live: The Collected Interviews of William S. Burroughs, 1960–1997,* edited by Sylvère Lotringer. Cambridge: Massachusetts Institute of Technology Press, 2001.

————. *Last Words: The Final Journals of William S. Burroughs, November 1996–July 1997,* edited by James Grauerholz. New York: Grove Press, 2000.

————. *The Letters of William S. Burroughs: 1945–1959,* edited by Oliver Harris. New York: Viking Press, 1993.

Campbell, James. *This Is the Beat Generation.* Berkeley: University of California Press, 2001.

Goldman, Michael B. *Contemporary Literary Censorship: The Case History of Burroughs'* Naked Lunch. Metuchen, NJ: Scarecrow Press, 1981.

Hibbard, Allen, ed. *Conversations with William S. Burroughs.* Jackson: University Press of Mississippi, 1999.

Morgan, Ted. *Literary Outlaw: The Life and Times of William S. Burroughs.* New York: H. Holt, 1988.

Russell, Jamie. *Queer Burroughs.* New York: Palgrave, 2001.

Michael D. Sollars

Busch, Charles (b. 1954)

Influential playwright and performer. Charles Busch grew up in New York mesmerized by theater. While home during vacations from Northwestern University, he witnessed experimental theater performed by **Charles Ludlam**'s Ridiculous Theatrical Company. Inspired by its cutting-edge style, incorporation of classic literature, and gender-bending emphasis, Busch returned to Northwestern and enrolled in independent studies in playwriting. It was during this time that Busch wrote and performed his first solo drag piece.

Shortly after graduation, Busch began to travel around the country performing solo performance pieces for almost eight years. Most of these pieces were directed by Busch's college friend and collaborator, Kenneth Elliott. At age 30, Busch returned to New York, tired of traveling and wanting to start his own theater company. Theatre-in-Limbo owner Michael Limbo agreed to let Busch mount a play at his theater, and two weeks later Busch wrote and produced his long-running hit *Vampire Lesbians of Sodom* (1986). The play was directed by Elliott and, after a successful run, moved to the Provincetown Playhouse where it played for five years, becoming one of the longest-running nonmusicals in off-Broadway history.

Soon, Busch's collaborators on *Vampire Lesbians of Sodom* became the resident company of the Limbo Lounge, performing a new show every three weeks. Busch wrote the plays with his company in mind and played the grande-dame role in each production. His next substantial success came in 1987 playing a psychotic Gidget character in *Psycho Beach Party*, a spoof of 1960s beach films. That production also moved off-Broadway.

In 1988, the Limbo Lounge closed and Busch and his company began an association with the WPA Theatre, where his first production, *The Lady in Question* (1990), brought him great acclaim. He also wrote an adaptation of the book for *Ankles Aweigh* for the Goodspeed Opera House, which became the first work he had written but not performed.

The 1990s saw more prolific works, including *Red Scare on Sunset* (1991) in which Busch portrayed a Hollywood star who names names at the McCarthy hearings of the 1950s, and Busch's first out-of-drag role as a **gay** man in his play *You Should Be So Lucky* (1995). He also began acting in film, notably as Countess Aphasia du Barry in *Addams Family Values* (1993) and a male role in the feature film *It Could Happen to You* (1994). In 1993, Busch published a novel, *Whores of Lost Atlantis,* inspired by his early days in New York City's East Village.

Commercial and critical acclaim came in 2000 with *The Tale of the Allergist's Wife*, a play that transferred to Broadway and earned Busch a Tony nomination for Best Play. That same year marked the first filmed adaptation of a Busch play, *Psycho Beach Party,* in which Busch created the role of police captain Monica Stark. He later played the lead in the adaptation of his play *Die, Mommie, Die!* (2001). On television, Busch played a recurring role as Nat Ginzburg on Home Box Office's *Oz* and the owner of a modeling agency on the soap opera *One Life to Live.* He continues to write and perform.

Whereas the plays of Charles Ludlam that influenced Busch in his college years were based on classic literary works, Busch is a child of the silver screen. His work embraces and exaggerates both acting style and characters from movies of the 1930s, 1940s, 1950s, and 1960s. Busch's popular hit *Vampire Lesbians of Sodom* shows his affinity for Hollywood. In it, Biblical epics, 1920s Hollywood divas, B-movie vampires, and Las Vegas reviews are the backdrop for Busch's allusions to the parallels of the secret lives of vampires and that of homosexuals.

In addition to incorporating familiar film styles into his work, Busch's work is often noted for its revelation of exposing a character's dual nature. In *Psycho Beach Party,* for example, which **camps** 1960s beach movies, with a little *Mommie Dearest* (1981) and *The Three Faces of Eve* (1957) thrown in, every character displays a dual nature. Chicklet's June Cleaver mother hides her past as a prostitute. Buff surfer Star Car is a brainy nerd. Hunk beach boys turn out to be gay lovers. Building on this idea, the lead character, Chicklet, a female character played by male actor Busch, has multiple personalities, some of whom are male or African American. Like all his early work, *Psycho Beach Party* ends with each character coming to terms with his or her multiple selves and finding happiness.

The Tale of the Allergist's Wife, Busch's first "respectable" play, was not as vast a departure from Busch's exaggerated and experimental style as some critics have noted. Although it presented a less episodic storyline and a smaller cast, it did not reflect a change in Busch's artistic integrity. Like much of his work, *Allergist's Wife* explores the duality of characters (a sweet-appearing old lady who talks graphically about her bathroom habits, for example); however, what makes it different from his earlier work is that he refuses to allow the dual natures to merge into a new self. Busch leaves the conclusion open-ended, asking the audience members to reflect on their own two-sidedness.

Busch's plays were exceptionally popular with gay audiences who recognized Busch's exploration of duality as a metaphor for the gay/straight struggle and his embracing of camp. Busch has also received tremendous acclaim for his drag performances. Although his plays have found a home in smaller fringe theaters across the country, particularly gay theaters, most major theaters ignore Busch's work. This changed with some of his later works, such as *Red Scare on Sunset,* and major theaters will surely continue to produce *The Tale of the Allergist's Wife*. In general, however, Busch's plays are produced primarily at smaller venues and are still categorized as both "camp" and "drag theater."

Further Reading

Brantley, Ben. "Between a Female Image and Fantasy." *New York Times,* December 20, 1996, C3.
Mendelsohn, Daniel. "Charles Busch: Some Kind of Diva." *American Theatre* (December 1993): 44.
Orloff, Rich. "A Conversation with Charles Busch." *The Dramatist* (January/February 2001): E5.

Tom Smith

Butler, Judith (b. 1956)

Postfeminist social theorist who developed the performance theory of **gender** among other concepts. Judith Butler earned a Ph.D. in Philosophy from Yale in 1984. Subsequently, she taught at Wesleyan University and Johns Hopkins University before obtaining her present position as the Maxine Elliott Professor in the Departments of Rhetoric and Comparative Literature at the University of California, Berkeley. She is a prolific author who has published extensively on the concepts of power, sexuality, gender, and identity, and the interactions of these various factors with race, class, ethnicity, and sexual orientation. More recently, she has turned to the personal-political realm for inspiration.

Butler's most influential book is *Gender Trouble: Feminism and the Subversion of Identity* (1990), for which she was inspired, at least in part, by the work of Michel Foucault. Throughout the course of her text, Butler challenges the notion of "woman" as a universal category, citing psychoanalysis as being primarily responsible for setting up this grand narrative. By eliding all women into one group, possibilities for difference are excluded. She implicates both Sigmund Freud and Jacques Lacan in this erasure, but also extends her criticism to feminist scholars such as Luce Iragaray and Simone de Beauvoir. Feminism reinforces patriarchal binaries, Butler claims, by insisting that "male" and "female" are socially inscribed upon bodies, leaving no room for any other gender.

Butler introduces her radical new concept: gender is part of a "continuum," in which sex causes gender, which causes desire. Thus, each of these is fluid and flexible, and not caused by any stable factor. Gender is a masquerade, a fantasy, and an act. Identity is therefore "performatively constituted," and never permanent; it is an effect, not an essential quality. Notions of stability, Butler claims, are rooted in internalized cultural ideals that reinforce hegemonic **heterosexuality**. She challenges the notion of the body, the subject, and language, destabilizing each to allow for gender to be radically reformed. She calls for subversive acts—gender trouble—that explode common notions of gender and emphasize it as an effect, not essential subjectivity.

Butler's work has had a tremendous impact on academic study. The concept of identity as being fluid is the basis of **queer theory**, since **queer** is seen as an identity without an essence. Identities can appear to be stable, but this appearance occurs through cultural signifiers, not through an essential expression.

Butler's next major work, *Bodies That Matter: On the Discursive Limits of Sex* (1993), attempted to clarify and expand ideas first presented in *Gender Trouble*. It both clarifies and equalizes Foucault's work, but Butler relies most heavily upon the theories of Jacques Derrida, particularly his theory of iterability (repetition of norms).

Admitting that she may have too quickly overturned sex as a category, Butler goes on to explore the materiality of sex, particularly as a construct of the "norm." Production of "natural" and "sexed" bodies is possible, even considering performativity; however, performance allows for destabilization of the subject, often in conjunction with social factors, such as race, class, ethnicity, and so forth.

In *Excitable Speech: Politics of the Performance* (1997), Butler examines the dynamics of hate speech and censorship. Butler argues that censorship has purpose; instead of eradicating certain viewpoints, for instance, censorship tends to generate the same language it purports to exclude. Hate speech exists only in retrospect and is solely dependent upon context for definition; however, it tends to demonstrate the limits of acceptable discourse.

Butler's books since these have included, among others, *Antigone's Claim: Kinship between Life and Death* (2000), which examines the incest taboo in relation to cultural change; *Hegemony, Contingency, Universality* (2000), an essay collection edited with Ernesto Laclau and Slavoj Žižek; *Precarious Life: The Powers of Mourning and Violence* (2004), an exploration of the Iraqi War's impact on language; *Undoing Gender* (2004), the first of Butler's works intended for a wide readership, includes her musings on gender and sexuality, revisits her ideas of performativity, and incorporates a look at intersexuality; and *Giving an Account of Oneself* (2005), which explores ethics in relation to self-knowledge.

Further Reading

Davies, Bronwyn. *Judith Butler in Conversation: Analyzing the Texts and Talk of Everyday Life*. London: Routledge, 2007.

Kirby, Vicki. *Judith Butler: Live Theory*. New York: Continuum, 2006.

Nussbaum, Martha. "The Professor of Parody." *The New Republic Online*, February 22, 1999. http://www.tnr.com/index.mhtml.

Osborne, Peter, and Lynne Segal. "Gender as Performance: An Interview with Judith Butler." *Radical Philosophy* 67 (1994): 32–39.

Salih, Sarah, ed. *The Judith Butler Reader*. Oxford: Blackwell, 2004.

Michelle M. Sauer

Butler, Octavia (1947–2006)

Influential African American science fiction writer. Butler is best known as one of the only African American women to gain success in the traditionally male-dominated literary genre of science fiction. Not only did Butler become commercially successful from the late 1970s onward, she also achieved a level of professional acclaim and recognition that few other science fiction authors have garnered. In 1995, she became the only science fiction writer to ever win a MacArthur Foundation "genius grant," which is an unrestricted fellowship awarded to individuals who have shown unique creative abilities and made significant cultural contributions. In addition, the science fiction community has recognized Butler many times over, awarding her short novel *Bloodchild* (1983) the prestigious Nebula Award for Best Novelette in 1984 and nominating her novelette *The Evening and the Morning and the Night* in 1987. Her novel *Parable of the Sower* was nominated best novel in 1994, and in 1999 *Parable of the Talents* was awarded the Nebula Award for Best Novel of the Year. She is one of a handful of authors to have won both the Nebula and Hugo awards, winning two Hugo awards, one in 1984 for her short story "Speech Sounds" and another in 1985, when the collection of short stories *Bloodchild* won for Best Novelette.

Octavia Estelle Butler was on born June 22, 1947, in Pasadena, California. Her father, Laurice, shined shoes for a living, but passed away when Octavia was still a very young child. Her mother, who was also named Octavia, was employed as a maid, sometimes bringing her daughter to work and other times leaving her in the care of her own mother, a strict Baptist. As a child, Octavia was known as "Junie," which was probably short for Junior, in order to distinguish her from her mother. As she grew up as part of a struggling family in the working-class section of Pasadena, Junie was exceedingly shy, standing out for being both very tall and very awkward. Although she was dyslexic, she was an avid reader who relied on cast-off books from the wealthy homes where her mother worked. She was particularly attracted to science fiction magazines, which in the 1950s had titles such as *Amazing, Galaxy,* and *Science Fiction.* These magazines were instrumental in popularizing the genres of science fiction and fantasy to many young people who would themselves grow up to be authors in subsequent years, including Butler. However, Butler would later state that it was her early consciousness of the fact that none of the characters in these stories were of African descent and the position of women was also marginal or nonexistent that led her to write her own stories. It was clear to her that even characters with whom she could have identified were excluded from the very works of fiction and fantasy in which she sought refuge from the world. In response to this lack of characters that she could identify with, Butler began writing her own science fiction stories at a young age.

She received a two-year degree from Pasadena College in 1968 and subsequently enrolled at California State University of Los Angeles, but rather than continuing toward a degree, Butler took classes through the adult education extension of the university. Throughout the 1970s, she participated in writing groups and workshops, which she credited with giving her the courage to continue writing and to view herself as a writer during a difficult period in which she was working low-paying jobs such as washing dishes, telemarketing, and working in a factory, getting out of bed before dawn so she could write before heading out to work. Although she was struggling, her writing came to the attention of noted science fiction and horror writer Harlan Ellison, who planned to include her short story "Childfinder" in a collection of short stories, which was never published. Nonetheless, Butler was encouraged to continue writing and submitting her work to publishers in spite of constant rejections. In 1976, her first novel, *Patternmaster,* was finally published. *Patternmaster* told the story of a hierarchical and dystopian civilization where humans known as patternists have evolved psychic abilities and subsequently are of a higher status than nonevolved, ordinary humans. Four other novels rounded out the series, *Mind of My Mind* (1977), *Survivor* (1978), *Wild Seed* (1980), and *Clay's Ark* (1984). The *Patternist* Series, as these novels are collectively known, introduced many of the themes that were to remain central to Butler's work throughout her life: notably, an exploration of the consequences of rigidly hierarchical societies, a belief in the interdependence of history and futurism, dystopianism, and the consequences of biological and genetic engineering.

In 1979, Butler's most famous novel, *Kindred,* was published, and it has retained a place in high school and college literature and African American studies courses ever since. *Kindred* is about Dana, an African American woman from the 1970s who is mysteriously and inexplicably transported back in time to the antebellum Southern United States, where she must live as a slave and save the life of her white, slave-owning ancestor, Rufus, in order to preserve herself in the future by ensuring that Rufus has a child with a female slave who is Dana's foremother. Presenting issues of race and the historical understanding of experiences of slavery in a unique way, Butler claimed that *Kindred* is her least science fiction novel, which is still highly speculative and as such it demonstrates how her more typically science fiction works raise similar issues of race, class, **gender**, and understandings of historical causality or determinism. Her other fictional works include the *Liliths Brood* Trilogy, which describes the results of an interplanetary war between humans and nonhuman beings who have three genders instead of two and trade in genetic engineering techniques; two novels that make up the *Parable* Series, and *Fledgling,* a vampire novel, in addition to many short stories.

Butler passed away on February 24, 2006, from a fall sustained at her home outside of Seattle, Washington. A scholarship foundation has been created in her name, for the purpose of assisting young science fiction writers of color to attend the annual Clarion science fiction writers' workshops, which Butler herself attended in 1970 and later taught for several years.

See also Science Fiction, Lesbian

Further Reading

Melzer, Patricia. *Alien Constructions: Science Fiction and Feminist Thought.* Austin: University of Texas Press, 2006.

Tucker, Jeffrey A. " 'The Human Contradiction': Identity and/as Essence in Octavia Butler's Xenogenesis Trilogy." *Yearbook of English Studies* 37, no. 2 (2007): 164–81.

Michele Erfer

C

Caffé Cino

Historical off-off-Broadway performance venue and birthplace of American **gay** theater. Joe Cino, a Sicilian American former dancer from Buffalo, New York, opened the Caffé Cino in 1958 in a tiny Greenwich Village storefront. His coffeehouse on Cornelia Street was meant to be a spot where locals could congregate and give expression to artistic impulses that were welcome at few other places in the city. Poetry readings and folk music concerts were among the types of performances staged there, but ultimately it was dramatic theater for which the Cino would become best known.

During the first years of its existence, the Cino had featured infrequent theatrical revivals. In 1960, however, the cramped performance space played host to its first original production: a play entitled *Flyspray*. The success of *Flyspray* prompted Joe Cino to book original plays with more regularity. This expanded performance schedule, along with an open invitation by the management to "do what you have to do," soon attracted the attention of a whole new generation of young, experimental playwrights. In fact, until its closing in 1968, the Cino served as a bastion for dramatists eager to stage productions considered too risky by mainstream theater companies.

With such a commitment to innovation, as well as with the backing of an openly gay owner, it is perhaps no surprise that Caffé Cino also earned a reputation as the birthplace of gay theater in the United States. Indeed dramas at the Cino often portrayed gay characters with great subtly and complexity, something that had never before been seen at any of the theatrical venues in New York. For it was in 1961 amid the closely gathered tables and chairs of the café that **Doric Wilson** premiered his one-act play *Now She Dances!*—the first American drama to provide a positive portrayal of a homosexual lead character. Other milestone productions reflecting gay themes soon followed, among them *The Madness of Lady Bright* (1964) by **Lanford Wilson**, *The Haunted Host* (1964) by Robert Patrick, and *The Bed* (1965) by Robert Heide.

But this haven for fringe artists could not go on forever. Continuous harassment by the police and the increasing migration of playwrights and performers to larger theatrical venues eventually contributed to the decline of the Cino. Moreover, because Joe Cino had consistently refused to charge patrons for admission to his plays, his establishment often suffered severe financial difficulties. The biggest blow, however, came on April 4, 1967, when the affable yet drug-addicted proprietor himself died of self-inflicted knife wounds. The Cino would not survive for much longer and closed a year later.

Nevertheless, the legacy of the little coffeehouse at 31 Cornelia Street endures. Despite its diminutive size and brief life span, Caffé Cino is now credited with having spawned the entire avant-garde theater movement that swept New York in the 1960s and whose influence continues to be felt to this day in the alternative arts scene known as off-off-Broadway.

Further Reading

Crespy, David A. *Off-Off-Broadway Explosion: How Provocative Playwrights of the 1960s Ignited a New American Theater.* New York: Back Stage Books, 2003.

Stone, Wendell C. *Caffe Cino: The Birthplace of Off-Off-Broadway.* Carbondale: Southern Illinois University Press, 2005.

Susoyev, Steve, and George Birimisa. *Return to the Caffe Cino.* San Francisco: Moving Finger Press, 2006.

Jules Hurtado

Camp

A pervasive sensibility, especially dominant in the **gay** male culture of the mid-twentieth century, camp comprises many aesthetic postures: irony, wit, role play, star worship, cross-dressing, bitchiness, and a love of "trash" and excess. As with any sensibility, camp is resistant to definition and has thus attracted legions of commentators attempting to articulate it. Is camp an attitude, an aesthetic, or a canon of objects? Is camp intrinsic to gay culture, or has it been co-opted by the mainstream? Is camp misogynist or does it celebrate femininity? And why does a sensibility that seems to insist on frivolity and play occasion so many attempts to make it a serious object of study?

Though the word's etymology is obscure, camp first appeared in the English language around the turn of the last century, perhaps deriving from the French verb *se camper,* meaning "to set up camp." (In seventeenth-century France, military camps were highly decorative spectacles, not the utilitarian khaki tents common today.) According to the *Oxford English Dictionary,* the first recorded uses of the word "camp" in English include mostly disparaging references to **queer**ness, infamy, and an exaggerated male performance of femininity. But if the word began as an epithet, it would eventually prove a nuanced sensibility and source of power to the homosexuals who embraced it. By 1954, when Christopher Isherwood limned the notion of camp in his novel *The World in the Evening,* the word had acquired two primary meanings, which, despite Isherwood's attempts to differentiate them, cannot ever be completely extricated. *Low camp,* writes Isherwood, is equivalent to female masquerade or drag (Isherwood's linking of effeminacy and debasement is a problematic gesture—though by no means atypical—that later critics redress). *High camp,* on the other hand, describes a sophisticated taste for artifice and play, an aesthetic sensibility that takes superficiality seriously and seriousness lightly. Though camp lies in the eye of the beholder, Isherwood suggests that there is a canon of artists whose works are particularly amenable to camp (ballet, Mozart, and El Greco, for example), while other artists' works (Beethoven and Flaubert) could never qualify as camp.

Isherwood's dichotomy between high and low was taken up by the next major critic of camp, **Susan Sontag**, whose essay "Notes on Camp" made her a literary celebrity when it was published in the *Partisan Review* in 1964. In the essay, Sontag writes that camp (that is, the connoisseurial mode Isherwood labels "high camp") is itself a reversal of high and low cultures. Camp, argues Sontag, is a way to be a dandy in an era of mass media, a way for an elitist temperament to enjoy the increasingly vulgar pop culture surrounding her. The phrase "it's so bad it's good" is, for Sontag, the backbone of camp connoisseurship, reflecting an impulse to find the success in certain aesthetic failures. Not any kind of badness, however, is available for a camp reading. As Sontag notes, artifice, excess, and mannerism are key characteristics of camp; she cites Josef von Sternberg's movies with Marlene Dietrich and Antoni Gaudí's Cathedral of the Sagrada Familia in Barcelona as examples of this "over-the-top" characteristic.

Both Sontag's and Isherwood's lists reveal an incoherence as to where camp should be located. Are certain artists, artworks, and artifacts intrinsically camp, or does the connoisseur herself camp them? Does camp reside in the *object* or in the *beholder?* (In other words, if a Tiffany lamp falls in the woods, but there is no one there to hear it, is it still camp?) Sontag attempts to address this incoherence by differentiating between intentional camp and naïve camp. Yet an immediate problem emerges with such a distinction, as later critics have pointed out: how can we ever determine an artist's intentions?

Esther Newton's 1972 study *Mother Camp* provides a different approach. Newton, an anthropologist, argues that camp does not live in the object or the spectator, but that camp is a mode of *relating*—between objects and persons but also between persons themselves. Restoring the breach between "low camp" and "high camp," between drag (female masquerade) and connoisseurial frivolity, Newton supposes that camp is a kind of social glue that binds queers together. (Eve Kosofsky Sedgwick later argues, in *Epistemology of the Closet,* that camp is a way of recognizing other gay artists in their creations. For Sedgwick, the animating question of the camp viewer is, "What if whoever made this was gay, too?") Camp, like the gay lingo Palare, seems to have operated, in certain historical moments, as a kind of subcultural code, legible only to those "in the know." Yet at other moments, in such safe spaces as the salon or the gay bar, camp is explosively theatrical and brazenly queer. For Newton, camp also describes a gay personality type: ironic, self-mocking, theatrical, and interested in all transformations and incongruities, not only the male-female incongruity of the drag queen. The camp queen performs the stigma of effeminate homosexuality, making sport of what others have deprecated. Here is where Newton's and Sontag's versions of camp intersect. Both Newton's "low" camp and Sontag's "high" camp find the success in failure, rendering "good" what was previously seen as "bad" (for example, homosexuality, the artistic failure).

Newton argues, from an anthropological perspective, that the "camp queen" is often the magnetic center of gay social groups (think of the flamboyant Emory in **Mart Crowley**'s *The Boys in the Band*). Indeed, camp seems to have been integral to the emergent identity politics that led to the **Stonewall Riots** in 1969, expressing and making visible a sexual identification that was previously kept **closet**ed. By functioning as a sign of homosexual culture, camp made a gay identity politics possible. Yet in the **gay rights**

movement that followed Stonewall, debate ensued among the Gay Liberation Front and the Campaign for Homosexual Equality as to whether camp was salutary for the gay cause or whether a more openly political, less ironic and "survivalist" mode was needed. Attendant to this debate was the question of whether camp—drag in particular—was subverting society's oppression of female identification and effeminacy, or whether it was simply replicating misogynist and thus, homophobic, attitudes. In 1978, Andrew Britton published an anticamp manifesto "For Interpretation: Notes against Camp," in which he argues that camp is only superficially transgressive and ultimately too cozy with bourgeois culture to effect social change.

The relationship between camp and femininity is a complex and vexed one. Is camp unkind to women? And are women ever camp? Though camp seems most often to denote a gay male mode, in *Camp: The Lie That Tells the Truth,* Philip Core argues that the Paris-based painter Romaine Brooks and other saloniste lesbians such as Djuna Barnes and Natalie Barney modeled a dandyish and camp relationship to cross-gender identification. And Sue-Ellen Case, in her essay "Toward a Butch-Femme Aesthetic," uses camp as a way of understanding the exaggerated performance of butch-femme roles in contemporary lesbian relationships. These performances can be seen as a kind of parodic, that is, camp, deconstruction of the heterosexual archetypes on which they are based. This line of inquiry would later be taken up by **Judith Butler** in her important book *Gender Trouble: Feminism and the Subversion of Identity* (1990). Butler argues that gender itself—not just sexual role play—is performative, and Butler uses drag to illustrate her highly theoretical position.

Because camp often involves a distancing or ironizing approach, it is often retrospective and nostalgic in orientation. What were once sincere artistic efforts—Busby Berkeley dance numbers, Art Nouveau, *Johnny Guitar*—can be enjoyed in hindsight as camp. Andrew Ross picks up this sense of historical revisionism in his essay "Uses of Camp" (1988). Writing from a Marxist perspective, Ross argues that camp flourishes when the outmoded products of the cultural industry are recovered and given new life. Camp can thus be understood as a recycling of history's waste products, in which an artwork that no longer makes sense as a tragedy can be reviewed as comedy. For Ross, *All about Eve* (1950) is an exemplary camp locus. Aside from its excessive, theatrical female performances, the movie takes up obsolescence itself as a subject. Just as Margo Channing (Bette Davis) faces obsolescence because of her advancing age and the threat of rival actress Eve Harrington (Anne Baxter), so in the larger scenario does theater face obsolescence at the hands of film; Eve plots to conquer not just Broadway but Hollywood. Yet even this plot reflects and refracts the external circumstances informing the production of the movie. *All about Eve* was in some ways the last gasp of Hollywood's declining studio era of production; television was the upstart fragmenting the media landscape. In Ross's view, when we enjoy *All about Eve* as camp, we affiliate ourselves with decline and attempt to rescue the film's endangered objects (Davis; the studio-era movie itself) from obsolescence. Accounting for this strong identification may be the nonreproductiveness of homosexuality. Are queers interested in history's waste products because our own desires are figured as unproductive?

Camp may look to the past, but what is the status of this sensibility today? Sontag's essay was a salvo against overt seriousness and sincerity. But she later lamented the effect her essay would have on a culture increasingly interested in entertainment at the expense of social engagement. In the intervening years, camp has become mainstream, the routine mode of Generation X. The clearest example of this co-optation is *Mystery Science Theater 3000,* a television series from the 1980s and 1990s in which a robot and a human marooned in space watch old B-movies ad infinitum. Installed as a permanent peanut gallery, their sarcastic comments are dubbed over the soundtrack of the films they and we watch together, thus implicating us as camp viewers. That these spectators are removed in time and space from earthly agency, powerless automatons in a distant echo chamber, reflects the degree to which camp has been vitiated of its subversive spirit.

Further Reading

Britton, Andrew. "For Interpretation: Notes against Camp." In *Camp: Queer Aesthetics and the Performing Subject: A Reader,* edited by Fabio Cleto, 136–42. Ann Arbor: University of Michigan Press, 1999.

Case, Sue-Ellen. "Toward a Butch-Femme Aesthetic." In *Camp: Queer Aesthetics and the Performing Subject: A Reader,* edited by Fabio Cleto. 185–99. Ann Arbor: University of Michigan Press, 1999.

Core, Philip. *Camp: The Lie That Tells the Truth.* New York: Delilah, 1984.

Cleto, Fabio. *Camp: Queer Aesthetics and the Performing Subject: A Reader.* Ann Arbor: University of Michigan Press, 1999.

Isherwood, Christopher. *The World in the Evening.* New York: Random House: 1954.

Newton, Esther. *Mother Camp: Impersonators in America.* Englewood Cliffs: Prentice Hall, 1972.

Ross, Andrew. "Uses of Camp." In *Camp: Queer Aesthetics and the Performing Subject: A Reader,* edited by Fabio Cleto, 308–29. Ann Arbor: University of Michigan Press, 1999.

Sedgwick, Eve Kosofsky. *Epistemology of the Closet.* Berkeley: University of California Press, 1990.

Sontag, Susan. "Notes on 'Camp.' " In *Camp: Queer Aesthetics and the Performing Subject: A Reader,* edited by Fabio Cleto, 308–29. Ann Arbor: University of Michigan Press, 1999.

Christopher Schmidt

Campo, Rafael (b. 1964)

Widely published and acclaimed Cuban American poet, essayist, memoirist, physician, and intermittent teacher of poetry. Rafael Campo was born in 1964 to Cuban-exiled parents and was raised in Elizabethtown, New Jersey. He is a graduate of both Amherst College (where he would later receive an honorary doctorate in literature) and Harvard Medical School (where he now is a practicing physician) in addition to his work at Beth Israel Deaconess Medical Center in Boston. His general physician's practice specializes in helping the **gay**, lesbian, bisexual and transgender community as well as the Latino and HIV-positive populations in the area. Campo's own rich history (in origin, profession, communities, and identity) has been the primary focus of his work as an author.

Rafael Campo's first collection of poems, *The Other Man Was Me* (1994), was selected as a winner of the National Poetry Series Competition. This respected collection of poems driven by the force of iambs tucked away in both his narrative poems and his sonnets was recognized for its accomplishments for several important reasons. Many critics have noted Campo's interesting relationship to formalist poetry. While he writes of contemporary and often emotionally and politically charged subjects (his generations of family, his complicated sense of homeland, and his own understanding of his gay identity), Campo employs formalism as a kind of container for what cannot seem to be contained—identity, suffering, healing, and hope. In this sense, his work is said to challenge and blur distinctions between narrative and lyric, form and content, the self and other. This collection exudes the sense of traveling and is still widely referenced and taught.

Campo went on to publish several more seemingly autobiographical (at least in their content's reflection of his life as a doctor, as a gay Cuban American, and as a writer) collections of poetry: *What the Body Told* (1996) was the recipient of a Lambda Literary Award for Poetry; *Diva* (1999) was understood as his most lyrical collection and included what some literary critics and writers deemed quite daring translations of Frederico Garcia Lorca's "Sonnets of Dark Love" because of their homoeroticism and lush language; *Landscape with Human Figure* (2002) appears to be his least recognized work though its framework—the fact that the book begins at the start of a new year and ends with its close—received some attention as an interesting way to record and document the year's time and the time's relationship to the book's subjects of race and identity. In 2007, Rafael Campo published his most recent collection of poetry entitled *The Enemy*. This collection is said to be the most overtly political of his collections, taking on not only his revisited subjects of identity, the AIDS crisis, and homeland, but also taking on the notion of "America" in a post 9/11 era, the debate about gay marriage, and the Iraq War.

As Campo is understood as a writer who explores human connection and the human condition as a complex web of intersections and crossover, it is no surprise that he would choose to write in more than one genre. Campo's work tries to express existence in more than one world: the world of healing *and* suffering, the world of science *and* art, the world of specificity *and* multiplicity, and finally the world of poetry *and* prose. His collection of essays, *The Desire to Heal: A Doctor's Education in Empathy, Identity, and Poetry* (1997), won his second Lambda Literary Award—this time in memoir. Marketed in bookstores as "Medicine/Literary Essays," Campo's lyrical collection of prose reveals him as a storyteller and as a poet. His long expressive and declarative sentences attempt to explore and study what Campo himself has called *layers of being*. The book makes clear Campo's understanding of his own layers of being by voicing the connections and disconnections between his vocations of poet and physician and between his role as an educator and healer. As with all of Campo's work, he focuses his attention, lyrically, physically, and spiritually, on the body—its fragility, its grace, its remarkable strength. His more recent prose collection, *The Healing Art: A Doctor's Black Bag of Poetry* (2003), which was first printed as a smaller volume entitled *The Poetry of Healing* in 1996, again reveals Campo as part literary critic and part philosopher, part poet and part physician; however, by the time the book is through, one cannot help but see that the physician, according to Campo, must always be a poet, a philosopher, and a profound thinker of literary thoughts. The collection of essays does also seem to have an argument; Campo believes that language has the power to heal suffering. He makes important distinctions between curing and healing while discussing his patients and their various stories. He argues for integrated medicine, for a blending of body and soul. He proposes language and poetry as one possible vehicle for change. More specifically, Campo gives attention to formal verse as a pathway to healing, a way for patients to make beautiful order from the chaos of their various afflictions. Discussing his sharing of poetry with his patients on rounds and the carrying of poems in the literal and metaphorical black bag, Campo understands poetry as a kind of internal ultrasound, a way to help patients see and feel the dimensions of both their illness and (hopefully) their healing.

It seems obvious, then, that Campo does get quite a bit of attention from literary critics and poetry journals; however, what is quite interesting about some of the scholars writing about Campo is that many of them are not writing in English Studies at all. Several medical journals have given attention not only to Rafael Campo, the physician, but also to his actual poetry. There has been some debate about Campo's eroticization of the doctor-patient relationship, and some critics in the medical field seem worried over a problem with "professionalization." It does seem, however, that Campo's poetry and prose have already answered these concerns. It is evident that Rafael Campo sees his life as a doctor and writer not as merely professions but as physical, emotional, and spiritual commitments to healing. His work seems to suggest sensuality and eroticism as pathways to that healing. This is part of the draw of his groundbreaking work.

Rafael Campo has been the recipient of many prizes and awards. He was the recipient of the Annual Achievement Award from the National Hispanic Academy of Arts and Sciences and the recipient of a Pushcart Prize. He has received fellowships from both the National Endowment for the Arts and from the Guggenheim Foundation. Campo, in addition to his work as a physician, has also served as a Visiting Writer at Amherst College, George A. Miller Endowment Visiting Scholar at the University of Illinois, Urbana-Champaign, and the Fanny Hurst Visiting Poet at Brandeis University. He has also given lectures at the Lannan Foundation, the Library of Congress, and other significant venues. He is, undeniably, one of the most celebrated contemporary poets.

Further Reading

Diedrich, Lisa. "AIDS and Its Treatments: Two Doctors' Narratives of Healing, Desire and Belonging." *Journal of Medical Humanities* 26, no. 4 (Winter 2005): 237–57.

Henderson, S. W. "Identity and Compassion in Rafael Campo's 'The Distant Moon.'" *Literature and Medicine* 19, no. 2 (Fall 2000): 262–79.

Lázaro, Lima. "Haunting the Corpus Delicti: Rafael Campo's *What the Body Told* and Wallace Stevens' (Modernist) Body." *Wallace Stevens Journal* 25, no. 2 (Fall 2001): 220–32.

Rendell, Joanna. "Drag Acts: Performativity, Subversion and the AIDS Poetry of Rafael Campo and Mark Doty." *Critical Survey* 14, no. 2 (2002): 89–100.

Stacey Waite

Cañón, James (b. 1968)

Colombian American novelist and short story writer. The third son of José Cañón and Blanca Vergara, James Cañón was born on June 19, 1968, in Ibagué, Colombia. Cañón's father was from a native Indian/peasant extraction in rural Colombia, an almost illiterate man who attended only two years of elementary school. However, he was a successful businessman. His mother was from working-class stock and never finished high school. She was his father's secretary before they fell in love and moved in together. His father continuously traveled; he grew up mostly in the company of his mother and his paternal grandmother, both of whom had a major influence on his early life and, later, on his writing. He moved to Bogotá in 1987 to go to college and graduated with honors in 1990 with a B.A. in advertising. After working for four years as a copywriter, he decided to move to New York City in 1994 to work and to study English for a year, but he decided to stay. Lacking both fluency in English and a resident card, his first job was cleaning the bathrooms and floors of a fast-food court in Manhattan. He moved from school to school and from job to job until the Spanish department of an advertising agency hired him in 1996. The following year, he decided to take an expository writing class at New York University. Every week he was asked to write three to five pages on any subject; he wrote short stories. Even though they showed glaring mistakes, his teacher loved them for his narrative voice and a style all his own. By the end of the quarter, he had already made up his mind: he wanted to be a writer. He quit advertising and started making a living as a part-time waiter, which allowed him time to write. He has been writing ever since.

His first short stories were autobiographical to some extent; two were published in anthologies of gay Latinos: "The Two Miracles of The Gringos' Virgin" in *Bésame Mucho* (1999), and "My Lessons with Felipe" in *Virgins, Guerrillas, and Locas* (1999). In 1999, he enrolled in the graduate program on creative writing at Columbia University, where he started working on his first novel, *Tales from the Town of Widows & Chronicles from the Land of Men* (2007), which has been translated into seven languages and published in more than 20 countries. It was originally inspired by an article he had read in a Colombian newspaper about a mountain village from which Communist guerrillas had taken most of the men away. The novel examines the lives of the women left behind—the virtual widows—how they survive without the men and how that process transforms them and the society. First he began to write the novel in Spanish but decided to abandon the effort and decided instead to tell the story in English. The English language, he believes, offers him an original and unbiased perspective on the Colombian conflict.

Articulate, funny, imaginative, sarcastic, sweet, and direct, Cañón's sweeping novel grabs you by the throat on a roller coaster of pyrotechnic verve and panache, where homosexuals and heterosexuals, pagans and believers concoct a better society where everyone is respected as equals. *Tales* was a finalist for the Lambda Literary Award as well as the 2008 **Edmund White** Debut Fiction Award.

He lives in New York City where he is working on his second novel. It is about religion, tolerance, and displacement; at the narrative center is a strong heroine who makes a perilous and life-changing journey.

Further Reading

Kirsch, Jonathan, "The Feminine Mystique." *Washington Post,* February 18, 2007, C6. www .jamescanon.com.

Miguel Falquez-Certain

Cappello, Mary (b. 1960)

Experimental prose writer, memoirist, poet, cultural and literary critic, and lecturer. Mary Cappello, a third-generation Italian American, was born in Darby, Pennsylvania. After earning a B.A. at Dickinson College in Carlisle, Pennsylvania, she worked as a teacher at Princeton High School in New Jersey for a short time. Cappello then went on to study for an M.A. and a Ph.D. in American Literature and Creative Writing at the State University of New York (SUNY) campus at Buffalo. Having completed her dissertation, which focused on literature and medicine, she was honored with the Richard Beale Davis Prize for the Best Essay published in Early American Literature. Cappello held her first academic position at the University of Rochester before becoming associate professor of English at the University of Rhode Island in 1991. She has won several awards for the high quality of her teaching and earned a Fulbright Fellowship that allowed her to teach at the Maxim Gorky Literature Institute in Moscow, Russia, in 2001. Cappello lives in Providence, Rhode Island.

Cappello's creative work, which has appeared in a variety of magazines, journals, and anthologies, is multifaceted and diverse, often transgressing the boundaries of disciplines, genres, and conventions and thus largely resisting classification. Cappello's manuscript, "Appearances: Scenes from a **Queer** Friendship," excerpts of which have appeared in *American Letters and Commentary* and in *Quarterly West,* is emblematic of her experimental approach. In it, Cappello creates a hybrid mixture of prose and poetry in order to grasp the dynamics of her "queer" friendship with a **gay** man with whom she is connected not only through her sexual orientation, but also her Italian heritage. The explicit autobiographical dimension of *Appearances* is characteristic of Cappello's work at large, in which the author's life regularly figures as a primary source of inspiration, calling for alternative and often radical forms of expression. Her study *Awkward: A Detour* (2007), a *Los Angeles Times* best seller, for instance, explores the multiple meanings and implications of the concept of "awkwardness" across a wide range of literary and cultural texts, while also drawing on Cappello's own everyday experiences and observations, not least as a lesbian and as a member of an immigrant family. Cappello's interest in immigrant identity is also expressed in her prize-winning collaborative project with photographer Paola Ferrario, *Pane Amaro/Bitter Bread: The Struggle of New Immigrants to Italy* (2001), which combines word and image to explore the lives of new immigrants to Italy.

The exploration of complex nonnormative sexual and ethnic identities runs like a red thread through Cappello's work and is central to her arguably most well-known publication, *Night Bloom: An Italian-American Life* (1998). The memoir met with great critical acclaim and was nominated for the 1999 Gradiva Award for Best Autobiographical Book by the National and World Associations for the Advancement of Psychoanalysis. *Night Bloom* is a complex and dense reflection of Cappello's own experiences of growing up in 1960s and 1970s Philadelphia as an Italian American, as a lesbian, and as an emerging scholar in the process of gaining the knowledge that would enable her to transcend her working-class origins. In addition, it is a family saga that comprises multiple voices and stories from previous generations: drawing on her maternal grandfather's bilingual journals, Cappello interweaves the struggles of a first-generation Italian immigrant to America with portraits of her agoraphobic mother, her violent father, and her depression-prone brother to underline the complexities of her family's history and her own heritage. Resisting the idea that memory works in a straightforward and linear fashion and emphasizing that remembering is a communal—or in this case familial—process that necessitates the awareness and acceptance of different perspectives, Cappello's text displays a "postmodern sensibility" and ultimately resists closure by pointing to the fact that "the search for knowledge of the self is ongoing" (Gillan 259). As such, *Night Bloom* is a prime example of Cappello's highly original writing, which succeeds in tackling the difficult questions of belonging and of how to remember and represent lives and relationships that do not easily "fit in."

Further Reading

Fortier, Anne-Marie. "Making Home: Queer Migrations and Motions of Attachment." In *Uprootings/Regroundings: Questions of Home and Migration,* edited by Sara Ahmed, Claudia Castañeda, Anne-Marie Fortier, and Mimi Sheller, 115–36. Oxford: Berg, 2003.

Gillan, Jennifer. Review of *Night Bloom: A Memoir,* by Mary Cappello. *MELUS* 26, no. 2 (2001): 258–60.

Giunta, Edvige. *Writing with an Accent: Contemporary Italian American Women Authors.* New York: Palgrave, 2002.

Jana Funke

Caschetta, Mary Beth (b. 1966)

Novelist, short story writer, and essayist. The youngest daughter and only female child in an Italian American family, Mary Beth Caschetta was born and raised in a suburb of Rochester, New York. Growing up with three brothers in a male-dominated household, Caschetta spent formative summers with female cousins and a beloved grandmother in a summer cottage on Lake Ontario built by her grandfather. Caschetta turned to religion to cope with childhood traumas and considered joining a convent, but instead the urge to write won out. In 1984, she enrolled at Vassar College, where she excelled academically. Moving to New York City, Caschetta worked briefly at the Virginia Barber Literary Agency, often reading new works by writer Alice Munro, which fueled her desire to write short fiction.

In 1989, with many friends dying of AIDS, Caschetta joined ACT UP (AIDS Coalition to Unleash Power). Working at an AIDS hotline, and later at **Gay** Men's Health Crisis, she honed her editing and writing skills, coping with writer's block by earning an advanced degree at the City University of New York (CUNY) Graduate Center. She authored several articles concerning women and medicine. Her master's thesis, "The Social Construction of Science as a Superior System of Knowledge: Activism, Women with AIDS, and Biomedical Research," was accepted by CUNY in 1994.

After AIDS activist Jon Greenberg's death in July 1993, Caschetta's writer's block finally broke, and she wrote her first complete short story, "Vanish," about her friend Greenberg's messiah complex. "Vanish" appeared in *Women on Women 3,* edited by **Joan Nestle** (1996), and later in Caschetta's debut short story collection, *Lucy on the West Coast: And Other Lesbian Short Fiction,* published by Alyson Publications in hardcover in 1996. Joan Nestle praised Caschetta's collection as ushering in "a wonderful new voice!" (dust jacket blurb). Writer **Paul Russell** noted that in the author's vivid fiction, "Catholic fervor, lesbian longings, and the shape of the dead all mingle with scrupulous regard" (dust jacket blurb). *Ms. Magazine* found it "a spectacular collection . . . Lucid, aching, often funny prose . . . A sensitive and telling portrait of contemporary American Life" (Razek). *The Lambda Book Report* called Caschetta's work "Heartbreakingly beautiful," adding that the author was "clearly on her way to becoming one of our finest storytellers" (Cassidy 14).

After the release of her debut collection, Caschetta continued to write and publish short fiction in such mainstream journals as the *Mississippi Review, Red Rock Review, Seattle Review, Small Spiral Notebook, Quick Fiction,* and *Eclectica,* as well as in gay literary journals: *Bloom Magazine, Lesbian Harrington Literary Quarterly,* and *Blithe House Quarterly.* Amassing two linked story collections, Caschetta won awards and honorable mentions for her fiction, including honors from the *Iowa Review, New Letters,* the *Mississippi Review, New Millennium Writing,* the *Potomac Review, Million Writers Award, New Century Writers,* and the *Dana Awards.*

At the same time, she started to explore the experience of growing up Catholic and Italian in personal essays dealing with identity. Her essay "The Seven Sacraments," published in *The Milk of Almonds: Italian American Women Writers on Food and Culture,* edited by Louise DeSalvo and Edvige Giunta (2002), explores her spiritual awakening and sexual self-affirmation in the context of her enhanced understanding of her ethnic heritage. "Italian Bride," Caschetta's poignant essay about marrying writer **Meryl Cohn**, the first day gay people were allowed to wed in Massachusetts (May 17, 2004), was the only openly lesbian work in *Our Roots Are Deep with Passion: Creative Nonfiction Collects New Essays by Italian-American Writers* (2006) and was a runner-up for the Laura Coen Pizer Nonfiction Award. Caschetta's deeply personal book-length meditation, written while retreating with silent nuns at a meditation center, entitled "Four Days in Silence: A Writer's Search for Meaning, or Get Me to a Nunnery," has yet to be published, but was the basis for a substantial financial grant from the Sherwood Anderson Foundation.

The years 1998–2008 were consumed with the writing of Caschetta's first novel, "Miracle Girl," an epic modern-day retelling of one of Chaucer's *Canterbury Tales.* In 2001, she left New York for Provincetown, Massachusetts, supporting her creative work as a freelance medical writer for the pharmaceutical industry. Despite receiving many honors during this time—including the W. K. Rose Fellowship for Emerging Artists (2000), the Sherwood Anderson Foundation Fiction Award (2004), a *Seattle Review* Fiction Award (2004), and a finalist grant from the Astraea Lesbian Foundation for Justice (2007)—Caschetta struggled with both the creative challenges of her novel and the narrowing of the publishing industry.

"Miracle Girl" brings Caschetta back to the trauma and transcendence of her childhood. The novel chronicles the short but faithful life of Cee-Cee Bianco from childhood to her adolescent demise. As a means of surviving a childhood trauma, Cee-Cee believes herself to be transformed into her namesake saint, St. Cecilia, a spotless virgin, whose faith endures suffocation in a burning bathtub and three bleeding whacks to the neck. After performing "miracles," Cee-Cee is proclaimed both freak and saint, a harrowing destiny she must find the courage to confront. The novel is yet to be published.

In 2004, filmmaker Amy Hobby and script editor Helen Eisenbach optioned the rights to "Nuclear Family," one of the stories in Caschetta's debut collection. The film is currently under development with Caschetta as the screenwriter.

Further Reading

Cassidy, Christine. "Securing the Borders." *Lambda Book Report* 5 (October 1996): 14.
Goeller, Allison D. "The Hungry Self." *Prose Studies* 27, no. 3 (2007): 235–47.
Razek, Rula. "Lucy on the West Coast and Other Short Fiction." *Ms Magazine* 8, no. 3 (1996): 32.

Meryl Cohn

Cassells, Cyrus (b. 1957)

African American poet and actor. Cyrus Cassells was born in Dover, Delaware. Author of four collections of poetry, his work is characterized by its lyricism, spiritual foundations, inventiveness with language, and the author's ability to assume multiple identities. Fluent in Spanish, Catalan, and Italian, Cassells has lived and traveled extensively outside the United States. His poetry is intimately linked to his travels and is reflected in its international range of references and multicultural humanity.

Cyrus Cassells's first book, *The Mud Actor* (1982, reissued 2000), was a National Poetry Series selection. Conceived as a single work with a tripartite structure, its poems use three identities—the poet's child-self, a nineteenth-century Frenchman, and an atomic bomb victim in Hiroshima, Japan—as metaphors for the need to confront both personal and world history to reconcile the past and the future.

Nominated for the Pulitzer Prize and recipient of the William Carlos Williams Award from the Poetry Society of America, *Soul Make a Path through Shouting* appeared in 1994. Informed by Cassells's travels in Europe and the Middle East and ranging in reference from classical Greek mythology to the United States civil rights movement, the poems use strong, precise, and elegant language to draw the reader into empathy with those who have suffered historical and personal violence. Many of the poems are dramatic narratives, using sensitive and ornate language to describe experiences of suffering and pain.

A sequence of love poems, the verse in Lambda Literary Award–winning *Beautiful Signor* (1997) echoes the medieval poet's role as troubadour while chronicling the affair of the American speaker of the poems with an ultimately unattainable young man from Venice, and their travels throughout the Mediterranean. The passionate and ecstatic lyrics intertwine the romantic settings with details of the pleasures of love, celebrating the mirroring of the self in nature and the beloved, as well as the both erotic and spiritual qualities of the union of two lovers.

Cassells's fourth volume of poetry, *More Than Peace and Cypresses* (2004), is an elegiac homage to his heroes and the sources of his inspiration. Written in response to his father's death as Cassells revisited Italy, France, and Spain, the countries that nurtured him as a young writer, the poems juxtapose mourning with love and eroticism, emphasizing the possibility of renewal. Writers and artists such as Vincent van Gogh, Cesare Pavese, Eugenio Montale, and Federico Garcia Lorca serve as touchstones in his search for expression.

Cyrus Cassells received a B.A. from Stanford University in 1979. He is the recipient of a Pushcart Prize, the Peter I. B. Lavan Younger Poets Award of the Academy of American Poets, Lannan Foundation Literary Award, and fellowships from the Rockefeller Foundation and the National Endowment for the Arts. He has worked as a translator, film critic, actor, and currently teaches poetry in the M.F.A. program at Texas State University in San Marcos. Author of a short film on Filipino American dancer Gregory Silva, *Bayok* (1980), he also appears as a minor character in the novel *Jack the Modernist* (1995) by Robert Gluck.

Further Reading

"Cassells, Cyrus." *Contemporary Authors, New Revision Series.* Vol. 49. Detroit: Gale Research Company. 1995. 82–83.
"Cyrus Cassells." Academy of American Poets. http://www.poets.org/poet.php/prmPID/215.

Reginald Harris

Champagne, John (b. 1960)

Contemporary **gay** American novelist, scholar, and professor of English. John Champagne grew up in Milwaukee, Wisconsin, graduated from Hunter College in Manhattan in 1986, received his master's degree in film studies from New York University two years later, and subsequently earned his doctorate in English and Cultural Studies from the University of Pittsburgh. Author of two novels and several scholarly works, he is currently an associate professor of English at The Pennsylvania State University at Erie.

Both of Champagne's novels—*The Blue Lady's Hands* (1988) and *When the Parrot Boy Sings* (1990)—examine gay urban lives in the 1980s. The protagonists search for love and stability in a hedonistic culture that revels in sexual promiscuity even as it is haunted by the frightening reality of the AIDS epidemic. The unnamed young protagonist of *The Blue Lady's Hands* narrates his often wounding search for love; at the center of his search is a deeply felt desire to find himself in a relationship that would resemble his parents' marriage: a relationship grounded in mutual love and monogamous commitment. His first love affair, however, proves disastrous. He falls in love with Michael who merely wants a summer fling. Sensing the narrator's vulnerability and emotional dependence on him, Michael manipulates and uses him. When the summer of their romance ends, Michael leaves the narrator and lets him know that he already has a lover with whom he goes to college. Devastated by the betrayal and the loss of his romantic dream, the narrator becomes withdrawn, begins therapy with a female psychologist, and refuses to act on his desire for love. Years later he falls in love with Daniel, a man a few years older than he. Daniel too proves disinclined toward monogamy: the narrator discovers that Daniel frequents jack-off clubs that had begun to proliferate in New York City as a response to the AIDS epidemic! This time, however, the narrator responds to his disappointment differently. Though he understands that he could never replicate the heterosexual paradigm of his parents' marriage in his relationship with Daniel, he begins to realize that he can now exercise a greater degree of sexual self-determination.

The quest for sustaining a meaningful love is also at the heart of *When the Parrot Boy Sings*. Will, the protagonist, is an artist who is a vegetarian and a Marxist. In his anarchic search for a perfect partner who would share his desire for monogamous commitment, Will sleeps with a variety of men. Then he meets Scott and Dennis, a couple who invite him for a ménage à trois. It is an invitation that Will accepts with reluctance and begins to hope that this arrangement could evolve into a "monogamous" threesome! Predictably neither Scott nor Dennis is interested in such a constraining situation, so Will, disappointed and lonely, withdraws from his two lovers. Like the narrator of *The Blue Lady's Hands*, Will is left facing the difficulty of finding the kind of devoted love that he seeks, yet beginning to realize the need for sexual independence in his life.

Both of Champagne's novels have provoked controversy and debate. Some gay readers find his agenda conservative and his politics assimilationist. They view his implied critique of gay promiscuity as a reflection of his internalization of conventional heterosexual models of romance and sexual conduct. Others, however, regard his protagonists' quests as intensely human and universal dramas. They also consider his criticism of pleasure seeking without emotional commitment a sensible response to the AIDS crisis and a call to live life more fully and meaningfully.

Further Reading

Nelson, Bill. Review of *The Blue Lady's Hands*. *Milwaukee Journal* (February 26, 1989): 9E.

Nelson, Emmanuel S. "AIDS and the American Novel." *Journal of American Culture* 13, no. 1 (1990): 47–53.

Piontek, Thomas. "John Champagne." In *Contemporary Gay American Novelists: A Bio-Bibliographical Critical Sourcebook* edited by Emmanuel S. Nelson, 65–69. Westport, CT: Greenwood Press, 1993.

Trevor A. Sydney

Chee, Alexander (b. 1967)

Korean American author and activist and professor of creative writing. Born in South Kingston, Rhode Island, Alexander Chee has traveled and lived in many different places throughout the United States. This can be attributed to his parents' passion for traveling. Prior to his matriculation at Wesleyan University from 1985 to 1989, he visited Korea and Hawaii, where Chee honed his writing skills under the tutelage of Anne Dillard. Subsequent to his graduate studies, he moved to San Francisco where he became involved in the **queer** activist organizations AIDS Coalition to Unleash Power (ACT UP) and Queer Nation.

Afterward, Chee made New York City his home while serving as assistant editor of *OUT* magazine. From 1992 to 1994, he attended the Iowa Writers' Workshop and received a Master's of Fine Arts in Creative Writing. He has taught at New School University, Goddard College, and Wesleyan University. Currently, he serves as instructor at Amherst College. He has received two fellowships from MacDowell Colony (2005, 2007), a National Endowment for the Arts Fellowship in Prose Fiction (2004), and a Whiting Writers' Award (2003).

Chee's first novel entitled *Edinburgh* (2001) is a winner of the Lambda Editor's Choice Prize. *Edinburgh* is a lyrical novel set in Maine. It consists of four parts. The first part is entitled "Song of the Fireflies." This section highlights the early life of Aphias Zhe who is also known as Fee. Fee is a Korean American adolescent who is one of a number of boys molested by a choir director who goes by the name of Big Eric. Compounding his dark secret of sexual abuse, Fee develops a romantic attachment for a fellow choirboy named Peter. The second part, "January's Cathedral," sheds light on Fee as he gets older and tragedy strikes when Peter and some of the choirboys commit suicide. As a result, Fee attempts suicide but does not succeed. The third section, "And Night's Black Sleep upon the Eyes," is narrated from Warden's point of view. Warden is a high school student and swim team member, who bears a ghostly resemblance to Fee's childhood beau, Peter. Part four of *Edinburgh,* "Blue," examines erotic desire and the complications of love. The novel is inspired by a Korean folktale of the fox-woman, Lay Tammamo, who transforms from a fox into a woman after falling in love with a woman. Currently, Chee is working toward completion of his second novel, "The Queen of the Night," which will appear in 2009.

Chee's shorter works, which include essays, short stories, and autobiographical sketches, have been published in a variety of mediums since 1990—works such as "These Trees Were Once Women" in *Boys Like Us: Gay Writers Tell Their Coming Out Stories* (1996), "A Pilgrimage of You" in *His 3: Brilliant New Fiction by Gay Writers* (1999), "Self Quiz" in *The Man I Might Become: Gay Men Write about Their Fathers* (2002), and "Best Fraudster Date Ever" in *Blithe House Quarterly* (2005). Like his novel, these stories explore the themes of desire, trauma, and queer identity.

Chee identifies several of his fellow writers as artists who have shaped his own work: Joan Didion, Anne Carson, Jeanette Winterson, Maxine Hong Kingston, **David Leavitt**, **Audre Lorde**, **June Jordan**, and **Ursula K. Le Guin**.

Further Reading

Cooper, Michael L. "Alexander Chee's Childhood Feels Like 'A Long Trip by Car, Plane, and Boat.'" *Lambda Book Report* 10, no. 8 (March 2002): 14–15.

Sarkessian, Juliet. "Artful Story about the Victims of Child Molestation." Review of *Edinburgh*, by Alexander Chee. *Lambda Book Report* 10, no. 8 (March 2002): 16–18.

Spinella, Michael. Review of *Edinburgh*, by Alexander Chee. *Booklist* 98, no. 6 (Nov. 15, 2001): 550.

Quianna Glapion

Children's Literature, Gay

Rather than being defined by a series of set generic conventions, **gay** children's literature is defined by its readership, targeted at preteens, and, as Donald E. Hall points out, "has become increasingly and explicitly politicized." Since childhood is a period of learning about the world, it is appropriate that much of gay children's literature serves such a didactic function, although a problem that still exists is of children not having access to these texts.

While there are numerous children's books that promote difference and tolerance in general terms, this entry concerns a selection of those that concern the issue of homosexuality more explicitly. Although children's literature is not defined by a series of specific generic conventions, authors of contemporary gay children's literature have appropriated some established genres for children. For example, there are coloring books and picture books that normalize same-sex parenthood. These include Michael Willhoite's *Families: A Coloring Book* (1991) and Sarita Johnson-Calvo's *A Beach Party with Alexis* (1993) and picture books such as Bobbie Combs's *123: A Family Counting Book* (2001) and *ABC: A Family Alphabet Book* (2001) and Barbara Lynn Edmonds's *When Grown-Ups Fall in Love* (1997), while, however briefly, Todd Parr's *The Family Book* (2003) and *It's Okay to Be Different* (2004) allude to same-sex parenthood. Other picture books include Michael Willhoite's *Daddy's Roommate* (1990) and *Daddy's Wedding* (1996); Forman Brown's *The Generous Jefferson Bartleby Jones* [with black-and white illustrations by Leslie Trawin] (1991), which has been described as Dr. Seuss-like with its rhyming verse to appeal to young children; Johnny Valentine's *One Dad, Two Dads, Brown Dad, Blue Dads* [illustrated by Melody Sarecky] (1994), written in a playful rhyme scheme; Andrew R. Aldrich's *How My Family Came to Be—Daddy, Papa and Me* [illustrated by Mike Motz] (2003); and Ann Heron and Meredith Maran's *How Would You Feel If Your Dad Was Gay?* [with black-and-white illustrations by Kris Kovick] (1991), targeted at older children with far more text. Meanwhile, Willhoite's other book, *Uncle What-Is-It Is Coming to Visit!!* (1993), uses the premise of a gay uncle's visit to explore **gay stereotypes**, while Judith Vigna's *My Two Uncles* (1995) involved a grandfather's refusal to invite a girl's uncle's gay lover to an anniversary and her father explaining that while some people have a problem with gay men, he does not. Justin Richardson and Peter Parnell's *And Tango Makes Three* [illustrated by Henry Cole] (2005), meanwhile, is based on real-life events and moralizes about humanity by depicting two male penguins who fall in love and start a family.

In picture books, other genres are inverted, normalizing same-sex parenthood. Before the sequel *King & King & Family* (2004), over in Holland, Linda de Haan and Stern Nijland appropriated the fairy tale in *King & King* (2002), where the standard heterosexual relationship between prince and princess is inverted. In the United States, Johnny Valentine had already inverted fairy tale/fantasy conventions, often found in children's literature, in his books *The Duke Who Outlawed Jelly Beans and Other Stories* (1991) and *The Day They Put a Tax on Rainbows and Other Stories* (1992), both illustrated by Lynette Schmidt. In the story titled "The Frog Prince," in the first collection, for instance, a boy kisses a frog, returning him into a prince (reminding one of *Beauty and the Beast* where Beauty kisses the Beast, returning him into an attractive man) with the two boys then living "happily ever after" with their fathers. In the story "The Ring of Consequence" included in the second collection, for example, a magic wish comes true (reminding one of the case of the mythological figure of King Midas whose wish that everything he touched turned to gold had negative consequences). But for a father, his wish that he fall in love was positive where he has been in a happy gay relationship ever since. We also find Peter Cashorali's nonpicture books for adults, *Fairy Tales: Traditional Stories Retold for Gay Men* (1995) and *Gay Fairy & Folk Tales: More Traditional Stories Retold for Gay Men* (1997), which draw on fairy tales by such writers as the Brothers Grimm and Hans Christian Andersen and recast them, sometimes humorously, so that they deal with other gay themes such as **coming out**, finding love, and coping with AIDS. Meanwhile, in the realm of factual books Aylette Jenness's *Families: A Celebration of Diversity, Commitment, and Love* (1990) saw 17 young people discussing different family structures, and there is also Judith E. Snow's *How It Feels to Have a Gay or Lesbian Parent: A Book by Kids for Kids of All Ages* (2004).

Other fantasy fiction includes Eric Jon Nones's illustrated *Caleb's Friend* (1993) and Bruce Coville's *The Skull of Truth* (1997); Coville's work is intended for older children up to age 12 and is not a picture book, although it contains a selection of illustrations by Gary A. Lippincott. Nones's book, however, concerns the not necessarily sexual bond between two males, one originating from the sea, when this mer-boy (the opposite of a mermaid) miraculously returns a harmonica dropped into the ocean. In Coville's novel, Charlie Eggleston discovers a talking skull in a magic shop that curses him to tell only the truth (an element of fantasy). As a minor subplot, it is revealed that his favorite uncle's roommate is his boyfriend, and Charlie is able to overcome his initial discomfort with this revelation.

While gay young adult (YA) works are sometimes included in the category of gay children's literature, it is being increasingly recognized that those works should be treated as distinct from children's literature (as indeed should **gay graphic novels**). Gay YA literature includes novels (such as those by **Alex Sanchez**, Brent Hartinger, Robin Reardon, Kim Wallace, Brian Sloan, and David LaRochelle who has also written for young children), edited collections of short stories and plays (such as by Jane Summer), and sometimes also falls into categories such as **gay sports literature**, as in the case of Chris Crutcher's *Athletic Shorts* (1991), Mark A. Roeder's *The Soccer Field Is Empty* (2001), and Joe Babcock's *The Boys and the Bees* (2005) among other texts noted elsewhere. But these books are targeted at an older readership and deal with more adolescent themes such as growing up gay and coming out and are often more "realist" in nature.

Further Reading

Day, Frances Ann. *Lesbian and Gay Voices: An Annotated Bibliography and Guide to Literature for Children and Young Adults.* Westport, CT: Greenwood Press, 2000.

Hall, Donald E. "Children's Literature," *An Encyclopedia of Gay, Lesbian, Bisexual, Transgender, & Queer Culture,* http://www.glbtq.com/literature/children_lit.html 2002.

Andrew O'Day

Children's Literature, Lesbian

Children's literature, which targets preteen readers, began to be published in the nineteenth century, and from its inception, relationships between same-sex pairs have been common in the genre. The jump from same-sex friendship to same-sex romance and partnership, however, has taken nearly two centuries to be accurately portrayed in children's literature. Now, books that recognize and celebrate diversity among families and individuals are on the increase. While male same-sex partners appeared first in the literature, themes and issues relevant to lesbians are evident in both classic and contemporary works of literature. Until the 1970s, children's literature that illustrated households with homosexual members was missing from classrooms, bookstores, and libraries, and the importance of children having access to books characteristic of themselves and their families was either dismissed, overlooked, or feared. Children's literature that includes lesbian parents in a major plot or subplot is more common than ever before. Lesbian characters now appear as major as well as minor characters and are more likely to be realistically represented.

Children's literature that contains lesbian characters falls under the category of diversity. The main theme running through books portraying diversity is that differences should bring distinction, not discrimination. Children's literature that includes lesbian characters in natural settings, where the focus is not based on the sexuality of the adult, but rather on delineating a wide range of types of families in a variety of socioeconomic settings, is an important part of educating for tolerance. The extant children's literature demonstrates that families cannot be easily categorized into either traditional or nontraditional and then dismissed. There is increasingly no one model of family life, no *normal* representing most families. Now, it is possible to find books that include a wide variety of family arrangements that illustrate parenting situations. Available books include representations of parental situations as varied as a communal women's group (*Lots of Mommies,* 1983), an artificially inseminated lesbian mother (*Heather Has Two Mommies,* 1989), divorced lesbian partners (*When Megan Went Away,* 1979, and *Saturday Is Patty Day,* 1993), as well as a book that includes the visitation by a noncustodial heterosexual parent of a child who is living with a lesbian parent.

In recent years, novels directly challenge sexist and heterosexist ideologies. Many of the works for the very young child, picture books, describe lesbian and gay relationships as a reality with happy families headed by two same sex parents. *Heather Has Two Mommies* (1989) by Leslea Newman is the story of a three-year-old who has both a carpenter mother and a doctor mother. The carpenter mother is artificially inseminated. The author explains the insemination that produced Heather. Published in 1989, it was the first picture book to portray an explicit lesbian-headed family. *Gloria Goes to Gay Pride* (1991) also by Leslea Newman deals with the issue of hatred and **homophobia**. Gloria celebrates holidays such as Valentine's Day and Mother's Day, but on Gay Pride Day, she encounters people who are openly hostile to her parents. Another book presents a nontraditional family, but does not address the relationship of the caregivers: *Lots of Mommies* (1983) by Jane

Severance is the story of Emily, a little girl with four female parental figures, again, a happy family.

One criticism of picture and children's books is that for the most part, they do not acknowledge that young children may be **gay**. The 1990s was a turning point, and there was a rise of lesbians in young adult literature. Public attitude is more open. We see heterosexuals trying to understand relatives who are lesbians, dealing with their feelings of embarrassment and sorrow. While children's literature and young adult literature will not eliminate homophobia, we can monitor the pulse of society by the rise of literature that includes a more diverse sexually oriented population.

Further Reading

Brogan, Jim. "Gay Teens in Literature." In *The Gay Teen: Educational Practice and Theory for Lesbian, Gay, and Bisexual Adolescents,* edited by Gerald Unks, 67–78. New York: Routledge, 1995.

Gallo, Don. "Bold Books for Innovative Teaching: The Boldest Books." *The English Journal* 94, no. 1 (2004): 126–30.

Goodman, Jan. "Out of the Closet by Paying the Price: Lesbian and Gay Characters in Children's Literature." *Interracial Books for Children Bulletin* 14, nos. 3–4 (1983): 13–15.

Grayson, Dolores A. "Emerging Equity Issues Related to Homosexuality in Education." *Peabody Journal of Education* 64, no. 4 (1987): 132–45.

Inness, Sherrie A. *The Lesbian Menace: Ideology, Identity, and the Representation of Lesbian Life.* Amherst: University of Massachusetts Press, 1997.

Jenkins, Christine. "Young Adult Novels and Gay/Lesbian Characters and Themes 1969–1992: A Historical Reading of Content, Gender, and Narrative Distance." *Youth Services in Libraries* 7 (1993): 43–55.

Rudman, Masha Kabakow. *Children's Literature: An Issues Approach.* 2nd ed. New York: Longman, 1984.

Sumara, Dennis. "Gay and Lesbian Voices in Literature: Making Room on the Shelf." *English Quarterly* 28, no. 1 (1993): 30–34.

Wolf, Virginia L. "The Gay Family in Literature for Young People." *Children's Literature in Education* 20, no. 1 (1989): 51–58.

Dianna Laurent

Chrystos (b. 1946)

Native American (Menominee) lesbian poet, visual artist, and activist. Born on November 7, 1946, in San Francisco to a Menominee father and a European immigrant mother, Chrystos grew up off-reservation and currently resides on Bainbridge Island, Washington. She authored five books of poetry: *Not Vanishing* (1988), *Dream On* (1991), *In Her I Am* (1993), *Fugitive Colors* (1995), and *Fire Power* (1995); she also designed some of the covers, co-edited *Best Lesbian Erotica 1999* with Tristan Taormino, and has been anthologized in such influential collections as *This Bridge Called My Back* (1981), edited by **Cherríe Moraga** and **Gloria Evangelina Anzaldúa**, and *Living the Spirit: A Gay American Indian Anthology* (1988), edited by Will Roscoe. Her poetry is political and erotic and tackles a multitude of issues, including colonization and indigenous genocide, lesbian sexuality, poverty, violence against women, and language. She writes in English, turning the colonizer's language against itself to speak truth about the colonization of indigenous land and genocide of indigenous peoples.

Not Vanishing is Chrystos's first book of poetry, and its title resists the colonial wish to think of indigenous peoples of the United States as vanishing Americans and makes visible the material circumstances of Native American lives. The language she incorporates within this work is highly visual and tactile, and she explores a wide variety of topics in this book with astute political analysis, humor, and great beauty. Poems such as "I Have Not Signed a Treaty with the United States Government" and "Savage Eloquence" expose the hypocrisy of a supposedly democratic nation founded on stolen land and genocide, while poems such as "Maybe We Shouldn't Meet If There Are No Third World Women Here" and "Poem for Lettuce" articulate with irony and sharp wit the racist and often self-righteous tone of left-wing political organizing that renders indigenous people and people of color invisible.

Dream On continues Chrystos's legacy of political poetry and weaves the intimate with the public, exploring the intersection of the personal with the political through lyric poetry and prose. Chrystos's environmentalist analysis of the exploitation of natural resources and animals is crystallized in "Impact" and "Song for a Doe." In "Na'Natska" and "Idyll: Four Days" she writes complex and stunning portraits of lesbian sex and relationships, and she perseveres with her task of making the genocide and continued colonization of North America visible in "Shame On!" (on the commodification of indigenous spirituality) and "Anthropology" (a satirical anthropological study of Caucasian peoples).

In Her I Am counters the middle-class sterility and pursuit of mainstream tolerance by some 1960s and 1970s lesbian feminists, articulating a specifically femme-butch erotic universe that refuses to give up sex for acceptance. Chrystos combines a critique of the racism, misogyny, and ableism of lesbian communities ("The Night Gown," and "Looking for a Blanket to Cover Myself after the Horses Are Free") with poems explicitly about lesbian sex that are vivid, rich, and full of humor ("Four Hours Later" and "We Pretended She Was a Young Boy" are just two of many examples).

Fire Power and *Fugitive Colors* speak a powerful political autobiography through Chrystos's self-positioning as a warrior for oppressed peoples and injustice. Many of the pieces in these works demand solidarity between indigenous people and people of color in struggling against racism and colonialism, because white supremacy stands to benefit from the oppression of both (examples include "The Roma Say," "Riding Up the Escalator," "In the Land of the Free," and "Gathering Words"). Part of her speaking truth about injustice includes state incarcerations: she reflects upon her time spent in the notorious Napa mental institution in California as well as engaging in prison and psychiatric survivor activism ("Going into the Prison," "I Have Three Names," and "The Man Who Had a Lobotomy").

While Chrystos has won prestigious awards such as the **Audre Lorde** International Poetry Competition Award in 1994 and draws large crowds to her readings, she has not received sufficient critical attention from the mainstream American poetry community. This problem has been exacerbated by the bankruptcy and closure of her publisher, Press Gang Publishers, in 2002. As a result, all of her books are now unavailable and out of print.

Further Reading

Bealy, Joanne. "An Interview With Chrystos." *off our backs* 33 (September–October 2003): 11–17.

Miranda, Deborah A. "Dildos, Hummingbirds, and Driving Her Crazy: Searching for American Indian Women's Love Poetry and Erotics." *Frontiers* 23, no. 2 (2002): 135–49.

Zeleke, E. Centime. "Speaking about Language." *Canadian Woman Studies/cahier de la femme* 16, no. 2 (Spring 1996): 33–35.

Rachel Hurst

Clarke, Cheryl (b. 1947)

African American lesbian poet, critic, and theorist. Cheryl Clarke, born in Washington, D.C., in 1947 and has been central to the tradition of black lesbian poetry in the United States. Clarke has published five volumes of poetry and was nominated for the Lambda Literary Award in 1993, among many other honors. Her poetry is characterized by representations of the multiple forms of violence that black women and girls experience even as it offers celebratory and explicit depictions of lesbian love.

Clarke has been involved in independent, feminist lesbian and women of color publishing as activism since the movement emerged in the late 1970s. She was also involved in the birth of Kitchen Table: Women of Color Press that was developed by the Combahee River Collective, a Boston-based black feminist lesbian organization in which she was active in starting in 1977. At the first black feminist retreat that the Collective held, in July 1977, Clarke encouraged the women gathered to discuss ways to extend the definition of family and to talk about the complexity of black lesbian "credibility" for black women in romantic relationships with white women.

Clarke contributed to Kitchen Table's definitive and enduring publications, *This Bridge Called My Back: Writings by Radical Women of Color* (1981) and *Home Girls: A Black Feminist Anthology* (1983), and published her first book, *Narratives: Poems in the Tradition of Black Women* (1983), through the same collective. In her piece "**Lesbianism**: An Act of Resistance," published in *This Bridge Called My Back,* she defines lesbianism as a political stance, not merely a personal lifestyle identification, and argues that lesbianism is productive of a radical structure of love that can dismantle and replace the structures of racism, sexism, capitalism, **homophobia**, and imperialism.

Clarke continues this line of argument in *Home Girls* with "Failure to Transform: Homophobia in the Black Community"; here she argues that homophobia is written into the very laws of the United States, but she also insists that these legal structures should not prevent black communities from fighting their own homophobia, since black existence is criminalized by the same legal framework. In this essay Clarke demonstrates her ongoing stance of double critique, her vigilance in calling out the racism of the women's movement and the homophobia and sexism of the Black Arts Movement from *within* both struggles.

In "Women of Summer," her fictional contribution to *Home Girls,* Clarke creates a narrative of two freedom fighters on the run, allowing readers to encounter generations of black women who relate as comrades and lovers, including an 80-year-old black woman named Nannie who carries a shotgun. "Women of Summer" participates in the tradition of Black Arts Movement literature epitomized by figures such as Toni Cade Bambara while invoking older traditions including the legendary Jamaican Maroon warrior "Nanny." Clarke's work maintains a fierce dialogue between the holistic critique designed to dismantle existing structures and the recuperation of submerged traditions of alternative power. In addition to her polemic and fictional demonstration of black lesbianism as a liberatory practice for black women, Clarke's enduring body of poetry produces a language in which the oppressions, possibilities, and choices facing black women meet the black vernacular languages of kitchen table storytelling.

Narratives: Poems in the Tradition of Black Women, which she also produced as a live performance in New York City and New Jersey in the 1980s, speaks of domestic violence and erotic love between women in a voice that publicizes the private conversations that Clarke suggests have been occurring all along. This collection documents the volatile environment of black Washington, D.C., in the wake of the murder of Martin Luther King, Jr., and participates in a wave of broken silences about violence against black women within black communities and also begins what Clarke calls a "mythology/genealogy" of black lesbian love.

Clarke's publishing choices say as much about where her political commitments reside as the brave content of her work does. Self-publishing *Narratives* and then reissuing it through Kitchen Table: Women of Color Press, Clarke also published three subsequent books, *Living as a Lesbian* (1986), *Humid Pitch* (1989), and *Experimental Love* (1993), through Firebrand Books, a lesbian publishing house with a commitment to ethnic diversity.

Clarke served on the editorial board of the radical feminist periodical *Conditions* from 1981 to 1990, where she demonstrated her commitment to bring black lesbian experiences to the forefront, battling the ways they were often submerged by the racism of the feminist movement. Clarke's interviews, recorded conversations, book reviews, and articles emerge as a trajectory of black feminist literary production and dialogue during her decade of work with *Conditions.*

In the contemporary moment, much of Clarke's activism and writing focuses on responding to the health, housing, and economic crises facing young people in black communities in the United States. Clarke is co-editor with Steven G. Fullwood of a journal called *NOW* published by AIDS Project Los Angeles, seeking new ways to talk about the AIDS crisis, women's health, and black cultural production in the current moment. Clarke also contributed a piece called "Lesbianism, 2000" to the 2002 tribute anthology *This Bridge We Call Home: Radical Visions for Transformation* created in honor of the 20-year anniversary of *This Bridge Called My Back,* and she appears in a forthcoming film featuring interviews with black lesbians called *Black/Womyn Conversations.*

In 2006 Clarke released a retrospective of her work over the past 25 years entitled *The Days of Good Looks: Prose and Poetry of Cheryl Clarke, 1980 to 2005,* and in 2007 she released her newest collection of poetry entitled *Corridors of Nostalgia* with Suspect Thoughts Press, the (self-proclaimed) "**queer**est little press on earth."

In "The Prong of Permanency: A Rant," a recent contribution to the Suspect Thoughts Press collection *I Do, I Don't: Queers on Marriage* (2004), Clarke articulates her radical stance on the transformative power of love, insisting that the pursuit of gay marriage actually "trivializes" queer partnerships. Clarke compares the "permanency" that she believes is the motivation behind the gay marriage movement to the "prong of love" that Zora Neale Hurston's character "Nanny" describes as the death of every woman. Clarke remains committed to the use of an intergenerational analysis toward a transformative present. Clarke therefore links her critical stance toward the contemporary lesbian and the **gay rights movement** to her earlier work as a radical black lesbian feminist, reminding readers that when she was part of a coming out movement in the 1960s, the intention was to dismantle the institution of marriage, not to earn inclusion within it.

Clarke, who earned a B.A. from Howard University and an M.A., M.S.W., and Ph.D. from Rutgers University, has also made a critical contribution to black and feminist literature on the level of analysis with her close attention to the **gender**ed politics *within* black radical movements. Her essays appear in *Callaloo* and *The Black Scholar* among many other journals, and she has published a critical monogram entitled *"After Mecca": Women Poets and the Black Arts Movement* (2000). Having worked at Rutgers University since 1970, Clarke currently serves as Director of Social Justice Education and LGBTQ communities, spearheading projects such as Q Safety Net, a program for LGBTQ students who become homeless due to their sexual or gender identities. Cheryl Clarke's body of work and her continued voice and vision exemplify a continued regeneration of radical response at the intersection of queer, black, and feminist trajectories of critique.

See also Lesbian Literature, African American

Further Reading

Hennessy, Christopher. Review of *The Days of Good Looks: Poetry and Prose of Cheryl Clarke,1980–2005. The Gay Lesbian Book Review Worldwide* 14, no. 2 (March/April 2007): 41–42.

Randolph, Elizabeth. "Cheryl Clarke." In *Contemporary Lesbian Writers of the United States: A Bio-Bibliographical Critical Sourcebook,* edited by Sandra Pollack and Denise D. Knight, 122–27. Westport, CT: Greenwood Press, 1993.

Alexis Pauline Gumbs

Clausen, Jan (b. 1950)

Poet, short story writer, novelist, editor, activist, and critic. Born in North Bend, Oregon, Jan Clausen and her sisters spent 10 years in Humboldt County, California, before moving with her family to the Puget Sound area in 1960. Clausen attended Reed College in Portland, Oregon, majoring in philosophy, but Reed left after her junior year. In 1973 at the age of 23, Clausen moved to New York City. There, she found a vibrant lesbian feminist community and became active in the poetry community and the small press movement.

Clausen cooperatively published her first poetry collection, *After Touch,* in 1975 with the small publisher Out & Out Books. Clausen's second book of poetry, *Waking at the Bottom of the Dark,* was published in 1979 by Long Haul Press, a small press that Clausen started herself to publish and distribute her work and work by other lesbian feminists. Long Haul Press published books by **Dorothy Allison**, Judith McDaniel, **Minnie Bruce Pratt**, Barbara Smith, and the first edition of *Yours in Struggle* (1984) by Elly Bulkin. Clausen's chapbook, *A Movement of Poets: Thoughts on Poetry and Feminism,* was published in 1982 by Long Haul Press and is a meditation on the role of poetry in the feminist movement and its impact. Clausen's third collection of poetry, *Duration,* was published in 1983 by Hanging Loose Press. It was nearly 25 years later before she published another full-length collection of poetry. In 2007, two collections of poems by Clausen were published. *From a Glass House* was released by IKON, and *If You Like Difficulty* was published Harbor Mountain Press in Brownsville, Vermont.

In 1976, with Elly Bulkin, Irena Klepfisz, and Rima Shore, Jan Clausen founded *Conditions,* a magazine of women's writing with an emphasis on writing by lesbians. *Conditions* published until 1990 and focused in particular on publishing work by lesbians of color and working-class lesbians. *Conditions* was recognized for the quality of writing that it published and for its commitment to including women of color. *Conditions: Five, The*

Black Women's Issue was edited by Barbara Smith and Lorraine Bethel; it was widely read and discussed. Clausen worked as co-editor on *Conditions* until 1981.

During the 1980s, Clausen's writing focused on fiction. She published a short story collection, *Mother, Sister, Daughter, Lover* (1980), and two novels, *Sinking Stealing* (1985) and *The Prosperine Papers* (1988), all with Crossing Press. She also published a collection of essays about lesbian literature, *Books & Life* (1985).

In 1999, Clausen published her memoir *Apples & Oranges: My Journey through Sexual Identity.* This book described her experiences in the lesbian-feminist movement and how she fell in love with a Caribbean male lawyer on a fact-finding mission to Nicaragua in 1987. She moved in with him and came out as bisexual, stunning many in the lesbian feminist community and earning her much derision. Her memoir served as a book to further understand the categories of sexual orientation, especially where they are limited and the effects of those limitations on people.

Reflecting on her body of literary work in a 2008 interview on Woman-Stirred Radio, a community radio show on the Plainfield, Vermont, station, Clausen said, "Now, the best way to describe my work is **queer**." All of Clausen's work is characterized by the examination of identity and how it is constructed, particularly at the fringes.

Clausen's poems have been anthologized in collections including *Amazon Poetry: An Anthology* (1975), *Cameos: 12 Small Press Women Poets* (1982), and *The World in Us: Lesbian and Gay Poetry of the Next Wave* (2000). She earned her bachelor of arts degree from the New School in 1994 and her master of arts degree in **gender** studies and feminist theory from the New School for Social Research in 1996; the topic of her thesis was "North American Feminists and the Sandinista Revolution."

Clausen has been awarded writing fellowships from the National Endowment for the Arts and the New York Foundation for the Arts. She is a regular reviewer for the *Women's Review of Books* and the *Lambda Book Report*. Since 1989, Clausen has taught creative writing at Eugene Lang College in Manhattan; she also teaches in the Goddard College MFA Writing Program. She lives in Brooklyn, New York.

Further Reading

Clausen, Jan. Interview by Merry Gangeni. *Woman-Stirred Radio.* WGDR, Plainfield, VT. June 26, 2008.

Griffin, Connie. "Forbidden Fruit: Review of *Apples & Oranges: My Journey through Sexual Identity.*" *Lesbian Review of Books* 6, no. 2 (Winter 1999–2000): 12.

Walter, Kate. "Jan Clausen: Radical Images from the 'Big Chill' Generation." *The Advocate* 413 (May 1985): 39.

Julie R. Enszer

Cliff, Michelle (b. 1946)

Jamaican American author of three novels, two short story collections, two poetry collections, and several essays. Michelle Cliff has held the Allan K. Smith Professorship of English Language and Literature at Trinity College, 1993–1999, and held academic positions at the University of Michigan, Emory University, and Johannes Gutenberg Universität, Mainz, Germany. The recipient of two National Endowment for the Humanities fellowships and other prestigious awards, she was twice visiting writer at the Vermont

Studio Center. The daughter of an American father and a Jamaican mother, Michelle Cliff was born in Kingston, Jamaica, on November 2, 1946. When she was three years old, her family moved to New York City for greater economic opportunity, where they remained for seven years—a move that Cliff in 1981 described as "disastrous" and more recently, in 2002, as "interesting" and, as budding writer, "enriching." After graduating from high school, Cliff earned her B.A. at Wagner College on Staten Island, New York, her M.A. in Philosophy at the University of London, and then returned to the United States, never again to reside in Jamaica.

Like many expatriates, Cliff imaginatively returned to her homeland in her writing, in which a postcolonial consciousness centrally figures. When Cliff was 22, her mother informed her that she was a person of color—a heritage that her family had suppressed but which the light-skinned Cliff had discerned—and which, as an adult writer, she embraced. In the course of her graduate studies, Cliff read the work of the neoplatonists on platonic—that is, same-sex love—and became romantically involved with another woman for the first time. Thus her conscious exploration of both racial and sexual identity coincided, precipitating her writing poetry for the first time and, in 1976, becoming the life partner of poet **Adrienne Rich**.

Cliff's first book, *Claiming an Identity They Taught Me to Despise* (1980), is a collection of poems that reflect her thoughts on racial prejudice and the politics of passing—that is, the cultural pressures for light-skinned people of color to "pass" as white. Along the same lines, these poems also address **homophobia** in Jamaica that motivates many **queer** people to hide their sexual orientation. Cliff's second book, *The Land of Look Behind: A Collection of Prose and Poetry* (1985), represents her movement from poetry to fiction; in her most recent interview (2002), she states, "I do not consider myself a poet at all" (Clawson).

Her next two books, *Abeng* (1984) and *No Telephone to Heaven* (1987), are novels for which Cliff became critically acclaimed and more widely known. *Abeng* introduces the autobiographical character Clare Savage. Along with *No Telephone to Heaven,* it focuses on Claire's quest for the suppressed history of Jamaica and her processual commitment to an anticolonialist politics. A light-skinned Jamaican daughter of parents who are, alternately, descended from the Maroons (early Jamaican resisters to plantation slavery) and brutal slaveowners, Clare, like Cliff herself, is a "white creole" who embodies hybridity. As she comes of age, Clare is drawn to her matrilineage and specifically her Afro-Jamaican grandmother, through whom Clare's personal history becomes intertwined with the mythology of Nanny, a legendary Maroon healer. Cliff connects Jamaica's layered slave and colonial past and its postcolonial present with Clare's effort to reconcile her split parts—"white and not white, town and country, scholarship and privilege" (*Abeng* 119).

In *No Telephone to Heaven,* Clare returns as a young woman who—coincident with Cliff's own development—achieves a more acute sense of the postcolonial condition and its relation to racism through her maturation in Jamaica, the United States, and England. Through Clare's eyes, the reader witnesses disturbing racial violence—first in Jamaica and then in the purported refuge of the "mother country" England—which moves Clare to work for social change before returning to her homeland. This return also involves Clare claiming her history and identity as a person of color. To apprehend her light skin as a legacy of the rapes of her grandmothers is to acknowledge that violence is the source of the privilege and power with which she has unwittingly grown up.

While the homophobic elements of Jamaican culture become perceptible to Clare, the sexual undertone of her feelings for her close friend Zoe remains inchoate. While critics have developed this aspect of Clare and Zoe's relationship, Cliff notes that "the lesbian subtext in *Abeng* was unconscious" (Schwartz 601). Elsewhere Cliff clarifies that

> for Caribbean women to love each other is different. It's not Vita-Sackville-West and Virginia Woolf, it's not Djuana Barnes or Natlie Barney, and it's not Sappho [...] Putting it into a Caribbean setting as part of a woman's self-definition, and as a way to value the female, which we've been taught so much to devalue, really makes it different. (Raiskin 69–70)

Free Enterprise (1993), Cliff's third and last published novel, resurrects the neglected alliances of women abolitionists prior to and during the Civil War. Through telling these unsung tales, Cliff continues "to value the female" (Raiskin 70), this time, for the first time in her career, in the form of a historical novel. If Cliff's early writing is a trenchant critique of colonialism and its bloody histories, *Free Enterprise* recognizes the overlapping histories of colonialism within which the cultures of the Americas have been shaped and implicitly questions modes of history that are delimited by the modern nation-state. *Free Enterprise* rewrites nationally delineated narratives of U.S. history that intersect in the Civil War, abolition, and nineteenth-century black women's lives. The novel is set both during and after the Civil War, yet it recontextualizes the War not as a nationalist narrative that consolidated the United States, but as a transnational slave revolt against imperialism in which black women, capital, and the discourse of "free enterprise" played a crucial role.

Free Enterprise marks a significant shift in Cliff's orientation: set in the United States, it features characters whose migrations from Jamaica, Europe, South America, and the Pacific Islands figure prominently in the narrative. Cliff's most recent publication, *The Store of a Million Items* (1998), is a collection of stories set in Jamaica, Europe, and the United States that also highlights transnational concerns. *Free Enterprise*'s North American setting and its explicitly "American" concerns (signaled immediately by the title) expand our sense of "America" to include a postcolonial perspective on U.S. history, complicating the "Caribbean" and "postcolonial" categories for which critics have appropriated Cliff from the beginning of her writing career. Central to *Free Enterprise*'s recasting of the Civil War as a major battle in a transnational war on slavery is its remembrance of a complex black female abolitionist history at the center of which is the enigmatic historical figure Mary Ellen Pleasant. A black entrepreneur, civil- and human-rights activist, and abolitionist, Pleasant was an unapologetic and successful capitalist who covertly dedicated her talent for personal profit within the system of "free enterprise" to undermining "the Trade" that thrived by it. At the center of Cliff's novel is the abolitionist venture of which the historical Pleasant was most proud, funding John Brown's raid on Harpers Ferry.

Republished in 2004 by City Lights as *Free Enterprise: A Novel of Mary Ellen Pleasant,* the novel invites its readers to view the untold story of Pleasant's historical role in abolition in a broader temporal and geographic context of underground resistance to colonization that precedes even Columbus's first voyage to the Americas, thus extending Cliff's attention to an anticolonialist politics. Its spatial narrative—distinct from her earlier novels—discloses the complex and entwined history of New World colonization, slavery, and counterhegemonic resistance, restoring the heterogeneous cultural histories and international struggles over slavery that precede and inform the U.S. Civil War. Not unlike the earlier novels' revisionist interpretations of colonialism and its discontents, *Free Enterprise* disrupts the essentialist identity of abolitionists and liberators of slavery in the United States as (primarily) white activist citizens and Union soldiers to carve a space in what it calls "the official version" (16).

A lesbian subtext also surfaces in *Free Enterprise*. Cliff's Pleasant associates with women almost exclusively; the novel suggests that Pleasant may have shared the same sexual orientation as the author. There does not seem to be evidence to support this characterization, although evidence exists that undermines it. While Cliff has undertaken the arduous task of researching the recondite history of Pleasant, she intentionally distorts and omits facts regarding Pleasant's second husband, daughter, and later relationship with a male lover in an effort to write lesbian desire into Pleasant's story. The same historical structures that conceal Pleasant as a (wealthy black female) historical subject would indeed conceal her as a lesbian. The suggestion of lesbian desire in *Free Enterprise,* however, seems to reveal more about Cliff's politics and Pleasant's performative strategies than Pleasant's sexuality.

Further Reading

Chancy, Myriam J. "Exile and Resistance: Retelling History as a Revolutionary Act in the Writings of Michelle Cliff and Marie Chauvet." *Journal of Caribbean Studies* 9, no. 3 (Winter 1993/ Spring 1994): 266–92.

Clawson, Jim. "Re-Visioning Our History: Interview with Cheryl Cliff." nidus (Spring 2002). http://www.pitt.edu/~nidus/archives/spring2002/cliff.html.

Raiskin, Judith. "The Art of History: An Interview with Michelle Cliff." *The Kenyon Review* 15, no. 1 (Winter 1993): 57–71.

Schwartz, Meryl F. "An Interview with Michelle Cliff." *Contemporary Literature* 34, no. 4 (Winter 1993): 595–619.

———. "Imagined Communities in the Novels of Michelle Cliff." In *Homemaking: Women Writers and the Politics and Poetics of Home,* edited by Fiona Barnes and Catherine Wiley, 287–311. New York: Garland, 1996.

Marni Gauthier

Closet, The

A popular metaphor to describe the silence and invisibility that inhere in sexual marginalization. The closet, or the status of being "closeted," generally refers to an otherwise "normal" appearing person's hidden, presumably transgressive sexual desires and/or practices. Until around the mid-twentieth century, the concept of closeting did not explicitly refer to sexuality but signified any deliberately hidden behaviors or predilections. According to George Chauncey, historian and author of the influential study *Gay New York* (1994), it was after World War II and in response to an increasingly regularized campaign of **homophobia** that the closet came to imply a person's efforts to hide sexuality considered shameful or perverse by the dominant society.

But it would be inaccurate to reduce the closet to a matter of a subject's personal choice to hide his or her sexual orientation. Eve Sedgwick's seminal work, *The Epistemology of the Closet* (1990), asserts that the closet helps to shape dominant understandings about sexuality and citizenship in the United States. Heteronormative culture demands that a sexually minoritized subject either "come out" by publicly announcing his or her (putatively perverse) sexual orientation or "stay closeted" by not disclosing what amounts to a dirty little secret in a homophobic world. As Sedgwick explains, the act of "coming out" of the closet is neither a singular act, nor is it ever fully complete. Rather, the compulsion to come out of the metaphorical closet continues to prevail on a subject as he or she encounters new and unknowing audiences, faced each time with the choice of whether to reveal or not.

Within this analytical framework, the closet works as a regime of power that privileges **heterosexuality** by raising it to status as original, authentic, and natural, indeed as the *default* state of being. So the logic goes: we are all heterosexual—"normal" in a world that privileges heterosexuality—unless we say or behave otherwise.

The closet as a spatial metaphor has its limitations when one considers its failure to contain the ambiguity of many audiences (Sedgwick describes a multiplicity of closets, some opening up into other closets), neither can it encompass the diversity of behaviors that serve, sometimes unconsciously, to conceal one's status as other than normal. Recent work by legal scholar Kenji Yoshino offers further insight into the operation of the closet, exposing the metaphor's limitations to depict the complexities of "choice" and self-depiction among minoritized subjects. Yoshino's work, *Covering: The Hidden Assault on Our Civil Rights* (2006), addresses the impact of the compulsion to hide, or as Yoshino asserts, to "cover," one's difference from the norm. Existing somewhere between the acts of either "coming out" or "staying in," "covering" occurs when one attempts to downplay a stigmatized feature, without denying or hiding it outright, in an effort to appear part of the mainstream community. In other words, one does not simply come out, nor does one "stay closeted"; instead, there is a liminal realm where dominant understandings of civic entitlement and belonging conspire to proscribe certain behaviors, without outlawing them explicitly, within particular contexts.

In Yoshino's analysis, the closet extends its powerful reach beyond those who work deliberately to conceal their differences; covering is something everyone does at one point or another because we are all united in our desire to appear normal and hence be entitled to the privileges and protections of citizenship. While his work explores how the nation's dominant assimilationist logic affects all stigmatized subjects, coercing them to cover parts of their identity, Yoshino focuses on its particularly insidious impact on sexual minorities. His work reveals the ways in which dominant society and the laws that govern civil rights assume that, unlike women (of all ethnicities) and nonwhites (of all genders), homosexuals, as unmarked individuals, have the ability to avoid the discriminations that prey on those with visible differences. Dominant reasoning presumes that sexually minoritized subjects may choose to remain closeted about their orientation (that is, to deny that they are anything but straight) or to downplay the behaviors that make them different. For example, a woman who may consider herself "out" as a lesbian may nevertheless feel she cannot demonstrate affection toward her partner in the company of heterosexual friends, so ingrained is her fear of homophobic violence as well as her concern that others may judge her as sexually deviant. Such compulsory assimilation masquerades as "choice" in a world where the law protects only those who cannot alter the physiologically "natural" differences that become the source of their discrimination. It is in this way that sexually minoritized people suffer more from the reach of the closet than others who occasionally feel compelled to hide their nonnormative differences.

Today the concept of the closet is increasingly used more generally to refer to nonsexual behaviors or identities kept intentionally hidden, as illuminated in the expression "I'm a closet sci-fi fan." Indeed, this seems to confirm Yoshino's assertion that we all participate in the assimilationist logic of covering, that we all experience, at one time or another, a fear that the predilection in question may invoke shame or ridicule from others. But as Yoshino's and Sedgwick's works make clear, the closet and the concomitant compulsion to cover, imposes additional layers of shame and danger upon those whose differences represent sexual deviance in the popular imagination. While our culture's assimilationist pressure weighs in daily on our decisions not to reveal certain aspects of our identity, and fear of embarrassment may drive us to occasional acts of subterfuge, it is often the forced invisibility of the differences in question that render sexually minoritized subjects most vulnerable to the coercive grasp of the closet.

See also Coming Out Narratives, Gay Male; Coming Out Narratives, Lesbian

Further Reading

Chauncey, George. *Gay New York: Gender, Urban Culture, and the Making of the Gay Male World, 1890–1940.* New York: Basic Books, 1994.

Eskridge, William N., Jr.*Gaylaw: Challenging the Apartheid of the Closet.* Cambridge, MA: Harvard University Press, 1999.

Humphreys, L. *Tearoom Trade: Impersonal Sex in Public Places.* Chicago: Aldine, 1970.

Sedgwick, Eve Kosofsky. *Epistemology of the Closet.* Berkeley: University of California Press, 1990.

Seidman, Steven. *Beyond the Closet: The Transformation of Gay and Lesbian Life.* New York: Routledge, 2003.

Seidman, Steven, Chet Meeks, and Francie Traschen. "Beyond the Closet? The Changing Social Meaning of Homosexuality in the United States." *Sexualities* 2, no. 1 (1999): 427–45.

Yoshino, Kenji. *Covering: The Hidden Assault on Our Civil Rights.* New York: Random House, 2006.

———. "Covering: Discrimination and Gay Assimilation," *Yale Law Journal* 111, no. 4 (January 2002): 769–939.

Caroline E. Light

Coe, Christopher (1954–1994)

Novelist and short story writer. Christopher Coe's short fiction has appeared in *Harper's Magazine* and has been featured in *Men on Men 2: Best New Gay Fiction* (1988). His first short novel, *I Look Divine,* was published in 1987 and was followed in 1993 by the longer *Such Times.* Both novels received positive critical attention in the mainstream press. Coe died of AIDS-related causes in New York City in 1994.

In *I Look Divine* Coe writes the story of Nicholas, a wealthy and narcissistic **gay** man whose avowed purpose in life is to be looked at and adored. The novel is narrated by his unnamed and less brilliant older brother, who is sorting through Nicholas's possessions following his death, apparently at the hands of a man whom he had paid for sex. The complex and interdependent relationship of the two gay brothers is at the heart of the novel's structure and is deeply implicated in its preoccupation with identity, surfaces, and mirroring. Nicholas's bedroom, in which the narrator is sitting as he relates the details of his brother's life, is furnished with mirrors, and with a life-size photograph of Nicholas at the height of his beauty. By the end of the novel, the narrator has drunk Nicholas's tequila, smoked his cigarettes, donned the Japanese robe that Nicholas is wearing in the photograph, and watched what Nicholas would have watched through his window. The narrator thus comes to literally inhabit his brother's life, as he allows the reader to do so through his narrative. The only portrait we are offered of the narrator is the one glimpsed through his portrait of his younger brother; the structure of the narrative replicates both

Nicholas's erasure of the identity of his older brother, and also of his dependence on him for his own sense of identity. The narrator is the suppressed but constitutive norm against which Nicholas's excess can be measured; they exist only in sexualized tension with one another. As William Clark Lane has noted, *I Look Divine* fits deftly into a Paterian and Wildean aesthetic tradition, and the novel clearly replicates the thematic concerns and narrative structure of Oscar Wilde's *The Picture of Dorian Gray* (72).

The wealthy, well-traveled, and idle lifestyle of the brothers in *I Look Divine* is very similar to that of the social milieu evoked in Coe's second novel, *Such Times*. Coe again deploys a first-person narrator and writes with precision about foreign travel and fine dining. While *I Look Divine* was written in the context of the AIDS crisis, Coe does not directly acknowledge it in his text, though the narrative certainly invites readings that draw on the historical context of its composition. *Such Times*, however, is a direct, detailed, and elegiac response to the effect that HIV/AIDS had on the gay male community. Timothy retrospectively narrates the history of his 18-year affair with Jasper, an older man who remained in a committed partnership with someone else, and who has recently died of what his partner insists on recording as heart failure. The novel documents both the gay nightlife of New York in the 1970s and the changes it undergoes as HIV/AIDS takes its toll, but Timothy is a distant narrator of these pleasures and is narratively, emotionally, and physically faithful to the lover with whom he owns an apartment in Paris, but whom he sees only on the weekends in New York. Through Timothy *Such Times* provides a detailed account of the nature of HIV/AIDS and the means of its treatment. Timothy himself has been hospitalized as a result of AIDS, is watching his friend Dominic die, and matter-of-factly details the exploitation of sufferers by those charged with their care. However, the novel is most powerfully a portrait of the demands, sacrifices, dishonesty, and self-interest at work in a long-term relationship, which the intrusion of HIV/AIDS only serves to further magnify.

Further Reading

Burgin, Richard. "Not Just a Pretty Face." *New York Times Book Review* 92 (August 30, 1987): 11.

Clark, William Lane. "Christopher Coe." In *Contemporary Gay American Novelists: A Bio-Bibliographical Critical Sourcebook,* edited by Emmanuel S. Nelson, 71–76. Westport, CT: Greenwood Press, 1993.

Hempel, Amy. "Talking to Christopher Coe." *Vogue* 438 (September 1987): 455–56.

Rosello, Mireille. "Pictures of a Virus: Ideological Choices and the Repesentation of HIV." *French Cultural Studies* 9, no. 3 (1998). 337–49.

Liz Vine

Cohn, Meryl (b. 1961)

Playwright, humorist, author, and syndicated columnist of *Ms. Behavior*. Meryl Robin Cohn was born in Brooklyn, New York, where she attended Yeshiva of Flatbush for several years before enrolling in public school. Her family's move to Long Island (Roslyn, New York) in 1972 was difficult for the 10-year-old Cohn, who suddenly found herself in unfamiliar territory. To survive suburbia, Cohn resorted to solitary reading and writing. She graduated from high school early—at the age of 16—eventually attended Smith College, where she majored in psychology and fell in love with playwriting. She studied with playwriting mentor Len Berkman and received the college's prestigious Denis Johnston Playwriting Award upon graduation in 1982. While freelancing for the *New York Village Voice*, Cohn attended New York University's Tisch School of the Arts and received an M.F.A. in Dramatic Writing in 1987.

Upon graduation, she began writing theater and film reviews and interviews in New York and Boston, eventually landing a health column for LGBTQ readers of *Bay Windows*. Offered the opportunity to create a new column in 1992, Cohn invented her beloved alter ego, humorous advice diva "Ms. Behavior." *Ms. Magazine* disputed her right to trademark *Ms. Behavior* as the name of her column, but once the **gay** and lesbian press began questioning the magazine's judgment, lawyers for *Ms. Magazine* dropped the case against Cohn. Soon Cohn's trademarked tongue-in-cheek advice was syndicated to as many as a dozen other LGBT newspapers, including the *Philadelphia Gay News*, the *Washington Blade*, the *Atlanta Southern Voice, Outfront*, and *Lavender Magazine*, reaching a readership of close to a million. Cohn's essays and articles also appeared in the *Washington Post*, the *New York Village Voice*, the *Boston Phoenix, 10 Percent Magazine*, and other publications.

In 1995, Houghton-Mifflin published Cohn's acclaimed book, *Do What I Say: Ms. Behavior's Guide to Gay & Lesbian Etiquette*. The book received praise from such **gay** and lesbian literati as **Rita Mae Brown**, **Lisa Alther**, and political comedian Kate Clinton. Author **Stephen McCauley** wrote, "Ms. Behavior's guide isn't so much a book of manners as a tongue-in-cheek tour through the contemporary gay and lesbian cultural landscape. Meryl Cohn is a shrewd, witty observer who knows when to balance the role of savvy sophisticate with that of a shocked lady. A fresh and funny book" (dust jacket blurb). Author Blanche McCrary Boyd added, "I'm not given to hyperbole, but this may be the funniest book I've ever read" (dust jacket blurb).

After an extensive book tour, Cohn appeared as Ms. Behavior on national television talk shows, including *The Oprah Winfrey Show, Lauren Hutton, Ricki Lake,* and *Rolanda*. She briefly performed a one-woman show entitled *Everyone Hates You When You're in Love*. Articles about Cohn's advice appeared in such mainstream media as the *New York Times*, the *Philadelphia Inquirer*, and the *Boston Globe*, as well as in the gay press. After marrying her partner, writer **Mary Beth Caschetta**, in Provincetown, Massachusetts, on the first day it was legally possible (May 17, 2004), Cohn was featured in a *Boston Globe* article, in which she dispensed gay and lesbian marriage advice.

Turning her attention back to playwriting in 2000, Cohn joined a playwright's lab at the Provincetown Theater. Her plays began premiering every year during Provincetown's legendary Women's Week, often to standing-room-only crowds. During these years, Cohn's plays were among the only lesbian comedies regularly produced in theaters in the United States. Early plays included *Funny, Sexy, Smart* (2002); *Almost Home* (2004); and *Ask Andrea Anything* (2004). Cohn's plays evolved toward family comedies with serious subject matters.

In *And Sophie Comes To* (2005), a semifinalist for the Eugene O'Neill National Playwrights Conference, the protagonist Barbara attempts to adopt a little girl from China, while arguing with her sisters about whether to revive their comatose mother who is bed bound in Barbara's living room. Of this play, the *Cape Cod Times* wrote, "Cohn's genius is drawing characters who manage to be simultaneously over-the-top and innately human" (Beardsley C2).

Naked with Fruit (2006) received glowing reviews, but also upset some mainstream reviewers by featuring a lesbian threesome. Judith Shaw Beardsley of the *Cape Cod Times* wrote,

> People are people, passion is passion, and Cohn is a fine playwright. Her central themes here are living while we're dying and connecting with others. The connection among three of the four major characters involve[s] a ménage à trois relationship. For me, the whole concept of a ménage à trois, whether gay or straight, denigrates the core of a loving relationship. (Beardsley C3)

In *Reasons to Live* (2007), considered Cohn's breakout work, the playwright hit her stride and struck a dazzling balance between comedy and tragedy. The play, also a semifinalist for the Eugene O'Neill National Playwrights Conference, received a rave review by the *Provincetown Banner*, stating Cohn "has transcended and crossed over into a whole new realm that is non-stop funny, wickedly insightful and infused with comedic brilliance" (Harrison 29). Turning her focus toward yet more serious topics in *Exposure* (2008), Cohn tackled three sisters facing their father's death and posthumous criminal accusations.

In addition to the O'Neill Conference honors, Cohn also received recognition from the Massachusetts Cultural Council, the Lark Theater Development Program, and *Curve* magazine. Her short plays were produced as part of Manhattan Theatre Source's HOMOgenius and Estrogenius festivals and in various festivals throughout the country. She is a member of the Provincetown Theater Playwrights Lab and a founding member of both the Northampton Playwrights Lab and the Wellfleet Harbor Actors Theater Playwrights Alliance. Her work is under development for a New York production of *Reasons to Live*.

Further Reading

Beardsley, Judith Shaw. " 'Sophie' a Cozy Laugh at Family Dynamics," *Cape Cod Times,* October 10, 2005, C2, C3.
———. " 'Naked' Thoughtful Look at Life," *Cape Cod Times,* October 9, 2006, B7, C3.
Harrison, Sue. *Provincetown Banner,* October 11, 2007, 29.

Mary Beth Caschetta

Cole, Henri (b. 1956)

Lyric poet, teacher, and administrator. The son of Crawford Lee Cole, an engineer, and Marianne Cole, a civil servant, Roger Henri Cole was born May 9, 1956, in Fukuoka, Japan. He became a naturalized U.S. citizen in 1970. Cole's growing up was not easy. In his personal essay, "How I Grew," Cole, raised as a Roman Catholic in a military and trilingual home, writes that violence at home between his parents was predictable, that he was whipped and beaten, and that he often prayed for a divine intervention that never came. While away in college, he wrote autobiographical poetry revealing the anger and yearning of a **closet**ed homosexual. This was the beginning of his attempt at the serious craft of lyric poetry, which he would go on to perfect during and after finishing multiple degrees: B.A. at the College of William and Mary in 1978, M.A. at the University of Wisconsin at Milwaukee in 1980, and M.F.A. at Columbia University in 1982. His graduate schools years were also busy with teaching and working as an editorial assistant at the *Paris*

Review in 1981, as the managing editor of *Columbia Magazine: A Magazine of Poetry and Prose,* 1980–1981, and then as editor from 1981 to 1982. Also during this time, he began to accumulate fellowships and awards, among them Bread Loaf Scholar, resident at the Virginia Center for the Creative Arts, and an award from the Ossabaw Island Foundation. After completing his final degree, he went on to serve as Director of the Academy of American Poets from 1982 to 1988.

It was during this time that Cole's first book, *The Marble Queen,* was published (1986). In 1989, his second book, *The Zoo Wheel of Knowledge,* came out, and he also won the Amy Lowell Poetry Travelling Scholarship. In 1993, Cole earned a National Endowment of the Arts Fellowship, and his third book, *The Look of Things,* appeared in 1995. His poetry from this time forward can be characterized as intensely lyrical and engaged with using language to understand the self in dialogue both with itself and the external realities of the world. These poems, beautiful and finely crafted, reveal a persona's dealings with desire, (un)requited love, classical learning, and fine art, in particular, painting. In 1998, Cole published *The Visible Man,* a collection that ends with the sonnet sequence "Apollo," which, as Cole said in an interview with Christopher Hennessy, is his attempt to understand the idea of manhood with which he grew up. Cole continued to earn prizes and awards, among them the Berlin Prize in 2000 and the Japan–United States Friendship Commission Creative Artist Fellowship in 2001. During his time in Japan he worked on *Middle Earth* (2003), a finalist for the Pulitzer Prize, which contains one of his more famous poems, "Blur," another exquisite, spare sonnet sequence. In 2004, he won the Kingsley-Tufts Poetry Award for this collection and also a John Simon Guggenheim Memorial Foundation Fellowship. In recent years he has taught at a variety of schools, including Reed College, Brandeis University, and Harvard University. Cole's most recent collection, *Blackbird and Wolf,* appeared in 2007.

Further Reading

Cole, Henri. "How I Grew Up." *The Borzoi Reader Online.* http://www.randomhouse.com/knopf/
authors/cole/poetsonpoetry.html (accessed December 14, 2007).
Hennessy, Christopher. "Henri Cole: An Interview by Christopher Hennessy." *American Poetry Review* 33, no. 3 (May–June 2004): 43–46.

Billy Clem

Color Purple, The

Alice Walker's exemplary text, *The Color Purple* (1982), may be seen as a response to traditional slave narratives, in which first-person factual narrative accounts by male and female former slaves about their experience of captivity were written in order to connect with other slaves and draw attention to their plight, serving to encourage social and political change toward the abolition of slavery. The literacy of slaves revealed in these narratives demonstrated the writers' intelligence and humanity, calling for consideration of their rights as God-fearing human beings. These slave narratives are part of a tradition of African American writing and charismatic Christian writing still resonating in more contemporary works. *The Color Purple,* structured in epistolary form as a series of "letters to God" by the central protagonist, Celie, moves far beyond the early slave narratives in its form, content, and effect.

It should be remembered that for centuries it was a crime for black people to read or write, thus the significance of Celie's act of writing herself into being through her letters to God. Across the text, Celie's language use develops and her ability to express herself is enhanced as she acquires self-esteem and her life expands through her relationships to other characters.

In her novel, *The Color Purple,* Alice Walker is writing back to a relatively recent period of American Southern history of slavery, from her contemporary standpoint as an articulate author. She is clearly mindful of the traditions and histories of her people who were silenced and unable to voice their experience through literature, and she is concerned with honest representation of a range of perspectives in her narratives. Her forthrightness has made her controversial as well, as Cheryl A. Wall points out:

> Among the group of black women writers who have remade the literary landscape of our time, Walker is by many accounts the most controversial. Perceived in some quarters as the exemplar of political correctness, Walker is often accused of sacrificing art to politics. But if she is deemed politically correct by more conservative white critics, within the African American literary community, not to mention among African Americans generally, her politics are often considered heretical. (211)

The effect of this novel is evident from the controversy that surrounded it at the time of its publication and in its immense and ongoing public appeal, echoed in the film and stage-play/musical adaptations. Criticism of *The Color Purple* was leveled at Alice Walker in three ways. First, Walker was criticized by the African American community for her portrayal of violent black male characters in the story. Depiction of black males by authors in the 1980s were seen as too frequently negative, reaffirming negative stereotypes that served to further alienate an already marginalized community. Walker's depiction of the novel's characters, Celie's stepfather, Pa, and husband, Mr . . ., and their brutal behaviors toward Celie were viewed by many as falling into this negative stereotype. Walker, however, has offered articulate defense of her novel and the politics that undergirds her representations in a variety of interviews and published commentaries.

The male protagonists in *The Color Purple* reveal a dynamic common to people who are oppressed and powerless, one in which the abuse that is leveled at them is often transferred to others perceived weaker than themselves. Further, Walker's characters are shown to transform across the course of the novel, evidenced by Celie's husband becoming a partner and companion, helping her with her tailoring business, and showing her some kindness in the final chapters of the work.

Second, Walker was criticized for her graphic depiction of a sexual relationship between black women (Celie and Shug), lesbian sexuality not being commonly represented in literature in the 1980s. Shug realizes that Celie is "virgin," in that she has never awakened to her sexuality, in spite of previous sexual relationships with her "Pa" and husband and having given birth to two children. Celie describes her relationship with Mr . . . as he beats her, demonstrating her disassociation from the brutality.

For Celie, the sexual act has been traumatic in the past, something she distances herself from psychologically in order to survive. Shug, however, teaches Celie that there is pleasure in the realization of her physical self, that acceptance of her sexuality can provide self-respect, fulfilment, and freedom. Further, Shug protects Celie by persuading Mr . . . to stop the beatings. This intervention allows Celie to move beyond the fragmentation of her inner self to a state in which she perceives herself as whole and of value. It is through Celie's relationships with the strong women of her tiny community that she is able to move beyond her "victim" status toward recovery of a unified sense of self.

Finally, Walker was criticized on racial grounds for her choice of film director, Steven Spielberg, to make the film version of the book. Black activists perceived him as an inappropriate choice of director for a film about an oppressed black woman (partly because Spielberg had stated that his favorite film was *Gone With The Wind,* an epic white-centered historical film on the South that continues to draw angry responses from the African American community). Although the film version of *The Color Purple* received 11 Academy Award nominations, it won no awards. Spielberg himself was not nominated for a Best Director award, with conspiracy accusations surrounding this omission. Spielberg's treatment of *The Color Purple* is seen by many to reduce the significance of the novel's complex social, racial and gendered positionings, and character interactions into universalizing stereotypes:

> The film version of *The Color Purple* . . . is informed by the phallocentrism, racism and regionalism inherent in most Hollywood productions. As de Lauretis argues, Hollywood functions as a technology system that reproduces the dominant ideology. Hollywood technologizes gender and, by extension, race and region as well. The emphasis on masculinist readings did not escape the making of *The Color Purple,* in which three out of the four producers were men, two of them white. Virtually all the important aspects of making the film were assigned to men. (Tate 155)

The Color Purple is set in the southern states of America during the first half of the twentieth century and follows the story of 14-year-old Celie who has been raped and impregnated by Pa, the man she believes to be her father. Her two children by Pa are taken from their mother and "given to God." Celie, abused, subjugated, and believing her children dead, is married off to a widower with four children, who further mistreats her. Celie is withdrawn and traumatized, with no sense of self-worth. It is through her relationships with three strong female characters, her husband's lover, Shug, her daughter-in-law, Sophie, and her sister, Nettie, that Celie begins to heal her fragmented self, is able to forgive those who have caused her harm, and is able to realize her potential as a woman capable of love and growth.

This novel is woman-centered, with a female author and central female protagonists. The theme of motherhood is an integral part of the work: not represented in a romanticized or idealized version of motherhood, but demonstrating the complexities associated with parenting within the framework of slavery and subjugation of women. Walker's characters are shown to nurture their own or other's children, depending on their circumstances. Celie rears the children of her widowed husband; Nettie mothers Celie's children; when Sophie is denied access to her children during imprisonment and servitude, they are mothered in her absence by her sisters; and Shug's children are reared by her parents.

Alice Walker utilized the term "**womanism**" to describe her perception of the ways in which women of color interact and form community within the constraints of oppression and racism. This term has been taken up by others and is demonstrated in her treatment of the female community within the novel:

> The women of *The Color Purple* contribute to Walker's textual encoding of her actual maternal relationships to produce a "womanist" prose fiction . . . to inscribe a place for women of color within a feminist culture that she finds overwhelmingly white and middle-class . . . For Walker, a "womanist" is synonymous with "responsible" and "serious" and indicates a variety of precocious behaviours: "outrageous, audacious, courageous or wilful." (Montelaro 12)

Celie's transformation from the oppressed victim of racism and domestic violence into a strong resilient woman of character and potential is beautifully realized in Walker's contentious, yet extremely popular text, providing a narrative that is harsh, but ultimately uplifting, illustrating the triumph of the human spirit through extreme adversity.

See also Lesbian Literature, African American; Novel, Lesbian

Further Reading

Bloom, Harold, ed. *Modern Critical Interpretations of Alice Walker's 'The Color Purple.'* Philadelphia: Chelsea House Publishers, 2000.

Hall, Donald. *Queer Theories.* New York: Palgrave, 2003.

Montelaro, Janet J. *Producing a Womanist Text: The Maternal as Signifier in Alice Walker's The Color Purple.* Victoria, BC, Canada: University of Victoria Press, 1996.

Tate, Linda. *A Southern Weave of Women: Fiction of the Contemporary South.* Athens: The University of Georgia Press, 1994.

Wall, Cheryl A. *Black Women Writers, Lineage, and Literary Tradition.* Chapel Hill: University of North Carolina Press, 2005.

Brenda Glover

Coming Out Narratives, Gay Male

Traditionally, the term "coming out" (short for "coming out of the **closet**") has meant the voluntary public announcement of one's true sexual orientation or **gender** identity. The experience of "coming out," as well as personal feelings toward one's sexual orientation, has varied widely among individuals based on the time period, society, and culture in which they lived. People of different age groups, ethnicities, and religions also undergo unique coming out experiences. Using fiction, nonfiction, drama, or film as their medium, many **gay** people want to share their coming out experiences with other people who may be afraid to go through that process. They will also share their personal coming out experience with straight audiences in order to educate them about homosexuality. In young adult fiction, coming out narratives are written by straight and gay authors, with different motives. Gay male coming out narratives, the focus of this entry, are best described as a body of literature that shares the common subject of a gay male adolescent or adult telling his personal story of coming to terms with living as a gay person.

Some literary scholars might view the coming out narrative as a form of *Bildungsroman,* or "novel of self-cultivation." A *Bildungsroman* can focus on the spiritual, moral, psychological, or social development and growth of the protagonist from childhood to maturity, or from adolescence to adulthood. The genre of *Bildungsroman* developed in the late eighteenth century, with the onset of the Industrial Revolution. For the first time in history, the majority of young men and women were leaving the safety of their homes and families to gain an education or learn a trade in the big cities. They encountered many dangers along the way and learned hard lessons on their roads to success. Writers of the *Bildungsroman* wanted to provide models of adolescents who overcame common adversities (poverty, illiteracy, and fear) to achieve a higher status in life, or a new level of self-fulfillment, in order to give hope to young audiences as well as to educate them about the challenges that they would face on their roads to adulthood. Today, the *Bildungsroman* is often called the "coming-of-age" story, and it remains an extremely popular genre of fiction in a world where more and more adolescents learn how to become healthy, productive adults from role models outside the home. This is especially so for gay male adolescents, who often learn about their sexual orientation from sources outside of the home. More conservative literary scholars consider coming out narratives as confessional stories, perpetuated by an American culture that loves the sensational while encouraging people to talk about their feelings in order to resolve their personal issues.

Prior to the late nineteenth century, gay men did not exist in literature except for government documents, church decrees, police records, and travelers' journals recording the behavior of tribal cultures. Men who had intercourse with other men were called *sodomites* or *pederasts* and were considered criminals based on religious and civil laws. The Industrial Revolution, which led to the rise of cities and a chance for anonymity, allowed men who loved men to find covert meeting places and form social networks. In 1869, Hungarian writer Karl-Maria Kertbeny coined the term *homosexual* as a neutral term to identify such men. Although Kertbeny did not identify himself as a homosexual, he worked tirelessly to decriminalize homosexuality after his best friend, a homosexual, was driven to suicide by an extortionist. In 1886, the Austrian psychiatrist Richard Freiherr von Krafft-Ebing interviewed many homosexuals, renamed their behavior *homosexuality,* and declared that they were neither criminals nor mentally ill. Kertbeny and von Krafft-Ebing's work allowed men who loved men to give a name to themselves, discard their shame, and begin their long struggle for visibility and human rights.

Over time, the term "homosexual" fell out of favor in the English-speaking world. In England, people associated the term with criminal activity, while in the United States it was associated with mental illness in psychiatry textbooks written by heterosexual males. Some literary scholars believe that American lesbian poet Gertrude Stein was the first to identify a nonheterosexual relationship as "gay" in a poem published in 1922. By the mid-twentieth century, the term "homosexual" had been replaced by "gay" in popular films and songs, although the exact date and source of a man's first self-identification as gay remains unknown. Nineteenth-century American poet Walt Whitman praised the male body and romantic friendships between men in "Song of Myself" (1855) and often spoke in favor of homosexuality for the promotion of democracy, but never "came out" as a homosexual in his writing. Perhaps twentieth-century African American author **James Baldwin** was the boldest of classic American writers; Baldwin's first novel, *Go Tell It On the Mountain* (1953) is autobiographical, recounting his own adolescent homosexual awakening. It is possible that the phrase "to 'out' someone" comes from Baldwin's short story "Outing" (1951) where Baldwin reveals one boy's increasing sexual feelings for another during a church picnic.

In the beginning, gay male coming out narratives were an oral tradition. American gay men did not officially come out until the sweeping civil rights movements of the 1960s and 1970s. The term "coming out" was coined by the Gay Liberation Front (GLF) during the late 1960s, when GLF activists would visit gay bars and shout at patrons to "come out of the closet." Later GLF activists regretted this consciousness-raising tactic and stated that people had to come out in their own time, on their own free will. With the support of gay activist groups and psychologists, Rob Eichberg, co-founder of the Experience group, developed a national workshop devoted to the coming out process, where he encouraged "straight acting" homosexuals to come out, as well as straight people who know a gay person. The first coming out stories led to parents telling stories about gay children, children telling stories about their gay parents, and gay men returning to their high schools and churches to tell about themselves. In fact, Eichberg declared October 11, 1988, as the first National Coming Out Day, honoring those who participated in gay rights marches and Pride Parades, as well as those who had died of AIDS.

Coming out stories help gay men discover their self-worth and confirm that they are not alone. Classic examples of gay male coming out narratives are depicted in two important films, *The Boys in the Band* (1970) and *Torch Song Trilogy* (1988). The traditional gay male coming out narrative begins in childhood and follows a linear, chronological progression. The narrator often describes his childhood as "unhappy" and that, as a child, he felt "different" from his peers. When looking back at his early adolescence, the narrator often remembers a great fear of the discovery of being gay, or a great fear of "becoming" gay, as well as his attempts—if any—to "act straight." At the same time, the narrator may recall his adolescence as the time when he searched for others like himself. He might have gone to the library to read about others like himself for a start, or he might have discovered a classmate or someone in his neighborhood who was gay. In extreme situations, the narrator might have experienced complete rejection from his family, eviction from home, and discovery of others like himself on the street. If the narrator has a positive experience meeting others like himself, and if he finds love, companionship, and common ground with those others, the narrator will affirm his gay identity.

Gay male coming out narratives did not exist in young adult fiction until the publication of John Donovan's *I'll Get There. It Better Be Worth the Trip* (1969). In this groundbreaking novel, narrator 13-year-old Davy Ross discovers that he is gay when he meets Douglas Altschuler, a boy at his new school who becomes his best friend. Davy and Douglas become quite intimate, and one day Davy's mother finds both of them on Davy's bedroom floor together. She becomes hysterical and gets Davy's father to deal with the situation. Unlike many fathers, Davy's father handles the situation calmly and rationally, stating that many people get upset when faced with people who are different from them. He also says that it is normal for boys to go through a phase where they "play around." At the same time, Davy's father does not tell Davy that it is fine to be gay; in fact, he says that "he shouldn't get too involved in some special way of life which will close off other ways of life." After this admonition, Davy and Douglas discuss their experience. Davy decides to follow his father's advice, while Douglas feels no remorse for what he has done and pushes Davy away. The original edition of the book included a blurb from the Gesell Institute of Child Development on the jacket flap, echoing Davy's father's stance on homosexuality. Considering that homosexuality was officially considered a mental illness in the United States until 1973, for its time Donovan's novel presents a progressive view of homosexual awakening. Unfortunately, it began a tradition of young adult novels where gay characters suffered because of their identity or decided to go back into the closet. Even in classic young adult novels written by gay male authors, such as Aidan Chambers's *Dance on My Grave* (1982) and Frank Mosca's *All-American Boys* (1983), the positive gay male protagonists end up dying in car accidents or in a hospital bed after a gay-bashing incident.

During the 1990s, more people in the United States came out of the closet than ever before. Music Television's *The Real World,* a pioneering reality show, portrayed real gay young adults such as Norman Korpi and Pedro Zamora coming out to their roommates on television. Teenagers could witness the drama unfold, then discuss their own feelings about sexual orientation with their peers or family members. In spite of the increase in positive gay role models, reports published by teachers' organizations and antihate crime organizations showed that **homophobia** still existed in public schools and that many gay or questioning youth were driven to drop out of school or attempt suicide due to bullying at school, lack of support from family or peers, and feelings of isolation.

For many gay people, the discovery of a "coming out story" in a public library is a defining moment of their lives; the story shows that they are not alone and that others have survived their adolescence. For this reason, gay men from all different backgrounds are choosing to publish their own unique coming out stories. Patrick Merla collected the coming out stories of 29 gay writers including **Samuel R. Delany**, **Edmund White**, and **Alexander Chee** in *Boys Like Us: Gay Writers Tell Their Coming Out Stories* (1996). Celebrities such as football player Roy Simmons, club diva RuPaul, and journalist/performer Kirk Read have published full-length autobiographies that describe their coming out experiences. Coming out narratives written by ordinary people who do not fit the **stereotype** of the gay male (construction workers, athletes, stockbrokers, and health care professionals, to name a few) also appear in nonfiction books for gay adolescents and adults on how to come out to themselves and others.

Further Reading

Berzon, Betty. "Developing a Positive Gay and Lesbian Identity." In *Positively Gay: New Approaches to Gay and Lesbian Life,* edited by Betty Berzon, 18–31. Berkeley, CA: Celestial Arts, 2001.

DeCrescenzo, Teresa, and Lombardi, Emilia. "The Brave New World of Gay and Lesbian Youth." In *Positively Gay: New Approaches to Gay and Lesbian Life,* edited by Betty Berzon, 360–77. Berkeley, CA: Celestial Arts, 2001.

Fuoss, Kirk. "A Portrait of the Adolescent as a Young Gay: The Politics of Male Homosexuality in Young Adult Fiction." In *Queer Words, Queer Images: Communication and the Construction of Homosexuality,* edited by R. Jeffrey Ringer, 159–74. New York: New York University Press, 1994.

Plummer, Christopher. *Telling Sexual Stories: Power, Change, and Social Worlds.* New York: Routledge, 1995.

Pullen, Christopher. *Documenting Gay Men: Identity and Performance in Reality Television and Documentary Film.* Jefferson, NC: McFarland & Company, Inc., 2006.

Rachel Wexelbaum

Coming Out Narratives, Lesbian

While women have lived openly as lesbians in the United States throughout the twentieth century, it was not until the 1970s that a combination of the **gay** liberation and lesbian feminist movements empowered lesbians to come out of the **closet** in large numbers and write their coming out stories. Lesbian coming out narratives traverse all literary forms, including short stories, autobiography, poetry, manifesto, comics, and graphic novels. They are coming-of-age stories in which the protagonist matures emotionally and sexually by going through a life-altering transition. The lesbian coming out narratives of today have a heritage in the 1960s and 1970s consciousness-raising practice of the second-wave of the women's movement. Consciousness-raising groups emphasized that a woman's personal experiences were inherently political, and lesbian coming out narratives of the time told of becoming conscious of a lesbian sexuality.

Lesbian coming out narratives play several important functions in lesbian lives, including building lesbian community, supporting women who are questioning their sexuality or coming out as lesbian, and empowering lesbians emotionally and politically. Because they document a shared experience for lesbians (as well as gay men), coming out narratives bind together the lesbian and gay communities. Some suggest that coming out narratives function like a founding myth, or origin story, for the lesbian and gay community. Coming out can be a difficult and painful, but also a liberatory and joyful, process. For most lesbians, coming out of the closet is an ongoing process involving not just family and friends, but bosses and co-workers, landlords, and other acquaintances. Lesbians who live outside of large urban centers may have difficulty finding a lesbian community for support, and coming out literature can offer this support. Coming out not only empowers the lesbian who is coming out by refusing to be ashamed or pathologized, but is also a political act that empowers the lesbian and gay community by making gays and lesbians visible in all areas of society.

The Politics of Coming Out. Historically, lesbian and gay activist groups, including the Gay Liberation Front, and **Queer** Nation have argued that coming out of the closet would lead to radical social change. They believed that coming out in large numbers would increase the visibility of lesbians and gay men in all walks of life, thereby challenging heterosexual privilege and ultimately leading to widespread acceptance by mainstream society. Similarly, lesbian feminists have argued that because lesbians challenge patriarchal definitions of family, marriage, and reproduction, lesbian personal narratives, including coming out narratives, are inherently political. In addition, many in the gay and lesbian movement argue that taking on gay and lesbian identities enables members to take hold of the power to name themselves and thereby redefine the negative stereotypes associated with those names. The lesbian and gay political movements share the hope that coming out as lesbian or gay could lead to equality and liberation.

Characteristics of Lesbian Coming Out Narratives. Lesbian coming out narratives share a number of characteristics. A common theme is that of a "journey" on a path of individual and sometimes collective growth. The narrative often begins with the narrator feeling "different" emotionally and sexually, which can be accompanied by a sense of alienation from family and friends. The narrative recounts the development of romantic feelings for other women or girls, which eventually leads to a first lesbian experience. The details of the story including setting, events, and characters vary widely, reflecting the diversity of lesbian coming out experiences. The coming out narratives by nonwhite lesbians often examine the difficulties of managing multiple communities and ethnic, cultural, religious, and racial identifications. The stereotype of lesbianism as a white phenomenon sometimes complicates these women's coming-out processes as does the prejudice or exclusion they often describe experiencing in lesbian communities.

The narrator eventually comes to recognize herself in the name "lesbian," a name that does not have the same meaning to all women. The process of this identification can involve a difficult struggle with internalized **homophobia**, which can sometimes lead to a phase of self-destructive behavior. The storyteller goes through a range of emotions, including shame, guilt, and fear, but usually the journey ends with feelings of freedom, pride, and empowerment. Some women decide not to come out to family members out of respect or for fear of rejection. For lesbians who do come out to family and friends, reactions range from painful rejection to tolerance to loving acceptance.

Criticism of Coming Out Narratives. Coming out narratives have received criticism on a few different levels. Some critics argue that the narrative structure of a journey to self-discovery imposes a false happy ending in the form of coming out to oneself and others. These critics argue that for most lesbians, coming out of the closet does not happen just once, but is an ongoing process over the course of their lives. Some also argue that coming out narratives ghettoize gay and lesbian literature by reducing the lives of lesbians and gay men to their sexual identity. These critics argue that it would be politically advantageous for lesbians and gay men to write about all the complex facets of their lives in such a way that will be compelling to mainstream as well as gay and lesbian audiences.

Other critics suggest that the narrative of self-discovery assumes that one's lesbian identity is an essential, but repressed part of the self that must be discovered. Critics argue that this aspect of coming out narratives reinforces the idea that a person's homosexuality defines the essential truth of his character. This "essentialism" is considered politically suspect by those who argue that a lesbian identity is a social construction that exists only in relationship to cultural and political definitions, as well as other facets of one's identity such as race, class, **gender**, or religion. They suggest that personal narratives are necessarily a reconstruction of past events. Looking back through the lens of either the dominant culture's definition of **lesbianism** or through a lesbian feminist political standpoint can change how one feels about and describes the experience of coming out.

The Anthologies. The 1980s saw the publication of a diversity of anthologies of lesbian coming out stories. These collections have been widely read and republished multiple times. Margaret Cruikshank's *The Lesbian Path* (1980) and Julia Penelope Stanley and Susan J. Wolfe's *The Coming Out Stories* (1980) contain the coming out narratives of some well-known and lesser-known women. *Nice Jewish Girls: A Lesbian Anthology* (1982) edited by Evelyn Torton Beck gives voice to the experience of coming out as lesbian and Jewish. *This Bridge Called My Back* (1983), edited by **Cherríe Moraga** and **Gloria Evangelina Anzaldúa**, is a collection of personal and political narratives by both lesbian and heterosexual women of color. Other notable publications include *Salir a la luz como lesbianas de color/Coming out colored* edited by Maya Chumu (1980) and *Testimonies: A Collection of Lesbian Coming Out Stories* (1988) edited by Sarah Holmes and Karen Barber.

Since the publication of these first anthologies, countless anthologies of lesbian and gay coming out narratives have been produced. These collections are often grouped according to the other intersecting identities of the contributors, including *Does Your Mama Know?: An Anthology of Black Lesbian Coming Out Stories* (1997) edited by Lisa C. Moore, *Chicana Lesbians: The Girls Our Mothers Warned Us About* (1991) edited by **Carla Trujillo**, and *Twice Blessed: On Being Lesbian or Gay and Jewish* (1991) edited by Christie Balka and Andy Rose. *A Lotus of Another Color: An Unfolding of the South Asian Gay and Lesbian Experience* (1993), edited by Rakesh Ratti, contains coming out narratives alongside essays, poetry, and fiction by South Asian gay men and lesbians living around the world. *Coming Out: An Anthology of International Gay and Lesbian Writings,* edited by Stephan Likosky, brings a collection of coming out stories from lesbians and gay men from around the world to an American audience. *Coming Out Young and Faithful* (2001), edited by Leanne McCall Tigert and Timothy Brown, is a collection of the coming out stories of Christian youth.

Lesbian Epiphanies: Women Coming Out in Later Life (1999) by Karol L. Jensen is a compilation of interviews with women who have come out as lesbians later in life. *Lesbian Motherhood: Stories of Becoming* (2007) by Amy Hequembourg presents the coming out narratives of lesbian mothers. *Liberating Minds: The Stories and Professional Lives of Gay, Lesbian, and Bisexual Librarians and Their Advocates* (1997), edited by Norman G. Kester, is a collection of coming out stories by librarians. *Lesbian Nuns: Breaking Silence* (1985), edited by Rosemary Curb and Nancy Manahan, tells the coming stories of lesbian nuns. *A Woman Like That: Lesbian and Bisexual Writers Tell Their Coming Out Stories* (1999), edited by Joan Larkin, is another collection of the coming out stories of women authors. *Early Embraces,* edited by Lindsey Elder, is a popular erotic anthology series in which contributors share their first lesbian sexual encounters.

The coming out stories of lesbian and gay youth are a common theme for anthologies. *Being Different: Lambda Youths Speak Out,* edited by Larry Dane Brimner (1996), contains personal narratives of young lesbians and gay men on coming out, sexual identity, and being gay in high school. *One Teenager in Ten: Testimony by Gay and Lesbian Youth* (1984) and the updated *Two Teenagers in Twenty: Writings by Gay and Lesbian Youth* (1993), both edited by Ann Heron, include personal narratives of gay and lesbian teenagers. In *Like Coming Home: Coming-Out Letters* (1988), editor Meg Umans presents a collection of letters between gay and lesbian children and their parents. And *Coming Out in College: The Struggle for a Queer Identity* (1994) by Robert A. Rhoads presents the coming out stories of college-age youth.

Nonfiction, Autobiography, and Memoir. Many authors have written their coming out stories into semiautobiographical coming-of-age novels. These include **Rita Mae Brown**'s ***Rubyfruit Jungle*** (1973), **Audre Lorde**'s ***Zami: A New Spelling of My Name*** (1983), **Elana Dykewomon**'s *Riverfinger Women* (1974), and British author Jeanette Winterson's *Oranges Are Not the Only Fruit* (1985). More recently some prominent lesbian authors have been writing their memoirs, which include their stories of coming out. These include *Naked in the Promised Land: A Memoir* (2003) by Lillian Faderman and *The Chelsea Whistle: A Memoir* (2002) by Michelle Tea. Most recently, **Alison Bechdel**, the creator of "Dykes to Watch Out For," published her memoir in the form of the highly acclaimed graphic novel *Fun Home: A Family Tragicomic* (2007).

In addition, many lesbian celebrities have co-written their coming out autobiographies. In 1986 Martina Navratilova co-authored her autobiography *Martina.* Patty Sheehan, the first out lesbian professional golfer co-wrote her autobiography, *Patty Sheehan on Golf,* in 1996. *Family Outing* (1998) by Chastity Bono (with Billie Fitzpatrick) weaves Bono's story of coming out to her famous parents together with the coming out narratives of other gay and lesbian youth. In *Love, Ellen: A Mother/Daughter Journey* (1999) Betty DeGeneres tells her famous daughter's coming out story and how she came to accept her daughter's lesbianism. In 2002, Melissa Etheridge co-authored her autobiography *The Truth Is . . .: My Life in Love and Music.*

Further Reading

Martin, Biddy. "Lesbian Identity and Autobiographical Differences." In *Life/Lines: Theorizing Women's Autobiography,* edited by Bella Brodziak and Celeste Schenck, 77–103. Ithaca, NY: Cornell University Press, 1988.

McRuer, Robert. *The Queer Renaissance: Contemporary American Literature and the Reinvention of Lesbian and Gay Identities.* New York: New York University Press, 1997.

Morris, Jessica F., Amy J. Ojerholm, Teri M. Brooks, Dana M. Osowiecki, and Esther D. Rothblum. "Finding a 'Word for Myself': Themes in Lesbian Coming-Out Stories." In *Dyke Life:*

A Celebration of the Lesbian Experience, edited by Karla Jay, 36–49. New York: Basic Books, 1995.

Salvatore, Diane. "What's So Bad About Being In Love? In Defense of the Coming-Out Novel." *Lambda Book Report* 4, no. 1 (November 1993): 6.

Torres, Lourdes, and Inmaculada Pertusa, eds. *Tortilleras: Hispanic and U.S. Latina Lesbian Expression.* Philadelphia: Temple University Press, 2003.

Zimmerman, Bonnie. "The Politics of Transliteration: Lesbian Personal Narratives." *Signs* 9, no. 4 (Summer 1984): 663–82.

Kristine Klement

Cooper, Bernard (b. 1951)

Contemporary American **gay** essayist and novelist. The youngest of four sons to second-generation Jewish parents, Edward Cooper and Lillian Harrison, Bernard Cooper was born in Hollywood, California, in 1951. Cooper's father, a successful divorce attorney, grew up in Chicago; his mother was born in Russia and immigrated to the United States at the age of two. His parents met at a party in Chicago and were married soon thereafter. Cooper's childhood in a middle-class neighborhood in Hollywood, California, was a happy one with his very lively and sometimes chaotic family. His father was particularly known for coming up with crazy schemes just for the fun of it, such as the time his father brought home a dog house to make a home movie of everyone moving into it. One painful memory in Cooper's life that has influenced much of his work is the death of his brother to leukemia while Cooper was a teenager. It was also during this time that Cooper began struggling with his own sexual identity, and he turned to architecture for solace. He attended the California Institute of the Arts and received a Master of Fine Arts in 1979. After graduation, however, he abandoned the visual arts and while supporting himself as a shoe salesman began to write. His primary subjects include growing up gay and middle class in the 1950s and 1960s, family relationships, sexuality, memory, loss, and AIDS. Cooper's works often blur generic boundaries: they blend fiction with autobiography, formal essay with personal revelation. In a 1997 interview with Richard Canning, Cooper offers this explanation for his writing style:

> I came out of an educational environment where iron-clad distinctions between genres weren't that important. I'd always used language in my own conceptual art, and I'd always been a reader —particularly of poetry. When I started thinking of writing as the most interesting avenue for me, a lot of my reading involved blurred boundaries too. (33)

Cooper has won numerous awards and prizes that include the 1991 PEN/Ernest Hemingway Award for his memoir, *Maps to Anywhere* (1990), the 1995 O. Henry Prize for *A Year of Rhymes* (1993), and fellowships from the Guggenheim Foundation and The National Endowment of the Arts. Cooper's most recent book, *The Bill from My Father: A Memoir* (2006) is being made into a Warner Bros. film by director Dean Parisot. His essays have been anthologized in *The Best American Essays* in 1988, 1995, and 1997 and have appeared in the *Oxford Book of Literature on Aging* as well as in *Harper's Magazine, Gentlemen's Quarterly* and *The Paris Review*. He has taught at the University of California at Los Angeles Writers' Program and the Creative Writing Program at Antioch University and currently resides in Los Angeles and is the art critic for *Los Angeles Magazine*.

Cooper's first book, *Maps to Anywhere,* features a collection of essays that capture snippets of everyday life from his father, architecture, and photography and freezes them in time. A conceptually unique text, it weaves autobiographical snippets, prose poems, brief humorous commentaries, as well as finely honed short essays into a dazzling collage. In 1993 Cooper published his first novel, *A Year of Rhymes,* a gripping narrative that tells the autobiographical story of a teenager in 1960s Los Angeles confronting his sexual identity while coping with the slow death of his brother from leukemia. The poignant text portrays the depth and honesty of the narrator's emotions while he is moving toward adulthood and learns to bear the sorrow of watching a sibling die. Cooper handles the delicate subjects of death and sexual identity with great care and sensitivity. *Truth Serum,* published in 1996, is another memoir of growing up gay in Los Angeles and showcases Cooper at his best. The book focuses on a concoction of sodium pentothal and amphetamine administered to Cooper by his therapist to reduce his attraction to men. Ultimately, Cooper is empowered by the same concoction to accept his homosexuality, leave his girlfriend, and expose the often graphic portrait of gay life among young professionals in Los Angeles. Cooper's fourth book, *Guess Again* (2000), features 11 expertly crafted stories, most of which were previously published in prestigious literary journals. Although many of the central characters are gay, his central themes are universal such as love, loss, aging parents, and many other rites of passages. Cooper's latest release, *The Bill from My Father: A Memoir,* was published in 2006 and had been suggested by an editor in New York City after she had read an essay by Cooper in a literary review. The book serves as an elegy to his father, who died in 2000, and chronicles their roller-coaster relationship over the years. The book's title refers to the real itemized bill of expenses Cooper received from his father concerning the cost of his upbringing.

Further Reading

Canning, Richard. *Hear Us Out [Conversations with Gay Novelists].* New York: Columbia University Press, 2003. 31–57.

Donna Dvoracek

Cooper, Dennis (b. 1953)

Extremist American novelist, poet, and playwright. Born to a wealthy Pasadena businessman, Dennis Cooper endured, by his own account, a troubled adolescence in which poetry and drug use provided succor and escape. After attending Pasadena City College and Pitzer College, Cooper founded the literary magazine *Little Caesar* in 1976, followed by Little Caesar Press in 1978, before going on to serve as director of programming for the arts center Beyond Baroque in Venice Beach, California. During this period, Cooper published several books of poems, including *Tiger Beat* (1978), *Idols* (1979), and *Tenderness of the Wolves* (1981). Though he considers poetry his apprentice work, Cooper's background as a poet clearly influenced the lyric, careful prose of his later novels. Airtight sentences, full of stylistic quirk but little excess, contain and make palatable the novels' sexual extremes and ethical malevolences.

Cooper moved to New York City in 1983, but it was not until 1985, on moving to Amsterdam, that Cooper was able to begin his first novel, *Closer* (1989). The novel was written as a paean to George Miles, a romantic fixation from Cooper's adolescence who figures as the central object of desire in *Closer*. Though *Closer* is the only novel in which Miles himself appears, his identity is refracted in the various characters of the five novels comprising Cooper's "George Miles Cycle": *Closer* (1991), *Frisk* (1991), *Try* (1994), *Guide* (1997), and *Period* (2000).

Cooper's novels of this period capture the self-destructive boredom and anomie of suburban adolescence. But the most salient feature of Cooper's novels is their frankness about sex, and the interrelation, in Cooper's imagination, of eros and thanatos, sex and death. In Cooper's novels, desire travels from age to innocence: the youths are often listless, disaffected, and motivated by a death wish—a drive that matches well the older man's desire to wreak havoc on a lithe and unspoiled body. Worship of doomed youth is a classic gay theme to which Cooper adds dark shadings, showing us how eroticism is itself often a source of ruin: our desires disfigure us.

Frisk, Cooper's second novel, is a horror fantasia whose murderous endgame is mostly staged in an Amsterdam ersatz windmill, where the line between reality and fantasy is smudged. Cooper's next outing, *Try* is by contrast a tender, almost romantic novel. *Try's* young protagonist, Ziggy, helps a friend through his heroin addiction while sorting through conflicted feelings for his two adoptive fathers, both sexually abusive. In *Try,* Cooper blurs the line between love and friendship, between love and abuse.

Guide, Cooper's fourth novel, is the most structurally ambitious of his works and also the most successful in marrying the cultural mores of late 1990s fan culture to Cooper's own erotic preoccupations. Cooper's canvas is large: in the novel a lesbian director runs a kiddie porn ring, a porn star acts out his suicidal impulses, the bassist from a popular rock-and-roll-band is drugged and molested, and a writer named Dennis breaks his journalistic objectivity by sleeping with an HIV-positive street hustler he is writing an article about. *Period,* Cooper's last novel in the George Miles cycle, is the most inscrutable and abstract of his works—a personal coda to the George Miles cycle.

Cooper's interest in youth culture allies him with Gus Van Sant; just as Van Sant's *Elephant* addresses the Columbine massacre, so does Cooper's next novel, *My Loose Thread* (2002), extrapolate from the Colorado school shootings. In *The Sluts* (2005), winner of the Lambda Literary Award, Cooper applies his usual sexual preoccupations—analerotic fixations and violence toward dissolute youth—to the virulent world of online sex. *The Sluts* is at once a thriller and an epistolary novel with unreliable, mutating narrators, with the fluidity of cyber-identity lending itself to deception and fiction making. *God Jr.* (2005) was Cooper's first novel set outside of a gay demimonde and seems to have garnered Cooper a new and diverse readership.

Cooper has recently taken a hiatus from writing novels, editing a series of books for Akashic Books and collaborating with Parisian director Gisele Vienne on a series of plays. Cooper is currently directing much of his creative energies toward his blog (http://denniscooper-theweaklings.blogspot.com/), a collaboration between Cooper and his fervently devoted, often adolescent readership.

Further Reading

Lev, Leora, ed. *Enter at Your Own Risk: The Dangerous Art of Dennis Cooper.* Madison, NJ: Fairleigh Dickinson University Press, 2006.

Stosuy, Brandon, ed. *Up Is Up, But So Is Down: New York's Downtown Literary Scene, 1974–1992.* New York: New York University Press, 2006.

Christopher Schmidt

Corn, Alfred (b. 1943)

Contemporary **gay** American poet. A master of poetic technique, much of Alfred Corn's work has an autobiographical component, dealing frankly with such issues as his marriage, divorce, and his homosexuality. His work connects personal details with historical, artistic, and literary concerns, and with the question of what it means to be an American. His poems display a sharp wit, strong sense of irony, an urbane worldview, and a strong visionary quality. Some of Corn's best-known work pays homage to such poets from the past as Walt Whitman, Wallace Stevens, and Hart Crane. Despite receiving high critical praise, however, as of this writing, Corn has yet to be nominated for a major poetry award.

Alfred Corn was born in Bainbridge, Georgia, and raised mostly in Valdosta, Georgia. He developed a strong attraction to religion in his late teens and early 20s and for a time considered becoming a Methodist priest. Corn studied the French language and literature at Emory and then Columbia University, where he earned a B.A. and an M.A.

Corn's first book of poems, *All Roads at Once,* appeared in 1976. Written in both free and formal verse, the poems display the poet's interest in describing how the mind works and what it is like to be alive, often with elements of loneliness appearing at their center.

Corn's next three books, *A Call in the Midst of the Crowd* (1978), *The Various Light* (1980), and *Notes from a Child of Paradise* (1984), are a poetic trilogy, retracing in different terms the journey followed by Dante in his *The Divine Comedy. A Call in the Midst of the Crowd* is subtitled "Poem in Four Parts on New York City." Its 26 lyrical sections depicting a young man walking the streets of New York are interspersed with prose "found objects," excerpts from various sources documenting the history and development of the city to create a portrait of an artist's struggle to connect with the city and find personal connections there. *The Various Light* continues the theme of a poet commenting upon his environment, using varying poetic forms and styles. The poems play with language and transform everyday observations into deep philosophical mediations. Two long poems, one in the voice of a traveler on a train about to move in with his lover, the other Corn's childhood memory of living in the South, dissect how the mind sorts and selects in the midst of action, and how Corn understands the world through language. The book-length narrative poem *Notes from a Child of Paradise* completes the trilogy. Modeled on the structure of *The Divine Comedy,* and often alluding to Dante, *Notes* explores the intellectual life, counterculture, and antiwar movements of the 1960s while chronicling Corn's courtship and marriage to Ann Jones, the recognition of his own homosexuality, and the unraveling of their marriage. One section recounts the couple's trip across country by car from New York to Oregon paralleled with the Lewis and Clark Expedition, raising their journey to a mythic voyage of discovery.

Dealing with the anxiety of writing about the self and turning life's details into art, *The West Door* (1988) also showed Corn's interest in religious themes. Displaying the wide range of the author's reading, the volume includes Corn's translations of Eugenio Montale, Rainer Maria Rilke, Pablo Neruda, and Sappho, as well as poems in voices of others. Corn continued his exploration of the possibilities of voice and personal stories made into verse in *Autobiographies* (1992). Here the poems give attention to both ordinary individuals and collective struggle. The 20 sections of the long poem "1992" that ends the volume are each titled for a different year in the past; beginning with a scene from the poet's life, the sections end with scenes from the life of another person representing a cross section of America.

In *Present* (1997), Corn's most varied book in its use of different forms and wide range of subjects, from poems inspired by music, ballet, places the author has visited to homelessness, and an autobiographical memoir of childhood, he uses classical and European influences to describe the lessons learned from being gay. After *Stake: Selected Poems, 1972–1992* (1999), Corn published *Contradictions* (2002), a finalist for the Oklahoma Book Award. Dealing with travel, memory, art, sexuality, AIDS, and other concerns, the collection continued his frank, autobiographical exploration of gay male life.

Corn's only novel to date, *Part of His Story,* also appeared in 1997. Its narrator, a successful New York playwright, travels to London to write a biography of an eighteenth-century English writer and grieve after the death of his younger lover from AIDS. When not doing research, he helps his lover's mother in her grief, reflects on the English social and literary scene, and begins a relationship with a young working-class Irishman. Corn uses the narrator's reflections on his experiences, emotions, and the AIDS epidemic to focus readers on the question of how one should live in the face of inevitable mortality.

Alfred Corn has also published a book of critical essays, *The Metamorphoses of Metaphor* (1987), a highly regarded study of prosody, *The Poem's Heartbeat* (1997), and a work of art criticism, *Aaron Rose Photographs* (2001). He has also written for *The Nation, Art in America, ARTnews* magazine, and other publications. Corn's poetry has been widely anthologized, included in such collections as *The Norton Anthology of American Literature,* (1985) and *The Paris Review Anthology* (1990).

He has received fellowships and prizes from the Guggenheim Foundation, the National Endowment for the Arts, the Academy of American Poets, the American Academy and Institute of Arts and Letters, the Rockefeller Foundation Bellagio Study and Conference Center at Bellagio, Italy, and *Poetry* magazine, among other honors. He has taught at numerous colleges and universities including the City University of New York, Yale University, Columbia University, the Ohio State University, and the Poetry School in London.

Further Reading

Hennessy, Christopher. *Outside the Lines: Talking with Contemporary Gay Poets.* Ann Arbor: University of Michigan Press, 2005. 40–56.

Martin, Robert K. *The Homosexual Tradition in American Poetry* Iowa City: University of Iowa Press, 1988. 208–17.

Smith, Ernest J. "Alfred Corn." In *Contemporary Gay American Poets and Playwrights: An A-to-Z Guide,* edited by Emmanuel S. Nelson, 87–91. Westport, CT: Greenwood Press, 2003.

———. "Alfred Corn." In *Dictionary of Literary Biography,* Vol. 282, edited by Jonathan N. Barron and Bruce Meyer, 41–49. Detroit MI: Thompson-Gale, 2003.

Reginald Harris

Cornwell, Patricia (b. 1956)

Novelist and nonfiction writer. A remarkably prolific and popular author, Patricia Cornwell is a pioneer in the genre of forensic science mysteries and the author of the best-selling series of novels featuring medical examiner Kay Scarpetta, as well as numerous other works of fiction and nonfiction for children and adults. By creating the uncompromisingly tough, fiercely independent, and unblushingly brilliant character of Scarpetta, Cornwell helped to create a new trend of strong and dynamic heroines in mystery fiction by demonstrating that a complex, difficult, and at times arrogant female protagonist could find favor with the American reading public. Cornwell's novels also played a significant role in sparking the creation of popular television shows such as *Crime Scene Investigation* (*CSI*), which focus on the work done by medical examiners. In addition to being a consistent favorite with the public, both nationally and internationally, Cornwell's work has also received significant critical acclaim. Among the many awards that she has won for her literary work are the Edgar Award, the Gold Dagger Award, and the Sherlock Award. Consistently spinning compelling narratives featuring fiendishly inventive villains, coolly competent heroines, and painstakingly (and, at times, gruesomely) detailed descriptions of medical examiners' work, Cornwell's novels are deeply grounded in the meticulous research that she conducts for her books and her own extensive knowledge about life in the fields of criminal investigation and forensic science.

Cornwell was born as Patricia Daniels in Miami, Florida, in 1956, and was raised largely in North Carolina. Cornwell's childhood was often a difficult one, as Cornwell had a troubled relationship with her father (he abandoned the Cornwell family in 1961), her mother suffered from (and was hospitalized for) severe depression, and she spent part of her life in the foster care system, frequently clashing with her foster mother. During her teenage years, Cornwell began to suffer from depression, as well as from anorexia. A key factor in Cornwell's recovery was the emotional support and encouragement that she received from Ruth Bell Graham, wife of evangelist Billy Graham, who encouraged the young Cornwell to pursue her interest in a career in writing. Cornwell subsequently published a biography of Graham, *A Time for Remembering: The Story of Ruth Bell Graham,* in 1983, for which she won an Evangelical Christian Publishers Association Gold Medallion Book Award.

Cornwell received her bachelor's degree in English from Davidson College in 1978, marrying one of her former professors, Charles Cornwell, soon after her graduation. The couple divorced in 1988. In 1997, Cornwell's name was linked to the scandal surrounding Eugene Bennett, a former Federal Bureau of Investigation (FBI) agent who asserted that Cornwell's affair with his wife, Margo Bennett, had been a primary motivation behind his plot to kidnap and murder his spouse. Quiet on the subject of her sexuality for much of her career, in an in-depth 2007 interview with the British newspaper the *Daily Telegraph* (London), Cornwell discussed her coming out process, her assertion of a lesbian identity, and her 2005 marriage to Harvard psychiatry professor Staci Ann Gruber in depth. Although not an active spokesperson for LGBTQ rights, Cornwell has nonetheless made public statements in support of gay marriage and against the persistent violence and discrimination that plagues LGBTQ people in American society. Cornwell is well known, not only for her literary work, but also for her work as a philanthropist and prominent donor to organizations and institutions focused on writing and forensic science, and her support of animal rights and victims' rights. The founder of the Virginia Institute for Forensic Science and Medicine, Cornwell has funded scholarships at institutions including National Forensic Academy at the University of Tennessee and the Creative Writing Program at Davidson College.

Part of what makes Cornwell's books so consistently popular is the high level of detail that she includes and the profound sense of realism that permeates her descriptions of life in police stations and medical examiners' offices. Prior to embarking on a career as a full-time novelist, Cornwell was herself a crime reporter and worked in a medical examiner's office, giving her a true insiders' perspective on the bleak and violent world depicted in her books. Between 1979 and 1984, Cornwell worked as a crime reporter for the *Charlotte Observer* in North Carolina. In 1980, she won an investigative reporting award from the North Carolina Press Association for a series of articles that she wrote about prostitution. Throughout her career as a writer, Cornwell has considered how violent crime impacts women's lives, using her work to consider the ways in which systematic sexism and persistent misogynistic violence shapes the lives of American women. In 1984, Cornwell transitioned from being a crime reporter to working as a writer and computer analyst in the Chief Medical Examiner's office in Richmond, Virginia, where she would remain until 1990. Hoping to write a novel about crime and its investigation, Cornwell used her time at the medical examiner's office to learn as much as possible about the intricacies involved in investigating violent crime. During this time, she also volunteered with the Richmond Police Department in order to gain insight into the experiences of police officers working on the streets. Drawing upon her experiences working with the police and at the medical examiner's office, Cornwell wrote and published her first novel featuring Kay Scarpetta, *Postmortem,* in 1990.

Postmortem was an immediate popular and critical success, quickly climbing the bestseller lists and garnering strong reviews from numerous critics. *Postmortem* introduced the character of medical examiner Kay Scarpetta, a complex, intellectual woman, with a complicated personal life and a fierce devotion to her chosen profession. Sometimes accused by readers of being unrealistically strong and implausibly free from any doubts or weaknesses, Cornwell gradually softened the Scarpetta character over the course of the novels, allowing Scarpetta increasingly vulnerability as the series progressed. As of 2007, there were 15 Scarpetta novels, each focusing on Scarpetta's efforts to use her remarkable skills as a medical examiner to solve violent crimes. The series features numerous recurring characters, including FBI agent Pete Marino, who is initially skeptical about Scarpetta's abilities, and Scarpetta's young niece, Lucy Farinelli. Marino is only one of several male characters whom Scarpetta encounters over the course of the series, who initially doubts her ability to function successfully in a "man's world" of crime and punishment. Ten years old in the first Scarpetta novel, the remarkably articulate and intellectually precocious Farinelli grows into a young woman as the series progresses, eventually coming out as a lesbian. Through the character of Farinelli, Cornwell explores the challenges facing young lesbian women negotiating sex and love in contemporary America (much as, through the character of Kay Scarpetta, she considers how single, heterosexual, middle-aged women navigate this same terrain). The novels also feature several different fiendish serial killers, including child-murderer Temple Gault and woman-killer Jean-Baptiste Chardonne, whom the brilliant Scarpetta (often successfully) outwits. The Scarpetta novels frequently focus on violent crimes against women, thus highlighting the persistent, violent misogyny that plagues American society. *Postmortem,* for example, focuses on Scarpetta's efforts to unmask a serial rapist and murderer terrorizing the city of Richmond, and *Body of Evidence* (1991) centers around a young female author murdered because of one of her controversial books. Permeated by brutal violence, the Scarpetta novels refuse to participate in the glamorization of violence against women and male serial killers common in the popular media, enlisting readers' sympathies for the justice-seeking Scarpetta rather than for the violent criminals whom she pursues. By the 2007 novel *Book of the Dead,* Scarpetta has left her job as a medical examiner, setting up shop as a private forensic pathologist, continuing to struggle against nefarious violent criminals, and to negotiate what it means to be a single, professional woman, in a society that still regards ambitious women alone with suspicion. Having created a heroine as deft in the kitchen as she is in the morgue, Cornwell published two cookbooks based on the Scarpetta character, *Scarpetta's Winter Table* and *Food to Die For: Secrets from Kay Scarpetta's Kitchen,* in 1998 and 2002, respectively.

In addition to her Scarpetta novels, Cornwell has also written three books, *Hornet's Nest* (1997), *Southern Cross* (1999), and *Isle of Dogs* (2001), which feature the young detective Andy Brazil, who draws upon his past experiences as a journalist in order to solve the crimes that he encounters. Significantly more lighthearted in tone (and less grisly in nature) than the Scarpetta novels, Cornwell wrote the Brazil novels as a much-needed break from the relentlessly dark world inhabited by Kay Scarpetta and the diabolical serial killers who pursue her. While by no means as successful as the Scarpetta books, Cornwell's Brazil books nonetheless proved to be popular with her readers.

In 2002, Cornwell published *Portrait of a Killer: Jack the Ripper—Case Closed.* The book presents Cornwell's theory that Jack the Ripper, the vicious serial killer who murdered at least five women working as prostitutes in London between 1888 and 1891, was post-Impressionist painter Walter Sickert. Cornwell builds her case based on a diverse assortment of evidence, including Sickert's troubled history with women and the unsettling similarities between Ripper's female victims and women depicted in Sickert's art. While the book was a best seller and generated significant discussion, not all experts on the Ripper case agree with Cornwell's conclusions. Cornwell herself, however, has continued to insist that her solution is, indeed, the correct one, and that in time, incontrovertible evidence will emerge that supports her theory. In 2006, Cornwell published her first novel featuring police investigator Win Garano and district attorney Monique Lamont, *At Risk.* The duo returned in Cornwell's 2008 novel *The Front.* Much like Kay Scarpetta, Lamont is a strong and ambitious female character, unafraid to alienate her at times sexist male co-workers in pursuit of justice for victims of violence.

A pioneer in the field of mysteries set in the world of forensic science, Cornwell's novels encouraged a new generation of mystery writers to set their stories in the grim but fascinating world of forensic investigation. Her books also helped to create a new type of female character in mystery fiction, a woman unapologetically passionate about her career, comfortable with her sexuality, unafraid to be single, who is as courageous as she is intellectual.

Further Reading

Bachrach, Judy. "Death Becomes Her." *Vanity Fair* 441 (May 1997): 146–50, 200–204.

Feole, Glenn. *The Complete Patricia Cornwell Companion.* New York: Berkley Books, 2005.

Gregoriou, Christiana. *Deviance in Contemporary Crime Fiction.* Basingstoke, England: Palgrave Macmillan, 2007.

Mizejewski, Linda. "Illusive Evidence: Patricia Cornell and the Body Double." *South Central Review* 18, nos. 3/4 (Autumn/Winter 2001): 6–20.

Palmer, Joy. "Tracing Bodies: Gender, Genre, Forensic Domestic Fiction." *South Central Review* 18, nos. 3/4 (Autumn/Winter 2001): 54–71.

Holly M. Kent

Covino, Peter (b. 1963)

Contemporary **gay** poet. Peter Covino was born in Sturno, Italy, and lived there through his early childhood before immigrating to the United States. After receiving his master's degree at Columbia University's School of Social Work, he spent more than a decade working as a social worker in New York City. While working full time, Covino earned a second master's degree in English/creative writing from City College of New York. Realizing that writing was his true calling, he enrolled at the University of Utah, where, as a Steffensen Cannon Fellow, he earned a Ph.D. in Creative Writing and English Literature.

Covino's poetry has appeared in well over 30 journals and anthologies, including *Colorado Review, Columbia, Italian Americana, The Journal, The Paris Review, Paterson Literary Review, Poet Lore, Verse, VIA,* and *The Penguin Book of Italian American Writing.* His *Straight Boyfriend* (2001) won the 2001 Frank O'Hara Chapbook Prize. His full-length book, *Cut Off the Ears of Winter* (2005), in turn, was a finalist for three awards (2007 Paterson Poetry Prize, the 2006 Publishing Triangle's **Thom Gunn** Award, and the 2000 Bordighera Poetry Prize), ultimately winning the prestigious 2007 PEN/Joyce Osterweil Award, which recognizes the literary merit of the work of a new, emerging American poet.

Cut Off the Ears of Winter is a fetching collection of poetry that speaks to the highs and lows of daily life in a language and vocabulary that reify such shifting thematics; its title, aptly so, references Van Gogh's attempt to deflect the negativity he felt overwhelming. The poem "April 18th—Thinking about Lionel, Recently Dead of AIDS" exemplifies Covino's keen rhetorical ability. It is a poem that shifts from a hopeful National Football League draftee who dies in a plane crash to a hopeless self-sabotaging drug addict and an abandoning alcoholic father, from the sacrificed St. Agatha to the oddly reassuring Lionel.

Cut Off the Ears of Winter is a lyrical journey just as much personal as it is universal. While "Pleiades," "No Standing Still," "Box of Broken Things," and "Poverty of Language" are most personal in content, to be sure, they also speak to those issues that, only until recently, have been discussed in a public forum: child abuse and its resultant despondency. The social and psychological complexities of immigration, fatherhood, and family constitute other themes that are all woven together in a most poignantly articulated poem entitled "An Offering." In it, the "half dream/half nightmare" of a "strange topography" speaks to the personal tragedy of a child juxtaposed to the conflicted and troubled existence of an immigrant father.

All of Covino's personal themes are often contextualized with the more universal issues of society: AIDS, art, history, literature, and religion. The prose poem "Caught" acutely underscores the onslaught of AIDS, when society was still ignorant of its existence. "Orchiectomy," in turn, nicely intertwines literary and historical references in an otherwise most personal narrative.

"Telling My Story" best underscores the personal conflicts the narrating I feels as he reexamines with distance his own personal tragedy. But what also comes to the fore is the continuum ("pathetic continuum") of abuse—spousal and/or parental—that can be passed down from one generation to the next. The passage of time, the father's denials, and the abused children's adult discussions only add to the contradictions of good versus evil and suffering versus healing.

Peter Covino has completed a translation project of Italian poets for an anthology titled *Contemporary European Poets* (2008). Covino is also a founding editor of *Barrow Street* and Barrow Street Press (established 1998). He is a professor in the English Department at the University of Rhode Island.

Further Reading

Giunta, Edvige. "Covino, Peter." In *The Greenwood Encyclopedia of Multiethnic American Literature.* Vol. 1, 509–10, edited by Emmanuel S. Nelson. Westport, CT: Greenwood Press, 2005.

Anthony Julian Tamburri

Cox, Christopher (1947–1988)

Influential editor, writer, and founding member of the **Violet Quill Club**. Born and raised in Gadsden, Alabama, Christopher Cox came from a middle-class southern family, in which his father was a friend of Governor George Wallace and served on the board of trustees for the University of Alabama. At the age of 16, Cox worked as a page for conservative Senator John Sparkman, which only served to galvanize him against the reactionary politics he experienced in the South. While Cox briefly attended the University of Alabama, he founded the local chapter of the Students for a Democratic Society, a progressive, left-wing student organization; **David Bergman**, in fact, characterizes Cox as the most radical of the Violet Quill members, a literary group of **gay** men. In the 1970s, however, Cox moved to Manhattan, where he first attempted careers as a writer and photographer, working for the *SoHo Weekly News,* before becoming an editor against the backdrop of the emerging post-**Stonewall Riots** gay literary scene; Cox was himself present at the Stonewall Riots. He entered publishing first with the E. P. Dutton Company before joining Ballantine Books, where he worked as an assistant to Bill Whitehead, the editor for **Edmund White** and **Robert Ferro** (companion members of the Violet Quill), and then become a senior editor himself. There, he strongly influenced the emergent group of young gay writers, who would both be decimated by and responsive to the AIDS epidemic.

Cox, however, remains most well known for his participation in the short-lived but highly influential group of gay writers known as the Violet Quill Club, who met between 1980 and 1981 in Manhattan to read aloud from their works in progress. Onetime lover of Edmund White during their time of membership in the Violet Quill, Cox published only one book during his lifetime, the nonfiction guide entitled *A Key West Companion* (1983), a guide to the Florida resort town, its historic buildings, and its contemporary cultural setting, but functioning more as a companion than a guide with its lack of didacticism and its emphasis on the colloquial. Rather than compiling a compendium of details concerning the logistics of travel, Cox constructs an engaging series of essays that evokes a sense of community and storytelling from an obviously engaged perspective. His ability as a creative writer, however, only fully emerges in his recently published short story "Aunt Persia and the Jesus Man," a humorous southern gothic tale that appears in *The Violet Quill Reader,* edited by David Bergman (1994). "Doe's Pillow," the title used by Cox during meetings of the Violet Quill, was itself never fully constructed during his lifetime; meticulous in his editing, Cox rewrote each of the paragraphs multiple times over the span of a decade, leaving the story itself strewn across numerous different papers before being amalgamated by David Bergman into the one piece published in his collection. This published story is based on the 1971 draft, the most complete intact version. The tale itself is set in rural Alabama and, while the text has no explicitly gay theme, Cox, in fact, uses small town American life to explore the close-knit societies of small communities in which annoyance and amusement collide in unexpected ways. In particular, Cox uses the first-person narrative voice of Persia and Doe's niece both to structure the story and to provide an audience for the embedded narrative in which the details of the farcical sibling rivalry between Aunt Persia and Aunt Doe are ultimately exposed; following the opening incident in which the dying Doe attempts to wrestle a necklace off the body of her estranged sister Persia, the narrative shifts into the narrator as audience for Persia's tale. Cox also wanted to write a book on the Chelsea Hotel, where he lived for many years, as a celebration of gay bohemian life, but unfortunately the book was never written; only a 30-page proposal remains.

Actively involved in the theater, Cox participated in the Broadway musical production of *Two Gentleman of Verona* and directed a number of plays at the Jean Cocteau Theater. He died of AIDS-related complications in 1988 at the age of 41. His manuscripts are housed at the Beinecke Rare Book and Manuscript Library at Yale University.

Further Reading

Bergman, David. "Race and the Violet Quill." *American Literary History* 9, no. 1 (Spring 1997): 79–102.
————. *The Violet Hour: The Violet Quill and the Making of Gay Culture.* New York: Columbia University Press, 2004.

Stephanie Youngblood

Crowley, Mart (b. 1935)

Playwright. Mart Crowley was born on August 21, 1935, in Vicksburg, Mississippi. He was raised Catholic, attended a parochial high school, and graduated from the Catholic University of America in Washington, D.C., in 1957. Following graduation Crowley moved to New York where he became a production assistant on the film *Splendor in the Grass* (1961). He then moved to Hollywood where he worked for several television production companies and eventually took a position as Natalie Wood's assistant. During that time he also worked on what would become his most famous play, a landmark in **gay** theater history, *The Boys in the Band*. With some help from Natalie Wood and an agent in New York City, the play eventually made its way into the hands of **Edward Albee** and Richard Barr at the Playwrights Unit, who decided to produce it.

The Boys in the Band premiered off-Broadway at Theatre Four on April 14, 1968. The play is a melodrama that depicts a birthday party thrown by Michael, a gay man who is a recovering alcoholic. The party is attended by several of Michael's gay friends who exhibit various degrees of comfort with their own homosexuality. The play begins with preparations for the party and ends after an arduous night in which the arrival of an unexpected guest from college sends Michael back into the throes of alcoholism and turns the party into an emotional bloodbath. *The Boys in the Band* was a groundbreaking piece because it was the first mainstream play that dealt so directly with homosexuality. While homosexuals had been featured on stage before, Crowley's play was the first to set the entire action of the play within the "homosexual subculture" and to give mainstream audiences an opportunity to see gay men as something besides flamboyant, comedic characters. While Crowley does include one "flaming queen," in the character of Emory, he also includes a wide array of others.

While the critical reception of *The Boys in the Band* was overwhelmingly positive, many in the gay community greeted it with scorn. They saw the play as an indictment of their lifestyle because some of the characters exhibit a great deal of internalized **homophobia**. They especially derided Michael's self-destructive tendencies. In Crowley's defense, however, it is important to remember that *The Boys in the Band* was written during a time before the **Stonewall Riots** when homosexuality was still considered a mental disorder by the American Psychiatric Association. (It was removed from the list of mental disorders in 1973, but was designated as "sexual orientation disturbance.") The play is a reflection of the time and context within which it was written. Even so, many in the gay community still find the play offensive, and it remains controversial.

Crowley's second play, *Remote Asylum,* was produced in Los Angeles in 1970. Unfortunately, it was not as well received by the critics and did nothing to further his reputation. The year 1970 also saw the release of a film version of *The Boys in the Band,* for which Crowley wrote the screenplay. The film was directed by William Friedkin and included all of the original cast members of the hit off-Broadway production. Crowley followed up next with *A Breeze from the Gulf* (1973) and then took a long hiatus from writing plays and spent much of his time traveling and partying. In 1984 he wrote *Avec Schmaltz* and then did not produce another piece until almost a decade later when he wrote *For Reasons That Remain Unclear* (1993). It is an autobiographical piece that presents a man's struggle to deal with a priest's sexual abuse that was perpetrated upon him as a young boy. In 2002 Crowley wrote a follow-up to *The Boys in the Band* that includes all but two of the original characters and also adds some younger characters. *The Men from the Boys* also takes place in Michael's apartment, but this time the event is a wake for Larry, one of the characters from the first play. While *Men* touches upon some of the same themes as *Boys,* the addition of younger characters and the difference in time period allows Crowley to touch upon things such as the generation gap and the effect of AIDS on the homosexual community. The play premiered in San Francisco in 2002 to generally favorable reviews. Although Crowley has produced a very small body of work throughout his career, he will forever hold an important place in gay theater history because of *The Boys in the Band.* Although he never considered himself an activist, by bringing *Boys* out of the **closet** and onto the stage and screen, he helped to raise awareness and ultimately contributed to increased visibility and acceptance of gay culture.

Further Reading

Clum, John M. *Still Acting Gay: Male Homosexuality in Modern Drama.* New York: St. Martin's Griffin, 2000.

Crowley, Mart. *The Boys in the Band: 40th Anniversary Edition.* Preface by Tony Kushner. New York: Alyson Publications, 2008.

———. *3 Plays by Mart Crowley.* Los Angeles: Alyson Publications, 1996.

Schiavi, Michael R. "Mart Crowley." In *Contemporary Gay American Poets and Playwrights: An A-to-Z Guide,* edited by Emmanuel S. Nelson, 93–100. Westport, CT: Greenwood Press, 2003.

———. "Teaching the 'Boys': Mart Crowley in the Millennial Classroom." *Modern Language Studies* 31, no. 2 (2001): 75–90.

Beth A. Kattelman

Cunningham, Michael (b. 1952)

Pulitzer prize–winning writer known for provocative, poetic fiction. Born in 1952 in Cincinnati, Ohio, Michael Cunningham has been publishing since the 1980s after graduating from the University of Iowa writing program. His work was recognized with a National Endowment for the Arts Fellowship in 1998, as well as the PEN/Faulkner Award for Fiction and the Pulitzer Prize for fiction for *The Hours* (1998). Currently a professor of creative writing at Brooklyn College, Cunningham has published five novels, a travelogue, and written a screenplay for the adaptation of *A Home at the End of the World.* Critics recognize Cunningham for his poetic and powerful narrative style that brings characters to life. His writings cohere through his focus on relationships, especially family dynamics, as well as the interweaving of **gay** characters and story lines that capture the early days of the AIDS crisis and its lasting legacy.

Cunningham's first novel, *Golden States,* was released in 1984. This novel received little critical notice, and Cunningham tends to overlook the novel, choosing instead to speak of *A Home at the End of the World,* published in 1990, as his first novel. *A Home at the End of the World* traces the friendship of Bobby and Jonathan. In many ways, the novel is a coming-of-age story as Bobby and Jonathan learn how to be adults in a world where they often feel isolated due to childhood experiences. Bobby carries the scars of his brother's accidental death and his mother's subsequent suicide, while Jonathan's childhood is marked by his longing for a father-son relationship and his mother's suffocating presence. The two meet as young boys who come together both platonically and intimately; they reunite as adults in New York City where Jonathan lives as an openly gay man and Bobby has chosen **heterosexuality** as he falls in love with Jonathan's roommate, Clare.

The subsequent birth of Clare and Bobby's daughter leads the three friends to move to Woodstock in search of an idyllic home that is shattered when Clare and her daughter leave and Erich, Jonathan's former partner who is dying of AIDS, needs a home. The novel concludes with Bobby and Jonathan taking care of Erich, while also building their restaurant business as Jonathan awaits the arrival of his own HIV symptoms. The story's power rests in Cunningham's skillful depiction of the transformation of the family from the nuclear unit of the 1950s to a nontraditional unit shaped by individual needs, as well as Bobby and Jonathan's realization that they must form their own family. In this way, the novel suggests that how families are created and defined has shifted in the 1980s in response to not only the failure of the traditional family, but also in response to the AIDS epidemic.

Flesh and Blood, published in 1995, traces three generations of Greek Americans, once again focusing on family dynamics. The novel presents a dysfunctional family with Constantine, an abusive family patriarch, and Mary, an addicted, kleptomaniac matriarch. The marriage disintegrates, leaving the three children to forge their ways in the world. Each child chooses an alternative family model to shape his or her adult life. Susan enters into an extramarital affair and has a son, while Billy builds a relationship with his male partner. Zoe turns to drugs and an interracial relationship that results in a child, Jamal, whom she raises with Cassandra, a transvestite living with AIDS. These atypical family models create happiness and stability, continuing a theme from *A Home at the End of the World* that the traditional family structure no longer works in contemporary times.

While Cunningham's early works were critically well received, it is with *The Hours* in 1998 that he moved to national recognition. This recognition increased when the novel received the Pulitzer Prize and was transformed into a film that received the Oscar for Best Film. The novel presents three separate but parallel stories. The novel opens with a fictionalized Virginia Woolf in the 1920s at work on her novel *Mrs. Dalloway,* dealing with her longing to escape her daily existence yet also longing to create something beautiful.

The second story follows Laura Brown, a mother in 1949 Los Angeles, caring for a young son, trying to create a perfect birthday cake for her husband, as she feels panicked and anxious about her life that is stifling her. With the third story line, the novel moves readers into 1990s New York City with Clarissa Vaughan, a book editor living in Greenwich Village, who is organizing a party for Richard, her best friend, who is dying of AIDS and has received a literary prize. The novel explores the question of how people find happiness, or at least contentment, as they move through life's daily hours. The characters' inner thoughts resonate through Cunningham's poetic language that heightens readers' experiences.

Land's End: A Walk in Provincetown followed in 2002. *Land's End* is both travelogue and memoir as Cunningham provides historical facts and personal reflections about the community and his friends. This work was followed by *Specimen Days* in 2005. The title comes from Walt Whitman's 1882 autobiography. Cunningham explains that for Whitman, a "specimen" is a heroic character, an individual who represents the whole. The title itself, then, creates a metaphor for the common human story rather than the individual story, which is developed through three stories that stand alone as novellas but are interconnected by common character names and the omnipresent words of Whitman from *Leaves of Grass*. The first story, "In the Machine," is set in the nineteenth century Industrial Revolution, with "The Children's Crusade" set soon after 9/11, and "Like Beauty" set in the twenty-third century. Cunningham suggests that the novel is about the need to examine technology and its uses before technology overtakes our humanity. In each story, new advances affect human relationships, most especially seen in the closing story as New York City has been transformed into a theme park where tourists pay to be mugged by "simulos." This novel continues Cunningham's preoccupation with relationships and demonstrates his lyrical language and unique narrative style.

See also Novel, Gay

Further Reading

Bahr, David. "The Difference a Day Makes: After Hours with Michael Cunningham." *Poets & Writers Magazine* 27, no. 4 (1999): 18–24.

Hughes, Mary Joe. "Michael Cunningham's *The Hours* and Postmodern Artistic Re-Presentation." *Critique* 45, no. 5 (2004): 349–61.

Karline, Danny. "Home-Breaking." *London Review of Books* 12, no. 10 (1991): 22–23.

Laurence, Patricia. "Homage to Woolf." *English Literature in Transition, 1880–1920* 43, no. 3 (2000): 370–76.

Peregrin, Tony. "Michael Cunningham after Hours." *Gay & Lesbian Review* 10, no. 2 (2003): 30–32.

Whitaker, Rick. "On the Beach." *Washington Post Book World* 32 (21 July 2002): 9.

Jeannette E. Riley

Currier, Jameson (b. 1955)

American novelist, short story writer, critic, and journalist. Jameson Currier was born on October 16, 1955, in Marietta, Georgia. In 1978, a year after graduating from Emory University with a B.A. degree in English, Currier moved to New York City to earn an M.A. in Dramatic Literature from New York University. He dropped out of the graduate program when he secured an apprenticeship with an entertainment publicity firm that handled theater accounts. Inspired by author **Armistead Maupin**'s *Tales of the City* (1978), Currier began writing short stories about the comic adventures of his itinerant theater friends. The subject and theme of the author's short stories changed as many of these friends became early casualties of the AIDS epidemic. Author **David B. Feinberg** brought Currier's AIDS stories to the attention of Edward Iwanicki, an editor at Viking Penguin who published the works of many gay male writers. Currier and Feinberg had become acquainted in the mid-1980s while participating in a gay writers' workshop in Manhattan, and Iwanicki had edited and published Feinberg's first novel, *Eighty-Sixed* (1989). Currier's first published collection of short stories, *Dancing on the Moon: Short Stories about AIDS* (1993), focused on the impact of AIDS on the families, friends, and partners of gay men who were facing the disease. Following the success of the short story collection, Currier began writing unbylined book reviews for *Publishers Weekly,* which led to further bylined reviewing assignments of gay-themed books with many local and national gay and mainstream publications, including the *Washington Post,* where he published a significant review for **Michael Cunningham**'s *The Hours* (1998). Currier continued to write about the impact of AIDS on the gay community in several ways, in monthly articles for *Body Positive* magazine, a magazine for the HIV-positive community, and by collaborating on the screenplay for the documentary *Living Proof: HIV and the Pursuit of Happiness* (1994), based on the portraits of HIV-positive people by photographer Carolyn Jones. In 1998, Currier published his novel *Where the Rainbow Ends* about a young gay man from the South who arrives in Manhattan in the late 1970s and falls in with a group of artistic friends who are pulled apart and pieced together by the unexpected challenges of the AIDS epidemic. Loosely based on the Biblical story of Job, Currier's version of the archetypal journey of a gay man from a small town to the big city stands out because of his strong portrayal of a gay man's reconfiguration of "family" and his protagonist's struggle with faith and his desire to find meaning within the randomness of life during the first decade of the AIDS epidemic. Currier continued to contribute short stories on AIDS issues and gay male relationships to literary journals and anthologies and new Internet ventures such as *Blithe House Quarterly* and *Velvet Mafia*. His second book of short stories, *Desire, Lust, Passion, Sex* (2004), collected many of these works. Currier has continued to work as a literary critic and journalist, including a stint in the late 1990s as an editor of the gay Manhattan weekly newspaper, the *New York Blade,* where he reported on the behind-the-scenes story of the **Stonewall** Inn being named to the National Register of Historic Places. Since 2001, Currier has reported on news items of interest to the LGBTQ publishing community, first in a column for the print journal *Lambda Book Review,* then in *QueerType,* his monthly Internet blog. Currier also worked directly with Anne-Laure Hubert, a Belgian university student whose master's thesis had been a French translation of *Dancing on the Moon,* on a new translation of his AIDS stories, which was published in France as *Les Fantômes* (2005), in cooperation with a national French AIDS organization.

See also AIDS Literature

Further Reading

Cady, Joseph. "AIDS Literature." In *Gay and Lesbian Literary History,* edited by Claude J. Summers, 16–20. New York: Henry Holt, 1995.

Kakutani, Michiko. "Critic's Notebook: For Gay Writers, Sad Stories." *New York Times,* March 12, 1993, C1.

Kruger, Steven F. *AIDS Narratives: Gender and Sexuality, Fiction and Science.* New York & London: Garland Publishing, 1996.

Verghese, Abraham. "Reports from the Front Lines." *Washington Post Book World,* April 25, 1993, 1.

Warner, Sharon Oard. "The Way We Write Now: The Reality of AIDS in Contemporary Short Fiction." In *The Tales We Tell: Perspectives on the Short Story,* edited by Barbara Lounsberry, Susan Lohafer, Mary Rohrberger, Stephen Pett, and R. C. Fedderson, 185–93. Westport, CT: Greenwood Press, 1998.

Tom Cardamone

Curzon, Daniel (b. 1938)

One of the most creative, controversial, and criticized **gay** novelists and playwrights of the late twentieth century. Daniel Curzon was born Daniel Russell Brown on March 19, 1938, to Ida and Russell Brown in Litchfield, Illinois. He attended the University of Detroit between 1956 and 1960 where he majored in English. After graduating, Curzon received a fellowship to Kent State University. Upon completing his master's degree, he returned to Michigan where he taught at the University of Detroit until 1964. In 1969 he obtained his doctoral degree from Wayne State University. After graduating he left Detroit and began teaching at the University of Maryland. He has also taught college English to American personnel in Vietnam, Japan, and Thailand and later taught English at City College of San Francisco.

Curzon's novels focus on the gay male experience, often in a world that is dark, ugly, and hostile to his gay male characters. His first published novel, *Something You Do in the Dark* (1971), is considered by some to be the first gay liberation novel. Curzon's second novel, *The Misadventures of Tim McPick* (1975), is one of the few comic novels to come out of the gay liberationist period in which the gay protagonist learns about life and defines himself through sexual experimentation amid the **homophobia** of the mid-1970s. *The Revolt of the Perverts* (1978) was his first collection of short stories. The 19 stories vary in style and subject matter from a mildly comic look at the struggle between romantic love and the need for sex to a child who molests older men. *Superfag* (1996) is a comedy about a semidivine being that is sent down from Heaven to rid the world of homophobia.

Along with his novels and short stories, Curzon is an award-winning playwright. *Last Call* (1981) was produced at the University of Calgary in 1982 and won the "best of series award." *Cinderella II: Happily Ever After* (1984) won an award from the Bay Area Theater Critics Circle. Other noteworthy plays include *My Unknown Son* (1987), *Sour Grapes* (1997), *Godot Arrives* (1999), and *A Fool's Audition* (2001), which won the Great Platte River Playwrights Festival Award the same year.

Daniel Curzon has received both praise and criticism for his work, but it is his refusal to stay within the confines of fictional genres and his dark, Gothic viewpoints to address homophobic attitudes that have set his writing apart from others. His work, while often filled with conflicted characters that face difficult situations, speaks universal truths and unapologetically advances a gay emancipatory agenda.

Further Reading

Curzon, Daniel. "Gay Literature after 'City of Night.'" *Los Angeles Times,* October 2, 1988, 15.

Gettys, John. "Daniel Curzon." In *Contemporary Gay American Novelists: A Bio-Bibliographical Critical Sourcebook,* edited by Emmanuel S. Nelson, 89–95. Westport, CT: Greenwood Press, 1993.

Kelly, Tom W. "Daniel Curzon." In *Gay and Lesbian Literature,* edited by Sharon Malinowski, 102–3. Detroit, MI: St. James Press, 1994.

William Holden

D

Dancer from the Dance

A landmark **gay** novel published in 1978. **Andrew Holleran**'s *Dancer from the Dance* dramatizes the beauty, pleasures, dangers, and dissolutions that mark the vibrant gay male subculture in the decade after the **Stonewall Riots**. Set in Fire Island and Manhattan, the novel centers on the elusive and magnetic Malone, an exceptionally handsome lawyer who decides to pursue a career in love. The novel records Malone's quest for meaning and connection in a nocturnal world that revels in music, youth, romance, gossip, parties, dance, drugs, and sex. As Malone's story unfolds, the novel raises enduring questions about what it means to live or die for transient beauty, fleeting unity, and impermanent joy.

Dancer chronicles Malone's odyssey from the awestruck perspective of an unnamed narrator on the same social circuit. The limited, third-person lens captures the outlines of Malone's short life and the mythology that surrounds it. Malone is both an idol and an everyman. His golden beauty, devotion to love, emotional fragility, and sensual excesses make him a complicated, charismatic ideal.

Although Malone has many lovers—and an intense first love affair—the most primary and enduring relationship in the novel is Malone's platonic connection to Sutherland, a **camp**y, exuberant queen. With Virgil-like insight, wit, and affection, Sutherland nurses Malone through his breakup and introduces him to the party circuit. The friendship is profound—supportive and transformative—and yet it is also fraught with irreconcilable tensions. Although Sutherland adores him, Malone may represent an apex of physical perfection, sexual adventure, and romantic idealism that consistently elude or confound Sutherland. Although Malone stays loyal to him, Sutherland, like the circuit and the city itself, becomes a paradoxical presence in the novel, implicated in Malone's imprisonment in habit, desire, sensation, and the promise of love. Ultimately, Sutherland and Malone remain powerfully connected and also alone, intimate, and still somehow estranged. Their simultaneous but separate deaths crystallize the intricate depths of their relationship: they both die on the same night—at the same party—and yet they both die alone.

Since its publication, *Dancer* has been celebrated as an unapologetic (though controversial) watershed of subcultural expression in the gay literary canon. **Edmund White** heralded the novel as *The Great Gatsby* of its generation, lauding its haunted glamorization of a beautiful and decadent age. Holleran himself has characterized the book as both satire and exposé. In the 1990s, critics questioned its interest in the more hedonistic or sordid dimensions of its characters' sexualities and life experiences. In style and content, the novel is a study in a gorgeous indeterminacy, conflicting truths, and savage bliss.

See also Novel, Gay

Further Reading

Bergman, David. *The Violet Hour: The Violet Quill and the Making of Gay Culture.* New York: Columbia University Press, 2004.

Leavitt, David. "Introduction." *The Penguin Book of Gay Short Stories.* New York, Penguin Books, 1994.

Schwartz, Michael. "David Leavitt's Inner Child." *The Harvard Gay & Lesbian Review* 11, no. 1 (Winter 1995): 39–44.

Woodhouse, Reed. *Unlimited Embrace: A Canon of Gay Fiction 1945–1995.* Amherst: University of Massachusetts Press, 1998.

Suzanne Ashworth

davenport, doris diosa (b. 1949)

Affrilachian (southern Appalachian African American) lesbian-feminist poet, performer, scholar, and ex-academic. davenport earned a Ph.D. in African American Literature from the University of Southern California in 1985, an M.A. in English from State University of New York at Buffalo in 1971, and a B.A. in English from Paine College in Augusta, Georgia, in 1969. The oldest of seven children, she was born in Gainesville, Georgia, and raised in Cornelia, Georgia. davenport's poetry speaks with a regional voice linked to northeastern Georgia and her history with the African American communities in which she was brought up. She is an emphatic voice for black lesbians, insisting upon whole scale social change and exposure of the difficultly gendered truths of American racism and **homophobia**.

A contributor to the immeasurably significant anthology *This Bridge Called My Back: Writings by Radical Women of Color* (1983), davenport's critical writing calls for a simultaneous rethinking of race and sexuality through community-based self-reflection. "The Pathology of Racism: A Conversation with Third World Wimmin," her contribution to *Bridge,* is a dauntless critique of white feminist racism and homophobia. davenport documents what she sees as a ubiquitous fear of difference within the white feminist community and calls for a feminism that eschews collaboration with movements disinterested in the needs of women of color. She envisions work focused acutely upon third-world women as a more productive direction for black activism. "Black Lesbians in Academia: Visible Invisibility," collected in *The New Lesbian Studies* (1996), describes the specific alienation of the lesbian student and teacher of color of literature within the academy. davenport insists that despite the continual fact of institutional resistance, a political black lesbian presence in academia is vital for the transformation of structural racism.

davenport's poetry collections include *It's Like This* (1980), *Eat Thunder & Drink Rain: Poems* (1982), *Voodoo Chile—Slight Return: Poems* (1991), *Soque Street Poems* (1991), and *Madness Like Morning Glories* (2005). As with much of her poetry, *Madness Like Morning Glories* is a recursive conversation with the people, places, and spirits of the southern Appalachian foothills, the Chattahoochee National Forest, and, specifically, of Cornelia, Georgia. The smoothness with which davenport inhabits her characters, spaces, and families encourages readers to understand each separate yet interconnected vignette as a vivid personal history and communal memory.

davenport has also published in journals and periodicals such as *Azalea, Matrix, Feminary, Callaloo,* the *Women's Review of Books, MELUS* (The Society for the Study of Multi-Ethnic Literature of the United States), *Black American Literature Forum, Black Music Research Journal,* and *Catalyst.* A member of Alternate Roots, an Atlanta-based southeastern organization for artists and activists, she continues to write, perform, and educate.

Further Reading

davenport, doris. "All This, and Honeysuckles too." In *Bloodroot: Reflections on Place by Appalachian Women Writers,* edited by Joyce Dyer, 87–97. Lexington: University Press of Kentucky, 1998.

Miller, James A. "Coming Home to Affrilachia: The Poems of Doris Davenport." In *Her Words: Diverse Voices in Contemporary Appalachian Women's Poetry,* edited by Felicia Mitchell, 94–106. Knoxville: University of Tennessee Press, 2002.

Melinda Cardozo

Davis, Christopher (1953–?)

Major **gay** American novelist and story writer. Christopher Davis remained reclusive during his short career. There is no information that reveals who he was aside from what is detailed in his novels and short stories. By viewing Davis's collected work as a window into the author's life, one can assume that he was a gay man in search of a way to articulate the contemporary urban gay experience. These primary sources also indicate that he once lived in Manhattan and wrote mostly toward the end of the 1980s. His final novel was published in 1994, ending a career that lasted only eight years. Due to the lack of information about the author, it is impossible to determine if Davis is still alive.

Joseph and the Old Man (1986), Davis's first novel, deals with ideas concerning true love in the face of death. Written in simple prose similar in style to Gertrude Stein's—who is mentioned frequently throughout the text—the story concerns the relationship between Joe Ross, a young history teacher, and an older man, Oswald Stevenson, who was once a well-known fiction writer. The two share a home together on Fire Island until one day when Joe is killed by a drunk driver on his way home from work in New York City. The old man faces turmoil when he is forced to contact the Ross family; the novel ends with his failed attempt at suicide by swimming out to sea, a passage that echoes the ending of Kate Chopin's *The Awakening.*

Valley of the Shadow (1988), Davis's second novel, represents the apex of the author's work. Written in the first person, Davis relates the story through the protagonist, Andrew John Ellis, a 28-year-old investment banker who operates out of New York City. Andrew and his lover Ted Erikson—who is five years his senior—have been diagnosed with AIDS resulting from very active and experimental sex lives. The story begins with Andrew recounting his childhood in Connecticut, where his family spent summers in a cabin on the lakeshore. It is here where Andrew comes to his sexual awakening at the age of 15 with an unnamed boy who lives nearby. Both boys manage to keep their tryst a secret by masking their activities as "doing the things boys do" (10). In public, they spend their time swimming and rock climbing, but when they are alone, they explore each other physically. It is at this point that Andrew becomes aware of his homosexuality. As time passes and Andrew's family starts spending the summers in the Adirondacks, Andrew develops a crush on the local tennis instructor. After being used and abused by this "Golden God" (15) of tennis, the narrator describes his descent into a world of uninhibited sexual activities. While a student at Columbia University, he remains determined in keeping physically fit, studies hard, and, at nights, navigates the gay bars searching for his next big thrill. One night he runs into Ted, an out-of-work actor who lives in Hell's Kitchen, and his life thereafter is never the same. The two fall in love with each other instantly—Andrew affectionately calls Ted his "Teddy Bear"—and, in contrast to Andrew's previous relationships, both express this love in public for all to see. The two spend their summers together on Fire Island, a noted gay community located far off the southern shore of Long Island, New York. Soon after the relationship with Ted begins, Andrew is confronted by his parents during Thanksgiving break in Connecticut. His mother knows, through motherly intuition, that he is gay and is accepting of the fact. However, his father is more apprehensive and expresses an initial disappointment. This does not last long; Andrew's father apologizes and assures him that he will always support him. His father also states his interest in meeting Ted. As a result, Andrew brings Ted to their winter house in Maine for Christmas, where his grandfather accidentally catches the two in bed making love. The grandfather condemns Andrew and never speaks with him again. The rest of Andrew's family gradually welcomes Ted despite his open homosexuality and promiscuity. As the years progress, Andrew and Ted face difficult times in their relationship, breaking up and getting back together frequently, experimenting with drugs and multiple partners, and generally losing touch with one another. It is during this turbulent time, which the narrator jokingly refers to as the "War Years," that Ted begins to show signs of having AIDS. When Andrew discovers that he also has the disease, the two come back together and support each other despite their differences.

As is the case with all of Davis's work, the plot of *Valley of the Shadow* focuses on a gay man who remains true to his passion in the face of great adversity. Although the protagonist is secure in his homosexuality, the social constructs of the society in which he lives force his relationships to exist in the shadow. In the beginning of the novel, Andrew relates his search for male companionship as "moving slowly from one shadow to the next" (18). This changes once he meets Ted. Through exploring the effects of their relationship on the microcosm represented by the Ellis family, Davis manages to show how an openly gay couple managed to challenge the views of the people around them. While the grandfather curses the relationship between Andrew and Ted, even until his own death, the rest of the family's acceptance represents a radical change in thought from one generation to the next. In this regard, *Valley of the Shadow* is a very hopeful novel. Even though it deals with themes of forbidden love, prejudice, the transition from youth to old age—represented by Andrew's rapid physical deterioration as a result of AIDS—and ultimately death, there is an overwhelming sense of triumph at the end. Andrew and Ted remain true to themselves and to each other, and though the world around them may not understand who they are and what they feel, there are those who stand with them. It would have been easy for Davis to write a vitriolic account of how AIDS affected the gay community given the zeitgeist of the 1980s (when it was largely known as "the Gay Disease") but, instead, he managed to challenge the conservative views held by much of society in relation to the subject by offering a heartfelt and human story.

These two novels, accompanied by his collection of short stories, *The Boys in the Bars* (1989), show the work of an author developing his craft. The stories contained in the latter work, particularly "Fireflies" and "History," offer much in the way of revealing the sources of his later material. Each details the devastating loss of "fallen comrades" (125): friends and lovers in the gay community who fall victim to AIDS. Also notable is the story "The Art of Criticizing Writers," which is the only text by Davis that mentions neither homosexuality nor the AIDS crisis. By examining the interplay between two different writers—one having a classic sensibility and the other leaning more toward the contemporary—the author reflects on the risk of being critical of others and offers insight into how people can learn from those who operate on completely separate levels.

Davis's final novel, *Philadelphia* (1994), works as a worthy companion piece to *Valley of the Shadow*. The story revolves around Andrew Beckett, a young, talented lawyer who has fallen ill with AIDS. An up-and-coming partner in the powerful Philadelphia-based law firm Wyant, Wheeler, and Hellerman, Andrew is fired by his superiors for circumstances that are beyond his control. During his time with the firm, Andrew managed to conceal the fact that he is a gay man, and although he worked hard, visible signs of his disease forced his employers' fears and prejudices to the forefront. With the support of his lover, Miguel, his family, and Joe Miller, a litigator for a much smaller firm, Andrew sues Wyant, Wheeler, and Hellerman for unfair practices. The novel ends with Joe Miller's victory in the courtroom and Andrew's death. There are very few differences between Davis's novel and the screenplay on which it is based (see the film *Philadelphia*, directed by Jonathan Demme), but the author manages to make the work his own by adding some minor flourishes and more depth to the relationship between Andrew and Miguel—a relationship that is frighteningly similar to that of Andrew Ellis and Ted Erikson in *Valley of the Shadow*.

Although Davis's presence in the literary community remained understated—even with the release of his debut novel in 1986—his works provide a keen insight into the collective mind of gay Americans in a time of persecution and epidemic. His novels and short stories are incisive in the ways that they deal with themes of prejudice, the pains of old age, and the fear of being alone in a world that remains uncompromising in its treatment of those who choose to live alternative lifestyles. They also reveal how natural it is for members of the same sex to fall in love and stay together. Davis may have stayed in the background with the release of three novels and a collection of short stories, but his small body of work offers an insightful glimpse into gay urban lives during the closing decades of the twentieth century.

Further Reading

Pearson, John. "Christopher Davis." In *Contemporary Gay American Novelists: A Bio-Bibliographical Critical Sourcebook,* edited by Emmanuel S. Nelson, 96–100. Westport CT: Greenwood Press, 1993.

Raphael Tombasco

De Angelis, Jacqueline (b. 1950)

Prolific author of short stories and other works of fiction and creative writing teacher. Because many of Jacqueline De Angelis's works are not concerned with a lesbian or feminist agenda, most of her work is not included in publications with such political agendas. But, because her works do include lesbian and **gay** content, many of her works are not included in mainstream literary journals. De Angelis was born March 21, 1950, and raised in Youngstown, Ohio. In 1969 she moved to Fullerton, California—a move she found traumatic—and eventually Los Angeles, where she has lived since. Her family, a mix of Italian and Polish, is mainly a working-class family. During high school De Angelis was involved in journalism and was the first female to cover athletic events. But, she never imagined she would be a writer. It was not until college that she met poets and began writing poetry herself. When De Angelis published her writings, she did so under pseudonyms, afraid to be identified by her friends. When she transferred to the University of California at Irvine, she fell in love with the form of the short story.

The loneliness De Angelis felt after moving to California sparked her to begin a journal and more poetry. In 1978 she became co-founder and editor of *rara avis* magazine, the focus being publishing literary works with a feminist, gay, lesbian, or multicultural theme, and Books of a Feather Press in 1981. De Angelis received a writer-in-residence fellowship from Dorland Mountain Arts Colony in 1984. From 1989 to the early 1990s De Angelis was a regular attendee of meetings for LGBTQ writers in Los Angeles hosted by Mark Thompson and Betty Berzon. The group was known as the Los Angeles Gay and Lesbian Writers Circle and included many renowned LGBTQ writers of the times. Since then, De Angelis has kept busy in publishing, advertising, public relations, and editing.

The Main Gate (1984), a lengthy short story published as a limited edition letterpress book, is De Angelis's first work of fiction. Unlike her later works of short stories, this is her only long work. This book was inspired by her time working at Disneyland. *The Main Gate* is a prime example of how De Angelis's writing is rooted in a powerful sense of place. This concept was translated to her cycle of poems from 1979 to 1985 titled "Interior Improvisations." The main focus of these poems is her father's death.

After a brief publishing hiatus, De Angelis started publishing short stories in anthologies fairly regularly. *Indivisible* (1991) is a collection of short fiction by West Coast gay and lesbian writers edited by Terry Wolverton. While the collection is varied in topics, the strongest selections are those based on themes that everyone can understand. De Angelis's short story "Baby" is such an example. "Baby" is about a woman who fears abandonment when her lesbian lover announces that she wants to start making plans for motherhood. "Baby" received praise by *Publishers Weekly*. De Angelis is featured in another anthology edited by Terry Wolverton, *Hers* (1995). Her short story in this collection is titled "Joshuas in the City with a Future." The following year, De Angelis was part of a new type of anthology. Amy Scholder's *Cooking with Honey: What Literary Lesbians Eat* (1996) contains not only recipes but also essays that correspond to each dish. The anthology focuses on the personal lives of lesbian writers and their perceptions of issues related to food. De Angelis offers "Jacqueline De Angelis' Rosemary Bread" to the cookbook anthology.

While De Angelis was noticed for her numerous contributions to anthologies and periodicals, one of her works received recognition before the contribution to the anthology. "Atwater" (1997), a short story, received the *International Quarterly* Crossing Boundaries Award. This short story proved to be exceptional in its use of experimentation, creativity, and innovation. The work later appeared as a contribution to *Another City: Writing from Los Angeles* (2001), yet another anthology. The premise of each selection is what it was like moving to Los Angeles or what it was like growing up in Los Angeles. De Angelis's inclusion is a natural one, since she experienced this back in the 1970s.

Further Reading

Wolverton, Terry. "Jacqueline de Angelis." In *Contemporary Lesbian Writers of the United States: A Bio-Bibliographical Critical Sourcebook,* edited by Sandra Pollack and Denise D. Knight, 164–67. Westport, CT: Greenwood Press, 1993.

Stephanie B. Crosby

Delany, Samuel R. (b. 1942)

African American author and professor. Samuel R. Delany is a prolific science fiction writer, memoirist, self-described "pornographer," literary critic, and social commentator. Since the publication in 1962 of his first book, *The Jewels of Aptor,* he has published numerous novels, short stories, essays, interviews, cultural commentary, and memoirs. What is most remarkable about this prolific output is its consistent quality, wide range, and continual development. Despite his numerous works in other genres, Delany has always strongly identified himself as a science fiction writer. But his work has always pushed at and expanded the boundaries and conventions of the field, constantly seeking out new forms, ideas, and themes. Indeed, his work has become more challenging and complex, and in some ways more difficult, over the course of his career.

Delany has also been an important figure in opening up the once almost exclusively white male world of science fiction to minority voices, both by being one of the first black science fiction writers and by writing about the experiences of nonwhite characters of all hues and backgrounds, of women, and of **gay** and bisexual characters. Almost none of his protagonists are heterosexual white men, but the racial identity of his characters is not made an issue in his books. He creates worlds in which race as we understand it is not a significant category and thus implicitly critiques our society's obsession with race and racial categorization. Delany has been a trailblazer for later black writers such as **Octavia Butler** and Steve Barnes, who have used science fiction as an arena in which to explore racial questions in a speculative and imaginative manner.

Samuel Ray Delany, Jr., was born in 1942 and raised among Harlem's black middle class. His position as both marginal (as a black man and a gay man) and privileged (in the economic and social opportunities available to him) is a major influence on his work. Delany graduated from the prestigious Bronx High School of Science and attended the City College of New York, though he did not obtain a degree. He has traveled and lived in Europe and Turkey and for many years made his living as a writer. Since 1988 he has been a university professor, at the University of Massachusetts Amherst, the State University of New York at Buffalo, and currently at Temple University. However, he still makes his permanent home in his native New York City, to which he has a great attachment and about which he has written powerfully and evocatively, most recently in his book-length essay *Times Square Red, Times Square Blue* (1999).

The power of language to shape human reality has been a strong theme of Delany's work since the beginning of his career. Much of his later work explicitly refers to literary and cultural theorists such as Roland Barthes, Jacques Derrida, and Michel Foucault, who sought to reveal and undo assumptions about language and communication. For such theorists, language is not a passive tool but an active social force. But Delany's work has always demonstrated a strong literary and linguistic awareness and even self-consciousness, both in its style and in its subject matter. He has always been fascinated by language's influence on the way we perceive and conceive of the world and ourselves. This may be related to his dyslexia, which he has said heightened his sense of the material reality of language.

Babel-17 (1966), inspired by the famous Sapir-Whorf hypothesis of linguistic determinism (that our language controls our thought), centers on the efforts of a poet to crack what is believed to be a military code used by an alien race with whom Earth is at war. What she finally discovers is that this code is, in fact, a highly exact and analytical language that has no word for "I", and thus no concept of individual identity. The novel examines the capacity of culture and language not only to condition the way people see the world, but also to determine who they are as persons. As the philosopher Ludwig Wittgenstein wrote, the limits of one's language are the limits of one's world: two different words imply two different worlds.

Dhalgren (1974), which is simultaneously Delany's most "difficult" and most popular novel, is about the efforts of a nameless (or many named: Kid/Kidd/The Kid) bisexual amnesiac to find his identity in the course of his wanderings through a postapocalyptic American city. He can find such an identity only by constructing one, and one of the ways he does so is through writing: he becomes a poet. By the end of the book (whose final phrase loops back to its opening words), the reader is left with the strong implication that the protagonist himself has written the novel that we have just finished reading about him. The novel is an enactment of the ways in which we create ourselves through our language and our ideas about ourselves.

Delany had earlier explored self-creation through self-narration in *The Einstein Intersection* (1967), a retelling of the ancient Greek myth of the poet Orpheus set in the far distant future. In the original myth, Orpheus descends into the underworld to bring his dead wife back to life by the power of his song, only to lose her again because of his own doubts. Delany's protagonist, Lo Lobey, is a member of an alien race that has come to Earth long after humanity has departed. These aliens live out human myths and stories in an attempt to understand what it meant to be human, trying to make sense of the world that they have inherited. By the end of his quest, the protagonist realizes that he and his people must create their own stories, rather than live out secondhand versions of someone else. He must become a new Orpheus, one who no longer sings the dead songs. Thus the novel is also an allegory about the power of art to create new realities.

Delany's work argues against the notion of a single, unified human nature. Instead, it celebrates difference, exploring the wide range of human possibilities that different languages and cultures can produce. However, Delany's work also delves into the complications and difficulties (up to and including war) that can result from such differences, especially when they are not acknowledged or recognized. His novel *Stars in My Pocket Like Grains of Sand* (1984) is largely about a clash of cultures, the conflict of incompatible assumptions about the universe and about people—including who and what (in a universe occupied by many different intelligent species) gets to be defined as "people." In this book, the conflict between the Family, a social ideal based on exclusion and hierarchy, and the Sygn, an ideal based on inclusion and free choice, almost ends with the destruction of a planet. The implication is that differences, even or especially the most radical differences, must be accepted if humanity is to survive, let alone to thrive. On a smaller scale, the antihero of *Trouble on Triton* (originally published in 1976 under the title *Triton*) makes himself and those around him miserable because he cannot reconcile his rigid, sexist ideas of the ways in which people should live and think with the variety and openness of his society's "ambiguous heterotopia" (in Delany's work, even utopia is plural).

Delany's celebration of difference particularly focuses on the celebration of sexual difference. Many of his protagonists are women, and most of his male protagonists are gay or bisexual. The exploration of sexuality is central to Delany's work. In his fiction, he not only presents universes in which homosexuality is completely accepted and women are fully equal members of society, but he also presents universes in which our familiar sexual categories do not apply at all. In his Nebula Award–winning short story "Aye, and Gomorrah" (1967), those people who are physically capable of deep space travel are neither male nor female and are eagerly sought after as sexual partners. In *Trouble on Triton*, it is as easy to change one's **gender** or one's sexual orientation as it is to change one's hair color.

Delany further explores the various ways and means of sexuality in the four-volume "Return to Nevèrÿon" series, which includes *Tales of Nevèrÿon* (1979), *Neveryóna* (1983), *Flight from Nevèrÿon* (1985), and *Return to Nevèrÿon* (originally published in 1987 under the title *The Bridge of Lost Desire*). Rather than being set in the future, these books are set in the distant past, in a world in which the rulers are dark-skinned and the barbarian lower classes are blonde and blue-eyed. These books are a deliberate revision of the sword and sorcery genre of which the Conan the Barbarian series is the most famous example. In them, Delany investigates the complex and contradictory realities of such a fantasized primitive world, examining the development of civilization in order to uncover the historical roots of our own culture. Among the topics these ambitious books address are the origins and development of language, the family, sexuality, gender roles, private property, commerce, social hierarchy, and the interconnections of sex and power and of language and power.

Slavery is a major theme of the Nevèrÿon series, with clear references to American history. The protagonist of the series, Gorgik the Liberator, is a former slave who rises to power and abolishes slavery. He is also a gay man whose sexual desires are all sadomasochistic, based on submission and domination. This is an example of the difficulty of separating sexuality and power in a hierarchical society in which, like our own, not all people are equal or equally free: slavery is both a sociopolitical phenomenon and a state of mind. But by making a mutually consenting game out of the power some people exercise over others, Delany's protagonist is able to defuse it to an extent and to create pleasure out of pain. In the third book of the series, Delany makes explicit the parallels between the ancient world he has created and our contemporary world by juxtaposing a plague that affects only homosexuals in his fictional world with the AIDS epidemic in 1980s New York City. In so doing, he directly addresses questions of **homophobia** and social stigma.

Delany is also an incisive literary critic and analyst of the process of reading and writing, which he points out are inextricably intertwined. Such books as *The Jewel-Hinged Jaw* (1977), *Longer Views: Extended Essays* (1996), *Shorter Views: Queer Thoughts & the Politics of the Paraliterary* (1999), and *About Writing: Seven Essays, Four Letters, and Five Interviews* (2005), among others, are filled with insights, unexpected yet apt connections, and practical advice for writers and readers.

Delany's most recent novel, *Dark Reflections* (2007), about an aging black bisexual poet in New York City's Lower East Side beset by loneliness and the fear of old age, is also a meditation on the place of the artist in a society that has no use for art.

As confirmed by his many awards, Delany has gained recognition and acclaim not only in the field of science fiction, but in those of literary theory and gay and lesbian literature. Despite controversies regarding the intellectual and stylistic challenges of some of his work (controversies that excite his critics more than his readers), and the graphic, deliberately perverse sexual content of novels such as *The Mad Man* (1994) and *Hogg* (1998), his reputation as an important writer and thinker is secure and growing.

See also AIDS Literature; Gay Literature, African American; Science Fiction, Gay

Further Reading

Barbour, Douglas. *Worlds Out of Words: The SF Novels of Samuel R. Delany.* Somerset, England: Bran's Head Books, 1979.

Broderick, Damien. *Reading by Starlight: Postmodern Science Fiction.* New York: Routledge, 1995.

Fox, Robert Elliott. *Conscientious Sorcerers: The Black Postmodernist Fiction of Leroi Jones/Amiri Baraka, Ishmael Reed, and Samuel R. Delany.* Westport, CT: Greenwood Press, 1987.

McEvoy, Seth. *Samuel R. Delany.* New York: Ungar, 1984.

Sallis, James, ed. *Ash of Stars: On the Writing of Samuel R. Delany.* Oxford: University Press of Mississippi, 1996.

Weedman, Jane Branham. *Samuel R. Delany.* Mercer Island, WA: Starmont House, 1982.

Reginald Shepherd

De la Peña, (Mary) Terri (b. 1947)

Mexican American novelist, short story writer, and essayist. (Mary) Terri de la Peña is known as an author who focuses on issues facing Chicana lesbians, such as sexual identity, gender roles, family relationships, **homophobia**, and cultural assimilation. She has written three novels and many short stories. Her short stories frequently consider contemporary social problems that affect the Chicano community. In her writing and in her selection of subject matter, she continues the literary tradition pioneered by writers such as **Gloria Evangelina Anzaldúa** and **Cherríe Moraga**.

De la Peña's first novel, *Margins* (1992), published when she was 45 years old, received many favorable reviews and established her as a respected Chicana writer. *The American Bookseller* selected it as one of 200 books that made up its core list of feminist books. *Margins* is the story of the sexual coming out of a young woman, Veronica Meléndez, and the simultaneous evolutions of her Chicana and lesbian consciousness. Veronica suffers the trauma of a car accident, witnessing the death of her lover, and endures unusual guilt over another accident that involves her nephew. While she personally works through these heartaches, she meets and forges relationships with two women who grant her the courage to talk to her family about her sexuality. Several themes are explored in this narrative that are crucial to the history of Chicano literature. One is the extensive use of Spanish mixed with English that de la Peña employs effectively. Another is the criticism of social institutions and practices within Chicano culture, such as the Catholic Church, the traditional family, the loss of the Spanish language, and the various levels of cultural assimilation found in the Chicano community. The novel presents two strong Chicana women who resist cultural assumptions about their sexuality and their individual social boundaries.

De la Peña's second novel, *Latin Satins* (1994), is the story of a Chicana lesbian singing group made up of four women, the Satins, who sing "oldies." The main character and narrator is Jessica Tamayo, the songwriter and a child care worker by day. The group advocates social change through its music, and the lyrics of its ballads are included in the narrative, in both English and Spanish. De la Peña presents important social issues, such as racism and misrepresentation of Chicano characters by the media, homophobia both within the Chicano communities as well as in the larger Anglo society, AIDS, and gentrification, in the lyrics of the Satins and also in the plot of the novel. One reviewer described the book as "sexy and fiery as its hot-blooded heroines" (76).

The 1994 Northridge earthquake in Southern California is one of the themes of de la Peña's third novel, *Faults* (1999). It is a story of women's relationships with one another and between an elderly mother and her adult daughters set in a working-class Mexican American home during and after the Northridge earthquake.

Terri de la Peña's reviews books for *Lambda Book Report*. Her work has been recognized and rewarded by the Chicano community and is considered essential to the Chicana literary canon. In 1986 she won third prize in the University of California, Irvine Chicano/Latino Literary Contest for her short story "A Saturday in August." Other awards include a Woman of Color Scholarship from the Flight of the Mind Women Writers' Workshop in 1988 and an Artistic Excellence in Writing Award from VIVA: Lesbian and Gay Latinos in the Arts in 1990. She works as a Senior Administrative Analyst for the College of Letters and Sciences at the University of California, Los Angeles.

See also Lesbian Literature, Mexican American

Further Reading

Fernández, Salvador C. "Terri de la Peña." In *Chicano Writers, Third Series. Dictionary of Literary Biography, Vol. 209,* 194–201, edited by Francisco A. Lomelí and Carl R. Shirley. Detroit: Gale Research, 1999.

Loya, Camille D. "Terri de la Peña." In *Contemporary Lesbian Writers of the United States: A Bio-Bibliographical Critical Sourcebook,* edited by Sandra Pollack and Denise D. Knight, 168–73. Westport, CT: Greenwood Press, 1993.

de la Peña, Terri. 'I Wrote This Book Because I Wanted to Read It.'" In *Happy Endings: Lesbian Writers Talk about Their Lives and Work,* edited by Kate Brandt, 237–246. Tallahassee, FL: Naiad Press, 1993.

Williams, Mary Elizabeth, "In and Out of the Genre Ghetto." *Belles Lettres* 10, no. 1 (Spring 1995): 76.

Rafaela G. Castro

De Veaux, Alexis (b. 1948)

Poet, playwright, teacher, activist, mentor, scholar, critic, and editor. Alexis De Veaux was born on September 24, 1948, in New York City to Mae De Veaux and Richard Hill. She grew up in Harlem and the South Bronx. She earned her B.A. from Empire State College in 1976 and her M.A. and Ph.D. in English at the State University of New York (SUNY) in Buffalo.

De Veaux's career is characterized by the brave creation of and intervention into literary institutions. The most striking example of this achievement is her 1985 publication *Blue Heat: A Portfolio of Poems and Drawings*. Standing out from the works of fiction and poetry that she published with Harper & Row (*Na Ni,* 1973, and *An Enchanted Hair Tale,* 1987) and with Doubleday (her noted 1973 *Spirits in the Street*), *Blue Heat: A Portfolio of Poems and Drawings* was composed, illustrated, and self-published by Alexis De Veaux and her Diva Publishing Enterprises. *Blue Heat* was an experiment in possible connection, tentative order, and unbound vision. Reviewer and fellow black lesbian poet **Cheryl Clarke** emphasized the boldness of De Veaux's insistence through the act of publishing *Blue Heat* that black women could publish themselves. Offering loose pages that implied that the reader was an editor, and metaphorizing Nicaragua as liberation and South Africa as struggle, *Blue Heat* exemplified black feminist production, an experiment in diaspora as a democratic intervention.

But *Blue Heat* is not the only example of De Veaux's versatility. In 1975 she wrote the play *The Tapestry,* which was performed the same year and broadcast on public radio the following year. A powerful piece of theater, *The Tapestry* maps the maturation and emotional liberation of its protagonist, Jet, as she learns to balance her individuality with her larger commitment to the black community. In 1977 De Veaux and Gwendolyn Hardwick co-founded The Flamboyant Ladies, a performance group that printed T-shirts and organized events about the implications of nuclear policies for black communities among other pressing issues. In 1980, De Veaux founded and led a black diasporic writing group for women in Brooklyn called the Gaptooth Girlfriends that went on to self-publish and perform their own work.

At the same time De Veaux infiltrated the pages of black fashion and beauty magazine *Essence* as poetry editor, contributing editor, and editor at large with a politics of black internationalist solidarity that confounded and contradicted the commercialized ideologies of the magazine. During her time at *Essence,* De Veaux worked with executive editor Cheryll Greene to feature work by black feminists such as **Audre Lorde** and **June Jordan** that contrasted sharply with the majority of the magazine's content.

Seeking her academic credentials at the State University of New York at Buffalo after an already rich career as a writer, performer, teacher, and institution builder, Alexis De Veaux focused on the understudied short stories of black women writers during a period that largely focused on the more marketable form of the novel. Providing an insightful analysis of black women's writing and reading practices, De Veaux's dissertation, on file at the Schomburg Library, near her place of birth, includes her original short stories and transcribed interviews with a number of black women in the Buffalo area.

As a scholar and critic and now a tenured professor at SUNY Buffalo, De Veaux emphasizes a radical approach to the academy, challenging her students to anaylze critically their relationships to systems of oppression.

De Veaux's *Warrior Poet,* the first biography of black lesbian literary legend Audre Lorde, is a priceless contribution to the study of Lorde as a human being and to the history of black feminist literary production during the twentieth century.

Further Reading

Gomez, Jewelle L. "Alexis De Veaux." In *Contemporary Lesbian Writers of the United States: A Bio-Bibliographical Critical Sourcebook,* edited by Sandra Pollack and Denise D. Knight, 174–80. Westport, CT: Greenwood Press, 1993.

Splawn, Jane P. "Re-Imaging the Black Woman's Body in Alexis De Veaux's *The Tapestry.*" *Modern Drama* 40, no. 4 (Winter 1997): 514–25.

Alexis Pauline Gumbs

Dhalla, Ghalib Shiraz (b. 1967)

Groundbreaking Kenyan Indian novelist, syndicated journalist, screenwriter, film producer, and activist. The only child of Parviz Virjee and Shiraz Dhalla, Ghalib Shiraz Dhalla was born on June 5, 1967, in Mombasa, Kenya. Dhalla's great grandparents were from the Ismaili faith and had immigrated to Kenya from India. His father was from the capital of Nairobi, and his mother was from a working-class family in Mombasa. During his early childhood, Dhalla saw his parents infrequently as they shuttled between Mombasa and Nairobi, where his father was employed. He was raised primarily by his maternal grandparents, uncle, and aunt. Dhalla's grandfather, Janoo Virjee, was renowned in the community as a songwriter and violin and harmonium player, and Dhalla's parents were avid fans of Bollywood's cinema and music. Influenced by them, Dhalla himself developed a passion for music, cinema, and literature and was barely five years old when he decided to be an author. In 1973, when Dhalla was five years old, his father was murdered by his mistress in Nairobi, and his mother relocated to Mombasa for good. The tempestuous relationship of his parents, its legacy on his own relationships, and his own "coming out" and acclimation to America would become the central themes of his upcoming creative works.

When Dhalla was 13, he got his first taste of being published when Kenya's national magazine, *Viva,* ran his article on the subject of "Infertility." By the time he was 18, Dhalla was a certified teacher and ordained as a priest in the Ismaili faith. He studied in the Aga Khan school system in Mombasa; upon graduation, he was awarded the "Student of the Year Award" and a partial scholarship by the Aga Khan Foundation to attend Woodbury University in Los Angeles as a Graphic Arts and Marketing major in 1987. To supplement the scholarship and financial assistance provided by his maternal family, Dhalla joined the banking industry and steadily climbed up to the ranks of a vice president. It was during his first few years as an entry-level banker that Dhalla finally began to write his debut novel, *Ode to Lata,* as a series of vignettes on an antiquated computer in the break room during his daily lunch hour. During the same time, Dhalla cofounded the South Asian program for the Asian Pacific AIDS Intervention Team, where a fellow writer and outreach worker encouraged him to submit his writing to an upcoming anthology focusing on South Asian literature. An excerpt from his yet untitled manuscript was published in *Contours of the Heart: South Asian Map North America.* His publication in this anthology led to his being signed by the William Morris Agency and eventually led to the publishing of his debut novel, *Ode to Lata,* in 2002.

Ode to Lata offers bold new representations of South Asian sexuality, challenges racial stereotypes, and introduced Ali, the first Muslim, Kenyan/Indian gay character in popular fiction. Nonlinear, and spanning three generations and two continents, the novel dared to unflinchingly chronicle the journey of its protagonist, Ali, through a dramatic and dysfunctional childhood, same-sex obsessions, and forays into sex clubs. Semiautobiographical in nature, the novel became a catharsis for Dhalla and innumerable South Asian gay men to whom Ali gave a face and who also related to the melodramatic Bollywood songs of the popular vocalist Lata Mangeshkar, to whom the title pays tribute. The *Los Angeles Times Book Review* hailed Dhalla's canonical debut "an accomplishment" and a book "that engages cultural differences and the loathing dismissal engendered by racism and intolerance" (12). Christopher Rice called it "a rare, great novel" (dust jacket blurb). *Ode to Lata* created milestones as the first South Asian gay novel ever to be reviewed by the *Los Angeles*

Times and to be excerpted by *Genre*. It was also the first account of the South Asian gay experience from an author from the African continent.

Although *Ode to Lata* was optioned for film even before it was published, it took several more years before the project passed from one producer to another and surmounted the challenges posed by the daring theme and the dark subject that Dhalla was unwilling to compromise. Dhalla helped produce and co-wrote the screenplay for the film adaptation called *The Ode*. Helming a stellar, multiethnic cast including Sakina Jaffrey, Wilson Cruz, and Sachin Bhatt, the film was shot on location in Dhalla's hometown of Mombasa, Kenya, and his current home, Los Angeles. The movie premiered at the Los Angeles Gay & Lesbian Film Festival in 2008. Dhalla has continued to contribute in the capacity of either a freelancer or editor to various regional and national publications including *Angeleno, Genre, Instinct,* and *Malibu;* in 2003, he founded *IndulgeMagazine.com,* a luxury travel and lifestyle e-zine. Presently, he is working on the completion of his second novel, "The Two Krishnas," and a screenplay based on his short story "A" from the *Love, West Hollywood* anthology (2008).

Further Reading

Carlile, D. J. "Song of Himself." *Los Angeles Times Book Review* March 24, 2002: 12.

Steve Valentine

Dixon, Melvin (1950–1992)

Gay African American writer and professor, who was torn between his academic and creative writing impulses. He published a variety of works, ranging from reviews and literary criticism to poetry and novels.

Melvin Dixon was born to working-class parents, Handy and Jessie Dixon, and although both of his parents were from the South, Dixon was raised in the black urban community of Stamford, Connecticut. His parents' familial roots, suggesting as they do the Great Migration of the mid-twentieth century where millions of African Americans migrated from the rural South to the urban North, created a highly mysterious and aesthetically productive geographic location for Dixon, who later used the South as a setting in several of his works. Dixon graduated from Wesleyan University in 1971 with a dual degree in English and Theater, and he attended Brown University, where he earned his Ph.D. in 1975. Although Dixon considered his creative writing pursuits to be his greatest achievement, he was additionally an accomplished academic. His numerous academic achievements include completing a Fulbright teaching award in Senegal, translating several books of French literary criticism and poetry, and producing numerous pieces of original scholarly work. Dixon also held a faculty position at Williams College before becoming a full professor at Queens College in Manhattan. He died from AIDS-related complications on October 26, 1992, in his hometown of Stamford.

Despite having been born and raised in New England, Dixon's critical and narrative purview extended from the historic oral tradition of Southern slaves to the contemporary concerns of the African American novelist. The productivity resulting from Dixon's wide-reaching interests can be readily seen in his study of the African American literary tradition, which was titled *Ride Out the Wilderness: Geography and Identity in Afro-American*

Literature (1987). Dixon's thesis examines the African American literary tradition, particularly as it varyingly reflects the narrative locations of the wilderness, the underground, and the mountaintop. This rigorous yet eloquently written book-length study opens with a consideration of slave songs and oral narratives and progresses to an analysis of 10 African American novelists. The breadth of Dixon's interests and critical engagement can also be clearly detected here, and the book ranges over an extensive range of novelists, including Jean Toomer, Richard Wright, Ralph Ellison, Gayl Jones, and Toni Morrison. Dixon's critical work continues to find an audience as late as 2006 with the publication of *A Melvin Dixon Critical Reader,* which collects eight of Dixon's critical essays for the first time.

Dixon began publishing poetry in magazines and journals in the late 1970s, and his work appeared in such titles as the *Beloit Poetry Journal.* His first book of poetry *Change of Territory* was published in 1983, and his chapbook *Six Poems for Senegal* was published in 1986. Dixon's final volume of poetry was posthumously published in 1995. As a collection, *Love's Instruments* reflects Dixon's geographic reach, which ranges from Paris to Provincetown, and it contains some of the poet's most powerful AIDS poetry, including the popular and impacting poem "Aunt Ida Pieces a Quilt." Dixon's interest in poetry extended to his translation work, and his French translation of the poems by Leopold Sedar Senghor was posthumously published as *The Complete Poems of Leopold Sedar Senghor* in 1998.

Dixon's first novel, which was published in 1989, explores the intersection of geography and identity. *Trouble the Water* reverses the established trajectory of the Great Migration when its protagonist flees the racial tensions in his adopted northern college town by returning to the southern hometown of his youth, only to find himself equally embroiled in the problematic conflicts that result from family history. *Trouble the Water* lightly touches on the topic of homosexuality, but this concern largely remains an actualized component from the protagonist's past. Dixon turns his narrative focus more fully on homosexuality in his second novel, *Vanishing Rooms* (1991), which innovatively narrates a brutal gay-bashing incident from three points of view—including that of the troubled gay basher. The novel also simultaneously grabbles with the complexities of racism and sexuality through the inclusion of an interracial gay love affair and a bisexual heterosexual romance.

As a gay African American, who wrote openly from the perspectives of his racial and his sexual identities, Dixon made important contributions to Joseph Beam's pioneering *In the Life: A Black Gay Anthology* (1986) and **Essex Hemphill**'s equally significant *Brother to Brother* (1991).

Further Reading

Koponen, Wilfrid. "Melvin Dixon." In *Contemporary Gay American Novelists: A Bio-Bibliographical Sourcebook,* edited by Emmanuel S. Nelson, 110–15. Westport, CT: Greenwood, 1993.

McBride, Dwight, and Justin Joyce, eds. *A Melvin Dixon Critical Reader.* Jackson: University of Mississippi Press, 2006.

Romanet, Jerome de. "A Conversation with Melvin Dixon." *Callaloo* 23, no. 1 (Winter 2000): 80–83.

Wallace, Maurice. "The Auotchoreography of an Ex-Snow Queen: Dance, Desire, and the Black Masculine in Melvin Dixon's *Vanishing Rooms*." In *Novel Gazing: Queer Reading in Fiction*, edited by Eve Kosofsky Sedgewick, 379–400. Durham, NC: Duke University Press, 1997.

Williams, Carla. "Melvin Dixon." glbtq, Inc. January 2003. www.glbtq.com.

Mark John Isola

Dlugos, Tim (1950–1990)

Significant **gay** experimental poet of the 1970s and 1980s. Tim Dlugos was an early poet to write in a thoughtful and artistic manner about the experience of living with HIV/AIDS, especially in such work as his long poem "G-9," named after the AIDS ward at Roosevelt Hospital in New York City, where Dlugos wrote some of his best-known poems while recovering from pneumonia.

Francis Timothy Dlugos was born in Springfield, Massachusetts, on August 5, 1950, and later grew up in Arlington, Virginia. In 1968 he joined the Christian Brothers, a Catholic lay order of religious men who took vows of chastity, poverty, and obedience and enrolled in their college, La Salle, in Philadelphia. He left the Brothers in 1971 to openly embrace a politically active gay life and eventually left La Salle College before graduating.

Dlugos began publishing his poems in the early 1970s while living in Washington, D.C., where he worked on Ralph Nader's *Public Citizen* and was heavily involved with the local poetry scene. He published five books and chapbooks of poetry during his lifetime, beginning with *High There* in 1973. His collection *Strong Place* (1992), named after both his address during its composition and the place that he felt he had reached in his poetry, was published posthumously, as was *Powerless* (1996), his volume of selected poems, edited by fellow gay poet **David Trinidad**.

Soon after his diagnosis as HIV-positive, Dlugos left his career as a fund-raiser to study for the Episcopalian priesthood at the Yale School of Divinity, which he was pursuing at the time of his death from AIDS-related complications in 1990. This strain of spirituality is a constant in his work, always in tension and dialogue with a strong commitment to the things of this world, no matter how quotidian and apparently insignificant (in both senses of the word). In an early artistic statement Dlugos said that his best work took the timeless and dragged it into the real world of everyday life, and this remained true throughout his writing career.

Many of Dlugos's poems revolve around memories, which often blur into both present realities and future possibilities. In these poems, memory is not fixed or static, but a mode of mental travel. Dlugos's poems are often strongly grounded in specific places and times, but they constantly remind us that this moment's present is yesterday's future and tomorrow's past: by being fully here now, one can be anywhere at any time. Any moment, any place, can become luminous, numinous even, if experienced in a properly receptive state of mind. Grace abounds in these poems, inhering in the smallest and the largest things.

Dlugos's poetry incorporates a wide variety of subjects, including literature, pop culture, visual art, classical and popular music, the textures and neighborhoods of New York City, contemporary urban gay life (and the traumas of gay adolescence), alcoholism, and AIDS. For Dlugos, however, style was as important as content: he wrote sonnets, sestinas, rhymed quatrains, and other formal poems (some of his own design), list poems, love poems, elegies, tight lyrics, and extended narratives. Dlugos's was a broad-ranging and eclectic sensibility, but he did not simply juxtapose disparate elements for their own sake. Instead, he synthesized those elements into new and unexpected wholes.

Poems like "Stanzas for Martina," "Day for Paul," and "Chez Jane" exemplify the collage-like technique of assembling sensory impressions and passing thoughts into a snapshot of the motions of a particular consciousness that Dlugos inherits and develops from gay New York School poet Frank O'Hara. Indeed, O'Hara is mentioned in "Day for Paul," and "Chez Jane" is named after a poem of O'Hara's. "Day for Paul" also explicitly mentions the gay French novelist Marcel Proust, whose multivolume novel *Á la Recherche du Temps Perdu* (usually translated as *Remembrance of Things Past*) explores the workings of memory and desire. The Proustian method of conjuring up panoramas of the personal past through sensory detail is an important component of Dlugos's work.

Much of Dlugos's later poetry dealt with his experiences of living with HIV and AIDS. The sense of the importance of the here and now is only sharpened by the poems' keen awareness of mortality not just as a universal human fact but as an imminent threat.

Further Reading

Cory, Jim. "Tim Dlugos: 1950–1990." *The James White Review* 10, no. 2 (Winter 1993): 18–19; Shepherd, Reginald. "Tim Dlugos." In *Contemporary Gay American Poets and Playwrights: An A-to-Z Guide,* edited by Emmanuel S. Nelson, 108–16. Westport, CT: Greenwood Press, 2003.
Koponen, Wilfrid. "Melvin Dixon." Beaudouin, David. "Tim Dlugos, an Appreciation." *Washington Review* (December 1982–January 1983): 28.

Reginald Shepherd

Donaghe, Ronald L. (b. 1948)

American novelist, essayist, technical writer, and editor; winner of the 2008 Jim Duggins Outstanding Mid-Career Novelist's Award. Ronald L. Donaghe was born on May 6, 1948, in the small town of Deming, located in the southwestern corner of New Mexico. His parents had six other children, four girls and two boys, one of whom died in infancy. Ron, the third in line, lived until age 7 in an adobe house in Deming built by his father and paternal grandfather. He then moved with his family to a farm outside of town.

Donaghe spent the rest of his growing-up years doing chores on the farm and attending a country school of about 110 students from first to eighth grade. He went to high school in Deming, where his attraction to a male classmate helped him begin to understand his sexual orientation. He kept his discovery to himself, however, and continued to date girls. At New Mexico State University in Las Cruces, he majored in education. There, he acknowledged his homosexuality to a few of his college friends and began frequenting the **gay** bars in El Paso, Texas, about 45 miles from Las Cruces. In 1970, though, after a couple of brief affairs with other men, he made what he now regards as a mistake and married a woman he had barely met. It took just six months for him to realize his mistake, after which he joined the U.S. Air Force as the war in Vietnam was winding down. He and his wife were divorced a few years later.

In the air force, Donaghe told everyone in his flight (called a "company" in the army) about his homosexuality and began a 14-year relationship with a fellow airman. He finished his bachelor's degree at Southwest Texas State University in San Marcos, returned to Las Cruces, worked in bookstores for a while, and then went to graduate school at New Mexico State, where he majored in technical writing and computer science. He started working as a technical writer in Las Cruces in 1980, ended his first long-term relationship in 1986, and published his first novel, *Common Sons,* in 1989.

This story, which takes place in 1965, tells of two high school boys, Joel Reece and Tom Allen, who meet, become friends, and fall in love. Two attributes make this book quite different from many others with the same theme: first is its setting, in the part of the country that Donaghe knows best, the little farming towns of southern New Mexico, far from the large gay urban enclaves of the East and West coasts where so much of America's gay fiction, before and since, has unfolded. Second is the fact that these two boys find the courage, almost unheard-of in those pre-**Stonewall** days, to defy the confusion of their parents and the hostility of their neighbors and insist on their right to love—and live with—each other.

Donaghe has moved this story forward through more than three decades in what he calls his "Common Threads in the Life" series. Three more novels—*The Salvation Mongers* (2000), *The Blind Season* (2001), and *The Gathering* (2006)—have been published, and Donaghe is working on a fifth, *A Summer's Change.* A second series, "The Continuing Journals of Will Barnett," includes the novels *Uncle Sean* (2001), *Lance* (2002), and *All Over Him* (2003). These three books have been translated into Spanish and published by Editorial Egales of Barcelona, Spain.

A fantasy series, called "Twilight of the Gods," has begun with the publication of its first novel, *Cinatis* (2004), to be followed by *Gwi's War* and *War among the Gods.* Donaghe's two autobiographical books are *Letters in Search of Love and Other Essays* (1998) and *My Year of Living Heterosexually: And Other Adventures in Hell* (2000). Essays by Donaghe appeared in two of John D. Preston's anthologies by gay writers—"Deming, New Mexico" in *Hometowns* (1991) and "My Sister and I" in *A Member of the Family* (1992).

Around 2000, Donaghe became disillusioned with conventional publishing and since then has been working as a technical writer. He continues to live in Las Cruces, New Mexico, with his partner Cliff, whom he met in 1991. Donaghe plans to retire in 2009 from his job as a technical writer and editor at New Mexico State University and will then concentrate on freelance editing and writing more fiction.

Further Reading

Selig, John R. Review of *Lance. ForeWord Magazine* (November/December 2002). http://www .forewordmagazine.com/reviews/printreviews.aspx?reviewID=978.
———. Rev of *All Over Him, ForeWord Magazine* (July/August 2003). http://www.foreword magazine.com/reviews/viewreviews.aspx?reviewID=1134.

Robert Taylor

Drake, David (b. 1963)

Award-winning playwright, performer, journalist, editor, activist, and director. David Drake was born David Drakula on June 27, 1963, and although he grew up in Baltimore, Maryland, Drake was born in Waynesburg, Pennsylvania. Best known for his one-man show, *The Night Larry Kramer Kissed Me* (1992), Drake began his illustrious career as an actor. He studied acting at Herbert Berghof Studio in New York City and went on to star in a string of hit off-Broadway shows including **Doric Wilson**'s *Street Theater* (1984), **Charles Busch**'s *Vampire Lesbians of Sodom* (1986), and the drag musical *Pageant* (1991). Then, as Drake recalls, he saw a performance of **Larry Kramer**'s ***The Normal Heart*** (1985), which, as a young adult coming-of-age at the dawn of the AIDS crisis, had a profound effect on him, leading him into activism. A member of ACT UP (AIDS Coalition to Unleash Power) and **Queer** Nation, Drake's work in activist groups heavily informed his creation of *The Night Larry Kramer Kissed Me,* which he began writing in 1990. *The Night Larry Kramer Kissed Me* opened at the Perry Street Theatre on June 22, 1992, and ran until June 27, 1993, Drake's 30th birthday and the 24th anniversary of the **Stonewall Riots**, winning Drake the *New York Village Voice* Obie Award, the 1994 Dramalogue Award for "Outstanding Solo Performance," and a Lambda Literary Award nomination for "Best New Play" in the process. Drake's theater career continued with performances in an all-star reading of *The Normal Heart* (1993), a revival of **Mart Crowley**'s *The Boys in the Band* (1996), *End of the World Party* (2000), and his second one-man show, *Son of Drakula* (2002). His film work includes roles in *Longtime Companion* (1990), *Philadelphia* (1993), *It's Pat* (1994), and the film version of *The Night Larry Kramer Kissed Me* (2000), directed by Tim Kirkman. Drake has written for several magazines including *Details* and *The Advocate* while also working as editor-at-large for *POZ,* a magazine focusing on HIV/AIDS, in 1996. But the theater has always been his first love, and when Drake is not acting in film and television, he is directing plays such as **Edmund White**'s *Terre Haute* (2005). Drake's own plays deal heavily with issues of **gay** identity, **gender**, politics, activism, and AIDS, and they are, for the most part, very well received by critics. Highly autobiographical, Drake's works, rhythmic in sound and motion, and episodic in form and content, often feature examinations of the "sissy" male child, a figure that is praised, defended, and loved. Drake is not one to run away from gay male effeminacy, nor is one to ridicule it, and instead of being a tragic figure, the "effeminate gay man" is portrayed as a character of great strength. But Drake's plays, created by a man who came into adulthood during the onslaught of AIDS in the early and mid-1980s, are still most notable for their very human connection to social awareness, activism, historical legacy, and a hopeful future.

Further Reading

Bruckner, D. J. R. "Of Gay Humor and Loss." *New York Times,* June 25, 1992, C18.

Drake, David. Introduction. *The Night Larry Kramer Kissed Me.* New York: Anchor, 1994. xii–xiv.

Feingold, Michael. "Normal Kisses." *New York Village Voice,* July 7, 1992, 81, 84.

Keehnen, Owen. "Footlight Activism: Talking with David Drake, Performer and Playwright of *The Night Larry Kramer Kissed Me*." In *glbtq: An Encyclopedia of Gay, Lesbian, Bisexual, Transgender, and Queer Culture,* edited by Claude J. Summers. September 30, 2005. http://www.glbtq.com /sfeatures/interviewddrake.html (accessed December 5, 2007).

Provenzano, Jim. "The Night Larry Kramer Kissed Me." *The Advocate* (July 30, 1992): 70–71.

Richards, David. "The Minefields of Monologue." *New York Times,* July 12, 1992, sec. 2:5.

Schiavi, Michael R. "Staging Effeminacy in America." Dissertation. New York University, 1998. 253–69.

———. "David Drake." *Contemporary Gay American Poets and Playwrights: An A-to-Z Guide,* edited by Emmanuel S. Nelson, 125–29. Westport, CT: Greenwood, 2003.

Solomon, Alisa. "The Performance Art That Dare Not Speak Its Name." *New York Village Voice* September 29, 1992: 104.

van Gelder, Lawrence. "A Gay Man's Awakening Captures the Spirit of a Time." *New York Times,* July 14, 2000, E21.

Willa, Julia. "Magic Time! *The Night Larry Kramer Kissed Me* by David Drake/*Jeffrey* by Paul Rudnick/*Angels in America Part II: Perestroika* by Tony Kushner." *Lambda Book Report* 4. no. 4 (May 1994): 24.

Winn, Steven. "A Tragicomic Look at Gay Culture: New York Hit 'Larry Kramer' at Life on the Water." *San Francisco Chronicle,* April 12, 1993, D1.

Damion Clark

Drama, Gay

One problem in discussing this topic is defining "contemporary." Un**closet**ed **gay** drama, as opposed to drama by gay playwrights, has been with us only for less than half a century. For our purposes, I am going to define "contemporary" as drama written in this century, though much of the work discussed here has been written by writers whose careers go back into the last century. "Gay drama" also could be defined in many ways, but I shall consider works that are gay created, speak directly to gay issues, and acknowledge that some of the audience is gay.

In the last decades of the twentieth century, drama was an important medium of expression and community solidarity for gay men when we were invisible in the mass media except for an occasional negative or stereotypical representation. Theater was the place where we could see aspects of our lives played out before an audience of fellow travelers. Beginning with experimental venues such as **Caffé Cino** in Greenwich Village in the 1960s to Theatre Rhinoceros in San Francisco and Bailiwick Repertory Theatre in Chicago in ensuing decades, theaters were founded in urban gay neighborhoods that were part of an emerging gay consciousness and pride. Other small theaters in major urban areas had a loyal gay audience. Gay drama hit its peak during the worst of the AIDS epidemic with works such as **William M. Hoffman**'s *As Is,* **Tony Kushner**'s *Angels in America,* and **Terrence McNally**'s *Love! Valour! Compassion!* that were created for regional or off-Broadway theaters, then had runs on Broadway, and subsequently played in small theaters around the country.

A number of factors led to the dwindling, if not demise, of gay drama. Such plays depended on a large gay audience as few straight people had any interest in seeing "gay plays," and fewer gay men are now invested in live theater, particularly when gay characters and openly gay actors appear regularly on television. Highly talented playwrights such as Alan Ball, Jon Robin Baitz, and David Marshall Grant who were once dedicated to writing for the stage moved to television and created shows like *Six Feet Under* and *Brothers and Sisters* with highly visible gay characters and narrative arcs. A British critic recently referred to the better Home Box Office and Showtime series as "America's national theater," and the treatment of the ups and downs of the mixed race gay couple on *Six Feet Under* was certainly as deftly handled as the relationships in most gay plays. The British and American versions of *Queer as Folk* were highly successful on television and through video distribution. Gay-oriented cable networks such as Logo and Here! offer continuous programming including the fine series about gay African Americans, *Noah's Arc.* Television drama certainly counts as drama—in fact, in the supposed "Golden Age of Television Drama" in the 1950s, teleplays by Paddy Chayefsky and Gore Vidal moved from television to Broadway. There are also a large number of independent gay films shown at gay film festivals, all of which seem to move quickly onto video. Granted the quality of these low-budget works is variable, but they do show that young writers and directors see film as the best way to mirror their experience as gay men.

Moreover, a number of gay men no longer find it necessary to live in urban gay "ghettoes" and have moved away from urban centers. Theater, then, is not the necessary source of gay expression it once was and, while some theaters in urban areas with large gay populations continue to thrive, they do so in part by offering plays with one thing that has not yet come to American television, male nudity. At times, as in *Take Me Out,* discussed below, nudity is crucial to the play. However, long-running commercials such as *Naked Boys Singing* could be summed up by the title. Nonetheless, some playwrights in New York and elsewhere around the United States are still interested in serious treatment of gay characters and situations. As you will see, most of these works had their first productions outside of New York City, many in London, another sign of the fact that Manhattan is far from the center of the theatrical world.

The only twenty-first century gay play thus far that has had the kind of success that 1990s plays such as *Angels in America* achieved has been Richard Greenberg's *Take Me Out,* which first appeared in London in 2002 in a co-production with the New York Public Theater where it was later produced before moving to Broadway. The title has multiple meanings. On one hand, the play tells the story of a talented, intelligent, mixed-race athlete who, because of his physical prowess, has never been anything but celebrated and privileged. The said athlete decides to break some of the longest-held taboos and myths of the hypermasculine world of baseball by coming out. The other central character is a lonely, nerdy gay accountant who, through being assigned to manage the athlete's considerable fortune, learns to love baseball, which takes him out of his loneliness and boredom. While *Take Me Out* has funny moments, it is really a bittersweet play about isolation and loneliness at the heart of the American Dream. The team does not function at all as a team off the baseball diamond. The celebrated athlete has no friends and even loses the romance of baseball. The two gay leading characters find no meaningful connection to what is called the "gay community," though they become unlikely friends. The original production, directed by Joe Mantello, had shower scenes with male nudity, but nothing sexual or romantic. If anything, they showed that men can be naked together while revealing little about themselves. Like much of Greenberg's work, this is a play about non-connection, about the power of language to wound. *Take Me Out* is a play that focuses on two gay characters—and one virulently homophobic one—but is about far more than coming out.

Two recent American plays attempt through a series of vignettes to capture a wider view of common experiences of gay men past and present. Terrence McNally has been writing plays about the gay community since the early 1960s. Indeed, his work offers a history of how gay men can be represented on the American stage. His play, *Some Men,* which premiered in Philadelphia in 2006 (before moving to New York a year later), is an attempt to write a history of love and marriage for American gay men in the twentieth and early twenty-first centuries. The play begins at a contemporary gay wedding, then travels back to scenes of love between men over the past century: from the fraught, furtive relationship of a master and servant on a Long Island estate in the 1920s to gay dads sitting on the beach of the same estate in 2007. McNally is not only interested in celebrating the fact that love between men has always been there, but also wants to examine the conflict between loving commitment and sexual desire. In the final scenes of the play, he also looks at the gay generation gap. In one scene, two young **queer** filmmakers give up filming an interview with older gay men who have fond memories of their lives in New York in a more repressive time because they see their elders politically incorrect and insufficiently "queer." A subsequent scene shows the tensions between a gay father and his adult gay son. McNally wants to celebrate the courage of men who dared to love other men before they could be as open as they now are in some cosmopolitan areas.

Joe DiPietro's *Fucking Men*, which had its first production in London in 2008, is a contemporary gay version of Arthur Schnitzler's early twentieth century play *La Ronde* that has already had an omnisexual musical version by gay composer Michael John LaChiusa (*Hello Again!*). Through the interlinked scenes (one partner in scene one becomes the partner of someone else in scene two, and so forth) of *Fucking Men*, DiPietro shows us a variety of men from different walks of life who look for love through sexual encounters. DiPietro is particularly interested in the mores of male-male relationships. Is sexual infidelity really a betrayal of love? The common thread through the various vignettes is loneliness and the need for love and companionship that is not often satisfied by sex alone.

Christopher Shinn's work, which is produced both in New York and London, is hard on gay men, a corollary to the sharp critique of heterosexual men found in the work of Neil LaBute, but he is also interested in the class divide in America and the ways in which the privileged, gay and straight, seal themselves off from any personal or social responsibility. Two of his plays are set in New York City around the time of 9/11. In *Where Do We Live* (London 2002; New York City 2004), even a well-meaning, politically correct, gay intellectual has problems breaking out of the prevailing hedonism and self-absorption and making the kind of connection to the people around him he claims people should have. Next door is a poor young African American whose chance of breaking out of a cycle of drug dealing is shattered by the disaster at the World Trade Center. There is only the slightest connection between the lives of privileged white gay men and those of their neighbors. *Dying City* (London 2006; New York City 2007), also set around 9/11, has one actor playing twin brothers, one gay and one straight, and their relationship with the wife of the straight brother. We see scenes before the straight brother returns to military service in Iraq where he sees not only the horror of war, but the horror of what he is capable of and, as a result, kills himself, and scenes a year later between the wife and the gay twin who has broken up with his partner. We see that both brothers are incapable of a loving relationship.

Like Tony Kushner's 1992 play *Angels in America*, which reached a nationwide audience via Mike Nichols's highly celebrated television production, Steve Yockey's daring, poetic *Octopus* (2008) presents a man who cannot deal with the fact that his lover may be HIV-positive as the result of a *ménage a quatre* he forced his lover to participate in. However, where Kushner's play leaves all its central characters alone, *Octopus*, subtitled "A Love Story," affirms the possibility of love and critiques men who want everything: a loving relationship but freedom to play around, a partner but nothing messy. Like Kushner's play, *Octopus* uses both theatrical realism and magic realism—and a lot of water on stage—as characters who are not loved enough disappear to the literal and metaphoric bottom of the sea. AIDS is not the deadly disease it was when Kushner first penned *Angels in America*, and Yockey's interest is not victimization from a disease, but from lack of love from those who claim to be in loving relationships. *Octopus* had its premiere at Actors Express in Atlanta, a theater that has premiered several successful gay-themed plays.

Yockey's fine play demonstrates that a lot of good drama, gay and otherwise, happens in small theaters outside of New York.

Douglas Carter Beane takes a lighter approach to gay theater in two 2008 works that demonstrate both continuity with gay works of the past and an ironic twenty-first century outlook. *The Little Dog Laughed* (2006) is on one hand a satiric comedy about a female Hollywood agent's relentless campaign to keep a male star in the closet. The answer to the question of whether his stardom or his love is more important (why not both?) should be obvious, but Hollywood still prefers that its leading actors be in the closet. The central character of Beane's comedy is not the star but the ruthless, foul-mouthed agent. In this and his earlier play, *As Bees in Honey Drown* (1998), Beane shows his mastery at writing old-fashioned **camp** diva roles that are not the least misogynistic. Beane's book for the musical *Xanadu* (2007) offers Broadway what is probably the most self-consciously camp musical in its history. In an era in which producers seem interested only in mounting stage versions of films, *Xanadu* puts one of the worst film musicals ever made onto the stage with an almost sadistic glee. Here is a contemporary, higher-budget version of the celebrations of kitsch and camp that the purveyors of Ridiculous Theater of the 1960s and 1970s presented in small theaters in Greenwich Village complete with chorus boys in drag portraying the muses. At one point, a character correctly acknowledges that she is performing in "children's theater for forty year old gay men." However, *Xanadu* is playing in a Broadway theater to a mixed audience suggesting that even the most outrageous camp is no longer only gay.

Further Reading

Clum, John M. *Still Acting Gay: Male Homosexuality in Modern Drama.* New York: St. Martin's Press, 2000.

Nelson, Emmanuel S., ed. *Contemporary Gay American Poets and Playwrights.* Westport, CT: Greenwood Press, 2003.

John M. Clum

Drama, Lesbian

Lesbian drama in the United States is a complex, historically rich component of the American theater. This pastiche of work includes plays written by and about lesbians, plays featuring lesbian characters, lesbian performance collectives, and one-woman shows by lesbian performance artists. Lesbian presence within American theatrical production also includes the history of lesbian actresses, choreographers, designers, and producers.

Pre-**Stonewall** theater is often dismissed as an era offering little more than pathologizing and stereotypical depictions of homosexuality, but recent interest in the history of **gay**s and lesbians in the theater has suggested a more complexly embedded legacy in early twentieth-century American theatrical production. Although many of this era's plays were written by men and performed by straight actors, some do indeed represent the possibility of tenacious, disruptive, and loving lesbian relationships. Some pioneering plays that enjoyed wide audiences and varying degrees of controversy include Sholem Asch's Yiddish drama *God of Vengeance* (1907), translated into English and performed in New York in 1923, *The Captive* (1926), an adaptation for Broadway of Edouard Bourdet's *La prison-nière,* and Lillian Hellman's *The Children's Hour* (1934). *God of Vengeance* is the story of a brothel owner whose presumably virginal young daughter has become the lover of one of the prostitutes from his brothel. Its New York performance dealt the cast members and producer a charge of indecency, and the play was shut down. *The Captive,* scandalized by its role in inaugurating a law in New York declaring that a theater—if found guilty by a jury of performing a work determined to be immoral—could be closed for a year, depicts a woman whose marriage falls apart because she cannot disengage from her lesbian lover. The two schoolmistresses in Lillian Hellman's *The Children's Hour* famously find themselves accused by a pupil of carrying on a lesbian affair, and the charge has tragic yet ambiguously provocative results.

Other plays from this era include *The Mothers* (1915), by British playwright and essayist Edith Ellis—open-marriage wife of British sexologist Havelock Ellis; Edna St. Vincent Millay's 1921 collegiate Sapphic love story *The Lamp and the Bell*—written and performed while she was a student at Vassar; and several works by Djuna Barnes: *Two Ladies Take Tea* (1923), *To the Dogs* (1923), and *The Dove* (1926). In December 1944 Dorothy Baker's adaptation of her novel *Trio* also began a very short run on Broadway. The play involved a middle-aged woman, a young woman, and a young man. The relationship between the women provoked a petition suggesting that the play was "injurious to public morals." By February 1945 the play had been shut down, and another confrontation between the courts and the theater began. Again, although many of these plays foreground lesbian "content," each approaches same-sex desire between women with varying degrees of sympathy and demonization.

A number of high-profile female playwrights and performers of the early twentieth century theater were known to have had female lovers and held long-standing relationships with women. A partial list of these women includes Mercedes de Acosta (Cuban American playwright, poet, and costume designer), Josephine Baker (dancer and actress), Tallulah Bankhead (actress), Djuna Barnes (writer), Gladys Bentley (Harlem drag performer), Katharine Cornell (Broadway actress, theater owner, and producer), Marlene Dietrich (actress), Isadora Duncan (dancer), Eleonora Duse (actress), Lynne Fontaine (actress), Eva La Galliene (Broadway star), Greta Garbo (actress), Alla Nazimova (theater and film actress, scriptwriter, and producer), Gertrude "Ma" Rainey (vaudeville performer and jazz singer), Bessie Smith (iconic blues artist and Broadway performer), and Estelle Winwood (prolific Broadway performer). As this list suggests, the American modernist movement was characterized by a bohemian climate. Especially in New York, both downtown and in Harlem, there were spaces for same-sex love between women; however, the citation of this community does not mean that the representation of lesbians in the theater at this time ever portrayed a cohesive, recognized lesbian identity. Furthermore, many of these women were married or carried on relationships with married women.

Although the overt depiction of homosexuality onstage was officially prohibited by New York state law until 1967, several plays in the 1960s featured lesbian characters with varying degrees of prominence. **Tennessee Williams** eased a love triangle between three female characters into his 1961 play, *The Night of the Iguana,* which was adapted into a critically acclaimed film in 1964. Frank Marcus's play *The Killing of Sister George* (1964), which debuted in London in 1964 and on Broadway in 1966, is a famously complicated precursor to post-Stonewall playwriting. Often derided by contemporary audiences for its stereotypical portrayal of butch/femme roles and manipulative, angry lesbians, this play also had the fortuitous effect of forcing the visibility of lesbian existence. The play was adapted into a critically acclaimed film by Robert Aldrich in 1968, becoming one of the first mainstream American movies whose central theme was the representation of conspicuous lesbian sexuality. African American playwright Ed Bullins included a minor lesbian character in *The Taking of Miss Janie* (1975); additionally, Jack, the protagonist of his earlier play, *Clara's Ole Man* (1965), is shocked to discover that "Big Girl," the butch lesbian he encounters in the home of a woman he is calling on, is actually the eponymous "old man." This play is often cited as the first nonhomophobic scripted play in African American theater.

These plays are documentations of the ways in which even stock or derogatory portrayals of lesbian characters are part of the archive of lesbian theatrical representation: they document historical understandings and popular misconceptions of lesbian identity during a time of nascent lesbian identity in the United States. Furthermore, they also provide interesting reference points for the ways in which patterns of lesbian social behavior, both in and out of the theater, are perceived as more or less viable performances of lesbian identity.

A more fully realized lesbian identity would not begin to gain representation in the theater until after the extended radical political work of gay and lesbian liberation, the women's movement and second wave feminism, radical lesbianism, and the Stonewall Riots of 1969. Post-Stonewall is how many descriptions now refer to the emergence of un-**closet**ed depictions of gay and lesbian identity. With the onset of gay liberation, the politics of representation became a serious component of gay and lesbian playwriting. The theater has a long history of gay and lesbian participation, but a short history of frank portrayals of same-sex relationships. In the United States, it is only in the post-Stonewall era that candid lesbian sexuality and identity artistically and legally became a possible theme in American theater.

Lorraine Hansberry, for example, is remembered as a very important yet closeted member of the lesbian theater. Hansberry's *A Raisin in the Sun* (1959) was the first play written by an African American woman produced on Broadway. She was also the first African American woman to win a New York Drama Critics' Circle Award. Her second play, *The Sign in Sidney Brustein's Window* (1964), featured a white gay male character. After her brief marriage to music producer Robert Nemiroff, Hansberry became a member of the early lesbian organization Daughters of Bilitis in 1957. She published two thoughtful letters under the initials L. H. N. in the organization's journal, *The Ladder*. Hansberry died of pancreatic cancer in 1965, at the age of 34, before completing another play. Her involvement in lesbian politics was not widely disclosed until the 1980s.

Since the 1970s and 1980s, a multitude of plays written and produced by lesbian writers, and plays with explicit lesbian content, have been widely produced throughout the United States. While lesbian playwrights have never enjoyed the visibility on Broadway experienced by their gay male counterparts, they have found wide representation in regional and experimental theaters. Generally recognized as the first self-identified lesbian to achieve mainstream success as a playwright, Jane Chambers wrote plainspoken love stories for lesbian characters. Her first play, *A Late Snow,* was produced by Playwrights Horizons in New York in 1974. Her best-known work, *Last Summer at Bluefish Cove* (1976), has become a classic "lesbian love story." Seven lesbian friends get together for a summer together in Long Island, and Lil, who is battling cancer, encounters Eva, a straight divorcee who has unwittingly rented a cottage at the lesbian beach resort Bluefish Cove. Lil befriends Eva and the friendship evolves into an intense lesbian relationship. It was produced by John Glines, one of the founders of The Glines, a nonprofit organization dedicated to the encouragement of gay art. The play's February 8, 1981, review by Alvin Klein in the *New York Times* ran with the title "Play's Theme: Lesbians without Apology." While this was a conventionally organized play considered to have been intended directly for gay and lesbian audiences, it helped pave the way for an abundant and varied lesbian presence in American theater.

Many female playwrights inaugurated prolific careers during this era and continue to pursue a woman- and/or **queer**-centered process of playwriting. British playwright Caryl Churchill's *Cloud Nine* (1979), a critique of British colonialism, features gay and lesbian characters and employs cross-gendered casting. *Top Girls* (1982) explores, with an all-female cast, the limitations of individualistic feminism. It also animates a variety of famous women from various historical junctures who testify to their own experiences with the complications of high-powered female subjectivity. Both plays were produced in New York; the latter enjoyed a critically acclaimed Broadway premier in 2008.

African American activist, writer, and academic **Alexis De Veaux** has written a number of plays that consider black female sexual identity, including *Circles* (1972) and *The Tapestry* (1986). Emily Mann, who describes her work as an attempt to "give voice to the voiceless," has garnered many awards including the Dramatists Guild of America Hull-Warriner Award for her work both as a playwright and a director. *Execution of Justice* (1984), in which Mann dramatizes the trial of Dan White for the killings of gay activist Harvey Milk and San Francisco mayor George Moscone, won a Playwrights USA Award.

Martha Boesing, author of many plays and founding member of the radical feminist theater At the Foot of the Mountain in Minneapolis, developed a woman-identified method of playwriting with work such as *Love Song for an Amazon* (1976) and *Antigone Too: Rites of Love and Defiance* (1983). *Love Song for an Amazon* is a one-act play written for two female performers that considers the importance of friendship between women. Her *Antigone* recognizes women throughout history who have also committed acts of civil disobedience, such as Mother Jones and Rosa Parks. Rebecca Ranson is perhaps best known for her play *Warren* (1984), which she wrote for a friend who died in San Francisco in one of the first AIDS wards. Ranson received a 2004 Publishing Triangle Lifetime Achievement Award for her oeuvre of more than 30 gay- and lesbian-focused plays. Lesbian feminist poet **Judy Grahn**, author of *Another Mother Tongue: Gay Words, Gay Worlds* (1985), adapted *The Queen of Wands* (1986) and *The Queen of Swords* (1987) from her poetry. Heavily rooted in goddess imagery, both are based on key principles of 1970s American feminism. Grahn received assistance from Adele Prandini, who would also produce the play, with the script for *The Queen of Swords*. Prandini was one of the first lesbian playwrights at the Theatre Rhinoceros in San Francisco, a queer theater founded in 1977, which is still active. Prandini first came to the Rhinoceros to produce her play *Safe Light* (1984), but she became involved with many of the theater's other projects and served as the artistic director from 1990to 1999. Kathleen Tolan's *A Weekend Near Madison* (1983) features a lesbian folksinger and her girlfriend, a domestic drama-inducing insemination plan, and post-1960s political processing. Many of Tolan's other plays, including *Kate's Diary* (1980), *Approximating Mother* (1984), *The Wax* (2000), and *Memory House* (2005), are women-centered, intimate dramas.

Cherríe Moraga, Chicana lesbian feminist playwright, poet, essayist, and artist in residence at Stanford University, has written and produced numerous queer plays. *Giving Up the Ghost,* which premiered at the Theatre Rhinoceros in 1989, is the story of Marisa, a Chicana lesbian in her late 20s, juxtaposed against Corky, a younger version or ghost of Marisa. Exchanges between the two characters merge to illustrate familial and cultural conflicts between her ethnic and sexual identities. Moraga's plays *Shadow of a Man* (1990) and *Watsonville: Some Place Not Here* (1995) each won the Fund for New American Plays Award. *Heroes and Saints* (1992) won the PEN West Award for Drama, and Moraga was also a recipient of the National Endowment for the Arts Theatre Playwrights' Fellowship.

Playwright Kate Moira Ryan won the Young Playwrights Festival prize in 1985 with *OTMA,* which imagines the Romanov sisters rehearsing Chekhov's *The Cherry Orchard* in the last days of the Russian Empire. Throughout her career she has produced work in a variety of genres, from the adventurous *Autobiography of Aiken Fiction* (1994) to her 2003 stage adaptation of **Dorothy Allison**'s 1998 novel *Cavedweller.* Ryan's other plays include a comedy about Jewish mothers, *G-d Doesn't Pay Rent Here* (2002), and the modern lesbian detective noir *Hadley's Mistake* (1998). Her collaboration with Linda S. Chapman to create *The Beebo Brinker Chronicles* (2007), an adaptation of Ann Bannon's 1950s and 1960s lesbian pulp novels, revisits McCarthy-era Greenwich Village.

Paula Vogel, playwright, out lesbian, and professor of Creative Writing and Comparative Literature at Brown University, won an OBIE Award for her 1992 AIDS-metaphor play *The Baltimore Waltz* and a Pulitzer Prize for her 1997 *How I Learned to Drive.* While Vogel is not known for authoring explicitly or singularly lesbian plays, her poignant representations of abusive, traumatic, and often taboo sexual experiences repeatedly think through the complications of sex and the limits of conventional heterosexuality. Animated by such themes as pedophilia, incest, pornography, AIDS, domestic violence, and gay parenting, her plays are unflinching considerations of desire.

Susan Miller, whose plays include *Confessions of a Female Disorder* (1974), *It's Our Town, Too,* (1992), *My Left Breast* (1994), and *A Map of Doubt and Rescue* (2002), has won two OBIE Awards, two Susan Smith Blackburn Prizes (1994/1995, 2002), and the Pinter Review Prize for Drama (2004). Wendy Hammond authored *Julie Johnson* (1994), a narrative about a New Jersey housewife who falls in love with her best friend and decides to pursue a lesbian identity after going back to college. Claire Chafee's first play, *Why We Have a Body* (1993), won *Newsday*'s George Oppenheimer Award, given each year for the most impressive debut of an American playwright. She has also received the San Francisco Drama-Logue Award and the Bay Area Critics' Choice Award. *Why We Have a Body* focuses on four women: Lili, a lesbian private investigator; her sister Mary, a high-minded robber of 7-Eleven convenience stores who is obsessed with Joan of Arc; Eleanor, their mother, who is a world-traveling feminist archeologist; and Renee, Lili's lover, a paleontologist who has recently separated from her husband. The play is a meditation on desire, the transformation of traditional gender roles, and the lack of female role models. Chafee has also written *Even among these Rocks* (1992), *Darwin's Finches* (2003), and *5 Women on a Hill in Spain* (2003). African American playwright and novelist Shay Youngblood is the recipient of many awards, including a Lorraine Hansberry Playwriting Award. She currently teaches creative writing at the New York School for Social Research. Her plays include *Shakin' the Mess Outta Misery* (1988), *Communism Killed My Dog* (1991), *Black Power Barbie* (1992), *Talking Bones* (1992), *There Are Many Houses in My Tribe* (1992), and *Amazing Grace* (1998). A founding member of the theater company The Five Lesbian Brothers, Lisa Kron teaches playwriting at Yale Drama School. Kron's solo plays include *Paradykes Lost* (1988), *Well* (produced on Broadway in 2006), and *2.5 Minute Ride* (2008).

A Broadway adaptation of **Alice Walker**'s 1983 Pulitzer Prize and National Book Award–winning novel ***The Color Purple***, produced by Oprah Winfrey, began a popular run in 2005. The novel was adapted for the stage by Marsha Norman, who has received many accolades for playwriting, including a Pulitzer Prize in 1983 for 'Night, Mother. The musical foregrounds the love story between the protagonist, Celie, and her abusive husband's lover, Shug. Shug eventually moves onto another relationship with a man after Celie, but the relationship permanently alters Celie's understanding of herself. The play, with its clear portrayal of same-sex desire between women, is billed as "The Musical about Love." The listing of these plays and awards is hardly a complete compilation of recent lesbian contributions to theater; however, it indicates the scope and seriousness with which post-Stonewall lesbian playwriting has been taken up and received.

Concomitantly establishing an intellectually rich niche for unconventional reinventions of lesbian drama, performance artists became a major theatrical presence in New York during the 1980s and well into the 1990s. In fact, the lasting influence of the WOW (Women's One World) Café cannot be stressed enough. This East Village performance space that opened in 1982 on East 11th Street, and later moved to East 4th Street between Bowery and 2nd Avenue, is still in operation. A vital outlet for women's experimental community theater, WOW was established by Peggy Shaw and Lois Weaver. Foundational fund-raising events such as a Freudian Slip party and a Debutante Ball raised the funds for rent, and the space quickly became home to early work by Split Britches, Holly Hughes, Sarah Schulman, Carmelita Tropicana/Alina Troyano, Reno, Terry Galloway, Danitra Vance, and The Five Lesbian Brothers. WOW performances also included stand-up comedy, but it mostly featured a kind of lesbian performance dedicated to reworking gender roles and conventionally gendered narratives. The theater encouraged a deconstructive approach to lesbian identity and desire and considered the influence of desire upon spectatorship through parody, unpolished scripts, outrageous costumes, and importantly—humor. Other performance spaces that housed many lesbian plays and performance pieces include La MaMa Café, founded in 1961 by Ellen Stewart, and P.S. 122 in the East Village, BACA Downtown in Brooklyn, and Josie's Cabaret in San Francisco.

Since 1981, Split Britches, a performance troupe primarily made up of Peggy Shaw, Lois Weaver, and Deb Margolin, has honed an original and now trademark style of postmodern lesbian performance. While many of Split Britches' early performances began at WOW, the group has also extensively toured the United States and Europe. The core Split Britches works are *Split Britches* (1981), *Beauty and the Beast; or, The One and Only World-Famous Vaudeville Review* (1982), *Upwardly Mobile Home* (1984), *Little Women: The Tragedy* (1988), and *Lesbians Who Kill* (1992). *Split Britches,* their eponymous inaugural work, is a piece about Weaver's female ancestors from Virginia. "Split Britches" refers both to the undergarments these women wore while working in the fields so they could urinate without disruption and to laughing so boisterously that one might end up with "split britches." These pieces are often pastiches of earlier plays. *Belle Reprieve* (1991), for instance, is a reconsideration of Tennessee Williams's *A Streetcar Named Desire* that alters the sexual preferences and **gender**s of the original play's characters. Stanley becomes "a butch lesbian" and Blanche is "a man in a dress." Their collaborations include *Dress Suits to Hire* (1987) with Holly Hughes, *Belle Reprieve* with Bloolips, *Salad of the Bad Café* (1999–2000) with Okinawan performance artist Stacy Makishi, and *Miss America* (2008) at La MaMa with Holly Hughes. Solo and duet pieces include *You're Just Like My Father* (1994), *Menopausal Gentlemen* (1999), *It's a Small House and We Lived in It Always* (1999), *To My Chagrin* (2003), and *What Tammy Needs to Know* (2004).

As she charts in *Clit Notes* (1990), Holly Hughes developed her style of performance art during early experiences at WOW. Hughes explains that the work put on at WOW was vastly different from the sort of playwriting being done by lesbian writers such as Jane Chambers. She describes a collective intention to build an unapologetic lesbian community inseparable from the production of plays: one could not happen without the other. *The Well of Horniness* (1983), her first play, premiered at WOW. This play is a lesbian murder mystery told in the style of a live-radio show. It makes use of a huge cast and often runs with the subheading "Where Women Are Women and so Are the Men." Other pieces by Hughes include *The Lady Dick* (1984), *Dress Suits to Hire* (1987) for Lois Weaver and Peggy Shaw, *World without End* (1989), and *Clit Notes*. Hughes's work, like that of Split Britches, Schulman, and The Five Lesbian Brothers, continues to be both widely discussed in academic contexts and regularly performed. Lesbian performance collective The Five Lesbian Brothers was made up of Maureen Angelos, Babs Davy, Dominique Dibbell, Peg Healey, and Lisa Kron. Their first play, *Voyage to Lesbos,* premiered at WOW in 1990. It implies that a reconsideration of the conventional heterosexual marriage plot is necessary for social change. *Brave Smiles . . . Another Lesbian Tragedy* (1993) is a pastiche of older plays and films including *The Children's Hour* (1961), *Cabaret* (1972), and *Mädchen in Uniform* (1931). *The Secretary* (1994) reconsiders the largely female world of secretarial work while rethinking misogynist and antifeminist clichés through a revisiting of a pastiche of films including *Nine to Five* (1980) and *The Texas Chainsaw Massacre* (1974). *Brides of the Moon* (1998) is a utopian spoof of sex and science fiction. These plays are collected in *The Five Lesbian Brothers (Four Plays)* (2000).

Novelist, playwright, and activist Sarah Schulman, an early member of ACT UP (AIDS Coalition to Unleash Power) and one of the co-founders of the Lesbian Avengers, occupies a unique place in the history of U.S. lesbian theater. *When We Were Very Young: A Walking Tour of Radical Jewish Women on the Lower East Side* (1982) was one of the first plays produced at WOW. She joined More Fire! Productions, a lower East Side experimental women's theater collective started by Robin Epstein and Dorothy Cantwell, in 1979. Schulman's collaborative work here included *Art Failures* (1983), *Whining and Dining* (1984), and *Epstein on the Beach* (1985). Her many novels represent lesbian community, AIDS, gentrification, and art on the Lower East Side in the 1980s and 1990s. *Stagestruck: Theater, AIDS, and the Marketing of Gay America* (1998) records Schulman's charge that Jonathan Larson's musical *Rent* (1996) blatantly plagiarized her novel *People in Trouble* (1990). Her play *Carson McCullers* premiered at Playwrights Horizons in 2002, as did *Manic Flight Reaction* (2006). She also authored an adaptation for the stage of Isaac Bashevis Singer's *Enemies, A Love Story*. In 1991 Schulman received a Guggenheim Fellowship in playwriting. She has also been awarded three residencies at Yaddo.

Current representations of lesbians in the theater are complicated by scholarship interested in sexuality as performance, which destabilizes the possibility of portraying cohesive, representative lesbian identities on stage and elsewhere. Therefore, as in its early days, lesbian theater remains very difficult to define. As this brief history suggests, its definition has changed drastically over the last century and continues to be constantly modified as lesbian existence in the United States becomes more possible and more varied.

Further Reading

Bennett, Suzanne, and Jane T. Paterson. *Women Playwrights of Diversity: A Bio-Bibliographical Sourcebook.* Westport, CT: Greenwood Press, 1997.

Harbin, Billy J., Kim Marra, and Robert A. Schanke, eds. *The Gay and Lesbian Theatrical Legacy: A Biographical Dictionary of Major Figures in American Stage History in the Pre-Stonewall Era.* Ann Arbor: University of Michigan Press, 2005.

Hodges, Ben, ed. *Forbidden Acts: Pioneering Gay and Lesbian Plays of the Twentieth Century.* New York: Applause Theatre and Cinema Books, 2003.

Hughes, Holly, and David Román, eds. *o solo homo: The New Queer Performance.* New York: Grove Press, 1998.

Lane, Eric, and Nina Shengold, eds. *The Actor's Book of Gay and Lesbian Plays.* New York: Penguin Books, 1995.

Marra, Kim, and Robert A. Schanke, eds. *Passing Performances: Queer Readings of Leading Players in American Theater History.* Ann Arbor: University of Michigan Press, 1998.

Sinfield, Alan. *Out on Stage: Lesbian and Gay Theatre in the Twentieth Century.* West Haven, CT: Yale University Press, 1999.

Melinda Cardozo

Duncan, Robert (1919–1988)

Experimental poet, essayist, and prodigious letter writer. The eighth surviving child of Marguerite Pearl and Edward Howe Duncan, Robert Duncan was born on January 7, 1919, in Oakland, California. His mother died only hours after the premature delivery; his father, a railroad engineer who was no longer able to support his large family, gave Edward and his two youngest sisters up for adoption. On August 4, the seven-month-old boy was taken in by Minnehaha and Edwin Symmes, members of an occult society who chose the child because his astrological chart indicated that he had played an important role in the destruction of the mythological continent of Atlantis. On March 10, 1920, he was legally adopted and renamed Robert Edward Symmes. Later that year, Minnehaha and Edwin Symmes adopted a baby girl, again on the basis of her astrological chart, and named her Barbara Eleanor Symmes. Even though Robert was intrigued by his parents' belief in the occult, he eventually rejected it as pseudoscience. Nevertheless, his poetry frequently shows the influence of hermetic and occult lore. When Robert was three years old, an injury to his left eye left him permanently cross-eyed. This traumatic event turned out to be crucial for Duncan's artistic development because it caused him to look beyond reality at what is hidden beneath the external. While in high school, Robert wrote his first poems and was encouraged by his English teacher, Edna Keough, an amateur poet. He also became aware of his attraction to boys and was derided by his classmates as "Sissie Symmes" because of effeminate traits. Between 1936 and 1938 Duncan was an English major at the University of California at Berkeley and published several poems in the school's literary magazine, *The Occident,* for which he also served as editor. He became involved with left-wing politics and joined the American Student Union, serving as its director of publications. He surrounded himself with a group of brilliant women, who served as his sounding board and whom he called his sisters. When it became clear to him that poetry was his true vocation, Duncan left Berkeley and, having been turned away by the experimental Black Mountain College in North Carolina, he moved to the East Coast. There he met up with Ned Fahs, a Berkeley alumnus and French teacher, with whom he had fallen deeply in love. It soon became obvious, however, that the two were incompatible and that Duncan's first attempt at a lasting relationship was doomed to failure.

During the next years Duncan roamed aimlessly between New York City and Florida and was involved in several brief homosexual affairs. When he was drafted in April 1941, Duncan declared his homosexuality, having spent a miserable month of boot camp in Kentucky. He was discharged with a Class 8 classification. A further indication that he felt a sense of rebirth and emancipation was the fact that he reclaimed his original name and broke with his adoptive family. Duncan subsequently experienced a creative breakthrough and published a large number of poems in quick succession. He also published the daring and revealing essay "The Homosexual in Society" in the August 1944 issue of the left-leaning journal *Politics*. While decrying the discrimination of minorities and demanding equal rights for everyone, Duncan also castigated the homosexual subculture, accusing it of elitism. The direct result of the essay was the rejection of Duncan's poem "An African Elegy" by the editor of *The Kenyon Review* even though he had previously accepted it for publication. Duncan was told that the poem represented an advertisement of overt homosexuality and that the journal did not condone such behavior. Having suffered a nervous breakdown in 1945, Duncan took a serious look at his poetic output, finding it sentimental and false, and decided to strive for authenticity in the future. In 1948 he moved back to Berkeley, where he surrounded himself with a group of likeminded poets and artists, such as Jack Spicer, Robin Blaser, **James Broughton**, and Paul Goodman, who became the core of the so-called San Francisco Renaissance and who established San Francisco State College's Poetry Center, for which Duncan served as assistant director in 1956 and 1957. Duncan was also associated with the Black Mountain poetry movement, teaching techniques of poetry at Black Mountain College in 1956, and befriending such poets as Charles Olson, Denise Levertov, and Robert Creeley.

In 1950 Duncan met the painter Jess Collins and the two artists established a marriage-like union that was to last for 37 years until Duncan's death of kidney failure on February 3, 1988. Their relationship not only provided Duncan with the personal stability he had yearned for, but it also profited his artistic vision: Duncan incorporated the collage, the technique favored by Collins, in his poetry and several of Duncan's collections featured the painter's work. The homosexual themes permeating Duncan's poetry also show a shift from restlessness and insecurity to domestic bliss. Before Duncan published the groundbreaking essay "The Homosexual in Society," he frequently obfuscated the homosexual elements in his poetry, fearing society's disapproval. The **gay** poet **Thom Gunn** has pointed out that Duncan frequently disguises the gay lover by turning him into a Christ figure, for example, in the poems "The End of the Year," "Random Lines: A Discourse on Love," and "The Silent Throat in the Dark Portends." The poems composed after the publication of the essay are to a large extent a reflection of Duncan's private life. In happy times he celebrated the beauty of his lovers in such highly erotic poems as "Night Scenes" or "The Torso: *Passages 18*," which can be read as the depiction of a sexual act. The suffering over failed love affairs is also expressed in numerous poems. "The Venice Poem," for example, is a reflection of the betrayal Duncan felt when his passionate affair with the Berkeley student Gerald Ackermann fell apart. This period of storm and stress ended when Duncan entered into the union with Jess Collins and the unalloyed pleasures of domesticity pervade such poems as "Homecoming" and "The Household." In "The Feast: *Passages 34 (Tribunals)*," Duncan describes a dinner he and his lover prepared for their friends. Most memorable are the poems in which Duncan expresses his love and devotion to Jess, such as "*Passages 36*," "These Past Years: *Passages 10*," and "From the Fall of 1950." Duncan's "Circulations of the Song," which is based on the thirteenth-century

Persian poet Rumi, has been called one of the best love poems in postwar American poetry. Despite the fact that Duncan was openly gay and his poetry was strongly influenced by his life, few studies have concentrated on the homosexual content of his works. The majority of critics has explored the experimental character of his poetry instead, such as its eclecticism and open form. It is high time that Duncan is not only recognized as one of the premier experimental poets of the second half of the twentieth century but also as one of its preeminent gay artists.

Further Reading

Faas, Ekbert. *Robert Duncan: Portrait of the Poet as Homosexual in Society.* Santa Barbara: Black Sparrow Press, 1983.

Gunn, Thom. "Homosexuality in Robert Duncan's Poetry." In *Robert Duncan: Scales of the Marvelous,* edited by J. Bertholf and Ian W. Reid, 143–60. New York: New Directions, 1979.

Rumaker, Michael. *Robert Duncan in San Francisco.* San Francisco: Grey Fox Press, 1996.

Stenger, Karl L. "Robert Duncan." In *Contemporary Gay American Poets and Playwrights: An A-to-Z Guide,* edited by Emmanuel S. Nelson, 130–40. Westport, CT: Greenwood Press, 2003.

Karl L. Stenger

Duplechan, Larry (b. 1956)

African American **gay** novelist. Larry Duplechan, in a 1987 interview with a fellow novelist, makes a candid admission: "I don't have a strong black identity. My gay identity is much more important to me. But much more than that, I am very much an assimilationist" (Davis 62). With equal candor he goes on to acknowledge his preference for well-built white male bodies and speaks of his "blond beefcake fantasies" (Davis 62). Some may find his declarations politically tasteless; some others might see his preoccupation with blond men as a sign of his colonized sexual imagination. Yet what is intriguing is that Duplechan's novels, despite the author's disclaimers, reveal a strong ethnic consciousness. Ethnic markers are ubiquitous in his narratives. Three of his four novels focus on young black, gay, male protagonists and thus simultaneously help inscribe a black presence in contemporary gay American fiction and a gay presence in contemporary African American literature. At times he beautifully evokes the texture of middle-class black family life, envisions the nuances of southern black rural communities, effortlessly captures the cadences of African American speech patterns, examines the impact of the black church on the formation of sexual attitudes, and poignantly re-creates memories of subtle and overt racial injury. Moreover, African American musical tradition—along with mainstream popular culture—is integral to his artistic vision. By his own admission **James Baldwin**, the legendary black gay writer, is a major source of inspiration for him.

Larry Duplechan was born in suburban Los Angeles on December 30, 1956, to Lawrence Duplechan, Sr., and Margie Nell Duplechan. After attending schools in Los Angeles and Sacramento, he studied at the University of California at Los Angeles (UCLA) and graduated in 1978 with a degree in English. He worked as a jazz vocalist for seven years but failed to secure even a single recording contract, so he decided, with some encouragement from friends, to write fiction. Now an author of four novels, he lives in Los Angeles, works part-time as a legal secretary, and occasionally teaches creative writing in the UCLA Continuing Education Program.

Eight Days a Week (1985), Duplechan's first novel, focuses on an interracial gay romance. Johnnie Ray Rousseau—an African American musician—and Keith Keller—a muscular, blond banker—fall madly in love with each other. Keith's whiteness fascinates Johnnie Ray; Johnnie Ray's blackness thrills Keith. Each is drawn to the other because of the racial difference, yet they are men with vastly different tastes and temperaments. The mutual sexual attraction alone, despite its explosive intensity, proves inadequate to sustain their relationship. The romance fails, but the novel ends on a teasing note that there is perhaps a vague possibility that Johnnie Ray and Keith might be able to resuscitate their friendship.

Duplechan's debut novel is a **camp**y, sexy, funny novel. It is one of the few gay American novels to depict candidly and elaborately an interracial romance. What is rather disappointing, however, is the novel's general superficiality. The theme of sexual desire across racial boundaries, for example, is treated in great detail, but Duplechan retreats from exploring the complexities and subtleties of such desire. Too, the novel so narrowly focuses on the relationship between the two men that it fails to position that relationship in any significantly larger social contexts. Johnnie Ray and Keith make love often, but how the politics of color informs sexual transactions remains largely unexamined. Nevertheless, Duplechan's first novel merits serious consideration, for it at least attempts a bold confrontation with a politically charged subject.

Blackbird (1986), Duplechan's entertaining second novel, maps Johnnie Ray's initiatory journey to young adulthood. A gay coming-of-age narrative, it has many of the stock characteristics of such works: disappointed parents who fail to accept or even understand their son's sexuality, the anxiety and sense of isolation that accompany gay adolescence, the liberating thrill of sexual discovery, and the gradual movement toward healing self-acceptance and at least quasi-public acknowledgment of one's sexual self. Like *Eight Days a Week,* Duplechan's second novel is narrated in the first person and appears to have considerable autobiographical content.

At the beginning of the novel Johnnie Ray is a high school student from a comfortable, middle-class, suburban Los Angeles family. His primary preoccupation, perhaps not so atypically, is sex. The objects of his affection are invariably young white males with bulging crotches. When Johnnie Ray goes to audition for an acting role, he meets Marshall, an aspiring young filmmaker, who becomes central to Johnnie Ray's sexual development. Marshall helps him realize his sexual fantasies for the first time, and Johnnie Ray proves to be an eager and competent learner. Though by the end of the novel Marshall has left Los Angeles in search of his own dreams, Johnnie Ray cherishes his memories of Marshall and a postcard without a return address that he receives from him. In the concluding pages of the novel we find that the protagonist has survived his adolescence: he is now a freshman at UCLA. Along the way he has lost a few friends, endured a failed romance, and lived through his parents' bizarre attempt to "deliver" him from his homosexual desires through a religiously inspired act of exorcism. We see him discovering a multicultural gay community on the university campus and exploring his own possibilities within that milieu.

In *Tangled Up in Blue,* published in 1989, Duplechan charts new territory. Abandoning the autobiographical-confessional, first-person narrative style of his earlier novels, here he opts to tell the story in the third person. Absent, too, is Johnnie Ray, Duplechan's alter ego; in fact, *Tangled Up in Blue* has no African American characters. The plot centers around three white characters: Daniel Sullivan, who considers himself straight but, in fact, is bisexual; Crockett Miller, Daniel's ex-lover and now a platonic friend; and Maggie Sullivan, Daniel's wife and Crockett's close friend. Maggie accidentally finds out that her husband has tested for AIDS antibody and, subsequently, discovers his bisexual past but also the fact that he and Crockett were once lovers. The ensuing crisis nearly destroys the Sullivans' marriage and their friendship with Crockett. Ultimately, however, love heals the ruptures.

The plot of *Tangled Up in Blue* is at times flimsy; it nevertheless is an important contribution to the genre of AIDS narratives. It remains one of the early novels in American literature to face the artistically and politically problematic task of fictionalizing an all-too-real epidemic that had, by the mid-1980s, begun to devastate gay communities. Unlike many other novels published in the 1980s, *Tangled Up in Blue* broadens the literary representation of AIDS by exploring the complex connections among gay, bisexual, and straight characters who are at risk.

Captain Swing, Duplechan's most recent novel, was published in 1993. Johnnie Ray Rousseau, the protagonist of Duplechan's first two works, resurfaces here, but now he is a widower: his lover, Keith, has died recently in an accident. The novel begins with Johnnie Ray's flight home to St. Charles, Louisiana, from Los Angeles to see his estranged father, who is now on his deathbed. It ends with Johnnie Ray's reluctant preparation to board a plane that will take him back to California. In between the two scenes is a personal drama that is enveloped in a larger familial drama. During the days he spends with his family in Louisiana, Johnnie Ray and his second cousin, Nigel, fall passionately in love with each other. Soon a disapproving family discovers the relationship. Meanwhile, Johnnie Ray's father dies, still resolutely rejecting his gay son. Prior to his departure from the South, Johnnie Ray invites Nigel to come with him to California. Nigel, though professing his love, declines but asks hopefully, "Can I come visit on summer vacation?" (182). Johnnie walks to the plane alone—a plane that he feels has "no business attempting to leave the ground" (184).

Captain Swing is a significant departure for both Johnnie Ray and Duplechan. Here the focus is on an intraracial romance. Such a focus, however, proves problematic: Duplechan is unable to write convincingly about two black gay men in love with each other. Nigel's character is wooden; the romance between him and Johnnie Ray lacks emotional authenticity. But the novel is hardly a failure. Duplechan succeeds in imagining a southern rural black family and community and capturing the moments of affection and elements of tension among their various members. The rhythms of southern black dialect come alive in the pages of the novel. The scenes of lovemaking are as elaborate as they are exquisite. Duplechan, as always, succeeds in entertaining his readers.

Among the post–James Baldwin generation of gay writers in the United States, Larry Duplechan is certainly an important figure. However, unlike **E. Lynn Harris**, who has managed to attract a considerable straight audience for his novels, Duplechan remains essentially a novelist with a primarily gay and predominantly white readership. All of his novels have generally received favorable reviews in the white-oriented gay press. Among his enthusiastic fans are other gay writers, such as **Michael Nava**, **Christopher Davis**, and Steven Corbin. For example, while commenting on *Blackbird,* Davis asserts that the novel made him "feel happy to be gay" (60). Charles I. Nero addresses one of the central features of Duplechan's work: interracial gay desire. About Johnnie Ray's compelling attraction to blond men in *Eight Days a Week,* Nero says that his "sexual attraction to white men . . . allows Duplechan a major moment of signifying in African-American literature: the sexual objectification of white men by a black man" (237). Duplechan's work is yet to receive significant academic attention, however. The only scholarly article devoted entirely to Duplechan's novel so far is John H. Pearson's chapter on Duplechan that appears in *Contemporary Gay American Novelists.* Pearson, who offers a favorable assessment of Duplechan's work, concludes that he is "warm, funny, poignant, self-assured, and utterly readable" (121).

Further Reading

Davis, Christopher. "CS Interview with Larry Duplechan." *Christopher Street* 10 (1987): 60–62.

Hannon, Charles. Review of *Captain Swing* by Larry Duplechan. *Booklist* (September 1, 1993): 33.

Nero, Charles. "Towards a Black Gay Aesthetic: Signifying in Contemporary Black Gay Literature." In *Brother to Brother: New Writings by Black Gay Men,* edited by Essex Hemphill. Boston: Alyson, 1991.

Pearson, John H. "Larry Duplechan." In *Contemporary Gay American Novelists: A Bio-Bibliographical Critical Sourcebook,* edited by Emmanuel S. Nelson, 116–21. Westport, CT: Greenwood Press, 1993.

Poulson-Bryant, Scott. Review of *Tangled Up in Blue* by Larry Duplechan. *New York Village Voice* 34 (July 18, 1989): 61.

Steinberg, Sybil. Review of *Tangled Up in Blue* by Larry Duplechan. *Publishers Weekly* 235 (January 6, 1989): 91.

Emmanuel S. Nelson

Durang, Christopher (b. 1949)

Playwright, satirist, actor, and educator. Christopher Ferdinand Durang was born on January 2, 1949, in Montclair, New Jersey. He endured a volatile childhood as his father was an alcoholic, and his parents fought a great deal. Although they tried to have additional children, a medical incompatibility between Durang's parents caused three babies to be stillborn, so Durang ended up an only child. Throughout her life Durang's mother fought bouts of depression, a condition that would also plague him at times. Durang had a strict Catholic upbringing, attending both a parochial elementary school and a parochial high school. It was in elementary school that he first began to write and produce plays. He sustained an interest in theater throughout high school and eventually decided to pursue playwriting as a career. He was admitted to Harvard University on a scholarship but had a difficult time there, as he sank into a deep depression. With the help of counseling, however, he finally managed to recover during his final year and to complete his B.A. During that year he also wrote *The Nature and Purpose of the Universe,* the piece for which he was accepted to Yale's prestigious playwriting program.

Durang really began to hone his playwriting while at Yale and had the good fortune to have several very talented classmates with whom to collaborate, including Sigourney Weaver, Meryl Streep, and **Albert Innaurato**. Durang graduated from Yale with an MFA in playwriting in 1974 but stayed in New Haven an additional year to take part in a production of his own play, *The Idiots Karamazov,* which was produced at Yale Repertory Theatre. He moved to New York City in 1975, and that same year his play *The Nature and Purpose of the Universe* was produced off-off-Broadway. The following year his musical *A History of the American Film* was accepted by the prestigious Eugene O'Neill National Playwriting Conference, and, as a result, in 1977 the piece received productions at the Hartford Stage Company in Connecticut, the Mark Taper Forum in Los Angeles, and the Arena Stage in Washington, D.C. In 1978 it opened on Broadway and he received a Tony nomination for Best Book of a Musical. About that same time Durang began work on his most controversial play, *Sister Mary Ignatius Explains It All for You*. The play is an indictment of Catholic dogma that grew out of his disillusionment with religion and with life in general. At its center is a caustic nun who delivers skewed religious dogma with a fanaticism that is both frightening and hilarious. In 1980 *Sister Mary* was presented off-off-Broadway at the Ensemble Studio Theatre. It received rave reviews and won Durang an OBIE Award for playwriting. The play angered some Catholic organizations, however, and subsequent productions in other cities drew protests. Durang was not deterred by the controversy, and the 1980s continued to be productive for him with several Broadway and off-Broadway productions including *Beyond Therapy* (1981), *Baby with the Bathwater* (1983), *The Marriage of Bette & Boo* (1986), and *Laughing Wild* (1987). *The Marriage of Bette & Boo* is Durang's most autobiographical play, with the central couple based directly upon his own parents. It chronicles three decades of Bette and Boo's relationship as they deal with stillbirths, alcoholism, madness, and death. The production won several OBIE Awards, including one for playwriting, and Durang also won a Drama Desk Award for Outstanding New Play. In the 1990s Durang's theater output slowed considerably, although he did pen *Sex and Longing* (1994), and *Betty's Summer Vacation* (1999) for which he won another OBIE. Throughout the 1990s Durang also worked extensively for television and film, writing several teleplays, screenplays, and sitcom pilots; in 1994 he was named co-chair of the Julliard School's Playwriting Program with Marsha Norman. He and Norman still co-direct the program, and in 2004 the two shared the Margo Jones Award for their contribution to the American professional regional theater. In 2006 Durang was awarded the prestigious Harvard Arts Medal.

Durang's plays consistently deal with issues of **gender** identity, dysfunctional family life, and religious disillusionment. His plays are comedies, but of biting satire that exposes the dark side of humanity. Durang defines his own style as "absurdist comedy married to real feelings" (Afterword 154). His characters are often caught in dysfunctional relationships and situations that are humorous, poignant, and sometimes painful. While Durang does touch upon issues of homosexuality in some of his works, he is not often included in the ranks of those who are immediately identified as **gay** playwrights because the theme of homosexuality is not central to many of his works.

Further Reading

Christopher Durang. http://www.christopherdurang.com (accessed November 15 2007).

Dukes, Thomas. "Christopher Durang." In *Contemporary Gay American Poets and Playwrights: An A-to-Z Guide*, edited by Emmanuel S. Nelson, 140–46. Westport, CT: Greenwood Press, 2003.

Durang, Christopher. "Afterword: Baby with the Bathwater." *Laughing Wild; and Baby with the Bathwater: Two Plays*. New York: Grove Press, 1989, 152–66.

Kattelman, Beth. "Sister Mary Ignatius Explains It All for You." In *Censorship: A World Encyclopedia*, edited by Derek Jones, 703–704. London: Fitzroy Dearborn, 2001.

Savran, David. "Christopher Durang." *In Their Own Words: Contemporary American Playwrights*. New York: Theatre Communications Group, 1988. 18–34.

Beth A. Kattelman

Dykewomon, Elana (b. 1949)

Award-winning Jewish American author, poet, teacher, and activist. Elana Dykewomon was born Elana Nachman to a large Jewish family on October 11, 1949, in New York City. Nachman's father had immigrated to the United States from eastern Europe in 1904, originally settling in Holyoke, Massachusetts. Both parents worked outside the home; her mother was a librarian and her father a lawyer. Little is known about Elana Nachman's childhood and upbringing; one could assume that having a librarian as a mother instilled a love of literature in the young girl and that she had developed a passion for justice from her father. When Nachman was eight years old, the family moved to Puerto Rico. Once she graduated from high school, Nachman moved to Portland, Oregon, to study fine art at Reed College, then received a Bachelor of Fine Arts in Creative Writing from the California Institute of the Arts. In 1997, Nachman (now Dykewomon) received a Master of Fine Arts in Creative Writing from San Francisco State University. Currently she teaches Creative Writing at San Francisco State University and also works as a writing coach and editor.

At the age of 21, Nachman wrote her first novel, *Riverfinger Women* (1974), which was published by the pioneering women's press Daughter's, Inc. It was Nachman's intention to write a lesbian novel that had a happy ending, as well as to portray a compassionate and courageous lesbian relationship. To this day, *Riverfinger Women* remains an extremely popular novel due to its positive lesbian content and young adult characters in a bohemian setting.

With the publication of a writing collection titled *They Will Know Me by My Teeth* (1976), Nachman changed her surname to "Dykewoman" to express her identification with the lesbian community, as well as to maximize her visibility as a lesbian author. When Nachman published her third work, a collection of love poems "for lesbians only" called *Fragments of Lesbos* (1981), she officially began to spell her new surname as "Dykewomon" to reject any connection with men.

From 1987 to 1994, Dykewomon worked as editor of the oldest surviving lesbian literary journal, *Sinister Wisdom*. From its inception, *Sinister Wisdom* has provided a space for the exploration, critical judgment, and advancement of diverse lesbian issues in poetry, prose, and art. Dykewomon demonstrated great passion and commitment to this mission not only by writing for the publication herself, but also in fund-raising, advertising, printing, mailing, and outreach. Women of color, including Jewish and Arab women, were encouraged to submit their work. To date, Dykewomon had the longest tenure as editor of *Sinister Wisdom,* still contributes her writing to the journal, and participates in operations.

While writing for *Sinister Wisdom,* Dykewomon admitted that she had spent many years distancing herself from her Jewish identity, more so than her lesbian one. She began to reembrace her Jewish identity in 1975, when she "heard" a woman sing of her life as a single Jewish immigrant coming to America. Twelve years later, she "heard" the same woman's voice again. Research on turn-of-the-century Russia and its Jews released a name and genealogy to the singing woman, Chava Meyer, who became the adventurous heroine in Dykewomon's classic historical novel *Beyond the Pale* (1998). The novel reveals the importance of Jewish lesbians and working-class women in Russia and New York between 1860 and 1912 and their role in fighting for worker's rights. *Beyond the Pale* has won the Lambda Literary Award for Best Lesbian Novel and the Ferro-Gumley Award for Best Lesbian Fiction, and it is the first of Dykewomon's works to reach a heterosexual audience. In 2007 it was republished as a young adult edition by Raincoast Books.

Dykewomon primarily uses her writing as a vehicle to unite the lesbian community. Through fiction, poetry, and personal essays, she illustrates the struggles and fears that all lesbians share regardless of race, religion, or class. Recurring themes in Dykewomon's writing include the lesbian as a proactive, dynamic, moral hero; the need for honesty and authenticity, no matter how difficult or painful; redefining standards of beauty and body image; and the belief that speaking out will encourage other women to do so, leading to social and political change. Using tales of wandering women isolated by culture, religion, or body shape, mythic lesbian communities, and creation myths for inspiration, Dykewomon encourages disenfranchised lesbians to find strength in their individual heritages, their physical bodies, and the common bonds of their experience as women to form their own communities where they could create functional alternatives to heterosexual, male-dominated systems of marriage, property ownership, health care, and education.

To date, Dykewomon has also published a short story collection, *Moon Creek Road* (2003), about Jewish lesbians on the road, and she continues to publish short works for various lesbian publications. Currently she is working on a novel about a lesbian gambler.

See also Lesbian Literature, Jewish American

Further Reading

Livia, Anna. "Dykewomon, Elana (1949–)." *glbtq: An Encyclopedia of Gay, Lesbian, Bisexual, Transgender, and Queer Culture.* http://www.glbtq.com/literature/dykewomon_e.html (accessed October 15 2007).

Roberts, Jenny. "Elana Dykewomon." http://www.libertas.co.uk/default-show-article-aid-2425.htm (accessed November 15 2007).

Wells, Jess. "Interview with Elana Dykewomon." *Lodestar Quarterly* 10 (Summer 2004). http://www.lodestarquarterly.com/work/208/ (accessed March 31, 2004).

Rachel Wexelbaum

E

Ellis, Bret Easton (b. 1964)

Controversial contemporary **gay** novelist and short story writer. Bret Easton Ellis was born in suburban Los Angeles to wealthy parents and attended exclusive private schools before enrolling at the prestigious Bennington College, from which he graduated in 1986. Though there are many gay and bisexual characters in his novels and short stories, Ellis denied he was gay until he formally came out of the **closet** during an interview in 2005.

Ellis began drafting his first novel, *Less Than Zero,* while still in high school; it was published in 1985 while he was an undergraduate student. A *Bildungsroman* narrated in the first person by its protagonist, Clayton, it offers a nihilistic view of modern life in pithy Hemingwayesque prose. Like the book's young author, Clayton is the only son of wealthy parents in California and he attends Camden College, an imaginary liberal arts college in New Hampshire that resembles Bennington College. Clayton returns to his family home during the Christmas holiday, and the narrative focuses on his experiences during a four-week period. He reconnects with his friends and resumes his life of drinking, using drugs, and going to late-night parties. He wants to rekindle his relationship with Blair, a young woman with whom he believes he is in love, but he has at least one casual homosexual encounter and forges a close bond with his childhood friend, Julian, who is now a drug-addicted gay prostitute. As Clayton descends deeper into the life of sex, drugs, and alcohol, he incrementally becomes disillusioned by his friends' casual attitude toward violence and sadistic sexuality. When his holiday ends he returns to his college campus numbed by the meaninglessness of what he has witnessed and experienced.

The Rules of Attraction, Ellis's second novel, was published in 1987; it chronicles the lives of a group of students from wealthy families who attend Camden College. A polyvocal text —the story is narrated by a chorus of characters in the first person, often in the form of personal journal entries and letters—the narrative centers on the lives of its three major characters: Sean Bateman, Lauren Hynde, and Paul Denton. All three have multiple sexual partners and Paul, in addition to sleeping with other men and women, offers in his diary entries descriptions of lovemaking sessions with Sean, who may or may not be bisexual. The nihilistic ennui in *Less Than Zero* is apparent in *The Rules of Attraction* as well; much of the narrative is about the characters' escapist retreat into sex, drugs, and alcohol.

It was *American Psycho* (1991), Ellis's third novel, that catapulted him into literary notoriety. Paul Bateman, its narrator, is simultaneously an investment banker and a sadistic serial killer. Like many of Ellis's characters, Bateman is sexually ambivalent, although he is primarily heterosexual. He chronicles in graphic details his many murders that often begin with shocking sexual violence and escalate into mutilation and cannibalism. Yet it is unclear if Bateman is a reliable narrator and if indeed his claims are real or delusional. The novel elicited calls for boycott from the National Organization for Women because of its misogynistic violence, and Simon & Schuster, the company that had initially planned to publish it, terminated its contract with Ellis. It was subsequently published by Vintage Press; in 2000, when the controversy surrounding the book had significantly waned, it was made into a film.

The Informers (1994) is a collection of 13 interconnected short stories. The setting is suburban Los Angeles that is presented as a moral and cultural wasteland. In this collection of short stories, much more so than in his earlier works, Ellis emerges as an incisive satirist. Rather than merely document the wasted lives of its characters who seek transcendence through alcohol, drugs, and promiscuous sex, Ellis examines the roots of their alienation and the sources of their disconnection from themselves and from the others around them.

Ellis's two most recent novels, *Glamorama* (1998) and *Lunar Park* (2005), are similar in tenor to his earlier works; they are marked by the same sense of inertia and peopled by characters who unsuccessfully seek meaning through often self-destructive means. From a narrative perspective, however, these two works reveal bolder postmodernist experimentation. *Glamorama* is a picaresque novel with a trans-Atlantic setting in which several contemporary American celebrities, including Ellis, briefly appear as characters. *Lunar Park* is a pseudoautobiographical narrative. The narrator is named Bret Easton Ellis, a well-known novelist; however, unlike the author, the character who bears his name lives with his movie star wife, their 11-year-old son, and the wife's 6-year-old daughter from a previous marriage. At the conclusion of the novel, Ellis, the protagonist, is falling in love with a man much younger than he. While there are some obvious parallels between Ellis the author and Ellis the narrator, there are also several disconnections. A poignant parallel is the novel's ending: in 2005 Ellis acknowledged that he had been in a relationship with Michael Wade Kaplan, a much younger man, who died of a heart attack in 2004 at the age of 30. *Lunar Park* is dedicated to Kaplan.

Further Reading

Flannigan, Roy C. "Bret Easton Ellis." In *Twenty-First Century American Novelists,* edited by Suzanne Dishroon-Green, 87–93. Detroit: Thomson Gale, 2004.

Trevor A. Sydney

Evans, Kate (b. 1962)

Poet, novelist, memoirist, and writing teacher. The middle daughter of Don Evans and Arlene Summers, Kathleen Mary Evans was born November 26, 1962, in Colfax, California. Evans's father, also an educator, was born in Cleveland to Hungarian parents. He met

Evans's mother—a San Francisco native—at Yosemite National Park where she was serving as a hospital nurse and he was driving a tour bus during college summer break. Her parents prized education and supported Evans's love for reading and writing.

Evans married a man at age 22, but five years later the union ended in divorce. After receiving a B.A. at California State University, Sacramento, she taught high school English in California and English to adults and children for a year in Japan. Living in Japan was the basis for one of her first published short stories, "City of Water," in the *Santa Monica Review.* This story was nominated for a Pushcart Prize. After pursuing a master's degree in English, she returned to the university to take a poetry class. There she met her life partner, poet and artist Susanne (Annie) Tobin, in 1993 in a course taught by the late lesbian poet Virginia de Araujo. In addition to de Araujo, two other former professors fostered Evans's love for writing: creativity expert Gabriele Rico and poet Dennis Schmitz.

Upon falling in love with a woman, Evans became aware of losing her "heterosexual privilege" as a teacher in the classroom. She learned that the ongoing process of censoring oneself or coming out as a teacher was fraught with tension. This fueled her Ph.D. work at the University of Washington, a study of lesbian and **gay** teachers, which was published by Routledge as *Negotiating the Self* in 2002. The book was widely praised. William F. Pinar, author of **Queer** *Theory in Education* (1998), wrote the introduction, calling *Negotiating the Self* an "exciting and important book" (ii).

Evans subsequently received an M.F.A. in Creative Writing and now teaches at San Jose State University, where she also co-directs the Center for Literary Arts. Her first poetry collection, *Like All We Love,* was published by Spirit Press/Q Press in 2006 and was nominated for the Los Angeles Times Book Prize and a Lambda Literary Award. The collection explores Evans's coming out as a lesbian and the struggles of caring for ailing parents. Poet Ellen Bass praised *Like All We Love* and Evans's ability to tell a "love story" with her work, while poet Dawn Trook described the poems as "luscious" and "moving" (dust jacket blurbs).

Evans has written a historical novel about three lesbian/bisexual women and a memoir; both are currently in circulation. A novel titled *For the May Queen,* which explores a straight woman's friendship with a gay man, has just been accepted for publication. The yet to be published memoir focuses on caregiving, telling the story of Evans's father's death after a long illness followed immediately by her mother's Alzheimer's diagnosis. She has published poetry, fiction, and memoir/essays extensively, including work in *Indiana Review, The Seattle Review, North American Review, Elixir, The National Poetry Review, Bellevue Literary Review, Harrington Lesbian Fiction Quarterly, The Cream City Review,* and *ZYZZYVA.*

Further Reading

Gunesekera, Manique, and Shaoxiang Wang. "Review of *Negotiating the Self* by Kate Evans." *Journal of Language, Identity & Education* 4 (2005): 77–83.

Kusiak, Karen. "Review of Kate Evans' *Negotiating the Self.*" *Education Review.* (2003). http://edrev.asu.edu/reviews/rev240.htm.

Lampela, Laura. "Review of *Negotiating the Self.*" *Teachers College Record.* (2003). http://www.tcrecord.org/Content.asp?ContentID=11035.

Collin Kelley

F

Feinberg, David B. (1956–1994)

Novelist, essayist, activist, and chronicler of the AIDS crisis, David Barish Feinberg was born on November 25, 1956, in Lynn, Massachusetts, and grew up in Syracuse, New York. His parents were observant Jews and his upbringing was a traditional one, but later in life he declared himself an atheist. In 1977 Feinberg graduated from the Massachusetts Institute of Technology (MIT) with a degree in mathematics and moved to Los Angeles shortly thereafter. The following year in Los Angeles he participated in the **Gay** Pride March, which became a defining moment in his life: it empowered him to acknowledge and declare his sexuality. In 1979 he enrolled at New York University and received a master's degree in linguistics in 1981. After graduation he began working as a computer programmer at the offices of the Modern Language Association in New York City; he held the job until a few months before his death from AIDS-related illnesses on November 4, 1994.

While a student at MIT, Feinberg took a course in creative writing taught by John Hersey and began writing a novel titled "Calculus." Although he completed the project, he never published it. In the mid-1980s he contributed several humorous and often autobiographical sketches to the magazine *Mandate;* those vignettes became the basis of his first novel, *Eighty-Sixed* (1989). The novel centers on the life and adventures of B. J. Rosenthal, a young Jewish gay man in New York City. Part I, titled "Ancient History," maps B. J's hilarious quest for enduring love in the bars, backrooms, and bathhouses; though he fails to find true love, he does succeed in having a voracious sex life. Part II, titled "Learning How to Cry," is sharply different in tone; it documents the apocalyptic arrival of an enigmatic new epidemic and its deadly impact on gay communities. B. J.'s world begins to collapse around him. Many friends, acquaintances, and former tricks become ill; disease and death begin to define his life. *Eight-Sixed,* which won major awards, remains one of the most compelling novels about AIDS and urban gay life of the 1980s.

B. J. Rosenthal is again the protagonist of Feinberg's second novel, *Spontaneous Combustion* (1991). In *Eighty-Sixed* B. J. was a shocked witness to the ferocity of AIDS; in *Spontaneous Combustion* he discovers that he is HIV-positive, battles various diseases by taking endless medications, and faces his death and the deaths of many around him. B. J.'s grim first-person narrative is laced with black humor, which only intensifies the poignancy of the story that he relates.

Queer and Loathing: Rants and Raves of a Raging AIDS Clone (1994) is a collection of 36 autobiographical vignettes and essays; it was published a few weeks prior to Feinberg's death. Some pieces carry the imprint of his impish humor and others articulate his activist rage at government agencies, pharmaceutical companies, and sanctimonious religious leaders. Unsentimental and devoid of self-pity, the testimonials stress the need for sustained political action even as they reveal the gallantry with which the author faces his own impending death.

Further Reading

Carducci, Jane S. "David B. Feinberg." In *Contemporary Gay American Novelists: A Bio-Bibliographical Critical Sourcebook,* edited by Emmanuel S. Nelson, 122–27. Westport, CT: Greenwood Press, 1993.

Kushner, Tony. "Introduction." *Queer and Loathing: Rants and Raves of a Raging AIDS Clone.* David B. Feinberg. New York: Penguin, 1995. n.p.

Emmanuel S. Nelson

Feinberg, Leslie (b. 1949)

Transgender author and activist. Leslie Feinberg is best known as the author of the seminal work of fiction *Stone Butch Blues* (1993), which tells the story of Jess Goldberg, an androgynously masculine Jewish girl growing up in the working-class neighborhoods of Buffalo, New York, in the 1960s. In the novel, Jess Goldberg goes from being a masculine-looking girl to living as a butch lesbian factory worker who eventually takes hormones in order to live completely as a man, passing at work and in public. However, the path to manhood proves difficult and Jess stops taking hormones, although her voice remains lowered and she continues to identify as a butch lesbian. She moves to New York City where she participates in the 1969 **Stonewall Riots**, a days-long rebellion that took place in response to a harassing police raid on a Greenwich Village gay bar. Many historians identify the Stonewall Riots as the beginning of the modern **gay rights movement** and the inclusion of the riots in the novel signifies Feinberg's overt political intentions as an author, as well as her belief that transgendered people's struggle for rights and recognition takes place both as a part of the movement for gay, lesbian, and bisexual rights and outside of the gay community. *Stone Butch Blues* is considered a classic of **queer** literature for many reasons, including its intimate portrayal of working-class butch/femme relationships in the 1960s period, a historical period that remained relatively unknown at the time of the novel's publication, as well as for the groundbreaking way that the fixed notions of **gender** roles are interrogated by the characterization of Jess Goldberg as someone who is always in between masculinity and femininity and thus must confront gender stereotypes for her entire life. Not only is Jess marginalized as both a child and an adult because of her atypical gender expression, she also experiences prejudice from other lesbians and within the gay community. In fact, the novel clearly contests all gender and sexual distinctions that take place both in heterosexual and queer society, portraying the division of masculinity and femininity, homosexuality and heterosexuality, as ultimately false dichotomies.

Stone Butch Blues has many narrative elements and plot twists that are also a part of Leslie Feinberg's own life history. Like the fictional Jess Goldberg, Feinberg identified as a butch lesbian while growing up in Buffalo, but later came to recognize a transgendered self-identity, undergoing sexual reassignment surgery twice. However, Feinberg insists that the book is not autobiographical and is rather a composite of experiences, both her own and those of other people. In 2006, Feinberg wrote another novel, entitled *Drag King Dreams,* which tells the dramatic story of Max Rabinowitz, a Jewish drag king (a woman who dresses and performs theatrically as a man) who works as a bouncer at a drag king bar in New York's East Village. The story details the complex relationships of employees, patrons, and performers of the bar, as well as the bar's sometimes strained relationship with hostile or bigoted neighbors who are unable to understand what motivates the patrons and performers at the bar. The narrative also focuses on the trauma and violence that is undergone by members of the non-gender-conforming community and espouses a message of tolerance in a post-September 11, 2001, New York City, in which the attack on the World Trade Center caused many previously peaceful communities to turn on people of Arab descent and recent immigrants from countries where Islam is practiced or which many Americans believe to be culturally Islamic in the days and weeks following September 11, 2001. Feinberg is also the author of several nonfiction books, including *Transgender Warriors: Making History from Joan of Arc to Dennis Rodman* (1997), *Trans Liberation: Beyond Pink or Blue* (1998), a compendium of talks and lectures given by Leslie in the 1990s, dealing with the history of people with gender-non-conforming behavior and appearances. Currently, Feinberg remains politically active, living with her partner, the poet **Minnie Bruce Pratt**, and endorses the use of gender-neutral pronouns *ze* and *hir,* instead of she, he, him, and her. Feinberg remains engaged in the fight for the social and political empowerment of all people regardless of their race, class, or gender, as a member of the socialist Workers World Party, the antiwar movement, and the struggle to free political prisoners incarcerated in American prisons.

See also Autobiography, Transgender

Further Reading

Bowen, Gary. "Transgendered Warriors: An Interview with Leslie Feinberg." *Lambda Book Report* 6, no. 6 (January 1998): 19.

Halberstam, Judith. "Lesbian Masculinity; Or, Even Stone Butches Get the Blues." *Women & Performance* 8, no. 2 (1996): 61–73.

Michele Erfer

Ferro, Robert (1941–1988)

Italian American **gay** novelist. Born on October 21, 1941, Robert Ferro grew up in Cranford, New Jersey, in an affluent family of conservative Catholics. Although Ferro's sexual orientation created occasional tension in his family, he remained emotionally close to his family members for his whole life. The bonds of family, particularly in the life of a homosexual man, became a prevalent theme in Ferro's works. Ferro remained in New Jersey for his undergraduate work at Rutgers University, where he received a B.A. in English in 1963. He attended the University of Iowa until 1967 and graduated with an M.F.A.

from the Creative Writing Program. Throughout the 1960s and 1970s, Ferro traveled frequently throughout Europe, an interest the protagonists of his novels also evince. In the late 1970s, Ferro's focus turned to New York, where he helped form the **Violet Quill Club**. The Violet Quill, a gay writers group, consisted of seven members: Ferro, **Edmund White**, **Christopher Cox**, **Andrew Holleran**, **Felice Picano**, **George Whitmore**, and **Michael Grumley**, Ferro's lover for more than a decade. The Violet Quill members played a pivotal role in the post-**Stonewall** renaissance of gay literature, particularly with their autobiographical fiction, which constitutes much of Ferro's writing. Ferro's popularity grew in the 1980s, especially after the publication of *The Family of Max Desir* in 1983, his most acclaimed work. He gave lectures and readings, published literary criticism, and taught at Hofstra University in the creative writing program. Ferro's blossoming career ended abruptly with a diagnosis of AIDS in 1984 and his subsequent death on July 11, 1988.

Ferro's first work of direct autobiographical fiction is arguably his greatest achievement. *The Family of Max Desir* centers on Max Desir, a gay man who struggles to find peace with his family and sexuality. As a child, Max lives in New Jersey with his affluent Italian American family. He enjoys "feminine" activities such as dancing, which terrifies Max's macho Italian father, John, and creates distance between the father and son. The tension is exacerbated when Max travels to Rome and meets a partner, Nick. Max writes home to John, bringing his homosexuality into the open and telling John of his male lover. Max's mother, Marie, accepts her son as a gay adult, as she did when he was a questioning child. When Marie becomes ill, she brings the family together once again. In illness, Marie attempts to unite John and Max, as she did when Max was a child. Max's siblings accept his sexual orientation and support him as he tries to make peace with his father, but the death of Marie complicates the process. In the meantime, Max seeks male affection elsewhere; besides Nick, Max develops relationships with other men who satisfy his artistic and spiritual curiosities. Max's most affecting relationship, besides his partner Nick, involves a man named Clive, whose mysticism first causes fascination and then estrangement. Max learns from his trials and encounters; he eventually matures into a man at peace with his family, spirituality, and sexuality.

In *The Family of Max Desir*, Ferro examines a homosexual man's partial departure from the constrictions of a heterosexual family, while still maintaining essential ties with the family. Through the anecdotes from Max's childhood, Ferro looks at the "nip-it-in-the-bud" mentality of some heterosexual fathers; this familial stifling of homosexuality can still be seen decades after the Stonewall Riots. In Rome, away from his family, Max finally acquires a sense of self-worth and social affirmation when he engages in sexual intercourse with a man. The semipublic sexual encounter attracts an audience, and Max feels that he finally did something that merits attention. Max seeks other partners and creative outlets for his sexuality, which leads him to his lifelong partner, Nick, as well as others, such as Clive. Mysterious, erotic, and sensual, Clive gives Max temporary escapes from the constrictions of the real world, a crossing that Max constantly seeks. Through this relationship, Max avoids the bonds of monogamy, and he immerses himself in mysticism, which is the polar opposite to the religion of Max's father: Christianity. The binary opposition exposes the different ways that the two men deal with the death of Marie and fail to connect, even in light of tragedy. While Max's father struggles to find peace through Christianity, Max finds comfort in writing, particularly through a story that he writes about a homosexual white man's journey into the Amazon, which, he claims, is a masque of his own story. Metaphysically, the story may be a reflection of Ferro's own cross-racial sexual relationships. In "Race and the Violet Quill," **David Bergman** brings to light Ferro's relationships with black men, but notes his resistance to writing about those relationships (79). Ferro felt close to his character Max Desir, as evidenced in Bergman's article. Ferro lived a "white" life of glamour and luxury in Europe, according to Bergman, but also enjoyed nights out at the bar, where he consorted with men of color and went by the name of "Max," as though "Max" Ferro was a separate person from Robert Ferro the author (89–90). The reader is left to speculate how closely the lives of Ferro and the character Max were intertwined. In *The Family of Max Desir,* through his sexual and creative encounters, Max discovers his own sexual and spiritual identity while maintaining a polite relationship with his dysfunctional, suffering family.

If *The Family of Max Desir* examines how homosexuality affects familial relations, *Second Son* (1988) pushes the theme miles ahead by adding AIDS into the family portrait. Written by Ferro after his own and his lover's AIDS diagnoses, *Second Son* shows the effect of AIDS on Mark Valerian and the Valerian family. The novel is more abstract than *The Family of Max Desir,* and, at points, reads more like a personal reflection than a novel. It begins by reflecting on the people and places of Mark's life. Ferro writes of Mark's family members as though he is creating character sketches and measures Mark against them as though the reader must understand each family member in order to understand Mark. Ferro also writes extensively about Cape May, a seaside house, which is equally divided among the family members after the death of Mara, Mark's mother. Mark wishes to keep the house, but his father, Mr. Valerian, wishes to sell it, causing tension between the father and his second son. After discovering he has AIDS, Mark departs for Italy to live as a gardener, a pathetic career in the eyes of Mark's father. Nevertheless, Mark lives happily as an aesthete in Italy and meets Bill, who also has AIDS, through a mutual friend. The two fall in love, support each other, and eventually accept their conditions. AIDS transforms Mark's life and he learns the true meaning of intimacy and love.

Second Son seeks to examine the idea of acceptance: acceptance of homosexuality and death. Although Mr. Valerian appears to accept his son and claims to want to find a cure for his illness, his actions suggest otherwise. Mr. Valerian ignores his son for years, failing to send flowers or visit with the rest of the family when Bill is ill in the hospital. In a sense, Mr. Valerian represents the government campaigns for abstinence, quarantines, and branding of the sick (Dewey 130). Through Mark, Ferro rejects such campaigns and shows how the acceptance of family and intimate companionship can have healing effects. Mark's other family members are more accepting, particularly his niece Sarah, who never hesitates to hug Mark or let him hold her baby. Companionship with Bill heals Mark the most, though. Since Bill also has AIDS, the two connect on emotional and physical levels, and eventually they come to terms with their fates. A mutual friend of Mark and Bill, Matthew represents a different end, as he cannot accept his pending death and seeks a fantastic escape through a science-fiction fantasy. In contrast, Mark and Bill represent the healthy ways that an ill, homosexual man might find peace with his family and his fate.

Ferro continues to trace the formation of identity in *The Blue Star* (1985), a beautifully lyrical and aesthetically pleasing novel, which follows the life and encounters of Peter Conrad. The novel begins with Peter's arrival in Florence from America. In Florence, he feels free to discover and explore his homosexuality, which leads him to Chase Walker, another gay man with a passion for gardening and a luxurious lifestyle. Both men establish ties in Florence before returning to the United States. Peter, however, falls in love with

Lorenzo, a young beautiful Italian, and Chase marries a woman, which brings him into Italian nobility and enormous wealth. These ties bring the two men back to Florence, more than 15 years later, for an extravagant and exotic cruise. By the end of the novel, both men come to accept their place in society and their enduring relationships. The story of Peter Conrad alternates with the novel's second plot: the construction of a Masonic temple beneath Central Park. This Masonic story ties into the main narrative thread, but many reviewers and critics have pointed out that Ferro does not entirely succeed in integrating it smoothly into the novel's primary plot. The Masonic tale reads like a summary of events, people, politics, and architectural logistics, which is starkly different from Ferro's lush European story. As a whole, the novel examines the privileged, upper-class, gay lifestyle; and Ferro accomplishes a gay novel of manners, a rich account of two American men, their travels, passions, surroundings, and dynamic acquaintances.

Ferro's other major works include *Atlantis: The Autobiography of a Search* (1970) and *The Others* (1979). Ferro co-authored *Atlantis* with his lover, Michael Grumley. It is a nonfiction retelling of their journey to the Bahamas and is told in alternating chapters from the perspective of each author. Grumley's chapters focus on the trip itself, but Ferro's chapters reflect upon broader topics, including time, civilization, writing, technology, imagination, and death. In *The Others* Ferro addresses some of the same topics, but uses an utterly different method. A radically experimental novel, *The Others* lacks a solid plot, structure, and even lacks a complete portrait of the main characters. It is composed as a series of fantasies and character sketches, and the protagonist wonders if he lives a real or imagined life. A significant departure from Ferro's other novels, *The Others* is a compelling narrative that resembles a strange and powerful dream.

As a writer and a member of the gay literary movement, Ferro helped push homosexual literature into the mainstream and publicize homosexual identity. His highly autobiographic novels read like extremely personal and realistic tales, which leave out no aesthetic or necessary detail. The elements of fantasy or mysticism in his books suggest a great imagination and hope for a more accepting society.

Further Reading

Bell, Chris. "Robert Ferro." In *The Greenwood Encyclopedia of Multiethnic American Literature,* edited by Emmanuel S. Nelson, 721–23. Westport, CT: Greenwood Press, 2005.

Bergman, David. "Race and the Violet Quill." *American Literary History* 9, no. 1 (Spring 1997): 79–102.

Dewey, Joseph. "Robert Ferro." In *Contemporary American Gay Novelists: A Bibliographical Critical Sourcebook,* edited by Emmanuel S. Nelson, 128–39. Westport, CT: Greenwood Press, 1993.

———. "Music for a Closing: Responses to AIDS in Three American Novels." In *AIDS: The Literary Response,* edited by Emmanuel S. Nelson, 23–38. New York: Twayne, 1992.

Allison Porzio

Fierstein, Harvey (b. 1954)

Award-winning Jewish American playwright, actor, and prominent **gay** rights activist, Harvey Forbes Fierstein was born in the Bensonhurst section of Brooklyn, New York, on June 6, 1954. He was the younger of two sons of Jacqueline, a school librarian, and Irving, a handkerchief manufacturer. Fierstein is one of the most well-known gay individuals in the arts community and certainly one of the earliest to herald his own sexuality. At age 11, he helped to found the Gallery Players Community Theatre (now known simply as The Gallery Players), and during his teens—around the time of the **Stonewall Riots**—he played drag queens in various clubs, leading to a role in Andy Warhol's play *Pork* in 1971. While continuing to perform at venues such as La MaMa, Fierstein went on to earn a B.F.A. in art from Brooklyn's Pratt Institute in 1973, though he was to pursue playwriting rather than painting.

Fierstein's early short plays (mostly unpublished) include *In Search of the Cobra Jewels* (1973), *Freaky Pussy* (1973), and *Flatbush Tosca* (1975), a transvestite version of Puccini's opera. But it was his groundbreaking *Torch Song Trilogy* (1982) that catapulted the playwright to fame, a series that evolved out of Fierstein's personal experiences. The cycle traces the development of Arnold Beckoff (played by Fierstein) through relationships, friendship, and death, and it also introduces the theme of family that permeates much of Fierstein's work.

The first play of the trilogy, *International Stud* (1978)—whose title derives its name from a Greenwich Village gay bar in the 1960s and 1970s—begins with an extensive soliloquy by Arnold in his dressing room, a monologue that expresses his sense of self as well as his needs and desires. In scene 2, Ed enters, and the remainder of the play revolves around the relationship between the two men as Ed struggles with his own bisexuality, a conflict that ends with him leaving Arnold for a woman named Laurel. *International Stud* is punctuated by a series of torch songs sung by Lady Blues that gives the trilogy its title as well as its tone.

Fugue in a Nursery (1979) picks up a year later when Ed and Laurel have established a fairly stable relationship. While at Ed's country house, Laurel calls Arnold—whom she has never met—to invite him up for a weekend, hoping to bring finality to the threesome's enmeshment. However, the 25-year-old Arnold's current partner, a gorgeous 18-year-old model named Alan, begs to go along, seeking from Arnold the same sort of affirmation that Laurel will seek from Ed. Not surprisingly, the weekend evolves into games of jealousy and comparison, as Ed probes for information about Alan, who in turn asks Arnold about Ed, while Laurel attempts to learn more of the connection between Arnold and Ed. When Ed seduces Alan, Laurel leaves; still, the play ends on a positive note as Ed and Laurel reconcile and become engaged, as do Arnold and Alan—inasmuch as they can. The musical divisions throughout *Fugue in a Nursery*—such as stretto, coda, subject, and countersubject—are designed, as Fierstein points out, to underscore its themes and moments rather than overpower or melodramatize them.

The final part of the trilogy, *Widows and Children First!* (1979), takes place five years later. Alan has died, the victim of gay bashing by a horde of teenage thugs, and Ed has separated from Laurel, having taken up temporary lodging on Arnold's couch. Arnold has begun adoption proceedings for a troubled, gay 15-year-old, David, following through on a decision that he and Alan had made to create a family unit. The mercurial aspect of the play comes with the arrival of Arnold's archetypal Jewish mother, who continually harps on her son's sexual talk and her belief that Arnold could renounce his homosexuality if he wanted to. Added to these conflicts is a bickering over whose grief is greater: Arnold's after a five-year relationship with Alan, or Mrs. Beckett's after a thirty-five-year marriage. Still, *Widows and Children First!*—like the entire trilogy—does conclude hopefully, with a tentative reconciliation between Arnold and his mother, an expression of David's love for his new father, and the possibility that Ed may rejoin Arnold to form the complete family that all the characters have yearned for. *Torch Song Trilogy* earned a raft of awards, including the OBIE, Oppenheimer Playwriting Award, two Tonys, and two Drama Desk Awards. Fierstein also won the Theatre World Award as outstanding new performer and the Drama Desk Award for outstanding actor. In 1988, the play was made into a film, for which Fierstein wrote the screenplay and in which he reprised his role as Arnold Beckoff.

Hard upon the heels of the success of *Torch Song Trilogy* came *La Cage Aux Folles* (1983), a French play adapted to a musical for which Fierstein wrote the book, earning him yet another Tony Award, while the play itself earned a raft of accolades. The first gay-themed production to appear on Broadway, *La Cage Aux Folles* centers around the relationship between a gay couple: a nightclub manager, Georges, and his primary star (let), Albin. Georges has a son from a youthful fling, Jean-Michel, who now informs him that he plans to marry a young woman, Anne, whose father is a pompous and pretentious but powerful political moralist. When Jean-Michel announces that his fiancée's parents wish to visit, catastrophe looms. The plot revolves around Georges's attempt to have Albin either disappear for a few days or masquerade as a macho uncle, while he also attempts to entice Jean-Michel's real mother to join him for the occasion. Despite an array of mishaps, all works out well in the end, with Anne's parents ironically avoiding the paparazzi by escaping through Georges's gay club, *La Cage Aux Folles,* dressed in drag. (In 1996, an American version of the play was filmed as *The Birdcage* (1996), starring Nathan Lane and Robin Williams.)

Following these dazzling sensations, Fierstein's playwriting career went into a downspin, and although he has continued to write, none of his works have attained the stature of those in the early 1980s. Despite the failure of subsequent works, including *Spookhouse* (1984), *Forget Him* (1988), and *Legs Diamond* 1988)—a musical for which Fierstein wrote the book—his 1987 trilogy *Safe Sex* does deserve some attention, not least for its bold, scathing confrontation of the AIDS crisis and its effect on the gay community. "Manny and Jake," the first work of the trilogy, focuses on characters of the same name: Manny, who is determined to love every man in the world but is haunted by being a carrier of the disease and obsessed with staying safe, and Jake, who is merely looking for a pickup while assuring Manny that he is clean. The centerpiece, titled "Safe Sex" like the trilogy itself, forefronts this concept even further, with one of the characters (Ghee) having made a list of safety practices that the other character (Mead) snidely refers to as the Ten Commandments of sex. The two men, former lovers who have reunited, discuss their various relationships as well as the fact that gays have now been publicly recognized— but only because of a disease. The final work of the trilogy, "On Tidy Endings," concerns a woman, Marion, whose husband, Collin, came out of the **closet** after 16 years of marriage. They divorced and he eventually found a companion, but only after he had contacted AIDS. The play opens after Collin's death, exploring the conflict and ensuing resolution between Marion and Arthur, Collin's lover, as they debate their roles in Collin's life. The trilogy—which, like *Torch Song,* has autobiographical roots for Fierstein— exposes how AIDS has brought gays both freedom and condemnation: though they are now "out of the closet," they are perceived and examined by the public as a kind of species.

Although Fierstein considers himself primarily a theater person, the gravelly voiced actor has become well known as a film star, with roles in movies including *Garbo Talks* (1984), *Mrs. Doubtfire* (1993), *Bullets over Broadway* (1994), and *Independence Day* (1996). He has also made several television appearances as well as doing voice-overs for film and TV. In 1984, he narrated the television documentary *The Times of Harvey Milk,* for which he won an Emmy Award. Fierstein also won a Humanitas Prize for his 1999 movie *The Sissy Duckling,* which he subsequently adapted to book form.

Fierstein made a glorious return to Broadway in 2002 in a musical revival of John Waters's film *Hairspray.* The play swept numerous awards, including a Tony for Fierstein in his role as Edna Turnblad, making him the first man ever to earn a Best Actor Award for playing a woman. In 2004, he performed in a revival of *Fiddler on the Roof,* and in 2008, he starred in the Broadway musical *A Catered Affair,* for which he also wrote the book, based on a teleplay by Paddy Chayefsky that was later adapted to film by **Gore Vidal**.

See also Drama, Gay; Gay Literature, Jewish American

Further Reading

Collins, Glenn. "In *Safe Sex,* Harvey Fierstein Turns Serious." *New York Times,* April 5, 1987, H5+.

Dukes, Thomas. "Harvey Fierstein." In *Contemporary Gay American Poets and Playwrights: An A-to-Z Guide,* edited by Emmanuel S. Nelson, 153–61. Westport, CT: Greenwood Publishing Group, 2003.

Hall, Ernest J. *Harvey Fierstein: A Prophetic Voice in the Gay Community.* Ann Arbor, MI: UMI Dissertation Services, 2001.

Rapp, Linda. "Fierstein, Harvey." GLBTW. http://www.glbtq.com/arts/fierstein_h_art.html (accessed August 18, 2008).

Stein, Harry. "*Playboy* Interview: Harvey Fierstein." *Playboy* (August 1988): 43–56.

Karen Charmaine Blansfield

Film, Gay

By the late 1980s, **gay** film was a broad category that included avant-garde films and videos, underground film cultures, a film festival circuit specializing in independent features and documentaries, activist films and videos, and a slowly increasing number of Hollywood narrative features. Filmmakers and producers built on the work done by gay filmmakers in the 1960s and 1970s. Jack Smith, Andy Warhol, Kenneth Anger, the Kuchar brothers, and Paul Morrissey developed the underground gay film scene in the 1960s and 1970s. In the 1970s, gay filmmakers began making the first feature-length narrative films and an explosion of activist films, videos, and documentaries were produced in the post-**Stonewall** era. Paul Morrissey's films for Andy Warhol crossed over from underground exhibition venues to commercial ones; the higher profile of these films inspired many gay filmmakers from the 1970s to the present, including John Waters and Gregg Araki.

By the 1980s, Hollywood was making baby steps in representing gay life on screen— even though films such as *Cruising* (1980) and *The Fan* (1981) portrayed gay men as pathological killers. In response to Hollywood misrepresentations of gay male life, gay directors and producers began producing more independent films—films made without the financial backing of Hollywood studios—and gay screenwriters, directors, and producers in Hollywood worked to push mainstream studios to do a better job representing gay characters on screen. Screenwriter Barry Sandler wrote the box office flop *Making Love* (1982), a film that dealt with a married man coming out of the **closet**. *Kiss of the*

Spider Woman (1985) also contained a gay character, but that character, like many gay and sexually ambiguous characters in Hollywood films from the 1930s to the 1980s, died at the end of the story.

Gay filmmakers reacted to stereotypical and demonizing representations of gay men in Hollywood film and to the AIDS epidemic by producing and distributing films that attempted to chronicle social and political struggles. There was a dramatic rise of documentaries dealing with gay history in the 1980s, including films such as *Pink Triangles* (1982), *Before Stonewall* (1984), *Silent Pioneers* (1985), and *The Times of Harvey Milk* (1984).

Gay filmmakers also began to make more narrative feature films, many of which represented gay male responses to the AIDS crisis. Arthur Bressan Jr.'s *Buddies* (1985) explored the relationship between an AIDS patient and the "buddy" assigned him by a local AIDS outreach group. Films such as Bill Sherwood's *Parting Glances* (1986) and Norman Rene and Craig Lucas's *Longtime Companion* (1989) focused on gay men's increasing efforts within urban gay communities to provide services to people with AIDS and to fight for federal AIDS funding.

Hollywood films also began to address the AIDS crisis, even though these films often marginalized gay characters. Ron Cowen and Daniel Lipman, who produced the American version of **Queer** *as Folk* for Showtime Networks, wrote the made-for-television movie *An Early Frost* (1985)—one man's coming out to his parents and revealing that he was HIV-positive. Television executives were so worried about one scene in which Michael's grandmother kissed him on the cheek that they pressured producers to get a green light for the scene from the Centers for Disease Control. Other made-for-television movies such as *Our Sons* (1991) and Home Box Office (HBO) Films' *And the Band Played On* (1993) would provide more mainstream visibility to the AIDS epidemic. *Philadelphia* (1993), directed by Jonathan Demme and written by out screenwriter Ron Nyswaner, became the first major Hollywood film to deal with gay men and the AIDS crisis.

Narrative features were not the only kinds of films that dealt with the AIDS crisis, however. Aesthetic collectives such as Gran Fury, Testing the Limits, House of Color, Paper Tiger Southwest, and DIVA-TV (Damned Interfering Video Activist Television) produced films and videos protesting the Reagan administration's lackluster response to the AIDS crisis, pressured the government to commit more research dollars to fight the epidemic, and gave people with AIDS an opportunity to tell their own stories. The most polished examples of these activist films and videos are Testing the Limits' *Voices From the Front: America 1988–1991* (1991) and Gregg Bordowitz's *Fast Trip, Long Drop* (1993).

Together, the rise in feature filmmaking and the stylistic experimentation in AIDS activist film and video contributed to the rise of New Queer Cinema. New Queer Cinema is a term coined by B. Ruby Rich to denote an emerging body of films by the early 1990s that challenged ideas about positive and negative images of queer men and women and experimented with new visual, sound design, and narrative techniques. Rich also argued that New Queer Cinema films represented political and social issues that feminist and queer theorists in the academy were also addressing, even though most New Queer Cinema films featured white male protagonists. Like **queer theory**, New Queer Cinema films examined the social construction of homosexuality and the ways in which gender and sexual performance were fluid and malleable concepts.

New Queer Cinema directors include John Greyson, Tom Joslin, Mark Massi, Tom Kalin, Todd Haynes, Gus Van Sant, Marlon Riggs, Isaac Julien, and Gregg Araki. John Greyson's *Zero Patience* (1995) reimagined Gaeten Dugas, the French Canadian flight attendant who was labeled patient zero of the AIDS epidemic in the 1980s. Harry M. Benshoff and Sean Griffin have called Greyson's film "a ghost story musical about AIDS" (235). Tom Joslin and Mark Massi's documentary entitled *Silverlake Life: The View from Here* (1993) chronicled the couple's losing battle with AIDS. Joslin began the documentary, Massi took over after his lover became too ill, and Peter Friedman, a friend of the couple, finished the project and released it on the festival circuit.

Tom Kalin's *Swoon* (1991) retold the 1924 Leopold and Loeb murder case. The film emphasized Leopold and Loeb's homosexuality more than other filmic accounts of the case. Kalin's decision to produce and direct a film that featured gay murderers as protagonists clashed with the idea that gay images needed to be positive images that would help gay men assimilate into mainstream society. Kalin's film helped set a tone for other New Queer Cinema filmmakers, who wanted to contest the necessity of positive images and represent queer men and women with more complexity.

Another major filmmaker in the New Queer Cinema movement is Todd Haynes. After getting his degree from Brown University, Haynes produced his first film, *Superstar: The Karen Carpenter Story* (1987), a biopic in which Haynes used Barbie dolls to tell the story of Karen Carpenter's rise to fame and her battle with anorexia nervosa. Mattel and the Carpenter estate's separate injunctions against the exhibition and distribution have made it difficult to view.

Poison (1991), Haynes's next film blended three stories. "Homo," the first story, is based on Jean Genet's work and expressions of homoeroticism between male prison inmates. The second story, "Horror," is about a scientist who ingests a sex hormone that makes him a killer and is shot in black and white. "Hero," the third story, deals with a boy who shoots his abusive dad and flies away; it is shot in a documentary style.

Haynes continued to play with genre and style in future films. Haynes cast Julianne Moore in *Safe* (1995) as a affluent California housewife who is made sick by her own home; many critics read the film as an AIDS allegory. *Velvet Goldmine* (1998) combined music video, the excesses of 1970s glam rock, and narrative film techniques. *Far from Heaven* (2002) queered the 1950s melodrama, especially Douglas Sirk's *All That Heaven Allows* (1955). In the Bob Dylan biopic *I'm Not There* (2007), Haynes cast eight men and women to play the rock legend, including British actress Cate Blanchett.

Gus Van Sant also started his career in the 1980s. Van Sant's *Mala Noche* (1985) dealt with queer life in Portland, Oregon. Future films such as *Drugstore Cowboy* (1989) and *My Own Private Idaho* (1991) continued to represent queer life in the Pacific Northwest. In *My Own Private Idaho,* Van Sant cast River Phoenix and Keanu Reeves to play leading roles. Van Sant has gone on to make both independent and Hollywood films such as *Even Cowgirls Get the Blues* (1993), *To Die For* (1995), *Good Will Hunting* (1997), *Gerry* (2002), *Elephant* (2003), and *Last Days* (2005).

Gregg Araki, the only Asian American gay male director included in the 1990s hype surrounding New Queer Cinema, studied film at the University of Southern California. Many of his films are set in Southern California and focus on teens and twentysomethings who speak in pop culture references, listen to rock and punk music, and feel cynical about their chances to lead full, happy lives as queer men and women. Araki's *The Living End* (1992) queered the buddy/road movie, featuring two HIV-positive lovers who leave a trail of violence in their wake. *Totally F***ed Up* (1994), *The Doom Generation* (1995), *Nowhere* (1996), *Splendor* (1999), and *Mysterious Skin* (2004) further represent Araki's cynical look at American pop culture, consumerism, and anger at the limited opportunities many gay and lesbian youths face.

Marlon Riggs and Isaac Julien are the two major black gay filmmakers of the 1980s and 1990s. Marlon Riggs's films such as *Ethnic Notions* (1987), *Tongues Untied* (1988), *Color Adjustment* (1989), *Anthem* (1993), and *Black Is . . . Black Ain't* (1994) dealt with issues of race and sexuality as well as with African American history and culture. Afro-British director Isaac Julien's film *Looking for Langston* (1989) and *Young Soul Rebels* (1991) also represented black gay sexualities on the screen. Other notable filmmakers in this period include Bruce LaBruce, Christopher Munch, and Derek Jarman.

In the 1990s and 2000s, gay films were more widely available than ever before. The rise of gay film festivals in major cities allowed gay filmmakers new venues for film exhibition. The formation and expansion of distribution companies such as Strand, TLA Releasing, Wolfe Video, Frameline, and Culture Q Connection allowed gay films to be seen outside the festival circuit. Within the mainstream film and television industry, Hollywood studios began producing films featuring gay characters and HBO, Showtime, the Independent Film Channel, the Sundance Channel, and gay networks such as Here! and Logo broadcast films with gay content.

Particularly on the festival circuit, an increasing number of documentaries dealt with gay culture and gay history. These films included *The Cockettes* (2002), *Trembling before G-d* (2001), *Daddy and the Muscle Academy* (1992), and *When Boys Fly* (2002). Arthur Dong's films *Coming Out under Fire* (1994), *Licensed to Kill* (1997), and *Family Fundamentals* (2002) won critical acclaim on the festival circuit.

Popular types of gay films included the coming out, buddy, and **camp** films. Lighthearted romantic comedies also proved to be popular. Coming out films such as *Edge of Seventeen* (1998) portrayed the struggles faced by gay teens. Romantic comedies included *Billy's Hollywood Screen Kiss* (1998), *Trick* (1999), *Big Eden* (2000), *All Over the Guy* (2001), and *Latter Days* (2003). Buddy films included *Love! Valour! Compassion!* (1997) and *The Broken Hearts Club* (2000), while camp and satirical films included **Charles Busch**'s *Psycho Beach Party* (2000) and *Die Mommie Die!* (2003). John Waters built on his 1970s and 1980s work in films such as *Serial Mom* (1994), *Pecker* (1998), *Cecil B. Demented* (2000), and *A Dirty Shame* (2004).

Gay directors such as John Cameron Mitchell, John Waters, Todd Haynes, and Gus Van Sant continue to make films that challenge audiences and help convince the industry to give new gay filmmakers a chance. Mitchell's *Hedwig and the Angry Inch* (2001) and *Shortbus* (2006) challenge audiences' comfort levels with on-screen sexuality. Ang Lee's *Brokeback Mountain* (2005), a romantic drama, was critically as well as commercially successful. These films, along with the work of established and emerging gay filmmakers, continue to push the envelope of what is acceptable on-screen.

Further Reading

Aaron, Michele, ed. *New Queer Cinema: A Critical Reader.* New Brunswick: Rutgers University Press, 2004.

Benshoff, Harry M., and Sean Griffin. *Queer Images: A History of Gay and Lesbian Film in America.* New York: Rowman and Littlefield, 2006.

Hays, Matthew. *The View from Here: Conversations with Gay and Lesbian Filmmakers.* Vancouver, BC: Arsenal Pulp Press, 2007.

Ben Aslinger

Film, Lesbian

While lesbian identity and desire have often been featured in or alluded to in film, they have not always been outwardly visible. Terry Castle, for instance, reads *Queen Christina* (1933), starring Greta Garbo, as having an underlying lesbian message. She points out that the lesbian is "always somewhere else: in the shadows, in the margins, hidden from history, out of sight, out of mind," which is to a certain extent applicable to the genre of lesbian film as a whole (Castle 2). An examination of lesbian film must therefore pay special heed to the invisible or implied forms of lesbian representation in film, for it is in the margins that the evolution of lesbian film begins.

As many films can be read as having an underlying lesbian message, it is impossible to pinpoint the beginning of lesbian film. An important early example of what is often viewed as a lesbian film is Ingmar Bergman's *Persona* (1966), which is interesting in that it dramatizes and cinematically visualizes the ambiguous relationship and unspoken passion between the two female main characters, without ever naming or defining it. Because the film does not offer a straightforward explanation of the women's affinity for each other, critics have come up with numerous different interpretations. **Susan Sontag**, for instance, has read the relationship between the two women as a play on the theme on the double as the two women seem to mirror each other. It is worth noting the similarities between *Persona* and the much more recent *Mulholland Dr.* (2001), a subversive and highly complex masterpiece directed by David Lynch, that—like *Persona*—has the desire between two women result in a bewildering confusion of identities and order.

As what constitutes a lesbian film is, at least partly, a "reading effect" in the sense that the viewer's sensibilities and awareness determine whether or not an implied relationship between two women is perceived as lesbian or not, there are many mainstream films that are viewed as lesbian by some, but not by others. *Fried Green Tomatoes* (1991), directed by Jon Avnet, is an interesting example. The film—based on the novel by Fannie Flagg in which the lesbian relationship between the main characters is made explicit—glosses over it, so that many viewers would be left unaware of this dimension of their relationship. Nevertheless, the film was perceived positively by the lesbian community and even won a GLAAD (Gay & Lesbian Alliance Against Defamation) Media Award. *Thelma & Louise* (1991) is another example of a mainstream film that has often been read as having an underlying lesbian message.

Since the 1980s, more and more films openly incorporated and depicted lesbian desire. An influential example is the fantasy vampire film *The Hunger* (1983) starring David Bowie, Susan Sarandon, and Catherine Deneuve, which includes a by now infamous kiss between Sarandon and Deneuve. It is noteworthy that many other films that were intended for a mainstream and, often, straight audience, included similar depictions of lesbian love that draw on a similar idea of the lesbian as associated with moral depravity, a lust for blood, and criminal tendency. Sharon Stone's character in *Basic Instinct* (1992), for instance, is a perfect example. And *Bound* (1996), a crime thriller in the tradition of film noir, directed by The Wachowski Brothers and starring Gina Gershon and

Jennifer Tilly, is another. It is about a woman who longs to escape her marriage to a Mafioso and falls in love with another woman who helps her to escape.

Other examples of the murdering lesbian include *Heavenly Creatures* (1994), directed by Peter Jackson, and starring Kate Winslet and Melanie Lynskey, which tells the true story of two New Zealand girls who become obsessed with one another and kill one of their mothers who is trying to keep them apart. The Academy Award–winning drama *Monster* (2003), starring Charlize Theron, is a biopic of serial killer Aileen Wuornos and a more recent example of the filmic link between lesbian identity and crime and murder.

In contrast to these often negative and bleak depictions of lesbian love, the by now classic *Desert Hearts* (1986) is often perceived as the first full-length filmic lesbian love story that depicts female same-sex desire in a realistic yet positive and affirmative light. The film, set in the 1950s, depicts the story of a female professor (Helen Shaver) who is divorcing her husband and falls in love with a younger casino worker (Patricia Charbonneau). In contrast to other early 1980s films such as *The Hunger* (1983), *Personal Best* (1982), or *Lianna* (1983), *Desert Heart* was the first overtly lesbian film to depict a happy ending. The 1990s marked a significant shift in lesbian film. Not only did films begin to focus more exclusively and explicitly on lesbian storylines, but they were often also written, directed, and produced by lesbians. Out writer and director Patricia Rozerma, who had already brought a lesbian love story to the screen with *I've Heard the Mermaids Singing* (1987), presented audiences with *When Night Is Falling* (1995), the unexpected love story between a frustrated college professor and a circus performer. Another important example of this wave of lesbian films in the mid-1990s is *Go Fish* (1994), an independent film directed and written by Rose Troche and Guinevere Turner, who were a couple at the time. The film follows the lives of a group of lesbian friends in Chicago and employs experimental techniques such as dream sequences or free verse poetry. Other important films from this era include *Better Than Chocolate* (1999) and the more gloomy *High Art* (1998).

A special subgenre of lesbian film that emerged during the time deals with lesbian young adults and focuses on the struggles of adolescent identity, first love, and coming out. While *The Incredibly True Adventures of Two Girls in Love* (1995) and *All Over Me* (1997) are ultimately positive in their depiction of teenage lesbian love, *Lost and Delirious* (2001) returns to the glum image of the celluloid lesbian as doomed as it ends with the suicide of the teenage protagonist Pauline (Piper Perabo), who cannot cope with the rejection by her best friend and ex-lover Victoria (Jessica Paré).

The 1990s also saw a series of films that depicted lesbian relationships outside of the Anglophone context and thus aim to reveal often underrepresented issues or concerns associated with lesbian identity and desire. A German movie entitled *Aimée and Jaguar* (1999), directed by Max Färberböck, depicts the true story of a love affair between a Jewish lesbian and a German housewife who is married to a Nazi in Berlin in the 1940s. *Fire* (1996) by Indian-born Canadian director Deepa Mehta is highly interesting in that it depicts the lesbian relationship between two married Indian women and draws attention to Western stereotypes of lesbian identity. The film was hugely controversial and resulted in death threats directed toward the director.

Since 2000, the genre of lesbian film has witnessed increasing success and popularity. *If These Walls Could Talk 2* (2000), for instance, traces how lesbian relationships and social attitudes toward them have changed over the years as it depicts three different couples in the 1960s, the 1970s and the "present day." The final segment, directed by Anne Heche

and starring her then-lover Ellen DeGeneres and Sharon Stone shows a lesbian couple trying and finally succeeding in having a child. The more lighthearted approach of the final
segment of *If These Walls Could Talk 2* is to a certain extent indicative of other recent
examples of films that depict love between women in accordance with the generic rules
of romantic comedies that are usually associated with straight relationships. Examples
include *Imagine Me and You* (2005), *Kissing Jessica Stein* (2001), and *Gray Matters*
(2006). This is not to say that lesbian film has lost its edge, but that it is more diverse.
Jamie Babbitt's comedy *Itty Bitty Titty Committee* (2007), produced by nonprofit organization POWER UP (Professional Organization of Women in Entertainment Reaching
Up) for instance, is a humorous take on radical feminism and **queer** politics that speaks
to a teenage audience. What this shows is that lesbian film continues to evolve by embracing new and interesting possibilities.

See also Film, Gay

Further Reading

Benshoff, Harry M., and Sean Griffin. *Queer Images: A History of Gay and Lesbian Film in America.*
    Lanham, MD: Rowman & Littlefield, 2006.
Castle, Terry. *The Apparitional Lesbian: Female Homosexuality and Modern Culture.* New York:
    Columbia University Press, 2005.
Darren, Alison. *Lesbian Film Guide: An Essential A–Z Guide to the Celluloid Lesbian.* New York:
    Continuum International Publishing Group, 2000.
Dyer, Richard. "Lesbian/Woman: Lesbian Cultural Feminist Film." *Now You See It: Studies on Les-
    bian and Gay Film.* London: Routledge, 1991. 174–210.

Sherri Foster

Finn, William (b. 1952)

Composer, lyricist, writer, and teacher. Best known for the trio of off-off-Broadway and
off-Broadway "Marvin" musicals that culminated in the Tony Award–winning Broadway
musical *Falsettos* (1992), the openly **gay** William Finn was one of the first artists to bring
gay subject matter into mainstream musical theater. In his works, he juxtaposes the families into which we are born with the families we choose as we grow.

Finn was born in Boston in 1952 and grew up in nearby Natick. The eldest of three
children, Finn received a guitar for his bar mitzvah and began composing, eventually
teaching himself piano. Despite this, he did not think of music as a career while growing
up. He attended Williams College and majored in literature and American civilization but
participated in musical theater, even composing musicals. He graduated with the prestigious Hutchinson Fellowship for Musical Composition, an award Stephen Sondheim
received from the same school years earlier. Finn then studied music for a year at the University of California at Berkeley before moving to New York in 1976.

Finn staged *In Trousers,* for which he wrote the music and complete libretto, in his
apartment for an audience of invited guests. The rough staging impressed a representative
from Playwrights Horizons, where *In Trousers* received a cabaret staging in 1979. In the
musical, Finn introduced Marvin, a young man struggling with growing up and coming
to sexual awareness. A few scathing reviews of the play briefly prompted Finn to consider
giving up the theater for medical school. Finn persevered, however, and continued

Marvin's story at Playwrights Horizon in 1981 with *March of the Falsettos*. In *March of the Falsettos,* Marvin leaves his wife Trina after he has an affair with Whizzer. Trina meanwhile begins a romantic relationship with her therapist Mendel. At the heart of the story is Marvin's relationship with his son Jason, who worries that he, too, will become a "homo" like his father. The production won the 1981 Outer Critics Circle Award for Best Off-Broadway Musical. Finn said that he referred to his characters as "falsettos" because they were living outside their normal range. After receiving a Guggenheim Fellowship in 1984, Finn continued Marvin's journey with James Lapine's help as co-writer in 1990 with *Falsettoland,* in which Marvin commits to a relationship with Whizzer just as Whizzer is stricken with the mysterious "gay cancer" (the musical is set in 1981). *Falsettoland* won the Outer Critics Circle Award for Best Musical, the Drama Desk Award for Outstanding Lyrics, and the Lucille Lortel Award for Outstanding Musical.

In 1992, Finn and Lapine reworked *March of the Falsettos* and *Falsettoland* as *Falsettos* for Broadway to great acclaim. Marvin's families come together as Whizzer faces death from the as-yet unnamed AIDS. Particularly touching is Jason's choice to celebrate his bar mitzvah in Whizzer's hospital room. Finn juxtaposes life and death in this scene while bringing Marvin's biological and extended family together with his chosen family. Even Trina uncomfortably but sincerely offers comfort to her ex-husband's lover as he faces a certain death in the early days of the crisis. The production received seven Tony nominations and won two for Finn's score and Finn and Lapine's book.

The joy of receiving Tony Awards, however, was marred by health problems. Doctors diagnosed Finn with an inoperable brain tumor around the time of the production of *Falsettoland.* Though the condition eventually proved to be an operable congenital arteriovenous malformation, the experience was traumatic enough to prompt Finn to write *A New Brain,* a musical about a composer of children's music who is diagnosed with an inoperable brain tumor. The show won the Outer Critics Circle Award for Best Musical.

Finn reached the height of his popularity so far with the Broadway production of *The 25th Annual Putnam County Spelling Bee,* a sweet and funny look at the outsiders in the finals of a spelling bee. The musical ran for 1,136 performances and received six Tony nominations with two wins for Rachel Sheinkin's book and Dan Folger's supporting performance. Like all of Finn's work, the show explores the conflict between intelligence and emotion.

Further Reading

Bordman, Gerald. *American Musical Theatre: A Chronicle.* 3rd ed. Oxford: Oxford University Press, 2001.

Hischak, Thomas S. "William Finn." In *Contemporary Gay American Poets and Playwrights,* edited by Emmanuel S. Nelson, 162–70. Westport, CT: Greenwood Press, 2003.

Rapp, Linda. "William Finn." In *The Queer Encyclopedia of Music, Dance & Musical Theater,* edited by Claude J. Summers, 105–6. San Francisco: Cleis Press, 2004.

Jeff Godsey

Forrest, Katherine V. (b. 1939)

Novelist, editor, and pioneering author of lesbian mystery fiction. Born in 1939 in Canada, Katherine V. Forrest emigrated to the United States in 1957 and subsequently became a naturalized U.S. citizen in 1976. Educated at the University of California at Los Angeles and Wayne State University, Forrest worked in the field of business management until she turned 40, after which she decided to devote herself to a career as a full-time writer. Her first novel, *Curious Wine,* appeared four years later in 1983, and quickly became a classic of lesbian romantic fiction. Forrest has gone on to publish many other successful novels in the romance, mystery, and science fiction genres, as well as editing numerous collections of lesbian erotica and fiction. She also served as editor of the influential Naiad Press between 1984 and 1994. Although Forrest has experienced significant crossover success with her books, attracting ardent straight as well as lesbian fans, she nonetheless explicitly and consistently defined herself as a lesbian writer. For Forrest, being a lesbian author—an author who identifies as a lesbian, and whose books are primarily intended for lesbian readers—has been an integral part of her literary career.

Forrest is the first author to write a mystery series centered around a lesbian police officer, the Kate Delafield mysteries. The first of these novels, *Amateur City,* was published in 1984 to both popular and critical acclaim. Between 1984 and 2004, Forrest published eight Kate Delafield novels, two of which (*The Beverly Malibu,* 1989, and *Murder by Tradition,* 1991) were awarded the Lambda Literary Award for Best Mystery. The protagonist of these novels, Kate Delafield, is a talented and ambitious ex-marine, who works as a homicide detective for the Los Angeles Police Department. Throughout the series, Delafield struggles with her decision to remain **closet**ed at her workplace, and Forrest sensitively and realistically explores the terrible toll that Delafield's denial of her lesbian identity takes on her both personally and professionally. Forrest uses the Delafield mysteries to explore many issues of concern to the LGBTQ community, including homophobic violence, the biases of the judicial system toward LGBTQ people, the coming out process, and parents' rejection of LGBTQ children.

In addition to her Delafield series, Forrest is perhaps best known for her perennially popular lesbian romance *Curious Wine* (1983). She wrote this novel, a passionate and affirming tale of an unexpected love affair between two women, because it was the sort of book that she wanted to read, but which no one had yet written. The novel tells the story of Diana Holland and Lane Christianson, two women who meet while on vacation by Lake Tahoe. Contrary to both of their expectations, the women fall in love, and the novel details their evolving relationship with great honesty and powerful sensuality. While some critics have seen *Curious Wine* as a simple love story, Forrest insists that the tale is a profoundly political one, about the radical transformative power of romantic and sexual love between women. Forrest is also the author of another romance novel, *An Emergence of Green* (1990), which explores the sexual awakening and coming out process of Carolyn Blake, an unhappily married woman who falls in love with her female neighbor.

In addition to her work in the genres of romance and mystery, Forrest is also the author of a three-book series of science fiction novels, *Daughters of a Coral Dawn* (1984), *Daughters of an Amber Noon* (2002), and *Daughters of an Emerald Dusk* (2005). A cult classic ever since its publication, *Daughters of a Coral Dawn* introduces readers to the planet Maternas, an all-female world created during the twenty-second century by a group of women who rebelled against Earth's patriarchal social order. By turns erotic, humorous, and suspenseful, the novel offers an intriguing vision of what a world without men— and male-created power structures—might be like. *Daughters of an Amber Noon* considers the lives of women left behind on Earth after the Maternas revolution, and *Daughters of an Emerald Dusk* explores how the second generation of Maternas women reshape and challenge their mothers' vision of a separatist feminist utopia. Throughout her literary work, Forrest offers daring and insightful reflections on the political, social, and personal significance of love between women.

Further Reading

Klein, Kathleen Gregory. *Great Women Mystery Writers: Classic to Contemporary.* Westport, CT: Greenwood Press, 1994.

Ware, Mary C. "Katherine V. Forrest." In *Contemporary Lesbian Writers of the United States: A Bio-Bibliographical Sourcebook,* edited by Sandra Pollack and Denise D. Knight, 196–201. Westport, CT: Greenwood Press, 1993.

Holly M. Kent

Fox, John (1952–1990)

Gay American novelist. John Fox was born on May 26, 1952, in the Bronx to conservative and devoutly Catholic parents. He received his undergraduate degree in English from Lehman College, moved to Manhattan, and enrolled in the Creative Writing Program at Columbia University in 1982. It was during that time he began to write *The Boys on the Rock* (1984), and it would be his only novel. Shortly after the publication of the work Fox was diagnosed with AIDS; he died of complications related to AIDS on August 14, 1990.

The Boys on the Rock is a classic coming-of-age story. Set in the Bronx in the politically turbulent 1960s, it is narrated by its protagonist, Billy Connors, who, like the author, comes from a large, close-knit Catholic family. On the surface he appears to be a typical teenager. He is a member of his school's swim team, has a girlfriend as well as many good friends, and he is a gifted student. As the narrative unfolds Billy begins to reveal his self-doubt and sexual confusion. He feels little sexual attraction to his girlfriend, and his fantasies often center around some of the male members of his swim team. Yet he is unable to define his sexuality. Gradually he begins a close friendship with one of his fellow students, Al DiCicco, who becomes an object of his frequent fantasies. Their friendship becomes a romantic relationship, and it serves as a catalyst to Billy's sexual self-understanding. He comes out to his swim coach, who reacts with consternation and faint hostility, but Billy seems unperturbed. He even insists on the naturalness of his desires. His relationship with Al, however, begins to falter as Al increasingly has difficulty coming to terms with his sexuality. Their friendship ends but by the end of the narrative Billy reveals a confident sense of who he is and a mature awareness of his sexual identity.

Fox's only novel remains a compelling gay *Bildungsroman.* It offers a map of its protagonist's often poignant journey of self-discovery. It is a journey that, despite struggles along the way, culminates in heightened and enabling self-awareness that becomes a basis for him to live his life authentically.

Further Reading

Bates, Mark E. "John Fox." In *Contemporary Gay American Novelists: A Bio-Bibliographical Critical Sourcebook,* edited by Emmanuel S. Nelson, 140–44. Westport, CT: Greenwood Press, 1993.

Henderson, David W. Review of *The Boys on the Rock*. *Library Journal* 109 (August 1984): 1466.

Trevor A. Sydney

Fries, Kenny (b. 1960)

Notable disabilities activist, memoirist, poet, and playwright. Kenny Fries was born with congenital deformities on September 22, 1960, in Brooklyn, New York, to Donald and Joan Fries, a lower middle-class Jewish couple. Donald was a kosher butcher, and Joan a housewife. Fries spent his first six weeks in the hospital, four of those in an incubator. His legs, without fibulae, have sharp anterior curves of the tibia and flexion contractures of the knees, as well as two missing toes and posterior calf bands on each foot.

Family sexual and physical abuse complicated Fries's search for self-identity and peace and helped forge his fearlessness as a writer. Fries holds an M.F.A. from Columbia University's School for the Arts (1983) and a B.A. in English and American Literature, graduating Phi Betta Kappa from Brandeis University (1981). He has been a visiting writer at numerous colleges and universities and held residencies at a number of artist foundations and retreats.

In 2002 Fries received a United States/Japan Creative Arts Program grant for a six-month stay in Japan from the Japan–United States Friendship Commission and the National Endowment for the Arts. He has also received grants from the Ludwig Vogelstein Foundation and the Massachusetts Cultural Council. *New Mobility Magazine* named him one of their 1997 Persons of the Year. Since the publication of his first memoir, Fries has become a notable and vocal spokesperson for disability rights, advocating a social instead of medical model to define disabled people. He writes editorials, makes speaking appearances, and teaches at Goddard College. Fries currently lives in Northampton, Massachusetts.

Fries's childhood details a litany of surgeries that allowed Fries to walk and to have relatively normal mobility for the first 40 years of his life. His physical disabilities and the psychological problems originating from them, familial dysfunctions, and the societal conflicts of being Jewish and **gay** became the sources of his work. The physical stress placed on his knees has begun taking its toll. Less mobile but ever forthright in facing hardship, he writes frequently about physical disability and the emotional illness that has periodically crippled him.

Fries maps the invasion of the AIDS virus into his lover and into their relationship in his second poetry collection, *The Healing Notebooks* (1990), which won the 1991 Gregory Kolovakos Award for AIDS writing. Fries's ability to mesh confession with objectivist distance, rooted in his struggle to embrace and objectify his own distorted body, makes for poetry that is angry and loving in turns, ambivalent, questioning, open, and ultimately affirmative. His first memoir, *Body, Remember* (1997), traces the physical and psychic scars that molded him, detailing the story of his disability and his family's history, recounting his unfolding gayness and his reflections on being Jewish and gay as experienced in Israel. Fries writes more and more about disability after the publication of this work.

In *Anesthesia* (1996), Fries's third book of poems, Fries confronts his body, its deformities, his Jewishness, and his gayness. A stunning achievement in gay literature, *Anesthesia* combines the best of poetic grace with the steely energy of gay liberation. *Staring Back: The Disability Experience from the Inside Out* (1997), a disability anthology edited by Fries, solidified and broadened the audience for his message. In *Desert Walking* (2000), the natural world becomes emblematic of a new search for spiritual awareness. Night and day, winter and spring, and rain and sun become frequent metaphors for opening and closing of the self and the search for awareness.

Fries's last book, *The History of My Shoes and the Evolution of Darwin's Theory* (2007), demonstrates his distinctive and creative skill at addressing disability and personal growth issues. Part travelogue, part history, it adeptly describes personal expeditions to Thailand, Bali, Maine, the Grand Canyon, and the Galápagos Islands while recounting the race between Charles Darwin and Alfred Wallace to formulate a theory of evolution. The journeys and evolutionary theory become vehicles for translating his physical and mental adaptations as symbolized by his custom-made, perennially metamorphosing orthopedic shoes. *History* affirms that variety and difference lead to adaptability and survival. The Gustavus Myers Center for the Study of Bigotry and Human Rights in North America gave it a 2007 Human Rights Book Award.

Fries's greatest critical acclaim has come through his capacity to define disability and being gay as a tool for personal growth, while simultaneously forming a body of criticism against society's prejudices. As a result he has become a major spokesperson for the disabled. Bringing sexuality into the forefront of such discussions has created a crossover of concerns, which places Fries in a distinctive position as poet and social critic.

See also Autobiography, Gay; Gay Literature, Jewish American

Further Reading

Beam, Jeffery. "Kenny Fries." In *Contemporary Gay American Poets and Playwrights: An A-to-Z Guide,* edited by Emmanuel S. Nelson, 171–77. Westport, CT: Greenwood Publishing Group, 2003.

Troxell, Jane. "Exposing the Scars: An Interview with Kenny Fries." *Lambda Book Report* 5, no. 8 (February 1997): 1–3.

Jeffery Beam

Fukaya, Michiyo (1953–1987)

Japanese American lesbian poet, writer, and antiracism and **gay** liberation activist. Michiyo Fukaya was born in Japan to a Japanese mother and a white American G.I. father. Her given name was Margaret Cornell, which she changed as an adult to Michiyo Fukaya, resuming her mother's family name. Raised in Massachusetts, she graduated from the University of Massachusetts with a B.A. in English Literature in 1975. Fukaya was a single mother to a biracial daughter whose father is African American. Through written work and activism, she exemplified the interstices of oppression she battled: rape, **homophobia**, poverty, sexism, childhood sexual abuse, mental illness, a dwindling community, and, as a mixed race Asian American lesbian mother, a precarious relationship to identity politics. Her work is widely referenced in bibliographies of contemporary anthologies of lesbian and Asian American women's writing. In 1987 she died of a self-inflicted gunshot wound to the head. Her ashes are buried on the grounds of Huntington Open Womyns Land, a 50-acre land trust for women in Vermont.

In 1981, Fukaya self-published a collection of poems entitled *Lesbian Lyrics*. Around this time she was also a frequent contributor to the local lesbian feminist newspaper in Burlington, Vermont: *Commonwoman* (1978–1984). Most of Fukaya's work is now out of circulation in its original form. Gwendolyn L. Shervington's memorial text, *A Fire Is Burning; It Is in Me: The Life and Writing of Michiyo Fukaya* (1996), is the only collection of her writing still in print. This anthology combines poetry, prose, autobiographical statements, book reviews, letters to various editors, and speeches delivered at political rallies with brief memories offered by women who knew Fukaya. One of the testimonies in this compilation indicates that she also composed a novel that was never accepted for publication. Another remembers Fukaya having a slew of various employments ranging from an administrative assistant, to a client advocate for Women Helping Battered Women, to a counter and grill person at a drive-in. From 1977 on, she was a freelance writer. What remains of this work provides an eloquent and singular description of a volatile yet utopian moment in **queer** history.

Despite its brevity at 181 pages, *A Fire Is Burning* is an affecting document. The text indicates that Fukaya's lesbian feminist community was both vitally supportive and protectively critical of this woman who is variously described as angry, volatile, abusive, diffident, passionate, articulate, accessible, courageous, and unlucky; however, *angry* is the most frequently used adjective. Women in the community helped raise Fukaya's daughter, and many of the concerns expressed address Fukaya's capabilities as a parent.

Fukaya's essays in the collection are carefully written analyses of cultural texts and events. Shervington includes a defense of Vermont's first Lesbian and Gay Pride March and rally—which Fukaya helped organize, a speech delivered at an abortion rights rally, and an argument against mainstream pornography. The poems throughout the volume, which engage topics including motherhood, nature, rape, incest, racism, creative writing classroom **gender** dynamics, and poetry, support Fukaya's reputation as a confrontational yet loving woman and committed thinker. The archive's title, for example, is taken from Fukaya's poem "The Rapist," in which the narrator describes castrating a white male rapist. In many of her poems, complicated juxtapositions use rage to invoke her most unjust opponent: structural inequality. Importantly, anger is not her only tactic. The poems are also erotic, gentle, hopeful, searchingly autobiographical, provocative, and funny. Some of the work plays formally with truisms about nature and the female body; others are loving tributes to her daughter and mother. As a whole, the poetry strives for clarity while asserting an evocative intermingling of frustration and delight.

The small yet instructional social foment Fukaya enacted offers a crucial window into LGBTQ history. If not for Shervington's honest and sensitive document, the unique space a community of women strove to create would easily be forgotten. Correspondingly, the distinctive yet truncated legacy of Fukaya's life and work remains a testament to the need for incessant reevaluations of prevailing social norms.

Further Reading

Chung, C., A. Kim, and A. K. Lemeshewsky, eds. *Between the Lines: An Anthology by Pacific/Asian Lesbians of Santa Cruz, California.* Santa Cruz: Dancing Bird Press, 1987.

Eng, David L., and Alice Y. Hom, eds. *Q & A: Queer in Asian America.* Philadelphia: Temple University Press, 1998.

Melinda Cardozo

G

Gambone, Philip (b. 1948)

Italian American novelist and lecturer. Born in Massachusetts, where he still resides, Philip Gambone earned a B.A. in English from Harvard University and an M.A. in Theology from the Episcopal Divinity School in Cambridge, Massachusetts. After teaching for 26 years at The Park School in Brookline, Massachusetts, Gambone accepted a position at the Boston University Academy (BUA), where he currently teaches and advises students. In addition to his full-time teaching responsibilities at BUA, he also teaches in the Creative and Expository Writing Program at Harvard University Extension School and has taught writing courses at the University of Massachusetts and Boston College. During a School Year Abroad Program in 1996, he also taught in Bejing—an experience that he credits for his developing interest in Asian literature and art. Gambone has twice been awarded Harvard's Distinguished Teaching Citation.

For the 2008–2009 BUA school year, Gambone has been awarded the sixth annual Metcalf Fellowship, which allows a faculty member to pursue a significant project of his or her choosing while teaching half-time. Gambone is working on a book, under contract with Random House/Doubleday, that is based on his own face-to-face interviews with prominent LGBTQ Americans from a variety of fields. This is his latest in an impressive list of literary projects and follows in the footsteps of his successful previous collection of interviews with **gay** writers, *Something Inside: Conversation with Gay Fiction Writers* (1999).

Gambone's short stories, essays, articles, and reviews have appeared in a wide variety of notable publications including *The New York Times Book Review,* the *Boston Globe, Bay Windows, Lambda Book Report, Frontiers,* and *The Advocate.* His essays have also been included in a number of anthologies: *Hometowns: Gay Men Write about Where They Belong* (1992), *A Member of the Family: Gay Men Write about Their Families* (1994), *Sister & Brother: Lesbians and Gay Men Write about Their Lives Together* (1994), *Wrestling with the Angel: Faith and Religion in the Lives of Gay Men* (1996), *Men on Men 3* (1990), *Men on Men 6* (1996), *His 3: Brilliant New Fiction by Gay Writers* (1999), *Boys Like Us: Gay Writers Tell Their Coming Out Stories* (1996), and *The Man I Might Become: Gay Men Write about Their Fathers* (2002).

His short-fiction collection *The Language We Use Up Here* (1992) was nominated for a Lambda Literary Award. Set in Boston, each of the 16 stories (10 of which previously appeared in journals) is concerned with what happens after the moment or process of **coming out**. Thus most of the characters are "thirtysomething," struggling to reconcile their lives and become adults in a world that does not always afford them the same luxuries and privileges that are available to others. The stories are concerned with very universal ideas: relationships, AIDS, and discrimination in one's own community (among others). As such, Gambone manages to move beyond the typical and situate these stories within a universal context.

Something Inside: Conversation with Gay Fiction Writers (1999), a collection of Gambone's interviews from 1987 to 1998 with some of the most gifted writers, was named one of the best books of 1999 by *Pride Magazine*. Twenty-one gay writers, including **Edmund White**, Alan Hollinghurst, Scott Heim, the late John Preston, and **Christopher Bram**, provide details about their work and their lives. What emerges through Gambone's questions is a chronological history of the development of gay fiction, told from the perspective of those writing it. In addition, Gambone asserts himself as a sensitive, provocative, and engaging interviewer.

Gambone's debut novel, *Beijing* (2003), records widower David Masiello's year in Beijing. To escape the life he once knew with his lover, his loneliness, boredom, and the realization that he is about to turn 50 and is stuck in a rut, David accepts a short-term position as an office manager at a medical clinic and begins to explore both the vibrant Beijing city —the one that everyone sees—and the gay culture that exists outside of the mainstream. During his adventures, in which he encounters many memorable and beautifully written characters, he meets a young artist, Bosheng. Promised to a woman that his parents have chosen for him to marry, Bosheng returns to his village out of familial obligation but eventually reconnects with David and spends a number of months with him. This novel is a collection of interconnected stories that come together to form David's rejuvenation. It was a Lambda Literary Award Finalist.

Further Reading

Hemrick, Stephen. "West Meets East." *Gay & Lesbian Review Worldwide* 10 (2003): 42.
Matthews, Lelley A. "Philip Gambone." In *The Greenwood Encyclopedia of Multiethnic American Literature,* edited by Emmanuel S. Nelson, 786–87. Westport, CT: Greenwood Press, 2005.

Sherri Foster

Garden, Nancy (b. 1938)

Margaret A. Edwards American Library Association Award winner in 2003 for lifetime achievement in writing for young adults as well as the Robert B. Downs Intellectual Freedom Award winner from the University of Illinois Graduate School of Library and Information Science. Nancy Garden, who has stated that she writes for the "invisible reader," addresses issues of adolescent homosexuality. Her young adult novels about **gay** and lesbian teenagers have brought her considerable acclaim from her peers, librarians, teachers, civil liberties groups, and young readers. Because of many of her novels' themes, she and her books are the brunt of controversy and even banning. Aside from her breakthrough work in writing about issues of homosexuality and **homophobia** in many of her novels, her writing also encompasses nonfiction and a range of fiction from historical to fantasy to realistic. Born in Boston in 1938, Garden was an only child born into a reading family. She received her B.F.A. from the School of Dramatic Arts at Columbia University and a Master's Degree in Speech Education from Teachers College. She began work as an editor at *Scholastic Parent & Child Magazine* and Houghton Mifflin Company. In addition to her long career as a novelist, she has been a teacher, a teacher of writing, a freelance writer, and a book reviewer. She currently lives with her partner of over 40 years, Sandra Scott. The couple married in Massachusetts when the Supreme Judicial Court ruled (2004) that it is unconstitutional to disallow homosexual couples the same right to marry as heterosexuals. They divide their time between homes in Massachusetts and Maine.

Publishing her first novel, *What Happened in Marston,* in 1971, Garden is the author of more than 25 published novels, but she is best known for the classic young adult title *Annie on My Mind,* which has never been out of print. Considered one of the most influential books of the twentieth century, *Annie,* one of the first young adult novels to dramatize a lesbian relationship, was first published in 1982, significantly in the same month that AIDS was named. The novel has been the target of numerous book banning attempts and became the subject of a nationally reported censorship controversy in 1993 when a Kansas school superintendent, Ron Wimmer of Olathe School District, ordered that the district's sole copy be removed from the school library after a fundamentalist minister publicly burned a copy. In that case, a judge ruled that the book had been unconstitutionally removed from the school shelves. The novel has been printed in a number of editions and languages with a range of covers that speak to the times and cultures in which they were drawn. The most recent reprinting in 2007 commemorates the 25th anniversary of the novel's publication. *Annie* focuses on two 17-year-old high school girls who meet at the Metropolitan Museum of Art, become friends, and then lovers. Initially their friendship is an unlikely pairing as Liza is student body president of her private school while Annie goes to public school and lives in a less desirable area of Brooklyn with her mother, cab-driver father, and grandmother.

The story is narrated in hindsight by Liza, now a student at the Massachusetts Institute of Technology, through a letter she struggles to write in response to the many Annie has sent her from her Berkeley campus. *Annie* is a love story that unfolds gradually in the novel; neither girl is initially aware of the depth of her own feelings for the other. Gardner sensitively chronicles the first awakenings of sexual awareness and identity between Liza and Annie. While the novel is not sexually explicit, an echo of its being published before authors were treating what had been a taboo subject in books for young adults, it does describe Liza and Annie's first kiss and the school officials' discovery of the half undressed girls when Liza house-sits for two of her vacationing teachers and invites Annie to stay over. The discovery precipitates a crisis, and Ms. Baxter's, the school administrator, exclamation on finding the girls, "there is ugliness and sin and self-indulgence in this house," is mirrored in Liza's private school board trying, albeit unsuccessfully, to expel her. She does, however, come out to her parents in the novel. The ending of the novel, in which Liza and Annie do reunite by telephone across North America, is, despite some critics' claiming that the novel is reputed to have the first "happy" ending with a gay-themed plot or subplot, not unequivocally a happy one. Liza's two favorite teachers, Ms. Stevenson and

Ms. Widmer, living quietly together themselves and presumed to be lesbians, are outed and fired from Foster Academy. Liza's musing that we still have "a range of [mountains] to climb" is as important to understanding Garden's ambivalence about the future as is Ms. Stevenson's admonition to Annie, "Don't let ignorance win. Let love." Despite what contemporary readers will see as Garden's mixed messages about being gay in a heterosexist culture in the early 1980s, the novel remains a landmark for making the invisible visible at a time when young gay and lesbian adults looked in vain for a literature that reflected their own struggles with who they are and who they can be.

Three more recent books by Garden are of special interest. In *The Year They Burned the Books* (1999), a Lambda Literary Foundation Award finalist the year it was published, the "maybe" heroine, Jamie Crawford, high school senior and editor in chief of the school newspaper, the *Telegraph,* finds herself in a battle with a conservative action group, Families for Traditional Values, that opposes newspaper content related to sex education, contraception, homosexuality, AIDS, and the school's health education curriculum. The group Jamie's mom calls the "stealth candidates" wins seats on the school board, and the whole New England town becomes embroiled in the controversy. Central to the plot is Jamie and Terry's, her sports editor, friendship, which becomes a journey they share from "maybe" to "absolutely [gay]," as they both struggle with same-sex attractions. Not surprisingly for this champion of the First Amendment, the novel has a strong anticensorship theme, but it avoids didacticism. Garden's characters do not read like mouthpieces for her political beliefs but rather like real people teenagers can empathize with. Focusing again on real people, just recently Garden published a collection of stories, *Hear Us Out! Lesbian and Gay Stories of Struggle, Progress, and Hope, 1950 to the Present* (2007), a book appropriate for middle and high school readers that tells the history of LGBTQ people in America in these years. Paired stories are preceded by a historical essay on each of the six decades that describes in broad political and social terms what life was/is like for the LGBTQ population in the United States and chronicles the history of that decade's gay civil rights movement. This is powerful history, ranging from the 1950s encyclopedia entry defining homosexuality as "sexual pathology," a "mental disorder," to the more contemporary "I'm gay and I'm proud" voices. *Hear Us Out* is an important book for all readers who do not know the history of what Garden herself, coming-of-age in the 1940s and 1950s and writing into the twenty-first century, lived. Finally, inspired by the shootings at Columbine High School in 1999, Garden takes on a new but related topic in her most recent novel, *Endgame* (2006), the story of 15-year-old Gray Wilton who lashes out with deadly violence against the bullying and harassment he suffers in high school. Gray recounts his story into his lawyer's cassette player from his detention cell. One by one all of Gray's potential support is removed or left untapped until he faces his enemies alone, crippling even the neighbor girl, Lindsay, who has tried to be his friend. Nothing alleviates the bleakness of this novel's vision. Facing the judge's sentence of life in prison for the school shootings, Gray remains unredeemed and unredeemable at the end as he thinks just before sentencing, "Look . . . I had to, anyone would've" (287) while fantasizing that he can still "go home to a life without 'Zorro,'" his harasser and tormentor.

Into her seventh decade now, Nancy Garden is continuing to write books for young readers that focus on themes of alienation, isolation, identity formation, freedom of speech and action, and the freedom to choose whom one loves.

See also Young Adult Literature, Lesbian

Further Reading

Broz, William. "Hope and Irony: Annie on My Mind." *English Journal* 90, no. 6 (2001): 47–53.

Garden, Nancy. "Nancy Garden, Author, Teacher, Speaker." http://nancygarden.com.

———. "Writing for the Invisible Reader." *The ALAN Review* 27, no. 2 (2000): 1–12.

Sutton, Roger. "A Second Look: Annie on My Mind." *Horn Book Magazine.* September/October 2007. http://www.hbook.com/magazine/articles/2007/sep07_sutton.asp.

Karen Stearns

Gardinier, Suzanne (b. 1961)

Poet and essayist. Throughout her career as a poet, Suzanne Gardinier has used the medium of poetry not only as a means of personal expression, but also as a tool of raising readers' consciousnesses, speaking out on behalf of activist causes, and affecting social change. Born in 1961 in New Bedford, Massachusetts, Gardinier did her undergraduate work at Drew University and the University of Massachusetts Amherst, subsequently receiving her M.F.A. from Columbia University. She has taught writing at institutions including State University of New York at Old Westbury, Rutgers University, and Sarah Lawrence College. Assistant editor of *Grand Street* magazine between 1988 and 1990, Gardinier's work has been nominated for awards including the Coordinating Council of Literary Magazines/General Electric Awards for Younger Writers, a PEN/Revson Fellowship, and a Pushcart Prize. She has also won awards from the New York Foundation for the Arts and the Lannan Foundation, among other institutions.

Gardinier is the author of several collections of poetry, including *Usahn: Ten Poems & A Story* (1990), *The New World* (1993), and *Today: 101 Ghazals* (2008). In its initial run, only 500 copies of *The New World* were printed, though the volume quickly excited interest, after receiving a glowing review from poet **Adrienne Rich** in the pages of *Ms.* magazine. Consisting of 100 poems divided into five books, *The New World* tackles the subjects of colonization, racism, and oppression with great passion, forcefulness, and insight. In *The New World*, Gardinier draws on sources including histories, biographies, and government reports to shape her subtle but deeply affecting poems about the invasion and colonization of the Americas, and the United States' long and painful history as an imperial power. Throughout this collection's poems, Gardinier adopts numerous different personae, including Christopher Columbus, and women and men from countries such as Vietnam, Nicaragua, and Zaire, considering these individuals' experiences with American imperialism and the day-to-day brutalities of life under a racist and repressive government regime. In the midst of these powerful, haunting poems about global injustice and racial oppression, Gardinier interweaves more personal poems about love, loss, identity, and discovery.

Gardinier's most recent collection of poetry, *Today: 101 Ghazals,* puts a fresh, modern spin on the ghazal, a traditional Arabic form of love poetry. Including references to a dizzying assortment of cultural texts, including the Bible, the literary work of **James Baldwin** and Herman Melville, and songs by folk artists such as Joni Mitchell, *Today* is a remarkably erudite, yet also persistently accessible, volume. In *Today*'s poems, Gardinier evokes both the pleasures and pains of sexual and romantic love in elegant, sensual language. As in *The New World*, in *Today,* Gardinier deftly blends the political with the personal, interweaving reflections about contemporary national and international events, with musings about romantic love and loss. In addition to her poetry, Gardinier is also the author of a collection of essays about poetry and politics, *A World That Will Hold All the People* (1996), a collection of essays about her work as a poet, the significance of poetry in modern American society, and the ways in which poetry can serve as a tool of political activism and social change. Throughout her work, Gardinier demonstrates the power of poetry both to illuminate personal experience and to speak out against injustice, oppression, and discrimination.

Further Reading

Nicholas, Christopher. *Under 35: The New Generation of American Poets.* New York: Doubleday, 1989.

Pollack, Sandra, and Denise D. Knight, eds. *Contemporary Lesbian Writers of the United States: A Bio-Bibliographical Critical Sourcebook.* Westport, CT: Greenwood Press, 1993. 202–4.

Prufer, Kevin, ed. *The New Young American Poets: An Anthology.* Carbondale: Southern Illinois University Press, 2000.

Townsend, Alison. "Review: Singing Back the World." *The Women's Review of Books* 12, no. 2 (November 1994): 19–21.

Holly M. Kent

Gaspar de Alba, Alicia (b. 1958)

Scholar, poet, and novelist. Born on July 29, 1958, in El Paso, Texas, to a Mexican Catholic family, Alicia Gaspar de Alba was raised by her paternal grandparents who sent her to a private Catholic girls' school. In 1977, Gaspar de Alba married her high school best friend and changed her name to Alice Noreen. In 1981 the marriage ended in divorce and Gaspar de Alba came out as a lesbian. In 1985 Gaspar de Alba changed her first name to Alicia and reclaimed her last name.

Gaspar de Alba earned her B.A. (1980) in English from the University of Texas at El Paso and graduated *magna cum laude.* She earned an M.A. (1983) in English from the University of Texas at El Paso, where she taught as a lecturer in English and linguistics for the next two years. Her first collection of poetry, also her M.A. thesis, was published in *Three Times a Woman: Chicana Poetry* (1989). In 1985 she began a Ph.D. at the University of Iowa, but quit after a year. She earned a Ph.D. (1994) in American Studies from the University of New Mexico. Her dissertation was published as *Chicano Art Inside/Outside the Master's House: Cultural Politics and the CARA Exhibition* (1998).

Gaspar de Alba taught as Minority Scholar in Residence at Pomona College from 1994 to 1995. She was hired to teach Chicana/o Studies and English at the University of California–Los Angeles in 1994 and was tenured in 1999. In 2003 she edited *Velvet Barrios: Popular Culture and Chicana/o Sexualitites* (2003), a series of essays that examine rasquache aesthetic via identity, sexuality, and gender. She has published critical essays in *Culture and Difference: Critical Perspectives on the Bicultural Experience in the United States* (1995), *The Latino/a Condition* (1998), and *Living Chicana Theory* (1998). Her creative works have been widely anthologized.

Gaspar de Alba's next collection of poetry, *La Llorona on the Longfellow Bridge: Poetry y otras movidas* (2003), contains poems and essays from 1985 to 2001 organized by locales lived. The essays contextualize her early life and her poetics.

Gaspar de Alba's first collection of short stories, *The Mystery of Survival and Other Stories* (1993), which won the Premio Aztlán Award (1994), examines the border between cultures, generations, and lovers. Her first novel, *Sor Juana's Second Dream* (1999), won the Best Historical Fiction Award in the Latino Literary Hall of Fame (2000). *Sor Juana's Second Dream* focuses on the life of Sor Juana Inés de la Cruz, a seventeenth-century nun in Mexico. Coupling Sor Juana's own writings with fictionalized journal entries, Gaspar de Alba imagines her daily thoughts, provocations, and desires.

Winner of the 2005 Lambda Literary Award for best Lesbian Mystery, Gaspar de Alba's second novel, *Desert Blood: The Juárez Murders* (2005), is an antidetective novel set in the border city of El Paso, Texas/Juárez, Mexico. Ivon Villa returns to her childhood home to arrange an adoption for herself and her partner. After arrival, Ivon learns the expecting *maquiladora* worker is brutally dismembered, murdered, and dumped in the desert. This fictionalized murder evokes the real murders of over 450 women that have occurred in Juárez since 1993. Within days of the murder, Ivon's younger sister is kidnapped after heading to the fair with Ivon's ex-girlfriend. Ivon becomes entrenched in the mystery and culture of silence on the murders and who is to blame (police, *maquiladoras,* drug traffickers, border patrol, snuff pornography, and others), as she seeks to save her sister.

Like *Sor Juana's Second Dream,* Gaspar de Alba's third novel, *Calligraphy of the Witch* (2007), is a historical drama set in seventeen-century Massachusetts Bay Colony. *Calligraphy of the Witch* tells the tale of Concepción, a 15-year-old indentured servant, who escapes to be captured by pirates and sold to a merchant entangled in the witch hunts.

Gaspar de Alba has won many other numerous awards, fellowships, and grants including the Massachusetts Artists Foundation Fellowship and Award in Poetry (1989), the Ralph Henry Gabriel Award for Best Dissertation in American Studies (1994), and the Border-Ford/Pellicer-Frost Award for Poetry (1998).

Further Reading

Marchino, Lois A. *The Oxford Companion to Women's Writing in the United States,* edited by Cathy N. Davidson and Linda Wagner-Martin, 915. New York: Oxford University Press, 1995.

Vivancos Perez, Ricardo F. "Los discursos sobre sexualidad en la obra de Alicia Gaspar de Alba." Ph.D. diss., Texas A & M University, 2002.

Laura Madeline Wiseman

Gay

The term "gay" refers to a self-identified man who is exclusively or primarily sexually and erotically attracted to other self-identified men. Today the term is not seen as inclusive and covers only one group within the larger sexual and **gender** minority populations. Acronyms such as LGBTQ (lesbian, gay, bisexual, transgender, and **queer**) have supplanted "gay" as an umbrella term to be more inclusive.

The word gay has a long and complex history. In addition to being a synonym for homosexual, it also has the meanings of happy and brightly colored. In earlier times it was a synonym for "prostitute" or meant promiscuous. In his seminal work on gay identity, George Chauncey traces the history of the term gay. "The term gay began to catch on in the 1930s, and its primacy was consolidated during the war. By the late 1940s, younger gay men were chastising older men who still used queer, which the younger men now regarded as demeaning" (19).

The 1960s was a pivotal time for oppressed groups in the United States. "The influence of the Black Civil Rights and Women's movements was tremendous. As feminists examined and challenged sexism, and Black activists fought racism under slogans such as "Black is Beautiful," it was indeed time to challenge the prejudice against homosexuals" (Baird 21). The earliest gay rights groups in the United States organized under the term "homophile." The gay male group was called the Mattachine Society (see Sears) and the lesbian group the Daughters of Bilitis (see Faderman). These early groups became more militant following the **Stonewall Riots** in 1969.

Sexologists and other "experts" often referred to gay people as "homosexuals." As Margaret Cruikshank asserts, "Homosexuals became gay when they rejected the notion that they were sick or sinful, claimed equality with heterosexuals, banded together to protest second-class citizenship, created a subculture, and came out in large numbers" (3). Gay was a political term meant to take away the stigma and clinical connotations of the term "homosexual."

The term gay originally was an all-inclusive term. Gay people, circa the 1960s and 1970s, meant homosexual men and women, and also included bisexuals and gender-variant people. "[O]ur older informants told us 'gay' in the 1930s, '40s, '50s, and '60s was the term that included homosexual men, lesbians, transgenders, and even bisexuals" (Faderman and Timmons 4). However, in the 1970s, as the **gay rights movement** progressed post-Stonewall, many lesbians became tired of the sexism and chauvinism they experienced in gay-male dominated activist circles. They formed their own lesbian organizations and spoke out against the sexism in the term gay. Although technically gender neutral, the term gay today is associated with male subjectivities.

The use of the term gay carries with it many potential problems. Critics have warned about the dangers of using the term cross-culturally and transhistorically. It is a truism that "homosexuality," as in the behavior, has existed throughout different time periods and across different cultures. However, as many postmodernists have pointed out, such as Michel Foucault, there is a vast difference between homosexual behavior and claiming a distinctly "gay" identity. Claiming a gay identity because one feels specific sexual desires and/or takes part in same-sex sexuality is a relatively new practice, starting in the United States and Europe in the early parts of the twentieth century. In addition, gay is a term that many associate with Western, industrial capitalism and white ethnic groups. Often, "gay" does not translate globally given the radical differences between and among cultures all over the globe and the specific ways that they organize notions of sex, gender, and sexuality. Some fear that the cross-cultural promotion of "gay pride" works to reinforce Eurocentrism and globalization.

Many have turned to literature for a better understanding of gay identity. "The coming-out stories gay people tell in the narratives of their own lives define and shape their adult identities. Gay novels also help gay people to find a sense of self and a feeling of belonging in the world" (Koponen 1). Gay literary critics have analyzed gay themes in literature and penned books and articles about the gay identities of past and present authors.

Further Reading

Baird, Vanessa. *The No-Nonsense Guide to Sexual Diversity.* London: Verso, 2001.

Chauncey, George. *Gay New York.* New York: Basic Books, 1994.

Cruikshank, Margaret, ed. *Lesbian Studies: Present and Future.* New York: The Feminist Press, 1982.

Faderman, Lillian. *Odd Girls and Twilight Lovers.* New York: Penguin Books, 1991.

Faderman, Lillian, and Stuart Timmons. *Gay L.A.* New York: Basic Books, 2006.

Griffin, Gabriele. *Who's Who in Lesbian and Gay Writing.* New York: Routledge, 2002.

Koponen, Wilfrid. *Embracing a Gay Identity: Gay Novels as Guides.* Westport, CT: Bergin & Garvey, 1993.

Sears, James. *Behind the Mask of the Mattachine.* Binghamton, NY: Haworth, 2006.

Joelle Ruby Ryan

Gay Literature, African American

The unique voice of African American **gay** men has been expressed through a vibrant literary tradition of fiction, poetry, drama, and autobiography. Including some of the most gifted authors of the twentieth century, the African American gay literary tradition straddles two centuries and spans approximately nine decades influenced by both **homophobia** and racism. The political and social perspectives of black gay literature in the twenty-first century extend far beyond social protest to narratives that tell new stories of black males coming-of-age in a world that allows more freedom of expression than any preceding era. Black gay literature explores race- and sexuality-based themes along with more universal human issues.

Much American literature about homosexuality from the Civil War to post–World War II (WWII) was concerned with homosexuality as a psychological deviation or condition. Blacks often mythologized homosexuality as a disease resulting from close interactions with white culture, or as a result of disfunctional, female-headed households. In addition, much of the African American Christian Church, which held the Bible to be a literal document, viewed homosexuality as a sinful, non-Biblical lifestyle. The Church tended toward rabid public homophobia while having homosexual members, employees, and leaders. Because of virulent homophobia in the black community, many authors dealt with homosexuality in veiled, fictionalized accounts. Only after WWII did homosexual males begin to self-identify as "gay," a description based on sexual orientation rather than sinful lifestyles or deviant behavior. Other writers leaned toward visible political action in the latter part of the twentieth century. By the first decade of the twenty-first century, young black gay men regularly began to share their literary voices using mainstream avenues.

The first widely visible expression of the African American homosexual male voice occurred during the Harlem Renaissance. Writers such as Wallace Thurman, Claude McKay, Langston Hughes, and Countee Cullen sought to portray the full range of black life. These bohemian writers sought to challenge the bland, one-dimensional "New Negro" whom leading black intellectuals felt was more acceptable to the white establishment. During the 1920s and 1930s, Harlem had a thriving gay community, and black writers found both veiled and explicit ways to deal with homoeroticism.

The first known gay short story, "Sadji" by Bruce Nugent, was published in Alain Locke's *The New Negro* (1925) anthology. However, most African American writers referred to homosexuality in coded form. Often, the inescapable and unavoidable issue of race trumped expressions of sexuality in the writings of black gay writers. The reality of black life during the post–World War I period makes it even more noteworthy when reading works that dealt not only with the overt issue of race but included a subtext of gay sexual orientation. Gays were usually secretive about their sexual orientation and found ways to disguise it. For example, shortly after marrying, Countee Cullen left his wife and moved with his male lover to Europe. He published a number of poems with homoerotic undertones such as "Every Lover" and "The Black Christ." Others, including Langston Hughes, were very careful in their treatment of homosexuality. While literary critics quieted questions about Hughes's sexuality, many of his poems are multilayered pieces in which the issue of race trumps but does not obliterate the homoerotic subtext.

The post–World War II period reflects a desire for integration on the political and social fronts, which was echoed in African American literature. Writers explored the conflicted lives of African Americans, particularly when assimilation was considered the solution to America's racial woes. Quiet conformity was the safest posture during times when homosexuality was often linked with communism. Fear of domestic communism led to intense scrutiny, persecution, and prosecution of those who were identified as having communist sympathies or membership. This atmosphere of witch hunts encouraged many gay writers to slide into invisibility, hide in plain sight, or become expatriates. Such investigations often had a chilling effect on authors and their writing, influencing writers to create negative, one-dimensional homosexual characters. Chester Himes, Owen Dodson, Richard Wright, and Ralph Ellison all created characters who struggled with internalized homophobia and the self-hatred it engendered. Showing homosexuality in a negative light was far safer in those perilous times. In spite of the poisonous atmosphere, by the late 1940s **James Baldwin** was becoming known on the national literary scene.

Baldwin's work became the crossroad of race and sexuality for gay African American writers. Born illegitimate, poor, and black, Baldwin became a defining figure in straight and gay African American literature with works such as *Go Tell It On the Mountain* (1953) and *Giovanni's Room* (1956). Both works address homosexuality, although in *Go Tell It On the Mountain* Baldwin carefully disguised the homosexual theme by including it in the young man's quest for personal identity. However, in *Giovanni's Room,* it is vastly different. The characters are white and based in Europe, and the struggle for gay self-acceptance is completely undisguised. The success of *Giovanni's Room* enabled Baldwin to openly address gay and bisexual themes in his later work, including *Another Country* (1962), *Tell Me How Long The Train's Been Gone* (1968), and *Just above My Head* (1979). Baldwin's work helped create the atmosphere that made the post-Baldwin generation of gay writers possible,

The civil rights era of the 1970s and 1980s introduced the Black Arts Movement that reflected the heterosexist and patriarchal values of the Black Power struggle. Black gay authors were often ridiculed by other black writers for being emasculated or inauthentic. In his "Notes on a Native Son" in *Soul on Ice* (1968), Eldridge Cleaver famously rejected Baldwin's work because he concluded that as a homosexual, Baldwin must be antiblack. Cleaver, while not alone in his homophobic views, did not represent the only perspective in the more radical arm of the Black Power movement. Huey Newton, co-founder of the Black Panther Party for Self-Defense, attempted to build coalitions with homosexual activists and to understand a more complete inclusive view of the African American community,

The **Stonewall Riots** of 1969 were a turning point in the LGBT community and were widely recognized as a catalyst for the increased public profile of gay authors in the larger literary community. In addition, in 1973 the American Psychological Association removed homosexuality from the *Diagnostic and Statistical Manual of Mental Disorders* (*DSM-IV*), the official manual for psychiatrists, psychologists, and therapists that lists all mental and emotional disorders. Gay men were publicly legitimized as normal individuals rather than sinful deviants. Both of these events contributed to increased publication of white gay authors by mainstream publishers. Black gay writers in the United States were unable to take advantage of this boon primarily because the gay community was dominated by and seen as a white community, with blacks paying a peripheral role at best. Not until black gay publishing houses and grassroots collectives and organizations began to publish their work did black gay writing become more widely available. In addition, the growth of gay-owned and -oriented independent bookstores and increased readership of gay authors by mainstream readers contributed to the larger numbers of published black gay writers. Two important anthologies were published by small gay presses in the 1980s, which gave wider visibility to gay writers who would later be published by mainstream presses: *Black Men/White Men: A Gay Anthology* by Michael J. Smith (1983) and *In The Life: A Black Gay Anthology* by Joseph Beam (1986). **Essex Hemphill**, **Larry Duplechan**, **Samuel R. Delany**, **Melvin Dixon**, and others gained recognition that led to mainstream publication. Desktop publishing and self-publishing have increased the number of gay authors who are being widely read. One of the most noteworthy authors who has achieved mainstream success using this route is **E. Lynn Harris**, who has written about straight, bisexual, and gay themes. Harris, whose first book was self-published before being republished by a mainstream publisher, has had five books on the *New York Times* Best Seller list. Since the 1990s, an array of literature by black gay authors has been published by black gay presses as well as mainstream and university imprints.

Further Reading

Bergman, David. *Gaity Transfigured: Gay Self-Representation in American Literature.* Madison: University of Wisconsin Press, 1991.

Carbado, Devin W., Dwight McBride, and Don Weise, eds. *Black Like Us: A Century of Lesbian, Gay, and Bisexual African American Fiction.* San Francisco: Cleis Press, 2002.

Harris, E. Lynn, ed. *Freedom in This Village: Twenty-Five Years of Black Gay Men's Writing, 1979 to the Present.* New York: Carroll & Graf Publishers, 2005.

Knadler, Stephen. "Africa American Gay Literature." In *The Greenwood Encyclopedia of Multiethnic American Literature,* edited by Emmanuel S. Nelson, 58–64. Westport, CT: Greenwood Press, 2005.

Nelson, Emmanuel S. "African American Literature, Gay Male." In *The Gay and Lesbian Literary Heritage,* edited by Claude J. Summers, 8–12. New York: Henry Holt and Company, 1995.

Nero, Charles I. "Gay Literature." *The Oxford Companion to African American Literature,* edited by William L. Andrews, Frances Smith Foster, and Trudier Harris, 311–12. New York: Oxford University Press, 1997.

Patricia L. T. Camp

Gay Literature, Jewish American

The first book in the canon of Jewish literature to address homosexuality is the Old Testament. The book of Leviticus states that "And with a man you shall not lie as with a woman. It is an abomination." Some Biblical scholars believe that this admonition was written to differentiate ancient Jews from their Gentile neighbors. According to Leviticus, the punishment for homosexual activity or sodomy was stoning until death, although there is no proof that any Biblical Jews had been stoned for consensual adult homosexual relations. Other Biblical scholars have noted homoerotic love in the Old Testament after the admonition against homosexuality had been written, particularly in the parable of

King David and Jonathan. This may indicate that, since ancient times, the Jewish community has had knowledge of gay men and that tolerance of gay men and their behavior has varied among Jews over time.

When Jewish people had to live among Christians, they were often subjects of persecution and second-class status. Cartoons, songs, and plays often transformed Jewish men into grotesque figures with perverse sexual appetites. For many centuries, Jewish men were often viewed as effeminate and soft by their male Christian counterparts. Religious Jewish men had to devote themselves to a lifetime of scholarship, while the more practical-minded worked as merchants, bankers, physicians, and lawyers—often the only professions available to them according to the laws of the countries where they resided. Jews were also depicted as creatures of "the underworld," amoral figures who sought to deceive innocent Christians. Fagin in Charles Dickens's novel *Oliver Twist* is a classic example of such a figure in British literature; the Jewish master of a band of prepubescent male pickpockets, Fagin was often accused of sleeping with his boys.

Because of these negative historical **gay stereotypes** of Jewish men, as well as the stigma against male homosexuality, many gay Jewish men feel that they live in a "double **closet**." They may perceive that living openly as a Jewish man in a non-Jewish society is dangerous or that living as a gay man in a heterosexual Jewish or heterosexual multicultural society is dangerous. A religious upbringing or the influence of antisemitic, homophobic media and authority figures may cause gay Jewish men to feel deep personal shame of their ethnicity, sexual orientation, or both. As a result, there have been few openly gay Jewish American writers or gay Jewish American literary characters as compared to Jewish American lesbians, who find strength in their individual identities as well as the community of women at large.

Many Jews who emigrated to North America sought to escape Old World religious persecution, while others wanted to escape the stifling confines of Orthodox Jewish society itself. Large Jewish communities in New York City, Chicago, and other major American urban centers supported the publication of Yiddish literature and Yiddish theater productions that attracted a wide audience. The Jewish desire to behave according to God's will often clashed with the desire for American freedom and self-expression, a major theme in early Jewish American literature and theater. This desire for freedom included freedom of sexual self-expression; the first Jewish gay and lesbian characters in Jewish American literature appeared in Yiddish theater productions at the beginning of the twentieth century. Although these characters were often comic or tragic figures, none of the Yiddish playwrights depicted their gay or lesbian characters as evil or sick, as the intent of the plays was not to condemn homosexuality.

Although not a gay man himself, Jewish American author Myron Brinig brought Harry Singermann, the first major gay Jewish character in American literature, to life in his novels *Singermann* (1929) and *This Man Is My Brother* (1932). Although Harry Singermann is characterized as effeminate, he is not ostracized by his family or the community of Silver Bow, Montana, at large as he is the head of his family's department store and is respected as an authority on money matters and art. Singermann, unfortunately, falls in love with an adopted nephew, leading to his eventual suicide. It is said that the inspiration for Singermann arose from Brinig's father, a Romanian shopkeeper.

The next major gay Jewish character in American literature, Stephen Wolfe of Sanford Friedman's novel *Totempole,* did not appear until 1965. (This gap in gay Jewish American literature could be attributed to the postwar McCarthy era, when Jews and homosexuals were often accused of being communists, as well as the "Muscle Jew" movement that arose with the formation of the modern state of Israel.) In *Totempole,* Friedman reveals Stephen Wolfe's development as a gay Jewish man, detailing his repressive childhood and coming-of-age. Friedman blames Wolfe's religious Jewish upbringing for his psychological problems; throughout the novel Wolfe considers himself "unclean" for masturbating and falsely believes that masturbation is what turned him into a homosexual. Finally, while Wolfe is a young man doing his military tour of duty in Korea, a Korean prisoner of war teaches him to love his body and to love himself as a gay man. Unlike the earlier award-winning novel *Wasteland* (1946) written by Jewish American lesbian author Jo Sinclair (Ruth Seid), which compared accepting one's Jewishness to accepting one's lesbianism, *Totempole* reflected Friedman's own internalized antisemitism, as the novel implied that gay identity and Jewish identity were irreconcilable. Fortunately, other gay Jewish American writers did not feel the same way. Poet **Allen Ginsberg** wrote countless works that incorporated both aspects of his identity in a positive manner.

After the **Stonewall Riots** of 1969, gays and lesbians across the United States encouraged one another to come out of the closet and take pride in their sexual identities. The civil rights movement also inspired Jewish people to fight against discrimination and find strength in their ethnic, cultural, and religious identities. Both events inspired an increase in the visibility of openly gay Jewish American novelists and characters. Post-Stonewall gay Jewish American literature often focused on the coming out process or discovering pride and strength in one's gay Jewish identity; two examples of such novels are Geoffrey Linden's *Jigsaw* (1974) where a gay Jewish man without positive role models slowly overcomes his shame through therapy, and Gary Glickman's *Years from Now* (1987) where a gay Jewish man decides to become a father in order to pass on Jewish traditions to the next generation. The AIDS epidemic caused some gay Jewish American writers to rethink gay pride, however: **Larry Kramer** predicted a Biblical doom for promiscuous, drug-using gay men in his novel *Faggots* (1978), while Douglas Sadownick writes about a gay Jewish journalist whose relationship with his lover is deeply affected by his in-depth coverage of the AIDS crisis in *Sacred Lips of the Bronx* (1994).

The most prolific post-Stonewall gay Jewish American novelist is Lambda Literary Award–winning **Lev Raphael**. The American-born son of Holocaust survivors, Raphael had grown up intimidated and ashamed of his parents and their strange ways, which originally caused him to reject his Jewish identity. After discovering his attraction to other boys as a young adolescent, he attempted to repress himself even further, to the point of attending a Christian school and purposely dating non-Jewish girls. In his memoir *Writing a Jewish Life* (2005), Raphael describes how learning how to embrace Judaism helped him come out and embrace himself as a gay man. Raphael's collection of short stories *Dancing on Tisha B'Av* (1990) and his semiautobiographical novel *Winter Eyes* (1992) all address the themes of embracing religious and sexual identity.

The most vibrant, provocative genre of gay Jewish American literature remains drama. **Martin Sherman** produced *Bent* (1979), which is about a gay man who decided to identify as a straight Jew rather than homosexual when captured by the Nazis and sent to Dachau, and the consequences of his actions. Gravelly voiced actor **Harvey Fierstein** wrote and starred in the classic *Torch Song Trilogy* (1979), a compilation of three short plays. In each play, Fierstein focuses on a different phase of hero Arnold Beckoff's life—finding a partner, raising a child, and finally coming out to his mother. The stage drama had so much success that it was turned into a full-length motion picture in 1988.

Playwright **Tony Kushner**'s *Angels in America* (1993), turned into a television miniseries and an opera, dealt with the darker side of being gay, Jewish, and politically involved during the mid-1980s. *Faggots*' author Larry Kramer is most famous for his plays about AIDS: ***Reports from the Holocaust: The Making of an AIDS Activist*** (1989) and the autobiographical plays ***The Normal Heart*** (1985) and *The Destiny of Me* (1993) all compare the AIDS epidemic to the Holocaust and depict the birth and development of Jewish gay radicals.

In the twenty-first century, the American Jewish community is becoming more tolerant of its gay family members and friends thanks to the increase of gay Jewish American voices in literature, drama, and film. This trend is sure to continue as LGBTIQ (lesbian, gay, bisexual, transgender, intersex, and **queer**) Americans of all ethnicities continue to make themselves visible in order to fight for state and federal antidiscrimination legislation as well as state and federal recognition of same-sex partnership.

Further Reading

Brinker, Ludger. "Jewish American Literature." *glbtq: An Encyclopedia of Gay, Lesbian, Bisexual, Transgender, and Queer Culture.* August 11, 2005. http://www.glbtq.com/literature/jewish_am _lit.html.

Friedman, Jonathan C. "Homophobia and Tolerance in Judaism." *Rainbow Jews: Jewish and Gay Identity in the Performing Arts.* Lanham, MD: Lexington Books, 2007.

Raphael, Lev. *Journeys and Arrivals: On Being Gay and Jewish.* New York: Faber Publishing, 1996.

Rachel Wexelbaum

Gay Literature, Mexican American

Mexican American (Chicano) **gay** literature came into its own in the 1980s. While gay Chicanos were certainly writing before this period, they were largely silenced by homophobic Chicano-nationalist and mainstream publishers; and while a post-1969 **Stonewall** gay/lesbian activism led to the founding of small presses that produced and disseminated larger numbers of white gay and lesbian authors, gay literature of color (Chicano especially) continued to receive scant attention.

The renaissance of gay Chicano literature in the 1980s owes much to the activist-intellectual work of lesbian feminists such as **Cherríe Moraga** and **Gloria Evangelina Anzaldúa.** The 1981 publication of *This Bridge Called My Back* by Persephone Press marked an important shift in the publishing of Chicano lesbian literature. Their various creative explorations and explosions of the traditionally straight Chicano versus Anglo fiction and poetics that defined a 1970s Chicano canon helped pave the way for the arrival of the gay Chicano author.

In 1986, foremost Chicano literary scholar Juan Bruce-Novoa published the seminal essay "Homosexuality and the Chicano Novel," wherein he naturalized the union of "gay" with "Chicano"; no longer could one read, for example, **John Rechy**'s novels as gay sex-shock narrative, but one had to read his work as fundamentally Chicano as well. Moreover, Bruce-Novoa remapped the existing straight Chicano/a literary canon, identifying its implicit homoerotic edge. For Bruce-Novoa, to ignore the gay Chicano voice was to miss the "dynamic and exciting" force at the core of Chicano literature.

Largely the result of such scholarly moves toward inclusion and the hard work of lesbian and gay activist intellectuals and writers—the establishment of independent publishing venues and the struggle to educate a New York publishing world—gay poets, playwrights, and novelists were coming into their own.

In the area of poetry we see a range of different voices, including Francisco X. Alarcón (b. 1954) who blazed new trails with his powerfully gay and indigenous poetic voice as seen in *Ya vas, Carnal* (1984) and *Tattoos* (1984). In both collections, Alarcón uses poetic rhythm and a penetrating, staccato voice to affirm his gay and Chicano identity within a racist and homophobic mainstream society. For Alarcón, the black marks on the page were more than just words; they formed images that lashed back at his racist world. In his *Body in Flames* (1991), Alarcón intermixes pre-Columbian myth with his inhabiting of a gay Chicano body in the present; he clears a space for a gay Chicano poetic where mind is no longer forced apart from body. In the mid-1990s yet another important gay Chicano poet arrived on the scene, the late Gil Cuadros. However, rather then unify a mythological past with a gay Chicano present, Cuadros sought to texture his childhood and coming out experience as a teenager in Los Angeles; to capture his feelings of estrangement both from the white gay community that exoticizes his brown body and from his Chicano community that promotes a **queer** hostile *machismo,* he intermixes poetry and prose in the writing of his memoir, *City of God* (1994)—a powerful testament to his struggle to humanize the gay Chicano experience before his death from an AIDS-related illness.

Gay authors have found a solid footing in other genres such as the memoir/essay form as well as drama. For example, one of the first on the drama scene was Los Angeles born and based Luis Alfaro. A self-identifying queer artist-activist, Alfaro's many performances and plays—*Downtown* (1980), *Cuerpo Politizado* (1996), and *Straight as a Line* (2000), to name a few—often employ a sharp-biting edge to express the multiform gay Chicano experience. And gay memoirist, journalist, and essayist **Richard Rodriguez** has made a name for himself nationwide. While his work for the Pacific News Service deals mostly with issues of race, his essayistic memoirs bring together issues of being gay and brown in the United States and Mexico; we see this faintly whispered in his best-selling ***Hunger of Memory: The Education of Richard Rodriguez*** (1982) and then more boldly in his *Days of Obligation* (1993) and *Brown* (2003). In *Days of Obligation,* for example, he makes public secrets otherwise kept in the **closet** by his Chicano upbringing: "to grow up homosexual is to live with secrets and within secrets. In no other place are those secrets more closely guarded than within the family home" (30). In *Brown,* he uses his trademark fast-paced and high-stylized journalese to render visible his experiences as queer and Chicano in a so-identified post-Protestant/Catholic postcolonial America.

Gay Chicano novelists have carved paths deep and wide into the Chicano and literary canons. We see this especially in the work of John Rechy, **Arturo Islas, Jr.**, and Michael Nava, who have variously used a number of different storytelling techniques and styles —the picaresque, the mystery suspense, stream of consciousness, and mixed media pastiche—to reframe one-dimensional representations of gay Chicanos. We see this, for example, with Rechy's use of the stream of consciousness form to tell the story of Amalia Gómez in his novel *The Miraculous Day of Amalia Gómez* (1991). Here, Rechy focuses on the psychological transformation of Amalia as she comes to terms with a contemporary racist and violent Los Angeles as well as her son's gay sexuality. And, we see in the novels of the late Arturo Islas, Jr.—*The Rain God* (1984) and *Migrant Souls* (1990)—how one can weave with great subtlety the gay voice into the texturing of Chicano family life along the United States/Mexico border. We also see how he complicates his vision of gay

Chicano identity and experience in his posthumously published novel *La Mollie and the King of Tears* (1996), where he uses a fast-paced first-person voice to tell the story of straight Louie Mendoza whose discovery of self includes his coming to terms with his own fluid sexuality as well as his brother's gay identity. And, ever since the appearance of the gay Chicano lawyer/detective character, Henry Rios, when Michael Nava published *The Little Death* in 1986, he published seven more novels in the series that finally ended in 2001 with *Rag and Bone*. Nava's self-identifying gay and Chicano character, Henry Rios, not only solves grisly murders and crimes but does so while dealing with affairs of the heart and with a constant sense of loss: friends and love interests lost to AIDS.

Gay novelists, playwrights, and poets such as Nava, Islas, Rechy, Alarcón, Cuadros, Rodriguez, and Alfaro, to name a few, have influenced many straight and queer Chicano writers since. Their creative visions celebrate the triumph of defying the odds while not losing sight of the goal to foster deep human empathy and understanding.

Further Reading

Aldama, Frederick Luis. *Arturo Islas: The Uncollected Works.* Houston: Arte Público Press, 2003.

Bruce-Novoa, Juan. "Homosexuality and the Chicano Novel." *European Perspectives on Hispanic Literature of the United States,* edited by Genvieve Fabre, 98–106. Houston: Arte Público Press, 1988.

Foster, David William, ed. *Chicano/Latino Homoerotic Identities.* New York: Garland Publishing, 1999.

Frederick Luis Aldama

Gay Literature, Puerto Rican

As Carlos Rodríguez Matos and others have noted, between the appearance of Carlos Alberto Fonseca's 1942 love poem to an "ephebe" and the 1973 publication of *El reino de la espiga* (*The kingdom of corn and grain*) by Victor Fragoso, there is no other reference to lesbian or **gay** subjects in Puerto Rican poetry. Arnaldo Cruz-Malavé asserts this deficiency is nearly true for all of Puerto Rican literature of the period in which the gay writing subject is absent. The major Puerto Rican writer of the late twentieth century, René Marqués (1919–1979), a fierce promoter of independence, also was the first to overtly depict male desire in his 1975 coming-of-age story *La mirada,* one of his last works of fiction, yet Marqués himself did not want to be identified as gay. Renowned storywriter, playwright, and essayist Luis Rafael Sánchez also was one of the first writers to depict homosexuality in his 1966 groundbreaking short story "Jum!," and later he broke more new ground for a Puerto Rican gay aesthetics in his most well-known work *La guaracha del Macho Camacho* (*Macho Camacho's Beat,* 1980), which in David William Foster's words "speaks of the primacy of a **queer** optics," rather than an explicit rendering of self-declared gay culture (17). In that work, Sánchez utilizes *la loca* (crazy woman) to represent the author's voice, and the burlesque drag show is a backdrop for the narrative.

The latter half of the twentieth century into the present has largely addressed the former absence of gay themes in literature, and since the 1995 publication of *¿Entiendes? Queer Readings, Hispanic Writings* there has been a flourishing of literary and critical texts both by and about Puerto Rican gays and lesbians. Although most of gay literary and cultural production has occurred off the island and on the United States mainland (because of self-imposed, but socially produced exile), the fluidity between United States and

Puerto Rican geographical places is very much evident as part and parcel of gay literary creation (not unlike Puerto Rican writing in general). Indeed, much of contemporary Puerto Rican gay literature has specifically sought to give emphasis to the unique cultural hybridism of Puerto Rican identity in its creation. Gay (and lesbian) writers have also stepped in to deconstruct the dominant heterocentered discourse of Puerto Rican nationhood that traditionally declared any effeminate nature as repulsive and that primarily conceived of the national Puerto Rican body and Puerto Rican nationalism as distinctly hypermasculine.

Critics such as Arnaldo Cruz-Malavé, Alberto Sandoval-Sánchez, and others have argued that in order to counter and compensate for the colonial in-between political status of Puerto Rico, which is both a nation (socioculturally) and not one (politically), established ideological norms of what constitutes Puerto Rico as a nation tended to be characterized by an overcompensatory identification with patriarchal, authoritarian, and paternalistic representations. Furthermore, the assertion of a *machista*-defined cultural independence as a unifying trope for the idea of national identity meant that Puerto Rican gays became the displaced target of frustrated nationhood. As writer Ángel Lozada's 1988 work *La Patografía* (an invented play on many words including "pato" (fag) and pathology), shows, in order to prove and assert their collective virility, Puerto Ricans kill *patos* (meaning both "ducks" and "fags") instead of gringos. His more recent work, *No quiero quedarme sola y vacía,* is a hyperimagined autobiographical story where all experience in the novel emanates from the repression and desire of the author but gets transformed through the creative process and through the authorial voice of the (feminine) transvestite.

While Puerto Rican **homophobia** has been complicated and confounded by the ambiguous nature of Puerto Rico's political status, it has also offered a space for the marginalized other, that is, the gay writer, to subvert that hypermasculinist discursive identity and offer new conceptualizations of what it means and does not mean to be Puerto Rican. As Cruz-Malavé asserts, Puerto Rican gay writers "have . . . conceived this uncovering of their sexual self as a search for a free authentic national space . . . they have set out to liberate both the sexual and national geography of their identity" (138), and later he asks, "What if in a colonial 'nation' like Puerto Rico—in that queer state of freedom within dependency, of nation without nationhood—impotence and lack were the only weapon, the ultimate ruse?" (140). And indeed that question seems to be answered in much late twentieth century queer Puerto Rican writing that focuses on abjection to work through and forge new identities, and where degradation and rejection are not only ways of destabilizing marginality, but are also turned on their heads as survival mechanisms (Sandoval-Sánchez 542–49). Alberto Sandoval-Sánchez's writing that moves between literature and criticism exemplifies this use of abjection as a liberatory practice where body and intellect are not dichotomous but rather are united through the writing process itself. By emphasizing abjection, Sandoval-Sánchez and others also critique the reductionism inherent in caricatured Latino types yet, unlike those types, their artistic production cannot be readily absorbed into mainstream U.S. culture. Manuel Ramos Otero (1948–1990), whose authorial guise was primarily that of a drag queen, is another important writer who candidly developed abjection "to free the body from the phallic representations of a national discourse" (Cruz-Malavé 156). His work exemplifies how the new generation both breaks with and allows continuity with previous generations of Puerto Rican gay writing.

Poet and playwright Abniel Marat, who began his writing career in Puerto Rico but moved to the mainland in the mid-1980s, directly challenges the patriarchal and oppressive social order of Puerto Rico, while also affirming that only when the marginalized individual is free can authentic national liberation be realized. His books of poetry include *Poemas de un homosexual revolucionario* and his plays such as *Dios en el Playgirl de noviembre* (1982–1983) and *Tres lirios de cala* (1987), while formerly meeting critical resistance in his homeland, are now being translated and performed in the United States. Similarly, Robert Vázquez-Pacheco's acclaimed short story "Brujo Time" seeks to reconcile his character's sexuality with his denied Boricua heritage. Puerto Rican writers, playwrights, and poets such as Manuel Ramos Otero (1948–1990), Víctor Fernández-Fragoso (1944–1982), Elliot Torres, Moisés Agosto Rosario, and **Emanuel Xavier**, whose works deal openly with homosexuality, often associate liberation of self with liberation of the nation and also rely on an autobiographical focus as a means toward realizing an authentic voice to marginality. One of the most important poets of the newest generation of diasporic writers is Rane Arroyo, whose nine books of poetry not only address ethnicity and sexuality but also critique cultural homogeneity. His poems have been characterized as a haunted writing in that he writes for and about "the impossible pueblo" (meaning both people and country)—the people that appear to him cannot be found on the screen, stage, or page: they are those lost to AIDS. He writes for the "coteries of ghosts" who come to him so that they may not be forgotten (Nelson).

The internalized homophobia within earlier Puerto Rican queer writing is being deconstructed by exiled writers whose genre-bending work is gaining a broader audience both within Puerto Rico and the mainland United States. One of the principal ways that this is occurring is through a creative repositioning and reconsidering of the diaspora. Larry La Fountain-Stokes, whose work investigates queer Latino performance, surveys this new conceptualization of diasporic and island Puerto Rican gay identities through clever wordplay both in his scholarship and creative writing. Likewise, new anthologies such as *Los otros cuerpos: Antología de temática gay, lésbica y queer desde Puerto Rico y su diáspora* will continue to add to the broadening of LGBTQ Boricua literature.

Further Reading

Agosto, Moisés, David Caleb Acevedo, and Luis Negrón. *Los otros cuerpos: Antología de temática gay, lésbica, y queer desde Puerto Rico y su diaspora.* San Juan: Editorial Tiempo Nuevo, 2007.

Arroyo, Rane. New Flash Fiction. http://www.ranearroyo.com/new%20works%20pg%204.htm.

Bergmann, Emilie, and Paul Julian Smith, eds. *¿Entiendes? Queer Readings, Hispanic Writing.* Durham, NC: Duke University Press, 1995.

Cruz-Malavé, Arnaldo. "Toward an Art of Transvestism: Colonialism and Homosexuality in Puerto Rican Literature." In *¿Entiendes? Queer Readings, Hispanic Writings,* edited by Emilie Bergmann and Paul Julian Smith, 137–66. Durham, NC: Duke University Press, 1995.

Foster, David William. *Sexual Textualities: Essays on Queer/ing Latin American Writing.* Austin: University of Texas Press, 1997.

Glave, Thomas, ed. *Our Caribbean: A Gathering of Lesbian and Gay Writing from the Antilles.* Durham, NC: Duke University Press, 2008.

La Fountain-Stokes, Lawrence. http://muse.jhu.edu.dbgateway.nysed.gov/journals/journal_of _lesbian_ and_gay studies/v008/8.1stokes.html.

Lozada, Ángel. *No quiero quedarme sola y vacía.* San Juan: Isla Negra Editores, 2006.

Nelson, Michael. "An Interview w/ Rane Arroyo." http://www.umkc.edu/ bkmk/interviews/ arroyor.html.

Ríos Ávila, Rubén. *La raza cómica del sujeto en Puerto Rico.* San Juan: Ediciones Callejón, 2002.

Sandoval-Sanchez, Alberto. *José, Can You See? Latinos On and Off Broadway.* Madison: University of Wisconsin Press, 1999.

———. "Politicizing Abjection: In the Manner of a Prologue for the Articulation of AIDS Latino Queer Identities." *American Literary History* 17, no. 3 (Fall 2005): 542–49.

Soto-Crespo, Ramón E. "Infiernos Imaginarios: Puerto Rican Marginality in Abniel Marat's *Dios en el Playgirl de noviembre* and Eugenio María de Hostos's *La Peregrinación de Bayoán.*" *Journal of Modern Fiction Studies* 44, no. 1 (1998): 215–39.

Torres-Padilla, José L. *Writing Off the Hyphen: New Critical Perspectives on the Literature of the Puerto Rican Diaspora.* Seattle: University of Washington Press, 2008.

Villanueva Collado, Alfredo, "René Marqués, Ángel Lozada, and the Constitution of the (Queer) Puerto Rican National Subject." *Centro Journal* 19, no. 1 (Spring 2007): 185–99.

Colleen Kattau

Gay Rights Movement

There are many social, political, and cultural groups and organizations that fall under the heading of the **gay** rights movement. However, the common goal uniting these disparate groups is the belief that gay, lesbian, bisexual, and transgendered people are entitled to equal protection, consideration, and rights of citizenship under the law. Gay rights are fundamentally human rights and for this reason the contemporary gay rights movement is often aligned with other social justice causes such as the protection of free speech and the fight against racism, classism, sexism, and xenophobia.

It is difficult to pinpoint exactly when a true gay rights movement can be said to have coalesced in Europe and the United States. Homosexuals (mainly men who had sexual relations with other men) were persecuted, tortured, and sentenced to death by hanging in Europe beginning in the twelfth century, and the violent persecution of homosexuals was generally perpetrated by the judicial system until the latter half of the nineteenth century when the more dramatic forms of corporal punishment were replaced by fines, prison sentences, and hard labor. It cannot be claimed that the men who were punished under antisodomy statutes of this time period possessed a "gay identity" in the modern sense of a cultural or social identity. Rather, the notion of homosexuality as anything other than a medical oddity, moral degeneration, or form of gender confusion did not emerge until the very end of the nineteenth century. A German doctor, Karl Heinrich Ulrichs, published several pamphlets about love between men using the term "Uranian" to refer to homosexuals as a third sex, neither men nor women, and the term was picked up in the English-speaking world by poet and literary figure John Addington Symonds who described Uranianism as an idealized Platonic form of love between men in the Greek tradition. The word homosexual was in popular use by 1869, coined by the Austrian Karl-Maria Kertbeny.

The notion of a "gay identity" became much more prominent around the turn of the century, with gay subcultures emerging in the larger cities of Europe and the United States. Perhaps the highly publicized Oscar Wilde sodomy trial of 1895 led to a new awareness of homosexuality as homosexuals were mainly cast as tragic figures of public ridicule and moral outrage. In 1897 a German physician and sexologist named Magnus Hirschfeld formed the first public gay rights organization, known as The Scientific-Humanitarian Committee, in response to a section of the German penal code that outlawed homosexual acts. Hirschfeld wanted to make scientific inquiry on the basis of his assertion that homosexuality was not a moral issue but rather a medical issue, claiming that homosexuality was analogous to a disease or a handicap and homosexuals should provoke sympathy and pity rather than punishment. He unsuccessfully fought to end the criminalization of homosexuality for the next 25 years and incurred the criticism of those who thought that casting homosexuality as a disease would not lead to more equal treatment under the law. Nonetheless, Germany remained at the forefront of research into homosexuality until the Nazi Party took control in 1933 and suppressed many such organizations.

Sexual and cultural liberation flourished in the cultural capitals of Europe in the 1920s. Homosexual authors and poets such as André Gide, Nathalie Barney, Marcel Proust, Gertrude Stein, and Radclyffe Hall wrote about the experience of gay life with varying degrees of openness. Radclyffe Hall's 1928 novel *The Well of Loneliness* asked society to tolerate homosexuality and **lesbianism** as a natural difference but ironically became the subject of a highly publicized obscenity trial in England in spite of its lack of explicitly sexual content. Hall's novel also sought to publicize the ideas of 1920s sexologists such as Havelock Ellis and Richard von Krafft-Ebing, both of whom believed that homosexuality was an inborn genetic trait, common in families with a history of mental illnesses and degenerative nervous disorders, although both men later modified their positions to a more moderate stance, asserting that homosexuality was not really a disease or a degenerative inferior condition, but rather a natural variation in human sexuality.

The years following World War II saw an increase in the number of gay and lesbian organizations, some of which were overtly political while others were more social and cultural in their aims and activities. These groups were known as "homophile" organizations; they sought to take homosexuality out of its sordid and tragic past of suicide, darkness, and despair into a better future of mainstream acceptance and assimilation. A postwar gay rights movement began to coalesce in both Europe and the United States in the 1950s and sought to rally democratic political processes around the cause of equal rights for homosexuals. They did so through the usual political means of letter-writing campaigns, small and orderly protests, petitions, and lobbying of politicians. However, gays continued to be harassed in both their public and private lives. In cold war America many suspected homosexuals lost their jobs when homosexuality was associated with communism in the furor of the Red Scare and McCarthyism. Police forces routinely raided and closed bars where gays and lesbians gathered and would publish the names in the newspaper of all the people found on the premises in order to publicly shame and humiliate them.

By the 1960s there were many homophile organizations in America, the most famous and lasting of which was the Mattachine Society, founded in Los Angeles in 1950 by Harry Hay and his circle of friends, who wanted to support the formation of a cohesive gay community, fight for gay rights, and provide social services to gay people who suffered as a result of their oppression. The group formally incorporated in 1954, and by the end of the 1950s there were chapters of the society in several cities. On July 4, 1965, the first American gay rights demonstration took place in Philadelphia, with a small group of people marching past Independence Hall and the Liberty Bell in support of gay rights; that same year saw progay picketing in front of the White House in Washington, D.C. The Daughters of Bilitis was another significant homophile organization, with a lesbian membership base, founded in San Francisco in 1955 by Del Martin and Phyllis Lyon, a lesbian couple who wanted to meet other lesbians outside of bars. Originally a social club, the group soon took on a more supportive role for women who were coming out as lesbians, providing outreach and education. Like the Mattachine Society, the Daughters of Bilitis had chapters in several cities and published a newsletter called *The Ladder,* which was distributed nationally until 1972.

The Philadelphia and White House demonstrations had been quiet and orderly, and the homophile organizations strove for assimilation with the wider heterosexual society. The **Stonewall Riots** of 1969 were anything but quiet. When New York City police officers raided a popular gay bar, the Stonewall Inn, on June 28, 1969, things got out of hand very quickly as patrons would not cooperate with the raid by producing identification in a docile and orderly fashion; the police began to get aggressive, arresting patrons as a crowd gathered to watch. After years of police harassment, the raid on the Stonewall Inn was the proverbial last straw. Several hundred Greenwich Village residents had gathered on Christopher Street, and as the crowd grew, many people spontaneously joined in what was to be known in the future as the Stonewall Riots. The raid touched off a week of confrontations between police and Village residents, and the riots are considered the beginning of the modern gay rights movement. Within a year of the riots, New York had several openly progay political organizations, three gay newspapers, and New York's first gay pride parade was held on June 28, 1970, the one-year anniversary of the Stonewall Riots.

The following year, 1971, gay pride parades were held in Paris, Los Angeles, and several other cities. Two years after that, in 1972, practically every metropolitan area had a gay rights organization; chapters of some of the groups formed after Stonewall, such as the Gay Liberation Alliance and the Gay Activists Alliance. This new movement differed from the homophile organizations of the past; these groups were more interested in confrontation than assimilation and were inspired by the civil protests and radical dissent of the African American civil rights movement and the anti-Vietnam War protests. In the 1970s the progress of the gay rights movement had a wider reach into the policy and politics of sexuality than ever before, as the increased visibility of homosexuals was accompanied by changes in societal views of gender and sexuality within the heterosexual community as well. The next major turning point for the gay rights movement was the advent of the HIV virus and AIDS, which first appeared in the gay community in the early 1980s. The failure of governments to act or even provide any resources to communities decimated by the virus led to a re-radicalization in the mid to late 1980s with groups such as ACT UP (AIDS Coalition to Unleash Power) staging dramatic protests in the form of "die-ins" and parades of mock coffins on the streets of cities. There was also a strengthening of gay social services within the community during this time, as organizations such as the Gay Men's Health Crisis were formed to deal with the sick and dying.

The gay rights movement has made tremendous progress culturally in the last 100 years, with a once marginalized and invisible minority becoming visible, self-sustaining, and global. However, on the juridicial front, it is only in the past few years that the gay rights movement is getting any real results in the realm of same-sex marriages and equal rights for homosexual and heterosexual couples. Of course, this is where the gay rights movement is facing its strongest opposition from counterorganizations that want to exclude homosexuals from the right to marry and equal protection under the law. Several countries, including the Netherlands, Belgium, Norway, Spain, and Canada recognize same-sex marriages, and the U.S. state of Massachusetts accepts gay marriages, while other municipalities have some sort of civil union available to homosexual couples. In the future, the extension of the gay rights movement as a global movement is to be expected.

Further Reading

Chauncey, George. *Gay New York: Gender, Culture and the Making of the Gay Male World, 1890–1940.* New York: Basic Books, 1995.

Deitcher, David, ed. *The Question of Equality: Lesbian and Gay Politics in America since Stonewall.* New York: Scribner, 1995.

Faderman, Lillian. *Odd Girls and Twilight Lovers: A History of Lesbian Life in Twentieth Century America.* New York: Penguin Books, 1991.

Michele Erfer

Gearhart, Sally Miller (b. 1931)

Essayist and author of lesbian-feminist science fiction. Born on April 15, 1931, in Pearisburg, Virginia, to Sarah Miller Gearhart and Kyle Montague Gearhart, her parents divorced when she was two years old, which introduced her to a world of women, where she experienced female friendship and support. In 1953, she completed an M.A. in Theater and Rhetoric at Bowling Green State University, and in 1956 a Ph.D. in Theater (with minors in rhetoric and philosophy) at the University of Illinois. She has taught at various colleges and state universities in the Midwest and Texas. While leading two lives, that of the popular professor of speech, debate, and theater and that of the **closet**ed lesbian, in the late 1960s, her conversion to feminism began. After being tenured in 1974 by the San Francisco State University as an open lesbian, she taught there until her retirement in 1992, helping to found its Women's Studies Program. She was also involved in political work on behalf of animals, civil rights, and fighting for a greater visibility for lesbian, **gay**, bisexual, and transgendered people, her best-known activity being her participation in the campaign to defeat the Briggs Initiative to bar lesbians and gays from teaching. Gearhart lives north of Willits, California.

The essay collection *Loving Women/Loving Men: Gay Liberation and the Church* (1974) that Gearhart co-edited with William R. Johnson presents one of the earliest lesbian and gay challenges to Christian religion. With her withdrawal from the church, Gearhart turned to themes of women's spirituality, authoring *A Feminist Tarot* (1976) together with Susan Rennie. Through her writing, Gearhart has contributed to the movements in which she has been involved, particularly by writing essays concerning feminist communication, such as "The Womanization of Rhetoric" (1979).

Gearhart has written numerous short stories, but her reputation as a fiction writer so far rests on the utopia *Wanderground: Stories of the Hill Women* (1979), which depicts an all-women Amazonian community. Whereas the women live in harmony with one another and nature, reproduce by ovular merging, and have developed telepathic powers, men are dependent on technology and are restricted to the cities where violence, crime, and poverty rule. The "Gentles," separatist men trying to live according to the women's values, challenge an essentialist assumption that violence is male; however, the belief in biologically determined sexual difference is never undermined in the text. According to the Hill Women's communal values, there is no single protagonist; *Wanderground* instead consists of separate episodes depicting the experiences of different women and was highly acclaimed as feminist speculative fiction providing an opportunity to experiment with alternative conceptions of an all-women society.

Gearhart's "Earthkeep" series further develops along the lines of the psychically enhanced communication depicted in *Wanderground,* but is set in a postapocalyptic world in which women fight for the survival of the planet. In the first volume, *The Kanshou* (2002), the inhabitants of "Little Blue" are faced with the disappearance of all animals, with natural disasters, and the effects of decades of political unrest. Gearhart herself explains her motivation for writing the Earthkeep series as attempting to explore three questions: (1) How would the world be different if women ran it? (2) Is violence **gender** related? (3) How should violence be addressed in the best of societies? The story of political struggle is seen from the perspective of two very different women, both political leaders, who love each other, but are divided by contrary convictions pertaining to the source of violence. In *The Magister* (2003), the second book in the series, the women are confronted with yet another disaster, the death of the children, which brings the human race close to extinction. The book concludes with an emerging vision of a peaceful society as well as a new relationship between human beings and animals. Challenging the readers to confront issues of gender differences, violence, and environmental concerns, the novels of the Earthkeep series have not yet received the critical attention they merit. A third volume with the title *The Steward* is forthcoming.

Further Reading

Andermahr, Sonya. "The Politics of Separatism and Lesbian Utopian Fiction." In *New Lesbian Criticism: Literary and Cultural Readings,* edited by Sally Munt, 133–52. New York: Harvester Wheatsheaf, 1992.

Foss, Karen A., Sonja K. Foss, and Cindy L. Griffin. "Sally Miller Gearhart." *Feminist Rhetorical Theories.* Thousand Oaks, CA: Sage, 1999. 257–92.

Secor, Cynthia. "Sally Miller Gearhart (1931–)." In *Contemporary Lesbian Writers of the United States: A Bio-Bibliographical Critical Sourcebook,* edited by Sandra Pollack and Denise D. Knight, 205–12. Westport, CT: Greenwood Press, 1993.

Miriam Wallraven

Geller, Ruth (b. 1945)

Fiction writer. Ruth Geller is the author of two novels and numerous short stories, many of which deal with the intersections of **gender,** sexuality, and Jewishness and which display an acute consciousness of the interlocking nature of gender, race, and class oppression. Geller's short fiction has been published in *The Things That Divide Us: Stories by Women* (1985), and in the groundbreaking collection *Nice Jewish Girls: A Lesbian Anthology* (1982). Geller self-published both *Seed of a Woman* (1979), a historical novel that records the beginning of the women's movement, and *Pictures from the Past* (1980), a collection of short stories. Crossing Press published her second novel, *Triangles,* in 1984.

In *Triangles,* Geller portrays several generations of the Rosenthal family, who are troubled by the emotional and physical violence of current political realities, their Eastern European Jewish heritage and the legacy of the Holocaust, and the personal decisions they themselves have made. Geller's protagonist is Sunny, who has divorced her husband following the accidental drowning death of their daughter and embarked on a relationship with another woman, Kay. *Triangles* is much concerned with the consequences of secrecy and openness, and it is a series of both casual and deliberate deceptions that motivates much of the narrative's dynamic tension. The Rosenthals keep secrets from one another, as do Kay and Sunny, and Sunny becomes increasingly critical of her own unwillingness to disclose her relationship with Kay to her family, and her Jewishness to her friends and co-workers. The characters' overlapping and mutually implicated deceits become untenable as the narrative progresses. Sunny increasingly recognizes both the personal and political needs for a greater degree of disclosure, which produces conflict, but also the possibility of new alliances and of positive change.

The novel's title refers both to the triangles that constitute the Star of David and the triangles by which the Nazi administration identified the various groups of people interned in concentration camps. Sunny comes to realize that the categories of the racially impure, religiously unacceptable, sexually deviant, and politically dissident are not mutually exclusive and that their common and overlapping exclusion and oppression is also at work in the contemporary United Sates. The narrative suggests that Sunny's sister's activism against the proliferation of nuclear weapons, her uncle's tales of the harassment of the political Left in the 1950s, the greenhouse effect, the derogatory stereotyping of the only African American employee at her place of work, the casual and idiomatic antisemitism that she encounters, and the gender conflicts within her family are interconnected in complex but powerful ways. Sunny's eventual response to the network of destructive hegemonic social norms and beliefs that surround her is a series of coming outs. She comes out as a Jew to her co-workers and landlords, as a lesbian to her siblings, and as colluding in a damaging family secret to Kay. These disclosures are not without consequences, and remain incomplete. It is indeed notable that the novel places more emphasis on antisemitism and coming out as Jewish than it does on **homophobia** and coming out as lesbian. However, near the end of the novel the Armory across from Sunny's apartment burns down; this destruction both of a symbol of military power and of a landscape feature that blocks Sunny's view of the river in which her daughter drowned suggests both an increasing reconciliation with her personal and familial history and a challenge to the daunting future.

While offering an affectionate if not uncritical portrait of working-class Jewish family life, the inclusive vision of *Triangles* has been questioned *en passant* by Barbara McDonald who suggests that on the back cover, and in the blurb and dedication of *Triangles,* Geller inappropriately makes her own grandmother the subject of a joke from whose humor she is excluded (24). In contrast, perhaps, to this position is the forceful character of Rose, Sunny's grandmother, whose negotiation of patriarchal family power and instinct both for survival and a good bargain, provide something of a model for Sunny. Nevertheless, the novel's most compelling character is Rose, Sunny's grandmother, whose negotiation of patriarchal family power and instinct for survival provide Sunny with a model of enduring female strength.

Further Reading

McDonald, Barbara. "Outside the Sisterhood: Ageing in Women's Studies." *Women and Aging: An Anthology by Women,* edited by Jo Alexander and Lisa Domitrovich, 20–25. Corvallis, OR: Calyx Books, 1986.

Zimmerman, Bonnie. "Out and About." *The Women's Review of Books* 2, no. 6 (1985): 14–15.

Liz Vine

Gender

What is gender? *Encyclopedia Britannica* defines gender as one's self-concept as being male or female, as different from biological sex. The *Merriam-Webster Dictionary* views gender as a set of behavioral, cultural, or psychological features associated with one's sex. The notion of gender clearly mixes distinct yet interconnected representations of an individual's self-image, that is, its biological, social, and psychological aspects. If gender is to be understood as a socially constructed model of masculine and feminine, then each individual has to negotiate not only his or her understanding of what it means to be masculine or feminine but also how such self-knowledge corresponds to the cultural expectations about masculinity and femininity at large. The definition of gender is further complicated by its interplay with sexuality, race, class, identity, social roles, power, and cultural behaviors assigned to the specific social groups in any historical moment. This multilayered tapestry of interwoven meanings reflects most of the scholarly and theoretical work on gender in the twentieth century.

Commenting on the differences between masculine and feminine sexual manifestations in his *Three Contributions to the Theory of Sex* (1905), Sigmund Freud stresses that "there is no pure masculinity or femininity either in the biological or psychological sense" (581). Freud's psychoanalytic approach acknowledges the artificiality of the divide between the sexes and focuses on how we unconsciously construct ourselves. In her groundbreaking and influential feminist work *The Second Sex* (1949), Simone de Beauvoir discusses the ways in which we become "gendered" in society, thus bringing forth the idea about becoming gendered (not born in gender) as part of social conditioning. For Beauvoir, society defines man as "the essential" and "the Self" while woman as "the Other" and "the inessential" (5). Such distribution of attributes disturbingly views women as the "second sex" physically, linguistically, and socially, and the author calls for granting that "the possible existence of differences in equality" (13).

The notion of difference takes on a new meaning when sexologist John Money, in his study "Hermaphroditism, Gender and Precocity in Hyperadrenocorticism" (1955), introduces the term "gender role" to signify all the peculiarities in behavior, clothing, language, and occupation that reveal someone as being identified a man or a woman.

Several decades later, Irene Fast's *Gender Identity: A Differentiation Model* (1984) develops the distinction of subjective and objective gender and postulates that objective demarcation of gender exhibits an individual's association with the notions of "feminine" and "masculine" within a particular social group. The author explains that subjective definitions refer to personal constructs of masculinity and femininity, that is, the individuals' own understanding, applied to themselves and others, of what it is to be masculine and feminine. The clash of personal and societal definitions of masculinity and femininity is prevalent throughout the history of gender in the twentieth century.

The ever-changing socioeconomic landscape of the first half of the twentieth century, including the 1920s suffrage movement and the liberties of the Jazz Age, the post–Great Depression industrial growth, the World War II labor force shortage, and the 1950s opportunities for the working-class family, all helped to shape the new image of a self-assertive woman, thus redefining the traditional gender roles based on female inferiority. However, the domestic revival of the 1950s also meant a temporal stall in a woman's growth as an educated professional.

Starting with the women's liberation movement in the late 1960s and 1970s and the gay movement with its interest in men and masculinity in the 1970s, traditional assumptions about gender identities and gender roles began to shift dramatically. Assertions about gender equality and sexual freedom displaced the worn-out models of masculinity and femininity as well as the notions of control over sexuality and socialization. Transformation and destabilization of gender binaries came not only from the subjective experimentations with sexuality but also from the explicit changes in cultural representation with its ambiguity and transgendered implications (Glam Rock, Andy Warhol's "The Factory," and pop cross-dressing). Michel Foucault's influential *The History of Sexuality: An Introduction* (1978) speaks of sexuality as a cultural mechanism of power. Foucault argues that power "is always-already present" through the discursive production of sexuality that is socially constructed, unstable, and historically situated (82). Like gender itself, sex embodies yet another manifestation of highly polarized cultural labeling and social conditioning.

However, with a growing interest in unpolarized gender dynamics and gender indeterminacy in cultural representations in the 1980s (androgynous artists as Annie Lennox, Boy George, and so forth), the theoretical considerations of gendered identity of difference become more prevalent. In her powerful and insightful inquiry into the dimensions of sexual differentiation, Luce Irigaray argues in her book *An Ethics of Sexual Difference* (1984) that "the meeting between the sexes" should stem from the dialogue between a man and a woman reaffirming their sexual difference, "voice in language," and unique "relation to the world" (140–41).

Since the 1990s, gender discussions reflect the feminist writers' interest in language, the unconscious, and the performance aspects of gender construction. In her groundbreaking book *Gender Trouble: Feminism and the Subversion of Identity* (1990), **Judith Butler** argues that gender serves a performative function; that is, it exists as a performance act in the interaction with others. Interestingly, the notion of gender as performance acquires a new dimension in the cybercentered, contemporary world where "gender is a virtual system" that "manipulates representations of the real but does not change the foundational perceptions of bodies upon which the 'real' depends," argues Bernice L. Hausman in her article "Virtual Sex, Real Gender" (192).

Another facet of contemporary studies on gender deals with gender as an extension of socially and personally constructed identity that exemplifies a complex negotiation of professional and racial self-realizations. According to Anne McClintock in her book *Imperial Leather: Race, Gender, and Sexuality in the Colonial Context* (1995), race, gender, and class "come into existence in and through relation to each other" (4–5). Gendered representations of race and labor reflect the traditional and provisional models of heterosexuality and institutionalized control. In *Gender and Power* (1987), R. W. Connell analyzes the interconnections between social structure (labor, power, and emotional relations) and an individual's personality. He focuses on the job allocations between men and women, organization of work, and personal and socially structured gender identities to ponder the specific power relations in which gendered inequalities are embedded.

As the various theoretical considerations show, the understanding of gender lies at the crossroads between our subjective self-image, cultural representation, and social construction of what it means to be a man or a woman. And whether we view gender as a cultural and/or self-imposed "fiction" or as a manifestation of sexual identity and difference, we are still left with an open-ended discussion about a complex negotiation of public and private meanings of "gender."

See also Androgyny; Transgenderism

Further Reading

Beauvoir, Simone de. "The Second Sex." *Key Concepts in Critical Theory: Gender,* edited by Carol C. Gould, 3–15. New York: Humanities Press, 1997.

Foucault, Michel. *History of Sexuality: An Introduction.* Translated by Robert Hurley. New York: Vintage Books, 1990.

Freud, Sigmund. *Three Contributions to the Theory of Sex.* From *The Basic Writings of Sigmund Freud.* Translated and edited by A. A. Brill. New York: The Modern Library, 1995. 521–97.

Hausman, Bernice L. "Virtual Sex, Real Gender." In *Virtual Gender: Fantasies of Subjectivity and Embodiment,* edited by Mary Ann O'Farrell and Lynne Vallone, 190–216. Ann Arbor: University of Michigan Press, 1999.

Irigaray, Luce. *An Ethics of Sexual Difference.* Translated by Carolyn Burke and Gillian C. Gill. Ithaca, NY: Cornell University Press, 1993.

McClintock, Anne. *Imperial Leather: Race, Gender and Sexuality in the Colonial Context.* London: Routledge, 1995.

Alla Boldina

Gidlow, Elsa (1898–1986)

Prominent lesbian poet, essayist, journalist, and activist, also known as the "poet-warrior." Elsa Gidlow was born in Hull, England, on December 29, 1898, as the eldest of seven children. In 1904, she emigrated to Tetreauville, a small French Canadian village near Montreal, Quebec, with her family. Gidlow's childhood and teenage years were troubled by financial problems, and she did not receive a formal education. Gidlow was self-taught and harbored the ambition of leading an independent life as a poet from an early age. When she was 19, she moved to New York City, where she worked for Frank Harris and his controversial *Pearson's Magazine.* When the magazine failed, Gidlow turned to working as an editor for a couple of years and took up freelance writing, a career that would allow her to make a living for the rest of her life.

In 1926, Gidlow moved to San Francisco together with her older lover, Violet Winifred Leslie Henry-Anderson, also known as "Tommy." The Bay Area became Gidlow's constant place of residence until her death six decades later. In 1946, she purchased five acres of land near the Muir Woods National Monument in northern California. Gidlow called her new home Druid Heights and began to establish a lively community for her friends among whom were some of the foremost artists and thinkers of her time, such as June Singer, Lou Harrison, Robinson Jeffers, Margo St. James, Ella Young, and Catherine A. MacKinnon to name but a few. Gidlow became an influential and active member of the political, cultural, and intellectual Bay Area scene. Among other pursuits, she joined the Daughters of Bilitis, the first lesbian rights organization in the United States, and co-founded the Society for Comparative Philosophy with her close friend and fellow Zen philosopher Alan Watts in 1962. After Tommy's death in 1938, Gidlow entered in a long-lasting relationship with Isabell Grenfell Quallo, a woman of color and Caribbean origin. It was arguably due to the openness with which Gidlow led her interracial lesbian relationship that she was investigated by the House Un-American Activities Committee. On June 8, 1986, Gidlow died on the Druid Heights premises after having suffered a series of strokes. The Druid Heights Artists Retreat has since become a nonprofit organization offering a retreat and sanctuary for women artists and writers.

During her lifetime, Druid Heights had played a similar role for Gidlow herself. Not only did Druid Heights allow her to create her own artistic and intellectual community, but it also offered her the privacy and solitude she sought in order to pursue her interest in creative writing. Gidlow is best known for her lesbian poetry, and her first publication, *On a Grey Thread* (1923), is often described as the first openly lesbian book of love poetry to appear in the United States. Drawing on her own experiences, Gidlow's poetry depicts lesbian experience and desire in a frank and outright manner that was groundbreaking at the time of publication. Gidlow continued to write lesbian poetry throughout her life and also produced several short stories, novels, and poetry dramas dealing with lesbian themes, some of which remain unpublished and form part of the collection of The Gay and Lesbian Historical Society of Northern California. Gidlow's book publications include *Wild Swan Singing* (1954), *Letters from Limbo* (1956), *Moods of Eros* (1970), *Sapphic Songs—Seventeen to Seventy* (1976), and the revised and extended edition *Sapphic Songs—Eighteen to Eighty* (1982). One of her most interesting nonfictional publications is the pamphlet *Ask No Man Pardon: The Philosophical Significance of Being Lesbian* (1975).

In the final years of her life, Gidlow began to work on her autobiography, which was published one month before her death in 1986 under the title *Elsa: I Come with My Songs.* Covering almost 90 years, Gidlow's memoirs give a vivid account of lesbian life throughout the twentieth century. She details her struggles to live openly as a lesbian and describes her desire to carve out a space for an independent and creative existence shared with other women. Even though Gidlow's style appears somewhat rushed, which is unsurprising given the fact that the author's health was deteriorating rapidly while she was in the process of writing the book, her autobiography is a fascinating piece of lesbian life writing and an important document of lesbian history. Even though the literary merits of Gidlow's work may be disputed, she emerges as a pioneering voice in lesbian literature.

Further Reading

West, Celeste. "In Memoriam: Elsa Gidlow." *Feminist Studies* 12, no. 3 (Autumn 1986): 614.

Jana Funke

Ginsberg, Allen (1926–1997)

Gay Jewish American poet and activist. Allen Ginsberg is best known as a founding member of the Beat Generation of the 1950s, although his life and work resonated throughout American countercultural movements from the 1950s heyday of the Beat movement until his death in 1997 and continue to do so in the present day. Born in Newark, New Jersey, and raised in the town of Paterson, as a child Allen was influenced by both of his parents. His father, Louis, was a high school English teacher who also wrote poetry, and his mother, Naomi, was actively involved in the Communist Party and many other left-wing political movements. She brought Allen and his older brother, Eugene (who was named after the socialist Eugene V. Debs), with her to meetings of the Communist Party in the 1930s and 1940s, and Allen was deeply influenced by his mother's left-wing political orientation. Even as a young boy he was dedicated to political causes such as communism, socialism, pacifism, and worker's rights. Allen was a bright and intellectually curious child, strongly moved by poetry, particularly the works of visionary poets such as Walt Whitman and William Blake.

By the time Allen reached adolescence, Naomi Ginsberg was in poor mental and physical health. While she had suffered various illnesses for most of her life, including epileptic seizures and episodes of paranoia and psychosis, her condition only worsened as she entered middle age. When he was still in high school, Allen accompanied her via the municipal bus as she voluntarily committed herself to a New Jersey hospital for the mentally ill, a traumatizing experience that would affect him for many years to come. Naomi's health never really improved, and, following her initial decision to commit herself, she spent the rest of her life in and out of various mental hospitals undergoing electroshock therapy and eventually a lobotomy. Naomi died in 1956 at the Pilgrim State Hospital, and Allen was haunted by her death for the rest of his life. His experience with his mother's mental deterioration led him to a lifelong fascination with mental illness and mentally ill people. In 1949 Allen spent six months in a mental hospital himself as a result of being in trouble with the law when stolen goods were stored in his New York City apartment. He would continue to befriend people who were mentally ill and always tried to question the very idea of mental illness, believing that there should be no real distinctions made between the sane and the insane, the normal and the abnormal.

Much of Ginsberg's artistic output was influenced by his mother's mental illness and featured his mother as its central subject matter—even where his mother is not directly alluded to, Naomi can be considered to affect his work more subtly. He eventually wrote an epic poem about his mother entitled *Kaddish for Naomi Ginsberg 1894–1956* (1961), which told the story of his mother's life beginning with her childhood in Russia, her emigration to America, and then incorporated Allen's point of view of her mental deterioration, narrating the bus ride he took with her to the mental hospital, as well as the circumstances of her eventual death and his perpetual mourning for his mother. As it is mainly a poem of loss and elegy, it took the form of the traditional Jewish mourners' prayer, the Kaddish and the word "kaddish" is repeated frequently throughout the work. In 1983, 25 years after writing *Kaddish,* Ginsberg wrote another poem about his mother, entitled "White Shroud" which was published in 1986. The poem reaffirmed his connection to Naomi and his continued mourning over her death.

While a student at Newark's Eastside High School, Allen distinguished himself academically; following his graduation in 1943, he began college at Montclair State University of New Jersey before winning a scholarship to Columbia University from the Paterson Young Men's Hebrew Association. While at Columbia, Allen was involved in various literary journals and clubs, including the *Columbia Review* and the university humor magazine. He also encountered several figures of New York's literary and bohemian underground including future Beat authors John Clellan Holmes, Gregory Corso, **William S. Burroughs**, Jack Kerouac, and Neal Cassady. Some of them became his lovers and most would remain lifelong friends. Allen was suspended from Columbia for graffiti and vandalism when he scratched a swastika in a window as an ironic statement against an antisemitic cleaning lady employed by the university who refused to go into his room because she knew he was Jewish. After the yearlong suspension, he went on to earn his B.A. in 1949 before embarking on a short-lived career as a Madison Avenue advertising copywriter. Living in New Jersey and commuting to Manhattan, he became friendly with the imagist poet William Carlos Williams, one of the most celebrated living American poets of the time. Williams lived nearby and became Ginsberg's artistic mentor, encouraging him to continue writing. On the advice of his psychoanalyst, Ginsberg quit his job and decided to pursue his passion. During this period of his life, he was also experimenting with psychedelic drugs and attempting to create poetry that mirrored the effects of these drugs by introducing a visionary state of consciousness to the reader. He delved deeper into experimentalism in both his life and work, traveling in 1953 to the Yucatan Peninsula of Mexico in order to try ayahuasca and peyote. After his time in Mexico, he settled in San Francisco, and the city remained his home for the next 25 years.

As Allen matured artistically, it became increasingly difficult for him to deny his homosexuality; in 1954 he met the man who would become his lifelong partner, a handsome model named Peter Orlovsky. These early years in San Francisco saw Ginsberg delve deeper into poetry; shortly after his arrival on the West Coast, he went on to compose his epic poem *Howl* and read it in public for the first time. *Howl* is a complex and lyrical masterpiece that tells the story of Ginsberg's life up until 1955, as well as the story of his contemporaries: the other Beat poets, artists, and personalities in his circle of friends, including the young schizophrenic Carl Solomon to whom the poem is dedicated, Neal Cassady, William S. Burroughs, and others. As the Beats were described in the poem, many had gone mad, committed suicide, or succumbed to drug addiction rather than adopt the conformist middle-class suburban lifestyle that was idealized in American popular culture of the time. The Beats saw the prevalent American way of life as essentially repressive and hypocritical. From its very first reading and publication, *Howl* would forever be considered the seminal work of poetry of the Beat Generation and would eventually make Allen Ginsberg a household name. *Howl* explicitly discussed prostitution, promiscuity, and homosexuality; for these topics it became the subject of a highly publicized obscenity trial in 1957. Lawrence Ferlinghetti, owner of San Francisco's famous City Lights bookshop and the publishing house that published *Howl,* was made to stand trial when a shipment of several hundred copies of the book was seized by customs officials as they arrived from the British printer. The obscenity trial became a cultural flash point in the late 1950s, and Ferlinghetti was defended by the American Civil Liberties Union while many prominent writers of the day wrote letters to the court defending the artistic merit of Ginsberg's work. Eventually, the case was concluded with the judge acquitting Ferlinghetti, declaring that the poem was indeed redeemed by its artistic merit.

Following the furor of the obscenity trial, Ginsberg decided to leave San Francisco and settled in Paris with Peter for the next year; in 1957 and 1958, many poets and artists associated with the Beat movement could also be found in Paris. Ginsberg continued to write, travel, and experiment with psychedelic drugs, becoming interested in Eastern philosophy and religion, most notably Buddhism. Paris was their home base for travels to Tangiers, which Peter and Allen visited with William S. Burroughs, who was writing his novel *Naked Lunch,* a story of life as a heroin addict. Ginsberg, Orlovsky, and Burroughs were fascinated by the squalor and corruption of Tangiers, where many drugs were readily available, and it was not unusual for adolescent boys to work as prostitutes employed by wealthy Europeans and Americans.

As the Beat movement of the 1950s gave way to the hippies and the antiwar protestors of the 1960s, it seemed that Allen Ginsberg was the common link between both decades' significant countercultural movements: both the Beats and the hippies considered Ginsberg to be something of an artistic leader and cultural figurehead. Although he often spoke about the spiritualism and politics that moved him, Ginsberg eschewed leadership and continued traveling and writing all throughout the 1960s. He went to India in 1962 and spent two years there seeking spiritual enlightenment, embracing Buddhism and trying to eradicate all traces of Western egotism in his life. His enthusiasm about Eastern religions was matched by the hippie culture's mystical beliefs and willingness to explore all ideas, philosophies, and religions equally in order to glean a mixed bag of beliefs that fit in with hippie ideals of peace, love, and brotherhood. Ginsberg became a Buddhist in India and is credited with introducing Hare Krishna to America; he could often be seen chanting Hare Krishna mantras at events and political protests in San

Francisco. Ginsberg's political engagement was not limited to the pacifist antiwar movement. He lived most of his life as a political exercise, participating in a multitude of social justice causes that would have made his leftist rebel mother proud: environmentalism, nuclear disarmament, racial equality, and anticonsumerism. Possibly due to the experience of the *Howl* obscenity trial, he became a vocal fighter for first amendment rights and free speech, and, although he had found it difficult coming to terms with his homosexuality as a young man, he became a firm supporter of the **gay rights movement**, often declaring a radical expression of nonmonogamous free love. For Ginsberg, love was the most important emotion and the love between members of the same gender deserved the same respect as heterosexual love. Throughout his life, he remained the poet and artist laureate of the underground and the Left. In the 1970s and 1980s, Ginsberg continued to travel widely, visiting with Buddhist spiritual leaders in China, paying his respects to fellow poet Ezra Pound in Italy, and lecturing students in Prague. Eventually, Ginsberg and his partner, Peter Orlovsky, settled in a loft in Manhattan's bohemian East Village.

In addition to being a prolific poet whose published works extend to hundreds of poems and several dozen collections, Ginsberg's many projects include collaborations and performances with rock bands and musicians such as The Clash, Bob Dylan, Philip Glass, and the Kronos Quartet. His many recorded readings of his own poems were collected in a four-volume CD collection that was released in 1994 by Rhino Recordings. He published several of his personal journals such as *Indian Journals: March 1962–May 1963* (1970) and *Journals: Early Fifties, Early Sixties* (1977). His most widely read collections of poetry are *Reality Sandwiches: 1953–1960* (1963), *Planet News: 1961–1968* (1968), *The Fall of America: Poems of These States 1965–1971* (1972), *Mind Breaths* (1978), *Plutonium Ode* (1982), and *Cosmopolitan Greetings* (1994); there was also an expanded and annotated edition of *Howl and Other Poems* published in 1986. Allen Ginsberg passed away on April 5, 1997, of liver cancer related to hepatitis. His passing was marked by vigils, poetry readings, and performances by his admirers all over the world. His final collection of poems was published posthumously as *Death & Fame* (1997); his continuing importance to radical political and artistic movements cannot be underestimated.

Further Reading

Charters, Ann, ed. *The Portable Beat Reader*. New York: Penguin Books, 1992.

Morgan, Bill. *Howl on Trial: The Battle for Free Speech*. San Francisco: City Lights Publishers, 2006.

Schumacher, Michael. *Dharma Lion: A Critical Biography of Allen Ginsberg*. New York: St. Martin's Press, 1994.

Michele Erfer

Gomez, Jewelle (b. 1948)

Acclaimed novelist, essayist, playwright, teacher, and poet, whose work reflects her racial and feminist consciousness as well as her lesbian identity. Her debut novel, *The Gilda Stories* (1991), depicts the first African American lesbian vampire heroine. While Gomez admits to being the product of various aspects of her upbringing and education —from "classic" European and American literatures to Catholicism and popular 1950s television serials—her major literary influences are Nikki Giovanni, Ntozake Shange, **Audre Lorde**, Chelsea Quinn Yarbro, **Octavia Butler**, and Joanna Russ. Her family heritage is a blend of ethnicities (Native American, African American, and Portuguese) and working class. She was born in Boston and spent her early childhood years with her mother in Washington, D.C. At age eight she returned to Boston, where she lived with her maternal great-grandmother until she graduated from Northeastern University at age 22. She earned her master's degree at the Columbia University School of Journalism in 1973.

As an undergraduate in the late 1960s, Gomez participated in her first demonstration for civil rights in Boston, in a march endorsed by Martin Luther King, Jr. She continued to be politically engaged throughout the Black Power movement, women's liberation movement, and into the **gay** rights era. Notably, she was on the founding board of the Gay & Lesbian Alliance against Defamation (GLAAD), the still highly influential media watchdog. She served as a researcher/interviewer on the U.S. gay and lesbian history documentary project *Before **Stonewall*** (1983). She was director of the Literature Program for the New York State Council on the Arts from 1989 to 1993 and has taught creative writing and women's studies courses.

Gomez's entry into the literary world began with self-published poetry collections, *The Lipstick Papers* (1980) and *Flamingoes and Bears* (1986), both of which are lesbian themed and woman centered. Her third collection of poems, *Oral Tradition* (a pun on lesbian sex), was published by Firebrand Books in 1995. She is best known for her fantasy/science fiction novel *The Gilda Stories.* Inspired by the intense mourning she experienced after the death of her great-grandmother, she based *Gilda* on her family's ethnic makeup and history. The creation of a black lesbian protagonist infuses vampire mythology with feminist politics and some of the particulars of African American culture and history. Gilda's 200-year trek from slavery to the year 2050 is propelled by entwining themes of moral consciousness, family and community, embracing death, and the struggle for survival by a racial minority in an increasingly antagonistic and violent world. For this work, Gomez was awarded two Lambda Literary Awards (one for fiction, the other for science fiction).

Gomez then published *Forty-Three Septembers,* a collection of nonfiction essays, in 1993. While it mostly contains autobiographical accounts of her family life and coming-of-age, it also displays her skills as an academician. She recounts her relationship with her father; explores the variations of influential womanhood and beauty in her family; recalls the firsthand experiences of protest marches and other momentous realizations that forged her feminist identity; connects her Catholicism to her attraction to vampire mythology; asserts the importance of black lesbian and gay public visibility in popular culture, history, and literature; and includes an exposition of the life and work of Lorraine Hansberry.

In 1996 she adapted *Gilda Stories* into a play entitled *Bones & Ash;* it was performed in 13 cities across the United States at such theaters as San Francisco's Yerba Buena Center for the Arts, the Walker Arts Center in Minneapolis, and the Joyce Theater in New York.

In her first collection of short stories, *Don't Explain* (1998), Gomez continues to explore black womanhood and freedom struggles, revisits the Gilda character, and further memorializes her great-grandmother. In the title story, a waitress in the 1950s forges an intimate bond with another woman through their mutual attraction to Billie Holiday, who also appears in the story. In "Lynx and Strand," citizens are controlled by a fascist government that prohibits even the minutest expression of individualism, such as tattoos. Gilda is featured in "Houston," where she finds a ruinous environment in which few humans are able to endure. "Grace A." is the imaginative retelling of how her austere great-grandmother reluctantly took on the duties of parenting in her old age. In "Water with the Wine," a 50-year-old African American professor confesses her affair with her younger, white student.

To date, her works in progress include a comic novel, *Televised,* about black activists of the 1960s as they face middle age and *Waiting for Giovanni,* a play based on the life of author **James Baldwin.**

Gomez has been a visiting writer at Menlo College and an instructor at New College of California. She was executive director of The Poetry Center & American Poetry Archives at San Francisco State University from 1996 to 1999 and, in 2001, became director of Cultural Equity Grants Program of the San Francisco Arts Commission. She is currently a member of the San Francisco Library Commission.

Her fiction, essays, criticism, and poetry have appeared in numerous periodicals, such as the *New York Village Voice, Essence Magazine, Callaloo, The Black Scholar,* and *The Advocate.* Her work has been featured in the following anthologies: *Home Girls* (2000), *Reading Black, Reading Feminist* (1990), *Dark Matter: A Century of Speculative Fiction from the African Diaspora* (2001), and *The Best American Poetry 2001.*

See also Lesbian Literature, African American

Further Reading

Bryant, Cedric Gael. " 'The Soul has Bandaged Moments' ": Reading the African American Gothic in Wright's "Big Boy Leaves Home," Morrison's *Beloved,* and Gomez's *Gilda. African American Review* 39, no. 4 (2006): 541–53.

Gomez, Jewelle. www.jewellegomez.com (accessed December 9, 2007).

Hall, Lynda. "Passion(ate) Plays 'Wherever We Found Space.' " *Callaloo* 23, no. 1 (2000): 394.

Palmer, Paulina. *Lesbian Gothic: Transgressive Fictions.* London: Cassell, 1999.

Marlon Rachquel Moore

González, Rigoberto (b. 1970)

Chicano poet, writer of fiction and nonfiction, children's book author, literary critic, and professor of creative writing. The eldest of two sons born to Rigoberto González Carrillo and Avelina Alcalá, Rigoberto González, Jr., was born in Bakersfield, California, on July 18, 1970. His parents were born in Mexico and raised in the small town of Zacapu, Michoacán; they were farmworkers who had little more than a third-grade education. With only a work permit, his father migrated back and forth to the United States to labor in the agricultural fields of Southern California. When his mother became pregnant, they relocated to the United States and worked in the grape fields in the Coachella Valley of California. González's mother, an undocumented immigrant, gave birth to him shortly thereafter and to his brother, Alexandro, two years later.

The family returned to live in Zacapu in 1972. In 1980, they relocated to the United States once again. They lived in a small apartment on top of a garage in Thermal, California. It was while living there and attending John Kelley Elementary that González developed a love for reading and writing.

His mother suffered from a weak heart condition and fragile health overall. Nevertheless, she continued working in the grape fields until she suffered a stroke. After undergoing open-heart surgery, the family returned to Zacapu—she died shortly thereafter, at the age of 31. González was only 12 years old, and his mother's tragic death would affect him deeply for years to come. Death, the absence of parental figures, poverty, and depression would become recurrent themes in his writing, along with themes related to crossing borders, fleeting love, and homoeroticism.

In 1983, his father returned to the Coachella Valley but abandoned his sons to be raised by their grandparents. There, González attended Indio High School until he left for the University of California, Riverside in 1988. He obtained his B.A. in Humanities in 1992, an M.A. in English (Poetry) from the University of California, Davis in 1994, and an M.F.A. in Creative Writing (fiction) from Arizona State University in 1997.

As is evident, González's childhood and young adulthood were far from blissful. He was often chastised for being effeminate and overweight, had a bipolar disorder, fell into deep bouts of depression, and was suicidal. In fact, he was hospitalized and treated for depression on three occasions between 1984 and 2006. His relationship with his father was always tumultuous. His father suffered from alcoholism, depression, and, later, Parkinson's disease, which would eventually lead him to take his own life. González sought affection from other men, but these relationships were also plagued with violence and abuse. All of these experiences have shaped his writing. His work is delicate, beautiful, and melancholic. He gives his readers vibrant portraits of bordered lives and takes them to places that are sometimes unsettling.

González's first book, *So Often the Pitcher Goes to Water until It Breaks* (1999), is a collection of poetry that was selected for the National Poetry Series in 1998. The poems are skillfully crafted vignettes that tell the stories of an array of people who live their lives on the border. His second collection, *Other Fugitives and Other Strangers* (2006), captures the intimacies and conflict that often exist between men who have sex with men. With rich lyricism and imagery, he describes a loving, gentle touch that is simultaneously dangerous and destructive. For González, these two seemingly disparate worlds are one in the same. There can be no love without pain.

Named *ForeWord Magazine*'s Best Book of the Year for Fiction, his first novel—*Crossing Vines* (2003)—is set in the grape fields of the Coachella Valley. Inspired by Tomás Rivera's . . . *y no se lo tragó la tierra* (1971), González pays tribute to Rivera and to all farmworkers by giving his readers a candid look at a day in the life of grape pickers.

His memoir, *Butterfly Boy: Memories of a Chicano Mariposa* (2006), was awarded the American Book Award by the Before Columbus Foundation in 2007. In it, he recalls his first years at college and a bus trip he took with his father to Mexico—a journey that takes him back to his painful childhood. The book is an unguarded look at a time in his life when he was the most vulnerable. As his readers learn about his childhood, they are better able to understand why he tolerates the verbal and physical abuse he suffers at the hands of a male lover who is almost twice his age. Fleeting happiness, lost love, and depression are topics with which González is all too familiar. These themes reemerge in *Men without Bliss* (2008), a collection of 13 short stories of a variety of men who suffer from emotional despair in deep-seated silence.

González has also written bilingual children's books: *Soledad Sigh-Sighs/Soledad Suspiros* (2003) and *Antonio's Card/La Tarjeta de Antonio* (2005). The first centers on how Soledad, a poor inner-city eight-year-old girl, handles coming home after school to an empty house because her parents are still at work. She uses her imagination and scarce resources to overcome her solitude. In the second book, Antonio is the only child of an interracial lesbian couple. As he becomes aware that his family is not like the typical nuclear family, he almost allows **homophobia** to interfere with his happiness. Art becomes his saving grace.

Since 2002, González has also written numerous book reviews for the *El Paso Times*. His column appears twice monthly and reaches thousands of readers. In it, González often highlights books that tend to be ignored by the mainstream press in an attempt to showcase emerging Chicana/o and Latina/o authors while also reviewing the works of established authors.

González is currently a professor of English at Rutgers University and has resided in New York City for several years. He has taught literature and creative writing at several universities and held a number of artist residencies outside of the United States, including Brazil, Switzerland, Scotland, Costa Rica, and Spain.

Besides the American Book Award, he has received a University Award from the Academy of American Poets, the Guggenheim Memorial Foundation Fellowship, and a National Endowment for the Arts Fellowship. He also serves on the Board of Directors for the National Book Critics Circle, is a contributing editor for *Poets and Writers Magazine,* and is on the Advisory Circle of Con Tinta—a collective of Chicana/o and Latina/o activist writers.

Further Reading

Olivas, Daniel. "Interview with Rigoberto González." *La Bloga.* Monday, November 19, 2007. http://labloga.blogspot.com/2007/11/interview-with-rigoberto-gonzlez.html.

Ortiz, Ricardo L. Review of *Butterfly Boy* and *Other Fugitives and Other Strangers. Lambda Book Report* 14, no. 3 (Fall 2006): 38–39.

Pérez, Daniel Enrique. "A Butterfly's Journey across Many Borders." Review of *Butterfly Boy. Chasqui: Revista de literatura latinoamericana* 36, no. 1 (2007): 152–55.

Daniel Enrique Pérez

Gould, Janice (b. 1949)

Poet and scholar whose creative and academic work focuses on issues of voice, identity, and familial and tribal ancestry. Janice Gould was born April 1, 1949, in San Diego, California, to Geoffrey H. Gould and Vivian Beatty. Gould is the second of three sisters born to a first-generation father of British descent and a mother of Koyangk'auwi (Concow Maidu) descent. Early in her childhood, Gould's family moved from San Diego to Berkeley, California, after her father lost his job at a naval laboratory where he helped to develop sonar. Shifting his focus from electronics to optometry, Gould's father attended the University of California (UC) at Berkeley in order to secure a better job. Educated at Julliard and Columbia, her mother taught music out of the home and was an accomplished seamstress and designer in later years.

Gould spent her formative years in her adopted grandmother's house (her orphaned mother was adopted by three white sisters) in the Berkeley hills, where she began to explore and embrace her cultural heritage. A number of family road trips exposed Gould to the landscapes of her northern Californian tribe at a young age. She recounts these travels in the introduction to her second book of poems, *Earthquake Weather: Poems* (1996). This inspirational connection to the land is a subject frequently explored in her work.

Gould was trained as a musician by her mother and continues to play at least six different instruments. Throughout her 20s, Gould performed folk music in coffee shops and self-published poetry. She roamed up and down the West Coast, putting in stints at small colleges and working as a ranch hand, waitress, and cannery worker, among other odd jobs. In her 30s, Gould rededicated herself to her education, transferring from Laney

College in Oakland to UC Berkeley as an affirmative action student. She graduated with high honors and distinction with a degree in linguistics, having completed fieldwork in Fairbanks, Alaska, on an Athapaskan language. Gould holds a B.A. in linguistics and an M.A. in English from UC Berkeley. She earned her Ph.D. in English at the University of New Mexico, with a dissertation focusing on Muscogee poet Joy Harjo. Gould is currently at work on an M.A. at the University of Arizona at Tucson's School of Information Resources and Library Science. She lives in Tuscon with her partner, scholar and writer Marie-Elise Wheatwind.

Among many professional and creative accomplishments, Gould received a National Endowment for the Arts grant in 1988, an Astraea Foundation Emerging Lesbian Writers Fund Award in 1992, and was Hallie Brown Ford Chair in Creative Writing at Willamette University.

Lesbian and feminist magazines such as *Calyx, Fireweed, Ikon,* and *Sinister Wisdom* were early publishers of Gould's work, circulating her poetry to audiences eager for autobiographical reflection on the nature of identity and oppression, politics, and love. Gould's first book of poetry, *Beneath My Heart* (1990), garnered positive critical attention, including a favorable review by well-known lesbian-feminist poet **Adrienne Rich** in *Ms.* magazine. The volume's thematic concerns center on grief and loss, dealing most locally with the death of Gould's mother and more broadly with cultural loss endemic to Native American life. Gould published both *Alphabet* (chapbook) and *Earthquake Weather: Poems* in 1996. *Earthquake Weather* consists of meditations on social identities and political change most often observed in the theater of personal interaction. Aside from cultural and identity politics, love poems represent a second significant preoccupation of Gould's poetic oeuvre. Her love poems are trademarked by the interplay of dualisms that love ignites in the intimate confrontation between self and other: alienation and connection, the spiritual and intellectual, and independence and mutuality. Taken together, Gould's poems testify to a lifetime of lovers and friendships, immortalizing these concurrent loves and struggles within a landscape of political upheaval, cultural colonization, and personal oppression.

Because of the encompassing scope of her work, Gould has been anthologized in several contexts, including a number of regional anthologies that spotlight work out of California. Gould is also co-editor with Dean Rader of the critical anthology *Speak to Me Words: Essays in American Indian Poetry* (2003) and has published widely in academic books and journals. Ultimately, Gould's scholarly and creative works offer thought-provoking commentary on ties between Native American and LGBTQ experience, drawing correlations between tribal and lesbian themes and rendering the search for spiritual, cultural, and sexual fulfillment in candid, yet lyrical verse.

Further Reading

Wheatwind, Marie-Elise. "Janice Gould." In *Contemporary Lesbian Writers of the United States: A Bio-Biographical Critical Sourcebook,* edited by Sandra Pollack and Denise D. Knight, 224–29. Westport, CT: Greenwood Press, 1993.

Emma Crandall

Grae, Camarin (b. 1941)

Writer of popular lesbian mystery, adventure, and science fiction novels. Because Camarin Grae chose to write under a *nom de plume* to separate her professional career from her lesbian identity as a novelist, little has been written about her private life. It is known that she was born on October 23, 1941, that she completed her public school education in 1959 in Chicago where she has lived most of her life, and that she was once married to a man with whom she has a daughter. The 10-year marriage ended when she came out as a lesbian; she lost her custody battle for her daughter because of her lifestyle, although she did not lose her relationship with her daughter.

Grae continued on with her education. She received her B.A. in 1968 from Roosevelt University in Chicago and began working on her M.A. in Clinical Psychology, which she received in 1971. She stayed on to complete her doctorate in 1974 and obtained a position as a staff psychologist at a Chicago university shortly thereafter. On campus, she is active in feminist groups and helped to establish the Women's Center. She is also active in the professional organizations in her discipline.

In addition to professional disciplinary activities, Grae writes lesbian fiction under her *nom de plume.* Her love of writing is intense; she has noted elsewhere that the enjoyment she gets from writing may actually be unhealthy (see Kate Burns). She began writing novels 10 years before she attempted publication and currently has eight novels to her credit. The works for which Grae has received the most critical acclaim are *The Secret in the Bird* (1988), which was nominated for the Lesbian Fiction Award for the first annual Lambda Literary Awards in 1989, and in 1991, *Slick* (1990), which received the nomination for the category of Lesbian Mystery novel. Given her professional leanings, it is not surprising that Grae's novels have a psychological edge. Themes in her work include the search for self, encompassing the search for a lesbian identity; power in relationships, often with sadomasochistic overtones; and the search for and workings of community and utopias. *The Secret in the Bird* revolves around all three of these themes as the protagonist, Rena, searches for herself and for a more stable relationship and harmony in her life. Rena is drawn to fantasies of being dominated and to domineering lovers—until she meets Lou, who helps her work through her dependency by helping her understand her need to kill and dissect birds. (The theme of a power imbalance in relationships, particularly with a strong sadomasochistic tone can also be found in Grae's earlier novel *The Winged Dancer* (1983)—an imbalance that was also resolved by the end of the novel.) Lou's utopian community, while imperfect with its dissenting members, is still a good place for Rena. Feminist utopias are a popular subject for Grae, who also includes them in *Paz* (1984), *Edgewise* (1989), *Slick* (1990), and *Stranded* (1991).

Slick is also a detective story in addition to being a novel about utopia. Characters from Grae's other novels reappear at a conference on feminist utopia communities. The Winged Dancer statue (from the novel of that name) on display at the conference as a symbol of what the women are trying to achieve is stolen, and a threatening message is left in its place. The protagonists must find it amid discussions of feminist community versus exploitative institutions.

Although Grae has been reviewed in mainstream venues and has been widely read by the gay/lesbian community and by the mainstream science fiction community, there is little if any serious critical attention. Her considerable work deserves greater academic attention.

Further Reading

Burns, Kate. "Camarin Grae." In *Contemporary Lesbian Writers of the United States: A Bio-Bibliographical Critical Sourcebook,* edited by Sandra Pollack and Denise D. Knight, 230–36. Westport, CT: Greenwood, 1993.

Reginald, Robert. *Science Fiction and Fantasy Literature, 1975–1991*. Detroit: Gale Research, 1992.
Sturgis, Susanna. "Women's Worlds." *Women's Review of Books* 3, no. 9 (June 1986): 13.

Althea E. Rhodes

Grahn, Judy (b. 1940)

Judy Grahn is a poet, writer, and social theorist. Her work has been formative to a variety of political and social movements in the second half of the twentieth century, including lesbian feminism, **gay** and lesbian studies, and women's spirituality.

Judy Grahn was born in Chicago, Illinois, on July 28, 1940. She grew up in New Mexico and at the age of 18 enlisted in the U.S. Army. At the age of 21, she was dishonorably discharged from the army for homosexuality. Interested in learning more about "who I might be, what others thought of me, who my peers were and hand been" (*Another Mother Tongue* xi), Grahn went to a library in Washington, D.C., to research homosexuality. There, she was told by the librarian that those books were locked away. This began Grahn's lifelong quest to make information, history, ideas, and opinions about homosexuality and lesbians widely available.

In 1963, Grahn picketed the White House to increase visibility of gay and lesbian people. A total of 15 people participated in this action organized by the Mattachine Society; three of them, including Grahn, were women. In 1964, using a pseudonym, Grahn published an article in *Sexology Magazine* saying that lesbians were normal, ordinary people. In 1965, Grahn wrote "The Psychoanalysis of Edward the Dyke," an angry satire about the ways that psychologists regarded lesbians and gay men. This poem would be the title poem of her first collection, published six years later. In the interim, Grahn published a few poems again using a pseudonym in the lesbian periodical published by the Daughters of Bilitis, *The Ladder*. By 1969, she was frustrated with the lack of publishing outlets available for her work and meeting other writers and activists in the San Francisco Bay area. With a mimeograph machine, Grahn began publishing her own work. With a group of women, she founded the Gay Women's Liberation Collective in 1969.

The Gay Women's Liberation Collective became one of the most influential West Coast organizations in the lesbian-feminist movement and the lesbian print movement. The collective founded a women's bookstore, called A Woman's Place in Oakland, California, which operated until the late 1980s. The collective also founded the Women's Press Collective, a publisher that operated until 1978. Women's Press Collective published many of Grahn's early chapbooks and poetry collections including *Edward the Dyke and Other Poems* (1971), *Elephant Poem Coloring Book* (1972), *The Common Woman,* (1973), and *A Woman Is Talking to Death* (1974). These early books were published as small print-run chapbooks. They were distributed by Grahn through readings and through women's bookstores around the country. The Women's Press Collective, Judy Grahn's involvement in it, and her poetry represent the spirit and practice of the feminist poetry movement during the 1970s. At this time, women and poets took control of the means of production and wrote, produced, and promoted their own work through small presses in which they were intimately involved in all aspects of the publishing.

Judy Grahn's poetry is plainspoken and grounded in the world of women in general and of lesbians in particular. Her work is also highly aural; she uses anaphora extensively, and much of her work can be appreciated best by reading it and also by hearing it. Grahn is a keen observer of how women live their lives. She writes about children, family, domestic scenes, but not to the exclusion of women's working lives. Grahn writes with compelling urgency about work, including the labor of secretaries, electricians, waitresses, and pipe fitters. Above all, Grahn infuses her work with humanity and a sharp, honest humor.

After the Women's Press Collective was closed in 1978, in part because of vandalism, Diana Press was created by Grahn and others from the remnants of the Women's Press Collective. Diana Press published Grahn's poetry as well, including *She Who: A Graphic Book of Poems with 54 Images of Women* and a new version of *A Woman Is Talking to Death*. Diana Press also published two volumes of short stories edited by Grahn titled *True to Life Adventure Stories volumes 1 and 2*. Grahn's subsequent books of poetry, *The Queen of Wands* and *The Queen of Swords*, were published during the 1980s by larger and more mainstream publishing houses that had developed an interest in lesbian and feminist work as a result of the demonstrated audience that writers and poets had created for their work.

In 1984, Grahn published *Another Mother Tongue*. *Another Mother Tongue* is a highly creative an imaginative account of gay and lesbian culture and history. Told in a personal and authoritative voice, *Another Mother Tongue* synthesizes Grahn's historical research and contemporary narrative accounts of gay and lesbian life throughout history. A year later, in 1985, Grahn published *The Highest Apple: Sappho and the Lesbian Poetic Tradition* with the San Francisco–based independent, feminist publisher Spinsters Ink. *The Highest Apple* provides a similarly styled history from Grahn's research in the history and literature of the Sapphic tradition. These two books establish the significance of Grahn's writing and thinking as a social theorist for the feminist and gay and lesbian movements.

Grahn published an anthology of Gertrude Stein's work, titled *Really Reading Gertrude Stein*, including her critical essays about Stein in 1989. This anthology made Stein more available to contemporary lesbian readers. Grahn has also published a novel, *Mundane's World* (1989), a feminist, ecological utopia set in an imagined prehistoric world. More recently, Grahn has been developing and teaching about her "metaformic" philosophy. This philosophy, rooted in her fiction and her research for *Another Mother Tongue*, was first articulated in Grahn's 1993 book, *Blood, Bread and Roses: How Menstruation Created the World*. In this book, Grahn reconceptualizes human history to place women at the center and explore ways to realign the values, ideologies, and beliefs shaping our world. Grahn continues this work in the online journal that she co-edits with Deborah J. Grenn, *Metaformia: A Journal of Menstruation and Culture*. The journal is available online at www.Metaformia.org.

Judy Grahn's work has received many awards and recognitions. She has won a National Endowment for the Arts grant, an American Book Review Award, an American Book Award from the Before Columbus Foundation in 1983, an American Library Award, a Lifetime Achievement Award (in Lesbian Letters), and a Founding Foremothers of Women's Spirituality Award. Triangle Publishers, a GLBTQ association of people working in publishing, features a "Judy Grahn Nonfiction Award" annually.

Grahn has appeared in two featured films: *Stolen Moments* (1997) about three centuries of gay life and *Last Call at Maud's* (1993) about a lesbian bar in San Francisco closing after operating since the 1940s. Whether studying history or participating in it, Grahn is often turned to as an expert on gay and lesbian experience. Throughout her writing career, Grahn has collaborated with a variety of artists, musicians, and dancers, and she has inspired many artists as well including Ani DiFranco. Grahn has taught extensively on feminism, gay and lesbian history and culture, and women's spirituality at colleges and universities in the San Francisco Bay area. Currently, she serves as Research Faculty for the Institute of Transpersonal Psychology in Palo Alto, California.

Further Reading

Backus, Margot Gayle. "Judy Grahn and the Lesbian Invocational Elegy: Testimonial and Prophetic Responses." *Signs: Journal of Women in Culture & Society* 18, no. 4 (Summer 1993): 815–37.

Henneberg, Sylvia B. "When Helen Awakens: Revisionary Myth in Judy Grahn's *The Queen of Wands*." *Women's Studies* 29, no. 3 (June 2000): 285–308.

Julie R. Enszer

Graphic Novel, Gay

Gay graphic novel is a recently emerged genre that describes narratives that deploy the visual layout and narrative conventions of the traditional comic book to explore the subculture and subjectivity of the gay male.

Although there is no standardized definition to describe the graphic novel, industry conventions and a review of published works suggest the following understanding: the term graphic novel suggests a unified story arc with a distinct beginning, middle, and end (as opposed to an episodic ongoing narrative), a storyline that falls outside the usual comic book genres, and a narrative trajectory that explores a mature theme and appeals to a mature audience. As such, the graphic novel can be understood as a self-contained narrative with a comic book layout in a single binding that sustains its narrative for at least 64 pages. Any such narrative that earnestly and significantly incorporates gay male characters and themes would further frame the understanding for the gay graphic novel. Using this definition, it is not until the 1995 publication of Howard Cruse's *Stuck Rubber Baby* that we can begin to discuss the gay graphic novel, for before Cruse's novel, gay visibility had itself only recently begun to appear in comics.

The comic industry's resistance to gays dates back to at least 1954 when the Comics Code Authority, a mandate from the Comics Magazine Association of America, was formed to regulate appropriate content for comic books. The Comics Code specifically prohibited alternative sexualities until it revised its policies in 1989 to allow for the non-stereotyped portrayal of gay and lesbian characters. This ban ensured the retardation of gay-themed comics, but it did not prevent Tom of Finland from passing his homoerotic drawings privately among his friends, and so gays in comics became an underground concern. Since the 1969 **Stonewall Riots**, gays started to fight for and achieve more visibility in comics. However, most of these successes were achieved in the gay publishing world and not in the mainstream comics publishing houses such as DC or Marvel. Nonetheless, in the post-Stonewall era, gay comics began to appear. Rick Fiala's work appeared in the revered gay magazine *Christopher Street*. Jerry Mill's "Poppers" began to appear in *In Touch*, and throughout the 1980s, Howard Cruse's comic strip "Wendel" appeared in *The Advocate*. This success eventually led to the annual publication of *Gay Comics*, which debuted in 1980 and ran for 25 issues until the early 1990s. This history goes a long way toward explaining why the gay graphic novel did not emerge until the end of the twentieth century.

Howard Cruse's *Stuck Rubber Baby* was originally published in 1995, and it was reprinted in 2000. *Stuck Rubber Baby* is a 210-page graphic novel that took some four years to produce, and it has won both the Wil Eisner and the Harvey comic industry awards. *Stuck Rubber Baby* narrates the story of a young white man's coming out, but it sets its coming out narrative against the turbulent context of the 1960s American Civil Rights Movement and the emergence of the feminist sensibility. Cruse's graphic novel serves as a productive model for the consideration of the gay graphic novel. Regarding content and structure, Cruse's novel successfully marries its visual narrative with an innovative and meritorious fictionalized autobiographical narrative that rises to the standard of a literary work. In some ways, this observation may be the most effective determinant for delineating the differences between the trade paperback comic and the original graphic novel. Cruse's work is decidedly the latter.

Since *Stuck Rubber Baby,* other gay graphic novels have appeared. One significant title is David Wojnarowicz and James Romberger's *Seven Miles a Second* (1996). This 64-page graphic novel serves as part of a trilogy of Wojnarowicz's autobiographical works, and it explores his time as an adolesent homeless hustler in New York City. Another recent title is Abby Densons's Shounen-ai manga inspired *Tough Love: High School Confidential* (2006), a young adult–aimed graphic novel about coming out. Interestingly, Denson's novel may show something of the future for the genre as American publishers become increasingly interested in merging the popular Japanese manga genre Yaoi with the post-Stonewall spirit of gay liberation.

Further Reading

Mccloud, Scott. *Understanding Comics: The Invisible Art.* New York: Harper, 1994.
Theophano, Teresa. "Comic Strips and Cartoons." glbtq, Inc. August 2005. www.glbtq.com.
Triptow, Robert, ed. *Gay Comics.* New York: Plume, 1989.

Mark John Isola

Graphic Novel, Lesbian

Historically, most comic strips and graphic novels have been created by heterosexual white male artists for a predominantly male audience. The term "graphic novel" was coined by male cartoonist Will Eisner in 1971, in the attempt to publish a comic book that would be as long as a novel. Prior to this date, comics had existed in the United States since 1827, appearing in various formats, from humorous one panel vignettes, episodic multipanel strips in newspapers or magazines, or cheaply printed booklets known as "comic books."

The Great Depression and World War II gave birth to comic book superheroes, as well as the first strong female characters in comics. In 1941, psychologist William Moulton Marston and comic book entrepreneur Max Gaines invented *Wonder Woman,* originally named "Diana the Amazon Queen," to open the comic book market to girls as well as to provide a strong female role model for them. Unlike other comic book heroes of the era, Wonder Woman single-handedly fought diabolical male and female villains and encouraged her female readers to exercise and stand up for themselves. Although Wonder Woman eventually fell in love with a male American intelligence officer, she had two "mommies"—the virgin Amazon queen Hippolyta and the goddess Aphrodite—as well as a series of female friends. Compared to male heroes Superman and Batman, who took a year before they could have their own comic books, Wonder Woman had such a rave following that her strip became a comic book in less than six months, and she remains a popular DC Comics superhero to this day.

In his book *Seduction of the Innocent* (1954), psychiatrist Frederic Wertham accused Wonder Woman of being a lesbian for her strength and independence and said that she was an extremely frightening image for boys. Wertham's general criticism of comic books as too violent, sexual, and perverse for children led to the formation of the Comics Code Authority (CCA) as part of the Comics Magazine Association of America (CMAA). The CCA regulated and censored any type of explicit or perceived violence, glorification of criminals, or "sexual perversion" in comic books. Crime and horror comics took a back seat to comics that depicted clean-cut American teenagers (such as *Archie* and *Katy Keene*) or mischievous little girls (such as *Little Lulu,* who continually attempted to crash the boy's club). Female teenage characters of 1950s romance comics primarily focused on beautifying themselves and finding male partners. Rarely did two attractive women share a friendship in 1950s romance comics; usually a shapely female was paired with a dumpy, nonthreatening sidekick who provided comic relief and undying loyalty through the female's single period. Attractive women rarely stayed friends, as they saw each other as competition for the desired male partner. The majority of these straight-laced comics were written by men, who may have been unaware that, during the 1950s, girls outnumbered boys as readers of comic books.

Lesbian-specific graphic novels arose from the underground comix movement (spelled "comix" to distinguish them from "comics" approved by the CCA), as well as the feminist and civil rights movements. In 1970, 10 female cartoonists including Trina Robbins gathered in San Francisco to form the Wimmen's Comix Collective, which published *Wimmen's Comix* anthologies that addressed political, cultural, and social issues specific to single working women. The collective remained too heterosexual for lesbian comic book artist Mary Wings, who published *Come Out Comix* (1972) and *Dyke Shorts* (1976). In 1980, gay cartoonist Howard Cruse established *Gay Comix,* providing a forum for lesbian cartoonists such as Jennifer Camper, Joan Hilty, and Cheela Smith.

Ironically, one of the most popular graphic novels series to feature lesbian characters was invented by men. In 1981, the Hernandez brothers Gilbert, Jaime, and Mario (also known as "Los Bros") self-published their first issue of *Love and Rockets.* The series includes several serial narratives, the most well-known being *Hoppers 13* (*Locas Stories*), which involves the ongoing love affair of Margarita Luisa "Maggie" Chascarrillo and Esperanza "Hopey" Leticia Glass, two Chicano girls from Oxnard, California, who come of age during the punk movement. This series is still published by Fantagraphics Books.

The "coming out" of gay comix, along with the burgeoning LGBTQ rights movement and Riot Grrrl Movement, paved the way for two of the most prolific lesbian comic book artists: **Alison Bechdel** (*The Essential Dykes to Watch Out For* and *Fun Home*) and Diane DiMassa (*Hothead Paisan: Homocidal Lesbian Terrorist*). While Bechdel is famous for her realistic portrayal of American lesbians and their concerns, DiMassa provides a cathartic release through Hothead Paisan's one woman rage against **homophobia** and the patriarchy, as well as the adventures of her lesbian fez-wearing cat Chicken. Up and coming lesbian cartoonists Carrie McNinch (*The Assassin & the Whiner*) and Erika Moen have both been influenced by their work.

As girls continue to outnumber boys in the consumption of graphic novels and comics, it is predicted that the number of lesbian cartoonists, as well as visibility of lesbian characters in graphic novels, will increase. In the meantime, nonprofit organization Friends of Lulu, established in 1994, continues to promote and encourage female involvement in the comic book industry.

Further Reading

Greyson, Devon. "GLBTQ Content in Comics/Graphic Novels for Teens." *Collection Building* 26, no. 4 (2007): 130–34.

Robbins, Trina. *From Girls to Grrrlz: A History of Women's Comics from Teens to Zines*. San Francisco: Chronicle Books, 1999.

———. *The Great Women Superheroes*. Northampton, MA: Kitchen Sink Press, 1996.

Weiner, Stephen. *Faster than a Speeding Bullet: The Rise of the Graphic Novel*. New York: Nantier Beal Minoustchine Publishing, Inc., 2003.

Rachel Wexelbaum

Graphic Novel, Transgender

Graphic novels are a type of comic book that usually has a traditional story arc and explores mature themes. They are typically bound in a more traditional book form that is more durable than regular comic books. The combination of text and drawings/graphics is a very popular form with a long history of devoted readership.

Although some graphic novels are comedic, many explore serious social themes. Graphic novels such as *Maus: A Survivor's Tale* by Art Spiegelman, which explores the Holocaust, and *Stuck Rubber Baby,* by Howard Cruse, which explores homosexuality and racism in the 1960s South, are part of a tradition of graphic novels to take on pressing cultural issues. Transgender themes have been featured in graphic novel of various types, including science fiction and more "realistic" texts.

One of the best-known graphic novelists, Neil Gaiman, featured a sympathetic portrait of a transsexual woman named Wanda in his *A Game of You* (which collects *The Sandman* #32–#37, 1991–1992). The character is best friends with Barbie and dies in a storm, only to be buried as a man by her parents and given a gravestone with her male name. Barbie crosses this out with lipstick and writes "Wanda" on the gravestone.

The Invisibles by Scottish writer Grant Morrison is a series of comic books that was collected into graphic novels. It also featured a transgender character. The books follow a group of people battling against oppression using a variety of tactics. One of the members is Lord Fanny. Lord Fanny is a transgender, Brazilian shaman who is instrumental in helping The Invisibles fight against the evil forces of oppression.

How Loathsome by Ted Naifeh and Tristan Crane is a truly important text in the small but growing graphic novel canon that features transgender characters. *How Loathsome* enters the gender and sexual underground of contemporary San Francisco. It features four chapters that explore cutting-edge identities and expressions that challenge hegemonic constructions of **gender** and sexuality. The main character is Catherine, a writer who falls in love with a trans woman named Chloe. Other characters include a male prostitute and a female-to-male-spectrum character. All of the characters eschew simplistic labels and are pioneers as they explore new possibilities for human expression.

A recent graphic novel geared toward youth is entitled *No Girls Allowed: Tales of Daring Women Dressed as Men for Love, Freedom and Adventure* by Susan Hughes and Willow Dawson. The book features text and illustration to transport young readers throughout history in order to illuminate the stories of various female-bodied people who lived and passed as men.

Transgender themes in graphic novels and comic books are also an international phenomenon. In particular, Japanese comics, known as manga, frequently feature themes of transgender and gender transformation. Manga artists known for exploring transgender themes include Takako Shimura and Emura and Taeko Watanabe. Chiyo Rokuhana has written a series of manga about the experiences of intersexed people.

Further Reading

Gravett, Paul. *Graphic Novels: Everything You Need to Know.* New York: Collins Design, 2005.

Joelle Ruby Ryan

Griffin, Susan (b. 1943)

Lesbian feminist poet, essayist, philosopher, and dramatist. Griffin was born on January 26, 1943, in Los Angeles, California, the second daughter of Sarah (Colvin) Griffin and Walden Griffin. When her parents divorced, Griffin lived alternately with her mother, father, and grandmother. After attending the University of California at Berkeley from 1960 to 1963, she graduated with a B.A. in English Literature and Ceative Writing from San Francisco State University in 1965. In 1966, Griffin married John Levy, whom she divorced in 1970; their daughter was born in 1968. After receiving her M.A. in English/ Creative Writing from San Francisco State in 1972, she taught English there (1974– 1975) and at Berkeley (1973–1975). She has continued to live in the San Francisco Bay Area, writing, lecturing, and teaching in workshops.

In *Made from This Earth: An Anthology of Writings* (1982), Griffin describes her evolving political consciousness, which was decisively shaped by the anti-Vietnam War, civil rights, and feminist movements, leading to her radical questioning of oppression and patriarchal authority. She also addresses the **closet**edness of **lesbianism**, since only after her marriage Griffin began to identify as a lesbian.

Her most famous nonfictional work *Woman and Nature: The Roaring inside Her* (1978) is a collage that dissolves genre distinctions and has decisively influenced the feminist movement by its depiction of women's role as earth nurturers versus men's role as destructors of nature and as makers of weapons. Throughout the 1980s and 1990s, Griffin has addressed many controversial topics, such as pornography, rape, and violence. All of her books are hybrid in genre, combining a lyrical prose with thorough academic analysis. *Rape: The Power of Consciousness* (1979) became a groundbreaking text for the antirape and women's shelter movements. Throughout the text, Griffin argues that rape, pornography, and the oppression of women are intertwined with racism, poverty, and the destruction of nature. In *Pornography and Silence: Culture's Revenge against Nature* (1981), Griffin elaborates on these subjects when she argues that pornography results from a fundamental fear of the natural body. After publishing *What Her Body Thought: A Journey into the Shadows* (1999), a book dealing with her own life with Chronic Fatigue Immune Deficiency Syndrome, Griffin wrote *The Book of the Courtesans: A Catalogue of Their Virtues*

(2001), where she presents the biographies of women who decisively influenced politics and culture.

In her play *Voices* (1975), for which she received an Emmy Award, as in her poetry, the search for a female identity and its expression in language is a central concern. The collection *Bending Home: Selected New Poems, 1967–1998* (1998) comprises more than 30 years of Griffin's career as a poet, which is yet to receive the scholarly and critical attention it deserves.

Further Reading

Adams, Barbara. "Susan Griffin (1943–)." In *Contemporary Lesbian Writers of the United States: A Bio-Bibliographical Critical Sourcebook,* edited by Sandra Pollack and Denise D. Knight, 244–51. Westport, CT: Greenwood Press, 1993.

Shima, Alan. *Skirting the Subject: Pursuing Language in the Works of Adrienne Rich, Susan Griffin, and Beverly Dahlen.* Uppsala, Sweden: Uppsala University Press, 1993.

Miriam Wallraven

Grimsley, Jim (b. 1955)

Southern playwright, novelist, and creative writing professor. Born September 21, 1955, dirt poor into a household riddled with alcoholism and abuse, Jim Grimsley never expected to live to see 30. As a hemophiliac in the 1950s and 1960s, he knew that he never had time to count on. During his childhood, he was a voracious reader who escaped into the world of comic books and adventure stories just to survive. At age eight, Grimsley began to write children's stories and fantasy material. His intelligence and perseverance enabled him to attend the prestigious University of North Carolina at Chapel Hill, where he studied with Doris Betts and Max Steele, which put him in the company of some of the most successful southern writers. In the past 20 years, Grimsley has earned his place in that pantheon.

After a brief stint in New Orleans, Grimsley settled in Atlanta, where he worked a desk job at Grady Hospital for almost two decades and wrote all the time. Grimsley's autobiographical first novel *Winter Birds* (1994) beautifully renders the story of the precariousness and vulnerability of his youth—and the level of violence and deprivation of his childhood. For 10 years, the manuscript was rejected by publishers as too dark and too grim, so he turned his attention to his other passion: playwrighting. In 1988, he became playwright in residence at Atlanta's 7 Stages, an avant-garde theater in the Little Five Points arts district. Four of Grimsley's plays have been published in *Mr. Universe: & Other Plays* (1998). It was through this theatrical connection that the manuscript of *Winter Birds* reached an enterprising German publisher, who finally put the book into print in 1992. It was subsequently published in French and was successful throughout Europe before eventually being published in the United States by Algonquin Books of Chapel Hill.

The novel is told in second-person narrative, as the adult Dan Crell tells his younger self the story of his survival. Stunning in its detail, *Winter Birds* takes its readers into a world of violence and deprivation on an almost dehumanizing scale. *Winter Birds* won the Sue Kaufman Prize for First Fiction and was a runner-up for the PEN/Hemingway Award.

Partly as a result of the circuitous journey of his first book, Grimsley was able to publish subsequent novels in short order. His novel of **gay** adolescent love and heartbreak, *Dream*

Boy (1995), won the American Library Association GLBTQ Fiction Award and has been made into a film by writer/director James Bolton. In this novel, Grimsley's immersion in southern Christian culture saturates a tale of sex, violence, death, and resurrection.

My Drowning (1997), which showcases some of Grimsley's most poetic, sophisticated writing, tells the story of Ellen Crell, Danny's mother. As a companion piece to *Winter Birds, My Drowning* shows the destructiveness of generations of the meanness of profound poverty. One fact readers learn from Grimsley's work is that the story of the poor is not just about having less material wealth than middle-class people. Few other writers—**Dorothy Allison**, **Sapphire**, and William Faulkner—have captured this stark reality.

The story of Dan Crell continues in *Comfort and Joy* (1999), in which the 30-year-old Dan and his lover Ford go to Ford's family's Christmas in the upscale world of Savannah. The novel addresses a couple dealing with HIV and other complications of a gay relationship, including family drama and marked social class differences.

Grimsley continues to write, teach, and thrive. He joined the Creative Writing faculty at Emory University in 1999, a move that underscored the wide-ranging talent and success he found in the 1990s. In recent years, he has continued to write plays and publish fiction, returning to the New Orleans of the late 1970s for his novel *Boulevard* (2002) and commenting on the world of media stardom, "infotainment," and delusions of fame and grandeur in the darkly satirical novel *Forgiveness* (2007). In addition to more than a dozen plays, Grimsley has written several award-winning science fiction/fantasy novels, including the Lambda Literary Award–winning *Kirith Kirin* (2000) and *The Ordinary* (2004). Throughout his work, there is a consistent intelligence, candor, and precision as Grimsley depicts a world in which the vulnerable suffer, where love cannot protect them, but still they survive, somehow intact.

Further Reading

Hermes, Richard. "The Ability to Imagine." *Emory Magazine* (Fall 1999). http://www.emory.edu /EMORY_MAGAZINE/fall99/grimsley.html.

Howorth, Lisa. "Jim Grimsley: Tales of Southern Courage." *Publishers Weekly* (November 15, 1999): 39–40.

Ricketts, Wendell. "Grimsley, Jim." www.glbtq.com/literature/grimsley_j.html.

Chris Freeman

Grumbach, Doris (b. 1918)

American novelist, memoirist, literary critic, and educator. Doris Grumbach was born in New York City to Leonard and Helen Isaac, is a Phi Beta Kappa graduate of New York University, and holds a master's degree in literature from Cornell University (1940). She was married to Leonard Grumbach for 30 years; the marriage produced four daughters. During World War II, Grumbach served in the United States Navy as part of the WAVES (Women Accepted for Volunteer Emergency Service). After her marriage ended in 1971, Grumbach served, among other notable positions, as literary editor at *The New Republic,* on the faculty of American University, and as a columnist for *The New York Review of Books.* She and her partner, Sybil Pike, relocated from Washington, D.C., to coastal Maine in the late 1980s. Grumbach is the author of roughly 20 novels and memoirs and a host of reviews and literary columns.

Grumbach's first novel, *The Spoil of the Flowers* (1962), was quickly followed by *The Sore Throat, The Tender Mouth* (1964), but it was *Chamber Music* (1979) that brought her recognition as a novelist. Though it is difficult to characterize her as a lesbian novelist, much of Grumbach's work deals with issues of sexuality. In *Chamber Music,* aged Caroline Mclaren looks back over her long life, richly evoking the life of a woman who sacrificed her own needs and passions for the career of a gifted husband. To a certain degree the novel has an autobiographical element because after the death of her husband Mclaren enters into a passionate relationship with the woman who nursed her dying husband and the two found an artists' colony, very much similar to Grumbach's own late-in-life relationship with partner Sybil Pike. There is also a suggestion that *Chamber Music* is based on the life of Marian McDowell, wife of composer Edward McDowell. Such biographical and autobiographical elements infuse much of Grumbach's work as she often uses real-life personages as the bases for her fiction: Marilyn Monroe in *The Missing Person* (1981) and Sylvia Plath in *The Magician's Girl* (1987), for example. *The Ladies* (1984) is Grumbach's fictionalized account of Eleanor Butler and Sarah Ponsonby, two Welsh women who lived together in a small village for over 50 years. Although not explicitly lesbian in the novel, Grumbach's delicately literary suggestion of such a relationship between the two women is characteristic of Grumbach's fiction as a whole in which ambiguity and subtlety are not evasive but evocative. Beginning in the 1990s, Grumbach began publishing memoirs in various forms. *Coming into the End Zone* (1991) is a prolonged meditation on the nature of aging and death, admittedly influenced by her own milestone 70th birthday and the loss of a number of friends, many due to AIDS. *End Zone* is notable for its decidedly unoptimistic approach to aging. *Extra Innings* (1993), Grumbach's second memoir, appears to have been published in response to the criticism of *End Zone,* though it, too, is frankly honest about the vagaries of age and of being a woman writer. In both memoirs, Grumbach blends memories with daily life, confronting missed opportunities and railing against the limitation of an aging body. The brute honesty with which Grumbach refuses to romanticize life is characteristic of her nonfiction work. In *Fifty Days of Solitude* (1995), Grumbach spends 50 days entirely alone in the woods of Maine while her partner is away. As daily life takes on nearly religious status in the absence of other people, Grumbach evokes both the stillness and the storminess that seem to reside in all humans. Similarly, in *The Presence of Absence: On Prayers and an Epiphany* (1998), Grumbach reflects on the nature of God and her own struggles with religion. What makes *Presence* so evocative is that it is almost hostile, not the sort of gently reflective book that the title would suggest. Grumbach rages against a physical ailment, wonders at the travails of other seekers, and emerges by noting that perhaps prayer is a state of mind rather than an action.

Though Grumbach has a large and loyal audience, her work suffers at the hands of many critics who find it too polite and too leery of offending. She is often criticized for not writing explicitly about issues of sexuality, but it is perhaps this exact quality that makes her work of such interest, especially to **queer** readers. The characters in her novels and the self she presents in her memoirs are self-reflective, but they are also cognizant of privilege and social limitation. This seems to speak to queer readers, most especially but not exclusively lesbians, eager to have their sexualities represented creatively but also matter of factly.

Further Reading

Grumbach, Doris. "Interview with Wendy Smith." *Publishers Weekly* 238, no. 40 (September 6, 1991): 84–85.

Waxman, Barbara Frey. "Nature, Spirituality, and Later Life in Literature: An Essay on the Romanticism of Older Writers." *The Gerontologist* 39, no. 5 (October 1999): 516–24.

Milton W. Wendland

Grumley, Michael (1942–1988)

American writer and artist. Michael Grumley was born and raised in Iowa and attended the University of Denver, the City College of New York, and the University of Iowa Writers' Workshop. Grumley was at the Workshop from September 1965 through May 1967, where he studied with Kurt Vonnegut and met fellow writers **Robert Ferro** and **Andrew Holleran**; Ferro and Grumley became lovers and lifelong companions. Through their relationship and continued correspondence with Holleran, Grumley and Ferro helped to start the **Violet Quill Club**, a **gay** writers club, in New York City in the late 1970s and early 1980s. There, Grumley, Ferro, and Holleran met with **Edmund White**, **George Whitmore**, **Christopher Cox**, and **Felice Picano** to discuss and to review the group's original writings. Throughout these years, Ferro and Grumley established a stable relationship, exploring interior design, New Age mysticism, and travel, especially to Italy, where they went regularly and where Grumley appeared in a number of films; all of these shared themes appear in their writing. Grumley died in New York of AIDS-related complications in April 1988 at the age of 46.

Grumley is best known for his work published in the 1970s. *Atlantis: The Autobiography of a Search* was co-written with Robert Ferro and published in 1970. Here, Ferro and Grumley give an account of what they claim is their discovery of the lost city of Atlantis off the coast of Florida. At the same time, the text follows the familiar trope of the American writer abroad; the book, in fact, opens as Grumley waits to hear about a possible supporting role in a film being shot in Italy; most of the narrative occurs, not in the vicinity of Atlantis, but instead in the Europe explored by Ferro and Grumley during the late 1960s. While lacking any explicit reference to their long-term relationship, *Atlantis* nonetheless chronicles Grumley and Ferro's companionable search for the legendary city toward which they claimed a specific destiny. Ironically, the focus of this search, Atlantis itself, occupies only the last dozen or so pages of the book. *There Are Giants in the Earth* (1975) continues the mythic emphasis explored in *Atlantis,* though here Grumley steps out on his own to explore the lives of legendary hominoid creatures such as Bigfoot, creatures whose existences may be doubtful but that indicate experience outside the mainstream.

This interest in the marginal continues in Grumley's *After Midnight* (1977), a series of sketches of people who work the night shift. From nighttime radio show hosts to struggling actresses to graveyard shift waitresses, *After Midnight* explores the overlapping discourses of **gender**, sexuality, and economics as they play out through both straight and same-sex relationships in a class of people who work while most of the world sleeps. Following this marginalized thematic, *Hard Corps: Studies in Leather & Sadomasochism* (1977) explores the world of leather and sadist/masochist relationships through a focus on the experience of male sexuality, broadly understood. Here, Grumley refuses to divide the men in his book into straight and gay groupings, thus producing an exploration of power and pleasure, without an emphasis on identity politics.

Most of Grumley's work was published before the Violet Quill met in the early 1980s, following which he wrote a column entitled "Uptown" for the *New York Native,* but did not publish another book until the posthumous appearance of *Life Drawing* (1991). This lyrical autobiographical novel represents his only extended fictional text; it emerged only after Ferro's extensive revisions. *Life Drawing,* set in the late 1950s, follows a 17-year-old boy named Mikey who travels down the Mississippi River from small-town Iowa to New Orleans, encountering an 18-year-old black man who becomes his central love interest. While in New Orleans, however, Mikey is unfaithful, thus destroying their affair, and prompting Mikey to follow Route 66 to Hollywood, before his eventual return to Iowa. Part road novel, part coming-of-age narrative, *Life Drawing* explores Mikey's burgeoning sexuality at the end of the 1950s within the context of same-sex desire and racial difference with a subtlety that marks Grumley as a talented and sensitive novelist.

The Ferro-Grumley Literary Awards, made possible by the estates of Robert Ferro and Michael Grumley, were first awarded for outstanding gay fiction in 1990 and have been presented annually as part of the Triangle Awards since 1994.

Further Reading

Bergman, David. "Race and the Violet Quill." *American Literary History* 9, no. 1 (Spring 1997): 79–102.

———. *The Violet Hour: The Violet Quill and the Making of Gay Culture.* New York: Columbia University Press, 2004.

Stephanie Youngblood

Guerra, Erasmo (b. 1970)

Essayist and novelist. Born and raised in the Rio Grande Valley of south Texas, of working-class immigrant Mexican parents, Erasmo Guerra's childhood, in many ways not unlike other Tejano children living on the border between Mexico and the United States, was profoundly affected by the death of his eldest sister, Diana Michelle, murdered at 18 soon after having graduated from high school. She was found dead not far from home, and no one was ever charged with the crime, leaving a deep psychological scar on both Guerra and his family. He moved to New York City in his early 20s and, later, graduated with a degree in creative writing from The New School's Eugene Lang College. The suicide of his 26-year-old, HIV-positive **gay** cousin pushed Guerra to finally come out of the **closet**, as well as to start writing.

Guerra's work often criticizes the "macho" culture in which many Latino gay men have to grow up in and offers a fresh, witty, and humorous counterdiscourse to it. He is mostly known as the editor of the nonfiction anthology *Latin Lovers: True Stories of Latin Men in Love* (1999) and the author of a novel, *Between Dances* (2000), which earned him the 2000 Lambda Literary Award in the "small press" category. *Latin Lovers* gathers a wide range of short stories focusing on Latino men as both objects and subjects of desire. The different interconnections among race, gender, and ethnicity portrayed in these stories are particularly compelling for their complex honesty. *Between Dances* explores the ambiguous world of male go-go dancers in Manhattan through the eyes of Marco, a young Latino gay man. The narrative exposes his anxieties and hopes leading to his final "redemption" and new start.

Guerra's work has also appeared in a number of journals and magazines, newspapers (such as the *Texas Observer*), and anthologies, including *New World: Young Latino Writers* (1996), and most recently *Hecho en Tejas* (2007), and *Fifteen Candles* (2007) in which Guerra pays homage to his sister, through the recollection of her "quinceñera," the traditional coming-of-age ceremony for Latina girls when they reach 15. His ethnicity, class, and sexuality are the primary marks of subjectivity in all his autobiographical writings. He runs a personal blog, "Mex & the City," featuring daily/weekly/monthly observations and considerations of his experiences, favorite books and exhibitions, family and friends, gay rights, and posts relating to Mexican American concerns. Departing from personal notes, his entries are always widened to include issues of general interest for which he provides a convincing approach. Guerra's fluid and poignant comments linger on his readers' minds, and though they show the immediacy and recklessness typical of blog entries, there is a narrative quality about them. Similar to many writers of Hispanic background, he intertwines English and Spanish together as one language, an idea reflecting his "border" position, often felt to be a space of anxiety and referred to as "a corridor of isolation and oppression" (Guerra) as in the descriptions of the borderland region in which he grew up. More recently his "mestizo" and "tejano" identity have been reappropriated as a subject position from which to speak proudly.

Further Reading

Guerra, Erasmo. "The Marrying Kind." *Texas Observer,* October 21, 2005. http://www .texasobserver.org/article.php?aid=2066.
http://erasmoguerra.blogspot.com.

Luisa Percopo

Guido deVries, Rachel (b. 1947)

Passionate poet, novelist, and feminist. All of Rachel Guido deVries's works concern her southern Italian heritage and lesbian identity. Rachel Guido deVries was born to southern Italian American parents on September 9, 1947, in Paterson, New Jersey. While Guido deVries grew up near Paterson, she has lived in central New York since 1970. Her father, a truck driver, was not a positive force in the household. Her mother, who was mainly a housewife but at times worked for the local supermarket, would often talk about family life, marriage, and the role of women. Rachel Guido deVries's **lesbianism**, especially her coming out, presented difficulties in her family life. Guido deVries does not exclude herself from the derogatory ethnic slurs that accompany her heritage or her sexuality. Rather, Guido deVries embraces these terms and often includes the taunts in her poetry.

Guido deVries has been a part of numerous writing projects. In 1984, Rachel Guido deVries founded the Community Writers' Project in Syracuse, New York, which she directed until 1995. From 1978 to 1982 she was co-director of The Women's Writers Center, formerly in Cazenovia, New York, and director of the Feminist Women's Writing Workshops at Wells College. While in these positions, she composed *An Arc of Light* (1978), now out of print, and had several works become part of anthologies. She currently is a poet in the schools in upstate New York and teaches creative writing through the Humanistic Studies Center of Syracuse University. Guido deVries offers readings and/or workshops in poetry, fiction, and autobiography. Her works are part of numerous anthologies, mainly those with an Italian American or feminist premise.

Tender Warriors (1986), her most widely read novel, is also her most autobiographical work. Guido deVries's siblings' and parents' reactions to her sexuality are captured in this semiautobiographical work. But her brother's words concerning her sexuality best exemplify how her decision would generally be accepted in her community. The novel follows three siblings, Rose, Sunny, and Lorraine, and their parents, Dominic and Josephine, as they confront life. Sunny, a short-order cook with a brain disease and representative of Guido deVries's brother, expresses how Rose's coming out is the worst issue the family has to deal with. Lorraine is a drug addict who marries a black man, Rose is a lesbian who works as a nurse and photographer, Dominic is an abusive father, and Josephine— dead for two years—acts as invisible support and motivation. The novel's main theme is survival in the face of personal and familial difficulties. *Tender Warriors* received much acclaim for being a novel with lesbian characters that nevertheless does not simply focus on lesbianism.

How to Sing to a Dago (1996) is one of many of Guido deVries's collections of poetry. One of the few published collections, it stays with Guido deVries's tradition of focusing on what she knows, her family and lesbianism. The poems in the collection are all about Italian American life and how her experience of being a lesbian fits within the Italian American tradition.

Guido deVries's most recent work, *Gambler's Daughter* (2002), is her second published collection of poetry; it was named a finalist in the 2002 Paterson Poetry Prize. The collection is quite autobiographical and includes a speaker who addresses memories of her violent father. While the father is deemed a negative influence, which sparks thoughts of a father the speaker would like, the speaker cannot help but consider how the good and bad times shaped her life. The collection also includes moments that capture how her mother and her mother's sisters would discuss the quality of their lives as women; it is those women who fundamentally shape the vision of the speaker.

Guido deVries's poems have appeared in magazines including *Yellow Silk, Voices in Italian Americana,* the *Paterson Literary Review,* and *Blueline.* She has also published an article, "Until the Voice Came"; published in *Breaking Open: Reflections on Italian-American Writers,* it gives her perspective on the literary tradition of Italian American women.

Further Reading

Sherman, Susan. "Rachel Guido deVries. In *Contemporary Lesbian Writers of the United States: A Bio-Bibliographical Critical Sourcebook,* edited by Sandra Pollack and Denise D. Knight, 181– 85. Westport, CT: Greenwood Press, 1993.

Stephanie B. Crosby

Gunn, Thom (1929–2004)

Anglo-American poet. Thom Gunn was a major **gay** poet whose life and career took him from the claustrophobic **closet**ry of pre-Wolfenden Cambridge, England, to San Francisco, where he experienced both the headiest days of gay liberation and the most extreme horrors of the worst years of the AIDS epidemic. Following the same trajectory, his poetry ranges across moods of scepticism and idealism, and through topics relating to both euphoria and grief, without ever losing its optimism and curiosity about human affairs. His typical early tone was one of laconic detachment, veering toward defensiveness; the later tones are much warmer and more casual.

Gunn was educated at University College School and Trinity College, Cambridge, before moving to the United States to be with his American lover, Mike Kitay. The move across the Atlantic held several layers of symbolic weight for Gunn. With the simple fact of following his heart came a cultural shift of broader significance to his writing: the move brought Gunn's poetry under the influence of Yvor Winters and, less directly, William Carlos Williams. His dedication to the formal measures and conceits of the English metaphysical poets of the seventeenth century began to melt, and he learned to write in a syllabic measure that gave an impression of casual ease. At the same time, his subject matter also took on some of the characteristics of the cultural revolution that was emanating from the Beat movement.

In Gunn's first two collections, *Fighting Terms* (1954) and *The Sense of Movement* (1957), sexual discretion finds its eloquent voice when repressively controlled by the poet's virtuosic use of traditional, rhyming, and metrical forms, borrowed, for the most part, from the English metaphysical poets. Although these forms may have been archaic, his subject matter is often thoroughly modern: *The Sense of Movement* daringly included poems about popular culture ("Elvis Presley"), bikers ("On the Move" and "The Unsettled Motorcyclist's Vision of His Death"), and the West Coast leather/sadist-masochist scene ("The Beaters" and "Market at Turk")—all without explicitly revealing that the central consciousness was gay. At times, Gunn adopts the tones of an aggressive masculinity that, later in life, he repudiated, unless it came festooned with the ironies of performativity. Among his favorite early topics is a virility whose chief defining characteristic was its self-restraint; it fits well, therefore, in the bondage of the tightest of metrical schemes. The laconic tone prevents the best of these poems from seeming to take themselves too seriously.

Gunn subsequently realized that his poem "The Allegory of the Wolf Boy," which characterizes puberty as a lycanthropic process, was about his own adolescence, when he was growing up gay but pretending to be straight. This closeted puberty can then be read as the prototype of his versions of adult virility, which keeps quiet about its own fears and insecurities while projecting a self-image of strength and confidence to the outside world.

When, in 1958, Gunn went to live in San Francisco with Mike Kitay, he took up a teaching position at the University of California, Berkeley. Like Christopher Isherwood before him, he found the physical and emotional warmth of California conducive to a life ostensibly unhampered by British inhibitions, stultifying class system, and obsolescent social convention. What he found on the West Coast, as well as a settled domestic life, were sexual freedom, a cornucopia of new recreational drugs, and a fresh approach to poetry most obviously displayed in his experiments with nonmetrical verse. The technical change suffuses both the structure and sensibility of his next collection, *My Sad Captains* (1961), which is structured in two separate halves, the first continuing in his (stylistically) metaphysical and English mode, the second showing the influence of Yvor Winters, and of life in the United States, in syllabic rather than metrical poems, much more relaxed and conversational in tone.

Topics by now becoming familiar to Gunn's readers included discipline, desire, and creativity. The indulgence of sensual pleasure—through sex and drugs, as well as the simpler joys of sea- and sun-bathing—was explored further when his Americanization continued apace in *Touch* (1967) and *Moly* (1971). The latter book, in particular, was ill received in Britain because of its supposedly "Californian" poems about sex and drugs and rock 'n' roll, but also because of its lack of rhyming poems. Yet Gunn rightly continued for the rest of his life to regard *Moly* as one of his strongest books. A further move into free verse completed his technical journey, but he never gave up on metrics or syllabics. One of the joys of his later books is their combination of methods perfected at different stages of his career.

Jack Straw's Castle (1976) broke new ground in both its sexual openness and its openness to looser poetic forms. Several of its poems attempt to capture the orgiastic pleasures of a generalized contact with other people, rather than with specific individual men. *The Passages of Joy* (1982) is another powerful book, woefully underrated by its early reviewers. It contains some of his best work. For instance, "Talbot Road" is one of his finest love poems, an elegy on his friend Tony White, who was heterosexual. There is no reason to find this ironic. The poem takes the two men's sexual difference as the pivotal aspect of their intimacy, almost as if sex might have gotten in its way.

Gunn's reputation in Britain had been languishing since his move to the United States. But the publication of *The Man with Night Sweats* (1992) abruptly changed that. It was clear from the reviews that, now that he was writing about AIDS, rather than merely about sexual pleasure, critics had found a way of taking him, as a gay writer, seriously. AIDS gave gay literature the gravitas that such readers imagined it had previously lacked. In some of these poems, Gunn laments the deaths of friends and erstwhile lovers in rigorously controlled poems reminiscent of his youthful mode, in part, because he wanted to avoid some of the emotional excess that had characterized other poetry about the epidemic; yet he managed to avoid the detached coolness of his earlier verse precisely by balancing emotional intensity with the restraints of form. The book was reviewed as if the epidemic was its only subject, whereas, in fact, it ranges across the gamut of his customary themes. He still had time to appreciate, and write about, a weed he had seen growing on a vacant lot.

The final volume, *Boss Cupid* (2000), ruffled a few feathers with its powerful sequence "Troubadour," spoken from the point of view of the gay serial killer Jeffrey Dahmer. Far from being sensationalistic, this sequence shows the best qualities of Gunn's inquiring humanism, unhampered by cliché or prejudice. His identification with the murderer, rather being exhibitionistic, is humble, acknowledging that such a man is no monstrous anomaly, but a variation on common themes: there, but for the grace of God, go all men. It is interesting to note that this last collection is, in many ways, Gunn's most sexual book; and it maintains a cheerfulness in the face of mortality that may be the sign of a man who, having personally survived the AIDS onslaught, yet having watched friends and lovers die painfully, saw no great fears in the approach of a death by old age.

Gunn was one of poetry's most elegant perfectionists, yet he never retreated from confronting imperfections both in his own character and in the social world at large. His communist mother had taught him that it ill becomes the comfortable to turn their backs on the destitute. ("The Gas-Poker," his eventual poem about her suicide, is one of the strongest pieces in *Boss Cupid*.) He identified with the homeless and downtrodden, yet never had the vanity, or the political naïvety, to think of himself as an outcast merely because he was gay. Indeed, he took the pleasures and pains that came with gayness as being signs of a commonality of human experience. More than many gay poets, he had a genuine interest in community, more than in the individualist pursuit of pleasure. The idea of isolation, whether in a wilderness or a crowded city, seems to have been his worst nightmare.

Gunn's *Selected Poems* was published in 1969 and 1979, and the *Collected Poems* in 1993. He was a rigorous literary essayist, and he also wrote several important autobiographical essays.

Further Reading

Agenda 37, nos. 2–3 (Autumn–Winter 1999). Special Issue on Thom Gunn.

Campbell, James. *Thom Gunn in Conversation with James Campbell.* London: Between the Lines, 2000.

Gunn, Thom. *The Occasions of Poetry: Essays in Criticism and Autobiography.* London: Faber, 1982.

———. *Shelf Life: Essays, Memoirs, and an Interview.* Ann Arbor: University of Michigan Press, 1993.

Hennessy, Christopher. *Outside the Lines: Talking with Contemporary Gay Poets.* Ann Arbor: University of Michigan Press, 2005.

Woods, Gregory. *Articulate Flesh: Male Homo-Eroticism and Modern Poetry.* New Haven & London: Yale University Press, 1987.

Gregory Woods

Gurganus, Allan (b. 1947)

Novelist, author of short stories, essayist, activist, and professor of creative writing. Allan Gurganus was born on June 11, 1947, in Rocky Mount, North Carolina, the oldest of four sons of Ethel and M .F. Gurganus. His father was the owner of stores and rental properties, and his mother was a schoolteacher who gave up teaching to raise her children. Whereas Ethel was a member of the Presbyterian Church, Gurganus's father converted to Baptist when Allan was nine years old and became a lay preacher, joining The Gideons International, the organization that distributes Bibles to hotels worldwide. Gurganus describes his childhood as blessedly schizophrenic: whereas he felt most at home in the Presbyterian Church, he was also drawn to the more physical and down-to-earth fundamentalist Baptist religion. Even though he ultimately cast his parents' religious beliefs aside, such religious elements as sermons and the Bible left an imprint on Gurganus's writings. While M. F. Gurganus had always been a rigid person, his conversion turned him, according to Allan, into a self-righteous dictator. The boys were frequently beaten by their father for no reason, and Allan developed a strong sense of justice and injustice and identification with those who cannot protect themselves. The boy exhibited a talent for painting early on, and some of his oil paintings were shown at a local art gallery when he was only 12 years old. After graduating from Rocky Mount Senior High School in 1965, Gurganus trained as a painter at the University of Pennsylvania and the Pennsylvania Academy of the Fine Arts. He has stated that the influence of the visual arts on his work is significant, that his writing is enormously painterly, and that he has learned as much from painters as he has from writers. Gurganus's studies were disrupted by the Vietnam War— he was drafted in 1966. Initially, he declared himself a conscientious objector but, facing conviction for draft evasion, he joined the U.S. Navy. After his training in cryptography in Monterey, California, Gurganus spent three years as a message decoder on the USS *Yorktown*. Being confined on the aircraft carrier for long periods and being surrounded by

4,000 young men proved to be a major turning point in Gurganus's personal and professional life. Whereas he had been sexually intimate only with women until then, he discovered that he was more attracted to men. However, he did not dare act on his desires outright, but instead he helped the men he fancied write sexually suggestive letters to their girlfriends and wives, becoming "the ventriloquist for these beautiful dummies," as he told Dwight Garner in an interview for Salon.com. In order to keep boredom at bay, Gurganus raided the ship's library, and his exposure to Henry James, Charles Dickens, and Honoré de Balzac came as a revelation. Gurganus remembers reading James's *The Portrait of a Lady* (1881) with suspended breath, discovering a world that was alien and magical and at the same time familiar, deciding on the spot that he would try his hand at writing fiction. He proceeded to write pastiches of his favorite nineteenth-century authors and continued to devour the 1,200 books of the ship's library, which earned him the nickname "Professor." His extensive reading also earned him two years of credit when he entered Sarah Lawrence College in 1970. There he studied under Grace Paley, one of America's preeminent short story authors, who weaned him from his nineteenth-century affectations and helped him develop a style of his own. Gurganus recalls during remarks he made in 1986 on the occasion of Paley's being named the first New York State author how, "awash in dependent clauses and authorial drag," he bolted up the stairs to his dorm room after a conversation with his teacher and typed out his first true work (www.slc.edu/grace-paley/Remarks_from_Allan_Gurganus.php). After his graduation in 1972, Gurganus attended the famous Iowa Writers' Workshop at the University of Iowa, where he was taught by Stanley Elkin and John Cheever. Cheever was romantically interested in his student, but Gurganus rejected his advances. In 1974 Cheever submitted one of his protégé's short stories, "Minor Heroism," to *The New Yorker* unbeknown to Gurganus; its publication made history as the magazine's first piece that openly treated homosexuality. The story, which Gurganus is still happy to call his own, explores the long-standing conflict between Richard, an insurance salesman whose role in bombing Dresden during the last days of World War II made him a minor celebrity, and his second son, Bryan, who refuses to follow in his father's footsteps. Having shown alarming artistic tendencies as a boy, Bryan eventually moves to New York City, where he works as a contributor to the magazine *Dance World* and lives with Jacques, an aspiring actor who earns a living as a model and who wears black nail polish. The simmering conflict between father and son erupts in an act of violence during one of Bryan's rare visits home when a drunken and resentful Richard swings at him and knocks him to the floor. This early story shows several elements that can be found in many of Gurganus's writings: autobiographical underpinnings, shifting narrative stance, and dissolution of chronological order.

After this auspicious debut, Gurganus contributed regularly to various magazines, was awarded numerous grants and prizes, and taught at Stanford University and Duke University. In 1979 he moved to New York City, which he experienced as his true home, as he told Dwight Garner: "This is it, this is mine, this is me, this is where I'll find others like me" ("The Salon Interview"). He taught part-time at Sarah Lawrence College and published over 20 stories, gaining a reputation in literary circles while remaining unknown to the reading public at large. This changed overnight in 1989 with the publication of the voluminous novel *Oldest Living Confederate Widow Tells All*. The seeds for this bestselling book were Gurganus's discovery that his forebears had been slave owners, as well as an article in the *New York Times* about surviving Confederate widows in Mississippi still receiving pensions, which had come to his attention in 1981 during a stay at the famous Yaddo artists' colony in Saratoga Springs, New York. In the novel 99-year-old Lucy Marsden, resident of a nursing home, tells a visitor the story of her marriage to William Marsden, a Civil War veteran more than three times her age. Lucy's narration spans over a century and includes stories that she knows only from hearsay, such as her husband's youth and traumatic war experiences and the life of her housekeeper Castalia, a former slave. As Gurganus told Richard Canning, he conceived of Lucy as "a Homeric repository for other people's tales" who is able to speak every language available to a person who lived in the hundred years she survived (226). The novel contains only a few homoerotic elements such as the emotionally and physically close relationship between William and his boyhood friend Ned Smythe, whose death in battle scars him for life, as well as some minor gay characters such as the choir director and Jerome, the nursing home orderly. By choosing a female who is neither rich nor beautiful as his narrator, Gurganus intended to present a new version of a pivotal period in U.S. history, namely, the death of the destructive patriarchy and the ascendancy of the nurturing feminine principle. Referring to the lack of homosexual themes in some of his works, Gurganus has stated on several occasions that he does not consider himself a **gay** or a straight writer but rather a pansexual writer who is able to write stories about outsiders honestly and with due consideration of all sides. In 2001 he told Joe E. Jeffreys, "I think I can treat gay and straight people fairly. I'm not a gay writer in the sense that I've never written about straight people. I find pathos in both camps. I wouldn't do anything different" (44).

The critical and financial success of *Confederate Widow*, which was translated into several languages and made into an Emmy Award–winning television miniseries, allowed Gurganus to turn to writing full time. It also facilitated the publication of *White People* (1991), a collection of previously published short stories and novellas. In addition to the aforementioned "Minor Heroism," *White People* contains three additional narratives with gay themes. In "Art History" a **closet**ed teacher is dismissed from his job in disgrace for inappropriate behavior with his pupils and eventually ends up in jail for propositioning a policeman in a park. In the similarly themed "Adult Art," Dave, a married superintendent of schools, who was an art history major in college and who experiences illegal feelings for young men every two or three years, invites Barker, a young man he has met in the street, to a bar for a drink. Eventually the two men end up in Barker's apartment, where they watch a straight porno film and Dave services the attractive stranger who looks as if he could have stepped out of an old navy recruiting poster. "Reassurance" consists of the original letter Walt Whitman wrote to the mother of the Pennsylvania soldier Frank H. Irwin, informing her of her son's death. The letter is supplemented with the mother's dream, in which Frank's spirit tries to ease her pain. Written in the midst of the AIDS pandemic, the piece can be read as Gurganus's elegy for friends and lovers who have died from the devastating disease, according to B. Austin Wallace (181). Having lost between 30 and 40 associates and having given 22 eulogies, Gurganus fled New York in 1993 and moved back to North Carolina, where he purchased a house in Hillsborough, a small town of 2,400. The emotionally painful act of purging his address book of the names of deceased friends led to the essay "On Whether to Purge the Dead from One's Address Book" and eventually to the comic novel *Plays Well with Others* (1997). The novel, which was inspired by F. Scott Fitzgerald's *The Great Gatsby* (1925), was conceived as a praise song to the friendship between gay men and straight women and to the heroism of those who cared for the sick and dying in the face of governmental apathy. *Plays Well* revolves around the lives of three friends who have come to New York to fulfill their artistic dreams. Hartley Mims, the book's narrator and aspiring writer, falls in love with bisexual Robert Christian Gustafson, a would-be composer who is also pursued by Angie "Alabama" Byrnes, a brilliant painter from Savannah. A large part of the novel replicates and celebrates the atmosphere of sexual abandon and freedom that characterized New York before the arrival of the virus. Gurganus has stated that he "wanted to write a comic aria about this immense, sickening loss" and has expressed his hope that the novel will eventually be one of the three or four texts that will be read about AIDS (Canning 244).

In 2001 Gurganus published *The Practical Heart,* a collection of four novellas, two of which feature gay characters. In "Preservation News" an elderly, genteel widow pays tribute to Tad Hunter, a young man who was instrumental in saving historical buildings in the fictional town of Falls, North Carolina, from the wrecking ball before he succumbed to AIDS. In "He's One, Too" the 40-year-old narrator remembers the public fall of his boyhood idol Dan R—, a married man and pillar of the community, who is entrapped by a detective and his 15-year-old son in the men's room of a Raleigh department store. Dan is convicted of indecent exposure and corruption of a minor and is forced to leave town. The narrator, who, as a nine-year-old boy, had a crush on "nearly too handsome" Dan and even approached him sexually, eventually leaves Falls for Boston and New York in order to avoid Dan's fate and to lead the life of an openly gay man. The fictional town of Falls, North Carolina, is also the setting for Gurganus's novel in progress entitled "The Erotic History of a Southern Baptist Church" and was conceived as the companion piece to *Confederate Widow* and second part of "The Falls Trilogy." The work, which Gurganus has characterized as a very comic, baggy monster of a novel, will trace the history of the United States from 1875 to 1975 from the point of view of a single rural church and pivot on the confusion between ecstatic religious experiences and ecstatic erotic experiences (Canning 258).

Further Reading

Canning, Richard. *Gay Fiction Speaks: Conversations with Gay Novelists.* New York: Columbia University Press, 2001. 225–59.

Garner, Dwight. "The Salon Interview: Allan Gurganus." http://www.salon.com/books/int/1997/12/cov_si_08gurganus2.html.

Jeffreys, Joe E. "What a Novelist Believes." *The Gay & Lesbian Review Worldwide* 8, no. 6 (November–December 2001): 43–44.

Ketchin, Susan. "When I'm Fog on a Coffin Lid: An Interview with Allan Gurganus." *The Southern Review* 29, no. 4 (Autumn 1993): 645–62. Reprinted in *The Christ-Haunted Landscape: Faith and Doubt in Southern Fiction* (Jackson: University Press of Mississippi, 1994).

Wallace, B. Austin. "Allan Gurganus." In *Contemporary Gay American Novelists: A Bio-Bibliographical Critical Sourcebook,* edited by Emmanuel S. Nelson, 178–82. Westport, CT: Greenwood Press, 1993.

Karl L. Stenger

H

Hacker, Marilyn (b. 1942)

Critically acclaimed Jewish American poet, editor, anthologist, translator, teacher, and **queer** activist. Born in Brooklyn, New York, the precocious single child of two Jewish parents, Marilyn Hacker entered New York University at the age of 15, where she honed the intellectual rigor, wide reading, and passion for poetic formalism that characterizes her poetry. One year before graduating, however, she relocated to Detroit in order to marry the famous African American science fiction writer **Samuel R. Delany,** since antimiscegenation statutes would not permit their union in New York. Both Delany and Hacker had same-sex extramarital affairs and separated years before they were divorced in 1980, although they have remained close friends and in 1974 had a daughter, Iva Hacker-Delany. Hacker's experiences of difference, as a Jew, a lesbian in an interracial marriage with a **gay** writer, a mother, an expatriate in Paris, and as a lover of history, remembrance, and traditions are exhibited in her use, quite uncharacteristic in modern lesbian poetry, of traditional poetic forms such as the sonnet, villanella, sestina, Sapphic stanza, haiku, and heroic couplet. These forms anchor her intense explorations of complicated love, lesbian eroticism, and mother-daughter relationships, as well as meditations on cancer, AIDS, friends, food, and books, and the urban landscapes of New York and Paris. In an ebullient language of slang, foreign phrases, allusions, ordinary scenes, and intense eroticism, Hacker's poetic corpus embodies the Jewish values of the redeeming ethical powers of *yizhor,* or remembrance, and *d'or-va-d'or,* the continuity between generations.

Hacker won the National Book Award for her first book of poetry, *Presentation Piece* (1974), which investigates exile, desire, and the unspoken experiences of the female body from a feminist perspective. *Assumptions* (1985) uses myth in a compassionate meditation on her relationships with her mother and daughter, and the processes through which conflict can transform into understanding, forgiveness, and new self-understanding. Her next book, *Love, Death, and the Changing of the Seasons* (1986), a masterpiece of lesbian poetics, uses Petrarchan sonnet cycle to narrate the course of her lesbian love affair with a younger woman. Replete with allusions to her queer forbear, Shakespeare, Hacker pays homage to his *Sonnets,* which also address a younger (male) lover. Filled with ironic **gender** play, in which Hacker often refers to herself in a masculine role to "represent" lesbian passion, this volume, like *Assumptions,* instructs the reader in how one can live beyond annihilating emotions. Her award-winning volume, *Winter Numbers* (1994), explores these themes of loss in far more somber contexts, setting illness, aging, and loss within political contexts of American imperialism, prejudice, and a looming sense of an uncertain future. Hacker describes her experiences with breast cancer and mourns friends who have died from AIDS.

Hacker uses wit to work through difficult emotions and has recently turned both to verse for healing and translations of French poetry. She has recently identified herself as a bisexual and lives in New York and Paris with her partner, Karyn London. Her work moves queers from the margins to the center by placing them in richly informed historical, political, cultural, and transnational contexts.

Further Reading

Biggs, Mary. "Present, Infinitesimal, Infinite: The Poetical Vision and 'Femin' Poetics of Marilyn Hacker. *Frontiers: A Journal of Women's Studies* 27, no. 1 (2006): 1–20.

Jagose, Annamarie. *Lesbian Utopics.* New York: Routledge, 1994.

Juhasz, Suzanne. *A Desire for Women: Relational Psychoanalysis, Writing, and the Relationships between Women.* New Brunswick, NJ: Rutgers University Press, 2003.

Corrine E. Blackmer

Hansen, Joseph (1923–2004)

Prolific and pioneering writer of **gay** mystery novels. Joseph Hansen was born in Aberdeen, South Dakota, and grew up in Minneapolis during the Great Depression. He married Jane Bancroft at the age of 20, and they remained married until her death in 1994. It was an open marriage; both Hansen and Bancroft, a lesbian, consented to each other's long-term affairs with others. Their only daughter, Barbara, underwent gender reassignment surgery and is now known as Daniel Hansen.

In the early 1960s, Hansen moved to Southern California and became increasingly active in the nascent **gay rights movement**. He was associated with the Mattachine Society, an early gay rights advocacy group. In 1965 he co-founded *Tangents,* a gay periodical; in 1969 he produced a controversial radio program titled "Homosexuality Today" in Los Angeles; in 1970 he was one of the organizers of Southern California's first Gay Pride March—an event intended to mark the first anniversary of the **Stonewall Riots.** Many of Hansen's novels reveal a distinct imprint of his activist consciousness. Even in his mystery novels, where the plots primarily pivot on solving murder cases, Hansen articulately engages a variety of political issues: the repressiveness of right-wing ideologies, Biblical liberalism and the bigotry and violence it spawns, pervasive **homophobia**, and racism in its subtle as well as overt manifestations.

Hansen began his career as a fiction writer by using the pseudonym James Colton. In 1965 he published *Strange Marriage* and later *The Outward Side* (1971) under his pseudonym. The central character in *Strange Marriage,* Randy Hale, marries a woman after being jilted by his male lover. His sexual secret, however, soon becomes public when another **closet**ed married man, with whom Hale has had an affair, commits suicide and leaves behind a note that alludes to Hale. Hale's wife is shocked and leaves him, but their family physician counsels her as well as Hale: he convinces Hale to come to terms with his sexuality and his wife to stay in the marriage. The novel's didactic intent is to normalize homosexuality. However, the intricate clinical explanation of the doctor, who serves as the author's mouthpiece, merely ends up contributing to the medicalization of homosexual desire. The tone of *The Outward Side,* in contrast, is less defensive. It is the story of a young married pastor in a small town who falls in love with a surprisingly self-assured gay teenager. The teenager helps the pastor to accept his sexuality and even announce it publicly.

Hansen's fame rests not on these early forays into fiction writing, but on the 12 mystery novels that constitute the Brandstetter series. The series begins with *Fadeout* (1970) and concludes with *A Country of Old Men* (1991). In these 12 installments Hansen creates one of the most compelling sleuths in American detective fiction: David Brandstetter, a ruggedly handsome, conventionally masculine, claim investigator for the Medallion Life Insurance Company. He is not unlike Mike Hammer, Philip Marlow, and Sam Spade—celebrated detectives familiar to the fans of mystery novels—but with one key difference: Brandstetter is a gay man who is entirely at ease with his sexuality.

Fadeout, the first work in the series, received surprisingly enthusiastic reception from the mainstream media. An elegantly crafted novel and written in lean and lively prose, *Fadeout* centers on the murder of Fox Olsen, a middle-aged married entertainer. Doug Sawyer, a childhood friend of Olsen, is charged with the murder. Brandstetter is assigned to investigate the insurance claim filed by Olsen's grieving family. During the course of his investigation he discovers the fact that Sawyer and Olsen were in fact lovers, and the murder was committed by Olsen's sister-in-law who was enraged by the gay relationship. Brandstetter clears Sawyer of all charges and by the end of the novel falls in love with the man whom he has saved.

In *Fadeout* the murder victim dies because of homophobic violence, but in *Death Claims* (1973) Hansen makes a daring move: the killer is a gay man. April Stannard, a young gay man, kills John Oats, his older lover, and attempts to blame Oats's son for the murder. Doug Sawyer resurfaces in the novel, this time as Brandstetter's lover, and assists him in solving the murder mystery. *The Man Everybody Was Afraid Of* (1978) tackles the subject of police brutality and corruption in a small California town. Ben Orton, the police chief, is savagely murdered; a right-wing zealot, he had many enemies and therefore there are many suspects. Cliff Kerlee, a local gay activist, is arrested and charged with the murder. Brandstetter comes to investigate the insurance claim filed by Orton's wife, and his investigation draws him into the town's complex political web. By this time his relationship with Sawyer has ended and the newly single Brandstetter falls in love with Cecil Harris, a young African American, who assists him in solving the murder case and exonerating Kerlee. *The Little Dog Laughed* (1986), in contrast to the earlier installments in the series, is an international intrigue. Adam Streeter, a California journalist, is found dead by his blind teenage daughter. His death is considered a suicide, but Brandstetter finds out the real cause: Streeter's investigative journalism had earned the murderous ire of a violent and corrupt politician from an imaginary Latin American country. Hansen's next work, *Early Graves* (1987), is arguably the first American mystery novel to deal with the AIDS crisis. In this compelling work Brandstetter tracks down an HIV-infected gay man who goes on a murder spree; to avenge his infection, he decides to kill all the men he has slept with. In *A Country of Old Men* Brandstetter, now in his

60s and in a stable relationship with Cecil Harris, comes out of his retirement to solve a murder witnessed by the adopted son of one of Brandstetter's close lesbian friends. At the end of the novel an exhausted Brandstetter suffers a massive heart attack. Since Hansen terminated the series with this 12th novel, one may assume that Brandstetter subsequently died of heart ailment.

Hansen's mystery novels have earned him a large and loyal fan base. Along with **Michael Nava** and **John Morgan Wilson**, he remains one of the most distinguished writers in the genre of gay detective fiction. What is significant also in Hansen's novels is the immense variety of gay characters who come from all walks of life. Some are stridently masculine while some others are flamboyantly effeminate. Some are murderers; some others are murder victims. Some are secretive and closeted whereas some others are confidently and comfortably gay. Creating such a wide range of gay characters helps Hansen advance one of his frequently articulated political goals: to disrupt and destabilize the commonly held monodimensional **gay stereotypes** about gay men by insisting on their complexity as well as their diversity. Often he emphasizes the ordinariness of his characters and presents their sexual identities as largely unremarkable attributes.

Further Reading

Baird, Newton. "Joseph Hansen." In *Twentieth Century Crime and Mystery Writers,* edited by John Reilly, 725–28. New York: St. Martin's Press, 1980.

Jones, James W. "Joseph Hansen." In *Contemporary Gay American Novelists: A Bio-Bibliographical Critical Sourcebook,* edited by Emmanuel S. Nelson, 189–96. Westport, CT: Greenwood Press, 1993.

Trevor A. Sydney

Harris, Bertha (1937–2005)

Novelist, biographer, editor, and scholar. Bertha Harris was born in Fayetteville, North Carolina, on December 17, 1937. She graduated from the Women's College of the University of North Carolina in 1959, when she moved to Manhattan. Harris is best known for her three works of experimental fiction, *Catching Saradove* (1969), *Confessions of Cherubino* (1972), and *Lover* (1976; 1993), and as co-author, with Emily L. Sisley, of the straightforward *The Joy of Lesbian Sex: A Tender and Liberated Guide to the Pleasures and Problems of a Lesbian Lifestyle* (1977). She has also authored a biography of Gertrude Stein for young adults and a few academic articles, co-edited *Amazon Expedition: A Lesbian Feminist Anthology* (1973) with a group of well-known second-wave lesbian feminists, and also regularly reviewed books for the *New York Times*. At the time of her death, Harris was working on her fourth novel, a comedy, *Mi Contra Fa*. Harris's *Lover* has been called "one of the finest examples of early post-**Stonewall** lesbian fiction" (Jay xv).

Throughout her life, Harris held a variety of jobs, including teaching appointments at various colleges and an assistant editorship at the briefly successful but immensely important Daughters Press—a radical, independent "Publisher of Fiction by Women." Harris describes her tempestuous relationship with Daughters' founders—business and domestic partners, June Davis Arnold and Parke Patricia Bowman—in her introduction to the 1993 reissue of *Lover.* Harris was the 24-year companion of Camilla Clay Smith. Harris died on May 22, 2005, in New York City at the age of 67.

Harris's first novel, *Catching Saradove,* was written to satisfy the degree requirements for her M.F.A., which she returned to the University of North Carolina to pursue. This semiautobiographical novel is dedicated to Harris's only child, Jennifer Harris Wyland, and focuses on the protagonist, Saradove Racepath, a young single mother brought up in the South who later moves to New York City. The novel's nonlinear narrative moves back and forth in time and place, from Saradove's contemporary situation living on Manhattan's Lower East Side before and after the birth of her child, to Saradove's southern childhood, where the characters of her brother, Duncan, her abused mother, abusive father, and the family's black maid and mother-figure to Saradove, Olympia, all loom large. The novel's narrative style ranges from realist to surreal, effects that Harris experiments with more fully in her later works.

In this early novel, Harris explores an extreme ambivalence about women's conventional roles, such as those embodied by Saradove's mother and, eventually, the unwillingly maternal Saradove. At the same time, however, Harris reveals deep skepticism about the merits of the women's, civil rights, and pacifist movements of the 1960s. That the novel's first image is of the stunned single mother, Saradove, as she sits around the city park sandbox with other similarly shell-shocked mothers and that its final image is of the temporarily lesbian and feminist but now pregnant and dependent Saradove, her head resting on the shoulder of the man who has just murdered the activist father of Saradove's unborn child (but has spared her life), bespeaks a troubled view of the women's liberation movement, to say the least.

In *Confessions of Cherubino,* published in 1972, Harris blends southern gothic with classical, baroque, and, again, surrealist traditions into a ribald, high-**camp**, melodramatic pastiche. The novel centers on Ellen Fairchild, a young woman who, at the beginning of the story, is enrolled at the all-female Redwing Academy for Music. Like Cherubino from Mozart's comedic *The Marriage of Figaro* for whom she is nicknamed, Ellen serves as both love object and subject within a tangled web of romantic and sexual relationships out of which the novel's plot is fashioned. Ellen is sought after by Margaret, her childhood friend and closest confidant at the academy; by Sanctissima, their crazy old lesbian music teacher whose penchant for seducing young pedagogues brings on her own fateful death; by Venusberg, Ellen's biracial half-sister, and daughter of the family maid; and by the nameless male soldier who impregnates her.

Like the characters in Djuna Barnes's *Nightwood* (1937), with whose author Harris's fictions are often associated, those in *Confessions of Cherubino* are all cultural outsiders in one way or another. This neo-**queer** motley crew also includes Ellen's oversexed southern belle of a grandmother, Miss Nina; her philandering and bisexual postman of a father (and his ghost); her pathetic excuse for a mother, Ellen-May; her effete uncle, Welch, and his delicate "Beloved," Darwin Waters; and America, the caricature of a southern Negro housekeeper, who is also mother to Ellen's half-sister, Venusberg. The novel closes with a queering of the prototypical heterosexual marriage plot: as Ellen approaches the threshold of her childhood home, carrying in her arms the now profligate and lunatic Margaret, piano music streams out the front door, while assembled on the porch sits the novel's entire cast of characters in an absurd rendering of domestic harmony, and Ellen cannot help but think "that they are approaching the conditions of perfect love."

The ending of Harris's third and most critically acclaimed novel, *Lover,* is clearly concerned with the same themes. *Lover* (originally published by Daughters Press in 1976) also ends on a hopelessly romantic note: "with Justice being done . . . true lovers united."

But in this case, lovers are literally conjoined because, throughout the course of the novel —the story of a/the novel being written—the lover has become the beloved and vice versa. Harris deliberately invokes this fluidity of character, form, and setting in order to challenge a patriarchal symbolic order in which women are objects and men, subjects (see Robinson; Smith; Stimpson). None of the novel's characters—Veronica, Flynn, Daisy, Maryann, Rose and Rose-Lima, Samaria, and even Bertha (yes, Harris), to name only a few—remain stable or discrete entities. They are all "manifestations of one protean consciousness" (18), according to literary critic **Wayne Koestenbaum**.

In this text, in which the frequent trope of "cancer of the brain," Harris explains, serves as a "memento mori" of the "imagination as death's head when contaminated by exegesis" (Introduction xxv), the reader has no choice but to heed the author's advice that the novel "be absorbed as if it were theatrical performance," as "delirious spin" (Introduction xix; xxvi). "There's tap-dancing and singing, disguise, sleights of hand, mirror illusions, quick-change acts, and drag," explains Harris (Introduction xix). One must surrender to the pleasure of the novel's performance to truly appreciate its theatricality, as Kostenbaum exhorts: "Read *Lover* to discover what it is like to be happy, to be lesbian, to be in love, to be discovering the size of one's voice, to be in love with the size of one's own lesbian voice" (18). If one could say anything definitive about this deliberately elusive text, it should be about the power of art to move and persuade its audience: "a vaudeville version of **queer theory**; presciently [*Lover*] explains everything that queer theory has come laboriously to know since 1976" (Koestenbaum 18).

Further Reading

Allen, Carolyn. *Following Djuna: Women Lovers and the Erotics of Loss.* Bloomington: Indiana University Press, 1996.

Harris, Bertha. Introduction. *Lover.* 1976. New York: New York University Press, 1993. xvii–lxxviii.

Jay, Karla. Foreword. *Lover.* By Bertha Harris. 1976. New York: New York University Press, 1993. xi–xv.

Koestenbaum, Wayne. "The Purple Reign of Bertha Harris: Excess Story." *New York Village Voice Literary Supplement* (October 1993): 18.

Robinson, Sally. "The 'Anti-Logos Weapon': Multiplicity in Women's Texts." *Contemporary Literature* 29, no. 1 (1998): 105–24.

Smith, Victoria L. "Starting from Snatch: The Seduction of Performance in Bertha Harris's *Lover*." *Sex Positives? The Cultural Politics of Dissident Sexualities.* New York: New York University Press, 1997. 68–94.

Stanley, Julia Penelope, and Susan J. Wolfe. "Consciousness as Style; Style as Aesthetic." In *Language, Gender and Society,* edited by Barrie Thorne, Cheris Kramarae, and Nancy Henley, 125–39. Cambridge, MA: Newbury House, 1983.

Stimpson, Catharine. "Zero Degree Deviancy: The Lesbian Novel in English." *Critical Inquiry* 8, no. 2 (1981): 363–79.

Wadsworth, Ann. "Bertha Harris." *The Gay and Lesbian Literary Heritage,* edited by Claude J. Summers, 337–38. New York: Routledge, 2002.

Cynthia Sarver

Harris, E. Lynn (b. 1955)

Best-selling African American novelist, editor of several collections of fiction, and professor of creative writing. Everette Lynn Williams was born on June 20, 1955, in Flint,

Michigan, and grew up in Little Rock, Arkansas, together with his sisters Anita and Zettoria. He was called Mike by his father, Ben Odis Harris, who considered the boy's given name not tough enough and who treated him as a punching bag whenever he acted like a "sissy." The frequent abuse caused E. Lynn to retreat into a world of silence and make-believe. When he was 12 years old, the boy discovered that his biological father was not Ben Harris but rather James Jeter from Union, South Carolina. Even though this knowledge made the frequent beatings somewhat easier to take, it came as a relief to E. Lynn when his mother, Etta Mae, divorced Ben in 1969 and, having given birth to a third girl, raised the four children on her own while holding down two jobs. E. Lynn attended the predominantly white Hall High School and gradually became aware of his sexual attraction to men. His first **gay** sexual encounter, however, proved disastrous. When he met an older, handsome black man and had sex with him in his car, his date suddenly turned on him, calling him "a goddamn faggot" and assaulting him. This traumatic experience taught Harris to be cautious; when he attended the University of Arkansas at Fayetteville, majoring in journalism, he fell into a pattern of dating female students while having crushes on unattainable straight men. He became the first black editor of *Razorback,* the university's yearbook, and the first black male cheerleader on the Razorbacks squad. As Harris reveals in his 2003 memoir *What Becomes of the Brokenhearted,* becoming a cheerleader proved to be the catalyst that led to his first serious and reciprocal relationship with a man. Eventually, this relationship fell apart when he graduated and moved to Dallas, Texas, where he worked as a computer sales executive for IBM (International Business Machines Corporation). In 1982 he moved to New York City to work for a telephone company after a two-year-long relationship with Andre, a Southern Methodist University law student, came to an abrupt and painful end. At the beginning of 1986 he moved to Chicago and, even though he was successful in his job, he felt unfulfilled, had bouts of depression, and started to drink heavily. In 1990 he experienced an emotional meltdown, came close to committing suicide, and left his lucrative job for an unsettled life in Washington, D.C. Eventually he moved to Atlanta, went into therapy, and turned to writing as his salvation. Even though he had been encouraged by Maya Angelou in 1983 to turn his experiences into fiction, Harris initially limited himself to writing sports articles. When a friend, who was dying of AIDS, urged him to give voice to the gay experience, he put pen to paper and wrote *Invisible Life* (1992) within a few months. When the novel, which is strongly autobiographical and whose title alludes to Ralph Ellison's *Invisible Man* (1951), was rejected by 12 publishers, Harris raised enough money to have 5,500 copies printed privately. Within nine months he managed to sell the entire print run in local bookstores and beauty salons, and his reputation as a new, exciting African American writer spread beyond Atlanta. In July 1992 Doubleday added E. Lynn Harris to its roster of authors and reissued *Invisible Life* as a paperback. Ever since then Harris has published entertaining and best-selling novels on a nearly annual basis. In 2003 he recounted his painful path to best-selling author in the memoir *What Becomes of the Brokenhearted,* coming out as a black gay man and confessing that writing has allowed him to change his self-hatred and doubt into true self-esteem and self-love (4). After publishing his memoir, Harris experienced a creative slump and turned to teaching creative writing at his alma mater in Arkansas. Being surrounded by talented and enthusiastic young people recharged his artistic batteries and he published *I Say a Little Prayer* after a three-year-long unofficial writing sabbatical. In order to support promising African American authors,

Harris established the Better Days Literary Foundation and edited several collections of fiction by emerging authors.

Each of Harris's nine novels can be read as a chapter of a continuing soap opera that explores the tumultuous and conflicted lives of a recurring cast of African American characters and that focuses on the search for racial and sexual identity. Even though Harris's goal is primarily entertainment, he injects such serious themes as homosexuality, **bisexuality**, AIDS, and racial and sexual discrimination in his romance novels. His first novel, *Invisible Life* (1992), for example, depicts the internal struggle of aspiring lawyer Raymond Tyler to accept the fact that he is sexually attracted to men. While dating Sela, a cheerleader, Raymond simultaneously has a relationship with the college football star Kelvin. This pattern of duplicity is repeated when Raymond graduates and moves to New York City, where he falls in love with Nicole, an actress, while dating Quinn, a married father of two. Torn between the desire for marriage and a heterosexual lifestyle sanctioned by society on the one hand and his homosexual urges on the other, Raymond eventually rejects a lifestyle "on the down low," which is led by men who have homosexual encounters while defining themselves as heterosexual. The turning point occurs when Raymond finds out that his former lover, Kelvin, has infected his fiancée with HIV and that he is responsible for her death. However, at this point in his life Raymond is not able to accept his homosexuality and he moves back to Alabama, where he commits himself to serving the black community while suppressing his sexual urges. In the sequel, *Just As I Am* (1994), Raymond still struggles with his sexual identity while working as a sports lawyer in Atlanta. As in *Invisible Life,* he is attracted to a football player who lives on the down low, and he is eventually forced by the specter of AIDS to reexamine his life. After spending the last months at the bedside of his friend Kyle and witnessing his death from AIDS, Raymond accepts his sexual proclivity and settles down with a male lover. Having shifted his focus in *And This Too Shall Pass* (1996) and *If This World Were Mine* (1997) to a group of new characters, Harris returns in *Abide with Me* (1998) to the trials and tribulations of Raymond, who is living with his lover, Trent, in Seattle, as well as to the continuing escapades of Raymond's former lover Basil Henderson, a football player on the down low. Henderson, one of Harris's most compelling and devious characters, takes center stage in *Not a Day Goes By* (2000) and is eventually reunited with Raymond in *A Love of My Own* (2002), upsetting his friend's hard-won emotional equilibrium after his relationship with Trent has failed. In *I Say a Little Prayer* (2006) Raymond and Henderson, who have become lovers, play a subordinate role to Chauncey Greer, a former member of a popular boy band, who brings about the downfall of a prominent fundamentalist preacher with whom he had a relationship as a young man. As in all of his novels, Harris combines a highly entertaining and breezy story line with controversial topics, in this case the relationship between fundamentalist churches and homosexuality. It is to his credit that he has exposed a large, predominantly black audience to such themes and, in doing so, perhaps he has fostered a more tolerant treatment of sexual minorities.

See also Autobiography, Gay; Gay Literature, African American

Further Reading

Frieden, Lisa. "Invisible Lives. Addressing Black Male Bisexuality in the Novels of E. Lynn Harris." In *Bisexual Men in Culture and Society,* edited by Brett Beemyn and Erich Steinman, 73–90. New York: Harrington Park Press, 2002.

Hardin, Michael. "Ralph Ellison's Invisible Man: Invisibility, Race, and Homoeroticism from Frederick Douglass to E. Lynn Harris." *Southern Literary Journal* 37, no. 1 (Fall 2004): 96–120.

Karl L. Stenger

Hayes, Penny (b. 1940)

Prolific author of nine lesbian historical novels. The majority of Penny Hayes's novels fictionalize aspects of American history, such as life in the Old West, immigration from Europe to America in the 1900s, and the institutionalization of women in mental asylums in the 1800s. Hayes thereby helps readers gain an understanding of the experiences of those who expressed same-sex desire and cross-gender identification in various past American contexts.

The historical anachronism associated with historical fiction is apparent in Hayes's depiction of various female characters who hold lesbian-feminist beliefs before the establishment of the lesbian-feminist movement. As many of her novels are steeped in lesbian-feminist theory, her explicit depictions of sexual encounters between women complicate understandings of lesbian feminists as asexual or sex-negative. Although historical fiction is often understood to be ahistorical because it embraces imaginative engagements with the past, like many authors of historical fiction, Hayes does extensive historical research before writing her novels. As she incorporates historical facts into her fictional narratives, her writing undermines the binary between fact and fiction.

Her first lesbian historical romance, *The Long Trail* (1986), which takes place in 1869 in Texas, examines the perils that a schoolteacher and a sex worker face when traveling from Texas to New England without male accompaniment. *Yellowthroat* (1988), which takes place in the Old West in New Mexico Territory, examines how internalizations of the feminine and heterosexual ideals may inhibit the development of relationships between women. Margarita, a Mexican bandit, initially resists her desire for Julia—a victim of one of Margarita's stagecoach robberies who later becomes Margarita's captive—because Julia is an Anglo like the men who murdered Margarita's husband. Although this novel contains many explicit lesbian-feminist commentaries, Hayes's examination of the power struggles between Margarita and Julia complicates the lesbian-feminist celebration of woman-loving relationships as egalitarian. *Montana Feathers* (1990), which takes place at the end of the nineteenth century, also highlights tensions between women as is seen in the tumultuous beginning to the relationship between Elizabeth, a city woman who decides to visit her aunt and uncle's ranch in Montana before marrying her fiancé, and Vivian, a sheepherder who grows increasingly jealous about Elizabeth's pending marriage.

Hayes's didactically lesbian-feminist novel *Grassy Flats* (1992), which takes place during the Great Depression, juxtaposes the egalitarian woman-loving relationship between Hayes's protagonists, Aggie and Nell, with oppressive heterosexual dynamics in order to celebrate the former. Hayes provides scathing commentaries on compulsory heterosexuality and male dominance that reflect critiques by lesbian-feminist theorists such as **Adrienne Rich** and Sheila Jeffreys. In the immigration narrative *Kathleen O'Donald* (1994), Hayes highlights the enduring trauma that results from colonization through her depiction of the open hostility that her Irish protagonist, Kathleen, feels toward her future lover, Rose, an Englishwoman whom she meets while on the voyage from Europe to New York in the early 1900s.

In *Now and Then* (1996), Elsa's obsession with Wild West shows during the late nineteenth century leads her to develop a relationship with the female trick rider Wynn Carson. This novel's compelling depiction of same-sex eroticism highlights the different forms that sexual encounters between women may take in various historical periods. For instance, Elsa and Wynn bring each other to orgasm without realizing that they are having sex and first kiss each other long after they have established a sexual relationship. In *City Lights, Country Candles* (1998), Hayes ventures into the realm of time-transgression fiction. When visiting her eventual lover, Eveleen, Hayes's protagonist, Laurie, is made to listen to stories that Eveleen's dying grandmother recounts about various women in the latter half of the nineteenth century who were punished by men for their gender and/or sexual transgressions by being imprisoned in an insane asylum. Grandma McNelly's stories that are told to Laurie in 1960 imaginatively transport Laurie back to the late nineteenth century.

Omaha's Bell (1999) examines how Keeley's relationship with her lover, Attie, is impacted by Keeley's desire for Prue, a beautiful restaurant owner who decides to raise money to purchase a bell for the local church. Hayes's most recent narrative, *The Tomstown Incident* (2004), is a time-trangression novel wherein Eloise, who lives in New England in 1977, travels back in time to establish a relationship with Marion who lives during the American Revolutionary War. Although Hayes's novels have received very little critical attention, her ability to vividly evoke historical periods and provide compelling examinations of the struggles faced by women in the past who desired other women make her one of the most powerful authors of LGBTQ historical fiction to date.

Further Reading

Alston, Jean. "Between Two Worlds: *The Tomstown Incident.*" *Lambda Book Report* 13, nos. 9/10 (2005): 49.

"Hayes, Penny." *Contemporary Authors.* Vol. 121, edited by Hal May. Detroit: Gale, 1987. 197–98.

Jones, Norman W. *Gay and Lesbian Historical Fiction: Sexual Mystery and Post-Secular Narrative.* New York: Palgrave Macmillan, 2007.

Mandy Koolen

Healy, Eloise Klein (b. 1943)

Eloise Klein Healy is a poet, teacher, editor, critic, environmentalist, activist, and naturalist. Born in El Paso, Texas, Eloise Klein Healy spent 10 years in Remsen, Iowa, before moving with her family to North Hollywood, California, in 1953. Her father worked as a special effects designer on television shows and films. Healy attended Providence High School, a private Catholic girls school, and she received a B.A. in 1965 and an M.A. in 1968 both from Immaculate Heart College in Los Angeles. In 1988, she received her M.F.A. from Vermont College.

Healy's first book of poetry, *Building Some Changes,* won the New Book Award from the Beyond Baroque Foundation. It was published in 1976 and 8,000 copies of the book were printed and freely distributed. These early poems by Healy are short, lyrical verses. Her second book, *A Packet Beating Like a Heart,* was published in 1981 by Books of a Feather Press. Her next book, *Ordinary Wisdom,* is based on a series of short lyrics based on Chinese ideograms; it was published in 1981 by Paradise Press and re-released in 2005 by Red Hen Press.

In 1991, *Artemis in Echo Park* was published by Firebrand Books. This book is an imaginative rendering of the goddess Artemis living in an older section of Los Angeles. It demonstrates the strength of Healy's work in bringing mythical archetypes into direct conversation with contemporary life. *Artemis in Echo Park* also demonstrates the impact of place on Healy's work. It was a finalist for the Lambda Book Award and was released as a spoken word recording by New Alliance Records.

Healy's fifth collection, *Women's Studies Chronicles,* was published in 1998. These poems give voice to Healy's experiences as a teacher. Healy has worked as a teacher throughout her adult life. She began by teaching high school for five years. In the late 1970s, involved in the feminist movement, Healy was a member of the core faculty in the Feminist Studio Workshop at The Woman's Building in Los Angeles, a pioneering feminist art center founded by Judy Chicago. At California State University at Northridge, Healy taught poetry and women's studies and was the director of the program. In 1992, Healy joined the faculty of Antioch University in Los Angeles and was the Founding Chair of the Creative Writing Program there. Today, she is Distinguished Professor of Creative Writing Emerita at Antioch University in Los Angeles.

In 2002, Healy's book *Passing* was published by Red Hen Press. This book addresses life's transitions: time passing, cars passing, and loved ones dying. In the collection, Healy demonstrates her formal skills in poetry as well as capturing lyrics that reflect life in the contemporary gay and lesbian community and her home of Los Angeles. In 2007, Red Hen Press published Healy's seventh book, *The Islands Project: Poems for Sappho.* This book takes up the long-term lesbian dialogue with Sappho, Healy's poetic mother, and it addresses the challenges of Sappho's work existing only in fragments. Healy uses Sappho to counterpoint her biological mother who at the time of her writing and publishing of these poems was ill and then passed away.

Healy has been awarded artist residencies at The MacDowell Colony and Dorland Mountain Colony. Recipient of numerous grants and fellowships, she was the Grand Prize winner of the Los Angeles Poetry Festival Competition.

Currently, Healy is working with her partner as the co-founder of ECO-ARTS, an eco-tourism/arts venture. She is the Guest Poet at the Idyllwild Summer Poetry Festival. In 2006, she initiated a special imprint with Red Hen Press, Arktoi Books, that specializes in publishing the work of lesbian authors. She lives in Los Angeles.

Further Reading

Gioia, Dana, Chryss Yost, and Jack Hicks, eds. *California Poetry: From the Gold Rush to the Present.* Berkeley, CA: Heyday Books, 2003. 242.

Sexton, Elaine. "Interview with Eloise Klein Healy" *Lambda Book Report* 15, no. 1 (Spring 2007): 3–5.

Julie R. Enszer

Hegnauer, Lilah (b. 1982)

Contemporary American poet. Daughter of Bruce and Kristy Hegnauer, Lilah Donnell Hegnauer was born on April 2, 1982, in Puyallup, Washington. Her father and mother work as a machinist and a physical therapist, respectively, and the family placed special emphasis on service, such as training guide dogs, which Hegnauer did for four years. As a child, Hegnauer read voraciously, studied and played the piano, and became thoroughly acquainted with the Washington landscape. In 2000, Hegnauer entered the University of Portland, a small Catholic college, where she explored multiple majors before settling on English. It was not until the fall of her junior year, however, that Hegnauer enrolled in a creative writing workshop. Under the guidance of Herman Asernow, Hegnauer studied contemporary poets such as C. K. Williams, Mark Doty, and **Adrienne Rich**—poets who continue to influence her work today. Between her junior and senior years of college, Hegnauer traveled to Uganda where she taught English and volunteered in a hospital. The intensity of her experiences in Uganda crystallized into Hegnauer's first book, *Dark under Kiganda Stars,* which she wrote in the fall semester of her senior year and published in 2005 with Ausable Press. After graduating from Portland, Hegnauer attended the Ohio State University's M.F.A. program for one year before relocating to the University of Virginia's M.F.A. program in 2005. While at the University of Virginia, Hegnauer completed a second book manuscript (*West: November,* yet to be published), served as poetry editor for *Meridian,* taught college-level workshops, and taught at a local Montessori school. Hegnauer was a finalist for the 2006 Astrea Lesbian Writers Fund. Her poems have appeared in a variety of journals, including *The Drunken Boat, FIELD, Harrington Lesbian Literary Quarterly, Identity Theory,* and *The Kenyon Review.*

Hegnauer's poems feature the often overlooked in language. They celebrate the mundane (vegetables, flowers, and city names) and moments that make up our daily lives; the humor and gravity that lie, latent, in our proverbs and colloquial expressions; the seeming non sequiturs in conversation or thought that subtly relate two distinct things. Although *Dark under Kiganda Stars* does not address **queer** identity, Hegnauer's first book examines ethnicity, race, **gender**, class, and faith—and our capabilities as well as responsibilities to sympathize with and care for others. Critics responded warmly to *Dark under Kiganda Stars,* amazed by the quiet confidence and skill in these poems. Roger Mitchell aptly compared Hegnauer's project to Walt Whitman's notion of sympathy in *Song of Myself* (1855) (dust jacket blurb)—but Hegnauer is more aware of the potential risks that accompany an imaginative blending of selves (for example, violation). In this way she recognizes that language can only partially bridge the distance between individuals—that the things that keep us together or drive us apart often resist precise naming. This combination of delight in language and respect for the invisible boundaries around the individual produce one of Hegnauer's most distinct techniques: a list that ends up describing what she chooses not to name. Hegnauer employs and perfects this technique in *West: November* in poems such as "Canary Bird Flower in Your Chaste Tree," where the speaker lists the female names of flowers to address being gay; "Like Music," where the tenor of the title simile is never named; and "Rain Two: Offut Lake," where "two women try to say the words [and] cannot." These techniques create a solid shape around the purposefully unnamed but clearly felt center of the poem.

Hegnauer's current manuscript, *West: November,* explores the personal and the political dimensions of sexuality. Through short lyrics, fractured narratives, a sequence of "Rain" poems, and prose poems, Hegnauer examines the quiet intimacies between lovers as well as friends, and the frustrations and sadness that result from being denied the same political protection and social recognition offered to heterosexual couples. These poems are more formally daring and subtle than the poems in *Dark under Kiganda Stars,* their subject matter more varied. The queer speaker across the collection lends additional significance to poems such as "When I Was a Boy" or "Like Music." Whereas *Dark under Kiganda Stars* is organized around the speaker's experiences in Uganda, the poems in *West:*

November draw on childhood memories, the Western landscape, the Midwest, Virginia, the joys of first love, the logistics of partnering, the desire to have a child, anger at the politics of marriage, and moving elegies for a deceased mentor and father figure.

Further Reading

Kanell, Beth Dugger. "Dark under Kiganda Stars." Review of *Dark under Kiganda Stars* by Lilah Hegnauer. *Kingdom Books.* June 2005. http://www.kingdombks.com (accessed May 6, 2008).

Julia Hansen

Hemphill, Essex (1957–1995)

African American poet, essayist, performance artist, and activist. Born in Chicago, Illinois, the oldest of five children, Essex Hemphill was raised in Anderson, Indiana; Columbia, South Carolina; and Washington, D.C., where he graduated from Ballou High School. He began writing poems at the age of 14 and attended the University of Maryland and the University of the District of Columbia, studying English and journalism. He spent most of his adult life in Philadelphia where he was a prominent member of the African American and **gay** political and artistic communities. His first book of poetry was the self-published *Earth Life* (1985) followed by *Conditions* in 1986, but Hemphill did not gain national acclaim until his work appeared in a seminal collection of writing by gay men of color edited by Joseph Beam, *In the Life* (1986). That same year Hemphill received a poetry fellowship from the National Endowment for the Arts. Following Beam's death from AIDS-related complications, Hemphill oversaw the completion of a follow-up anthology entitled *Brother to Brother: New Writings by Black Gay Men* (1991) that was honored with a Lambda Literary Award. His work also appeared in many other poetry and essay collections including *Gay and Lesbian Poetry in Our Time* (1986) and *Life Sentences: Writers, Artists, and AIDS* (1993). In 1992 he won the National Library Association's Gay, Lesbian, and Bisexual New Author Award for a collection of poetry and prose entitled *Ceremonies: Prose and Poetry* (1992). He also contributed work to magazines and journals such as *Obsidian, Black Scholar, Callaloo, Painted Bride Quarterly, The Advocate,* and *Essence* and was a co-founder of the *Nethula Journal of Contemporary Literature* while still in college in 1978.

Essex Hemphill is also known for his contributions to two award-winning documentaries: *Tongues Untied* (1991), which was directed by Marlon Riggs, and *Looking for Langston* (1989), directed by Isaac Julien. Both of these projects addressed the issues that predominated in Hemphill's poetry: notably, the ways in which different forms of prejudice and oppression intersect and overlap. For Hemphill, racism, sexism, **homophobia**, and classism are never to be understood in isolation but rather in their relation to one another. For example, Hemphill was highly critical of racism within the gay community itself, particularly the sexual objectification of black gay men, which he believed undermined their rights to be valid speaking subjects. He raised this point in "Does Your Mama Know About Me?" (*Ceremonies,* 1992), a polemical piece that spoke out against the work of photographer Robert Mapplethorpe in which black men's faces are obscured in favor of close up shots of their genitalia, chests, and other anatomical features. Hemphill also spoke against racism and sexism within the African American community, both of which he believed contributed to the disenfranchisement of blacks. However, the most pressing issue that traversed much of his work was the lack of brotherhood among gay men of color. He also wrote extensively about the toll that the AIDS virus was taking in both of his communities and the disease would eventually claim his life as well. Hemphill felt that the specific needs of the black gay community were neglected by mainstream AIDS activism and health care, which were addressed mainly to the white population. He also believed that projects such as the NAMES Project AIDS Memorial Quilt, which sought to memorialize those lost to the virus, did little to halt the spread of the virus or to educate people about their own vulnerability.

While he was still in good health, Hemphill was a popular guest speaker at universities, performing readings and lecturing in institutions such as Howard University, Harvard University, MIT, and the University of Pennsylvania. He participated in the National Black Arts Festival at the Whitney Museum in New York and was a visiting scholar at the Getty Center for the History of Art and the Humanities. He was honored with a Lambda Literary Award for Excellence and received four grants from the District of Columbia Commission for the Arts. At the time of his death, on November 4, 1995, Hemphill left three unfinished projects: *Standing in the Gap* (1999), a novel about a mother defending her gay son who has AIDS from religious condemnation; "Bedside Companions," an anthology of short stories by gay men of color; and a collection of narratives by older gay black men titled "The Evidence of Being." He posthumously received the **James Baldwin** Black Quill Award.

Further Reading

Flannigan-Saint-Aubin, Arthur. "Black Gay Male Discourse: Reading Race and Sexuality within the Lines." *The Journal of the History of Sexuality* 3, no. 3 (1993): 468–90.
Glave, Thomas. "(Re-)calling Essex Hemphill." *Callaloo* 23, no. 1 (2000): 278–84.
Steward, Douglas. "Saints Progeny: Assotto Saint, Gay Black Poets and Poetic Agency in the Field of the Gay Symbolic." *African-American Review* 33, no. 3 (1999): 507–18.

Michele Erfer

Heteronormativity

A term that is widely used in **queer theory**, heteronormativity refers to a foundational belief that heterosexuality is natural and normal, and, therefore, all nonheterosexual attractions, desires, and practices are unnatural and abnormal. It is deeply grounded in the notion that human beings can be categorized into two sexes—male and female— and that men are sexually attracted to women and women are sexually attracted to men. Such an attraction is perceived to be inherently biological and therefore fundamentally natural. Any sexual attraction outside the heterosexual frame is considered deviant and unnatural. The ideology of heteronormativity is pervasive and powerful; it informs a variety of social institutions, belief systems, and cultural practices. Dominant discourses— such as the discourses of law, religion, medicine, and education—collude in the normalization, institutionalization, and perpetuation of heterosexuality as well as in the pathologization of all forms of nonheterosexual desires and behaviors. Heteronormativity, therefore, privileges individuals who view themselves as heterosexuals. It marginalizes people who are homosexual, bisexual, intersexed, or transgendered. Such marginalization, historically, has led to systemic discrimination against nonheterosexuals; it has encouraged mistreatment, abuse, and even violence against them.

In the last two decades or so, queer theorists and many **gender** theorists have sought to disrupt and destabilize the assumptions on which heteronormativity is founded. They argue that gender and sexual identities are, to a considerable degree, performative. Identitites are not natural but socially constructed and culturally reinforced: they are not fixed but fluid; they are not permanent but provisional, contingent, and shifting. Queer theorists assert that heteronormativity is based on a false binary gender system that is repressive and severely stigmatizes a wide range of emotional, affectional, and sexual self-expressions that human beings are capable of. Elimination of beliefs and practices grounded in heteronormativity, they insist, will lead to a more humane and equitable society that acknowledges the legitimacy and validity of human sexual diversity.

See also Heterosexuality; Homophobia

Further Reading

Farrell, Kathleen, Nisha Gupta, and Mary Queen. *Interrupting Heteronormativity.* Syracuse, NY: Syracuse University Press, 2007.

Hall, Donald E. *Queer Theory.* New York: Palgrave Macmillan, 2003.

Katz, Jonathan Ned. *The Invention of Heterosexuality.* Chicago: University of Chicago Press, 2007.

Trevor A. Sydney

Heterosexuality

The most basic definition of heterosexuality (slang "straight") is the state of erotic attraction and/or erotic actions between individuals of the opposite biological sex. Whether or not this is an exclusive state or a fluid one is debatable. Even more problematically, however, heterosexuality commonly becomes interpreted as the "correct" sexual expression and is often defined in opposition to what it is *not*. Thus, heterosexuality's more pernicious connotation as normal, natural, and right is predicated upon a larger system of social injustices, namely, sexism, racism, and **homophobia**—including irrational reactions toward bisexuals, transgendered people, intersex individuals, **gender** benders, and anyone else deemed "**queer**" and "abnormal."

Heterosexuality as a concept arose out of the sexological discourses of the nineteenth century. In 1892, James G. Kiernan defined "heterosexual" as a perversion similar to some modern conceptions of **bisexuality**—a subject who desired both women and men. One year later, heterosexuality's status as a perversion changed with the American publication of *Psychopathia Sexualis, with Especial Reference to Contrary Sexual Instinct: A Medico-Legal Study* (1893, originally published in Europe in 1886) by Richard von Krafft-Ebing, who uses the term "hetero-sexual" to define an individual who desires only one, different sex. Krafft-Ebing implies that sexuality is always reproductive in instinct even if not always in practice, and "hetero-sexuals" were proposed as the "normal" standard against which "homo-sexuals" and other perverts could be measured. The third, and perhaps most influential, use of "heterosexuality" came from psychoanalysis, when Sigmund Freud employed the term in his *Three Essays on the Theory of Sexuality* (1905). For Freud, a heterosexual not only desires the opposite sex, but also is the right and "normal" kind of person to be.

Based on these normative perceptions, procreation is intrinsic to heterosexuality. Early discourse located the urge to reproduce as one of the main reasons for the dominance of heterosexuality and further centered this desire primarily within women. Though this prevailing view came to be challenged by the radical practice and theorization of a new sexual ideal based on the opposite sexes of the individuals involved, reproduction and family—alongside marriage—remain the basis of what **Judith Butler** calls the "heterosexual matrix" (*Gender Trouble,* 1990) and a source of controversy in today's political arena. Further, it becomes the foundation for the concept of "compulsory heterosexuality," a term introduced by **Adrienne Rich** to indicate society's expectation that every human being is initially raised to expect marriage and family—the trappings of heterosexuality —as part of a "normal" life. In other words, not only is every individual presumed to be heterosexual until proven otherwise, but heterosexuals are also never invited to question their (hetero)sexual orientation. Moreover, since heterosexuality is integral to societal organization, it becomes naturalized as well as assumed.

Early twentieth-century studies suggested that genetic bisexuality was the standard genetic and psychological makeup of human beings. Alfred C. Kinsey's famous reports seemingly confirm the genetic disposition by affirming that the majority of people have had both homosexual and heterosexual erotic encounters. Science and theory both seem to agree that human sexuality should be presented on a fluid scale rather than a binary opposition. Whether or not sexual orientation is socially constructed or biologically determined is a related factor. Historically, Freud and many other psychoanalysts and developmental psychologists speculated that formative childhood experiences helped produce sexual orientation and that all individuals experience unconscious same-sex desires to some degree. Though there is currently no general medical consensus, the dominant theory today suggests that biological factors—whether genetic (chromosomal) or acquired *in utero* (exposure to hormones or lack thereof)—at least contribute to atypical gender behaviors. Current American Psychology Association regulations state that sexual orientation is not chosen and cannot be changed and should no longer be considered the basis for deviancy.

Heterosexuality has had a troubled history with the feminist movement. Early liberal feminists criticized Freud for his demeaning and deterministic ideas about women, along with advertisers, magazine writers, and other cultural producers for spreading stereotypes that coerce women into accepting the traditional role as housewife and mother, locked into a position predetermined by heterosexual function. However, many of these liberal feminists also felt that the visibility of lesbians within the women's movement was a hindrance to the cause because heterosexual women were stigmatized as lesbians. Lesbian feminists vehemently disagreed, and for the first time, heterosexuality as an institution came under concentrated attack, though it was still viewed as the norm. With the term "heteropatriarchy," feminists further linked patriarchal oppression to the normativizing of heterosexuality, outlining marriage as slavery for women, with childbirth being a mark of male ownership.

More recently, queer theorists have problematized heterosexuality in two key ways: first, by coining the term "heteronormativity" to refer to the ideological institutionalization of heterosexuality (as distinguished from "heterosexuality," which describes only opposite-sex eroticism); second, by pointing out that heterosexuality, like any other identity, is subjective. For instance, while most Western societies believe that heterosexuals exclusively prefer erotic attachments to members of the opposite sex, some cultures accept that individuals are heterosexual if they maintain their standard societal gender role while receiving sexual gratification through nonheterosexual means. Further, many societies that vilify homosexuality are tolerant of (or turn a blind eye to) "situational homosexuality," since the participants generally define themselves as heterosexual and either practice heterosexuality along with homosexuality or experience a brief period of homosexual relations followed by a much longer period of heterosexuality, and often marriage. That the participants are often referred to as "straight" people who have "gay" sex and then go on to live "normal" (heterosexual) lives only shows how, at times, heterosexuality is defined by the erasure of homosexuality and/or other nonnormative sexualities.

Assumptions such as these—that all people are and should only be "straight"—are indicative not of heterosexuality but of heterosexism—the pervasive prejudice and discrimination against queer people, including unconventional heterosexuals such as single parents and child-free couples. Rather than an individual prerogative, heterosexuality is constrained into the hegemonic cultural imperative of heteronormativity, which is said to be constitutive of "civilization." From the popular wisdom that "opposites attract" to orthodox injunctions against same-sex marriage, "heterosexuality" becomes the prime signifier of Western thought—the central principle of intelligibility in a symbolic of hierarchically arranged binary oppositions that privileges men over women, heterosexuals over homosexuals, whites over people of color, and so forth. That this pervasive system of inequality grossly misrepresents the everyday desires and practices of most ostensible heterosexuals, however, has not impeded its persistence throughout time and across cultures. Thus, for many feminist scholars, gender critics, and queer theorists, disentangling "heterosexuality" from "heteronormativity" has been an urgent and highly contentious endeavor.

Further Reading

Katz, Jonathan Ned. *The Invention of Heterosexuality.* Chicago and London: University of Chicago Press, 1995, rpt. 2007.

Kinsman, Gary William. *The Regulation of Desire: Homo- and Hetero-Sexualities.* 2nd ed. Montreal, QB, Canada/Cheektowaga, NY: Black Rose Books, 1996.

Lochrie, Karma. *Heterosyncracies: Female Sexuality When Normal Wasn't.* Minneapolis and London: University of Minnesota Press, 2005.

Masters, William H., Virginia Johnson, and Robert Kolodny. *Heterosexuality.* New York: Harper-Collins, 1994.

Rich, Adrienne. "Compulsory Heterosexuality and Lesbian Existence." *Signs* 5, no. 4 (1980): 631–60.

Thomas, Calvin, ed., with Joseph O. Aimone and Catherine A. F. Macgillivray. *Straight with a Twist: Queer Theory and the Subject of Heterosexuality.* Urbana and Chicago: University of Illinois Press, 2000.

Michelle M. Sauer

Highsmith, Patricia (1921–1995)

American novelist. Patricia Highsmith was born Mary Patricia Plangman in Ft. Worth, Texas, in 1921. Raised by her mother and stepfather, she earned her bachelor's degree from Barnard College in 1942, after which she spent several years writing stories and plotlines for comic books. Highsmith's first novel, *Strangers on a Train* (1949), has been adapted to the big screen several times, the most notable adaptation being Alfred Hitchcock's 1951 film of the same name. The Hitchcock film brought to Highsmith a great deal of publicity, and in fairly rapid success she continued to publish over 20 novels and several collections of short stories, although the true scope of her work has only recently been fully recognized. Though her novels might be cast as mysteries, Highsmith's fiction reworks that genre in important ways by using psychological and moral ambiguity to heighten the suspense, blending the line between good and evil so that moral judgments must be suspended. In *Strangers,* the two murderers meet each other quite by accident, and the intermingling of their crimes makes it difficult to determine if either or both (or perhaps neither) is morally guilty. Rather laughingly agreeing that if Bruno will kill Guy's wife, Guy will return the favor by killing Bruno's father, the complication becomes not the act of murder itself or who committed the deed but the ethics and execution of the deal itself. What violence does occur in Highsmith's fiction often occurs rather clumsily, the logic and planning of the characters stymied by the messiness of overturned vases and unexpected visitors. Much of her work also employs a homoerotic subtext as a way of further complicating the relationship between good and evil, as is the case with *Strangers* and the Tom Ripley series. In *The Talented Mr. Ripley* (1955; most recently adapted for the screen in 1999), the sexuality of con artist Tom Ripley is as ambiguous as his morals, and he plays both against the privileged backgrounds and desires of his victims. Indeed, Tom Ripley becomes a sort of amoral hero, and some have suggested that Highsmith's Ripley is the progenitor of such cult-like killer figures as Hannibal Lecter, who both attract and repel. Highsmith's refusal to dwell on the simple who and why of the mystery forces readers to identify with Ripley's stern logic. **Queer** readers might find that Highsmith's characters and their ambivalent status as both insiders and outsiders speaks to queer identity and the question of where desire and logic meet. Highsmith's protagonists are at once both unsympathetic and intensely personal, and it this mixture of desire and repulsion that propels most of her work.

Highsmith led a relatively solitary life in exile in Switzerland and France due in part to what biographers have termed a "difficult personality." Nevertheless, she had a number of affairs with both men and women, and one might believe that her own bisexual attractions played some role in shaping the narrative ambiguities that are characteristic of her published work. Using a pseudonym, she did write one novel that can certainly be termed lesbian: *The Price of Salt* (1952; later republished as *Carol*). In *Price of Salt,* Highsmith presented a picture of lesbian life that was not overladen by depression or suicide. The novel is, nonetheless, typical Highsmith in its interest in the complexity of desire and attraction and the messiness of daily life. The two main characters, Carol and Therese, come from different class backgrounds (also a staple in many Highsmith novels) but experience an attraction toward each other that neither is fully able or willing to acknowledge as lesbian. Carol is in the midst of a divorce and custody proceedings, while Therese must deal with a dismissive boyfriend who treats her like a child. The two grow closer both physically and emotionally. Although the novel does not end on an entirely happy note (Carol loses custody of her children), for its day the novel was one of the few that depicted lesbian sexuality as something other than depraved or illicit. Highsmith's work continues to be read and adapted for film. Highsmith died in Switzerland in 1995, leaving the bulk of her estate to the Yaddo writing colony where she received her start.

Further Reading

Cassuto, Leonard. "Reality Catches Up to Highsmith's Hard-Boiled Fiction." *The Chronicle of Higher Education* 50, no. 24 (February 20, 2004): B12.

Cochran, David. "'Some Torture That Perversely Eased': Patricia Highsmith and the Everyday Schizophrenia of American Life." *Clues: A Journal of Detection.* 18, no. 2 (Fall 1997): 157–80.

Wilson, Andrew. *Beautiful Shadow: A Life of Patricia Highsmith.* New York & London: Bloomsbury, 2003.

Milton W. Wendland

Historical Fiction, LGBTQ

LGBTQ historical fiction generally refers to literature that depicts a time period that precedes the period in which the text was written and also contains representations of same-sex desire and/or cross-**gender** identification. By encouraging readers to identify with characters who resemble lesbian, **gay**, bisexual, transsexual, transgender, and/or **queer** people, this literary genre works to undermine homophobic, biphobic, and transphobic beliefs. LGBTQ historical novels "queer" the genre of historical fiction by replacing traditionally "heterosexual" (as I, like many LGBTQ historiographers, am critical of the tendency to use contemporary terminology when speaking of the past, when I use sexual identity labels or other terms anachronistically, I enclose them in quotation marks to signal that this usage is ironic) characters with those who express desire for members of the same sex. Isabel Miller's *A Place for Us* (1969), later republished as *Patience & Sarah* (1972), which is set in early nineteenth-century America, is widely viewed as one of the first and most influential LGBTQ historical novels to date. Miller is generally understood to be the first writer to put historical fiction to "queer" uses. Not only did Miller's powerful novel, *Patience & Sarah,* help define the genre of LGBTQ historical fiction, it also encouraged queer and trans authors to adopt this literary genre. Other American authors such as Sarah Aldridge, **Penny Hayes**, **Christopher Bram**, **Leslie Feinberg**, **Mark Merlis**, and **Tom Spanbauer** have also written influential historical novels that examine the experiences of those who had same-sex desires and/or expressed cross-gender identification in various historical periods.

Like traditional heterosexual historical fiction that often takes the form of historical romance, most LGBTQ historical novels focus on romantic relationships. Yet the romance depicted in LGBTQ historical literature is generally politicized as is seen in texts that represent same-sex relationships in a positive manner and thereby counter the view that LGBTQ people are doomed to lives of misery and depression. The ability of historical romance to convey powerful political statements is also apparent in many lesbian historical novels that depict long-lasting relationships between women and thereby undermine the notion that lesbianism is an infantile state of sexual immaturity that must be superseded by **heterosexuality**.

By focusing on characters who desire members of the same sex, LGBTQ historical fiction also addresses the heterosexism and/or **homophobia** of traditional historical records. LGBTQ historical fiction deviates from traditional heterosexist, "objective" historical accounts by openly exploring same-sex eroticism and encouraging readers to form emotional connections with "queer" and "trans" characters. This literary genre thereby challenges the erasure of LGBTQ pasts and works to fill in gaps in the historical record. While many authors of historical fiction partake in intense historical study and weave historical facts into their narratives, informed speculation is also central to the writing of historical fiction. As the often private and taboo nature of same-sex dynamics generally makes it difficult to know the forms that sexual encounters between members of the same sex took in various past contexts, informed speculation is a central part of historical literature that explicitly depicts sexual acts between same-sex couples. Authors such as Penny Hayes—one of the most prolific writers of lesbian historical fiction—counter the belief that women in the past did not engage in sexual acts with each other by providing explicit depictions of sex between women in their historical novels.

In addition to speculating about past sexual encounters between members of the same sex, many authors of LGBTQ historical fiction hypothesize about both the difficulties experienced by those in the past who expressed same-sex desire and/or cross-gender identification and their survival strategies. For instance, authors of lesbian and queer historical fiction often depict women adopting male disguises in order to avoid sexism and homophobia. Much historical literature represents cross-gender identification as solely an expression of "**lesbianism**" and thereby fails to acknowledge the possibility of "transgender" experience. In contrast, authors of trans historical fiction, such as American novelists Leslie Feinberg and Frankie Hucklenbroich, work to legitimize cross-gender identification as an experience that is separate from, although often related to, same-sex desire. Trans historical novels examine not only past expressions of "homophobia" but also the way that "transphobia" was manifested in various historical periods.

As historical fiction exists in the space between fiction and history, it is widely dismissed for lacking both literary and historical merit. While historical fiction is generally considered to be a low-brow form of literature due to its reliance upon realism and romance, it is also often viewed as ahistorical because it embraces fictionalizations of the past and encourages anachronistic cross-temporal identifications. Although historical fiction predates the postmodern period, this literary genre may be understood as a decidedly postmodern form of literature as it highlights the difficulty of differentiating between fact and fiction and thereby reflects postmodern understandings of history *as* fiction. With the rise of postmodernism, this widely denigrated literary genre has slowly gained critical attention. Many contemporary writers of historical fiction—such as British authors Jeanette Winterson, Jackie Kay, and Sarah Waters—incorporate postmodern literary techniques, such as magic realism, temporal playfulness, and representations of sexuality and gender as shifting and unstable, into their narratives.

"Time-transgression" fiction, one of the subgenres of LGBTQ historical fiction, reflects the playful depictions of time apparent in much postmodern literature. This subgenre includes texts that depict shifts between various time periods as seen in **Michael Cunningham**'s *The Hours* (2002), which examines the lives of three women who live at different times during the twentieth century. Although written during the modernist period, British author Virginia Woolf's *Orlando* (1928) provides an even clearer example of this type of historical fiction as this novel documents the life of a character who lives from 1588 to 1928 and transforms from a man to a woman in the late seventeenth century. Time-transgression novels make connections between the past and the present explicit and demonstrate that there are queer ways of representing and understanding time and our relationship to time. In contrast to the temporal playfulness of time-transgression fiction, "period-portraying" fiction focuses on a single specific historical period and generally uses more realistic plots and representations of time. An example of period-portraying fiction is Sarah Aldridge's *Madame Aurora* (1983), which examines the class struggles faced by women who chose to have same-sex relationships in late nineteenth-century America.

In addition to undermining stereotypical understandings of LGBTQ people, historical fiction helps counter the collective trauma that results from LGBTQ history being neglected or lost. LGBTQ historical literature encourages readers to think critically about dominant heterosexist versions of history and recognize the limits of traditional historical studies. These texts also reveal the interconnectedness of the past and the present since their depictions of past forms of discrimination raise awareness of the ongoing struggles of LGBTQ people while also encouraging challenges to contemporary forms of discrimination.

Further Reading

Jones, Norman W. *Gay and Lesbian Historical Fiction: Sexual Mystery and Post-Secular Narrative.* New York: Palgrave Macmillan, 2007.

Mandy Koolen

Hoffman, William M. (b. 1939)

Award-winning playwright, director, educator, and critic. William Moses Hoffman is a New York City native with a degree from City College. Long a vital presence in New York's experimental and off-Broadway theater scenes, Hoffman is most notable for his pioneering play *As Is* (1985), one of the first major plays to deal with the subject of AIDS. Other major works include *The Ghosts of Versailles* (1991), an opera for which Hoffman wrote the libretto, *Cornbury: The Queen's Governor* (1976), co-written with Anthony Holland, and the seminal *Gay Plays: The First Collection* (1979), for which Hoffman served as editor and wrote the introduction. A prolific writer, works by Hoffman include *Thank You, Miss Victoria* (1965), *Good Night, I Love You* (1966), *Saturday Night at the Movies* (1966), *Incantation* (1967), *Spring Play* (1967), *Three Masked Dances* (1967), *The Cloisters: A Song Cycle* (1968), *Uptight!* (1968), *XXX* (1969), *Luna* (1970), *A Quick Nut Bread to Make Your Mouth Water* (1970), *The Children's Crusade* (1972), *From Fool to Hanged Man* (1972), *Gilles de Rais* (1975), *Cornbury: The Queen's Governor* (1977), *The Last Days of Stephen Foster* (1977), *A Book of Etiquette* (1978), an adaptation of *Gulliver's Travels* (1978), *The Cherry Orchard Part II* (1983), also with Anthony Holland, *Whistler: 5 Portraits* (1984), *Wedding Song* (1984), *As Is* (1985), *The Ghosts of Versailles* (1991), and *Riga* (1995). Most of his early work received its development and support from **Caffé Cino** and La Mama Experimental Theatre Club. Currently an Associate Professor of Journalism, Communications, and Theatre at City University of New York (CUNY), Hoffman has also served as an editor at Hill and Wang, working to develop the work of other playwrights, and he served as a writer for the television hit soap opera *One Life to Live* in the 1990s. But it is 1985's *As Is* that leaves the biggest mark on the theater world. Centering on the relationship between Saul and his lover Rich, the play really seeks to reveal the human costs of AIDS and the vital importance of family and community. The play was an enormous hit and went on to win the Drama Critics Award for Best Play, the Village Voice Obie Award, and it was nominated for the Tony Award for Best Play. Clearly widely loved and respected, garnering mostly positive reviews, the play would also go on to be filmed by director Michael Linsday-Hogg in 1986 and aired on television, winning two nominations for the CableACE Awards. Part of a duo of important plays that hit at the same time, *As Is* is in many ways the more accessible play, **Larry Kramer**'s *The Normal*

Heart (1985) is the other play, but it tends to have much more of an activism focus than *As Is,* which keeps its scope tightly on human relationships. But lest he be known as only an AIDS playwright, it should be noted that the subjects of Hoffman's works vary widely from literary adaptations and sequels to experimental works of the occult and librettos to soap operas. Still a large focus of Hoffman's body of work as writer, editor, and educator has been a historic preservation and contemporary fostering of specifically gay work. The importance of *Gay Plays: The First Collection* really cannot be underestimated, as it would go on to inspire other **gay** playwrights and preserve plays that might otherwise have disappeared once they left the stage. And while *As Is* is overt, if at times experimental, in its depiction of a gay male couple, other works by Hoffman, especially *Cornbury: The Queen's Governor,* are more tongue-in-cheek, alluding to the homosexuality of its title character, but also throwing it into question. Nevertheless, Hoffman's *As Is,* along with Kramer's *The Normal Heart,* broke the silence and taboo around the subject of AIDS in American theater and together demonstrated the complexity of living and dying with the disease and the ramifications of the illness on partners, family, doctors, community, and the nation. Hoffman's work is indispensable to American theater and to the history of the gay and lesbian communities that battled on the front lines during the initial height of the AIDS pandemic in America. It is his work with *As Is* that put a very human face on a mysterious disease and made the audience confront it, and also confront themselves, while simultaneously providing the frightened gay male community with a voice and a venue.

See also AIDS Literature

Further Reading

Baker, Rob. "Early Stages: Larry Kramer, William M. Hoffman, and Robert Chetey." *The Art of AIDS: From Stigma to Conscience.* New York: Continuum, 1994. 175–87.

Carlson, Marvin. "*The Ghosts of Versailles.*" *Theatre Research International* 25, no. 1 (Spring 2000): 3–9.

Clum, John M. *Still Acting Gay: Male Homosexuality in Modern Drama.* New York: St. Martin's Griffin, 2000.

DiGaetani, John L. "William M. Hoffman." *A Search for a Post Modern Theater: Interviews with Contemporary Playwrights.* Westport, CT: Greenwood, 1991. 133–38.

Gross, Gregory D. "Coming Up for Air: Three AIDS Plays." *Journal of American Culture* 15, no. 2 (Summer 1992): 63–67.

Hoffman, William M. "Introduction." In *Gay Plays: The First Collection,* edited by William M. Hoffman, vii–xliv. New York: Avon, 1979.

Lawson, D. S. "Rage and Remembrance: The AIDS Plays." In *AIDS: The Literary Response,* edited by Emmanuel S. Nelson, 140–54. New York: Twayne, 1992.

Plooster, Nancy. "Toxic Bodies and Performance of Mourning in American AIDS Drama." *JAISA: The Journal of the Association for the Interdisciplinary Study of the Arts* 1, no. 2 (Spring 1996): 103–10.

Shackelford, Dean. "William M. Hoffman." In *Contemporary Gay American Poets and Playwrights: An A-to-Z Guide,* edited by Emmanuel S. Nelson, 205–11. Westport, CT: Greenwood, 2003.

Shatzky, Joel. "AIDS Enters the American Theatre: *As Is,* and *The Normal Heart.*" In *AIDS: The Literary Response,* edited by Emmanuel S. Nelson, 131–39. New York: Twayne, 1992.

Sohn, Dong-Ho. "Theory and Practice in Teaching Gay, AIDS Dramas: The Case of *As Is.*" *Journal of Modern British and American Drama* 15, no. 2 (August 2002): 77–107.

Damion Clark

Holleran, Andrew (b. 1943)

Major late-twentieth century novelist, essayist, and cultural critic. Through his use of both humor and pathos, Andrew Holleran has become one of the most prominent chroniclers of **gay** life, documenting both the pleasure and the hedonism of the 1970s and the subsequent impact of AIDS on that community through the 1980s and into the present. More broadly, Holleran's fiction documents the complications of integrating homosexuality with other facets of identity, given the marginalization of alternative sexualities. While Holleran has not published a large quantity of texts, those he has produced have been widely recognized and broadly influential.

Holleran's biographical details are themselves notoriously obscure, given his assumption of a pseudonym and his zealously guarded privacy, although his interview with *Publishers Weekly* in 1983 and *Bookslut* in 2007 provide a few details. Born and raised as Eric Garber in a white, middle-class, American family living in Aruba, Holleran soon moved to the southern United States, attended an exclusive prep school, and graduated from Harvard University in 1965. During the Vietnam War, Holleran was drafted into the army and subsequently served in West Germany; upon his return to the United States he briefly attended law school at the University of Pennsylvania before dropping out in order to enter the Iowa Writers' Workshop. He took the pseudonym Andrew Holleran before the publication of his first book.

After moving to New York in 1971, Holleran began writing for the *New York Village Voice* and *Christopher Street* before achieving an early commercial success with the publication of the satiric **Dancer from the Dance** (1978), ranked as number 15 in *The Advocate*'s 1999 listing of the 100 best gay novels. Structured through the exchange of letters between two gay men, one in New York and one in the Deep South (and inspired by Holleran's own long-term correspondence with **Robert Ferro**), Holleran reformulates the relationship between text and audience as he documents the lives of young homosexual men in their movements among the Everard Baths, the Greenwich Village disco circuit, and the Fire Island house parties. Narrated through emphatically **camp** language by a narrator not directly friendly with the protagonist himself, the novel focuses on the alluring and mysterious Malone, who, accompanied by the wisecracking queen Sutherland, travels through these circles, Dante-like, enticing desire and speculation without ever achieving intimacy. The epistolary framing positions the text as a direct address to a presumably gay audience, an innovative and defiant choice in an industry that, at the time, directed its texts to a presumptively heterosexual reading public. The migration of Malone, moving from an upper-middle-class, traditionally suburban family to the urban hedonism of sex, beauty, and drugs mirrors the evolution of a gay culture obsessed with beauty and youth; more than one commentator has positioned the novel within the literary heritage of F. Scott Fitzgerald's *The Great Gatsby*. Often read as a glamorization of gay promiscuity in the 1970s, in his interview with *Bookslut* Holleran himself characterizes the text as a critical or satiric work in response to a cultural obsession with beauty and anonymous sex.

While the novel received many important reviews, the reception was conflicted and often linking Holleran's text with the similarly controversial publication of *Faggots* in that same year, in which **Larry Kramer** critiques the centrality of beauty, youth, and promiscuity in contemporary gay culture (**Edmund White**'s *Nocturnes for the King of Naples,* released at roughly the same time, is also drawn into the debate). While *The New Republic* and *The New York Times Book Review,* among others, gave Holleran generally positive comments, *Harper's Magazine* leveled a combined assault against both Holleran and

Kramer, for what it characterized as their lack of style and, perhaps more tellingly, their overt attachment to homosexual themes and representations.

Following his success with *Dancer from the Dance,* however, Holleran continued to function as an important cultural critic and social commentator in the New York of the late 1970s. He was an active member in the short-lived but abidingly influential **Violet Quill Club**, a group of gay writers living in New York who met to discuss their work during the years 1980 and 1981, all of whom positioned homosexuality as central to their political and aesthetic ideologies. He and six other men—Edmund White, **Felice Picano**, Robert Ferro, **Michael Grumley**, **George Whitmore**, and **Christopher Cox**—met eight times during that one-year period, reading aloud from their work, emphasizing their own identities as gay men, and writing to an audience they acknowledged as being composed of other gay men. Holleran had been friends with Grumley and Ferro since their days at the Iowa Writers' Workshop in 1965; four of the seven members died of AIDS-related complications by 1989. They have since been celebrated both as constituting a post-**Stonewall** renaissance in writing by gay men and as documenting a specific historical moment before the onset of AIDS. After Ferro's death, *Christopher Street* published Holleran's remembrance of his longtime friend.

His next ostensibly autobiographically inflected creation, *Nights in Aruba* (1983), centers on the relationship between Paul, a young gay man, and his family, inhabitants of rural Florida. The novel is another coming-of-age tale, though here charting the development of an individual rather than the group focus of *Dancer from the Dance.* The novel follows its protagonist Paul through his upbringing on Aruba, his service in the army in West Germany, his subsequent move to New York, and his occasional visits to his retired parents' home in Florida. Again contrasting the urban life of New York with the more rural aspects of life outside the city, Holleran reflects on the varying modes of gay male life, structured through friendship, sex, and the irretrievable past.

After *Nights in Aruba,* the rapidly spreading consequences of the AIDS epidemic prompted Holleran to begin his long-running series of monthly essays for *Christopher Street* as a compromise between the production of fiction and the seeming meaninglessness of writing altogether. Holleran, as well as many other gay authors, was not only confronted with the personal consequences of HIV but was also forced to negotiate its literary implications, in terms of whether anything but AIDS could be a suitable focus of artistic creation. Although Holleran moved to Florida in 1983 to take care of his parents, his removal from New York City did not separate him from the effects of HIV and AIDS. *Ground Zero* (1988) collects 23 of his short essays written in response to AIDS, most notable of which are the twin texts "Notes on Promiscuity" and "Notes on Celibacy," collections of various culturally inflected aphorisms concerning their respective subjects. Here, Holleran challenges the use of fiction in response to AIDS, positioning the autobiographical as the point from which a response to AIDS would most effectively emerge, while at the same time remaining skeptical of the ability of writing to evoke any helpful response, especially in terms of a cure. In the ongoing debate about the role of writing in relation to the AIDS crisis, Holleran strongly challenged writing on anything that did not take AIDS as its explicit theme. While Holleran himself characterizes these essays as mere elegies for friends, they, in fact, confront major literary figures such as F. Scott Fitzgerald, Marcel Proust, Henry James, and George Santayana, as well as broad-ranging cultural themes, such as gay baths, urban and rural life, promiscuity, celibacy, and anger.

In *The Beauty of Men* (1996), Holleran traces the story of 47-year-old Lark, one of the few survivors of a group of AIDS-decimated friends in Manhattan in the early 1990s, who has moved to Florida to care for his paralyzed mother. Following the toll of AIDS, Lark must also confront the implications of aging as a gay man, which brings with it not only the general conditions associated with growing older but also an increased invisibility specific to a gay culture that prizes youth and beauty. Again establishing a contrast between the rural and the urban, here Holleran emphasizes a potentially diasporic gay community wrought through the urban onslaught of HIV. *The Beauty of Men* won the Ferro-Grumley Award for excellence in fiction and experimentation in 1997 and was a finalist for the American Library Association's Gay, Lesbian, Bisexual, and Transgendered Book Award.

In September, the Light Changes (1999) is a collection of 16 short stories, only three of which were previously published, but all of which, taken together, were written over the course of more than 20 years. Here, Holleran explores the experiences of aging as a gay man, continuing his use of varying locales to trace the connections among love, age, lust, and friends. At the same time, the stories all connect to a New York that disappeared decades ago and are thus infused with both grief and nostalgia as they trace the city as much as they do the individuals who once lived within it. Before turning to his next novel, Holleran also wrote the foreword for *The Man I Might Become: Gay Men Write about Their Fathers* (2002), edited by Bruce Shenitz, and co-edited *Fresh Men 2: New Voices in Gay Fiction* (2005) with Donald Weise.

While less explicit in its confrontation of AIDS and its continuing aftermath, Holleran's next work, *Grief: A Novel* (2006), explores the complexity and necessity of varying modes of grief and mourning. The narrator has moved to Washington, D.C., from rural Florida following the death of his mother in order to take a temporary job teaching AIDS literature at Georgetown University. There, he becomes obsessed with Mary Lincoln's letters and consequently ponders the value of grief and the comfort of mourning. Ultimately, Mary Lincoln herself, in her sorrow and pain, dominates the novel, posing the question as to whether grief is powerfully tragic, inevitably comic, or a mixture of both. Interwoven with Mary Lincoln's self-conscious commitment to grief, however, is the narrator's own dilemma concerning his mourning for both his mother and the friends he lost to AIDS. *Grief* won the 2007 Stonewall Book Awards–Barbara Gittings Literature Award.

Holleran has also published works under the name Eric Garber. In 1986, he co-edited with Camilla Decarnin and Lyn Paleo *Worlds Apart: An Anthology of Lesbian and Gay Science Fiction and Fantasy,* followed by the anthology *Swords of the Rainbow* (1996), co-edited with Jewelle Gomez, which was a finalist for the Lambda Literary Award. Garber also published the novel *Embracing the Dark* (1991), another finalist for the same Lambda Literary Award, and co-wrote with Lyn Paleo the nonfiction *Uranian Worlds: A Guide to Alternative Sexuality in Science Fiction, Fantasy, and Horror* (1983).

In 2007, the Publishing Triangle, an association of gay men and lesbians in the publishing industry, founded by Felice Picano, presented Holleran with the Bill Whitehead Lifetime Achievement Award. He is currently working on another collection of essays, tentatively entitled *Sheridan Square,* which brings together his continuing responses to the AIDS crisis. Holleran divides his time between rural Florida and Washington D.C., where he currently teaches at American University.

See also AIDS Literature; Novel, Gay

Further Reading

Bergman, David. *Gaiety Transfigured: Gay Self-Representation in American Literature.* Madison: University of Wisconsin Press, 1991.

———. *The Violet Hour: The Violet Quill and the Making of Gay Culture.* New York: Columbia University Press, 2004.

Denneny, Michael. "AIDS Writing and the Creation of a Gay Culture." In *Confronting AIDS through Literature: The Responsibilities of Representation,* edited by Judith Laurence Pastore, 36–54. Urbana: University of Illinois, 1993.

Sherry, Michael S. "The Language of War in AIDS Discourse." In *Writing AIDS: Gay Literature, Language, and Analysis,* edited by Timothy F. Murphy and Suzanne Poirier, 39–53. New York: Columbia University Press, 1993.

White, Edmund. "Out of the Closets, Onto the Shelves." *Newsweek* (March 21, 1988): 72–74.

Stephanie Youngblood

Homophobia

In 1971, K. T. Smith ushered the word "homophobia" into the academic lexicon with an article titled "Homophobia: A Tentative Personality Profile," and in 1972, George H. Weinberg solidified its scholarly currency with *Society and the Healthy Homosexual.* From its first usages, homophobia signified an aversion to homosexual persons, anti**gay** rage, and an acute dread of homosexuality. Homophobia still carries those connotations; generally, it names feelings of fear, anger, prejudice, and antipathy toward homosexuality (Fone 4–6).

Nonetheless, psychologists maintain that homophobia is not a "true" phobia. As David Plummer summarizes, a typical phobia is driven by fear, but hatred and anger collude with homophobic anxiety. In addition, homophobic attitudes are frequently deemed justified and reasonable while a classic phobia recognizes that the fear is distorted and illogical. Also, homophobia can inspire aggression and violence, where a phobia tends to elicit avoidance. Finally, homophobic discrimination abounds with a cultural significance that does not attach to the standard phobia. To introduce more clarity, various researchers have argued for alternative terms, including "antihomosexual prejudice," "homosexism," "heterosexism," and "homonegativism" (Plummer 4–5). These concepts want to acknowledge the bigoted realities that the "phobia" in homophobia can mask or misname. That said, no proxy has gained currency, and homophobia remains idiomatic.

Homophobia thrives on the stereotypes and logical fallacies that haunt same-sex desire: that homosexuality is "unnatural," "abnormal," "sinful," "immoral," "criminal," "diseased," "disordered," "contagious," "disabled," "predatory," and "gross." The intensity and scope of such assumptions gives homophobia a pervasive cultural reach. Homophobia infiltrates schools, the family, child rearing, police services, laws, public policies, zoning ordinances, court cases, jury verdicts, health care systems, religious institutions, business practices, employee benefit packages, and so forth. Likewise, some thinkers contend that homophobia permeates the search for the biological and social "cause" of homosexuality: the quest for causation tangles with a sociopolitical interest in treatment, correction, and regulating "deviance." Subcategories—such as "institutional homophobia" and "cultural homophobia"—underscore the more public or political manifestations of hatred and intolerance. "Personal homophobia" and "interpersonal homophobia" capture the psychological and communal dimensions of the 'ism, denoting privately held beliefs, name-calling, bullying, social exclusion, gay bashing, and assault.

Without minimizing its genocidal impact on LGBTQ persons, Warren J. Blumenfeld and other scholars have argued for the ways that homophobia also damages members of the straight majority. Because homophobia valorizes unyielding **gender** roles, it constrains the heterosexual subject in rigid notions of "masculinity" and "femininity" and obstructs close, intimate same-sex relationships. Because it nurtures injustice and bigotry, homophobia compromises the humanity of heterosexual persons. Because homophobia works through silence and censorship, it stifles open, healthy conversations about sex and sexuality and effaces mainstream knowledge of the intellectual, spiritual, and creative contributions LGBTQ persons have made.

Despite its usefulness as an inclusive, catchall term, LGBTQ individuals face unique— though interrelated—forms of homophobia. **Lesbianism**, for example, bears specific stigmas: that lesbians either hate men or want to be men; that lesbian desire emanates from failed or abusive heterosexual relationships; that lesbians are unfulfilled and incomplete without heterosexual love, sex, or marriage; that lesbians are not authentic or legitimate "women." Homophobia assumes that gay men are weak and sissified; that they are sex obsessed, irresponsible, and promiscuous; that they are essentially failed men—unathletic, effeminate, flamboyant, excessively interested in fashion, art, or interior design. The most gender-transgressive sexual citizens—"butch" lesbian women and "femme" gay men—are often vulnerable to the most overt and violent forms of homophobic intolerance. Terms like "biphobia" and "transphobia" avow interlocking forms of oppression, but affirm that bisexual and transgender persons shoulder distinct prejudices and stereotypes.

Within the literary tradition, the impact of homophobia is vast and multivalent, shaping canon formation and reader reception. For instance, Henry Abelove and Michael S. Sherry explore the homophobic impulses that shadowed American literary studies in its foundational moments. Given that historical context, in the 1970s and 1980s writers such as **Adrienne Rich** called for a revolutionary approach to creative and critical labor, spurring work that recovers lost voices, re-sees the writing of the past, and shatters an old homophobic world order. Because sexual prejudice and male privilege had rendered much of lesbian history and literature invisible, that call was especially important to galvanizing a lesbian feminist aesthetic. For Rich, sexual identity was essential to discovering and creating a literature that confounds patriarchy and "compulsory **heterosexuality**." In the 1990s, Reed Woodhouse's taxonomy of gay male fiction deployed a text's relationship with homophobic discourse as an aesthetic measuring stick and a categorical tool. "**Closet** literature," for example, recognizes a "gay" selfhood but emphasizes a thematic of shame, isolation, loss, and fear. In contrast, Woodhouse valorizes an "identity literature" that is most resistant and subversive, most impervious to assimilation, most challenging to a homophobic sensibility.

Gloria Evangelina Anzaldúa and others, however, complicate an implicit insistence that "gay" literature take recognizably (or even stereotypically) "gay" forms. That insistence can mean that sexual identity must trump other facets of selfhood (gender, race, class, ethnicity, religion, age, nation, and so forth). That insistence can reduce a text to its sexuality and confine both writer and text to normative or limiting notions of identity. Many **queer** theorists argue that homophobia was a formative precursor to our culture's conceptions of "homosexuality" and "heterosexuality"; thus, some writers caution us against an uncritical relationship to its discourses and paradigms.

Further Reading

Abelove, Henry. *Deep Gossip.* Minneapolis: University of Minnesota Press, 2003.

Anzaldúa, Gloria. "To(o) Queer the Writer." In *InVersions,* edited by Betsy Warland, 249–63. Vancouver: Press Gang, 1991.

Blumenfeld, Warren J., ed. *Homophobia: How We All Pay the Price.* Boston: Beacon Press, 1992.

Faderman, Lillian. *Surpassing the Love of Men.* New York: William Morrow, 1981.

Fone, Byrne. *Homophobia: A History.* New York: Picador, 2000.

Halberstam, Judith. *Female Masculinity.* Durham, NC: Duke University Press, 1998.

Plummer, David. *One of the Boys.* New York: Haworth Press, 1999.

Rich, Adrienne. "When We Dead Awaken." *College English.* 34, no. 1 (October 1972): 18–30.

Sherry, Michael S. *Gay Artists in Modern American Culture.* Chapel Hill: University of North Carolina Press, 2007.

Woodhouse, Reed. *Unlimited Embrace.* Amherst: University of Massachusetts Press, 1998.

Suzanne Ashworth

Homosociality

The term homosociality is used to refer to social relationships among individuals of the same sex, and most typically among men, that are neither intended to be romantic nor sexual in nature. The term is distinguished from homosexuality to reflect that men who engage in homosocial relations derive satisfaction, pleasure, and enjoyment from spending time in the company of members of the same sex without desiring, or taking part in, homosexual relations of any kind with those same individuals. Men typically seek and derive approval of other men through such same-sex social relations, and masculine social hierarchies within groups of men who interact together regularly emerge from those relations. As such, homosociality represents a historically influential form of **gender**ed power because of its emphasis on relations between and among males. The resulting male-male social bonds frequently become valued more highly than male-female relationships.

The concept of homosociality in literary works and other media texts is frequently traced back to the pioneering writing of Eve Kosofsky Sedgwick and her influential book *Between Men: English Literature and Male Homosocial Desire* (1985). The framework she develops in that book, which focuses on the existence of homosocial desire evident in pre-twentieth-century literary texts, has since been applied to all kinds of texts, ranging from Greek poetry to contemporary works of fiction. In her discussion of homosociality, Sedgwick identifies various forms of male bonding that involve male-male interaction and are sometimes associated with societal fears pertaining to homosexuality, such as complex male-bonding rituals or participation in homoerotically charged organizations (such as fraternities or branches of the military). In addition, she demonstrates that the boundaries between the social and the sexual are never entirely clear and are continually in flux. For example, it is common for men engaged in homosocial relationships to demonstrate various forms of physical affection with other men in ways that are not regarded as, nor intended to be, overtly sexual.

Although homosociality is readily evident in literary works geared primarily toward heterosexual audiences, it has also been a common attribute of various forms of LGBTQ literature, past and present. It is frequently used to demonstrate the strong bonds of companionship, caring, and competition that occur among groups of individuals, such as close-knit groups of **gay** men. It also frequently involves sexual rivalry, such that two men who are engaged in a homosocial relationship frequently compete for the affections of another individual, at least in part, because they actually desire one another on some meaningful level and use that motivation to propel their sexual competition.

In literary works, homosociality has functioned somewhat differently in different historical eras. For example, in the post–World War II era, men who preferred to remain engaged in regular forms of homosocial behavior, rather than settling down and taking part in heterosexual marriage and child rearing, were coded in literary works as "gender deviant," a shorthand way of suggesting that they were likely nonheterosexual in an era when such a topic was not always readily and blatantly addressed. In more contemporary works, homosocial practices among men that involve genital exposure or genital contact (such as the occasional penis grabbing) in group settings are sometimes utilized to represent a kind of homoerotic desire that is not regarded as socially acceptable for men to express regularly.

In an insightful analysis stemming from the ideas of Sedgwick, Mary E. Pagano has demonstrated that contemporary media texts featuring homosociality at their core, whether geared to LGBTQ or mainstream audiences, frequently invoke noteworthy aspects of homoeroticism and homoerotic behavior among men while at the same time ensuring that their narratives do not cross over into actual homosexual behavior, even when they initially appear to be destined to do so. In doing so, such offerings generate audience member interest and suspense by teetering on the edge of provocative and potentially subversive behavior before refusing to cross the boundary into the homosexual domain, thereby ultimately disseminating information about and reinforcing acceptable forms of legitimate homosocial bonding that remain somewhat reassuring and uncontroversial.

Further Reading

Pagano, Mary E. " 'Tell Me I'm a Man!': Homoeroticism and Masochism in *Jackass the Movie.*" In *Film and Sexual Politics,* edited by Kylo-Patrick R. Hart, 135–43. Newcastle, UK: Cambridge Scholars Press, 2006.

Sedgwick, Eve Kosofsky. *Between Men: English Literature and Male Homosocial Desire.* New York: Columbia University Press, 1985.

Van Leer, David. "The Beast of the Closet: Homosociality and the Pathology of Manhood." *Critical Inquiry* 15, no. 3 (1989): 587–605.

Waugh, Thomas. "Homosociality in the Classical American Stag Film: Off-Screen, On-Screen." *Sexualities* 4, no. 3 (2001): 275–91.

Kylo-Patrick R. Hart

Howard, Richard (b. 1929)

Influential contemporary American poet, editor, and academic. Shortly after his birth on October 13, 1929, Richard Howard was adopted by the Josephs, a prosperous and prominent Jewish family in Cleveland, Ohio. His adoptive parents inculcated in him an early love of the arts and actively nurtured his childhood fondness for books and poetry. After graduating from Shaker Heights High School in suburban Cleveland in 1947, Howard enrolled at Columbia University. In 1951 he was awarded a B.A. in French and

English and an M.A. the following year. Subsequently he won a fellowship to study at the Sorbonne (1953–1954). The year in France enabled him to refine his command of the French language and develop his lifelong interest in French literature.

After Howard returned to the United States, he worked as a lexicographer for four years. During that time he began to write poetry and to translate major French literary texts to English. Soon he distinguished himself in both efforts. Now Howard, who has published 11 volumes of verse, ranks among the most accomplished contemporary American poets. His creative work has earned him numerous awards, including a Pulitzer Prize (1970) and a MacArthur Foundation Fellowship, often called a "genius grant," in 1996. In 1993 he was appointed the Poet Laureate of New York State. As a translator, his range and prolixity are astonishing: he has translated nearly 160 literary and theoretical works—including works by André Gide, Albert Camus, Simone de Beauvoir, and Roland Barthes—from French to English. He is a fine critic as well; his *Alone with America* is a wonderfully eccentric collection of essays on American poetry since 1950.

For 10 years, beginning in 1987, Howard was a Distinguished Professor at the University of Houston. Currently he lives in New York City, serves as the poetry editor for *The Paris Review,* and teaches at Columbia University.

Erudition is clearly the defining feature of Howard's poetry. An urbane and cosmopolitan poet, his intellectual sophistication is manifest in his densely allusive poetry. Since his frame of reference includes an intimate familiarity with a wide range of contemporary and classical writers, painters, dancers, sculptors, and other artists, his poetry at times is inaccessible to most readers. This obtrusiveness of content, which is further complicated by technical intricacy, renders his poetry largely unappealing to many readers outside academic circles.

The complex nature of the creative process is a central concern in Howard's poetry. He explores the subtleties of this theme by often adopting the voices of major American as well as European modern and premodern artists and speaking through those voices. Such artistic impersonation, or what Norman Friedman aptly characterizes as "literary ventriloquism" (564), has resulted in dozens of exquisitely chiseled dramatic monologues that appear in many of Howard's books of poetry, such as *Untitled Subjects* (1969) and *Two-Part Inventions* (1974). Some readers may view such extended and frequent poetic masquerades—Howard's insistence on concocting multiple identities and voices in his poetry—as an elaborate attempt on his part to submerge, even conceal, his own subjectivity. That he largely eschews the autobiographical-confessional stance so popular among contemporary **gay** American poets certainly reinforces such a perception. However, Howard's penchant for adopting the voices of other artists may indeed be an attempt to inscribe his own selfhood in a subtle yet powerful way in his poetic compositions. Like Robert Browning, whose work has considerably shaped his craft and poetic sensibility, Howard stages his own self seemingly through the voices of others in his dramatic monologues, dialogues, and epistolary poems. As David Bergman astutely argues, the multitude of historical figures who populate Howard's poetry help construct "a cultural and historical matrix in which his own depersonalized work may be located and against which it can resonate" (397). In other words, Howard creates "a cosmopolitan linguistic community" (Bergman 401) of many voices and selves within which he forges his own singular selfhood and distinct poetic voice.

Gay voices are central to this cosmopolitan community that Howard builds in his oeuvre. In fact, a sustained evocation of European American gay men's heritage is a salient feature of his poetry. He recalls and celebrates that cultural legacy as a way of defining himself as an intellectually refined gay man in the postmodern world and, more specifically, as a means of locating his own poetic self in that grand aesthetic tradition. "Decades," the first poem in his collection *Fellow Feelings* (1976), is especially illustrative of this approach that Howard adopts in his work. The poem is an elegiac statement that memorializes Hart Crane's untimely death. What is noteworthy, however, is that here Howard, by imaginatively linking his personal history to Crane's biographical details, firmly plants himself in the gay male tradition in American poetry that began with Walt Whitman. The poem is as much a tribute to Crane, a fellow gay poet, as it is Howard's explicit self-identification as a figure in the gay poetic tradition.

Such obvious gay markers are ubiquitous in Howard's post-**Stonewall** poetry, although subtle gay references are discernible even in his two earliest works: *Quantities* (1962) and *The Damages* (1967). But it is in *Fellow Feelings* (1974) that Howard's self-consciousness as a gay artist first becomes clearly evident. Comprising six lengthy poems, each of which can be defined as a dramatic dialogue in verse, *Two-Part Inventions* (1974) is a tribute to some of the defining figures in the gay artistic culture. "Wildflowers," for example, is a splendid recreation of an imaginary conversation between Walt Whitman and Oscar Wilde. "Contra Naturam," a poem that identifies homosexuality as a fount of creativity, is about Rodin and a male traveler who remains anonymous. "The Lesson of the Master" is a **camp**y narrative that charts a conversation between Edith Wharton and Gerald Roseman in which Wharton, for the first time, learns of her recently dead male lover's homosexuality.

Howard's self-understanding as a gay artist is even more obvious in his *Fellow Feelings* (1976). As the title itself signifies, this collection of poems is an acknowledgment of his "fellows," an impressive gathering of other gay artists, such as W. H. Auden, Marcel Proust, Hart Crane, and Walt Whitman among others. In his subsequent volumes, *Misgivings* (1979) and *Lining Up* (1984), the theme of mutability, accompanied by an elegiac sense of personal and collective loss, surfaces with particular insistence. Those themes and mood dominate Howard's most recent collections—*Like Most Revelations* (1994) and *Trappings* (1999)—in which the haunting presence of AIDS and its attendant loss figure evocatively.

Although Howard's poetry has not elicited extensive critical response—there are, for example, no published book-length studies of his work yet—the reception he has received so far is respectful, even enthusiastic. Daniel Kane's entry on Howard in *Contemporary Jewish-American Dramatists and Poets* is a concise yet informative introduction to the poet's life and work. Kane specifically attempts to locate Howard in the Jewish tradition in American literature. An equally good introduction to Howard is Norman Friedman's chapter in *Contemporary Poets*. Friedman emphasizes the technical aspects of Howard's poetry and praises him for his "learning, sophistication, and brilliance" (564).

James Longenbach's article "Richard Howard's Modern World" offers an excellent survey of Howard's poetry and criticism, while Jerome Mazzaro provides an immensely useful close reading of Howard's famous poem "Even in Paris." Richard Howard's and James Merrill's treatment of the past is the focus of Jeffery Donaldson's fine comparative commentary on the two gay poets.

Michael Lynch's and David Bergman's articles are among the best scholarly readings of Howard as a gay poet. Their sentiments are echoed in Robert K. Martin's enthusiastic assessment of Howard's poetry. Martin finds Howard's verse "elegant and cultured, tasteful and erudite" and adds that he "brings to his poetry a mind trained in the rigors of French politics and ear attuned to the rhythms of Ronsard as well as those of Browning." In our obscenely self-confessional age, Martin asserts, "[Howard] remains a voice of civilization, a man trained in an old tradition. His poems speak clearly of his commitment to the mind and to precision in expression" (109).

Further Reading

Bang, Mary Jo. "An Interview with Richard Howard." *Boulevard* 15, no. 3 (Spring 2000): 37–47.

Bergman, David. "Choosing Our Fathers: Gender and Identity in Whitman, Ashberry, and Howard." *American Literary History* 1, no. 2 (Summer 1989): 383–403.

Donaldson, Jeffery. "Going Down in History: Richard Howard's *Untitled Subjects* and James Merrill's *The Changing Light at Sandover.*" *Salmagundi* 76–77 (Fall 1987–Winter 1988): 175–202.

———. "Physical Measures." *Salmagundi* 88–89 (Fall 1990–Winter 1991): 486–95.

Friedman, Norman. "Howard, Richard (Joseph)." *Contemporary Poets,* 7th ed. London: St. James Press; New York: St. Martin's Press, 2001. 562–65.

Friedman, Sanford. "An Interview with Richard Howard." *Shenandoah* 24, no. 1 (1973): 5–31.

Gray, Paul. "A Conversation with Richard Howard." *Literature in Performance* 2, no. 1 (1981): 76–88.

Greenberg, Martin. "Howard's Rendering." *New Criterion* 18, no. 5 (Jan. 2002): 63–66.

Kane, Daniel. "Richard Howard." In *Contemporary Jewish-American Dramatists and Poets,* edited by Joel Shatzky and Michael Taub, 306–11. Westport, CT: Greenwood Press, 1999.

Longenbach, James. "Richard Howard's Modern World." *Salmagundi* 108 (Fall 1995): 140–63.

Lynch, Michael. "The Life below the Life." In *The Gay Academic,* edited by Louie Crew, 178–92. Palm Springs, CA: ETC Publications, 1976.

Martin, Robert K. "The Unconsummated Word." *Parnassus: Poetry in Review* 4, no. 1 (1975): 109–18.

Maxwell, Mary. "Richard Howard's *Trappings.*" *Raritan: A Quarterly Review* 20, no. 4 (Spring 2001): 139–47.

Mazzaro, Jerome. "Fact and Matter: Richard Howard's 'Even in Paris.'" *Salmagundi* 76–77 (Fall 1987–Winter 1988): 159–74.

Ramke, Bin. "Reading off the Wall: Recent Books by Richard Howard." *Denver Quarterly* 30, no. 2 (Fall 1995): 125–29.

Richman, Robert. "A Chronicle of Vanishings." *The New Criterion* 8, no. 4 (Dec. 1989): 72–73.

Rick, Christopher. "Conspicuous Consumption." *Parnassus: Poetry in Review* 3, no. 1 (1974): 58–64.

Sloss, Henry. "Clearing and Burning: An Essay on Richard Howard's Poetry." *Shenandoah* 29, no. 1 (1977): 85–103.

Sontag, Susan. "The Writer, the Work: Thrown Voices." *PEN America: A Journal for Writers and Readers* 1, no. 1 (Winter 2000): 99–114.

Trevor A. Sydney

Howe, James (b. 1946)

Celebrated author of humorous children's picture and chapter books, including the popular Bunnicula series as well as numerous mysteries and young adult novels. James Howe's contributions to the field of LGBTQ literature began with the publication of his young adult novel called *The Misfits* (2001), a book that became Howe's coming out story. The novel, which tells the story of several young people who decide to take a stand against the name-calling and harassment they have endured for all of their schooling, was followed by its continuation in *Totally Joe* (2005). Joe, a young **gay** boy in both of the novels, is the character that Howe claims was based somewhat on his own story.

Howe, born on August 2, 1946, in Oneida, New York, claims to have always loved playing with words and remembers using them to get attention from his three older brothers. His father, Lee Arthur Howe, was a clergyman and his mother, Lonnelle Crossley Howe, was a teacher. Howe began writing at age seven and continued with articles for the school newspaper in high school. He received his B.F.A. from Boston University in 1968, but he took a job as a social worker after graduation as civilian public service during the Vietnam War. After working for a few years as an actor and director, Howe entered graduate school and received an M.A. from Hunter College in 1977. While in a playwriting seminar Howe rediscovered his love of writing.

He wrote his first children's book, *Bunnicula: A Rabbit-Tale of Mystery* (1979), with his first wife, Deborah Smith, whom he married in 1968. Smith also was a writer and actor, and the two collaborated on many book projects until her death in 1978. Howe continued his children's book career, married Betsy Imershein in 1981, and had a daughter. The couple divorced in 2002, and Howe now lives with his partner, Robert Mark Davis.

The years 2001–2002 marked important points in Howe's life and career as he published *The Misfits* as his coming out story. The story of young teens fighting against name-calling has become a national phenomenon with schools across the country establishing "no name-calling" weeks. What makes the story even more appealing is its lighthearted humor and quirky characters, especially in the character of Joe, perhaps one of the most self-accepting gay teenagers in literature. Joe's assurance of his **gender** identity as well as his sweet gay teen romance as part of normal existence make the story an important text for young adults.

Further Reading

"James Howe."*Contemporary Authors Online,* Gale, 2008. Reproduced in *Biography Resource Center.* Farmington Hills, MI: Gale, 2008.

"James Howe." *Major Authors and Illustrators for Children and Young Adults,* 2nd ed., 8 vols. Gale Group, 2002. Reproduced in *Biography Resource Center.* Farmington Hills, MI: Gale, 2008.

"James Howe." *St. James Guide to Children's Writers,* 5th ed. St. James Press, 1999. Reproduced in *Biography Resource Center.* Farmington Hills, MI: Gale, 2008.

Ruth R. Caillouet

Hunger of Memory: The Education of Richard Rodriguez

This widely taught self-representational text by **Richard Rodriguez**, published in 1982, chronicles the author's coming-of-age as a first-generation American of Mexican descent. As its subtitle implies, this *Bildungsroman* concentrates upon the "history of [Rodriguez's] schooling" (4), a focus accounting, in part, for the book's critical success: its timely publication during the early 1980s provided ideal fodder for culture wars raging within U.S. institutions of higher education—over literary canons, affirmative action, and bilingual education. Controversial for its conservative stance on these issues, the book was roundly praised by the popular but decried by the more liberal academic press. Although Rodriguez is careful to say that he does not "intend to model [his] life as the typical

Hispanic-American life" (6), this pledge of circumspection seems not to apply to the several occasions upon which he critiques educational equity policies based solely upon his own experience in schools. His claims that such identity-based policy actually impeded (rather than enhanced) his personal and academic success quickly elevated him to the status of "poster child" for conservatives on these issues. It is significant that Rodriguez's homosexuality is never overtly mentioned in the autobiography.

The book was a critical success in its own right, however, earning several awards including the Anisfeld-Wolf Book Award, the Christopher Prize for Autobiography, and the Gold Medal for Nonfiction from the Commonwealth Club of California. Rodriguez also won the Frankel Medal from the National Endowment for the Humanities and the International Journalism Award from the World Affairs Council of California for his work on the book. *Hunger of Memory* is the first in a trilogy made complete by two later autobiographies, *Days of Obligation: A Conversation with My Mexican Father* (1992) and *Brown: The Last Discovery of America* (2002), publications that resulted in Rodriguez's nomination for the National Book Critics Circle Award and the Pulitzer Prize in Nonfiction.

Hunger of Memory comprises, in fact, several shorter autobiographical essays. However, unlike Rodriguez's two later autobiographies, similarly composed but more stylistically experimental, the essays in this volume are arranged in rough chronological order. As such, they trace Rodriguez's educational path from his days in the 1960s and 1970s at predominantly white middle-class primary and secondary Catholic schools in suburban Sacramento, through his undergraduate years at Stanford University, to his graduate studies at Columbia University and the University of California at Berkeley in the late 1970s and early 1980s, to the abrupt ending of his sojourn in U.S. higher education with his rejection of the several job offers he received from some of the nation's most elite universities, to end with his days as an independent scholar writing this book.

The book's first and now widely anthologized essay, "Aria," tells of Rodriguez's struggle to negotiate home and school cultures as a young student, a heartbreaking narrative of what Rodriguez deems "inevitable" cultural assimilation and one that he uses as a basis for denouncing bilingual education. In the second essay, "The Achievement of Desire," Rodriguez endeavors to understand this painful assimilation experience through British sociologist Richard Hoggart's notion of "the scholarship boy," a narrative foray through which Rodriguez implicitly impugns affirmative action. In the third essay, "Credo," Rodriguez reflects upon the role that the Catholic Church—one of the sole cultural constants throughout his childhood and adulthood—has played in forming his identity. "Complexion," the book's fourth chapter, reflects upon class and racial identity and Rodriguez's own struggle to identify with those working-class Mexicans whom his mother disparagingly calls "*los pobres.*" In chapter five, "Profession," Rodriguez explicitly takes affirmative action to task and, in so doing, separates himself from many Chicanos and members of other politicized minority groups who insist that one can maintain one's ethnic heritage while being educated in mainstream schools: "The child who learns to read about his nonliterate ancestors," Rodriguez counters, "necessarily separates himself from their way of life" (173). The book's final chapter, "Mr. Secrets," offers a personal reflection upon self-disclosure and the autobiographical act itself.

The third of four children born to Mexican immigrants, Rodriguez was the first among a slew of critically successful authors who emerged during the 1980s and 1990s to relate the now familiar tale of the "hyphenated American": the first-generation child of parents who abandoned well-established careers, family, and friends in their homeland, all to afford their children access to the American Dream. Like Maxine Hong Kingston, Amy Tan, and other prominent authors writing in this genre, Rodriguez reflects upon his struggle to balance the cultural values of home with those of the dominant, white middle-class (and implicitly, in his case, heteronormative) "American" culture. But unlike the stories of some of his counterparts, Rodriguez's is admittedly rife with nostalgia, longing, and an insatiable "hunger" for ties to a past that grow increasingly more tenuous as the years wear on. "What preoccupies me is immediate: the separation I endure with my parents in loss" Rodriguez discloses in the book's prologue. "That is what matters to me: the story of the scholarship boy who returns home one summer from college to discover bewildering silence, facing his parents. This is my story. An American story" (4).

On one hand, Rodriguez acknowledges that his story embodies themes common to all coming-of-age stories: moving "from the company of family and into the city. This was my coming-of-age: I became a man by becoming a public man" (5–6). But on the other, Rodriguez recasts a story partially about emergent language and identity development— what philosopher Jacques Lacan calls the human subject's developmental progression away from the "real" and into the "symbolic order"—as one almost exclusively about cultural and linguistic assimilation. Rodriguez maintains that "Bilingualists scorn the value and necessity of assimilation . . . . They do not realize that while one suffers a diminished sense of *private* individuality by becoming assimilated into public society, such assimilation makes possible the achievement of *public* individuality" (26; emphasis in original). Thus Rodriguez's understanding of his loss in terms of a neat Spanish/English, private/public analogy reduces what should *also* be understood as an effect of childhood and cognitive development to a strictly sociocultural phenomenon.

This criticism, however, is intended neither to diminish the pain and genuine loss of language and culture that Rodriguez experiences nor to ignore his incisive critique of institutionalized racism. Indeed, Rodriguez's candid reflections upon his experiences in schools do expose many of the difficulties and dilemmas faced by nonnative speakers and people of color. Rodriguez should also be celebrated for bravely exposing the hypocrisies and racist behaviors of white liberal academe (and, in so doing, wittingly burning bridges between himself and those cultural institutions with which he shares the most affinity). But it *is* to point out the heavy-handed and, ultimately, unscientific nature of Rodriguez's criticism of educational equity policies.

To put it more plainly, Rodriguez suggests that nonnative speakers must choose English only and complete cultural assimilation if they are to maximize their opportunities for success, since practicing a first language or one's cultural traditions essentially compromises one's access to mainstream institutions of power. However, this argument ignores scholarship that clearly contends otherwise. Educational researchers such as Jim Cummins have shown the cognitive and psychological benefits of allowing students to continue to build upon "underlying proficiencies" in their first languages while developing their English language skills. And in recent years, as teachers are increasingly expected to practice more "culturally responsive" pedagogy, the benefits of such a more democratic pedagogical approach have also been shown (see **Gay**). To be fair to Rodriguez, however, much of the richest research in these fields was only developing as *Hunger of Memory* was published in 1982, emerging, much like the autobiography, out of climate of debate over the Bilingual Education Act of 1981 and California's Proposition 227 (1998).

Of course, the proverbial elephant in the living room throughout Rodriguez's coming-of-age story is his emergent (homo)sexuality. One cannot help but wonder how the combined influences of what Rodriguez later calls his "sexually secretive" youth and the homophobic values of Mexican Catholics depicted by Latina lesbian authors, such as **Gloria Evangelina Anzaldúa** and **Cherríe Moraga**, contributed to the painful alienation from his family that Rodriguez describes. In other words, it is well worth considering what role, if any, *heteronormative* assimilation may have played in the feelings of "loneliness" and never being able to "go home again" that Rodriguez attributes, in *Hunger of Memory,* to cultural and linguistic assimilation alone.

Further Reading

Anzaldúa, Gloria. *La frontera/Borderlands.* San Francisco: Aunt Lute, 1987.

Cummins, Jim. "Primary Language Instruction and the Education of Language Minority Students." In *Schooling and Language Minority Students: A Theoretical Framework,* edited by Charles F. Leyba, 3–46. Los Angeles: Evaluation, Dissemination and Assessment Center, 1994.

Gay, Geneva. *Culturally Responsive Teaching: Theory, Research, and Practice.* New York: Teachers College Press, 2000.

Moraga, Cherríe. *Loving in the War Years.* Boston: South End Press, 1983.

Olivas, Michael A. Review of *Hunger of Memory: The Education of Richard Rodriguez,* by Richard Rodriguez. *The Chronicle of Higher Education* 54 (1983): 472–75.

Staten, Henry. "Ethnic Identity, Class and Autobiography: The Case of *Hunger of Memory.*" *PMLA*113, no. 1 (1998): 103–16.

Torres, Hector A. "'I Don't Think I Exist': Interview with Richard Rodriguez." *MELUS* 28, no. 2 (2003): 165–202.

Cynthia Sarver

I

Indiana, Gary (b. 1950)

Writer, director, actor, journalist, playwright, photographer, critic, and musician. Gary Indiana, born Gary Hoisington, does not talk much about growing up in Derry, New Hampshire. Born in 1950 into a working-class family, Indiana has referred to his early life simply as "turbulent," "strange," and "provincial." The life he has led since his escape from suburban New England, however, can also be described as turbulent and strange, but it has certainly been anything but provincial. Over the past few decades, Indiana has assumed the reputation of a worldly if jaded jack-of-all-trades. His boundless intellectual energies and willingness to take chances have allowed him to move among the fields of literature, film, theater, music, photography, and art with relative ease. And yet, while the medium often changes, the message has remained very much the same. For all his generic variability, Gary Indiana is, in fact, an artist focused on a single quest to expose the moral corruption and absurdity that lies at the heart of contemporary America.

After leaving Derry to attend Berkeley in the late 1960s, Indiana dropped out of college and settled for a while in Los Angeles. Following an automobile accident in 1974, he decided to start afresh in New York City, where he immediately became immersed in the **gay** and bohemian underground of downtown Manhattan. Indiana began directing plays for small theater companies, performing in a punk band called The Boners, and appearing regularly as an actor in low-budget art films. But it was art criticism for which he would become better known. The publication of a succession of highly regarded essays in the journals *Art in America* and *ArtForum* led to a job in 1985 as senior art critic at the *New York Village Voice*. What makes this hire remarkable is the fact that Indiana had actually had no formal training in either the theory or practice of art. In many ways, Indiana was a new kind of art critic, one whose unique journalistic style featured sharp insight as much as it did personal reflection, cultural critique, literary flair, and a vicious wit.

Examples of his work during this time were later collected in a volume entitled *Let It Bleed: Essays 1985–1995* (1996). But restlessness and disillusionment soon set in, and, after three controversial years at the *Voice,* Indiana decided to abandon his high-profile post in order to pursue other writing projects.

From the late 1980s to the present, Indiana has produced two collections of short stories, six novels, dozens of articles, and three books of nonfiction. His literary output as a whole is marked by a deeply cynical tone and an obsessive preoccupation with, among other issues, the superficiality of modern life, the hypocrisy and selfishness of human beings, and the damaging effects of media and celebrity on American culture. All of these elements perhaps find their greatest expression in what Indiana has called his "American crime trilogy." Each piece of this unofficial trilogy involves the fictionalization of the lives of infamous personalities whose crimes have been sensationalized by the American mass media. The first in the series, *Resentment: A Comedy* (1997), is a novel based loosely on the trial of Erik and Lyle Menendez, the Beverly Hills brothers convicted of murdering their wealthy parents. In *Resentment,* Indiana presents a biting satire of modern-day Los Angeles, turning his unrelenting critical gaze upon everything from television to gay subculture to the U.S. justice system. Similar themes are taken up in the next installment, *Three Month Fever: The Andrew Cunanan Story* (1999). *Three Month Fever* is a hybrid of fiction and nonfiction that closely documents the life and death of the young gay man accused of murdering Italian fashion designer Gianni Versace. Indiana uses both factual evidence and creative license to humanize Cunanan who, as his author argues throughout the book, had been unfairly demonized by an ignorant and unsympathetic media. The last in the trilogy, *Depraved Indifference* (2001), returns to a more traditional novelistic form. Here Indiana depicts the criminal exploits of a pair of mother-and-son con artists modeled on the real-life con artist team of Sante and Kenneth Kimes. As with every book in the series, *Depraved Indifference* manages to put on trial not only its criminal protagonists, but also the very moral indifference of America itself.

While he continues to write in a wide range of styles, from film studies and art monographs to cultural commentaries and even the occasional autobiographical novel, Gary Indiana has remained true to his protean nature and has not limited his work solely to the literary medium. In 2002, for instance, Indiana debuted his first photography exhibition and, in 2007, he directed two feature films: *Pariah* and *Soap.* Once the product of a "provincial" upbringing, Indiana now finds himself on a ceaseless odyssey of artistic exploration and discovery. Indeed, he seems to have rightly earned his reputation as a jack-of-all-trades, but whether he proves to be a master of any, only time will tell. What is certain, however, is that Gary Indiana is today one of the most vocal and one of the most relevant commentators on the corrupted state of the contemporary American milieu.

Further Reading

Cartwright, Garth. "The King of Blood and Mischief." *Guardian* (Manchester), February 19, 2000, 11.

Press, Joy. "The Laws of Depravity." *New York Village Voice,* February 12, 2002, 53–54.

Jules Hurtado

Inman, Will (b. 1923)

Noted antiwar, labor, civil, and **gay** rights activist/poet. William Archibald McGirt, Jr., was born May 4, 1923, in Wilmington, North Carolina, to William A. McGirt, who worked in the insurance and real estate business, and Delia E. Inman, a registered nurse. Inman worked in a shipyard during World War II and graduated from Duke University in 1943. His activism as a tobacco union organizer led to being called before the Un-American Activities Committee in 1956. After that he worked in libraries in New York City and began writing. In the mid-1960s he was vice-president of the Free University of New York. Inman was appointed poet in residence at American University in 1967 and taught there and at Montgomery College (1969–1973). He married Barbara Ann Sherman in 1969, and they divorced in 1973, at which time he took his mother's maiden name. Author of numerous books and chapbooks of poetry, a few stories, and many essays, Inman is also a prolific correspondent and diarist, serving as editor for a number of literary journals, most notably *Kauri,* and columnist for the *Franklin (PA) News Herald* (1960s). Inman's papers are collected at Duke University. In 2005 the Tucson Poetry Festival, which he co-founded, established the Will Inman Award. He currently resides in a nursing home in Tucson, Arizona.

In 1956 Inman quit the Communist Party and the War Resisters League after becoming disenchanted with ideology at the expense of humanitarianism. He stresses the hidden meaning of his name "Will In-Man" to reflect his aesthetic—each human being's individual spark demonstrates and powers the whole and organizes life-force into spiritual insight and collaborative growth. Inevitably, he was led to work with the disabled, prisoners, and the homeless through workshops stressing the healing nature of poetry and instinctive encounters with the world acting as a studio for the sacred.

Metaphoric excess, churning with dazzling images and brilliant self-questionings, characterizes Inman's poetry. It celebrates psyche unfolding into universal, even Promethean, elevations of language within which the human spirit might thrive. Social engagement and biographical reminiscence aid in realizing these pyrotechnical arguments for wholeness and responsibility.

Reminiscent of *The Song of Solomon,* the chapbook *A Resonance of Begetting* (2001) narrates the unifying fecundity between the poet and an Indian-Cherokee lover through images of tides, bridges, serpents, and turtles. The poem "Lazarus" (*Mad Window* journal, 1969) recasts Jesus as a holy being who first passes his physical love around to everyone, but particularly to Lazarus ("our man-love fertilizing the olive bloom"), and his sisters, Martha and Mary. When Jesus leaves to begin his mission, Lazarus—brokenhearted—dies. Jesus revives him, renewing their love, foretelling the Passion. The poem ends with a prayer to "open the narrows" of the poet's "to the timeless verge" that love is. Unfortunately, most of Inman's obviously gay poetry remains unpublished; however, Leyland Publications is currently working on a collection. Until then *Surfings: Selected Poems* (2005) offers a small selection from Inman's enormous output.

Further Reading

Gargan, William. Review of *Memoirs of an Activist Poet.* by Will Inman. *Library Journal* 123 (November 15, 1998): 67.

Review of *Memoirs of an Activist Poet.* By Will Inman. *Publishers Weekly* 245 (October 19, 1998): 68.

"Will Inman." *Contemporary Authors Online,* 2002. Literature Resource Center. Gale. University of North Carolina at Chapel Hill Library. http://galenet.galegroup.com (accessed November 11, 2007).

Jeffery Beam

Innaurato, Albert (b. 1948)

Italian American playwright, director, television writer, essayist, and professor. Best known for his Broadway smash *Gemini* (1976), Albert Innaurato explores issues of sexuality, social and generation gaps as well as the bridges between them, second- and third-generation Italian American experiences, and issues of physical weight. Indeed, food often serves as a major plot device in his work, used to great comic effect in *Gemini* and with haunting and painful consequence in his short play *The Transfiguration of Benno Blimpie* (1977).

Innaurato was born in 1948 to Italian immigrants and grew up in South Philadelphia, which provides the settings for much of his work. He received a B.A. in theater from Temple University and spent some time at the California Institute of the Arts before joining the playwriting program at the Yale School of Drama, receiving his M.F.A. in 1974. His class at Yale was awe-inspiring: its students included actors Meryl Streep and Sigourney Weaver and playwright **Christopher Durang**, with whom Innaurato developed a friendship and working relationship. At Yale, the two co-wrote the farce *The Idiots Karamazov* (1974), starring Streep. Seen by many influential critics and theater makers, the farce helped launch the careers of the two young playwrights. During their stay at Yale, they both spent time at **Edward Albee**'s writers' retreat. While there, Innaurato began working on *The Transfiguration of Benno Blimpie,* a play that Innaurato claims appeared to him in a dream that demanded to be solved onstage.

Innaurato received a Guggenheim Fellowship in 1975. Despite undergoing serious health problems stemming from an operation he underwent while a student at Yale, Innaurato used the Guggenheim to work full time on *Gemini.* Indeed, his hemorrhaging from the initial surgery led to a second surgery, which resulted in an infection. Uninsured, Innaurato turned to former Yale Dean of Students Howard Stein for assistance. Stein sought financial help for Innaurato, and the young playwright was able to finish *Gemini.* Playwrights Horizon held a workshop of the play with Sigourney Weaver in the cast in December 1976. It subsequently enjoyed a short run at Long Island's PAF Playhouse before moving to off-Broadway's Circle Repertory Company and eventually to Broadway's Little Theatre, where it ran for four years and 1,819 performances. Though Sigourney Weaver left the show before it arrived on Broadway, up-and-comers Danny Aiello and Robert Picardo were in the original Broadway cast, and young actors Jeff Daniels, Wayne Knight, and Kathleen Turner would be part of the cast during its lengthy run. Innaurato won a 1976–1977 Obie for playwriting and Aiello and Anne De Salvo won Obies for their performances in the show. On the way, Innaurato also received a Rockefeller grant.

Gemini is Innaurato's greatest commercial success to date. Helped no doubt by a notorious New York television ad campaign emphasizing the more vulgar aspects of the show, the production enjoyed large audiences that thought they would perhaps be spectators to an evening of burlesque. Critical response was mixed, and Innaurato claims that the production suffered from a cartoonish production style devised to offset the late 1970s Broadway audience's reluctance to accept the play's profane language and misfit characters in a realistic style. Set in South Philly on the day of Francis Geminiani's 21st birthday in the summer 1973, *Gemini* is at heart the story of Francis and his father, Fran, as they work to strengthen their father/son bond despite Francis's struggles with his sexuality and his Italian American heritage, problems exacerbated by the arrival of his white Anglo-Saxon Protestant friends Judith and Randy from Harvard, where Francis dates Judith but is attracted to her brother Randy. Also thrown into the mix is Fran's girlfriend, the restrained Lucille, and randy neighbor Bunny and her overweight, eccentric son Herschel. The play climaxes at a painful birthday party at which truths are revealed and food is flung, apparently even into the audience during the play's Broadway run. During the play's denouement, Fran assures his son that he will always love him, no matter what his sexual orientation may be, an issue left undecided at the play's end.

As *Gemini* opened on Broadway, Innaurato's haunting and much darker work, *The Transfiguration of Benno Blimpie*, was beginning its off-Broadway run at the Astor Place with James Coco in the title role. Seated apart from the rest of the actors, the enormous Benno begins the play with his declaration that he is eating himself to death. Surrounded by family members who stop obsessing about their own problems only long enough to tell Benno that he is fat, the boy eats to fill the emotional void that his angry mother, negligent father, and pedophiliac grandfather have torn open in him. Benno is rendered passive to the point of putting up no fight as he is raped in the local schoolyard by three local bullies. In the final scene, a grotesque parody of the Eucharist, Benno is draped in a white robe upon which a butcher's chart is drawn. As the play ends, Benno brandishes a meat cleaver as he prepares to hack and literally eat himself to death. The play, along with *Gemini*, won a playwriting Obie, and Coco won an Obie for his performance. Both plays also received 1977 Drama Desk Award nominations for Outstanding New Play.

Though Innaurato has not yet again achieved the commercial success of *Gemini* or the critical success of *Gemini* or *The Transfiguration of Benno Blimpie*, he has continued to write for the theater and for film and television, garnering an Emmy nomination for his 1978 screenplay *Verna: USO Girl*. He lectures on opera throughout the country, and he writes frequently for the *New York Times* and *New York Magazine*.

Further Reading

Ahearn, Carol Bonomo. "Innaurato and Pintauro: Two Italian-American Playwrights."*MELUS* 16, no. 3 (1989–1990): 113–25.

Clurman, Harold. "Theatre." *Nation,* April 2, 1977, 410–11.

Innaurato, Albert. Introduction. *Best Plays of Albert Innaurato.* New York: Gay Presses of New York, 1987. iii–xvi.

Lange, Alexandra. "The Other Philadelphia Story." *New York Magazine* June 14, 1999. http://www.nymag.com/nymetro/arts/features/805 (accessed January 21, 2008).

Jeff Godsey

Islas, Arturo, Jr. (1938–1991)

Mexican American novelist, poet, and professor. Arturo Islas, Jr., was born to Arturo Islas and Jovita La Farga on May 25, 1938, in El Paso, Texas. His parents named him to honor the memory of the first Arturo Islas, who was an intellectual, poet, and hero shot dead by a Federalist bullet in the Mexican Revolution of 1918. In many ways, Islas lived up to this memory, becoming himself a poet, novelist, and intellectual who cleared new paths of expression and thinking in the late twentieth century.

Born the first of three sons, Islas (or, "Sonny," as his family called him) grew up in a racially divided and divisive El Paso during the late-1930s and 1940s. This was a time when signs such as "No Mexicans Allowed" were posted in shop windows and when the public swimming pool was open to Mexicans only just before emptying and cleaning. Needless to say, the Islas family—especially the paternal grandmother, Crecenciana Sandoval Islas—espoused bicultural Anglo and Mexican values and encouraged bilingual Spanish/English fluency, providing Islas with the tools necessary to sidestep prejudice from an early age. So, while many of his Mexican American peers struggled with English-only classes in elementary school, Islas excelled. While Spanish was spoken at home, Islas became an avid reader and writer in English from an early age. If he was not under the great oak at the back of the family's house on Almagordo Street, he was to be found at the library or with this grandmother doing homework. Any spare time he had, he spent as an alter boy at the local parish.

Islas's childhood became even more ascetic after he contracted the polio virus just after turning eight years old and just before returning to school after summer break. The polio virus was caught early enough to curtail an untimely death, but not fast enough to prevent the uneven growth of his legs; even after a surgery during his teenage years, he would not only have to buy two separate pairs of shoes to match the different sizes of his feet, but he would walk with a decided limp for the rest of his life.

Throughout high school, Islas's passion for knowledge continued unabated; he excelled especially at science and English. And while a shorter left leg left him with a limp, this did not stop him from dancing a mean jitterbug at school socials. And his charm and good looks made him extremely popular. Graduating from El Paso High as class valedictorian in 1956, Islas became the first Chicano to attend Stanford University on an Alfred P. Sloan scholarship. Although Islas entered Stanford with the idea of becoming a neurosurgeon, by the time he graduated in 1960 with a degree in English and a minor in religion, it was with the firm conviction that he would pursue literary studies and creative writing. That fall, Islas returned to Stanford to embark on his Ph.D. studies in English. Here he studied with Ian Watt, Wallace Stegner, and Yvor Winters—the most influential of his mentors. However, during the height of the civil rights movement and worker and student protests worldwide (Mexico, Paris, and Czechoslovakia), he decided to take some time out of the program to find use outside the Ivory Tower. After working for about a year, including as a speech therapist at the Veterans Administration Hospital in Menlo Park, California, Islas suffered from an ulcerated intestine that led to a brush up against death and, after three major surgeries, an ileostomy. After recuperating from his surgeries and learning to live with a colostomy bag, Islas finished his Ph.D. and secured a tenure track position in the English department at Stanford in 1971.

During the next five years on the Stanford campus, Islas developed path-breaking courses on Chicano/a literature, established a Chicano/a literary journal, worked to open scholarly spaces for incoming Mexican American undergraduates, and wrote reams of poetry as well as his first novel, *Día de los muertos/Day of the Dead*. Much of his writing during this period not only textures the experiences of a Chicano, but absorbs his full exploration of life as a **gay** man living in a San Francisco bursting at the seams with same-sex exuberance, including cruising and the frequenting of sadomasochistic clubs and bathhouses. In 1976, Islas's creative work and tremendous dedication to teaching and his students was recognized by the university by promoting him to associate professor. During this period, he dedicated much time to writing, revising, and sending out the manuscript of *Día de los muertos* to try to secure a contract with a New York publisher. By the early 1980s, *Día de los muertos* had been rejected by over 30 different publishers; as the letters from publishers such as HarperCollins, Farrar Straus and Giroux, and so on attest, editors objected either to his excessive use of Spanish (a quick glance at the original manuscript shows the contrary) and/or to his too strong presence of a gay Chicano protagonist. Islas finally published the novel, much transformed, as *The Rain God* in 1984 with a small local publisher, Alexandrian Press in Palo Alto, California. It immediately achieved a word-of-mouth eminence within university and high school classrooms and journalistic acclaim in such newspapers as the *San Francisco Chronicle* and the *Los Angeles Times.*

Islas had finally realized his dream of publishing a Chicano novel that spoke with great subtlety and nuance not only to the ins and outs of a Chicano family life, but also to the interiority of a gay Chicano. That the novel did well—it was also translated into Dutch as *De Regen God*—spurred Islas on to write the next novel. During a visiting professorship (1986–1987) at the University of El Paso, Texas, Islas wrote a draft of the novel he ultimately titled *La Mollie and the King of Tears.* In a sharp turn from the mythopoetic voice of *The Rain God,* he uses a fast-paced first-person narration told from the point of view of Louie Mendoza—a musician from El Paso living in San Francisco's mission. Islas employs the noir genre to frame Louie's adventures and his coming to terms with his past (a lost daughter), his brother's **queer** sexuality, and his internalizing of self-destructive values. When Islas sent the manuscript out, he again met with great resistance. The novel was eventually posthumously published in 1996 by the University of New Mexico Press—a press that had rejected the manuscript when he first sent it.

While Islas's experience with trying to get *La Mollie* published met with dead ends, *The Rain God* was selling well, in fact, too well for the small Alexandrian Press to keep up with demand. Islas knew that he needed to reach back out to New York, so he signed on with famed literary agent Sandra Dijkstra, who shopped it around for paperback rights and also secured him a contract with William Morrow to write a sequel. With his advance contract in hand, and later Avon's purchase of the paperback rights to republish *The Rain God,* Islas began typing out the story of characters from the fictionalized town of "Del Sapo" (an anagram of El Paso that also playfully translates from the Spanish as "From the Toad") and set during a period earlier (1950s–1960s) than that of *The Rain God.* Between late 1987 and early 1989, the novel that would be published as *Migrant Souls* took shape. Here, Islas focused less on the Angel family and the gay character Miguel Chico and more on the women in the family—especially that new generation of women willing to act and speak against the family's restrictive sexist and racist codes of conduct. As such, Islas tells the story through the filter of such women as Miguel Chico's cousin, Josie Salazar. The protagonist of *The Rain God,* Miguel Chico, still appears, but less as consciousness that controls the flow of events and more as a secondary figure that can relate to the other outcast characters from the sidelines. Here again, Islas blurs the border between biographical fact and narrative fiction. And, his intertextual play—figures from *La Mollie* appear as minor characters and French lesbian writer Colette as well as Chicano authors Rolando Hinojosa and Américo Paredes appear in disguised form—serves as a metafictional device that announces its fictionality. Upon publication, *Migrant Souls* (1990) proved another success for Islas. It sold out within a month and ranked at the top of the *San Francisco Chronicle*'s top-10 best-seller list. And Anglo and Chicano writers and scholars alike sung its praises. Poets Denise Levertov and **Adrienne Rich** gave it their seal of approval. Chicano scholar Roberto Cantú identified it as a dramatic move away from an Us/Them understanding of Chicano and Anglo race relations. For Cantú, Islas "advances other narrative dimensions to a higher aesthetic level" (153) to open his readers' eyes to different ways of understanding complex social relations and hybrid cultural phenomenon.

Although mostly known for his two novels, *The Rain God* and *Migrant Souls,* Islas's creative drive and output was immense. We see this not only with the posthumous addition of *La Mollie and the King of Tears* to his opus, but also with the many unpublished short stories, poetry, and beautifully wrought scholarly essays that are now published with Arte Público Press. Though Islas's life was radically cut short when he died of AIDS-related pneumonia on February 15, 1991, his impact as a gay Chicano writer, teacher, and intellect has been tremendous. Many of his former Ph.D. students such as José David Saldívar and Rafael Pérez-Torres are now leading scholars in Chicano/a studies. His unyielding drive to confront and overcome a bigoted publishing industry and his dedication to crafting rich and nuanced Chicano/a (gay and straight) poetry and narrative fiction has stretched wide the horizon of the American and world literary landscape.

See also Gay Literature, Mexican American

Further Reading

Aldama, Frederick Luis. *Critical Mappings of Arturo Islas's Narrative Fictions.* Tempe, AZ: Bilingual Review Press, 2004.

———. *Dancing With Ghosts: A Critical Biography of Arturo Islas.* Berkeley: University of California Press, 2004.

———, ed. *Arturo Islas: The Uncollected Works.* Houston, TX: Arte Público Press, 2003.

Cantú, Roberto. "Arturo Islas." In *Chicano Writers: Second Series,* edited by Francisco A. Lomeli and Carl R. Shirley, 146–54. Detroit: Gale, 1992.

Frederick Luis Aldama

J

Johnson, Fenton (b. 1953)

Novelist, autobiographer, and professor of creative writing. Fenton Johnson is the youngest of nine children and was born in New Haven, Kentucky. His father was Catholic and his mother a Protestant, whose conversion to Catholicism for the sake of love was considered scandalous in the rural hill country. In keeping with the family's history of bootlegging, Johnson's father worked for Seagram's Distillery while his mother tended home.

Religion was a major influence in Johnson's life. Everything from his name—bestowed by Trappist monks located near his home—to his education centered on Catholicism. An introverted child, he spent a great deal of time reading, which was primarily limited to the Bible, and listening to family stories. Enthralled by the family stories, he wrote them down, honing the skills that would lead to a writing career.

After high school, Johnson fled Kentucky to attend Stanford University on a scholarship from his father's employer. He majored in English, encountering many of the authors that would later influence his writing: William Faulkner, Flannery O'Connor, Eudora Welty, **Tennessee Williams**, Carson McCullers, and Wendell Berry.

His postcollege career included a job as press secretary for a congressman in Washington, D.C. It was during this time Johnson met his first love, resolved to lead an honest, open life as a **gay** man, and pursue a career in the arts. He returned to California and committed himself to publishing at the national level within two years and, if he failed, going to law school.

Success did not arrive in the allotted two years. Undaunted, Johnson attended the prestigious Iowa Writers' Workshop, obtained a Master's Degree in Fine Arts, and held a Wallace Stegnor Fellowship at Stanford University. Later, while teaching creative writing at San Francisco State University, he obtained his original goal, publishing an article about Kentucky in the *New York Times Magazine.* In addition, he contributed articles to *The Virginia Quarterly Review, Mother Jones, Los Angeles Times Magazine,* and *Harper's Magazine.*

That same year, Johnson published his first novel, *Crossing the River* (1989). The story concerns Martha Pickett, a Baptist who marries a Catholic. Martha realizes marriage and motherhood offer few rebellious opportunities, but she seizes those moments, finding her choices intertwined with and reflected back by her son's choices. Clearly a fictionalization of his parent's story, the autobiographical elements escaped reviewers, who rated the novel a satisfactory first effort.

Kentucky author Wendell Berry's influence is obvious in Johnson's next novel, *Scissors, Paper, Rock* (1993), which captured the attention of reviewers and awards committees. The book focuses on an HIV-positive gay man who returns to his native Kentucky to confront mortality and complex familial relationships. Johnson tells the story in episodic fashion, focusing on male characters dealing with aging and death yet united by strong female characters. Reviewers praised the work for its wisdom and compassion and the American Library Association's Gay, Lesbian, Bisexual, and Transgendered Round Table (ALA-GLBTRT) nominated the title for its annual book award.

In *Geography of the Heart* (1996), the persistent presence of autobiographical elements came to fruition as Johnson switched from fiction to memoir. Setting aside storytelling to embrace autobiography was never Johnson's intent; rather, he found the story in the course of writing the eulogy for his partner, who died of AIDS-related complications. The tender rendering of their relationship met with critical success. Hailed by reviewers as "lyrical" and "graceful," the book won ALA-GLBTRT's Gay and Lesbian Book Award and a Lambda Literary Award. Johnson continued his autobiographical disclosure in the Lambda Award–winning memoir *Keeping the Faith: A Skeptic's Journey* (2003).

Currently Johnson is at work on a third novel, *The Man Who Loved Birds,* about an encounter between a Trappist monk, an immigrant Bengali woman doctor, and a Vietnam veteran marijuana grower. He is also researching and writing for "Desire in Solitude," a book-length essay about writers and artists who achieved their greatest work while living alone.

Johnson's faith, Kentucky upbringing, and family are frequent touchstones in his writings. While his work features strong autobiographical elements, the characters and stories are amalgamations of various persons and circumstances in his life. His conscious decision to write from his heart has resulted in an oeuvre that stands between various worlds: Protestant and Catholic; rural and urban; gay and straight. Although only a portion of his writing explicitly addresses gay issues, being a gay man informs all of his writing.

Further Reading

Creadick, Anna. "Fenton Johnson." *Appalachian Journal* 22, no. 2 (Winter 1995): 160–73.

"Fenton Johnson." http://www.fentonjohnson.com/ (accessed June 18, 2008).

Miller, Laura. "Litchat: Fenton Johnson." *Salon.com.* Salon Media Group, Inc. http://www.salon.com/weekly/litchat960916.html (accessed June 18, 2008).

Ellen Bosman

Jordan, June (1936–2002)

African American poet, essayist, activist, and professor of English. Born on July 9, 1936, in Harlem and raised in Brooklyn as the only child of Jamaican immigrants, June Jordan was a powerful force in the movements for racial, sexual, economic, and feminist liberation. A survivor of child abuse and sexual assault and eventually a victim of breast cancer, Jordan reveals in her work the sensibility of a fighter and survivor. For Jordan, who skipped two grades and was almost always the smallest person in any given room due to her small build, being a fighter meant believing that those who were called "minorities" could move beyond mere survival through passionate collaboration and poetic faith.

Jordan's first collection of poetry, *Some Changes,* was published in 1967, but broader recognition of her achievement came in 1969 with her long poem "Who Look At Me," published alongside paintings, dedicated to her son, and marketed for children. Jordan emerged as a poet in the context of the Black Arts Movement, which Jordan both participated in and expressed distance from due to her political stance, her poetic style, and her refusal of the boundaries of black nationalism. Though Jordan wrote *Some Changes* before the years that she spent co-directing a poetry workshop for children, co-editing *The Voice of the Children* anthology, and visiting public libraries and public schools all over the city of New York to read "Who Look at Me" aloud, it was her cultivation of a youth audience that sustained Jordan's career as a poet and teacher.

Though the first edition of *Some Changes* received little notice, it reappeared in a critically acclaimed second edition the same year as her young adult novel *His Own Where* (1971), written almost entirely in African American vernacular English. In the early 1970s, Jordan also published two children's books. The republication of *Some Changes* represented a moment where Jordan could use the leverage she had gained as a black woman poet creating positive images *for* black children and to publicize her critical analysis of the positionality of black motherhood in relationship to black freedom. *Some Changes* was the first in a long series of collections of poetry by Jordan that would critique political structures including marriage, capitalism, and imperialist foreign policy through deeply embodied and formally experimental invocations of love.

While leading writing workshops for young people and creating books marketed to public schools and libraries, Jordan boldly asserted the need for Black English to be respected as a language with a grammar reflective of the survival skills of black people under oppression. Jordan went on to publish books targeted toward children about the life of Fannie Lou Hamer, the failures of the civil rights movement, and the struggles of black families in urban environments at the same time that she published collections of poetry and essays about fierce political love. Jordan's calling as a teacher informed her relationship to writing, audience, and accountability throughout her lifetime.

Though Jordan left Barnard College without completing her degree in the late 1950s, her publications eventually earned her a brilliant academic career. In 1967 she went on to teach at the City University of New York alongside **Audre Lorde**, **Adrienne Rich**, Barbara Christian, Addison Gayle, Jr., and Toni Cade Bambara. During a student uprising, she stood in solidarity with the students who insisted that the public educational system in New York City, including secondary and university units, needed to reflect the predominantly "minority" student population of New York City in its admissions structures and the content of its curriculum. She went on to teach at Yale University, Sarah Lawrence College, and the State University of New York before moving to the University of

California where she developed her revolutionary model of community poetry called Poetry for the People.

Through poetry, Jordan asserted that language was political in its very structure. In one of her most often quoted poems, "Poem about My Rights," Jordan describes the link between the way she is made to feel "wrong" by her father for not being a boy and "wrong" under racism for being black to the mode through which rape is justified on the levels of individual bodies and nation-states. Visiting socialist states including Cuba and (at the time) Nicaragua, she emphasized and revealed social alternatives in poetry from around the world including Chinese T'ang poetry. In a review of June Jordan's 1985 poetry collection *Living Room,* Arab American feminist Carole Haddad praises Jordan's pursuit of a truly livable and demilitarized world. Jordan strongly advocated the end of the occupation of Palestine and American intervention in Lebanon until the end of her life.

Jordan's prolific journalism created a platform through which she could write political essays on figures from Phyllis Wheatley to O. J. Simpson. She advanced propositions on urban architecture designed to empower the dreams of the children of Harlem and Black English school curriculums that asserted the poetry of black vernacular speech. Through her relationships with Susan Taylor, Cheryll Greene, and **Alexis De Veaux** at *Essence Magazine,* Jordan was able to reach the large audience of black women who read this fashion and beauty magazine with her writing in support of the socialist revolution in Nicaragua.

In her extensive work as a public speaker, Jordan was also among the first to theorize the politics of **bisexuality** as the embodied exemplification of choice. In her 1991 keynote address to the Bisexual, Gay and Lesbian Student Association at Stanford University, titled "A New Politics of Sexuality," Jordan explained her belief that "the Politics of Sexuality is the most ancient and probably the most profound arena for human conflict" and explicitly stated that when she talks about a politics of sexual oppression she includes "gay and lesbian contempt for bisexual modes of human relationship."

June Jordan died of breast cancer in 2002, but up until the end of her life she advocated antimilitaristic alternatives to terror and terrorism. Her words continue to be invoked by contemporary **queer** activists and musicians including Meshell Ndegeocello, who included Jordan's voice reading her poem "In Memoriam: Martin Luther King, Jr." on her album *Cookie: The Anthropological Mixtape,* released just 10 days before Jordan died. Jordan's phrase "We are the ones we've been waiting for" was the opening headline of *Between Our Selves: Women of Color Newspaper* in Washington, D.C., and became one of the most well-known refrains sung by the musical group Sweet Honey in the Rock. Publishing 28 books and making lasting contributions to fields as various as architecture, journalism, poetry, activism, and academia, Jordan received many awards and honors including a National Endowment for the Arts Fellowship, the Achievement Award for International Reporting from the National Association of Black Journalists, and the Chancellor's Distinguished Lectureship at the University of California at Berkeley.

See also Lesbian Literature, African American

Further Reading

De Veaux, Alexis. "Creating Soul Food: June Jordan" *Essence* (April 1981): 82–150.

Grebowicz, Margaret, and Valerie Kinloch. *Still Seeking an Attitude: Critical Reflections on the Work of June Jordan.* Lexington, MA: Lexington Books, 2005.

Muller, Lauren, ed. *June Jordan's Poetry for the People: A Revolutionary Blueprint.* New York: Routledge, 1995.

Sutton, Soraya Sablo. "In Remembrance of June Jordan: 1963–2002." *Social Justice* 29, no. 4 (December 2002): 205.

Alexis Pauline Gumbs

K

Keenan, Joe (b. 1958)

Award-winning American screenwriter, playwright, novelist, and television producer. Born in Cambridge, Massachusetts, in 1958, Keenan is best known for his work on the popular television sitcom *Frasier,* for which he won five Emmy Awards as a writer and producer over his 10-year tenure (1994–2004).

While a student at New York University, Keenan and fellow student Brad Ross wrote the musical comedy *The Times,* which won the 1991 Richard Rodgers Development Award and the 1993 Kleban Award (for Keenan's lyrics). Although he has written no further stage musicals, references to musical comedy pervade Keenan's other work.

Keenan has written three novels that explore the relationship of two **gay** best friends: Philip Cavanaugh, a playwright and lyricist, and his former lover Gilbert Selwyn. A third recurring character is Clair, a straight woman who works with Philip. All three novels are heavily influenced by the British humorist P. G. Wodehouse (as acknowledged by Keenan) and feature farcical plots, stereotypical characters, and rapid-paced action. In *Blue Heaven* (1988), Gilbert plans to marry a woman in order to receive wedding gifts, but a series of complications lead him instead to rekindle his relationship with Philip. *Putting on the Ritz* (1991) is set in New York's high society and has Philip and Claire spying on a powerful business couple; it won a Literary Award from the Lambda Literary Foundation (which honors gay and lesbian writing) for humor. *My Lucky Star* (2006), set in Los Angeles, involves (among other things) a plagiarized screenplay, an ambitious madam, and a **closet**ed gay movie star.

Blue Heaven attracted the attention of the producers of the successful television sitcom *Cheers,* who asked Keenan to collaborate on a pilot for a planned new series, *Gloria Vane.* Although *Gloria Vane* was not put into production, the contact led to another opportunity for Keenan, who joined the staff of *Frasier,* a spin-off of *Cheers,* in 1994.

The first episode Keenan wrote for *Frasier,* "The Matchmaker" (October 4, 1994), was nominated for an Emmy and won the 1994 Gay and Lesbian Alliance against

Defamation award for outstanding comedy episode. The episode was based on a series of incorrect assumptions made by the characters about other characters' sexual preferences and capitalized on the fact that the straight characters Frasier and Niles Crane were metrosexuals before the term existed. A recurring theme on *Frasier* is the fact that their fashion sense, eye for interior decoration, and fondness for musicals, opera, fine food, and wine frequently cause other characters on the show to assume that Niles and Frasier are gay.

In another *Frasier* episode, Keenan takes aim at the homophobic right-wing radio celebrity Dr. Laura Schlessinger. The episode "Dr. Nora" (April 29, 1999) features a hypocritical radio host and rival of Frasier who advocates on the air for traditional heterosexual marriage and "family values" while her own family is in disarray and she has been divorced twice.

Keenan worked on several other television series as well. Of these, the most successful was *Desperate Housewives,* for which he produced 32 episodes and wrote four in the years 2006–2007. Keenan created the series *Bram & Alice* in 2002 with Christopher Lloyd, who also worked on *Frasier:* it featured the relationship between a young woman and her long-estranged father and ran for only one season. Keenan and Lloyd also created the series *Out of Practice* (2005), a comedy about a family of doctors that included one lesbian character; this series also ran for one season only.

Keenan won the 2007 Annie Award for best writing in an animated feature production, given by the l'Association Internationale du Film d'Animation for his work on the 2006 film *Flushed Away* (2006). He also contributed a scene to the romantic comedy *Sleep with Me* (1994), which consisted of six scenes by six different writers centering on the same three characters: Sarah and Joseph, who are married, and Frank, who is in love with Sarah. This film includes many cameos by Hollywood stars, including director Quentin Tarantino, who expounds at length on the homoerotic subtext of film *Top Gun* (1986).

Keenan lives with his life partner, Gerry Bernardi, in Studio City, California, whom he refers to in the acknowledgements to *My Lucky Star* (2006) as his husband.

Further Reading

Durade, Alonso. "Pretty Witty—and Gay." *The Advocate,* January 17, 2006. http://www.advocate .com/issue_story_ektid24417.asp (accessed July 5, 2008).

Melloy, Kilian. "Our Lucky Star: An Interview with Joe Keenan." *AfterElton,* March 2, 2006. http://www.afterelton.com/archive/elton/print/2006/3/keenan.html (accessed July 5, 2008).

Sarah Boslaugh

Kelley, Collin (b. 1969)

Neo-confessional poet, playwright, journalist, and political activist. The only son of Linda Graves (a homemaker) and Harold Kelley (a plumber and contractor), Collin Mitchell Kelley grew up in Fayetteville, Georgia, a suburb of Atlanta. Two major events that later informed his confessional-style poetry were the death of his uncle Terry Graves due to AIDS complications and his mother's extramarital affair. When his mother planned to meet with her lover, she would leave 10-year-old Kelley at the library or local movie theaters, which fostered his love of the arts. As a boy and adolescent, Kelley was a voracious reader and lover of music, especially artists such as Kate Bush, Peter Gabriel,

Fleetwood Mac, and Laurie Anderson. It was a musician who led him to the poetry of his greatest literary influence when he discovered the poetry of Anne Sexton after hearing Peter Gabriel's musical tribute to her, "Mercy Street."

Kelley always sensed he was **gay** and had his first sexual experience with a friend at age 12. Around that time, he discovered a writer in his lineage when his grandmother gave him a notebook of poems that had belonged to his great-great-great-grandmother and namesake, Julia Collinsworth, a Civil War–era poet who had lived in Covington, Georgia. He also developed an interest in another distant relative, Margaret Mitchell, author of *Gone with the Wind* (1936). At one time, Kelley worked part time at the Margaret Mitchell Public Library in Fayetteville. He also wrote an article that appeared in the *Atlanta Journal-Constitution* about the efforts to restore Mitchell's apartment where she wrote her famous novel. This publication at age 16 led to Kelley's freelancing for regional magazines. In high school, he became a part-time reporter for the local newspaper, the *Fayette Sun,* and served as editor for his high school newspaper.

After high school graduation, Kelley attended Clayton State College in Morrow, Georgia, for one semester, planning to major in English, but he left school for newspaper work. Soon he became a reporter for the *Marietta Daily Journal* and *Neighbor Newspaper* chain in suburban Atlanta, where he worked for 12 years, eventually becoming an executive editor. Currently he serves as managing editor of *Atlanta Downtown,* a monthly arts and culture magazine.

While working as a journalist, Kelley has written plays and poetry. In 1994, Kelley's first published poem appeared in *Welter.* He was inspired to write his first play, *Porcelain,* while watching Jill Godmillow's film *Waiting for the Moon,* which is about Gertrude Stein and Alice B. Toklas. *Porcelain* portrays two sisters who try to reconnect after years of separation and sexual abuse at the hands of their father in 1950s Louisiana. Kelley's second play, *The Dark Horse,* won the Deep South Writers Award from the University of Louisiana in 1994 and a Georgia Theater Conference Award in 1997. In *The Dark Horse,* a young artist and his mother search for a reclusive artist who lives on a deserted Canadian beach that is haunted by a spectral horse.

After a failed love affair in the early 1990s, Kelley began traveling extensively throughout the United States and abroad, which became the basis for his first poetry collection, *Better to Travel* (2003). The collection's narrative arc of a dissolving relationship is set against an international backdrop of New York, London, Paris, Berlin, Africa, and New Orleans. Kelley self-published *Better to Travel* in 2003 despite warnings from other poets that a self-published book would never be taken seriously. The book, however, went on to receive favorable reviews and sold hundreds of copies.

In 2004 he recorded *HalfLife Crisis,* a spoken word and music album that features poems in *Better to Travel* as well as some newer work. In 2006, MetroMania Press brought out Kelley's poetry chapbook *Slow to Burn,* a cycle of poems about growing up gay, suicide, and failed relationships. He writes a popular blog, *Modern Confessional,* discussing everything from politics and poetry to music and pop culture. With Kodac Harrison, Kelley co-edits the *Java Monkey Speaks* anthologies. In 2007, he won the 2007 Georgia Author of the Year/Taran Memorial Award. His second chapbook, *After the Poison,* was published in 2008. The poetry in this collection skewers conservative politics in the wake of September 11, the war in Iraq, and Hurricane Katrina. Praising *After the Poison* on the book jacket as a "must-read," Jim Elledge describes the poems as pointing an "unfliching gaze [at] . . . every imaginable form of human-cause and human-condoned tragedy."

Further Reading

Greenstreet, Kate. "First Book Interview with Collin Kelley." 2007. http://www.kickingwind.com/081407.html.

Herrle, David. "Interview with Collin Kelley." http://www.subtletea.com/collinkelleyinterview2.htm.

Selman, Sean. "Love Hurts: But for Atlanta Poet Collin Kelley, Pen and Pain Earn Praise." *David Magazine* (May 26, 2004): 28.

Vogeltanz, Kathy. "Review of *Better to Travel* Review." *Lambda Book Report* 12, no. 7 (Winter 2004): 31.

Kate Evans

Kenan, Randall (b. 1963)

American author of fiction and nonfiction. Born March 12, 1963, in Brooklyn, New York, Kenan was raised primarily in the North Carolina countryside and has focused his literary works on a black, **gay** identity centered in the South. He grew up under the watch of his great-aunt in the farming community of Chinquapin, North Carolina, which is where many of his stories are set. He called this fictional location of many of his stories "Tims Creek," which is loosely based on Chinquapin.

Kenan remained in North Carolina for his undergraduate education, attending University of North Carolina (UNC) at Chapel Hill, where he graduated in 1985. Though he initially majored in physics, Kenan eventually earned his degree in English and Creative Writing. While at school, he worked under the tutelage of Doris Betts. After graduation, and with the assistance of Nobel Prize–winning novelist Toni Morrison, Kenan gained employment with Random House in New York City. After working for a spell at Random House, he began working on the editorial staff at Alfred A. Knopf, Inc., where he remained until 1989. Upon leaving the publishing world, he entered into academia through teaching jobs at both Sarah Lawrence College and Columbia University. In 1994, Kenan was hired as the William Blackburn Visiting Professor of Creative Writing at Duke University. He later held the Lehman Brady Professorship at the Center for Documentary Studies there. He taught urban literature at Vassar College as well, before returning to his alma mater, UNC Chapel Hill, as the Edouard Morot-Sir Visiting Professor of Creative Writing in 1995. Kenan left UNC Chapel Hill to become the John and Renée Grisham Writer-in-Residence at the University of Mississippi, Oxford, in 1997–1998 and taught for a brief stint at the University of Memphis before returning to UNC Chapel Hill. Kenan currently works as an Associate Professor of English at the University of North Carolina.

He has published several works, of both fiction and nonfiction; he has been versatile in his approach to the written word, equally adept at both short stories and oral histories. His first novel went to press in 1989; though *A Visitation of Spirits* was reviewed highly in select instances, it otherwise garnered little attention. *A Visitation of Spirits* received recommendations by accomplished authors Gloria Naylor and Adrienne Kennedy, which is quite an accomplishment for a first-time author, yet it failed to give Kenan the recognition he deserved. Split into five sections, the plot is centered around the Cross family, and it is set in the fictional Tims Creek. Kenan addresses racism in the South through the interactions of the children in the schoolyard. The 16-year-old Horace Cross is the main character of the novel, and Kenan focuses on Horace's mental trajectory as he attempts to come to terms with his homosexuality. He hopes to reverse his homosexual tendencies by morphing into a red-tailed hawk; when this fails, Horace becomes delirious and finds little redemption. Intense and dramatic, the novel races toward a screeching climax.

His second book, a collection of short stories, launched his career. This publication, *Let the Dead Bury Their Dead,* was honored as a *New York Times* Notable Book in 1992. These stories are set in his invented landscape known as Tims Creek, and the collection was nominated for several other awards as well, including the *Los Angeles Times* Book Award for Fiction and the National Book Critics Circle Award. Most of his works emphasize the black and gay experience of the southern United States. In *Let the Dead Bury Their Dead,* some of Kenan's characters from earlier works reappear; yet aside from the characters and the location, the 12 stories are fundamentally disparate. Using the township as a common ground, Kenan capitalizes on the opportunity to discuss, for instance, an older woman grappling with the knowledge that her grandson, now dead, was gay; moreover, his partner was white. There is also the mixing of realism and myth, which is displayed in the farm animal that can talk. Another story in the collection addresses the emotions of an attorney unwilling to wrest himself away from his incestuous interactions with his half-sister. Clearly Kenan does not shy away from difficult issues in contemporary society, but addresses them with earnestness and elegance.

After his collection of short stories came out, Kenan moved into the realm of nonfiction and published a biography: ***James Baldwin***: *American Writer (Lives of Notable Gay Men and Lesbians),* edited by Martin Duberman in 1995. The book was developed for a young adult audience, and Kenan writes with admiration on the work of the skilled gay and black author James Baldwin, with whom he shares considerable personal, cultural, and intellectual affinity. In addition to his longer works of fiction and nonfiction, Kenan's shorter works have appeared in magazines and anthologies. He has appeared in numerous interviews as well, discussing contemporary issues such as hip-hop music. Influenced by Nobel Prize–laureate Toni Morrison, Kenan's work mixes folklore with the supernatural. His understanding of the human psyche is cutting and sharp, perceptive. As a skilled black author openly discussing gay issues, Kenan's career looks promising.

Kenan followed his James Baldwin biography with the descriptions to a book of photographs by Norman Mauskopf, *A Time Not Here: The Mississippi Delta* (1997). After his foray into nonfiction, Kenan continued down that path with a collection of oral histories, titled *Walking on Water: Black American Lives at the Turn of the Twenty-First Century* (1999). Prior to publishing the work, Kenan spent eight years traveling across the United States and Canada to record the oral histories and collected over 200 personal accounts, delineating the multifarious experiences of black Americans. He was rewarded for his hefty research with a nomination for the Southern Book Award. His latest work, written in 2007, is *The Fire This Time,* which derives its title from a work by James Baldwin, *The Fire Next Time* (1963). This novel continues to explore the characters within Kenan's invented locale, Tims Creek.

Kenan has been the recipient of numerous awards, including the Whiting Writers' Award, the John Dos Passos Prize, and the Sherwood Anderson Award, in 1995. Furthermore, he was honored with a prestigious Guggenheim Fellowship, and in 1997 Kenan won the Rome Prize from the American Academy of Arts and Letters. He was awarded the North Carolina Award for Literature in 2005.

Further Reading

Betts, Doris. "Randall Garrett Kenan: Myth and Reality in Tims Creek." In *Southern Writers at Century's End,* edited by Jeffrey J. Folks and James A. Perkins, 9–20. Lexington: University Press of Kentucky, 1997.

Ketchin, Susan. *The Christ-Haunted Landscape: Faith and Doubt in Southern Fiction.* Oxford: University Press of Mississippi, 1994. 277–302.

McRuer, Robert. "Randall Kenan." In *Contemporary Gay American Novelists: A Bio-Bibliographical Critical Sourcebook,* edited by Emmanuel S. Nelson, 232–36. Westport, CT: Greenwood Press, 1993.

Rowell, Charles H. "An Interview with Randall Kenan," *Callaloo* 21, no. 1 (Winter 1998): 133–48.

Laura Blosser

Killian, Kevin (b. 1952)

Prolific San Francisco–based playwright, novelist, poet, art critic, teacher, actor, biographer, reviewer, and editor. Kevin Killian was born and grew up in Smithtown on Long Island, New York. His parents worked very hard in that suburban environment and were immersed in traditional bourgeois family values within a Catholic context that encouraged Kevin to become an altar boy. He moved to New York City to get a B.A. degree at Fordham University and subsequently an M.A. and an A.B.D. at the State University of New York, Stony Brook. He has taught as an Adjunct Professor of Visual and Critical Studies in the M.F.A. Graduate Program at the California College of the Arts. In 1980 he settled permanently in San Francisco, where he met Dodie Bellamy in 1981 at poetry and prose workshops in the city and in Noe Valley. In 1985 he married her, though his homosexuality had been clearly established since his high school years, as shown in his autobiographical novel, *Shy* (1989). This marriage has proven successful. Bellamy and Killian have collaborated as editors of over 140 issues of the xeroxed magazine *Mirage #4 Period(ical)* since 1992.

The 1980s were for Killian a period of productive creativity in San Francisco. He acted in Carla Harryman and Tom Mandel's play, *Fist of the Colossus* (1984), published a chapbook, *Desiree* (1986), a novel *Shy* (1989), and a book of memoirs, *Bedrooms Have Windows* (1989). He began attending workshops taught by Bob Glück, one of the leaders of the neo-narrative school, which included other writers, such as Bruce Boone, **Dennis Cooper**, Dodie Bellamy, Camille Roy, and intermittently Kathy Acker. Here, transgression, confession, and the pursuit of truth were accompanied by a focus on themselves as **queer** outlaws. Despite Killian's emphasis on the theme of love that is present in the background of his stories, **gay** eroticism and porn practices are considered the constructedness or high artifice of his fiction. This is exemplified in *Shy, Bedroom Have Windows,* and *I Cry Like a Baby* (2001), where fiction becomes memoirs permeated by both experience and sublimation of sexual acts.

Since the early 1990s, Killian has achieved considerable literary recognition. In 1993 he received the California Arts Council Award for Fiction, and in 1996 he was the winner of the PEN Oakland/Josephine Miles Award for his book of stories, *Little Men* (1996), and in 1998 he and his wife won the *San Francisco Bay Guardian* "Goldie" Award for Literature. In this decade he published the books *Brothers and Sisters Retold from the Brothers Grimm* (1994), *Arctic Summer* (1997), and *The Kink of Chris Komater* (1999). More recently he has published a collection of stories titled *I Cry Like a Baby* (2001), his first full-length book of poetry, *Argento Series* (2001), and the autobiographical *Islands of the Soul* (2004). He has also written over 35 plays presented by the San Francisco Poetry Center, co-written plays with Leslie Scalapino, *Stone Marmalade* (1996); with Barbara Guest, *Often* (2001); with Wayne Smith, *Fascination* (2002); and with Karla Milosevich, *Love Can Build a Bridge* (2003), *Is It All Over My Face?* (2004), *The Red and the Green* (2005), and *Celebrity Hospital* (2007). As an actor, he has performed in video and theater extensively.

As a biographer, Killian co-edited with Lew Ellingham the widely acclaimed volume *Poet Be Like God: Jack Spicer and the San Francisco Renaissance* (1998), considered as Spicer's definitive biography and a significant exploration of the San Francisco Renaissance and its contacts with the Berkeley Renaissance, Beat, and New York School poets. Killian's work has been widely anthologized in *Men on Men* (1986, ed. George Stambolian), *Best American Poetry* (1988, ed. **John Ashbery**), *Farm Boys* (1990), *Discontents* (1992, ed. Dennis Cooper), and *The Best American Erotica* (1999, ed. Susie Bright).

His poems in *Argento Series* are his most forceful exploration of the horrors of the HIV virus fatally affecting many of Killian's close friends since the mid-1980s. On Kathy Acker's suggestion, the landscape of these poems is based on the Italian director Dario Argento's horror films, which help establish a tone of terror as well as the heroic attitude of those afflicted. Killian is also an insightful and sensitive reviewer. His copious reviews for Amazon.com have become the favorite of many readers. Some of those 1,791 reviews have been collected in *Selected Amazon Reviews* (2006), and they testify to Killian's dramatization that language is his home.

Further Reading

Gilbert, Alan. "Fade to Black: Kevin Killian's *Argento Series*." *Another Future: Poetry and Art in a Postmodern Twilight*. Middletown, CT: Wesleyan University Press, 2006. 37–62.

Jackson, Earl, Jr. "Scandalous Narratives: Appearing as Oneself: Countermimetics in Kevin Killian." *Strategies of Deviance: Studies in Gay Male Representation*. Bloomington: Indiana University Press, 1995. 216–54.

"Kevin Killian Webpage." Electronic Poetry Center at the State University of New York, Buffalo. December 17, 2007. http://epc.buffalo.edu/authors/killian/.

Lawson, D. S. "Kevin Killian." *Contemporary Gay American Novelists: A Bio-Bibliographical Critical Sourcebook,* edited by Emmanuel S. Nelson, 237–43. Westport, CT: Greenwood Press, 1993.

Manuel Brito

Koestenbaum, Wayne (b. 1958)

Queer Jewish American author of genre-bending poetry, fiction, and criticism. Wayne Koestenbaum is a Distinguished Professor of English at the City University of New York Graduate Center. He graduated from Harvard with a B.A., the Johns Hopkins University with an M.A. in Creative Writing, and Princeton University with a Ph.D. in English. He has also held a visiting professorship in the painting department of the Yale School of Art and frequently publishes as an art critic and reviewer. A recipient of a Whiting Writers' Award in 1994 for nonfiction/poetry, Koestenbaum composes with a scholarly yet self-referential and anecdotal voice that creatively queers his objects of scholarship and poetics. Koestenbaum's perusals of sexual identity, language, literature, musicology, psychoanalysis, visual art, and pleasure animate his oeuvre.

The Queen's Throat: Opera, Homosexuality, and the Mystery of Desire (1993), Koestenbaum's inquest into the singularity of **gay** opera fandom, was a National Book Critics Circle Award finalist. Perhaps the most well known of his books of criticism, *The Queen's Throat* weaves Koestenbaum's inveterate history as an "opera queen" into a pastiche of documents and episodes describing affiliations among fans, opera, and a historically specific possibility of visible gay identity. He folds a vivid cache of details from his lifelong fascination with opera into quotations from both fictional and journalistic chronicles of fans who develop febrile attachments to individual divas, to the obliquely gay pomp of the opera, and to the often irrational and occasionally ruinous draw of celebrity. Koestenbaum uses this text not only to investigate the gayness of opera, but also to retrace his own early fears of queer identity. Rethinking a practice now often dismissed as retrograde, his text embraces the secretive identifications necessarily performed by pre-**Stonewall** opera queens. In its introduction, Koestenbaum describes this text as a "scrapbook," and Tony Kushner applauds it as "the queerest political treatise I have read."

Koestenbaum's other works of criticism include *Double Talk: The Erotics of Male Literary Collaboration* (1989), *Jackie under My Skin: Interpreting an Icon* (1995), *Cleavage: Essays on Sex, Stars, and Aesthetics* (2000), *Andy Warhol* (2001), and *Hotel Theory* (2007).

Hotel Theory—a thorough commingling of fiction and theory—reconsiders conventional approaches to scholarship. The entire text runs theoretical "dossiers" alongside a novel called *Hotel Women*. On the left side of each page, the dossiers discuss hotels, the metaphorical implications of their parlance, and the transience they enable. Ultimately, these components create a heady episodic manifesto for the permanently temporary identities made possible by the public home life of hotels. Theory all-stars including Martin Heidegger, Gertrude Stein, and Walter Benjamin are cited here for their relevance to the epistemology of hotel living, but the dossiers are far from conventional critical discourse. Somewhere between a bizarre method of travel writing and innovative Marxism, *Hotel Theory* reads like well-theorized narrations of vividly recounted dreams. The text's embedded novel, *Hotel Women,* tells the story of a hotel called Hotel Women, home to Liberace and Lana Turner. The characters on this half of the page likewise give voice to provocative ruminations on the implications of their transient abode.

To date, Koestenbaum has published one novel: *Moira Orfei in Aigues-Mortes* (2004). This virtuoso text, narrated by pianist Theo Mangrove, is organized into 25 chapters labeled as notebooks. As with much of Koestenbaum's work, the novel is sprinkled with studied references to classical music, opera, idolatry, hustling, and complex mother-son dynamics. Theo's primary obsessions are his famous pianist mother Alma, sex, his own career as a pianist, recovering from a nervous breakdown, and the mandatory diva: circus performer Moira Orfei. The notebooks document Alma's performances and philosophical musings of advice, letters between Theo and Moira Orfei, Theo's encounters with escorts, and his daily assessments of music and family.

The *New York Village Voice Literary Supplement* named Koestenbaum's first book of poetry, *Ode to Anna Moffo and Other Poems* (1990), one of its "Favorite Books of 1990." Koestenbaum, who has described his poetry as an attempt at making a private history, followed this success with four more collections: *Rhapsodies of a Repeat Offender* (1994), *The Milk of Inquiry* (1999), *Model Homes* (2004), and *Best-Selling Jewish Porn Films* (2006). *Best-Selling Jewish Porn Films* is worldly, common, practiced, and funny. The eponymous porn from the poem "Best-Selling Jewish Porn Films" is a stark naming of 56 film titles. Producing a familiar sensation evoked by Koestenbaum's work, the titles are at once humorous and impossibly absurd. Regardless of whether they are actual films or not, the list's pointed enumeration invokes a poignant naming of cultural fantasies surrounding gay Jewish men. As with *Model Homes,* the collection's title carries an overarching metaphor for the collection. Whereas in *Model Homes* Koestenbaum's exploration of form, language, and the mundane events of routine home life offers variations on the theme of "home," in *Best-Selling Jewish Porn Films* "porn" stands in for narcissism, indulgence, compulsion, and the frenzy of familiar tendencies.

Koestenbaum enacted a similar organizing principle in the form of spatial performance in 1998 at a gallery in New York where he curated a group show simply called "Bathroom." The show juxtaposed photograph, painting, and sculpture in order to imply the limits and demands of the body, spatial answers to this dilemma, and the psychic complications such frank recognitions might produce. Koestenbaum's unique archival of iconic fixtures of gay culture continues to transform subjects that might easily be dismissed as cliché into profound reconsiderations of the fragmentation of the self through art, reflection, identification, and desire.

See also Gay Literature, Jewish American

Further Reading

Bankowsky, Jack. "Story of A." Review of *Andy Warhol* by Wayne Koestenbaum. *Bookforum* (Spring 2002). http://www.bookforum.com/archive/spr_02/bank.html (accessed July 1, 2008).

Kakutani, Michiko. "Jackie Oh, Oh, Oh, Oh, Oh, Oh." Review of *Jackie under My Skin: Interpreting an Icon* by Wayne Koestenbaum. *New York Times,* May 5, 1995, C29.

Koestenbaum, Wayne. "Queering the Pitch: A Posy of Definitions and Impersonations." *Queering the Pitch: The New Gay and Lesbian Musicology,* edited by Philip Brett, 1–8. New York: Routledge, 1994.

Melinda Cardozo

Kramer, Larry (b. 1935)

Jewish American activist, essayist, novelist, and playwright. A founder of both the **Gay** Men's Health Crisis (GMHC) and the AIDS Coalition to Unleash Power (ACT UP), Larry Kramer has often drawn the ire of the gay community by criticizing the promiscuity through which homosexuals have often asserted their identity and by being one of the first to suggest that safe sex and monogamy should be practiced to slow the spread of AIDS. He also enraged the Jewish community by comparing the early days of the AIDS epidemic to the early days of the Holocaust, saying that homosexuals were doing nothing to save themselves just as many Jews turned a blind eye during the 1930s as Hitler began putting his "Final Solution" into effect.

As a writer and as a speaker, Kramer has always allowed his personal and political lives to intersect as he has addressed themes of the difficulties people have in loving each other, how people use sex as a weapon, and how people respond to crisis, making great use of angry hyperbole throughout his career. He bears witness to history and provides his testimony, insisting that the rest of us accept personal responsibility for our world just as he feels he has done. According to Kramer, each individual's actions matter.

Born to an American Jewish father and a Russian Jewish mother during the Great Depression, Kramer and his family lived with his mother's parents. He spent much of his time in the grocery his grandparents owned while his mother was out seeking odd jobs and his father, an attorney, was often away on cases requiring travel. When Kramer was six, his father landed a job in Mount Rainier, Maryland, where the Kramers were part of a Jewish minority. At age eight, Kramer saw his first play; and a love affair began with the theater, a love affair that brought ridicule from Kramer's father, who thought he should be more interested in sports and other more traditionally "masculine" activities. In 1950, the family moved to Washington, D.C.

Kramer entered Yale University in 1953. Yale had not been Kramer's first choice of schools, but his father, brother, and uncle had all attended, and his father all but forced him to go to the university. While there, Kramer became extremely depressed, falling behind in his studies and attempting suicide during his freshman year. Kramer began seeing a psychiatrist and remained at Yale, where he began an affair with his male German professor in the spring. Kramer ended the relationship but confided in his brother about it. His brother convinced their parents that Kramer should continue seeing a psychiatrist because of his homosexuality. The relationship between Kramer and his brother would later be highlighted in Kramer's plays. Kramer graduated from Yale with a degree in English in 1957.

Kramer began working in the teletype room of Columbia Pictures in 1958. Though his employment status and job description at Columbia changed often, he worked with the company throughout the 1960s. By the end of the 1960s, Kramer had gone to work for United Artists, where he wrote the Academy Award–nominated screenplay for *Women in Love* (1969). Despite the film's critical success, Kramer did not enjoy the experience and was further disappointed in the industry with the now-legendary failure of the movie musical *Lost Horizon* (1971), for which Kramer had written the screenplay.

Playwrights Horizons premiered Kramer's first play, *Sissies' Scrapbook,* in 1973. The play, about one gay and three straight male friends, was a success in its original run but was destroyed by a hostile Clive Barnes review in the *New York Times* a year later when it was remounted in Greenwich Village under the title *Four Friends.*

In 1978, Kramer published *Faggots,* his first novel. Chronicling four days in the life of Fred Lemish, a gay screenwriter dealing with turning 40 in the heyday of emotionally detached gay sex in New York in the late 1970s, the novel suggested that promiscuous homosexuals who denied the importance of love in personal relationships were responsible for their own unhappiness rather than the disapproving heterosexual world. The novel sold well but received mixed reviews, with the gay press labeling Kramer as a self-loathing, homophobic homosexual. This criticism would continue to dog Kramer throughout his career, particularly when he began a grassroots campaign to collect funds to combat the new "gay cancer" that had begun to kill people in Kramer's circle two years after the publication of *Faggots.* Standing outside gay bars in Manhattan and on the beach at Fire Island, Kramer began collecting dollar bills and spare change to research the as-yet-unnamed disease and subsequently began the newest and most important phase in his career—that of an AIDS activist.

Kramer's first published work on the disease appeared in August 1981 in the *New York Native.* Asking for funds for research into Kaposi's sarcoma, the skin cancer killing many gay men, Kramer was immediately attacked in the letters column by writers calling him alarmist and homophobic. In January 1982, Kramer and five other men, including novelist **Edmund White**, formed the GMHC to educate gay men about the disease and its spread. The GMHC set up a telephone information line, published a newsletter, held public information sessions, and established a crisis-intervention program. Though the

GMHC became incredibly successful, raising funds, building a volunteer base, and educating the public about the growing epidemic, Kramer's involvement with the organization ended within a year and a half due to infighting and fears within the group that Kramer's aggressive politics and strident attacks on indifferent government officials would hinder the GMHC's efforts. Kramer had been vocal and highly critical of New York City Mayor Ed Koch's lack of attention to the problem and had published the article "1,112 and Counting" (1983) in the *New York Native*. The article not only attacked the government and the health care system but also the gay community itself for its lack of assertiveness in fighting the disease. Kramer later attacked Koch again along with the entire Reagan family in his satirical farce *Just Say No* (1988). The GMHC attempted to distance itself from "1,112 and Counting" and from Kramer, so he angrily resigned his position on the GMHC board. The article became one of the most important documents of the AIDS epidemic, and Kramer's experience with the GMHC became the basis of his play ***The Normal Heart*** (1985).

The original production of *The Normal Heart* ran for over a year at Joseph Papp's Public Theatre—the longest run of any play there—in New York City and has since been produced all over the world. The play is at once virulently polemic and extraordinarily compassionate, dealing with the problems of the GMHC as well as with Kramer's own family issues, especially the difficulties his brother had accepting Larry's sexuality. Kramer derived the play's title from W. H. Auden's poem "September 1, 1939," itself a reference to the day Germany invaded Poland and began World War II while most of the world watched impassively. *The Normal Heart* was revived at the Public in 2004 with Raúl Esparza and Joanna Gleason in the cast. Though the production itself received mixed reviews, critics agreed that it is still a relevant piece, addressing issues of same-sex marriage and gay identity as well as the simple truth of frightened people reaching out to each other. Twenty years after the premiere of *The Normal Heart,* the journey of its main character Ned Weeks, a doppelganger for Kramer himself, has become archetypal.

In 1987, Kramer, disappointed with the lack of progress he perceived the GMHC had made in the fight against AIDS, called a New York meeting that led to the formation of ACT UP. Decidedly more radical than the GMHC, ACT UP's first act was to stop traffic on Wall Street during the morning rush to protest the U.S. Food and Drug Administration's lack of attention to the AIDS problem. This and other similar acts brought ACT UP the national attention that GMHC, despite its many successes, had never managed to attract and led to many victories in the fight against AIDS. ACT UP is also notable for mobilizing young homosexuals in their 20s, a group that had generally been absent from earlier homosexual activist movements.

Kramer was diagnosed with chronic hepatitis B in December 1988, when he entered a hospital for a hernia operation. Upon further testing, Kramer tested positive for HIV. He did not allow his HIV status to halt his activism but instead incorporated it into his activism, implying in his speeches that the movement had let him down and that now he would die. In 1989, his speeches were collected in the volume ***Reports from the Holocaust: The Making of an AIDS Activist***.

The autobiographical play *The Destiny of Me* opened off-Broadway in 1992, earning an Obie and a spot on the short list for the Pulitzer. A sequel to *The Normal Heart, The Destiny of Me* continues the story of *The Normal Heart*'s Ned Weeks, now sick and trying to get into an experimental treatment program at the National Institutes of Health (NIH) while once again dealing with his relationship with his brother, events drawn directly from

Kramer's life. The play also draws on Kramer's college suicide attempt and violent relationship with his father. It earned Kramer even better reviews than *The Normal Heart* had. Together, the two plays make it clear that the crisis in contemporary gay life is a synecdoche for the human experience as a whole.

In 2001, despite reports from *Newsweek* and the Associated Press that Larry Kramer was either dead or dying, Kramer successfully underwent a liver transplant following end-stage liver disease caused by hepatitis B. During the same year, his brother Arthur gave Yale University $1 million to establish the Larry Kramer Initiative for Lesbian and Gay Studies.

Still going strong in 2004, Kramer spoke in front of a capacity crowd at Cooper Union in Greenwich Village, berating gays who were continuing to practice unsafe sex practices and castigating them for their seeming refusal to organize to combat an American right wing happy to let homosexuals kill themselves through sex. The speech was published in its polemic yet humane entirety in *The Tragedy of Today's Gays* (2005). During this time, Kramer also helped the late C. A. Tripp publish his notorious assertion of Abraham Lincoln's homosexuality, *The Intimate World of Abraham Lincoln* (2005); Kramer has always propounded the importance of the gay community's reclaiming of its historical figures. In 2006, he called for a public series of trials similar to the Nuremberg Trials, in which public figures such as Ed Koch, Nancy Reagan, and researchers from the NIH would be tried publicly for their lack of appropriate action in halting the AIDS epidemic in its early days.

Often referred to as the single-most important and certainly the loudest voice of the AIDS movement, Larry Kramer is currently working on *The American People: A History*. He has spent 25 years writing the book, the research of which has convinced him that the HIV/AIDS plague has been intentionally allowed to happen.

See also AIDS Literature

Further Reading

Bergman, David. "Larry Kramer and the Rhetoric of AIDS." In *AIDS: The Literary Response*, edited by Emmanuel S. Nelson, 175–86. New York: Twayne, 1992.

Mass, Lawrence D. *We Must Love One Another or Die: The Life and Legacies of Larry Kramer*. New York: St. Martin's Press, 1999.

McFarlane, Roger. Afterword. *The Tragedy of Today's Gays*. Larry Kramer. New York: Jeremy P. Tarcher/Penguin, 2005. 91–105.

Wolf, Naomi. Foreword. *The Tragedy of Today's Gays*. Larry Kramer. New York: Jeremy P. Tarcher/Penguin, 2005. 3–11.

Jeff Godsey

Kushner, Tony (b. 1956)

Award-winning, prolific American playwright, screenwriter, and activist. Tony Kushner was born to William Kushner and Sylvia (Deutscher) Kushner in New York City on July 16, 1956. When Kushner was two, his parents, both classically trained musicians, moved from Manhattan to Lake Charles, Louisiana, in order to run the Kushner Lumber Company. In 1974, Kushner returned to New York, where he received his bachelor's degree in Medieval Studies from Columbia University in 1978; he graduated from New

York University (NYU) in 1984 with a master's degree in theater directing. His work has been produced in over 30 countries, as well as at the New York Shakespeare Festival, the Mark Taper Forum, New York Theatre Workshop, Hartford Stage Company, Berkeley Repertory Theatre, and the Los Angeles Theatre Center. He is the recipient of a 1990 Whiting Writers' Award and playwriting and directing fellowships from the New York Foundation for the Arts, the New York State Council on the Arts, and the National Endowment for the Arts. In April 2003, he and his longtime partner, Mark Harris, had a wedding ceremony in New York. Kushner is currently an adjunct faculty member of New York University's Dramatic Writing program.

Throughout his career, Kushner has confronted contemporary social concerns—AIDS and the conservative politics of the 1980s, Afghans and the West, racism and civil rights, the rise of capitalism—through the embodiment of marginalized voices in a dramatic style that mixes a deft attention to dialogue with a combination of the real and the phantasmagoric. Following his graduation from Columbia, Kushner worked at the Governor's Program for Gifted Children in Lake Charles, Louisiana, in the summers between 1978 and 1981, directing his original works (such as *Masque of Owls and Incidents* and *Occurrences during the Travels of the Tailor Max*) and Shakespearean plays (*A Midsummer Night's Dream* and *The Tempest*). During his graduate work at NYU in the early 1980s, Kushner also founded a theater group, for which he continued to write and produce his own plays. After receiving his master's degree, Kushner then became the assistant director of The Repertory Theatre of St. Louis in 1985, where he produced *Yes Yes No No: The Solace-of-Solstice, Apogee/Perigee,* and *Bestial/Celestial Holiday Show,* which were later published as *Plays in Process* in 1987.

His first major release, *A Bright Room Called Day,* was produced in New York in 1985, with eventual publication in 1991. Like much of Kushner's work, *A Bright Room Called Day* explores the relevance of art to contemporary social and political concerns. The work, set in the Weimar Republic immediately before Hitler's rise to power, follows a group of left-leaning friends who gradually realize their socialist cause is losing to fascism. Using a mixture of comedy, drama, and philosophical-political commentary, Kushner traces the force of personal resolution against a seemingly unavoidable political catastrophe. Furthermore, through the insertion of monologues from a modern woman in 1990, Kushner also establishes a parallel with what he saw developing in the United States with the election of Ronald Reagan as president in 1980 (a theme developed in a different direction in **Angels in America**).

In 1987, Kushner became the artistic director for the New York Theatre Workshop, producing *Stella* (adapted from the play by Johann Wolfgang von Goethe) and *Hydriotaphia or the Death of Dr. Browne,* based on the final days in the life of Sir Thomas Browne (1605–1682). *Hydriotaphia* is itself the title of an essay Browne wrote in which he concludes that God does not necessarily promise immortality to man. Here, Kushner uses ghosts, souls, and witches to explore a world of emergent capitalism within the context of politics, **gender**, and a prolonged meditation on death. *The Illusion* (adapted from Pierre Corneille's *L'Illusion Comique*) appeared in New York City in 1988 and was published in 1991; *In That Day (Lives of the Prophets)* was produced at New York University in 1989. In 1990, Kushner was appointed the director of literary services for the Theatre Communications Group and the playwright in residence for Juilliard School of Drama.

Angels in America: A Gay Fantasia on National Themes, Kushner's most well-known work, was written and produced in the early 1990s. The play is divided into two parts, the first entitled "Millennium Approaches," the second "Perestroika." The two parts were produced individually in 1992, the first in San Francisco, the second in New York, with both plays produced together in 1995. The play traces three households as they encounter and confront HIV and AIDS in the early to mid-1980s. The work focuses on a gay couple, one of whom has AIDS; a Mormon man coming to terms with his sexuality; and the lawyer Roy Cohn, a historical figure who denied his homosexuality until his death of AIDS-related complications in 1986. Kushner was awarded the Pulitzer Prize in 1993 for "Millennium Approaches," as well as two Tony Awards, two Drama Desk Awards, the Evening Standard Award, two Laurence Olivier Award nominations, the New York Drama Critics' Circle Award, the Los Angeles Drama Critics Circle Award, and the LAMBDA Liberty Award for Drama. The television production of *Angels in America* won an Emmy for Outstanding Writing for a Miniseries, Movie or Dramatic Special in 2004.

Slavs!: Thinking about the Longstanding Problems of Virtue and Happiness (1995) chronicles the demise of the Russian Communist experiment while mourning the loss of idealism this failure wrought. Using a moving and hilarious combination of burlesque and satire, Kushner sets this dark fantasia in a gloomy setting that resembles a city following an earthquake, evoking the death of the Russian Revolution through a wide range of voices that include Communist Party members, minor functionaries, and dead children. *Homebody/Kabul* premiered in New York in December 2001. The title character, Homebody, is a London housewife who muses on the troubled history of Afghanistan, dominating the subsequent monologues despite her relatively short stage time. The play then follows Priscilla, Homebody's daughter, as she searches for her missing mother in Kabul, where most of the play takes place. His new translation of Bertolt Brecht's *Mother Courage and Her Children* was performed at the Delacorte Theater in the summer of 2006 starring Meryl Streep and directed by **George C. Wolfe**.

Kushner's creative talents also extend into the genres of opera and musical theater. *La Fin de la Baleine: An Opera for the Apocalypse* emerged in 1983 during Kushner's early professional days in New York. Kushner also wrote and produced *St. Cecilia, or The Power of Music,* an opera libretto based on Heinrich von Kleist's eighteenth-century story *Die heilige Cäcilie oder die Gewalt der Musik, Eine Legende.* In 2002, he wrote the book for the musical *Caroline, or Change,* which was nominated for two Tony awards and later won the Laurence Olivier Award for Best New Musical in 2007. *Caroline, or Change* uses a mixture of spirituals, blues, Motown, classical, Jewish klezmer, and folk music to tell the story of a young woman named Caroline who works as a maid for a Jewish family in Lake Charles, Louisiana, during the American civil rights movement, during and after the Kennedy assassination.

Kushner's commitment to AIDS activism and political justice extends beyond his work for the stage, as is evident in the numerous introductions and essays he has published. Kushner has written new introductions for a number of texts by prominent gay authors, such as **David B. Feinberg**'s *Queer and Loathing: Rants and Raves of a Raging AIDS Clone* (1995) and David Wojnarowicz's *The Waterfront Journals* (1996). Furthermore, Kushner has published many essays, such as "Three Screeds from Key West: For **Larry Kramer**," in *We Must Love One Another or Die: The Life and Legacies of Larry Kramer* (1997), and a number of his own books, including *A Meditation from Angels in America* (1994), *Save Your Democratic Citizen Soul!: Rants, Screeds, and Other Public Utterances for Midnight in the Republic* (2003) and *Wrestling with Zion: Progressive Jewish-American Responses to the*

Israeli-Palestinian Conflict, with Alisa Solomon (2003). In 2003, he published the children's book *Brundibár* (illustrated by Maurice Sendak), an adaptation of a children's opera originally performed in the Theresienstadt concentration camp; Kushner wrote the libretto for a performance of the opera later that year. He also wrote the introduction for *Peter's Pixie,* by Donn Kushner, illustrated by Sylvie Daigneault.

Kushner is co-author, with Eric Roth, of the screenplay for the 2005 film *Munich,* directed by Steven Spielberg, which earned Kushner and Roth Academy Award and Golden Globe nominations for Best Adapted Screenplay. He has contributed to numerous magazines, including the *New York Times, The Times Literary Supplement, Theater, The Kenyon Review,* and *The Nation.* In January 2006, a documentary feature entitled *Wrestling with Angels,* directed by Freida Lee Mock, debuted at the Sundance Film Festival.

See also Gay Literature, Jewish American

Further Reading

Bloom, Harold, ed. *Tony Kushner.* New York: Chelsea House, 2005.

Fisher, James, ed. *Tony Kushner: New Essays on the Art and Politics of His Plays.* London: McFarland & Company, 2006.

Geis, Deborah R. *Postmodern Theatric(k)s: Monologue in Contemporary American Drama.* Ann Arbor: University of Michigan Press, 1995.

Stephanie Youngblood

L

Lara, Ana-Maurine (b. 1975)

Afrodominicana novelist, poet, essayist, performance artist, and social justice activist. Ana-Maurine Lara's life and work have been a story of transcending and transgressing borders. Born in Santo Domingo, Dominican Republic, on September 22, 1975, to an American mother and a Dominican father, Lara moved with her family to Mount Vernon, New York, at age five, before leaving to spend her formative years in Nairobi, Kenya. At age 12, she returned to Mount Vernon and graduated from Mount Vernon High School. Lara attended Harvard University, studying Social Anthropology and Archaeology, with an emphasis on race and ethnicity in the Dominican Republic and women in the Mayan records of the Yucatan. In college, Lara began writing performance poetry and performing in slams in Boston, where she first began to think of herself as a poet. At age 22, she became part of a LGBTQ Latino/a social justice/arts group in Boston, called Mango con Pique, which staged community arts performances, workshops, and events. After studying in Brazil, at the School for International Training, she graduated *cum laude* from Harvard-Radcliffe and began working in HIV/AIDS research and political education.

Lara spent six months in East Timor as a UN volunteer before returning to San Francisco to work in youth development while expanding her focus on arts as a crucial element in social justice activism. In 2004, she completed *Erzulie's Skirt*. This lush, spiritually rich love story, based in the sugarcane harvesting bateyes of El Sur, Dominican Republic, explores how two poor, black, female lovers confront poverty and come to define freedom on their own terms. Published by RedBone Press in 2006, this first novel was a finalist for the Lambda Literary Award. The social, spiritual, and political place of El Sur also finds voice in her short fiction, and in Lara's second novel, *Anacaona's Daughter* (2008), which incorporates a deeper exploration of the region's Taino history. Lara's poetry and fiction have appeared in numerous publications, both print and online, including *To Be Left with the Body, Sable Lit Mag, Encyclopedia—A Literary and Visual Arts Journal, Blythe House*

Quarterly, Torch Magazine, Stanford Black Arts Quarterly, Tongues Magazine, and *Radcliffe Magazine.*

Lara's life and work are shaped by multiple cultural, linguistic, and historical reference points. Her artistic influences are equally as diverse. Writers from Jorge Luis Borges, Albert Camus, and Fyodor Dostoyevsky mix with Isabelle Allende, Zora Neale Hurston, **Audre Lorde**, **Cherríe Moraga**, Ben Okri, Louise Erdrich, Joy Harjo, and Sherman Alexie as well as visual and performing artists including Mark Rothko and Ana Mendieta. She has deliberately defined her role within social justice activism as an artist and writer. Her critical writing addresses the shifting topography of these experiences and provides a thoughtful balance to her creative and organizing work. Her essays have appeared in *Telling Tongues: A Latino Anthology on Language Experience, Blackberries and Redbones: Critical Articulations of Black Hair/Body Politics in Africana Communities, Phoebe Journal of Gender & Cultural Critiques,* and *Canadian Woman Studies Journal.* Her interviews have appeared in *Torch Magazine, Carry the Word: A Bibliography of Black LGBTQ Books,* and *A Gathering of Tribes Magazine.* Lara co-founded bustingbinaries.com as a space for analyses of intersectionality within the multi-identity framework of U.S.-based social justice work. In 2005, Lara founded "We are the Magicians, the Path-breakers, the Dream-makers LGBTQ POC Oral History Project," which collects oral histories of lesbian, **gay**, bisexual, transgender, two-spirit, **gender** nonconforming/gender**queer** artists of color. In 2007, she founded The Austin Salon Sit-Down, featuring presentations, interviews, and community dialogues with local and international artists.

Lara has performed, read, and spoken at artistic and scholarly venues internationally. She has served as an artist in residence at Cave Canem, Can Serrat, Atlantic Center for the Arts, The Austin Project, Hedgebrook, OurWords Workshop, and VONA/VOICES. Her performance work includes online, interactive, multimedia performance such as *Pёnz (It's Pronounced Pants)* and *Written on the Body,* and performance dinners, Serving Desire, and Dinner at the Crossroads, held in private homes and galleries. Lara has also shown installation work including *Gagá,* a photo installation, and *Sugarcane Dance,* an interactive installation. She has won numerous awards for her work including the Barbara Deming Memorial Fund for Women, the 33rd Annual Chicano/Latino Literary Prize, PEN/Northwest Margery Boyden Davis Residency, Puffin Foundation Creative Nonfiction Grant, and Goelet Fund Research Fellowship.

Further Reading

Allen-Agostini, Lisa. "Erzulie's Skirt." *Caribbean Review of Books* 13 (August 2007): 11.
Miller, Martha. "East of Haiti." *The Gay & Lesbian Review Worldwide* 14, no. 3 (May 2007): 43–44.

Samiya Bashir

Larkin, Joan (b. 1939)

Prominent poet, essayist, editor, and playwright. Joan Larkin was born on April 16, 1939, in Boston, Massachusetts. She received her bachelor's degree from Swarthmore College and went on to complete two master's degrees: an M.F.A. from Brooklyn College and an M.A. in English from the University of Arizona. In 1961, Larkin married the painter Robert Ross and lived for several years as a teaching assistant at the University of

Arizona in Tucson. Once the marriage ended, Larkin moved to New York City where she met her second husband, Jim Larkin. Her daughter, Kate, was born in 1967, and her marriage to Jim Larkin ended in 1969. Larkin has said that she had several intermittent lesbian relationships but did not begin to come out publicly and seek out the lesbian community until the 1970s. However, when Larkin did enter the community, she entered in with power and grace. She, along with Irena Klepfisz and Jan Clausen, formed a lesbian writer's group called Seven Women Poets. In 1976, she founded an independent women's publishing collective called Out & Out Books. Out & Out Books published both her first book of poems and her popular anthology, *Amazon Poetry* (1975), co-edited with Elly Bulkin.

Housework (1975) is Larkin's first published collection. It is a small book that contains not only stark, declarative, and confessional poetry, but it also becomes a small canvas for the watercolor painter Mimi Weisbord. The poems in *Housework* have short lines. The sentences are simple, yet the territory explored by the poems is the complicated and heartbreaking web of family, of love, and of the body. The poems seem to challenge binaries and try, again and again, to understand and interrogate what we know of **gender** itself. The poems can also be seen as a series of dedications—to her daughter Kate, to friends and lovers, and finally to herself. Larkin explores the pleasure and suffering of being alone. In a section entitled "True Stories," Larkin quite specifically tells the stories of family, moving from images of childhood to the image of her adult self who writes this book. Her final section, "A Certain Kind of Strength," resembles an incantation, and the book ends by repeating the line *go down to the water and look.* The repetition becomes a chant, its force seeming to gather up the strength it had taken Larkin to write the book and to the live her life, the strength it takes all women.

Larkin's second collection of poems, *A Long Sound* (1986), is seen by most critics as some of the best, most honest, and complicated work on alcoholism and recovery. Larkin offers no sentimental or easy solutions and tries to represent her struggles with alcoholism and its connection to all other aspects of life. There are a variety of voices in this book, voices of recovery, of love, of the **gay** and lesbian communities in which Larkin lives. She would then go on to publish two more collections of original poetry, *Cold River* (1997), which was a recipient of the Lambda Literary Award for Poetry, and finally *My Body: New and Selected Poems* (2007). The most recent collection is said to be a wonderful representation of her life's work in poetry and includes several new poems that have arrived as Larkin's sharpest and most lyrical poems as of yet.

Larkin's literary work does move far beyond her poetry. She has written several plays—among them a play called *The Living,* which takes on the subject of HIV and has even been produced in Boston and New York. She was the translator, along with Jaime Manrique, of *Sor Juana's Love Poems* (2003) and was the co-editor, along with Carl Morse, of *Gay and Lesbian Poetry in Our Time* (1988), which won a Lambda Literary Award for Poetry. She has served as the co-editor of the Living Out series at the University of Wisconsin Press and as the poetry editor for the literary magazine *Bloom.*

She has been teaching writing and poetry for over 40 years and is currently a member of the core faculty at New England College.

Further Reading

Bulkin, Elly. "Joan Larkin on Poetry and Recovery." *Sojourner* (February 1987): 21–22.

Hacker, Marilyn. "A Pocketful of Poets." Review of *A Long Sound. Women's Review of Books.* (July 1988): 23–34.

Rich, Adrienne. "There Is a Fly in This House." Review of *Housework. Ms.* (February 1977): 46–106.

Stacey Waite

Larson, Leslie (b. 1956)

Contemporary American novelist. Leslie Larson was born in San Diego, California, on February 17, 1956, the oldest child and only daughter of Thomas Larson, a printer, and Joan Marsh, a housekeeper in a convalescent home. Coming from Norwegian immigrants on her father's side and "Okies" who migrated to California during the Great Depression on her mother's, Larson grew up during the height of the Cold War—an atmosphere that had a profound effect on her writing and personality. An avid reader from a very young age, she attended public schools in San Diego, where she experienced many of the tumultuous events of the 1960s and 1970s, including the assassination of John F. Kennedy, Martin Luther King, Jr., and Robert F. Kennedy, and the Vietnam War. In the sixth grade she decided to be a writer; in seventh grade she attempted her first novel. She was a reporter and editor for her high school newspaper. The first in her family to attend college, she supported herself with scholarships and by working in the campus dining commons. She received a degree in English and American Literature at the University of California, San Diego, in 1980.

A week after graduating from college, Larson fulfilled her long-held ambition to leave Southern California and move to London, where—because of obsessive youthful reading of Charlotte Brontë, Thomas Hardy, Charles Dickens, and Virginia Woolf—she believed a writer *should* live. She landed a job with a small publisher, Marion Boyars Publishers Ltd., where she worked for the next two years. She did everything—typed, answered phones, read manuscripts, edited books, and wrote promotional copy, an experience that laid the groundwork for her long connection with independent publishing. She shared a house with immigrants from Ireland, South America, and India, which greatly expanded her horizons. Ironically, her work left little time or energy for her own writing. Hoping to work less for more money, she returned to California, this time to San Francisco.

Larson moved to Haight-Ashbury, came out of the **closet**, and thrived in the freedom that the Bay Area offered. For the next 15 years she did freelance work: writing advertising copy, television spots, feature articles, book reviews, and short stories. Her first novel, *The Season before Dawn* (2000), focuses on two children who try to sabotage their mother's disastrous relationship with a man they detest. Like the novels that were to follow, this one delves into the lives of working-class characters pushed to the margins of society.

Her next novel, *Slipstream,* published in 2006, is set in and around the Los Angeles International Airport. An intricately crafted tale integrating the lives of five people who are drawn toward a fateful collision in a post–9-11 world, deftly weaves suspense, humor, and revelation. With its rich characterization and breathless pacing, *Slipstream* blurs the edges between thriller and literary fiction. It was critically acclaimed and named a BookSense notable book and Target Breakout Book. It also won the Astraea Award for Fiction and was a finalist for the Lambda Literary Award.

Her third novel, *Breaking Out of Bedlam* (2008), introduces the unforgettable character of Cora Sledge, an 82-year-old woman forced into an assisted living facility by her children. Cora takes revenge by keeping a tell-all journal that is by turns profound, profane, gossipy, and confessional. This novel is a unique portrait of the human condition confronting many aging Americans who begin to lose their self-sufficiency while still retaining their will to keep their own ways of existence. It captures the loneliness and secrets that lurk within families, the hardscrabble reality facing women with limited choices, and the triumph of the human spirit that survives, despite all the odds, through an unlikely combination of humor, faith, and acceptance.

Larson's dedication to writing about the lives of the working class caught the eye of other notable working-class writers, such as **Dorothy Allison**, who indicates that Larson writes about "the lives of people used to being looked past, over, or beyond," and Sandra Cisneros, who says "Larson writes with an intimate eye and heart about citizens so familiar to the American landscape, we don't even see them." Yet her novels, and the characters in them, reflect a sense of hope for the reader, as they elicit an underlying purpose to surviving and ultimately redemption. Jim Shepard addresses this in his comments about Larson's work by stating that she "renders beautifully a lower middle class California that's being squeezed out of a place to live . . . yet provides an intricate and moving sense of the way in which such characters' lives go wrong, and the persistence of their resolve to turn them around" (all quotes from dust jacket blurbs).

In addition to creating unforgettable characters, Larson is a wonderful storyteller. Her voice resonates with a deep and detailed knowledge of the nuances of American life. Readers are captivated by her superb craftsmanship. Larson's work never hesitates or refrains from giving the reader all the possibilities and from putting her spirit, heart, and commitment to great writing on the page.

Further Reading

Elson, Rachel F. "Comings and Goings at an Airport." *San Francisco Chronicle,* May 28, 2006, M2.
Faderman, Lillian. "The New Normal." *Gay & Lesbian Review Worldwide* (September–October 2007): 37.
Pepper, Rachel. "Paperback Writers." *Curve* 14, no. 3 (April 2007): 60.

Carla Trujillo

Lassell, Michael (b. 1947)

Award-winning author, publisher, critic, and editor of various magazines, articles, anthologies, and journals. Michael Lassell boasts a literary career that spans over 20 years. Hailed as one of the most prolific writers of his generation, Michael Lassell's collection includes multigenre works of fiction and nonfiction ranging from books on decorating and design, to his sexual and emotional encounters as a **gay** man in New York City, to nonfiction books on the production and design of Disney plays on Broadway. Son of Michael Joseph Lassell and Catherine Elizabeth Lassell, he was born in New York City on July 15, 1947. Many of his works are inspired by his experiences growing up and residing in Manhattan. Despite his educational endeavors and extensive travel, Lassell's home base is always Manhattan as he writes fondly and romantically of the city in many of his poems and essays. Lassell earned degrees from Colgate University, the Yale School of Drama (where he was awarded the John Gassner Prize for Criticism), and California Institute of the Arts, where he became a professor in the School of Theater and Division of Critical Studies. Lassell has won awards including the Lambda Literary Award for Poetry for his collection of poems entitled *The World in Us* (2000) and the Society of American Travel Writers Foundation Lowell Award for his travel writing.

Lassell's first collection of poetry, *Poems for Lost and Un-Lost Boys* (1985), won the Amelia Award in 1986. *The Hard Way* (1994), his second publication, is a collection of poetry, prose, and essays regarding the joys and heartaches of living and loving as a gay man who is at once self-centered yet self-loathing. His works, written like songs, are lyrical and passionate accounts of his sexual encounters during the gay liberation movement of the late 1960s and early 1970s. Although he claims his works to be neither fiction nor nonfiction, it becomes evident to the reader that *The Hard Way* is an account of a man who is, at times, saddened and at odds with a culture that is becoming increasing superficial. Despite his trenchant criticism of some aspects of urban gay life, Lassell maintains a witty combination of humor and anger in his writing that has earned him a reputation in the literary world as being one of the most honest and heartfelt writers of his time. Lassell's next publication, *The Name of Love: Classic Gay Love Poems* (1995), is an anthology of gay male love poetry.

Lassell published a number of collections of poetry and prose from 1996 to 2001 including *Eros in Boystown: Contemporary Gay Poems about Sex* (1996) and *A Flame for the Touch That Matters* (1998), a vibrant and visionary collection of poems about male gay sex and love. Lassell's graphic accounts of gay desire and passion mixed with his sexual fantasies are deeply honest, and at times, startling accounts of a society obsessed with sex. *Men Seeking Men* (1998), *Certain Ecstasies* (1999), and *The World in Us: Lesbian and Gay Poetry of the Next Wave* (2001) are Lassell's most current publications of poetry and prose. *Lesbian and Gay Poetry of the Next Wave* is an anthology Lassell co-published with friend and colleague Elena Georgiou. The anthology consists of 40 poets of multicultural and multiracial backgrounds and their accounts of living and loving in the lesbian and gay community. The poems are nontraditional in that few are metered or use rhyme and make up a refreshing sampling of poets and poems at the beginning of the twenty-first century.

The millennium came with a shift in Lassell's career and writing. He began to focus on his background in theater and dramatics with an emphasis on Disney productions. In 2000 he co-published *Elton John & Tim Rice's Aida: The Making of the Broadway Musical,* a celebrated book about the Disney Broadway play including songwriter Elton John and acclaimed lyricist Tim Rice. Lassell writes of the production and action that occurs in front of and behind the curtain. With colorful pictures and detailed accounts of the excitement and energy that goes into creating and producing a Broadway musical, Lassell's book became widely popular. His success with Disney led him to publish numerous other works on the accounts of production life on Broadway. In 2002 he published *Disney on Broadway,* a colorful collection of photographs and staff commentary on *Beauty and the Beast, The Lion King,* and *Aida,* three of Disney's most popular Broadway plays. *Celebration: The Story of a Town* (2004) explores the planned community of Celebration, Florida, Walt Disney's idea for what later became Epcot Center. Lassell compiles accounts of architects that helped design the community, local residents' trials and tribulations within the community, and beautiful illustrations of Florida's most unique neighborhoods. In 2007, Lassell published *Tarzan: The Broadway Adventure* and co-published *Mary Poppins: Anything Can Happen If You Let It* with Brian Sibley. Lassell continued to expand his variety of nonfiction writing with his book *Decorate: Insider's Tips from Top Interior Designers* (2005). Lassell has been writing for the *Metropolitan Home* magazine since 1992 and is currently the Features director. The book was created around the concept of how some of the best designers came up with their ideas for decorating and includes personal design secrets and key concept ideas behind the creations.

Lassell has worked as a journalist, theater critic, and arts features writer for *LA Weekly* and the *Los Angeles Herald-Examiner* since 1992 and an editor to the *New York Native* and *The Advocate* magazines. His literary career includes a variety of poems, short stories, and essays published in magazines, newspapers, anthologies, and literary journals as well as his extensive list of books of poetry, prose, essays, and nonfiction. Lassell's works have been translated into many languages including French, Spanish, and German.

Further Reading

Gambone, Philip. Review of *The Hard Way*. *Lambda Book Report* 4, no. 8 (Spring 1995): 31–32.

Klein, Michael. Review of *The Name of Love: Classic Gay Love Poems*. *Lambda Book Report* 4, no. 11 (Summer 1995): 33–34.

Olson, Ray. Review of *The World in Us: Lesbian and Gay Poetry of the Next Wave*. *Booklist* 96, no. 114 (2000): 1317.

Suzanne C. Farah

Leavitt, David (b. 1961)

Prominent **gay** author of both fiction and nonfiction. David Leavitt was born June 23, 1961, in Pittsburgh, Pennsylvania, to Harold Jack Leavitt and Gloria Rosenthal Leavitt. His father was a professor at Stanford University, and his mother was an activist in their community. After growing up in Palo Alto, California, he attended Yale University, graduating with a degree in English in 1983. He has gone on to teach at Princeton University and the University of Florida, where he is a professor today. He acts as editor of the magazine *Subtropics,* a literary journal featuring fiction and poetry. He often collaborates with his partner, Mark Mitchell; they currently split their time between Florida and Tuscany, Italy, where they own property.

A prolific author, his works comprise collections of short stories, novels, and nonfiction. His collections of stories include *Family Dancing* (1984), *A Place I've Never Been* (1990), *Arkansas* (1997), and *The Marble Quilt* (2001). His novels include *The Lost Language of Cranes* (1986), *Equal Affections* (1989), *While England Sleeps* (1993; revised and reissued 1995), *The Page Turner* (1998), *Martin Bauman; or, A Sure Thing* (2000), *The Body of Jonah Boyd* (2004), and his most recent novel, *The Indian Clerk* (2007). His works of nonfiction include *Italian Pleasures* (1996) with Mark Mitchell, *Pages Passed from Hand to Hand: The Hidden Tradition of Homosexual Literature in English from 1748 to 1914* (1997) co-edited with Mark Mitchell, *In Maremma: Life and a House in Southern Tuscany* (2001) with Mark Mitchell, *Florence, A Delicate Case* (2003), and *The Man Who Knew Too Much: Alan Turing and the Invention of the Computer* (2005).

Although Leavitt's works often deal with the lives of gay characters, his audience includes a large number of straight readers. His work has been influenced by some of the most prominent authors of the twentieth century, such as Virginia Woolf and Ford Madox Ford. For Leavitt, his influences may appear on the subconscious level, filtering through authors he has read, though not admired, such as Henry James. Such accidental influences are countered by his more conspicuous **queer** influences: E. M. Forster, Oscar Wilde, and Marcel Proust. Of his contemporaries, Leavitt has developed relationships—

both positive and negative—with many of them. He admires the critical work of **Edmund White**, but dismisses many other gay authors as overly pandering to the market.

Leavitt began publishing his work while still a student at Yale. He published "Territory," a short story, in *The New Yorker,* which was directly followed by "Out Here." These stories, published as a student, later served as the seed for his first collection of short stories, *Family Dancing,* which received accolades, including garnering nominations for the National Book Critics Circle Award and for the PEN/Faulkner Award. After this collection of stories, his first full novel emerged in 1986, *The Lost Language of Cranes.* In 1992 his novel *The Lost Language of Cranes* was converted into a television movie. This book examines homosexuality from the perspective of both the father and son: the son's gayness forces his father to confront his own latent feelings of attraction toward men. Following the success of *The Lost Language of Cranes,* Leavitt produced another novel, *Equal Affections,* which also dealt with parent-child relationships. In it, a gay attorney must grapple with his mother's 20-year battle against cancer. Some read this as an autobiographical narrative, but Leavitt has denied these claims. In 1989, Leavitt was the recipient of the prestigious John Simon Guggenheim Memorial Foundation Fellowship and worked as writer in residence at the Institute of Catalan Letters in Barcelona. His second collection of short stories, *A Place I've Never Been,* gains traction through his studies abroad, considering that many of those stories discuss American adventures in Europe.

His next novel, *While England Sleeps,* was a hotbed of controversy after allegations emerged that Leavitt had copied pieces of a memoir almost verbatim. As Leavitt's first foray into historical fiction, the storyline centers on the gay romance of an aristocratic author and a blue-collar Communist in 1930s England. Stephen Spender, the subject of *While England Sleeps,* sued Leavitt in 1991 on charges that Leavitt had copied portions of his memoir, *World within World* (1951), without properly crediting it. Furthermore, Spender accused Leavitt of using falsified, sexually graphic fantasies attributed to his character. For Spender, this was the most infuriating aspect of the plagiarism: the misrepresentation of his identity. The matter was settled out of court, with Viking Press agreeing to delete certain problematic segments. The novel was withdrawn and republished two years later, in 1995. Despite the plagiarism scandal, the novel went on to be a finalist for the *Los Angeles Times* Fiction Prize.

After *While England Sleeps,* Leavitt published *Arkansas* (1997), a compilation of three novellas: "The Term Paper Artist," "The Wooden Anniversary," and "Saturn Street." Another novel by Leavitt emerged this same year, chronicling the sphere of classical music, *The Page Turner. Martin Baumann* came next, in 2000, followed by *Florence, A Delicate Case* in 2002 and his *Collected Stories* in 2003. *The Body of Jonah Boyd* came out in 2004, and the story tracks a family's search for answers in grappling with the effects of a stolen manuscript. Somewhat of a misnomer, the "body" in the title refers to the body of the manuscript, rather than a physical body. In 2005 he made another attempt at historical writing with *The Man Who Knew Too Much: Alan Turing and the Invention of the Computer.* His most recent novel is *The Indian Clerk,* which was published in 2007.

Following his early success and subsequent litigative struggles, Leavitt has continued to produce new work and maintains a steady career. Following his stint in Spain, Leavitt returned to New York City for a spell, but later settled in southern Tuscany, Italy. He and his partner, Mark Mitchell, published a book documenting the process of restoring their 1950s farmhouse and Italian life there, titled *In Maremma: Life and a House in Southern Tuscany* (2001). He remains active in the literary world and displays his commitment to encouraging young writers through his role as editor of the literary journal *Subtropics.*

Further Reading

Alexander, Jonathan. "One Gay Author, One Straight Author, and a Handful of Queer Books: Recent Fiction of David Leavitt and Bruce Hornby." *Harrington Gay Men's Fiction Quarterly* 4, no. 1 (2002): 111–20.

Bleeth, Kenneth, and Julie Rivkin. "The 'Limitation David:' Plagiarism, Collaboration, and the Making of a Gay Literary Tradition in David Leavitt's *The Term Paper Artist.*" *PMLA* 116, no. 5 (Oct. 2001): 1349–63.

Harned, Jon. "Psychoanalysis, Queer Theory, and David Leavitt's *The Lost Language of Cranes.*" *South Central Review* 11, no. 4 (Winter 1994): 40–53.

Lilly, Mark. *Gay Men's Literature in the Twentieth Century.* New York: New York University Press, 1993.

Laura Blosser

Le Guin, Ursula K. (b. 1929)

Science fiction, fantasy, children's books and realistic writer, essayist, and poet. She was born October 21, 1929, in Berkeley, California, where she also grew up. Daughter of writer Theodora (Kracaw) and anthropologist Alfred Kroeber, she was educated at Radcliffe College (B.A., 1951) and Columbia University (M.A., 1952), where she studied French and Italian literature. She later won a Fulbright scholarship to continue her studies on French and Italian Renaissance literature in France. She met Charles Le Guin, a fellow scholar from Georgia, and they married in 1953. They afterwards moved permanently to the United States, living first in California and later in Portland, Oregon. The couple has three children and four grandchildren. Ursula K. Le Guin is an extremely prolific writer whose career began in 1966, when she published her first novel, *Rocannon's World,* and spans to the present moment. Her 1968 novel, *A Wizard of Earthsea,* became a best seller. Her latest book is *Powers,* a fantasy book for young adults published in September 2007. In all, she has published over 30 volumes, including fiction and poetry, and this has been recognized in the numerous awards and prizes she has received. Among them, she received the 2004 Margaret A. Edwards Award for lifetime achievement and the 2002 PEN/Malamud Award for Short Fiction.

Ursula K. Le Guin is primarily a fantasy and science fiction writer who began to write in the 1960s out of her feminist interest in a new world where **gender** equality could be achieved. Science fiction and utopian literatures provided women writers with adequate spaces to explore liberating possibilities, if only imaginatively. Much of her writing continued to have a political undertone as far as science fiction allowed her to create alternative societies based on nonsexist, pacifist values.

Ursula K. Le Guin does not address homosexual issues directly, but does call into question prevalent gender and identity structures, reexamining our assumptions about sex roles and stereotypes. In *The Left Hand of Darkness* (1969) Le Guin creates a society with a different construction of sexuality with **androgyny** as its norm. The Gethenians are "ambisexual" and their unconventional sexual physiology is explained by the "Envoy" from an interplanetary union, who travels there with the mission of convincing the governments in Gethen to join this union. Gethenians have a sexual cycle of 26 to 28 days, and during most of them (21 or 22 days) the person is "somer," that is, sexually inactive and androgynous. Hormonal changes bring about a new phase, "kemmer," characterized by the appearance of the sexual impulse. In this phase the individual finds a partner in kemmer and hormonal secretion determines male and female dominance in each of the partners. The genitals adopt the form most suited to performing the male and female sexual roles, either engorging or shrinking, and the sexual relationship is fulfilled. It is important to emphasize that Gethenians do not have a preestablished preference for either sexual role, and once they have achieved a concrete sexual form, it cannot be changed during the kemmer period. After five days of maximum sexual capacity and drive, the kemmer phase ends abruptly and the person returns to the somer period. If there was conception, the individual who was impregnated remains female for 9 months, and "her" male sexual organs remain retracted. After giving birth, she reenters somer and becomes androgyne once more. What is striking about the sexual physiology of Gethenians is the fact that the mother of several children may be the father of several more. The adoption of sexual identity and role in Gethenians happens thus completely at random. However, the Gethenians are not neuters, but potentials.

In *The Dispossessed* (1974), Le Guin's second major science fiction novel, Shevek is a scientist who travels from his utopian world, called Anarres, to Urras, the planet that symbolizes Earth, characterized by all the evils that the 1970s social movements fought against, that is, militarism, sexism, hierarchism, and so forth. Shevek's aim is to reestablish contact with Urras, interrupted seven generations back. He witnesses the sexual objectification of women in Urras, evident in their going around with bare breasts. In Urras, women are completely subordinated to their sexual role. Shevek contrasts this with the culture of his planet, which allows women to perform the same social roles as men. His own father, and not his mother, was the one who looked after him and brought him up. It is significant the way Le Guin explains how civilization in Anarres came about: female philosopher Oddo's ideas triggered a revolution in Urras and her followers (founders of the Odonian Movement) had to abandon it and colonize another planet (eventually "Anarres"), where they established a society based on Odo's precepts, which emphasized a holistic approach to life and avoided pyramidal hierarchy. In this new society, there are no restrictions in sexual relationships, homo or heterosexual. Marriage does not even exist and, in short, the relations between the sexes are egalitarian. Through the example of Urras, Le Guin attacked all the wrong notions about women that Betty Friedan had analyzed in her 1963 book *The Feminine Mystique*. Thus, although Le Guin does not provide solutions, she certainly incorporates a feminist consciousness into her writing.

See also Science Fiction, Lesbian

Further Reading

Bernardo, Susan M., and G. J. Murphy. *Ursula K. Le Guin: A Critical Companion*. Westport, CT: Greenwood, 2006.

Bloom, Harold, ed. *Ursula K. Le Guin*. New York: Chelsea House, 2000.

Cummins, Elizabeth. *Understanding Ursula K. Le Guin*. Columbia: University of South Carolina Press, 1992.

Fayad, Mona. "Aliens, Androgynes and Anthropology: Le Guin's Critique of Representation in *The Left Hand of Darkness*." *Mosaic: A Journal for the Interdisciplinary Study of Literature* 30, no. 3 (1997): 57–73.

Haley, Guy. "Interview: Ursula K. Le Guin." *Death Ray* (October 2007): 76–82.

Pita, Marianne. "Gender Bending: Ursula K. Le Guin's *The Left Hand of Darkness.*" In *Women in Literature: Reading through the Lens of Gender,* edited by Jerilyn Fisher. Westport, CT: Greenwood, 2003. 166–68.

Rochelle, Warren. *Communities of the Heart: The Rhetoric of Myth in the Fiction of Ursula K. Le Guin.* Liverpool, UK: Liverpool University Press, 2001.

Matilde Martín González

Lesbianism

Lesbian refers to a woman-identified person whose exclusive or primary emotional, erotic, and romantic attractions are to other women-identified people.

Lesbian derives from the name of the Island of Lesbos, in ancient Greece, where poet Sappho was known to write sexually graphic love poems to other women. Throughout the ages, much of lesbian love, desire, and life has been rendered invisible, buried beneath a sea of sexism and **homophobia**. As Lillian Faderman writes, "It was not until the second half of the nineteenth century that the *category* of the lesbian—or the female sexual invert—was formulated" (1991). Like the term **gay**, lesbian is a socially constructed identity that differs widely based on geographical space and temporality.

While in the 1950s and 1960s it was not uncommon to hear terms like "gay girls" and "female homosexuals," the late 1960s and 1970s political environment changed the landscape of sexual identity politics. On the one hand, the second wave of the women's movement was in full swing. Since the publication of Betty Friedan's *The Feminine Mystique* (1963), feminists had been engaged in a variety of projects to win full equality for women. However, some saw the full integration of lesbians in the movement as a liability, even referring to it as "the lavender menace." Due to this marginalization, lesbians worked to challenge heterosexism and homophobia within the women's movement and to demand that lesbian rights were an integral part of the feminist agenda for social change. While some stayed to advocate for full lesbian inclusion within feminism, others were so disgusted by the homophobia from straight women that they formed their own lesbian-feminist groups.

In addition, after the **Stonewall Riots**, many organizations and groups formed to work for the civil rights of gay, lesbian, bisexual, and transgender people. However, it quickly became apparent that these groups had a problem with sexism, whereby lesbians were not given a full seat at the table. Due to this bigotry, many lesbians decided it was time to separate from gay male–dominated groups and work on their own. Between the sexism of gay male groups and the homophobia of straight women's groups, the ground was fertile for the growth of lesbian feminism.

One of the founding papers of lesbian feminism was "Compulsory **Heterosexuality** and Lesbian Existence" by **Adrienne Rich**. First published in 1980, this essay put forth a vision of lesbianism that was not based solely, or even primarily, on female-to-female genital contact. Sexuality was decentered in favor of the emotional, spiritual, and psychological bonds that many women form. The "political lesbian" was born to refer to a woman who actively chose lesbianism in conjunction with her radical feminist politics and her desire to be a "woman-identified woman." Lesbian feminism also included a desire by some women to be separatists (see Hoagland 1988), to live communally on lesbian land, and to replace the spelling of "women" with "womyn."

However, beginning in the 1990s and beyond, many younger lesbians began to challenge the radical orthodoxies of the lesbian foremothers. The "sex wars," for instance, exploded in feminist and lesbian communities as women disagreed vehemently about issues such as pornography, bondage and domination, sadomasochism, and prostitution. In addition, the emergence of the third wave, the terminology of "**queer**," prosex feminism, and the transgender rights movement helped to shift ideologies within the lesbian community once again.

As with their gay male counterparts, lesbian literary critics have been working for decades to find and expose lesbian content in novels, as well as research the lesbian lives of novelists, poets, and essayists. Books such as *The Lesbian History Sourcebook* go back through history and try to replace the intentionally erased, distorted, and ignored figure of the lesbian woman. The LGBTQ political movement, in conjunction with queer and allied scholars, has made formidable progress toward weaving the lesbian back into history, literature, society, and culture.

Further Reading

Aragon, Angela Pattatucci. *Challenging Lesbian Norms.* Binghamton, NY: Haworth Press, 2006.

Cornwell, Anita. *Black Lesbian in White America.* Tallahassee, FL: Naiad Press, 1983.

Faderman, Lillian. *Odd Girls and Twilight Lovers.* New York: Penguin Books, 1991.

Hoagland, Sarah Lucia. *For Lesbians Only: A Separatist Anthology.* London: Onlywomen, 1988.

Kleindienst, Kris. *This Is What Lesbian Looks Like.* Ithaca, NY: Firebrand Books, 1999.

Oram, Alison, and Annmarie Turnbull. *The Lesbian History Sourcebook.* New York: Routledge, 2001.

Rich, Adrienne. "Compulsory Heterosexuality and Lesbian Existence." In *The Lesbian and Gay Studies Reader,* edited by Henry Abelove, Michèle Aina Barale, and David M. Halperin. New York: Routledge, 1993.

Joelle Ruby Ryan

Lesbian Literature, African American

Literary historians are uncovering a wealth of pre-twentieth-century literature written by African American women. Perhaps soon to be found is an early African American lesbian novel. Women's slave narratives certainly demonstrate women who were aware of the sexual violence done to them not only through rape and forced reproductive acts, but also through the requirement that they be either martyrs to chastity or else available to every man, extreme versions of compulsory **heterosexuality**.

In early twentieth-century African American women's writing, discomfort with the available marriage options can be read as a foil for lesbian desire. Thus in Nella Larsen's *Passing* (1929), we can find a simmering relationship between Irene Redfield and Clare Kendry. As its title indicates, *Passing* belongs to a common subgenre of African American literature: the passing novel that tells the tale of light-skinned African Americans who pass for white. Larsen's novella indeed focuses on two light-skinned African American women, Irene who does not pass for white, and Clare who does. The possible relationship between Irene and Clare haunts the text. Critics note that the very unclear and unknown quality of desire between the women in the novel points to how, in the first half of the twentieth century, African Americans may have passed not only racially but also sexually, asking us not to identify lesbian characters but to think about the many desires and identities that intersect and that mask one another in the first centuries of African American literature and culture.

During the Harlem Renaissance, out of which *Passing* emerged, African American authors articulated a politics and an aesthetics that were uniquely Negro and deeply American and that looked to staking out not only the humanity and freedom of African Americans but also an identity replete with intellectual and artistic traditions. The literature of the Harlem Renaissance put into fictional form W. E. B. Du Bois's theories about the double consciousness of African Americans. It also celebrated African heritage and its contribution to contemporary art forms such as jazz. The Harlem Renaissance is famous for its sexual permissiveness, and most of the authors who explored same-sex desire were men, such as Langston Hughes and Countee Cullen; Larsen is one of the few women writers of the Harlem Renaissance who even alluded to **lesbianism**.

The Harlem Renaissance gave way to the Protest Era with the civil rights movement, the Black Arts Movement, and the Black Power movement. The great focus of the African American community turned to the urgent need to secure equal rights. The reliance of the civil rights movement on Christian ministers and of the Black Power movement on Muslim clerics established for both profoundly heterosexual value systems. A fear of taking attention away from the movement's antiracist message blocked serious consideration of the ways that race, **gender**, sexuality, and class implicate one another, of the ways in which the civil rights movement might not only support but also be supported by women's rights and lesbian rights. Furthermore, throughout African American history the mother stands as the holder of tradition, the connection to Mother Africa, so that women who might be perceived as untraditional threaten the entire community. African American lesbian writers found little place to express their sexuality that was not considered marginal or even antithetical to the civil rights movement and the great literature that surrounded it. At the same time, the women's and homosexual movements that emerged in the 1960s prioritized gender and sexuality, respectively, over race, ignoring the ways that by virtue of their different races some women experience different oppressions, and refusing to acknowledge the racism within their own ranks. Thus African American lesbian authors often kept their lesbianism hidden in their lives and in their works well into the 1970s.

A certain reticence to identify African American authors or characters as lesbian may also, however, indicate not **homophobia** or fear of coming out, but rather an attempt to express desire between women outside the category "lesbian" that can be taken to be marked white by its allusion to European history (the Greek island of Lesbos) and by its connection to a predominantly white movement. Perhaps the most important example of this, after Larsen's *Passing,* can be found in **Alice Walker**'s epistolary novel, ***The Color Purple*** (1982). Walker refers to herself as a womanist, a term that for her expresses a primary commitment to women that may take any form, from political activism to erotic relationships, but that also always attends to race. Set in rural Georgia in the early twentieth century, *The Color Purple* recounts the troubled lives of sharecropping families through a series of letters written by Celie and her sister Nettie. While Celie marries, leaves, and then reconnects with Mr. _____, she finds herself through a relationship with Shug, a blues singer with whom both she and her husband are in love. To both Celie and Shug, the relationship that they share is of primary importance in their erotic and emotional lives, but to neither is it exclusive nor does it stop both women from having subsequent relationships with men. The relationship between Shug and Celie provides an essential alternative to the sexual violence and abuse that Celie suffers with men, but Celie learns not to turn away from men but to embrace them differently. Celie's relationship with Shug brings Celie to a consciousness about her power as an African American woman and allows her to formulate an identity that cannot be organized by any single marker.

Prior to *The Color Purple,* however, a few novels by African American women had begun to claim lesbianism for themselves. The first novel written by an African American woman with a self-identified lesbian protagonist is **Ann Allen Shockley**'s *Loving Her* (1974), though Shockley did not label her own sexual identity. Rosa Guy's *Ruby* (1976) offers another early portrayal of an African American protagonist whose primary love relationship was with another girl, but *Ruby* ends with an apparent universal turn to heterosexual adulthood. **Octavia Butler**'s science fictions, spanning the late 1970s through her death in 2006, do not depict lesbianism per se, but they often explore nonheterosexual reproduction, including a pregnant man ("Bloodchild"), third-gendered aliens who mate with humans (the Xenogenesis series), and body- (and gender-) shifting autogeneraters (the Patternist series).

Around the same time, African American lesbian poetry provided a space for much more radical expressions of lesbianism. **Pat Parker**, in *Child of Myself* (1972), *Pit Stop* (1974), *Womanslaughter* (1978), and *Jonestown and Other Madness* (1985), playfully and explicitly describes lesbian lovemaking, coming out of the **closet**, and black lesbian feminist politics. **Cheryl Clarke** has devoted herself to assuring that Parker's work continues to be remembered while also publishing her own poetry. In collections including *Living as a Lesbian* (1986) and *Experimental Love* (1996), Clarke writes with openness, humor, sensuality, and profanity about lesbianism in a violent, underprivileged, urban environment that is nonetheless marked by hope as well as by struggle.

The most well-known African American lesbian writer, **Audre Lorde**, in her "biomythography" ***Zami: A New Spelling of My Name*** (1982), comes up with a novel way to negotiate the apparent disjoints between African American and lesbian identification. By 1982, Lorde was already an accomplished poet and essayist who in *The First Cities* (1968), *Cables to Rage* (1970), *From a Land Where Other People Live* (1973), *The New York Head Shop and Museum* (1974), *Coal* (1976), and *The Black Unicorn* (1978) expressed herself as an African American lesbian. In *Zami,* she traces how she came to that identity and what it means to her. Zami describes Lorde's coming-of-age in a Granadian immigrant family in New York in the 1950s. Lorde/Zami initially connects to her Caribbean heritage, finding in it a strong assertion of women's sexuality and power, although not any women lovers. However, the relative invisibility of black, be they Caribbean or African American, lesbians in New York in the 1950s leads Lorde/Zami to discover her sexuality with white women in the burgeoning lesbian community. After an initial exuberance, however, Lode/Zami finds the racism of white lesbians as stifling as the homophobia of the African American community. She continues to search for a space where she can be black and lesbian without needing to prioritize either. This she finally finds with another black lesbian, Afrekete, and also with the change of her name to Zami. Zami is a term used in parts of Grenada to refer to lesbians and thus asserts the existence of a historical Afro-Caribbean lesbian community. Furthermore, Lorde argues that the very tradition of black mothering is one of "black dykes," so that even married mothers who never have sexual relationships with other women can be part of a community and a history of Afro-Caribbean and African American lesbians. But as a young African American lesbian in New York in the 1950s, Lorde remains a lonely trailblazer, establishing rather than joining a community. By the time that *Zami* reaches the presses, however, and certainly aided by the novel's tremendous critical and popular success, an African American lesbian community does exist. And thanks to Lorde, Walker, Parker, and others, a variety of identity positions seem increasingly available to African American lesbian writers.

Also in the 1980s, another lesbian straddling Caribbean and African American communities, **Michelle Cliff**, began to publish semiautobiographical novels and essay and poetry collections. In numerous works including *Claiming an Identity They Taught Me to Despise* (1980), *No Telephone to Heaven* (1987), and *Free Enterprise* (1993), Cliff describes the experiences of an Afro-Caribbean girl discovering her cultural and sexual identities between New York and Jamaica. Cliff's work joins a growing body of not only novels and poetry but also critical and anthological work by African American lesbians. These women brought the issues of African American lesbian literature and its relative absence into the critical debates surrounding feminism and lesbianism and also African American Studies. Literary and cultural critics such as Barbara Smith, Ann Allen Shockley, Cheryl Clark, and **Jewelle Gomez** wrote about how although women, lesbians, and African Americans had made great steps forward in the arenas of civil rights and/or artistic recognition between the 1950s and the 1980s, African American lesbians still often found themselves in the untenable position of needing to proclaim themselves either lesbian or African American, as if the two could be separated.

In the 1990s, African American lesbian writing again turned away from predominantly lesbian-themed novels but now rather than avoiding explicit lesbianism or the term lesbian, authors such as Helen Elaine Lee, April Sinclair, and **Sapphire** integrated lesbian characters and themes into their treatment of the multiple questions of race, class, gender, place, sexuality, religion, motherhood, and family on which African American literature turns. At the same time, a growing body of literature also focused on lesbian characters involved not only in staking out a place for themselves to exist but also negotiating the many parts of their lives as African American lesbians. Jewelle Gomez in *The Gilda Stories* (1991) and *Don't Explain* (1998) plays with history and literary genre in a series of romance–science fiction–historical-vampire stories that consider how to articulate African American lesbianism even as they do so. The first novel by Odessa Rose, *Water in a Broken Glass* (2000), traces a young African American sculptor's coming out in the context of her homophobic family but also of an out and proud African American lesbian and gay community. Laurinda D. Brown's first novel, *Fire and Brimstone* (2001), depicts a relationship between a single mother and a minister as the two explore what it means to be an African American family and to have religion in the South. Lesbianism has become not the unspoken and unspeakable shadow but rather one of the many spoken pieces of African American literature.

See also Womanism

Further Reading

Carbado, Devon, Dwight McBride, and Donald Weisse, eds. *Black Like Us: A Century of Lesbian, Gay, and Bisexual African American Fiction.* San Francisco: Cleis Press, 2002.

McKinley, Catherine, and Joyce DeLaney, eds. *Afrekete: An Anthology of Black Lesbian Writing.* New York: Anchor Books, 1995.

Nelson, Emmanuel S. *Critical Essays: Gay and Lesbian Writers of Color.* New York: Haworth Press, 1993.

Smith, Barbara, ed. *Home Girls: A Black Feminist Anthology.* New York: Kitchen Table Women of Color Press, 1983.

————. *The Truth That Never Hurts: Writings on Race, Gender, and Freedom.* New Brunswick, NJ: Rutgers University Press, 1998.

Keja Lys Valens

Lesbian Literature, Jewish American

This brilliant, prolific, affirming body of literature has called consistently for social change and justice, has written the body with joy, originality, and rapture; it has articulated itself powerfully in the historical contexts of lesbian modernism, lesbian feminism, narratives that reinscribe identities as aleatory forms and sexual identity as having a social as opposed to a private identity; and it has lifted powerful poetic voices rich in prophecy, and the accents of Yiddish and Hebrew, and remained passionate in claiming the most capacious forms of Jewish identity, sexual practice, and **gender** identity. The Jewish lesbian Gertrude Stein identifies as Jew and marries another Jewish lesbian, Alice B. Toklas, but dispenses with religious Jewish culture but can be seen in her writing as using Talmudic-like processes of discovery, division, definition, and lesbian narratives that counter Freudian and medical sexologist views of lesbians as maladjusted. Stein also grapples with the relations between prostitutes and lesbians, and the dependent role of women in patriarchal society. In a moment of post–World War II exuberance, Jo Sinclair's *The Wasteland* (1946) containing the first realist and in-depth portrait of a Jewish lesbian character is published, but the 1950s and 1960s restrain lesbian voices in this era of McCarthyism, views of lesbians as mannish or maladjusted, and conformism. Betty Friedan's *The Feminine Mystique* (1963) foreshadowed the renaissance of 1970s lesbian feminism and the major work of poets such as **Adrienne Rich**, Irena Klepfisz, and **Marilyn Hacker**, all of whom wrote about **lesbianism** in direct political, ethical, or cultural-historical contexts, connecting it to the legacies of the Holocaust and the development of antipatriarchal and antihomophobic practices in Judaism, Jewish intellectual history, and the Israeli-Palestinian conflict. In subsequent decades, Jewish American lesbian writers such as **Alice Bloch** and **Joan Nestle** redefined the meaning of being Jewish and lesbian in the face of violence, censorship, fragmentation, and the pressure to assimilate.

The striking differences between Sigmund Freud and Sholem Asch, two Jewish men who wrote on lesbian subjects in the time period this literature begins, reveal the divergences and discontinuities in "tradition." Sigmund Freud, modeling his psychological theories on ancient Greek myth, posited that just as Electra plots to murder her mother Clytemnestra for having her father Agamemnon killed, so do daughters wish to kill their mothers so that they might have sex with their fathers. In contrast, the lesbian daughter, although first desiring her father, experiences disappointment in him, and so turns back to her mother in lesbian regression. With Freud, a lesbian subject cannot have the right desires or destinations. In contrast, Sholem Asch in his play *God of Vengeance* (1914) presents Yankl, a procurer, husband, and father, and Sorre, a procuress, wife, and mother—and also a former prostitute—in their brothel, also their Jewish home. The parents repeatedly exhort their daughter, Rivkele, to remain chaste *and* contract a marriage with a rich man that will make her (and them) prosperous and respectable. But Rivkele falls in love with one of her father's prostitutes and has no consciousness of wrongdoing. Yankl has commissioned the *mitzvah* of writing a Torah, which he intends for the marriage of his daughter. Instead, Rivkele and her *bashert* make love in the room where the Torah rests. The link between prostitution and lesbianism developed by Asch becomes a theme for Jewish American lesbian writers too. Prostitution paid far more than other kinds of work available to women, and this fact could recommend it to all those, including lesbian subjects, searching for independence from dependence. Stein pondered the nature of the relationship between lesbian desire and prostitution when she fell in love with a woman while studying medicine at Johns Hopkins University. In her posthumously published autobiographical novel, *Q.E.D.* (1903), Stein parodies her earlier self in the character Adele, who cannot have sex with her lover, May, because her moral training teaches her she must own (marry) May before she can have sex (own) with May. May becomes impatient and has sex with another woman who lavishes her with presents but sees her as a fling. Adele accuses May of acting the part of a prostitute, but women are defined consistently as objects of ownership, a system of thought incompatible with lesbian relations and identity.

In 1946, shortly before her death, Stein wrote *Brewsie and Willie* (1946), which celebrates the expansive sense of freedom at the end of World War II by portraying the camaraderie of **gay** and lesbian American soldiers in clear, direct, slangy speech. In the United States, this exuberant spirit prompted the publication of Jo Sinclair's novel, *Wasteland* (1946), which contains the first clear, realist, and humane portrait of a lesbian character, an American Jewish woman in New York City. An exploration of the love and support between a sister and brother, the brother suffers from his internalized antisemitism and the sister from internalized **homophobia**. They turn to helping each other confront their fears, and they learn to accept themselves. The oppressive ambiance of coercive assimilation and the first shocking blows of the Holocaust transform the conjunctions between homophobia and antisemitism into mutual corollaries and consequents, under the ethics enjoined in the post-Holocaust world.

The silence of the two decades following World War II was enforced through psychiatry theories of maladjustment, political hysteria, and witch hunts. For their part, in this period many American Jews relocated to the suburbs, celebrated the State of Israel, assimilated into the mainstream, found traditional Judaism embarrassing, and knew Yiddish and European Jewish civilization to be dead. Betty Friedan first denounced the appalling idea that babies and suburban life fulfilled women in *The Feminine Mystique* (1963). Many Jewish women, most of whom were married, rejected the entire premise of suburban life. In "Reflections of a Jewish Lesbian Feminist Activist-Therapist" (1983), Adrienne J. Smith finds the suburbs antithetical to Judaism and Jewish values, tradition, and *halachah* (law). Indeed, lesbian feminism, which defined lesbianism in ethical and political terms and fostered open communication and meaningful action among women, could readily be seen as a form of *taken olam,* or world repair. **Elana Dykewomon**, who changed her last name from Nachman so that no one could mistake her books, creates a heroic and compassionate lesbian feminist heroine in her novel *Riverfinger Women* (1974), who stands apart (as kosher) from the *treyf* (nonkosher) of heterosexual prostitution, abuse, and violence from which she helps women escape.

However, the most accomplished figures who emerged in this period are Adrienne Rich, Irena Klepfisz, and Marilyn Hacker. Rich, already a renowned poet when she came out as a lesbian feminist, enjoined women in academia to find the lesbian within and dispense with lies, secrets, and silences. In *Diving into the Wreck* (1971), the work of assessing the damage, counting the losses, and restoring what can be salvaged from the ruins of historical violence begins. In *The Dream of a Common Language* (1974), Rich finds this common language still mainly a private language between women and women endangered if they cannot articulate it with other women. Putting historical recollection in the service of interpretation that illuminates what has or has not been learned from history, Rich sees Ethel Rosenberg, executed for treason, as not much in control of her life or political decisions. The work of Jewish writers to counter antisemitism in the lesbian world, homophobia in Jewish law and practice, and divergent positions within Yiddish, Holocaust, and other perspectives informs the three important anthologies *Nice Jewish Girls* (1982), *The Tribe of Dina* (1986), and *Twice Blessed* (1991). These and other works give context to Rich's intense engagement with her Jewish identity and legacy in "Split at the Root: An Essay on Jewish Identity" (1983). Rich, still split by the patriarchal face of Judaism, and its homophobia and sexism, takes compassion on her assimilated father and assumes a Jewish identity she feels to be split at the root. Rich's poem "Yom Kippur: 1984," an extraordinary meditation on the figure of the stranger in the Bible and on the plight of gays, blacks, and Jewish lesbians, ends with a prophetic scene in which Israeli and Palestinian children open the closed city of Jerusalem.

Rich endows the act of these children into what might be called the transcendent figuration of the solitude she figures as especially **queer** in the post-Holocaust world. But what Rich sees prophetically, a number of other Jewish lesbian writers have made opposition to the post-1967 Israeli occupation of Palestinian territories an important aspect of their historical, Jewish ethical, and lesbian political identities. Irena Klepfisz, one of the few Polish Jewish children who survived the Holocaust that took her father, escaped with her mother to America and adopted Yiddish as her *mame-loshn*. In the 1970s, she began to write poems in Yiddish about her witness to the Warsaw Ghetto, the destruction of her secular Yiddish European culture, and her sense of herself as an exile who could never go home. Addressing love poems to a woman who committed suicide, her most famous poem, "Bashert," which means fated or intended, is a love poem to all who died or survived in the Holocaust. In *Etlekhe verter oyf mame-loshn/A Few Words in the Mother Tongue* (1990), Klepfisz says Yiddish makes her feel alive, but different from what she was. In many respects, Klepfisz's ability to articulate pure pain over the losses she suffered in the Holocaust are balanced by her affirmations and moral refusals, a tonal range that she shares with the honored and award-winning language poet Marilyn Hacker, whose frolicsome, witty rhythms are philosophical paeans to the profundities of everyday pleasures of food, sex, books, conversation, family, lovers, friends, walks through the streets of Paris and New York, and language that articulates its pleasures. Justly renowned for her sonnet cycle, *Love, Death, and the Changing of the Seasons* (1986), *Winter Numbers* (2003) should be judged as her most accomplished volume of poems. Mourning friends lost to AIDS, her own suffering with breast cancer, and the oppressive atmosphere caused by American imperialism and consumer capitalism, she rages against the waste, the brutality, and the protests against the mistreatment of Algerians in Paris.

Other Jewish lesbian writers, particularly those who perceive their Jewish identities as a historical manifestation of the ethical impossibilities of violence, rather than a religious or political Zionist identity, also situate themselves in opposition to Israeli policies toward Palestinians. Joan Nestle, a self-declared femme working-class Jewish lesbian who has written about the historical movement for queer rights in *A Fragile Union* (1991), defines her Jewishness through her feminism, her ethics, and her historical perspective as the founder of the Lesbian Herstory Archives. For Nestle, what she perceives as cruel domination and unmerited aggression ignores the values of Jewish culture and the lessons of history. Alice Bloch makes related points about Jewish identity and belonging in *The Law of*

Return (1983), which refers to the 1950 Israeli law giving Jews—defined as those with a Jewish mother or grandmother or married through Orthodox Judaism—the right to return to their homeland and become Israeli citizens. The protagonist, Elishiva Rogin, has returned to Israel and is exploring Orthodox Judaism but finds her real being not with her boyfriend but a woman, making lesbian identity her actual law or condition of return. Indeed, Melanie Kaye/Kantrowitz, an activist academic, has argued that the histories and cultures of nonwhite Jews have been overlooked by racist constructions of Jewish identity, as implicit in Zionism, against which she champions Palestinian rights and an international multiracial Jewish diasporic culture that does not see exile as an affliction. In her story collection *My Jewish Face and Other Stories* (1990), she represents, in an admixture of humor and earnestness, her experience of the conflict-ridden terrain of Western and American Jewish identities. Her construct of Ladino, Sephardic, African, and Arabic-Islamic-Middle Eastern cultural milieu of Jews of color—a radical diaspora —provides affirmation and repose from the clamors of her anti-Zionist and anti-Israeli Nationalist views that make her diasporic lesbian identity feel exilic.

Not all Jewish American writers experience Jewish history as an onerous ethical demand, the Israeli-Palestinian conflict insupportable—or legibly black and white—or American Judaism as other than as inclusive places for lesbians, feminists, and queers. The prolific and mindfully accessible self-described Jewish lesbian femme writer Lesléa Newman graciously and sociably affirms her many identities and roles as a writer, reaching out to communicate "controversial" material to wide audiences with winning directness and oneself-consciousness in her landmark and politically controversial children's book *Heather Has Two Mommies* (1989). This first representation of lesbian mothers in a children's book generated widespread right-wing hysteria. In her adult/young adult novel *Letter to Harvey Milk* (1988), Newman uses the epistolary form to good effect, using the Yiddish-inflected language of a Jewish man who, in the course of his letters to Harvey Milk, discourses on lesbian Jewish identity, the dramatic nature of mother-daughter bonds, the relations between antisemitism and homophobia, the Holocaust, and affirmations of his love for Milk combined with scenes from a Shabbos (Sabbath) dinner. Her volume of poetry, *Still Life with Buddy* (1997), chronicles the friendship between a loving woman friend and a gay man dying of AIDS. Her scores of other books deal with Jewish identity in terms of a character struggling with her attraction to women and bulimia, an ethnic Yiddish *schtick,* the Holocaust (as symbol), or fond childhood memories of *Bubbe.* Such ornamental accessories are suitable for beginners, but the lack of further development and growth indicates the conviction of limit, beyond which the reader or her culture or the writer cannot imagine progressing beyond. Indeed, therapeutic language can constitute an artistically powerful mode of addressing common manifestations of distress such as bulimia and poor body image. But the premises of the therapeutic encounter, involving an "artistic" collaboration between the healer and the sufferer, leading to cognitive and behavioral modification, becomes an embarrassing misconception, an obscenity, a sacrilege, and a disavowal of the historical annihilation of a human civilization. It speaks of the good intentions of the author and the intoxication of the trope of life-conferring power of the erotic and spiritual bonds of women to *heal.* In her strenuously titled novel *Running Fiercely toward a High Thin Sound* (1987), Judith Katz creates an elaborate historical *mythos* wherein a host of powerful, compassionate, and efficacious historical Jewish women—both lesbian and heterosexual—*heal* the Jewish women—more exactly, Yiddish-speaking Polish Jewish women—suffering the unspeakable horror and vacancy of slow starvation, random killing, disease, and, for those who had survived, the *Umschlagplatz* or removal to Treblinka. Beneath the *chutzpah* one wonders if the Jewish women feel impelled to break the chains of what amounts to an idolatrous mythic treatment of their beings. However, the historical contexts of this novel were the intoxications of coming out, of communal belief in the mythic figure of the female healer, who stood as authentic redemption from patriarchal medicine, and the antihumane cult of scientism.

There are invocations of coming out in **Andrea Freud Lowenstein**'s collection of quasiautobiographical short stories, *The Worry Girl* (1992), which celebrates an adolescent Jewish girl who achieves authentic creative identity by coming out of the **closet** and confronting the pressure to assimilate and class prejudice. And, in the midst of concerns about the Middle East, Edith Konecky brings these concerns about what forms of life can contain and transmit meaning through narrating the story of a late-middle-age Jewish woman in *A Place at the Table* (1990). The title refers to the Jewish custom of leaving a place at the table of Sabbath dinners for strangers. Rachel Levin, long divorced and with grown children, has a younger woman lover leaving her, a friend whose marriage is dissolving, and another, a lesbian artist, descending into madness. What becomes of lesbian and Jewish identities in the face of such individualistic strains and lack of cohesion?

Sarah Schulman, the most accomplished and innovative contemporary Jewish lesbian writer, creates narrative trajectories that question the linear model of identity and that make community building and political activism essential for survival. Her lesbian characters struggle to articulate themselves through divided and multiple identities that have endured betrayal, rejection, death, and poverty. *After Delores* (1988) depicts the emotional annihilation, loneliness, and rage of having your lover leave you for another woman and never apologize or empathize. *People in Trouble* (1990) uses narrative realism to critique the aesthetic disengagement of a husband and wife who attempt to arrange and control their lives in the face of the political emergencies of AIDS and a world crumbling from neglect and greed. In *Empathy* (1992), frequently described as her best novel, Schulman again depicts Jewishness not through ethnicity but rather through intellectual, political, and ethical history. Freud had argued that lesbians either hate or want to be men, a position that makes it impossible for a lesbian to be a woman. Anna, the protagonist, develops a split personality, but gets relief from a nonlinear narrative filled with dialogue, poems, ads, movies, essays, and personal ads. Schulman rejects the private view of sexuality and locates lesbianism in the social world, representing it as a part of the inimical social mechanisms and ideologies that produce racism, classism, ageism, and so forth. In *Empathy,* Schulman moves the question of sexual identities from the family to the social sphere, arguing that it is as adults, not children, that people negotiate their sexual identity. *Rat Bohemia,* which uses rat extermination as a metaphor for unwanted minorities in New York, represents the waning days of ACT UP (AIDS Coalition to Unleash Power), where the protagonist is exhausted by endless hospital visits and is worried that, in the face of ongoing death and the indifference of others, death will lose its meaning. Schulman's incisive analysis of the role of sibling rivalry expands our vocabulary and social understanding of familial homophobia.

Schulman also writes plays, and her most notable success has been the production of her adaption of Isaac Bashevis Singer's *Enemies: A Love Story* (1946) as a play. The invocations of Yiddish theater and the dramatic world of performance are the brilliant work of one of the most deliciously enjoyable, funny, and witty Jewish bisexual artists, Sandra Bernhard. Within her signature send-up of celebrities, kitsch culture, and commoditized mass art forms, Bernhard combines **camp** burlesque and pure evocations of lyrical sweep. Bernhard recites the Kaddish, memorializes Patti Smith, and imitates herself as Nina Simone, crooning about her lesbian lover Carlotta. Her most recent film, *I'm Still Here . . . Damn It,"* which begins with her on a stage bathed in radiantly gorgeous light and wearing nothing but a sheer slip over her very pregnant stomach, provides the most stunningly beautiful picture of lesbian motherhood as one might imagine. Artists such as Schulman, Bernhard, and Hacker, as well as others will blossom abundantly in relation to the legacies they have inherited, and this literature will continue its innovative celebration of the new and its capacity to support major new voices.

Further Reading

Alpert, Rebecca. *Like Bread on a Seder Plate: Jewish Lesbians and the Transformation of Tradition.* New York: Columbia University Press, 1998.

Balka, Christie, and Andy Rose. *Twice Blessed: On Being Lesbian or Gay and Jewish.* Boston: Beacon Press, 1991.

Beck, Evelyn Torton. *Nice Jewish Girls: A Lesbian Anthology.* 2nd ed. Boston: Beacon Press, 1983.

Kaye/Kantrowitz, Melanie, and Irena Klepfisz. *The Tribe of Dina: A Jewish Women's Anthology.* Boston: Beacon Press, 1989.

Shneer, David, and Caryn Aviv. *Queer Jews.* New York: Routledge, 2002.

Corrine E. Blackmer

Lesbian Literature, Mexican American

Prior to the 1980s, straight men dominated Mexican America literature. A few bold women such as Bernice Zamora, Lorna Dee Cervantes, and Alma Luz Villanueva explored female sexuality in their poetry and short stories. A few daring **gay** men such as **John Rechy** and Francisco X. Alarcón wrote openly about homosexuality. In 1976 Estela Portillo Trambley's play *The Day of the Swallows* featured Josefa who rebels against marriage and falls in love with a woman. In 1982, Sheila Ortiz Taylor published *Faultline,* the first novel by a Chicana lesbian about a Chicana lesbian. Then two radical Chicanas drove **lesbianism** to the front and center of Chicana literature: **Gloria Evangelina Anzaldúa** and **Cherríe Moraga**. They hail from different backgrounds and represent different aspects of the Mexican American community, but the anthology that they co-edited, *This Bridge Called My Back* (1981), and each woman's first work, Moraga's *Loving in the War Years* (1983) and Anzaldúa's *Borderlands/La Frontera* (1987), changed the face of Chicano literature. Anzaldúa and Moraga provide frank narrations of lesbianism and careful considerations of its place in Chicano literature and culture. Anzaldúa's and Moraga's works mix the genres of essay, short story, poetry, and memoir; they are radical in their form as well as their content, suggesting that Chicana lesbian literature not only tells a new story, it also offers a new way of telling stories.

This Bridge Called My Back presents Chicana lesbianism in the context of the radical women of color movement in the United States in the 1980s. Radical feminism, antiracism, and challenges to the dominance of **heterosexuality** fit together, the anthology proclaims. Chicana lesbians work with Chicana feminists such as Norma Alarcón and with radical women of color from bell hooks to **Chrystos**. Together, they critique the ways in which patriarchy operates in the guises of colonialism, racism, male dominance, and compulsory heterosexuality to deny women access to the full and free exploration and expression of their sexuality and of their personhood. Under the editorial hand of Moraga and Anzaldúa, the anthology stakes out a space of Chicana feminists and lesbians who were previously unknown not only in Chicano circles but also in women of color circles.

Moraga and Anzaldúa's work is intimately tied to the Chicano/a movement that, beginning in the late 1950s, asserted Chicanos as not immigrants, not hyphenated Americans, but native people of the Southwest, colonized first by Spaniards and then by North Americans. They trace their heritage as *mestizos* (mixed people) to include Aztec, Spanish, and Anglo strands. Moraga and Anzaldúa's Xicanisma (Chicanisma) critiques the male dominance and heterosexual order of the Chicano movement, but from within the movement.

Like the Chicanos, Moraga and Anzaldúa claim their Aztec heritage, although Moraga and Anzaldúa single out La Malinche and La Llorona as their spiritual ancestors. La Malinche was the Aztec woman who supposedly served as Cortez's translator and lover. La Malinche regularly suffers accusations of being a traitor and a whore. Moraga and Anzaldúa portray her as the sacrificial lamb to Spanish colonialism and as the mother of all mestizos. They do not claim La Malinche as a lesbian, but rather as a woman who refused the two options standard in Chicano culture—virgin (mother) or whore—and exemplified how existing between two supposedly irreconcilable identities is a classically Chicana position. La Llorona stands as the archetypal bad mother in Chicano folklore, legendary for having killed her own children to wander forever crying and in search of young souls to snatch away. Again, Moraga and Anzaldúa claim not that La Llorona was a lesbian but that she exemplifies the ways in which all Chicana women are expected to become mothers or be forever damned. In La Llorona, they find an ancestor who can be rehabilitated as an emblem of women who stand outside of Chicano sexual and familial mores.

In the essays that make up her memoir-like book, *Loving in the War Years,* Moraga uses an English strongly marked by Spanish, but she also discusses how she was raised monolingually, taught that English was the language of progress. English was also her father's native language, for Moraga is from a half-Chicano half-Anglo family. For these reasons, Moraga was from a young age acutely aware of concerns about selling out, about losing Chicano culture through an embrace of all things Anglo that, she thought, included lesbianism. Paradoxically, Moraga feels herself to be an outsider both as half-Anglo and as the darkest person in her family. She discusses how skin color as well as sexuality must complicate understandings of "the Chicana." For Moraga, a surprising realization was that while male domination serves men, women, and specifically mothers, play a primary role in perpetuating it. Thus she describes how her own mother tried to teach her to be always subservient to her brothers and tried to show her through her own example that an unsatisfactory marriage was preferable to no marriage at all. Moraga refuses her mother's lessons in women's oppression just as she refuses to believe that lesbianism is by definition foreign and antithetical to Chicano culture. *Loving in the War Years* represents her effort to stake out a space within Chicano history and culture for Chicana lesbians.

Anzaldúa in *Borderlands/La Frontera* shares Moraga's project of rewriting Chicano history to include Chicana lesbians and of considering exactly what it means to be a Chicana lesbian. The language of *Borderlands/La Frontera* combines Spanish and English, even more than does *Loving in the War Years,* and also discusses the different variations of Chicano "Spanglish." Anzaldúa describes how not only languages such as Spanish and English become embattled, but also how tongues and thus bodies and language about bodies and sexuality are subject to policing from both within and without the borderlands. Anzaldúa writes more explicitly than Moraga of women's sexuality both in terms of the sexual violence that all Chicana women risk and in terms of the sexual pleasure that Chicana lesbians can find with other women. *Borderlands/La Frontera* finds the borderlands that are such an important paradigm in Chicano studies to be also the paradigmatic site for Chicana lesbianism: it is indeed a site of contact between tongues, between cultures, and between people. It is the periphery that is the center of Chicana identity. But Anzaldúa also advocates for radical change in Chicano and in Anglo culture, a restitution of what she sees as the repressed Indian part of the *mestizo* identity and an accompanying reconfiguration of the roles of women.

Although they remain the most famous, *This Bridge Called My Back, Loving in the War Years,* and *Borderlands/La Frontera* are not Moraga and Anzaldúa's only collaborative or respective works. Moraga has also written a number of plays and short stories and two memoirs about mothering. Anzaldúa has also written several short stories, edited another radical women of color anthology, *Making Face, Making Soul/Haciendo Caras* (1990), and with AnaLouise Keating edited a follow-up to *This Bridge Called My Back, This Bridge We Call Home* (2002). Anzaldúa's last anthology marks the arrival of Chicana lesbian literature in a location where it can move beyond self-preservation and into exploration and expansion.

A next generation of Chicana authors push at the definitions of lesbian, and in the process ask us to reconsider whom we may have excluded and why. In the 1980s, the act of explicitly naming lesbian desire was crucial, for without being named and claimed as such it was much too easily overlooked. But in the 1970s and 1980s other Chicanas were refusing traditional **gender** and sexual roles and describing polymorphously perverse desires that in retrospect already qualified as **queer**. These include Zamora's poems of autoeroticism and Villanueva's depictions of mother-daughter eroticism. And perhaps we should extend our purview to include Sandra Cisneros, whose *The House on Mango Street* (1984) and *Woman Hollering Creek* (1992) tell stories of tomboys and rebel women who refuse the sexual mores that they encounter; she, in an author's biographical note appended to the book, described herself as "nobody's wife and nobody's mother," pointedly outside of a heterosexual norm. These women, as much as Moraga and Anzaldúa, laid the groundwork for the explorations of Chicana lesbian authors at the turn of the century.

Many authors who have not published independent books have outstanding poems and short stories in anthologies such as *Compañeras: Latina Lesbians* (1994), *Chicana Lesbians: The Girls Our Mother Warned Us About* (1991), and *Tortilleras: Hispanic and U.S. Latina Lesbian Expression* (2003). The first traditional Chicana "coming out novel" that traces a girl's discovery and declaration of her lesbianism is **Terri de la Peña**'s *Margins* (1991). De la Peña also writes of lesbianism in *Latin Satins* (1994) and *Faults* (1999). **Alicia Gaspar de Alba** is a Chicana critic and creative writer whose collection *The Mystery of Survival and Other Stories* (1993) considers the importance of history and of memory as well as the inventive possibilities of collaboration between women across cultures and times. Gaspar de Alba's second book, *Sor Juana's Second Dream* (1999), claims this grande dame of Mexican letters as a foremother to Chicana lesbians. Ana Castillo is famous not only for her lesbian poems and stories, some of which are collected in *My Father Was a Toltec: And Selected Poems* (1995) and *Loverboys* (1997) where some, but not all, of the lovers are boys, but also for her novels where lesbianism is less explicit, including *So Far from God* (1993) and *Peel My Love Like an Onion* (2000). Demetria Martínez has published a novel, *Mother Tongue* (1994), as well as several collections of poetry, most recently *The Devil's Workshop* (2002). Emma Pérez explores racism and **homophobia** in rural Texas in *Gulf Dreams* (1996), while her forthcoming historical novel *Forgetting the Alamo, or Blood Memory* features an avenging baby butch vaquera. Laura del Fuego's first novel, *Maravilla* (1998), brings Chicana lesbian literature into East Los Angeles, while her second novel, *Carmen García Was Here 'c/s'* (2003), travels up and down California's Central Valley and all around Carmen García's complex sexual identification. Mónica Palacios's plays and performance art offer forthright and sexy humor about queer Chicana identity. **Carla Trujillo**, a scholar responsible for bringing to light the work of many Chicana lesbian writers, has herself published a novel, *What Night Brings* (2003). And Ortiz Taylor continues to write, most recently a lesbian comedy, *Outrageous* (2006), and the lesbian thriller *Assisted Living* (2007).

While major publishers now regularly pick up LGBTQ Latino/a authors, Chicana lesbians are strikingly absent from their lists. Even in the face of the body of Chicana lesbian literature and an accompanying scholarly apparatus, there is an overwhelming tendency for Chicana lesbian authors to be published by small presses dedicated to bringing to light the work of women of color. It is then perhaps all the more noteworthy that Chicana lesbians hold a significant place in Chicana literature and in LGBTQ literature. Chicana lesbians and queers may always exist pulled between apparently competing loyalties, but they know that they have a right to claim that liminal space as their own and continue to build their community there.

Further Reading

Anzaldúa, Gloria, and Cherríe Moraga, eds. *This Bridge Called My Back: Writings by Radical Women of Color.* New York: Kitchen Table, Women of Color Press, 1983.

Arredondo, Gabriela F. et al., eds. *Chicana Feminisms: A Critical Reader.* Durham, NC: Duke University Press, 2003.

Esquibel, Catriona Rueda. *With Her Machete in Her Hand: Reading Chicana Lesbians.* Austin: University of Texas Press, 2006.

Ramos, Juanita. *Compañeras: Latina Lesbians.* New York: Latina Lesbian History Project, 1987.

Torres, Lourdes, and Inmaculada Pertusa, eds. *Tortilleras: Hispanic and U.S. Latina Lesbian Expressions.* Philadelphia: Temple University Press, 2003.

Trujillo, Carla. *Chicana Lesbians: The Girls Our Mothers Warned Us About.* Berkeley, CA: Third Woman Press, 1991.

———. *Living Chicana Theory.* Berkeley, CA: Third Woman Press, 1997.

Keja Lys Valens

Lesbian Literature, Native American

With the resurgence of Native American writing in the mid to late twentieth century that some critics call the Native American literary renaissance came the first native writers to have lesbian themes in their works. Notable among these is **Paula Gunn Allen**, Laguna/Métis novelist, poet, theorist, and professor. In 1986, Allen published her germinal essay, "Hwame, Koshkalaka, and the Rest: Lesbians in American Cultures" in her *The Sacred Hoop: Recovering the Feminine in American Indian Traditions.* This essay signaled the beginning of a shift in research perspectives on sexuality and **gender** among tribal groups as it pulled together a number of studies on what came to be termed two-spirit people, approaching them in a positive way. Further, Allen has published poetry with lesbian themes, and her novel *The Woman Who Owned the Shadows* (1983) has as its main character a woman who reclaims her Native American spiritual traditions that include being open to same-sex relationships. Allen is also well known for her work with **gay** and lesbian communities on the West Coast and activism with antinuclear, antiwar, feminist, and gay and lesbian movements.

Beth Brant, Mohawk, is another Native American who writes with a lesbian perspective. As the first native to edit an entire collection, she produced the groundbreaking collection of fiction, poetry, and narratives, including the work of native lesbians, *A Gathering of Spirit: A Collection by North American Indian Women* (1984). She also has a book of personal narrative and poetry, *Mohawk Trail* (1985), that contains an often-anthologized poem with a lesbian theme, "Her Name Is Helen," and a trickster story in which Coyote is tricked by her own lesbian trick. She has a book of short stories, *Food & Spirits: Stories* (1991) that contains one of the first short stories about AIDS. In *Writing as Witness: Essay and Talk* (1994), she takes on the topic of **homophobia** as introduced by colonialism into the tribes and other topics related to two-spirited people.

Before the collection *A Gathering of Spirit,* there was *This Bridge Called My Back: Writings by Radical Women of Color* (1981), edited by **Cherríe Moraga** and **Gloria Evangelina Anzaldúa.** This collection included Native American lesbian writers and activists such as Barbara Cameron (Lakota) and **Chrystos** (Menominee). Cameron's "Gee, You Don't Seem Like an Indian from the Reservation" discussed particularly difficult topics —not only the problem of racism and homophobia outside and targeting the Native American community, but also inside the Native American community. Cameron had an illustrious career as an activist (she died at age 48 in 2002). She was a delegate for Jesse Jackson's Rainbow Coalition to the 1988 Democratic Convention and was appointed by the mayor to the San Francisco Human Rights Commission and the Commission on the Status of Women.

Chrystos is well known for both biting political and lyrical erotic poems. She has five books of poetry: *Not Vanishing* (1988), *Dream On* (1991), *In Her I Am* (1993), *Fugitive Colors* (1995), and *Fire Power* (1995). These illustrate her identification with victims of violence, and her themes include the silencing and abuse of Native Americans. She won the **Audre Lorde** International Poetry Competition in 1994 and the Sappho Award of Distinction from the Astraea National Lesbian Action Foundation in 1995.

Sharon Day, Ojibwe, is a poet, activist, and the executive director of the Indigenous Peoples Task Force. She identifies herself as a two-spirit person and does readings on this topic. She is one of the editors of *Sing, Whisper, Shout, Pray! Feminist Visions for a Just World* (2002), a compilation of essays that addresses the politics of race, class and gender. Another Ojibwe author, Carole LaFavor, wrote the first Native American lesbian murder mystery. *Along the Journey River* (1996) features an Ojibwe two-spirit detective as the protagonist. *Evil Dead Center* (1997) is the second in the series. LaFavor served on the President's Advisory Council on HIV/AIDS from 1995 to 1997 and is featured in a film about women living with AIDS.

Vickie Sears (Cherokee) is a writer of short stories. *Simple Songs* was published in 1990, addressing particularly "all of the children who ever lived in an orphanage or foster home and had a dream." This book was designed to be accessible for women with limited reading skills and as such it translates the oral/plain speaking into written text. The stories, written in the first person, present tense, are especially moving as Sears addresses the joys and sorrows of children often abused and culturally confused.

Janice Gould (Maidu) is a widely anthologized lesbian poet with two books of poetry: *Beneath My Heart* (1990) and *Earthquake Weather* (1996). Gould writes about issues of voice and identity firmly rooted in the California landscape where she was born and where her Native American ancestors lived. Her first book of poetry was completed with a poetry fellowship from the National Endowment for the Arts for 1989. In 1992 she won the Astraea Foundation grant and a Ford Foundation Fellowship in 1994–1995. She teaches creative writing at various college workshops and Native American literature.

In her commentary on Gould's *Beneath My Heart,* Beth Brant sums up the underlying importance of writing for Native American lesbians:

> All is important, all makes the whole, all is to be honored. When one is a Two-Spirit Woman, the desire to connect all becomes an urgent longing. Faced with homophobia from our own communities, faced with racism and homophobia from the outsiders who hold semblances of power over us, we feel that desire to make connections between oppressions in a primal and necessary way. (945)

Further Reading

Allen, Paula Gunn. *The Sacred Hoop: Recovering the Feminine in American Indian Traditions.* Boston: Beacon Press, 1986.

Brant, Beth, ed. *A Gathering of Spirit: A Collection by North American Indian Women.* Ithaca, New York: Firebrand, 1984.

———. "Giveaway: Native Lesbian Writers." *Signs: Journal of Women in Culture and Society* 18, no. 4 (Summer 1993): 944–45.

Roscoe, Will, ed. *Living the Spirit: A Gay American Indian Anthology.* New York: St. Martin's, 1988.

Annette Van Dyke

Lesbian Literature, Puerto Rican

Like other Latina writers, Boricua lesbian writers confront the complexities of race, ethnicity, and class within a dual cultural identity defined between the homeland of Puerto Rico and the "mainland" of the United States. The duality of two cultures, exemplified in the nation's two names (the colonial one of "Puerto Rico"—meaning "rich port," and its indigenous Taíno one of Borinquen) is a recurring theme in Puerto Rican literary production in general. For many lesbian writers, the notion of exile becomes a metaphor for the double and triple diaspora that they experience as both migrants between two geographic spaces and as marginalized voices within two heterosexually dominant patriarchal worlds. Many work through both a sense of urgency to address sociopolitical issues such as independence versus colonization yet also are compelled to speak to the double silence surrounding women's voices generally and lesbian voices in particular. Given these personal and political exigencies, contemporary Puerto Rican lesbian texts represent the self, family, friends, and the larger world through a lens of social critique and rebellion that often defies traditional literary genres and language boundaries. Both defined and not defined by borders, Puerto Rican lesbian writing is fluid and multifaceted, reflecting the many levels of self to be negotiated in the creative process.

As part of Latino/a cultural production, Boricua lesbian writing is necessarily bilingual; texts may be exclusively in Spanish or in English, or may move between the two languages in a creative play of difference and invention. The bilingual nature of many of these texts not only structurally challenges difference, it also provides an innovative avenue of resistance to cultural assimilation. As linguistic alienation and isolation give way to linguistic liberation, so too does lesbian existence gain a space for authentic expression through that language play. Contemporary self-identified Puerto Rican lesbian writers not only connect sexual and sociocultural identities through multiple languages, but also by blurring the lines around their literary production as essayists, short story writers, playwrights, filmmakers, spoken word artists, and poets, and their work as sociopolitical activists and intellectuals. Given the immediacy and accessibility of these genres, the cultural production of contemporary Puerto Rican lesbians is most prominent in these areas of artistic and social expression. Juanita Díaz-Cotto's 1987 important anthology *Compañeras: Latina Lesbians* (published under the pseudonym Juanita Ramos), which documents (primarily working-class) Puerto Rican lesbian experience from the 1950s to the 1980s, is a vital contribution to lesbian writing and is illustrative of the diversity of creative forms of expression among the *puertorriqueñas* represented there: Rota Silverstrini is a poet, editor, and writer; Brunilda Vega, a poet and social worker; Cenen, an African-Boricua short story writer and poet, to name only a few. In her own coming out story, "Bayamón, Brooklyn y Yo" (1987), Juanita Ramos's public proclaiming of her lesbian identity is likened to revealing her Puerto Rican heritage. She, like Vega, also criticizes the **homophobia** and sexism of the traditional male-centered Left in Puerto Rico that further complicates progressive lesbian political involvement and allegiances.

As with other rights movements that gained ground from the civil and social transformations of the late twentieth century, the 1970s and 1980s marked the moment when self-identified Boricua lesbians began to produce and publish works that reached a wider audience. Rather than give up multiple identities of color, *raza,* African roots, and the diasporic condition, these writers sought to articulate and explore those differences. Nemir Matos Cintrón's *Las mujeres no hablan así* (1981) and *Proemas para despabilar cándidos* (1981) and **Luz María Umpierre**'s texts including *The Margarita Poems* (1987) and *For Christine: Poems and One Letter* (1995) are late twentieth century poetic contributions that challenge the tradition of censure and prejudice that women loving women experience. While Matos Cintrón utilizes a direct vocabulary that relies on metaphors of nature to create a highly eroticized poetry, Umpierre's work largely connects sexuality and issues of personal oppression to racism and colonization. Both poets necessarily challenge and transgress phallogocentric discourse by daring to name the previously unnamable. Umpierre, in particular, has been the subject of much critical inquiry especially because her work's form and content was one of the first to militantly defy boundaries of language and ritual. Boricua poet and photographer Samantha Martínez, who primarily publishes in online venues, echoes this need to write for sanity and for herself.

More recently, Aixa Ardín's sensual and political collection of poetry, *Batiborrillo* (1998; meaning "Hotchpotch"), continues the themes expressed by her precursors in a poetry marked by rebellion and open expression of lesbian desire. Like many Puerto Rican writers, Ardín relies on references and vocabularies specific to island culture to bring her underground poetry to the surface. In the first poem of the collection, "Poesía para Mayra Montero," Ardín playfully calls herself a *"plátano"*—but one that cannot be used for traditional dishes. In "Pa-ul" the great island rainforest of El Yunque provides a metaphor of healing for one who dies of AIDS. As is the case with many Latina writers, Ardín plays on the **gender**ed nature of Spanish grammar, anthropomorphizing words like "la imaginación' into a girlfriend, a best friend. Informed by lesbian sexuality and also by a rejection of colonization, these poems are out and proud and are representative of both the rage and celebration found in writings by women-identified women.

Family is central to Latino culture and thus is also an important theme in Puerto Rican lesbian writing. Radical lesbian feminist and Puerto Rican poet Teresita Bosch explains in her work how familial estrangement is overcome by identifying and working through common spaces of oppression. For Bosch coming out as a lesbian is parallel to the repression of language that her mother experiences as the price to be paid for striving toward a middle-class lifestyle within an Anglo culture that demands assimilation of difference. Puerto Rican and Cuban performance artist Marga Gómez's plays (*Memory Tricks, A Line around the Block,* and *Marga Gomez Is Pretty, Witty & Gay,* all performed during the 1990s), deal with the difficulties of sexual identity and assimilation through the use of family memories and humorous reminiscence. Taboo subjects such as sexuality or leftist politics are fleshed out often concurrently in nuanced (and not so nuanced) dialogue among family members whereby the audience deciphers the playwright's ultimate intended critique.

Since the publication of Ramos's anthology, online journals and Web sites such as *Conmoción* (which published between 1995 and 1996) have begun to provide forums for Latina lesbian writing. Yet, the most visible cultural production has been in terms of theater and spoken work, especially within the Nuyorican context. Among the most notable figures here are Bronx-born Puerto Rican lesbian writer, actor, and producer Janis Astor del Valle, who founded Sisters on Stage, and Brenda Cotto, who with Noelia Ortiz wrote the wholly woman-identified 1996 play *Motherlands,* which also explores the complexities of mother-lesbian daughter relationships. Astor del Valle's one-woman play *Transplantations: Straight and Other Jackets para Mí* (2004) explores the many ways biracial **queer**s pass and **closet** or uncloset themselves while it also calls into question the idea of a single Puerto Rican nation. For Mí, *Transplantations'* light-skinned femme character (whose name plays on the meaning of the Spanish object pronoun "me"), it is the Bronx that is home whereas visiting Puerto Rico among relatives only approximates "being home." The switching of the nostalgic homeland is a transgressive act in and of itself, but also opens spaces for making other transgressions more palatable. Lourdes Torres's important article "Boricua Lesbians: Sexuality, Nationality, and the Politics of Passing" (2007) explains how this play links racial passing with sexual passing to expose the arbitrariness of racial as well as sexual categories. Interracial graphic novelist Erika López also deals with passing and outing in her text *Flaming Iguanas* (1998) where the protagonist, Tomato Rodriguez, a biracial queer, articulates her ambivalent subject positions: "I don't feel white, gay, bisexual or like a brokenhearted Puerto Rican in West Side Story, but sometimes I feel like all of them."

Since Puerto Rican lesbian artistic production often goes beyond strictly literary genres, it is also important to mention Frances Negrón-Montaner's 1994 film *Brincando el Charco: Portraits of a Puerto Rican,* which was the first film to openly address Boricua lesbian sexuality. The title, which means "jumping over the pond," refers once again to the negotiations the lesbian subject must make between national and personal identity further problematized in the Puerto Rican case where one cannot really claim an actual "nationality" (because of the island's colonial status), nor a conformist straight identity—the expectation within its Catholic, patriarchal, and still traditional cultural milieu.

Further Reading

Bergmann, Emilie, and Paul Julian Smith. *Entiendes?: Queer Readings, Hispanic Writings.* Durham, NC: Duke University Press, 1995.

Blasius, Mark. *Sexual Identities, Queer Politics.* Princeton, NJ: Princeton University Press, 2001.

Chanady, Ameryll, ed. *Latin American Identity and the Construction of Difference.* Minneapolis: University of Minnesota Press, 1994.

Costa, María Dolores. *Latina Lesbian Writers and Artists.* New York: Harrington Press, 2003.

Cruz-Malavé, Arnaldo, and Martin F. Manalansan IV, eds. *Queer Globalizations: Citizenship and the Afterlife of Colonialism.* New York: New York University Press, 2002.

Gómez, Alma, Cherríe Moraga, and Mariana Romo-Carmona, eds. *Cuentos: Stories by Latinas.* Brooklyn, NY: Kitchen Table Press, 1983.

Martínez, Elena. *Lesbian Voices from Latin America: Breaking Ground.* New York: Garland Publishing, 1996.

Ramos, Juanita. *Compañeras: Latina Lesbians.* New York: Routledge, 1994.

Rivera, Carmen. *Kissing the Mango Tree: Puerto Rican Women Rewriting American Literature.* Houston: Arte Publico Press, 2002.

Romo-Carmona, Mariana. *Conversaciones: Relatos por padres y madres de hijas lesbianas y hijos gay.* San Francisco: Cleros Press, 2001.

Sánchez González, Lisa. *Boricua Literature: A Literary History of the Puerto Rican Diaspora.* New York: New York University Press, 2001.

Torres, Lourdes. "Boricua Lesbians: Sexuality, Nationality, and the Politics of Passing." *Centro Journal* 19, no. 1 (2007): 230–49.

Torres, Lourdes, and Inmaculada Pertusa. *Tortilleras: Hispanic and U.S. Latina Lesbian Expression.* Philadelphia: Temple University Press, 2001.

Colleen Kattau

Levin, Jenifer (b. 1955)

Fiction writer. Jenifer Levin is the author of four novels and a collection of short stories; her work appears in several anthologies and she is co-editor, with Tristan Taormino, of *Best Lesbian Erotica 1998.* Levin's novels have been published by and reviewed in the mainstream press, but she chose to publish her 1996 collection of short stories, *Love and Death, & Other Disasters,* with Firebrand Books, a feminist and lesbian publishing house. Her first novel, *Water Dancer* (1981) was published when she was 26 and was nominated for the PEN/Hemingway Award; her most recent, *The Sea of Light* (1993), was a Lambda Literary Award finalist. *Water Dancer* and *The Sea of Light* both locate lesbian-based narratives in the context of competitive swimming, drawing on Levin's own experience as a competitive swimmer. Of the two intervening novels, *Shimoni's Lover* (1987) is set in Israel and focuses on the lives of the brothers of the deceased Shimoni Kol, all sons of an Israeli military commander; *Snow* (1983) details the conflict between a chemical corporation and insurgent forces opposed to the puppet government on the fictional island of Bellagua, which rally around the mysterious figure of the White Goddess.

Water Dancer tells the story of Dorey Thomas, a long-distance swimmer seeking to resurrect her career after having suffered a nervous breakdown. Dorey is intent on swimming the 32-mile San Antonio Strait, off the Washington coast, for which she trains with a coach whose son died attempting the same feat. The novel introduces a number of themes that recur in Levin's fiction: emotional isolation and the search for a means to bridge it; personal trauma and survival; family histories, and their impact on characters' interpersonal relationships and identities; the detailed agonies and rewards of competitive sports and of the body in general; the negotiation and acknowledgment of a lesbian identity; and the complex interaction of racial, cultural, and sexual identities. These elements are similarly important in *The Sea of Light,* whose more ambitious structure sees Levin narrate the novel's action from the first-person perspective of multiple characters. Here again Levin's characters are trying to survive a series of personal and historical traumas. Babe Delgado is the only survivor of a plane crash that has killed the rest of her elite university swim team; before the crash she was considered an Olympic hopeful, but now she is attempting to overcome her mental and physical scars to make a comeback at a Division II state school. Brenna Allen, the coach at that school, is coming to terms with her lover's death from cancer and the fact that as a **closet**ed lesbian she cannot mourn her publicly. Ellie Marks, the captain of the women's swim team, is the child of Holocaust survivors and is in the process of wrestling with her lesbian identity. Levin relates the novel's action through the interior voices not only of these three principal characters, but also via a number of more peripheral figures. Often writing the same event from multiple perspectives, she emphasizes the subjectivity of experience, and the nature of her characters' relationships with one another.

The death of lovers, the emotional legacy of the Holocaust, and sports and bodies are again important in *Love and Death, & Other Disasters.* These stories were written between 1977 and 1995 but, as Levin notes in her preface, for much of that time they proved difficult to place because of their everyday portrayal of butch-femme relationships and lives. Levin does not explain or apologize for the butch-femme identities and relationships that these stories depict—they exist as an uncommented-upon given for the women involved. The collection also includes a rewriting of the story of the Pied Piper, and of an Inuit myth, that suggests a fabulous, transhistorical, and transcultural element to lesbian desire. At the conclusion of *The Sea of Light,* Levin approaches the idea of lesbian family and parenthood; it is a theme also affirmatively present in a number of these stories and a subject on which Levin has been published in other forums.

Further Reading

Carson, Sharon, and Brooke Horvath. "Sea Changes: Jenifer Levin's *Water Dancer* and the Sociobiology of Gender." *Aethlon: The Journal of Sport Literature* 9, no. 1 (1991): 37–48.

Oriard, Michael. "From Jane Allan to *Water Dancer:* A Brief History of the Feminist (?) Sports Novel." *MFS: Modern Fiction Studies* 33, no. 1 (1987): 9–20.

Liz Vine

Levithan, David (b. 1972)

Author and editor of young adult fiction, many centering on **gay** teens and love stories. As an editor for Scholastic Books, Levithan searches for fresh, new young talent for publication in the annual PUSH edition, but he is also well known for his own fiction. His lighthearted novels feature gay teens who are usually quite comfortable with their own identities and place in society. Born in Short Hills, New Jersey, in 1972, Levithan graduated from Millburn Senior High School in Millburn, New Jersey. He received his B.A. from Brown University in 1994 and now works as an editor for Scholastic's PUSH.

Levithan's characters are not struggling with decisions about coming out but are instead working through the same issues as other teens—love, the prom, friendship, and the usual pains of adolescence. *Boy Meets Boy* (2003), his first novel, is set in what some have labeled a utopian existence, but the story is more important for its lighthearted tale of love and relationships between gay teens rather than as a political or social text. The story of Paul and his infatuation with Kyle is the primary plot, but along the way Levithan introduces the reader to several other intriguing teens including the cheerleader who is also a football player. The upbeat tale of teen romance, which began as Levithan's Valentine's Day gift to friends, portrays homosexuality as part of the norm in a very accepting school and community environment.

Levithan's next book, *The Realm of Possibility* (2004), is told in many voices and in the form of verse poetry. The 20 students from the same high school include a gay couple, but the story also illustrates the lives of other individuals and a unique blend of interconnected worlds. Other novels include *Are We There Yet?* (2005), *Marly's Ghost: A Remix of Charles Dickens's A Christmas Carol* (2005), and *Wide Awake* (2006), a futuristic tale of a gay Jewish man elected president, are all written for a young adult audience. Levithan has also written many short stories featured in a variety of anthologies. Another important contribution to gay young adult fiction is *The Full Spectrum: A New Generation of Writing about Gay, Lesbian, Bisexual, Transgender, Questioning, and Other Identities* (2006), a collection of stories that Levithan edited with Billy Merrell. The book won the Lambda Literary Award for the best children's/young adult title of 2007.

Levithan's contributions to gay young adult fiction have earned him honors and recognition as well as a devout following among gay teens. His books and characters offer laughter and hope not only for homosexual young adults but also for anyone who appreciates a sweet romance, quirky characters, or a gay utopia.

Further Reading

"David Levithan." *Contemporary Authors Online,* Gale, 2008. Reproduced in *Biography Resource Center.* Farmington Hills, MI: Gale, 2008.

Ruth R. Caillouet

Liu, Timothy (b. 1965)

Prominent Asian American **gay** poet. Timothy Liu has published five books since his award-winning first collection, *Vox Angelica* (1992). He is also the editor of *Word of Mouth* (2000), an anthology of modern American gay male poetry.

Liu's first book showed the strong influence of his mentor Linda Gregg, with whose work his shares the search for a place for the spiritual in a quotidian world often hostile to the transcendent. As in the poems "Aphrodite as I Know Her" or "The Kore," most of the traces of the numinous in Liu's work are broken or in ruins; there is little wholeness to be found. *Vox Angelica*'s main subjects, sometimes intertwined, are the speaker's struggles with his sexuality, with his repressive religious background (the dual sense of religion as promise and prohibition is strong in Liu's work), and with his mother's lingering illness (mental and physical) and death.

Homosexuality is a pervasive topic and theme in the poems, as a force both of connection and of alienation. It simultaneously joins and separates sexual partners, and it estranges the speaker and his partners from the larger world of socially dictated normality, including his family, while at the same time connecting him to a subculture with its own rituals and norms. The human body, the body of the speaker's dying mother and the bodies of his lovers and sexual partners, is both numinous and endangered, especially by the pervasive presence of AIDS, whose massive effects on gay lives and gay sexuality are strongly reflected in Liu's work.

Liu's first three books, including *Burnt Offerings* (1995) and *Say Goodnight* (1998), were more personal in tone and topic, more lyrical in style, and more linear in syntax than much of his later work. Starting with his fourth book, *Hard Evidence* (2001), much of Liu's more recent work has been more experimental, moving him closer to the poetic avant-garde. The poems are more fractured and disjointed, juxtaposing phrases and images. There is a deliberate roughness to the poems, as if to make too smooth and polished an object would be a betrayal of the messy, contradictory, and often brutal reality of the contemporary world, saturated in violence and mass-mediated illusions, which the poems both engage and recoil from.

The focus on sexuality remains unwavering, though the vision of sexuality is a harsh and unforgiving one, and one clouded by the continuing social stigmatization of homosexuality. In many of Liu's poems, sex, far from being a mode of transcendence or even intimate communication, is yet another vehicle of degradation and alienation. Even the body betrays, with its unruly and unreasonable hungers. But the haze of desolation sometimes clears to reveal a tender erotic pastoral with the war between body and soul, between different bodies, briefly held in abeyance.

The poems are crowded with the detritus of contemporary commercial society and pervaded by the sense that all this (mis)information has overwhelmed individuality, crushing or erasing an interior life that can serve as a refuge from or counterpoint to the lies and demands of the world. In many of the poems the individual voice has been drowned out by the loud and multifarious voices (noises) of the mass media; there is only the pile-up of verbal and material debris. In a somewhat self-reflexive move, the speaker of the poems often turns to poetry in an attempt to heal the self, to provide a psychic and emotional breathing space, though this quest for a safe harbor for the self is not always successful.

Liu has been called an apostate who cannot stop praying, and this sense of spiritual quest informs all his poems. Having lost his faith in the transcendent, he is constantly searching for the sacred immanent in the earthly, and though he knows it cannot be found, he sometimes stumbles upon it anyway. No matter how broken and corrupted the world as he finds it is, Liu never gives up the impulse to sing or the will to connect.

Without surrendering any of its intensity, Liu's more recent work, in the books *Of Thee I Sing* (2004) and *For Dust Thou Art* (2005), returns to a more lyrical, less syntactically fractured mode, though still one informed by what has been called the broken lyric.

Further Reading

Hennessy, Christopher. *Outside the Lines: Talking with Contemporary Gay Poets.* Ann Arbor: University of Michigan Press, 2005.

Huot, Nikolas. "Timothy Liu." In *Gay American Poets and Playwrights: An A-to-Z Guide,* edited by Emmanuel S. Nelson. Westport, CT: Greenwood Press, 2003.

Van Cleave, Ryan. *Contemporary American Poetry: Behind the Scenes.* New York: Longman, 2003.

Zhou, Ziaojing. *The Ethics and Poetics of Alterity in Asian-American Poetry.* Iowa City: University of Iowa Press, 2006.

Reginald Shepherd

Lockhart, Zelda (b. 1962?)

Poet, publisher, and teacher. Zelda Lockhart earned her B.A. from Norfolk State University and a master's degree in Literature from Old Dominion University and is currently an active cultural worker in Durham, North Carolina, where she lives with her two children. Lockhart has earned broad critical acclaim for her artistic bravery in tackling difficult topics, her carefully molded characters, and the lyricism of her prose.

Lockhart's first novel, published in 2003 when Lockhart was 41 and entitled *Fifth Born,* is a faintly autobiographical work about a young girl growing up in Mississippi and Missouri who survives sexual violence and witnesses a murder in her large rural household. Protagonist Odessa struggles to create a truthful life despite the lies her family is committed to protecting. *Fifth Born* was a finalist in the "debut fiction" category of the Zora Neale Hurston/Richard Wright Award competition.

Her most recent novel is *Cold Running Creek* (2006), a historical novel that brings life to generations of Native American and African American women struggling for freedom from displacement and slavery in the period surrounding the Civil War. A Choctaw woman, Raven, survives the murder of her parents, only to become entrapped as the wife of a slave-holding white/Choctaw man. She adopts a young black/Choctaw girl, Lilly, whom she raises to be heir to the master's wealth, but who in turn is kidnapped into slavery and then kidnapped into an abusive marriage when she escapes. Lockhart drew on the untold stories of her own maternal grandmother for the roots of this novel, which gained considerable critical acclaim.

When her former publisher, Simon & Schuster, missed multiple publishing dates for *Cold Running Creek,* possibly due to the recent controversial decision by the Cherokee Nation to deny any rights or benefits to descendents of slaves owned by Cherokees, Lockhart founded her own publishing company, LaVenson Press, which she operates with the help of an intern. LaVenson Press is named in honor of her late brother LaVenson who encouraged her to achieve her dreams and move past fear.

Lockhart is also the author of a number of novellas, essays, and poems that appear in anthologies including *Present Tense: Writing and Art by Young Women* (1997) and *When I Was a Loser: Stories of (Barely) Surviving High School* (2007). Her work also appears in national magazines including *WordWrights, Sojourner, Calyx,* and *Sinister Wisdom.* Lockhart's serial novella, *The Evolution* (2003), a speculative fiction adventure full of futurism, strange clawed creatures, and lesbians and part of *USA Today*'s "open book" project, provides a strong contrast to her other works and demonstrates Lockhart's versatility as a fiction writer.

Lockhart's writings, which foreground young women's experiences with violence and survival, extend into her cultural work with people of all ages through which she seeks to empower people to take command of their own destiny through creative arts. Lockhart leads writing classes for home-schooled children in the North Carolina area, workshops about self-esteem and writing for adolescents, a writing intensive series for women, and workshops all over the country for writers about how to get their books published.

She encourages writers to remember that their writing has purpose or as she frequently says, "your writing is food, medicine and water for somebody." Lockhart consistently uses her skills as a writer to sustain her community. In 2004 in partnership with SpiritHouse, a Durham, North Carolina–based nonprofit organization, Lockhart designed and facilitated an ongoing after-school workshop for elementary school children at the Lyon Park Community Center entitled "Love Circles." During the workshop, Lockhart led the children in writing exercises designed to enable them to talk about the cycles of love in their lives in a way that was inclusive of community and family structures outside of the heteropatriarchal family norms that children consume in the media daily. The participants in the class created a book of their illustrated stories dedicated to their beloved friends, teachers, and family members.

Lockhart also remains active in her local literary community. She has been the final judge in the local poetry contest administered by the weekly free newspaper the *Durham Independent Weekly* and is also a consistent supporter of local bookstores and coffee shops in her local area. Lockhart has also been an honored speaker nationwide at places as varied as Chicago's Newberry Library and Nyack's African-American Authors Symposium. Zelda Lockhart uses her voice to awaken forgotten histories and encourages empowered futures for the countless writers and readers she has nurtured with her example.

Further Reading

Greenlee-Donnell, Cynthia. "The Red and the Black: Zelda Lockhart Explores the Shared Histories of Native and African Americans." *Independent Weekly,* March 28, 2007, C1.

Lockhart, Zelda. "Biography." www.zeldalockhart.com.

Alexis Pauline Gumbs

López Torregrosa, Luisita (b. 1945)

Editor, journalist, and autobiographer. Born in Puerto Rico into a middle-class family, Luisita López Torregrosa's father was a doctor, and her mother, a practicing lawyer from a very distinguished upper-class family in San Juan. The eldest of six children, she moved to the United States at the age of 14 to a girls-only boarding school in Pennsylvania, and later to college in North Carolina, never to return to Puerto Rico except to visit. Unlike many Puerto Ricans who migrated after World War II, she was the first family member to leave the island to fulfill her mother's middle-class dream to have her children educated abroad. She has since traveled extensively and lived in Tokyo, Manila, and New York City.

Her main work *The Noise of Infinite Longing: A Memoir of a Family—and an Island* (2004) is an attempt to reconcile herself with her family and the island after long periods of absence. It is an autobiographical text; however, rather than focusing exclusively on López Torregrosa's life experience, the narrative describes her as part of a large extended family held together by an extraordinary mother, who embodies the spirit of vibrant Puerto Rican culture and its middle-class social milieu of the second half of the twentieth century. The Puerto Rico evoked here is very different from the ones described in similar memoirs, and the narrative stands out for its lyrical, yet clean, direct, and very detailed prose. The book opens with López Torregrosa's mother's death and the reunion of all six of her scattered children after 10 years apart. The setting is Texas, where their mother had remarried and lived for the previous 30 years, and spans the four days of the funeral. Though a terminal moment in López Torregrosa's life, her mother's death marks the beginning of a reminiscent process about her childhood on the island: its infinite illusions and its bounded realities. Moving from present to past and focusing on one sibling at a time, López Torregrosa reveals the shaping forces in her childhood: the security of an extended loving upper-class family, the fears of her parent's ill-sorted marriage, and those of her tyrannical, womanizing, and drunkard father. Most importantly, out of the singular, often contradictory, memories of her six siblings, the multifaceted portrait and comforting presence of a strong and exceptionally gifted mother emerges from this auto/biography. Interestingly enough López Torregrosa's **lesbianism** is only briefly mentioned throughout the narrative.

Further Reading

Ortiz, Roberto Carlos. "Lopez Torregrosa, Luisita." *The Greenwood Encyclopedia of Multiethnic American Literature,* edited by Emmanuel S. Nelson, 1362–63. Westport, CT: Greenwood Press, 2005.

Volk, Patricia. "A Place and the Family That Left It but Never Forgot It." *New York Times,* April 23, 2004, A35.

Luisa Percopo

Lorde, Audre (1934–1992)

African American poet, essayist, autobiographer, and activist. Audre Lorde astounded and awakened generations of women with her writing, and her legacy continues to inspire a new generation of young writers today. She was born Audrey Geraldine Lorde in Harlem on February 18, 1934, to Caribbean immigrants Frederic Byron from Barbados and Linda Belmar Lorde from Grenada. Lorde's early childhood had significant ramifications for her later development. Her extreme nearsightedness went undetected until she was almost four years old—a fact that impacted her perception of the world from the time she was a child through her adult life. She recalls that she began talking at age five only when she discovered the magical possibilities of the written word. Her first memories of Catholic school were about knowing how to write her name but being chastised by authoritarian teachers for not following directions. Lorde was a precocious child with an ambiguous relationship to her mother. She states, in her autobiographical ***Zami: A New Spelling of My Name*** (1982), "I am the reflection of my mother's secret poetry as well as of her hidden angers." She recalls the nuns telling her mother not to put heavy clothes on her because then she would not feel the strap they used to punish her. Even before grammar school Audre preferred to drop the "y" from her name, loving the "evenness" of that spelling in relation to her last name.

Lorde began writing poetry in her teens and published her first poem (a love sonnet) in *Seventeen* magazine while still in high school, but even before that, poetry was central to her life. She attended Hunter High School and graduated from Hunter College in 1959 with a degree in philosophy and literature. She received her master's degree in library science from Columbia University in 1961 and worked as a librarian for several years thereafter. Lorde came of age and discovered the lesbian community both as a student in Cuernavaca, Mexico, where she lived for several months, and in Greenwich Village where she lived on her own "proud and poor" for a time. In 1962 she married Edwin Rollins, a legal aide, and had two children with him, Johnathan and Elizabeth. During this time her poems were anthologized in two volumes of black poetry including Langston Hughes's anthology *New Negro Poets,* and Lorde also left her librarian career to teach creative writing. Lorde's first poetry volume, *The First Cities,* was published in 1968, and this same year she obtained a National Endowment for the Arts writer-in-residence grant to teach at Tougaloo College in Jackson, Mississippi, where she met her partner, psychotherapist Frances Clayton. Her experience there teaching aspiring but at-risk young black artists was a pivotal experience for Lorde as she began to see the power and possibilities of her art to impact the lives of others, while also more deeply recognizing that to be a black lesbian poet in the 1960s was to endure a triple kind of invisibility.

Lorde divorced her husband in 1970 and moved to Staten Island where she and Clayton raised her children. Between 1970 and 1976, Lorde published four more volumes of poetry and gained greater recognition for her work, including being named Staten Island Community College Woman of the Year. She received the National Book Award in 1974 for *From a Land Where Other People Live* (1973). At the awards ceremony Lorde's close friend and fellow poet **Adrienne Rich** read a collective statement of acceptance written by Lorde, Rich, and **Alice Walker** (all three of whom had been nominated that year), in response to the competitive patriarchal rewards structure of the arts.

In 1974 Lorde made her first trip to Africa with her children. Her seventh poetry volume *The Black Unicorn* is highly influenced by her experience of the legends and landscapes of Dahomey (now Benin), and many of these poems reference African mythology and female deities and call upon ancestral knowledge as a way to reclaim women's power as warrior and sage. Severed from the ritual language of her foremothers, the poet here creates a new way to honor those ancient traditions through her poetic voice. These poems proclaim sisterhood and female connection now made more realizable through the infusion and creative potential of African myth.

Lorde was keynote speaker and guest lecturer at many conferences and colleges, including being a featured speaker at the first national march for **gay**s and lesbians in Washington D.C., in 1979. Many of her speeches and essays are collected in *Sister Outsider* (1985). One of Lorde's most important essays, "The Uses of the Erotic: The Erotic as Power," was first given at Mount Holyoke College and later published by Crossing Press. In this essay she talks about the danger (and thus the promise) that women's erotic power represents for dominant power relations, and its crucial role in enacting authentic social change. For Lorde, the spiritual (psychic and emotional) should not be separate from the political, and likewise the erotic should not be separate from the spiritual: this erotic power is conceived and realized always in relation to another and can lead to self-realization and attainment of real understanding. Lorde, perhaps more than any other writer of her time, emphasizes the value of feeling and emotion for empowerment. Deriving power from within, she argues, makes us better able to challenge oppression from without. Although Lorde has been criticized by some literary critics of essentialist thought, it is more important to consider her work as one continuous work of poetry with one idea always leading to another, being realized through the process of its articulation. Considered as a whole, Lorde's writing continuously works through contradictions and thus avoids essentialist traps.

A critical moment in Lorde's life came in 1978 when she was diagnosed with breast cancer. This experience is documented in her first nonfiction book *The Cancer Journals* published in 1980, the same year in which she was inducted into the Hunter College Hall of Fame. With this text, Lorde brought to light the otherwise hidden epidemic of breast cancer in women, relating both its personal toll and critiquing the sociocultural and environmental factors that underlie its causes. Declaring that "our bodies have an imprint of the connection between work and life," Lorde empowered other women by not wearing a prosthesis after her mastectomy—transgressing and challenging once again sexist ideas of women's physical appearance. *The Cancer Journals* marks a shift in Lorde's writing in which the immediacy of priorities and the urgency to be vocal and visible become apparent. Lorde comes to terms with the enormity of the work that still needed to be done and uses the impetus of her own mortality as a source of power in her writing and activism. As **Alexis De Veaux** states in her 2004 definitive biography of Audre Lorde, "The Impact of cancer performed a transfiguration not only of Lorde's physicality, but of her personality, creativity and social activism" (xii). Lorde aligned her struggle with cancer with struggles against racism, capitalism, and **homophobia**. Living with cancer, she declared, made her "more able to touch her power because she does not have to reckon with fear." Indeed survival is a recurring theme in Lorde's work. On the one hand, she recognizes that "we were never meant to survive," while at the same time she advocates the need to create and to give voice in order to endure. Indeed for Lorde, poetry is "not a luxury" but rather itself a means of survival. Lorde further explores the impact of cancer on her life in *A Burst of Light* (1988), which won a Before Columbus Foundation Award in 1989. That anthology of interviews and essays by Lorde includes "A Burst of Light: Living with Cancer," a series of journal entry excerpts written over three years in reaction to being diagnosed with metastasized liver cancer in 1984 two weeks before her 50th birthday.

Lorde's ability and advocacy in making connections among disparate women's communities is legendary. For Lorde, differences of class, race, **gender**, sexuality, and ethnicity make interdependence all the more necessary, and so she adamantly argued that we must move beyond mere tolerance of difference but rather strive to gain an integral understanding of how we differ from and come together with others. This insight in turn will provide yet another source of authority that is enough to challenge power relations of dominance within capitalist patriarchal structures. She pits language and community against fear, arguing that we all must bridge our experiences together manifestly and vocally. In *Sister Outsider* (1984), Lorde declared that "there are no hierarchies of oppression"; she was one of the first to perceive all oppressions as equally injurious. Eminently quotable, Lorde also declared to progressive feminist communities that "the master's tools will never dismantle the master's house," that is, until each of us recognizes our own part in oppression and strives to build authentic coalitions based on difference, we will be complicit in perpetuating patriarchal power relations. Lorde enacted this belief in both her writing and in activist commitment. Kitchen Table Press exemplifies her philosophy of interdependence and connectedness. Inspired by a conversation between Audre Lorde and Barbara Smith in 1980 about the need for women of color to have access to publishing, the Kitchen Table Press became the first U.S. publishing company run by and for women of color. It was the first to forge connections among Asian, Native, African, and Latina American women regardless of sexual orientation who before that had primarily worked separately in media and publishing.

In 1984 Lorde traveled to Germany as a visiting professor at the Free University of Berlin where she taught seminars on poetry and black women poets. Lorde's visit inspired the publication of the Afro-German anthology *Farbe bekennen* (translated into English as *Showing Our Colors: Afro-German Women Speak Out* (1991) for which she wrote the introduction). Her European tour underscored for her the importance of transnational African women's solidarity and the interwoven struggles of all women throughout the world. Without that union with others, her work was meaningless. And it was this interconnective value that made Lorde's work have profound resonance for women from the United States to Europe to South Africa, Australia, and Cuba. The value of her work is recognized in Jennifer Abod's film *The Edge of Each Other's Battles: The Vision of Audre Lorde* (2002), which documents a four-day Boston conference, "I Am Your Sister: Forging Global Connections across Differences," where 1,200 women and men and activist youth from 23 countries relied on Lorde's work to examine cross-cultural awareness of race, gender, sexuality, and class divisions.

Lorde's 1982 innovative life narrative, *Zami: A New Spelling of My Name* altered notions of autobiography. Subtitled "A Biomythography," this textual memoir explores the mythic and actual parameters of identity formation. Lorde takes Zami, "a Corriacou name given to women who work together as friends and lovers" as a title metaphor for her own name to denote the collective of women within one individual name. In this way, the autobiographical "I" becomes a collective "we," and she is able to (re)create how other women shaped her identity while simultaneously establishing her own.

Two years after Lorde was diagnosed with metastasized liver cancer, she returned to the Caribbean where she moved to St. Croix with her then partner Gloria Joseph. There she continued her activism and writing while also struggling with her disease. After Hurricane Hugo devastated the Virgin Islands in 1989, Lorde and Joseph published *Hell under God's Orders: Hurricane Hugo in St. Croix, Disaster and Survival.* Both she and Joseph continued to work with local and international women's organizations. Shortly before she died, Lorde took the African name "Gamba Adisa," meaning "Warrior: She Who Makes Her Meaning Clear." In 1991 she was named New York State Poet Laureate. Audre Lorde's papers are officially archived at Spelman College in Atlanta.

Further Reading

Brodzki, Bella, and Celeste Schenck, eds. *Life/Lines: Theorizing Women's Autobiography.* Ithaca, NY: Cornell University Press, 1988.

De Veaux, Alexis. *Warrior Poet: A Biography of Audre Lorde.* New York: Norton, 2004.

Griffin, Ada Gay, and Michelle Parkerson. *Litany for Survival: The Life and Works of Audre Lorde.* New York, Third World Newsreel, 1995.

Munt, Sally, ed. *New Lesbian Criticism: Literary and Cultural Readings.* New York: Columbia University Press, 1992.

Wiley Hall, Joan, ed. *Conversations with Audre Lorde.* Jackson: University Press of Mississippi, 2004.

Colleen Kattau

Lowenstein, Andrea Freud (b. 1949)

Jewish American novelist, academic, and literary critic. Born in Boston and raised in Lincoln, Massachusetts, Andrea Freud Lowenstein records her adolescent experiences with coming out, and battling against assimilation, class prejudice, and conflicts, with her well-meaning mother in her second book, an autobiographical series of short stories, *The Worry Girl* (1992), whose title derives from the Yiddish word *sorgenkind*. A greatgranddaughter of Sigmund Freud, her mother, Sophie Freud, Professor Emeritus of Social Work at Simmons College, wrote *Living in the Shadow of the Freud Family* (2007), which chronicles her escape from the Nazis and her alienation from the Freud family and Freudian psychology. Freud Loewenstein credits her mother with her love of literature, and Loewenstein established innovative writing programs for incarcerated and low-income women. Her feminist dedication to the support of women—African American, lesbian, poor, disadvantaged—and to the elucidation of the relationships among **homophobia**, antisemitism, misogyny, and social stereotypes of madness has characterized all her work.

Her experiences with women on the margins inform her brilliant first novel, *This Place* (1984). Set in the enclosed world of a woman's correctional institution, Loewenstein interweaves the voices of four major characters: Candy, a former prostitute in a butch-femme relationship with Billie; Ruth Foster, a therapist; Sonya Lehrer, a Jewish art therapist; and Telecea Jones, a black woman whose "mad visions" paint an eerily accurate view of their world. While the setting enables Loewenstein to focus on the manifold dynamics of lesbian relationships, the novel underscores the points made in her later scholarly article "From the Literature in Search of Madness" (2004). For Loewenstein, "madness" is a social—not individual—product of power relations that produce marginalizing languages of **lesbianism**, race, and **gender**.

Loewenstein addresses these dynamics in her acclaimed scholarly study *Loathsome Jews and Engulfing Women* (1993). Here she argues that the British modernist writers Wyndham Lewis, Charles Green, and Graham Greene obsessively represent Jews and women as victims, villains, and social outcasts because of *their* traumatizing prison-like experiences of dominance, humiliation, and rape in the British public school system. Forced to remain "in the **closet**" about their experiences, they project hatred onto **queer**s, Jews, and women as the visible "outsiders" and representatives of their public school selves.

Loewenstein, a tenured academic, teaches and produces a writing project that can imagine others' perspectives and contexts and model creative social communication free from secrets and closets, margins and centers, and violence and domination.

Further Reading

Freud, Sophie. *Living in the Shadow of the Freud Family.* London: Praeger, 2007.
Stratton, Jay. *Coming Out Jewish.* New York: Routledge, 2000.

Corinne E. Blackmer

Lucas, Craig (b. 1951)

Major American playwright, screenwriter, and director. Found in an abandoned car in Atlanta, Georgia, Craig Lucas was born in 1951. He attended Boston University, and, free from the sphere of his conservative adoptive parents, discovered both his left leanings and his emerging homosexuality. Lucas was encouraged by poet Anne Sexton to move to New York after graduating in 1973. He soon found work as an actor, most notably in Broadway productions such as *Sweeney Todd, Shenandoah,* and *On the Twentieth Century.*

In 1991, Lucas wrote a play entitled *Missing Persons,* which was later directed by Norman René, with whom he would have a 15-year artistic collaboration. Lucas would go on to author critically acclaimed plays such as *Reckless* (1983), *Blue Window* (1984), and *Prelude to a Kiss* (1990) and the book to the Tony-nominated *The Light in the Piazza* (2007). Lucas eventually settled in Seattle, assuming the Associate Artistic Directorship of the Intiman Theatre under collaborator Bartlett Sher. He has since begun directing both for stage and screen.

Lucas's reputation is that of a plot-driven writer who is unapologetic for his inclusion of **gay** and lesbian themes. Much of his work seems to echo important parts of his life, particularly confusions about personal identity. In *Reckless,* for example, housewife Rachel is forced to leave her life and family and forge a multitude of new identities as she encounters character after character who are also not what they appear. *The Dying Gaul* (1998) finds a woman hiding online behind the identity of a screenwriter's deceased male lover in order to exact revenge. In many ways, this journey to find and create an identity not only reflects the struggles of many in the LGBTQ community, but also reflects the abandonment issues with which Lucas himself encountered as a baby.

Sexuality is viewed in a magical and metaphoric manner in *Prelude to a Kiss.* The play poses the question of whether or not gender is an important element of identity as Rita, a newlywed, transfers souls with an elderly, dying man. Can Rita's husband Peter not only recognize that transition, but love Rita outside of her physical age and gender? Can we be attracted to a soul, rather than a body? In *Prelude to a Kiss,* the answer is yes, and the kiss between Peter and the old man is the fairy-tale-like means to bring Rita's soul back into her body.

Prelude to a Kiss and *The Dying Gaul* also deal with AIDS, a disease that affected many of Lucas's friends. In *Prelude,* a seemingly healthy young woman is suddenly transformed into a frail and dying man, much like AIDS ravaged the bodies of healthy young men in the 1980s and 1990s. In *Gaul,* Robert is unable to move forward with his life after the death of his lover from AIDS, holding onto the hope that he can communicate from the dead. Lucas's 1990 screenplay, *Longtime Companion,* deals frankly and directly with AIDS and its devastation to the gay community and is respected as one of the pivotal films about the disease.

Lucas's political voice deepened in the late 1990s. His work, which often was categorized as madcap romantic comedy, took on a decidedly sharper and edgier tone. With his trademark use of fantasy, *Singing Forest* (2005), an exploration of a Viennese family in the 1930s and in contemporary New York, looks piercingly at gay relationships and the duality of the helpfulness and hurt of psychotherapy. His play *The Dying Gaul* is a searing look at Hollywood's dark side and the lengths we go to exact revenge.

Toward the latter part of his career, Lucas has split his time between writing for the stage and writing for the screen. His films include adaptations of his plays *Reckless, Blue Window, Prelude to a Kiss,* and *The Dying Gaul* and original screenplays such as *The Secret Life of Dentists* (2002). He also directed *The Dying Gaul* (2005) and *Birds of America* (2008).

Lucas's work has been critically acknowledged with a Tony nomination, a National Endowment for the Arts grant, a Drama Critics' Circle Award, a Lambda Literary Award, an Obie, and a nomination for the Pulitzer Prize, among others.

Further Reading

Bernstein, Robin, ed. *Cast Out: Queer Lives in Theater.* Ann Arbor: University of Michigan Press, 2006.

Lucas, Craig. "Equality in the Theatre." *Bomb* 57 (Fall 1996): 66–70.

Swartz, Patti Capel. "Craig Lucas." *Gay & Lesbian Literature, Volume 2,* edited by Tom Pendergast and Sara Pendergast, 232–34. Detroit: St. James Press, 1998.

Tom Smith

Ludlam, Charles (1943–1987)

Influential playwright, director, designer, and performer. Charles Ludlam was raised across the street from a movie theater on Long Island. His mother took him to see every new movie as it came, and by age 10, Ludlam was well versed in Hollywood film. Years earlier, he got lost at the Minneola State Fair. He wandered into a Punch and Judy Show and soon began staging puppet shows in his basement. These events, in addition to his family's devout Catholicism, influenced Ludlam's artistic aesthetic.

Ludlam's family moved when he was 10, and in lieu of seeing movies every week, Ludlam immersed himself in reading classics. At age 15, he accepted an apprenticeship at the Long Island summer stock, the Red Barn Theatre. There he met artists who embraced a more free-spirited way of life, which intrigued Ludlam who had grown up in a conservative town. With encouragement from friends in the company, he later traveled to New York City to see productions, including The Living Theatre's *The Connection* and *Tonight We Improvise.*

By age 17, fueled by his interest in classic literature and avant-garde theatrics, Ludlam founded the Students' Repertory Theatre in an abandoned Odd Fellows' meeting hall. As artistic director, he acted in and directed obscure plays, such as the modern Noh drama *Madman on the Roof* and *Theatre of the Soul,* a Russian romantic work set inside the human body.

In 1961, Ludlam entered Hofstra University on an acting scholarship. He struggled with what seemed like the mundane and traditional methods of his instructors. Seen as too over-the-top acting-wise and too opinionated in his beliefs, the Hofstra theater faculty encouraged Ludlam to consider writing or directing, where he could have more artistic control. During this time, Ludlam was also coming to terms with his homosexuality and wrote his first play, *Edna Brown,* an expressionistic and semiautobiographical work never performed and subsequently destroyed. Upon graduation with a degree in dramatic literature, he moved to New York City where he hoped to find other artists with whom he could experiment and explore theatrically.

Briefly after his arrival, Ludlam was cast in Ronald Tavel's *The Life of Lady Godiva* (1966), playing Peeping Tom. The play was directed by John Vaccaro at the Play-House of the Ridiculous, and the group's aesthetic of mixing high and low culture, **camp**, drag, and pageantry proved to be what Ludlam was searching for back at Hofstra. Another Play-House piece, a 30-minute curtain-raiser called *Screen Test,* gave Ludlam his first foray into drag while wearing a wig once owned by Salvador Dali. In it, Ludlam improvised Gloria Swanson's Norma Desmond character, making the play into a star turn. This gave him the courage to write his own work for the Play-House: *Big Hotel,* which drew upon dozens of movies, songs, classical literature, and comic books, and was staged by Vaccaro in 1966. A success, Ludlam was encouraged to write another play, and he began work on *Conquest of the Universe,* based loosely on Christopher Marlowe's *Tamburlaine the Great.* During rehearsals, Ludlam, who was to star as Tamburlaine's twin opponents, got into an altercation with Vaccaro, who eventually fired him. Half the company walked out with Ludlam, and they encouraged him to start his own company and stage the play himself. Thus was born The Ridiculous Theatrical Company.

The Ridiculous Theatrical Company's first full season of plays began in 1968; among them were a revival of *Big Hotel* in repertory with *When Queens Collide,* Bill Vehr's *Whores of Babylon,* and a Ludlam/Vehr collaboration called *Turds in Hell.* Unable to find much of an audience, Ludlam temporarily renamed his company the Trocadero Gloxinia Magic Midnight Mind Theatre of Thrills and Spills. When this did not work, he reinstated the group's original name. The year 1969 brought *The Grand Tarot* and the group's first bit of notoriety: a *New York Village Voice* Obie Award for distinguished achievement in the off-Broadway theater. Throughout the late 1960s, The Ridiculous Theatrical Company had no permanent location and struggled both critically and financially.

The early 1970s brought Ludlam's first popular success with *Bluebeard* (1971). Critics began taking notice of Ludlam's company, and soon so did audiences. A Guggenheim Fellowship in Playwriting, two European tours, New York City and National Endowment for the Arts (NEA) grants, an Obie for acting, five new plays, and a permanent location to the Evergreen Theater quickly followed.

In 1975, Ludlam published his "Manifesto: Ridiculous Theatre, Scourge of Human Folly" in *The Drama Review* in which he clarified the core beliefs and ideals of Ridiculous Theatre. Critics and scholars could now look at this as a legitimate theatrical genre. He also achieved critical and commercial acclaim for his adaptation of *Camille* (1973), based on Alexandre Dumas's fils's *The Lady of the Camellias*. *Camille* embraced the elements of Ridiculous Theatre that Ludlam advocated: revaluing pop culture, especially simplistic or irrelevant pop culture; use of humor, drag, and homosexual undertones to reexamine relationships between the sexes; exploration of the dichotomy of personal art versus academic art; and the glorification of artifice. In brief, it attempts to create high art out of low trash.

Ridiculous Theatre culls most of its inspiration and content from pop culture: opera, cherished for its melodramatic emotional nature and its ostentatiousness of design; B movies, noted for their earnest but unsuccessful attempts at melodramatic emotional nature and ostentatiousness; and classical plays. This is wholly apparent in *Camille*.

The production provided Ludlam his most acclaimed drag role and also provided an ideal example of the dichotomy of Ridiculous theatre. He appeared onstage the epitome of the nineteenth-century heroine, complete with styled wig, lavish gown, expensive jewelry, and a fan. He also, however, revealed masculine chest hair underneath his dress. The forbidden love of Marguerite and Armand is paralleled by the forbidden love of a man in drag playing love scenes with another man. The result proved to be funny and moving, real and artificial, beautiful and grotesque. Camille became the most revered performance in Ludlam's career and was a role with which he became inextricably associated.

The year 1976 marked the beginning of the artistic and personal partnership of Ludlam and Everett Quinton. Quinton, an actor and designer, collaborated with Ludlam throughout the remainder of Ludlam's career. This time period is also noted for masterworks such as *Der Ring Gott Farblonjet,* national grants, an Obie for design, a fellowship to coach graduate playwriting students at Yale University, Ludlam's first film, *The Sorrows of Dolores* (1987), and a new permanent home at One Sheridan Square.

The 1980s culminated in recognition of Ludlam's numerous contributions to the world of theater. In addition to two NEA Fellowships in Playwriting and a Drama Desk Special Award for Outstanding Achievement in the Theater, Ludlam wrote his most produced play, *The Mystery of Irma Vep*. Written as a quick-change show for two actors playing four roles apiece, *Irma Vep* pulls from disparate sources such as the Alfred Hitchcock film *Rebecca* (1940), Emily Brontë's *Wuthering Heights* (1847), Henrik Ibsen's *Ghosts* (1881), and Edgar Allan Poe's poem "The Raven." It opened in 1984 to unanimous praise, and Ludlam found his play reviewed for the first time by *Time* magazine. *The Mystery of Irma Vep* was named among the year's best plays for 1984 by both the *New York Times* and *Time* magazine, and Ludlam and his partner Everett Quinton won Obie and Drama Desk awards for their performances. The success of this play made film and television producers take notice, and this led to a guest-starring role on a short-lived sitcom co-starring

Madeline Kahn. Following its cancellation, Ludlam was cast in the title role in *Hedda Gabler* for the American Ibsen Theater in Pittsburgh.

By 1986, Ludlam had found critical acclaim, had written 29 plays, performed in countless more, received almost continuous support through the NEA, performed in television and film, directed opera, begun work on a production of *Titus Andronicus* for New York Public Theater's Shakespeare in the Park, and was negotiating for a Broadway run of *Der Ring Gott Farblonjet*. At Thanksgiving, he was diagnosed with AIDS. Six months later, on May 28, 1987, at the age of 44, Charles Ludlam died of pneumocystis pneumonia and other AIDS-related complications. Posthumously, his work has been carried on by Everett Quinton, published by Samuel French in a volume of collected works, and the street in front of his theater was renamed "Charles Ludlam Lane."

The legacy of Charles Ludlam lies in both the extreme outrageousness of his plays and the literary merit they possess. He came from an educated background through both his college courses and his own continual self-education. For example, when deciding to produce his foray into children's theater, *Professor Bedlam's Educational Punch & Judy Show*, he extensively researched the history of Punch and Judy, created historically accurate reproductions, and tracked down famed puppeteer Al Fossi to work one-on-one with him on the manipulation of the puppets. It was vitally important for him to be accurate in theatrical forms.

Ludlam was also well versed in classical dramatic literature, which he often used as the basis of his plays. He knew "academic art" and detested its passivity. Ludlam wished to challenge the audience's perceptions of "good" art by mixing it with "bad" art, thus making all art valued equally. He often underplayed his own skills as a playwright, often telling people that in terms of writing he was a craftsman rather than an artist: able to pull, manipulate, and restructure existing materials into a new form. Yet through his creation of a collage of characters, plots, and styles, Ludlam reexamines views of high art and pop culture.

Reconsidering relationships between the sexes is at the core of Ludlam's works, and Ludlam played many leading female roles himself. Drag is, by its nature, politically charged. It forces observers to question the function of **gender** and sexual orientation. It also layers reality. On one level, we have the character of Camille, falling in love with a man. Is it a traditional heterosexual love story? On another level, we have a man playing the character of Camille, falling in love with another man. Are we then to interpret that this play is now a comment on homosexual love? On yet another level, we have a man, dressed like a woman but not totally convincingly, playing a woman in love with a man. What gender are we to associate with this character now? Is it a feminine man or masculine woman or some third gender? Which reality do we believe? In Ludlam's plays, the answer is all of them.

Perhaps the most pervasive theme in Ludlam's works is the idea of liberation from societal expectations of what constitutes happiness, morality, and propriety. This theme can been found most clearly in his major works, including *The Mystery of Irma Vep, Der Ring Gott Farblonjet, Camille,* and *Bluebeard,* which were all staged in the 1980s. Ridiculous Theatre challenges audiences to be accepting of all art, of all lifestyles, of all people, no matter how "ridiculous." It is a challenging style for most traditional theatergoers, and because of this Ludlam's plays are largely praised critically and academically but often overlooked artistically in the American repertory.

Of Ludlam's 29 plays, 12 received positive reviews, 8 received mixed reviews, and 9 received poor or no reviews. Critics were often harshest when Ludlam wrote conservative plays, like *Stage Blood* (1979), which had more literary than Ridiculous value. Audiences seemed more fickle, and positive reviews did not always translate to better box office. By his final plays, however, Ludlam had hit his artistic stride whereby he was able to play to full houses consistently. His final completed work, *The Artificial Jungle* (1987), opened to positive reviews and good audiences and closed early only because of Ludlam's failing health due to complications from AIDS. Critics concur that Ludlam's legacy is great and lasting, inspiring future theater artists and defining a theatrical style for the ages.

Further Reading

Bernard, Kenneth, and John Vacarro. "Charles Ludlam." *Theatre of the Ridiculous.* Baltimore: Johns Hopkins University Press, 1998.

Dasgupta, Gautam, and Bonnie Marranca, eds. *Theatre of the Ridiculous.* Baltimore: Johns Hopkins University Press, 1998.

Marranca, Bonnie. *American Playwrights: A Critical Survey.* New York: Drama Book Specialists, 1981.

Roemer, Richard. *Charles Ludlam and the Ridiculous Theatrical Company: Critical Analyses of 29 Plays.* Jefferson, NC: McFarland & Co., 1998.

Tom Smith